PHILIP'S

STREET ATLAS

UNRIVALLED DETAIL FROM THE BEST-SELLING ATLAS RANGE*

NAVIGATOR® WILTSHIRE

& SWINDON

www.philips-maps.co.uk

Philip's, a division of
Octopus Publishing Group Ltd
www.octopusbooks.co.uk
Carmelite House
50 Victoria Embankment
London EC4Y 0DZ
An Hachette UK Company
www.hachette.co.uk

First edition 2024
First impression 2024
WILDA

ISBN 978-1-84907-639-5 (spiral)

© Philip's 2024

Ordnance Survey
Licensed Data

This product includes mapping data licensed from Ordnance Survey® with the permission of the Controller of His Majesty's Stationery Office. © Crown copyright 2024. All rights reserved. Licence number 100011710.

CONTENTS

III **Key to map symbols**

IV **Key to map pages**

VI **Route planning**

X Major administrative and Postcode boundaries

1 **Street maps** at 3½ inches to 1 mile

163 **Street maps** at 1¾ inches to 1 mile

213 **Street maps** at 3½ inches to 1 mile

218 **Town maps** of Andover and Frome

219 **Index** of towns, villages, streets, hospitals, industrial estates, railway stations, schools, shopping centres, universities and places of interest

T0329516

Key to map symbols

Motorway with junction number	
Primary route – dual/single carriageway	
A road – dual/single carriageway	
B road – dual/single carriageway	
Minor road – dual/single carriageway	
Other minor road – dual/single carriageway	
Road under construction	
Tunnel, covered road	
Rural track, private road or narrow road in urban area	
Gate or obstruction to traffic – may not apply at all times or to all vehicles	
Path, bridleway, byway open to all traffic, restricted byway	
Pedestrianised area	

BS22	Postcode boundaries
	County and unitary authority boundaries

Railway with station
Tunnel
Railway under construction
Metro station
Private railway station
Miniature railway
Tramway, tramway under construction
Tram stop, tram stop under construction
Bus, coach station

♦ Ambulance station
♦ Coastguard station
♦ Fire station
♦ Police station
✚ Accident and Emergency entrance to hospital
Ⓗ Hospital
✛ Place of worship
ℹ Information centre – open all year
🛒 Shopping centre
Ⓟ Parking
P&R Park and Ride
PO Post Office
Ⓧ Camping site
🚐 Caravan site
▶ Golf course
⊠ Picnic site
Church Non-Roman antiquity
ROMAN FORT Roman antiquity

Univ Important buildings, schools, colleges, universities and hospitals

Built-up area

Woods

River Medway Water name
River, weir
Stream
Canal, lock, tunnel

Water

Tidal water

Adjoining page indicators

112

58 ◄ ► 87

The small numbers around the edges of the maps identify the 1-kilometre National Grid lines

The dark grey border on the inside edge of some pages indicates that the mapping does not continue onto the adjacent page

Abbreviations

Acad	Academy	Meml	Memorial
Allot Gdns	Allotments	Mon	Monument
Cemy	Cemetery	Mus	Museum
C Ctr	Civic centre	Obsy	Observatory
CH	Club house	Pal	Royal palace
Coll	College	PH	Public house
Crem	Crematorium	Recn Gd	Recreation ground
Ent	Enterprise		
Ex H	Exhibition hall	Resr	Reservoir
Ind Est	Industrial Estate	Ret Pk	Retail park
IRB Sta	Inshore rescue boat station	Sch	School
		Sh Ctr	Shopping centre
Inst	Institute	TH	Town hall / house
Ct	Law court	Trad Est	Trading estate
L Ctr	Leisure centre	Univ	University
LC	Level crossing	W Twr	Water tower
Liby	Library	Wks	Works
Mkt	Market	YH	Youth hostel

The map scale on the pages numbered in green is 1¾ inches to 1 mile
2.76 cm to 1 km • 1:36 206

0	½ mile	1 mile	1½ miles	2 miles

0	500m	1 km	1½ km	2km

The map scale on the pages numbered in blue is 3½ inches to 1 mile
5.52 cm to 1 km • 1:18 103

0	¼ mile	½ mile	¾ mile	1 mile

0	250m	500m	750m	1km

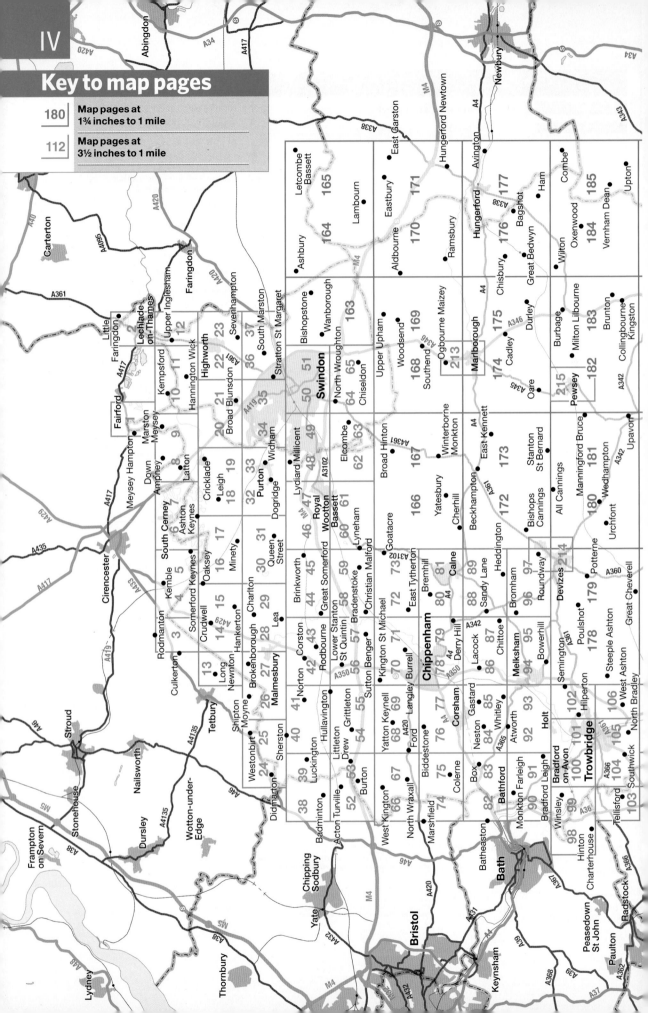

IV

Key to map pages

180	**Map pages at** **1¾ inches to 1 mile**
112	**Map pages at** **3½ inches to 1 mile**

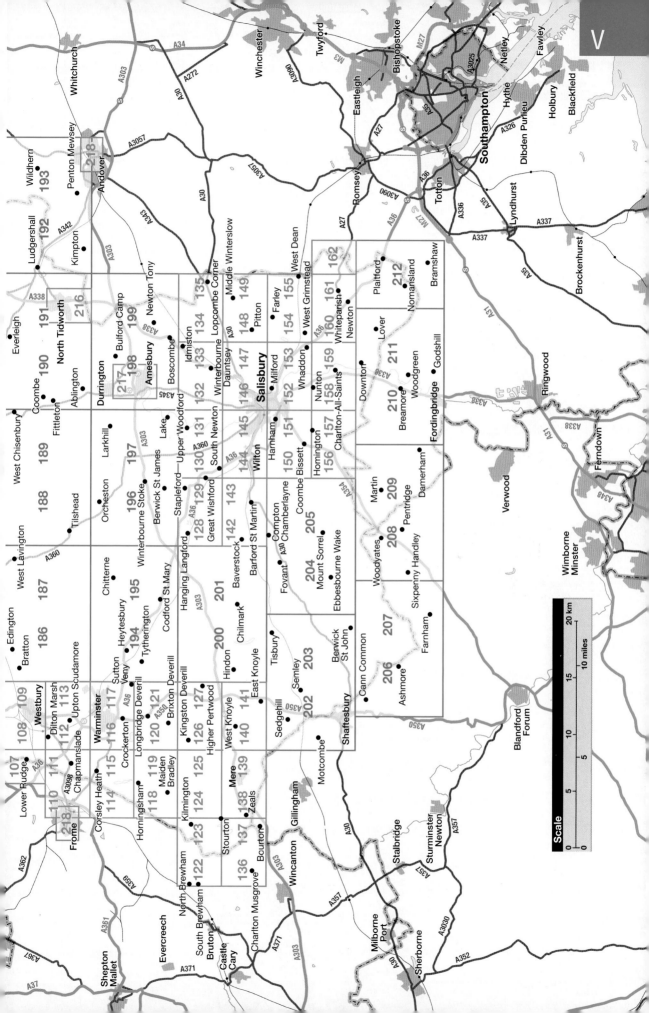

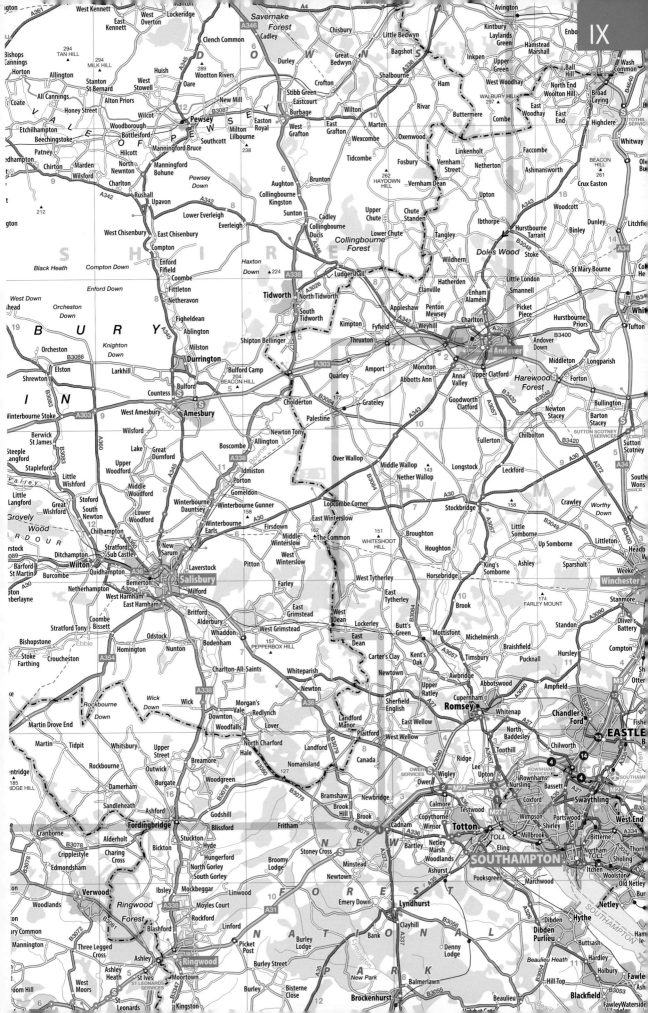

Major administrative and Postcode boundaries

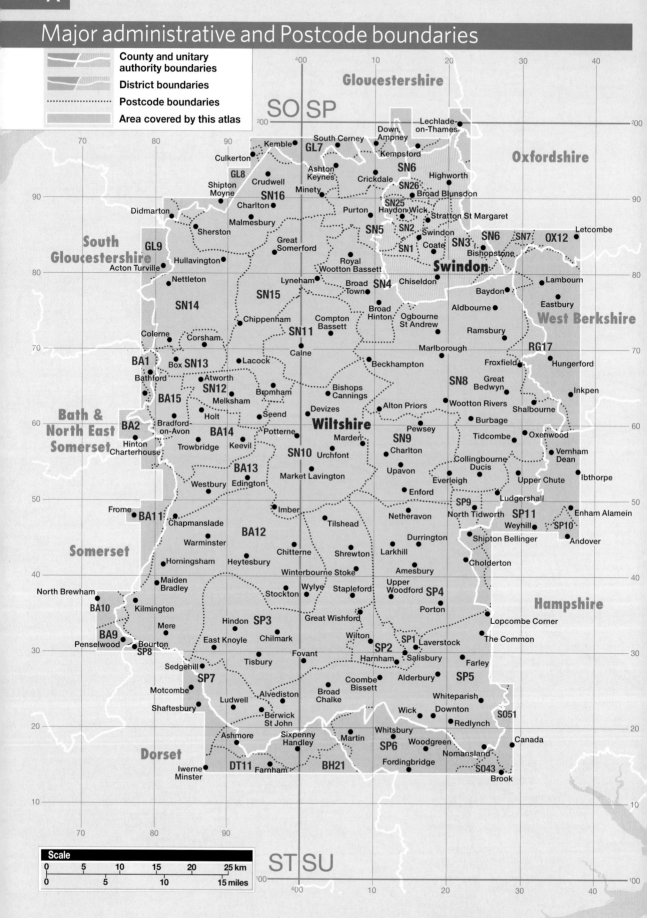

Legend:
- County and unitary authority boundaries
- District boundaries
- Postcode boundaries
- Area covered by this atlas

Scale

| 0 | 5 | 10 | 15 | 20 | 25 km |

| 0 | 5 | 10 | 15 miles |

Gloucestershire

Oxfordshire

SO | SP

South Gloucestershire

West Berkshire

Bath & North East Somerset

Wiltshire

Somerset

Hampshire

Dorset

ST | SU

Kemble, GL7, Culkerton, GL8, Crudwell, Shipton Moyne, SN16, Charlton, Didmarton, Malmesbury, Sherston, Great Somerford, South Cerney, Ashton Keynes, Minety, Purton, Crickdale, Down Ampney, Kempsford, Lechlade-on-Thames, SN6, Highworth, SN26, Broad Blunsdon, SN25, Haydon Wick, Stratton St Margaret, SN5, SN2, Swindon, Coate, SN1, SN3, Bishopstone, SN6, SN7, OX12, Letcombe

GL9, Acton Turville, Hullavington, Nettleton, SN14, Colerne, Corsham, Chippenham, SN11, Calne, Lyneham, Royal Wootton Bassett, Broad Town, SN4, Broad Hinton, Ogbourne St Andrew, Chiseldon, Baydon, Aldbourne, Ramsbury, Lambourn, Eastbury, Compton Bassett, Marlborough, Froxfield, RG17, Hungerford

BA1, Bathford, Box, SN13, Lacock, Atworth, SN12, Melksham, Bromham, Holt, Bishops Cannings, Beckhampton, SN8, Great Bedwyn, Inkpen, Wootton Rivers, Shalbourne

BA15, Bradford-on-Avon, Seend, Devizes, Alton Priors, Burbage, Tidcombe, Oxenwood

BA2, Hinton Charterhouse, BA14, Trowbridge, Keevil, Potterne, SN10, Marden, Urchfont, SN9, Charlton, Pewsey, Collingbourne Ducis, Vernham Dean, Upper Chute, Ibthorpe

BA13, Westbury, Edington, Market Lavington, Upavon, Everleigh, Ludgershall, Enford, SP9, North Tidworth, SP11, Weyhill, SP10, Enham Alamein, Andover

Frome, BA11, Chapmanslade, Imber, Netheravon, Durrington, Shipton Bellinger, Cholderton

BA12, Warminster, Tilshead, Larkhill, Amesbury

BA10, Kilmington, Horningsham, Heytesbury, Chitterne, Shrewton, Winterbourne Stoke, Upper Woodford, SP4, Porton, Lopcombe Corner, The Common

North Brewham, Maiden Bradley, Stockton, Wylye, Stapleford, Great Wishford, Wilton, SP1, Laverstock, Farley

BA9, Penselwood, Bourton, SP8, Mere, Hindon, SP3, Chilmark, East Knoyle, Fovant, SP2, Harnham, Salisbury, Alderbury, SP5

Sedgehill, SP7, Motcombe, Ludwell, Tisbury, Alvediston, Broad Chalke, Coombe Bissett, Wick, Downton, Whiteparish, SO51

Shaftesbury, Berwick St John, Ashmore, Sixpenny Handley, Martin, Whitsbury, SP6, Woodgreen, Redlynch, Canada

Iwerne Minster, DT11, Farnham, BH21, Fovington, Fordingbridge, Nomansland, SO43, Brook

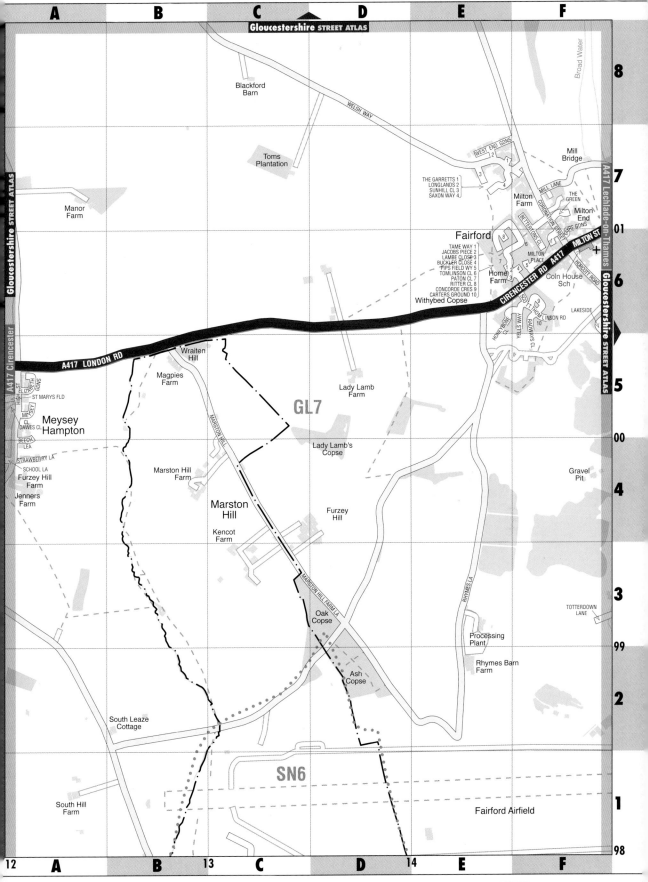

Gloucestershire STREET ATLAS

8

Blackford
Barn

WELSH WAY

Broad Water

Toms
Plantation

Mill
Bridge

WEST END GDNS

Manor
Farm

THE GARRETTS 1
LONGLANDS 2
SUNHILL CL 3
SAXON WAY 4

Milton
Farm

MILL LANE

THE
GREEN

7

CORONATION STREET

Milton
End

01

Fairford

TAME WAY 1
JACOBS PIECE 2
LAMBE CLOSE 3
BUCKLER CLOSE 4
PIPS FIELD WY 5
TOMLINSON CL 6
PATON CL 7
RITTER CL 8
CONCORDE CRES 9
CARTERS GROUND 10

MILTON ST

MILTON
PLACE

Home
Farm

CIRENCESTER RD A417

Coln House
Sch

6

HORCOTT ROAD

Withybed Copse

LAKESIDE

A417 LONDON RD

Wraiten
Hill

Magpies
Farm

Lady Lamb
Farm

HONEYBONE CL

YELS WAY

TOM LINSON RD

RADWAYS CL

A417 Cirencester

ST MARYS FLD

GL7

5

00

Meysey
Hampton

MARSTON HILL

Lady Lamb's
Copse

Gravel
Pit

DAWES CL
BEECH
LEA

Marston Hill
Farm

Furzey
Hill

4

STRAWBERRY LA

SCHOOL LA

Furzey Hill
Farm

Marston
Hill

Jenners
Farm

Kencot
Farm

RHYMES LA

3

TOTTERDOWN
LANE

MARSTON HILL FARM LA

Oak
Copse

Processing
Plant

99

Ash
Copse

Rhymes Barn
Farm

2

South Leaze
Cottage

SN6

1

South Hill
Farm

Fairford Airfield

98

12 **A** 13 **B** **C** 14 **D** **E** **F**

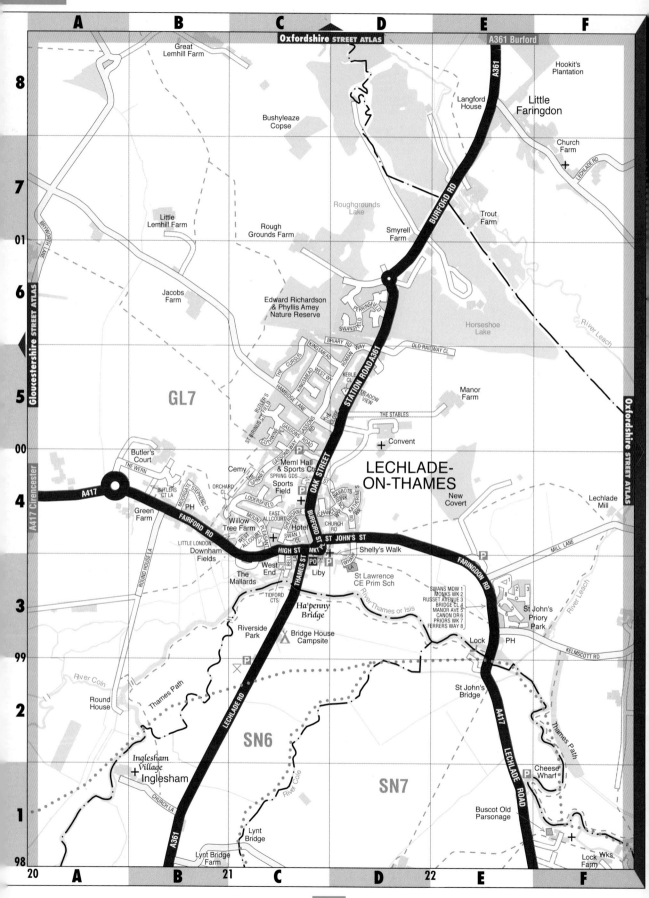

A361 Burford

8

Great
Lemhill Farm

Hookit's
Plantation

Bushyleaze
Copse

Langford
House

Little
Faringdon

Church
Farm

7

01

Little
Lemhill Farm

Rough
Grounds Farm

Roughgrounds
Lake

Smyrell
Farm

Trout
Farm

Jacobs
Farm

Edward Richardson
& Phyllis Amey
Nature Reserve

BURFORD RD

River Leach

6

SWANSFIELD

PERINSFIELD

Horseshoe
Lake

BRIARY RD

ROMAN WAY

OLD RAILWAY CL

5

GL7

THE CURSIS

KINGSMEAD WEST WY

KINGSMEAD RD

STATION ROAD A361

KEBLE CL

MEADOW
VIEW

Manor
Farm

BUTLER'S

ST BRINIS CT FIELD

BYZANTINE

HAMBIDGE LANE

GASSONS WAY

GASSONS RD

THE STABLES

Convent

00

Butler's
Court

THE WERN

BUTLERS CT LA

MOORGATE STEPHENS CL

PH

ORCHARD CL

THE SPINNEY

SPRING GDS

GASSONS WAY

LODERSFIELD

OAK STREET

ABBOTS WK

LAWN PARK

LANTHONY

CHANCEL

KATHERINES

LECHLADE-
ON-THAMES

New
Covert

Lechlade
Mill

4

Cemy

Meml Hall
& Sports Ctr

Sports
Field

Green
Farm

FAIRFORD RD

WILLOW Tree Farm

MOUNT PLEASANT

EAST ALLCOURT

SHERBORNE

BURFORD ST

SWAN CL

Hotel

CHURCH RD

ST JOHN'S ST

FARINGDON RD

MILL LANE

A417 Cirencester

A417

ROUND HOUSE LA

Downham
Fields

LITTLE LONDON

WEST ALLCOURT

HIGH ST

MKT PL

Shelly's Walk

River Leach

3

TIDFORD CTS

The Mallards

West
End

BELL

THAMES ST

PO

Liby

WHARF LA

St Lawrence
CE Prim Sch

River Thames or Isis

SWANS MDW 1
MONKS WK 2
RUSSET AVENUE 3
BRIDGE CL 4
MANOR AVE 5
CANON DR 6
PRIORS WK 7
FERRERS WAY 8

St John's
Priory
Park

KELMSCOTT RD

Ha'penny
Bridge

99

River Coln

Round
House

Riverside
Park

Bridge House
Campsite

Thames Path

Lock

PH

St John's
Bridge

Thames Path

2

SN6

LECHLADE RD

SN7

A417

Thames Path

Inglesham
Village

Inglesham

CHURCH LA

River Cole

Cheese
Wharf

1

Buscot Old
Parsonage

98

A361

Lynt Bridge
Farm

Lynt
Bridge

LECHLADE ROAD

Lock Wks
Farm

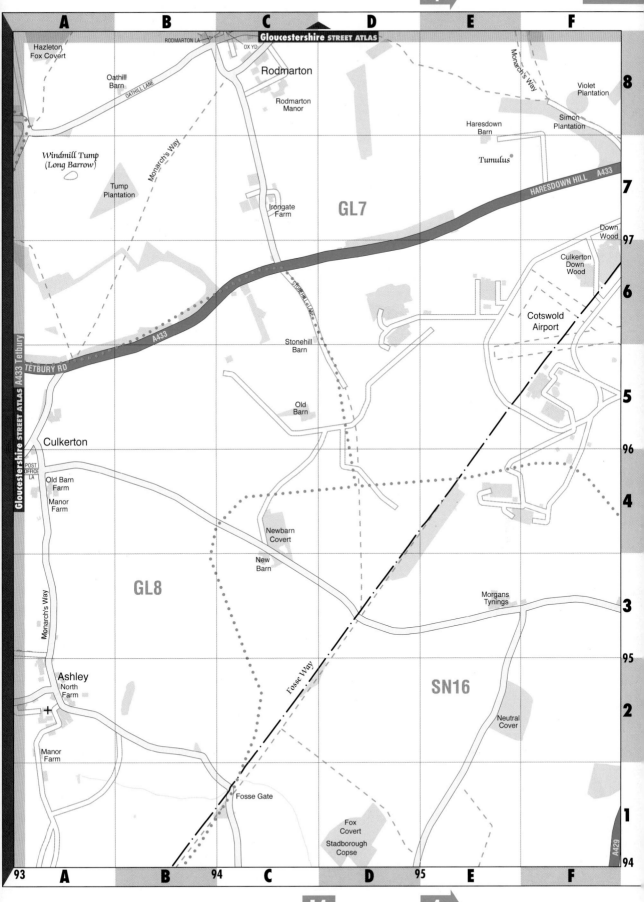

Gloucestershire STREET ATLAS

A **B** **C** **D** **E** **F**

Hazleton
Fox Covert

Oathill
Barn

OATHILL LANE

RODMARTON LA

OX YD

Rodmarton

Rodmarton
Manor

Monarch's Way

Violet
Plantation

8

Simon
Plantation

Haresdown
Barn

Windmill Tump
(Long Barrow)

Monarch's Way

Tumulus

HARESDOWN HILL A433

7

Tump
Plantation

Irongate
Farm

GL7

Down
Wood

97

STONEHILL LANE

Culkerton
Down
Wood

6

A433

Cotswold
Airport

TETBURY RD

Stonehill
Barn

5

Old
Barn

96

Gloucestershire STREET ATLAS A433 Tetbury

Culkerton

POST
OFFICE
LA

4

Old Barn
Farm

Manor
Farm

Newbarn
Covert

New
Barn

Morgans
Tynings

3

GL8

Monarch's Way

95

Fosse Way

SN16

Ashley

North
Farm

Neutral
Cover

2

Manor
Farm

Fosse Gate

Fox
Covert

Stadborough
Copse

1

A429

94

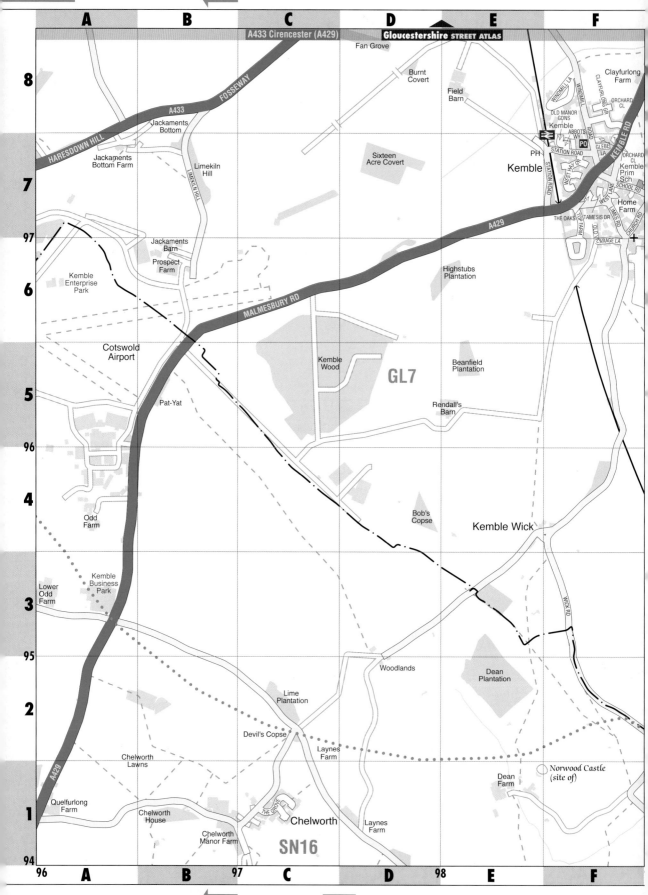

3

A433 Cirencester (A429)

Gloucestershire STREET ATLAS

A **B** **C** **D** **E** **F**

8

FOSSEWAY

A433

Fan Grove

Burnt Covert

Field Barn

Clayfurlong Farm

WINDMILL LA

WINDMILL

OLD MANOR GDNS

ORCHARD CL

Kemble Abbots

Jackaments Bottom

HARESDOWN HILL

LIMEKILN HILL

Jackaments Bottom Farm

Limekiln Hill

7

Sixteen Acre Covert

WEST WAY GR

GLEBE LA

KEMBLE RD

PO

STATION ROAD

PH

Kemble

WEST LANE

SCHOOL RD

LIMES RD

Kemble Prim Sch

ABBOTS WY

ORCHARD CL

Home Farm

97

Jackaments Barn

Prospect Farm

A429

THE OAKS

TOP FARM

TAMESIS DR

OLD WY

CHURCH RD

CARAGE LA

Kemble Enterprise Park

Highstubs Plantation

6

MALMESBURY RD

Kemble Wood

Beanfield Plantation

GL7

Cotswold Airport

Pat-Yat

5

Rendall's Barn

96

4

Odd Farm

Bob's Copse

Kemble Wick

Kemble Business Park

Lower Odd Farm

3

WICK RD

95

Woodlands

Dean Plantation

2

Lime Plantation

Devil's Copse

Laynes Farm

Norwood Castle (site of)

Chelworth Lawns

Dean Farm

1

Quelfurlong Farm

THE GROVE

Chelworth

A429

Chelworth House

Laynes Farm

Chelworth Manor Farm

SN16

94

96 **A** **B** 97 **C** **D** 98 **E** **F**

3 15

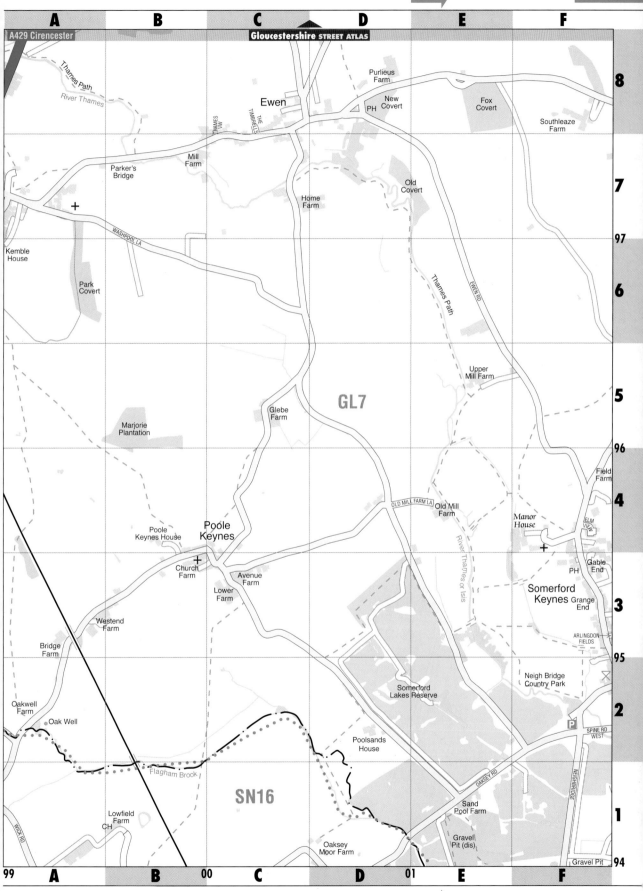

Thames Path

River Thames

Purlieus Farm

Ewen

PH
New Covert

Fox Covert

Southleaze Farm

THE TIMBRELLS

THAMES VW

Parker's Bridge

Mill Farm

Home Farm

Old Covert

WASHPOOL LA

Kemble House

Park Covert

Thames Path

EWEN RD

Upper Mill Farm

GL7

Marjorie Plantation

Glebe Farm

OLD MILL FARM LA

Old Mill Farm

Field Farm

Poole Keynes House

Poole Keynes

Manor House

ELM VIEW

PH

Gable End

Church Farm

Avenue Farm

River Thames or Isis

Somerford Keynes

Grange End

Lower Farm

ARLINGDON FIELDS

Westend Farm

Bridge Farm

Neigh Bridge Country Park

Oakwell Farm

Oak Well

Somerford Lakes Reserve

P

SPINE RD WEST

NEIGHBRIDGE

Poolsands House

OAKSEY RD

Flagham Brook

SN16

Sand Pool Farm

Lowfield Farm

CH

WICK RD

Oaksey Moor Farm

Gravel Pit (dis)

Gravel Pit

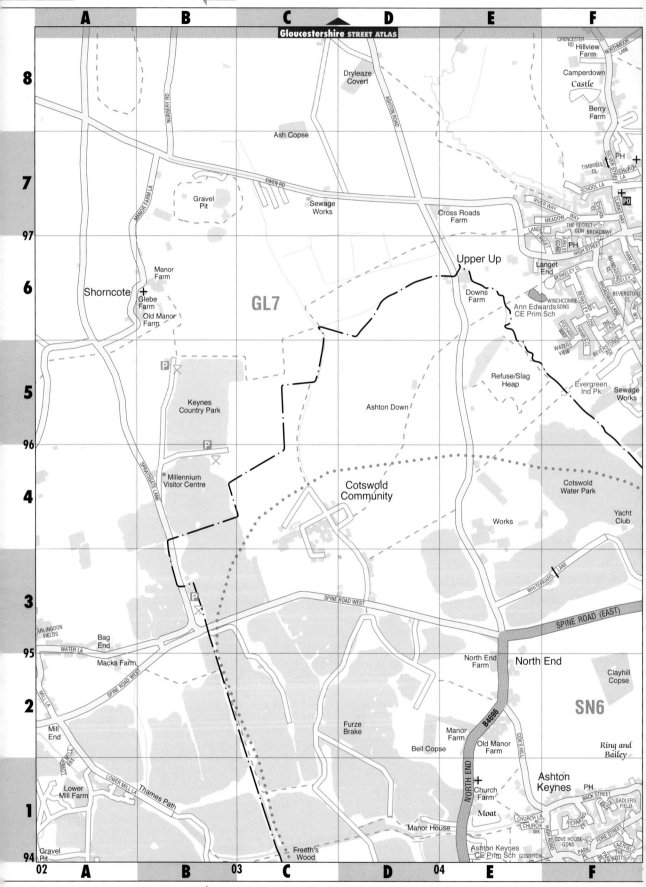

Gloucestershire STREET ATLAS

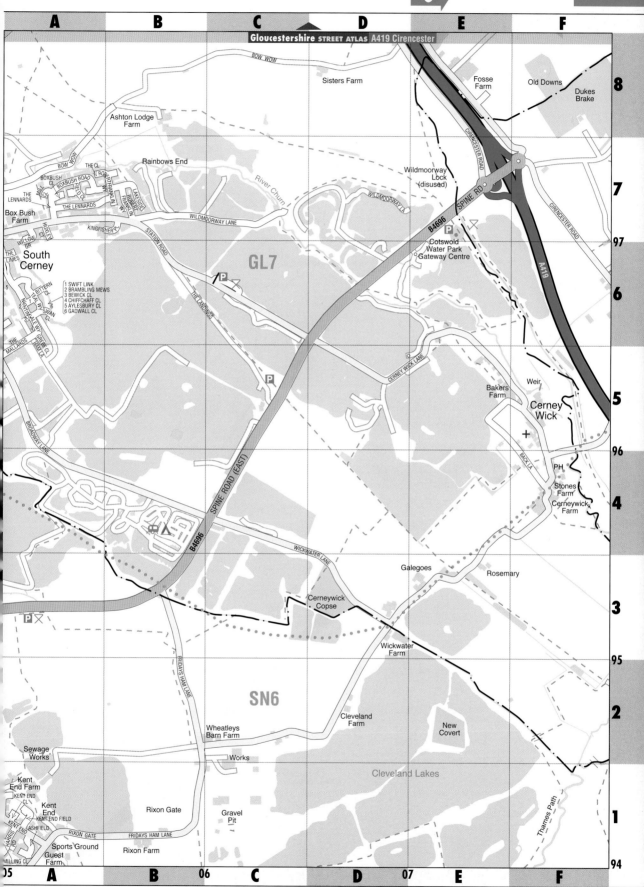

Gloucestershire STREET ATLAS A419 Cirencester

A · B · C · D · E · F

Bow Wow

Sisters Farm

Fosse Farm

Old Downs

Dukes Brake

8

Ashton Lodge Farm

Rainbows End

River Churn

WILDMOORWAY LA

Wildmoorway Lock (disused)

CIRENCESTER ROAD

7

BOW GR

THE CL

BOXBUSH CL

BOXBUSH ROAD

FIELD CL

R ROBERT FRANKLIN W

R ROBERT FRANKLIN CL

THE LENNARDS

HUXLEY

WILLOW GR

KINGFISHER

Box Bush Farm

THE LENNARDS

WILDMOORWAY LANE

STATION ROAD

SPINE RD

B4696

Cotswold Water Park Gateway Centre

A419

CIRENCESTER ROAD

97

South Cerney

THE LIMES

BITTERN

RLWY

SWAN

6

THE LANDMORS

GL7

1 SWIFT LINK
2 BRAMBLING MEWS
3 BEWICK CL
4 CHIFFCHAFF CL
5 AYLESBURY CL
6 GADWALL CL

6

THE MALLARDS

GREBE CL

TEAL CL

NORTHSCALE W

CERNEY WICK LANE

Bakers Farm

Weir

Cerney Wick

5

BROADWAY LANE

SPINE ROAD (EAST)

B4696

BACK LA

+

96

PH

Stones Farm

Cerneywick Farm

4

WICKWATER LANE

Galegoes

Rosemary

FRIDAYS HAM LANE

Cerneywick Copse

3

Wickwater Farm

95

SN6

Cleveland Farm

New Covert

2

Wheatleys Barn Farm

Sewage Works

Works

Cleveland Lakes

Thames Path

Kent End Farm

KENT END

KENT END FIELD

Rixon Gate

Gravel Pit

1

HARRIS RD

MILLING CL

Kent End

ASHFIELD

KENT END

RIXON GATE

FRIDAYS HAM LANE

Rixon Farm

Sports Ground Guest Farm

94

05 · A · B · 06 · C · D · 07 · E · F

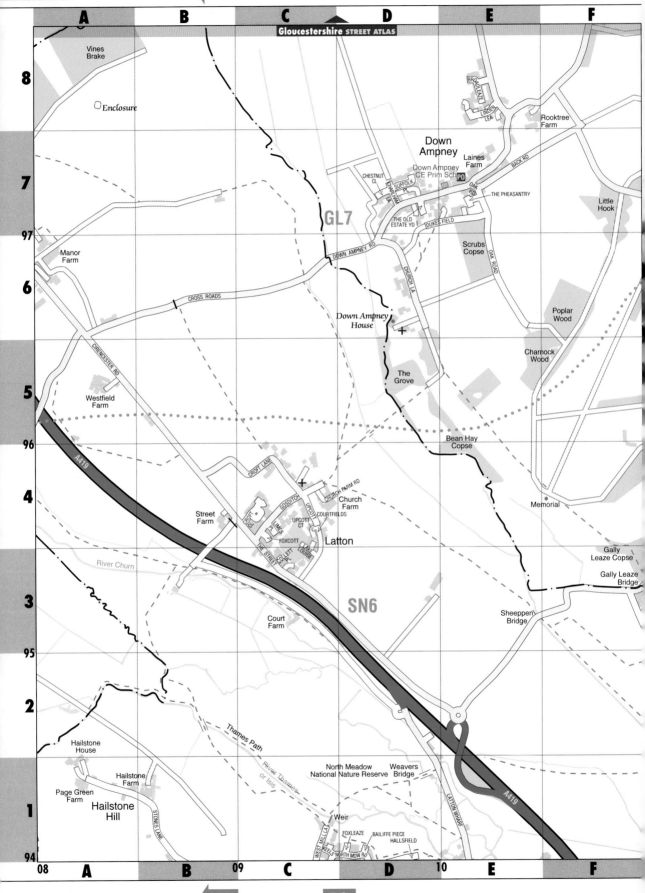

Gloucestershire STREET ATLAS

Vines Brake

Enclosure

Down Ampney

BROADLEAZE

LINDEN LEA

Rooktree Farm

Laines Farm

Down Ampney CE Prim Sch

CHESTNUT CL

PO

BACK RD

OAK RD

THE PHEASANTRY

Little Hook

GL7

SUFFOLK

CAROLINE

PL

V

LA

THE OLD ESTATE YD

DUKES FIELD

Scrubs Copse

OAK ROAD

Manor Farm

DOWN AMPNEY RD

CHURCH LA

Poplar Wood

CROSS ROADS

Down Ampney House

Charnock Wood

CIRENCESTER RD

The Grove

Westfield Farm

Bean Hay Copse

A419

Memorial

River Churn

CROFT LANE

CROFT CRES

GOSDITCH

CHURCH FARM RD

Church Farm

UPCOTT

COURTFIELDS

Gally Leaze Copse

Street Farm

THE STREET

LIMES

UPCOTT CT

Latton

Gally Leaze Bridge

FOXCOTT

COXLETT

CLOSE LOUISE

SN6

Sheeppen Bridge

Court Farm

Thames Path

Hailstone House

North Meadow National Nature Reserve

Weavers Bridge

LATTON WHARF

A419

Hailstone Farm

River Thames or Isis

Page Green Farm

Hailstone Hill

STONES LANE

Weir

FOXLEAZE

BAILIFFE PIECE

HALLSFIELD

WEST MILL LA

NORTH MOW RD

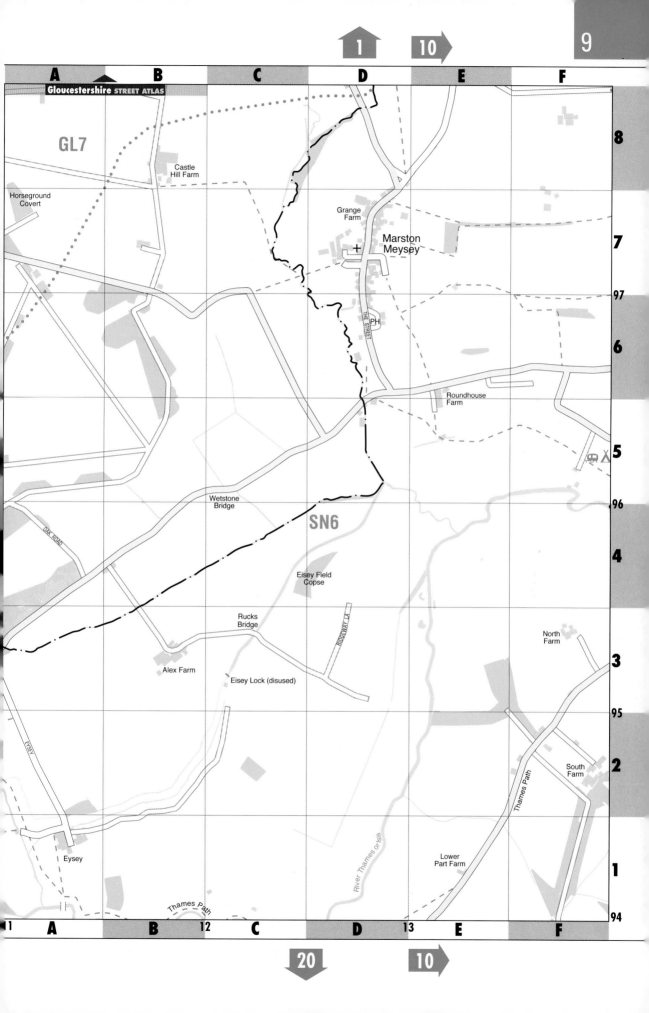

Gloucestershire STREET ATLAS

GL7

Horseground Covert

Castle Hill Farm

Grange Farm

Marston Meysey

THE STREET

PH

Roundhouse Farm

OAK ROAD

Wetstone Bridge

SN6

Eisey Field Copse

RIDGEWAY LA

Rucks Bridge

North Farm

Alex Farm

Eisey Lock (disused)

EYSEY

Thames Path

South Farm

River Thames or Isis

Eysey

Lower Part Farm

Thames Path

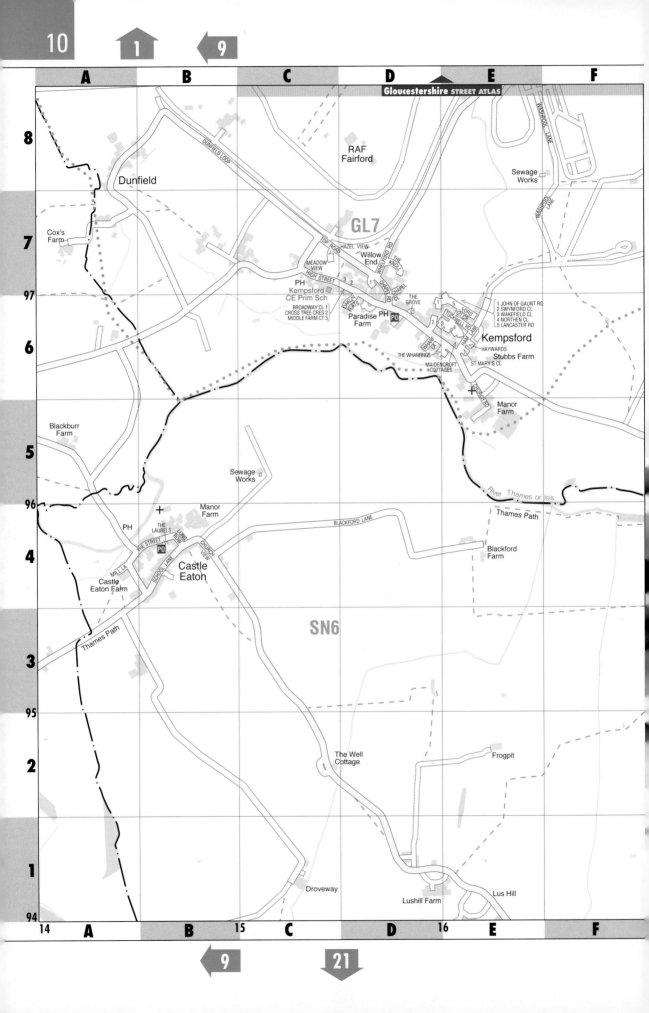

Gloucestershire STREET ATLAS

A **B** **C** **D** **E** **F**

RAF Fairford

Dunfield

DUNFIELD LOOP

GL7

Cox's Farm

HAZEL VIEW

WHELFORD RD

TOP ROAD

MEADOW VIEW

HIGH STREET

WILLOW End

THE KNOL

PH

Kempsford CE Prim Sch

OAKLEY PLACE

BROADWAY CL 1
CROSS TREE CRES 2
MIDDLE FARM CT 3

3
2

CHAPEL RD

THE GROVE

PH

PO

FORD
2 CR

TUCKWELL RD

HAM LANE

1 JOHN OF GAUNT RD
2 SWYNFORD CL
3 WAKEFIELD CL
4 NORTHEN CL
5 LANCASTER RD

Paradise Farm

Kempsford

THE WHARFINGS

MAIDENCROFT COTTAGES

MANOR LA

HAYWARDS

Stubbs Farm

ST MARY'S CL

CHURCH RD

Manor Farm

Blackburr Farm

Sewage Works

River Thames or Isis

Thames Path

Manor Farm

PH

THE LAURELS

THE STREET

LONG ROW

PO

SCHOOL LANE

MILL LA

Castle Eaton Farm

Castle Eaton

CHURCH VIEW

BLACKFORD LANE

Blackford Farm

Thames Path

SN6

The Well Cottage

Frogpit

Droveway

Lushill Farm

Lus Hill

Sewage Works

WASHPOOL LANE

8
7
97
6
5
96
4
3
95
2
1
94

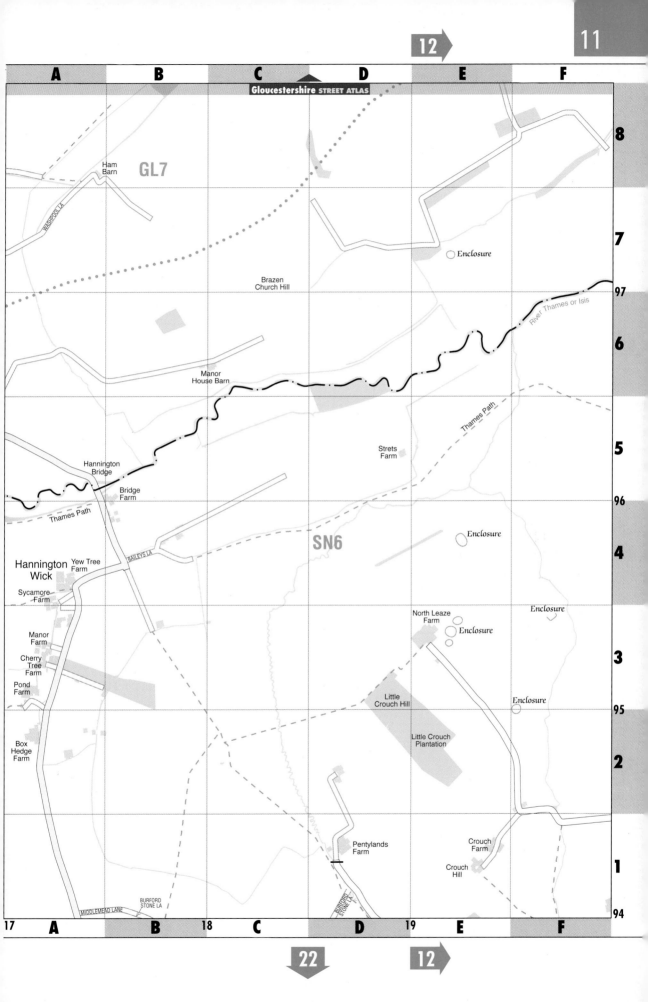

Gloucestershire STREET ATLAS

A   B   C   D   E   F

8

7

97

6

Enclosure

Brazen
Church Hill

River Thames or Isis

5

Manor
House Barn

Thames Path

Strets
Farm

Hannington
Bridge

96

Bridge
Farm

Thames Path

Enclosure

SN6

BAILEY'S LA

Hannington
Wick

Yew Tree
Farm

4

North Leaze
Farm

Enclosure

Enclosure

Sycamore
Farm

Manor
Farm

Enclosure

3

Cherry
Tree
Farm

Pond
Farm

Little
Crouch Hill

Box
Hedge
Farm

Little Crouch
Plantation

95

2

Pentylands
Farm

Crouch
Farm

Crouch
Hill

1

MIDDLEMEAD LANE

BURFORD
STONE LA

BURFORD
STONE LA

94

Ham
Barn

GL7

WISHPOOL LA

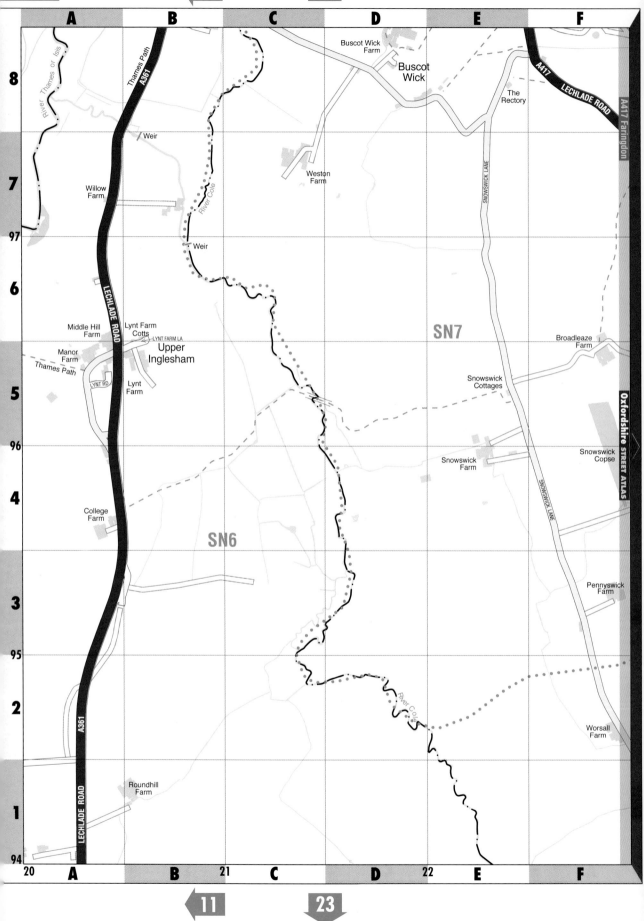

A B C D E F

8

7

97

6

5

96

4

3

95

2

1

94

20 21 22

A B C D E F

River Thames or Isis

Thames Path
A361

Weir

Willow Farm

River Cole

Weir

Buscot Wick Farm

Buscot Wick

Weston Farm

The Rectory

SNOWSWICK LANE

A417 LECHLADE ROAD

A417 Faringdon

SN7

Broadleaze Farm

Oxfordshire STREET ATLAS

LECHLADE ROAD

Middle Hill Farm

Manor Farm

Thames Path

LYNT RD

Lynt Farm Cotts

LYNT FARM LA

Upper Inglesham

Lynt Farm

Snowswick Cottages

Snowswick Copse

Snowswick Farm

SNOWSWICK LANE

College Farm

SN6

Pennyswick Farm

A361

River Cole

Worsall Farm

Roundhill Farm

LECHLADE ROAD

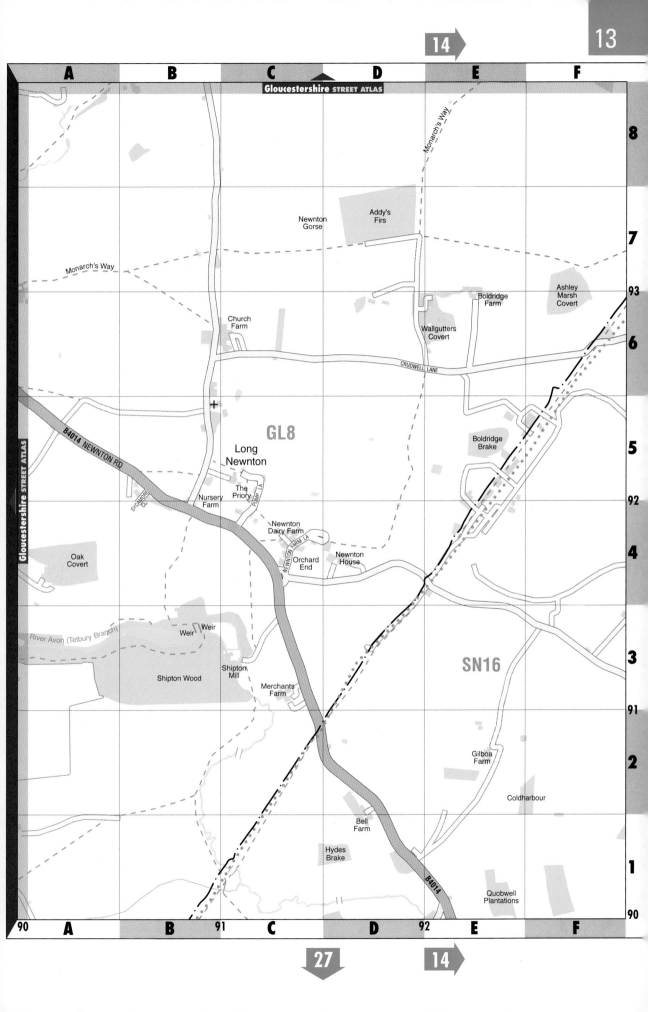

13
3

A
B
C
D
E
F
8
7
93
6
5
92
4
3
91
2
1
90
93
94
95
GL8
Ashley Marsh
Ash Bed
Withy Bed
West Crudwell
Chedglow
Crudwell Court Farm
Hotel
Crudwell CE Prim Sch
Manor Farm
PH
Crudwell
CRUDWELL LANE
Chedglow Barn
Gallops
TETBURY LANE
CHAPEL WAY
THE RIDGEWAY
TUNERS LANE
DAYS CT
BROOKSIDE
THE DAWNEYS
THE BUTTS
THE STREET
Ravenhurst
KINGS MD
GOOSELANDS
PO
PH
Hayleaze Farm
Village End
A429
SN16
Murcott
Murcott Park Farm
Murcott Farm
Meadow End
Upper Marsh Farm
Marsh Farm
Ashlands Court
CRUDWELL RD
Hankerton Field Farm
Bishoper Farm
Messels Plantation
Five Lanes Plantation
Five Lanes
Bishoper Plantation
The Wedge
The Cleaver
Grandchild Plantation
CHARLTON PK
TETBURY LA

13
28

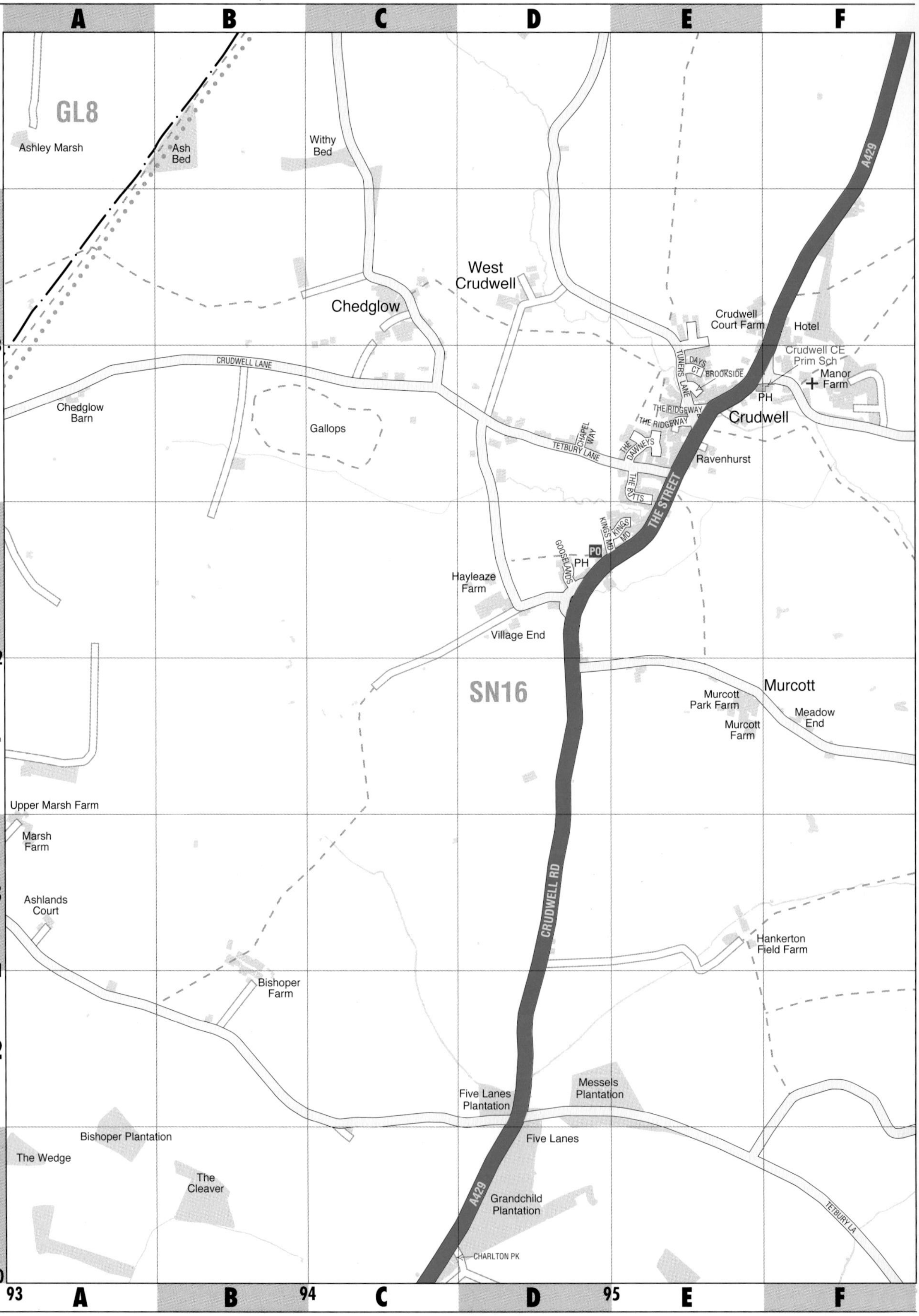

A   B   C   D   E   F

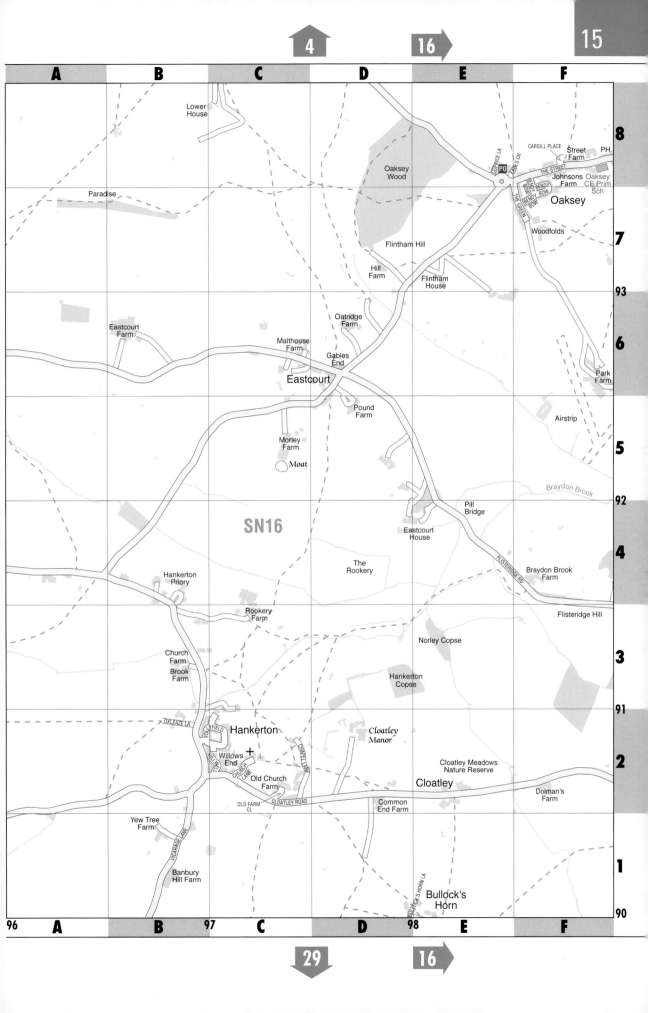

Lower House

Paradise

Oaksey Wood

CARGILL PLACE
Street Farm   PH
PO
Johnsons Farm   Oaksey CE Prim Sch
COPPICE LA
CATH.S CR
THE STREET
BENDY BOW
BENDY BOW
THE GREEN
Oaksey

Woodfolds

Flintham Hill

Hill Farm

Flintham House

Eastcourt Farm

Oatridge Farm

Malthouse Farm

Gables End

Park Farm

Eastcourt

Airstrip

Pound Farm

Morley Farm

Moat

Braydon Brook

Pill Bridge

SN16

Eastcourt House

The Rookery

FLISTERIDGE RD

Braydon Brook Farm

Hankerton Priory

Flisteridge Hill

Rookery Farm

Norley Copse

Church Farm

Hankerton Copse

Brook Farm

OXLEAZE LA

FOLLYFIELD

Hankerton

Cloatley Manor

HILL LA

Willows End

CHAPEL LANE

Cloatley Meadows Nature Reserve

CHURCH LANE

Old Church Farm

Cloatley

Dolman's Farm

OLD FARM CL

CLOATLEY ROAD

Common End Farm

Yew Tree Farm

VICARAGE LANE

Banbury Hill Farm

BULLOCK'S HORN LA

Bullock's Horn

A | B | C | D | E | F

8

Wheatsheaf LA
PH
WICK RD
THE STREET
Oaksey
THE STREET
Oaksey Bridge
Lower Moor Farm
Gravel Pit
Gravel Pit

Court FARM Farm
Oaksey CE Prim Sch
Mallard Lake

Swillbrook Lakes Nature Reserve

Clattinger Farm Nature Reserve

7

MINETY LANE

Clattinger Farm

Swillbrook Bridge

Lower Swillbrook Farm

93

Oaksey Ford Bridge

Swill Brook

Park Farm

6

Stert Farm

Cooles Farm

Barn Cooles Farm

Airstrip

RIGSBY'S LA

5

Lyngrove Farm

TIDLING CORNER

Oaksey Nursery

92

Upper Lyngrove

SN16

Brandiers Farm

LC

THE CROSSING

Field End

Ash Bed

Flisteridge Wood

Oakwood Farm

Row Ash Farm

4

OAKSEY ROAD

Maskelyne's Copse

Flistridge Farm

Mansells Farm

Upper Minety

CROSSLING LANE

Tellings DR

ST LEONARD'S CL

THE MOOR

3

FLISTERIDGE ROAD

PH
ST LEONARD'S ROW

Osbourne Farm

Cowleaze Farm

91

Thistledown
COPENACRE

Home Farm

Wellfield Farm

MEADOW CL

Cockrode Farm

Mill Farm
ELM FARM CLOSE

Laurel Farm

Alsperes Farm

Cloatley End Farm

HANKERTON ROAD

Elms Farm

The Elms

Buxwell Farm

2

Brookside Farm

BAKET HILL

HORNBURY HILL

Cloatley End

Emmett Hill Meadows Nature Reserve

Fairholme Farm

Brownockhill Plantation

DOG TRAP LANE

1

Woodward Farm

90

99 | A | B | 00 | C | D | 01 | E | F

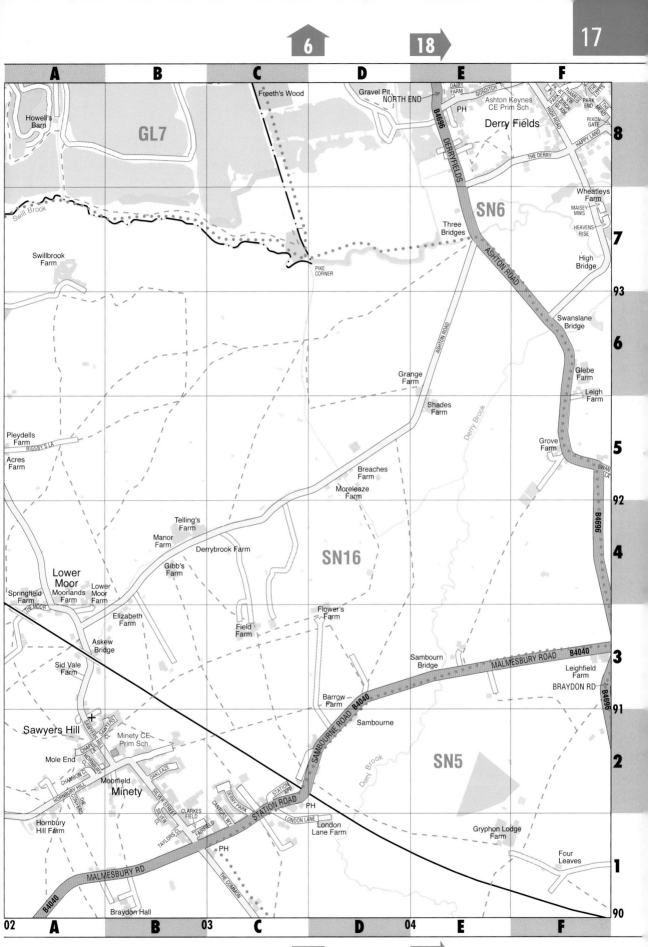

A B C D E F

8

Rixon Gate
Four Acre Cl
The Mead
Westfields Farm
Ashton Keynes
Happy Land
Thames Path
Gravel Pit
Manorbrook Lake
Thames Path

7

P
Waterhay Bridge
Waterhay Farm
Sewage Works
Waterhay
Upper Waterhay Nature Reserve
Brook Farm
River Thames or Isis
Manor Farm
Bournelake Farm

93

Upper Waterhay Farm
Johnnys Farm
Bourne Lake Pk
Chelworth Rd
Crossroads Farm

6

Archer's Farm
Malmesbury Road
Greenfield View

5

Cove House Farm
Home Farm
Brookside Farm
SN6
Meliot Farm
Cross Lanes Farm
Leigh
Stocks Farm
Leigh Hall Farm
Chelworth Rd

92

Knapp Farm
Swan Lane
Hillside
Bowood Angus Farm
PH
Purley Farm

4

Malmesbury Road
Mast

3

B4040
Greenacres
Blakehill Farm

91

Southleigh Farm
Leighfield Lodge Farm

2

B4696
Hardings Farm

Cox Hill
Stoke Common Meadows Nature Reserve
Stoke Common Farm
Stokecommon La

1

Braydon Rd
Bridge Farm
Bury Hill
P
Lower Farm
SN5

90

Bury Hill (Settlement)

05 A B 06 C D 07 E F

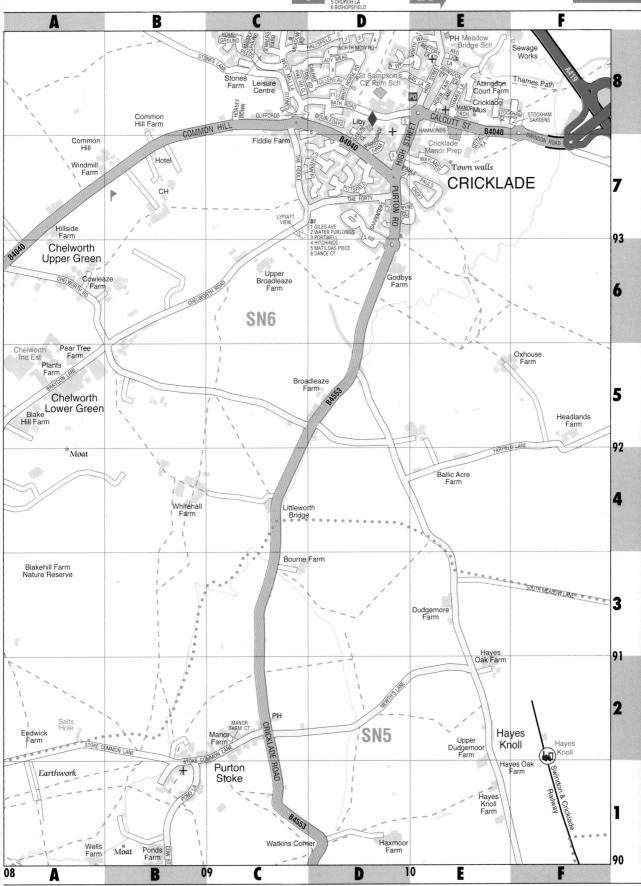

D8
1 FAIRFIELD
2 KITEFIELD
3 PLEYDELLS
4 BRANDERS
5 CHURCH LA
6 BISHOPSFIELD
7 BRAMBLE CT
8 CLOVER LA
9 WILLOW GRO
10 BLYTHE CL
11 SKYLARK RISE

CRICKLADE

SN6

SN5

A B C D E F

8

SWINDON RD

Water
Eaton
House

Thames Path

Manor
Farm

Calcutt

7

Calcutt Ct
Farm

Calcutt
Farm

Manor Farm
Cottages

A419

Port
Farm

93

SN6

Enclosures

6

Mast

Seven Bridges
Bridge

Seven
Bridges
Farm

GREAT ROSE LA

Kingshill
Farm

ROMAN BUILDING
(site of)

LITTLE ROSE LANE

5

Farfield
Farm

FARFIELD LA

92

4

Lower Widhill
Farm

Newlands
Farm

3

SOUTH MEADOW LANE

Weir

SN26

Chapel
Farm

BLUNSDON HILL

91

River Ray

LOWER WIDHILL FARM LA

William
Morris
Prim Sch

Blunsdon
Hill

A419

BLUNSDON HILL

SN5

Churchward
Sch

Upper Widhill
Farm

2

SOUTHALL CL 1
MERCER CL 2
BAYES CL 3
ARMFIELD RD 4
FAULKNER RD 5
SELWYN RD 6
LUMB CL 7
ARTISANS LA 8
WOOLNER RD 9
MILLAIS CL 10
TRELLIS ST 11
BALLIE CL 12
Tadpole Farm CE Prim Acad 13

Gravel
Pit

Shepherd's
Copse

WILLIAM MORRIS WAY

Great
Western
Acad

Upper
Widhill
Copse

Blunsdonhill
Copse

SHERRER LA

KEOHLER

IMAGE RD

DRESSER CL

CHERWELL

IRVINE CL

HORTA CL

LALIQUE CL

STEINLEN CL

1 HANKER CL
2 NEWLYN CL
3 JEFFREYCL
4 FELSTEAD
5 JOHN RUSKIN RD
6 DEMORGANCRES
7 SIDDAL ST
8 BURDEN RD
9 BEARDSLEY LA
10 NEWILL CL
11 KEMPE LA
12 DEARLE RD
13 JEBB CL
14 EGLANTYNE AVE
15 BURNE JONES AVE

PARSONS
PL

BLANCHARD RD

STICKLEX
CL

COOPER CL

SHAPLAND

EASTLAKE

MACKAN RD

MUCHA

SN25

RODMARTON
CL

LYTHM

SCLTON

BARNSLEY

VAN ERP CL

JEKYLL

HEYGATE

MATHEWS
CL

PEARSON RD

CHATFIELD

HORNE TIFFANY
CL

CRESWICK

Abbey Farm
Prim Sch

1

Grove
Farm

CITRINE CL

RUBY CL

STONEYWELL
CL

HIGH GROUND

DANEWAY

THE LEASOWES

GIMSON CRES

GREENE ST

MAIZEY RD

MALLORY
CL

DIAMOND CRES

BLACKWELL CL

A LETT CRES

MACKAY CRES

BRANTWOOD CL

TOWBREE AVE

90

05 A B 06 C D 07 E F

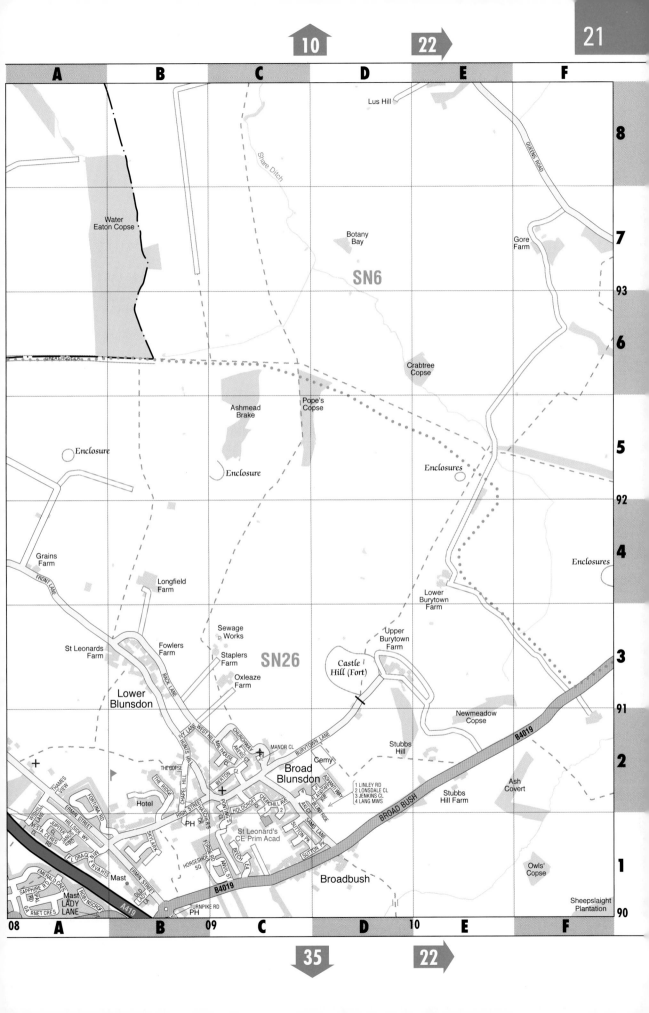

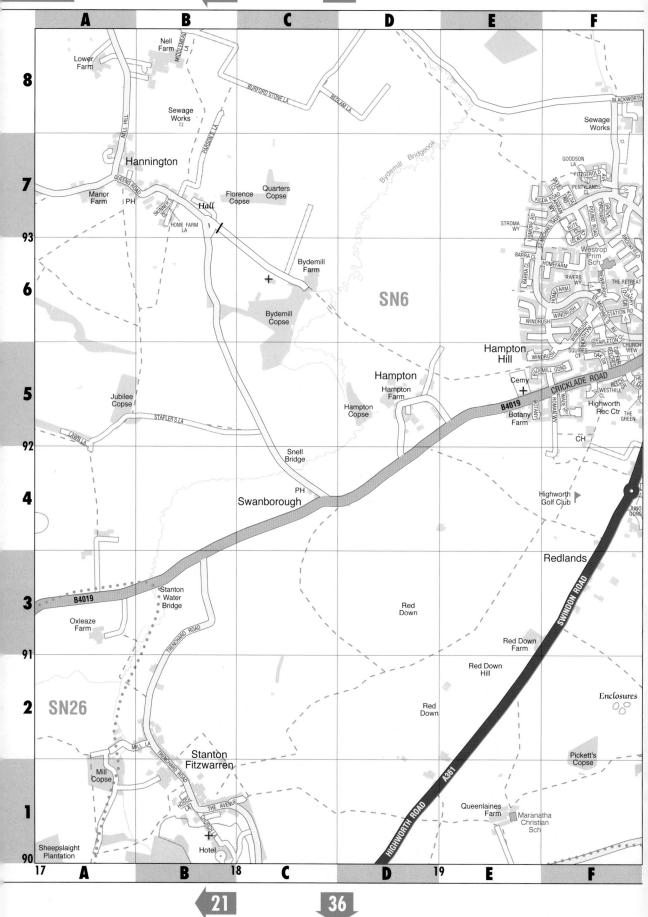

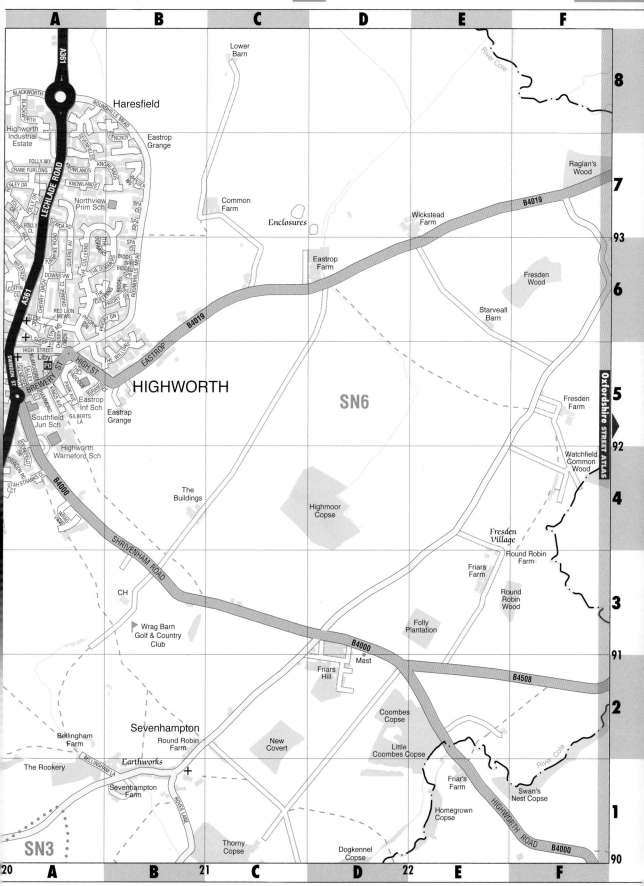

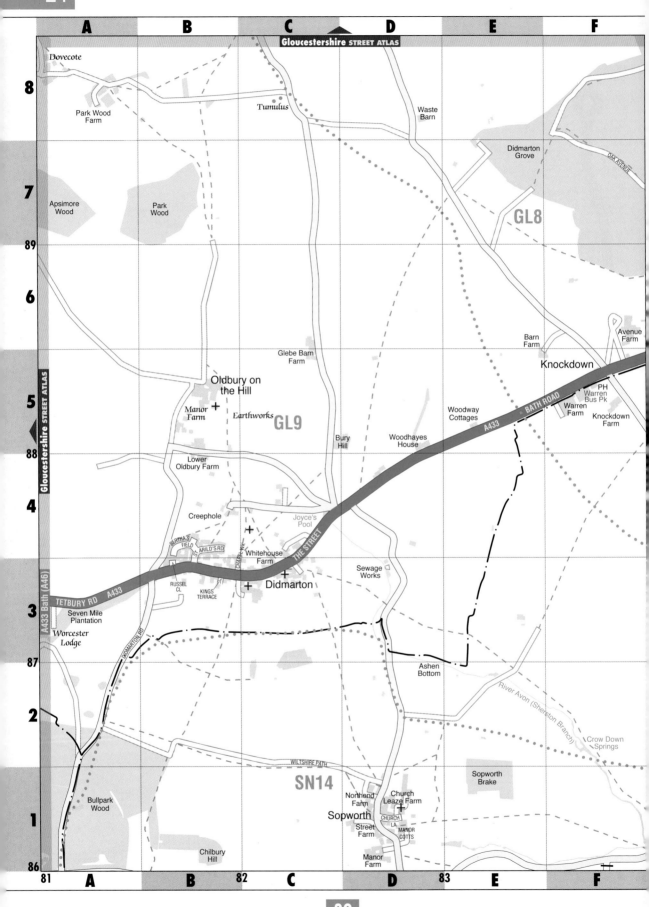

8
7
89
6
5
88
4
87
2
1
86
81   A   82   B   82   C   D   83   E   F

Dovecote

Park Wood
Farm

Tumulus

Waste
Barn

Didmarton
Grove

OAK AVENUE

Apsimore
Wood

Park
Wood

GL8

Gloucestershire STREET ATLAS

Glebe Barn
Farm

Barn
Farm

Avenue
Farm

Knockdown

Oldbury on
the Hill

Manor
Farm

Earthworks

GL9

Bury
Hill

Woodway
Cottages

Woodhayes
House

BATH ROAD

A433

PH
Warren
Bus Pk

Warren
Farm

Knockdown
Farm

Lower
Oldbury Farm

Creephole

Joyce's
Pool

BERTHA'S
FIELD

ARILD'S RD

CHLEBE WK

Whitehouse
Farm

THE STREET

Sewage
Works

A433 Bath (A46)

TETBURY RD   A433

RUSSEL
CL

DIDMARTON RD

KINGS
TERRACE

Didmarton

Seven Mile
Plantation

Ashen
Bottom

River Avon (Sherston Branch)

Worcester
Lodge

Crow Down
Springs

WILTSHIRE PATH

SN14

Sopworth
Brake

Bullpark
Wood

Northend
Farm

Church
Leaze Farm

CHURCH
LA

Sopworth

Street
Farm

MANOR
COTTS

Chilbury
Hill

Manor
Farm

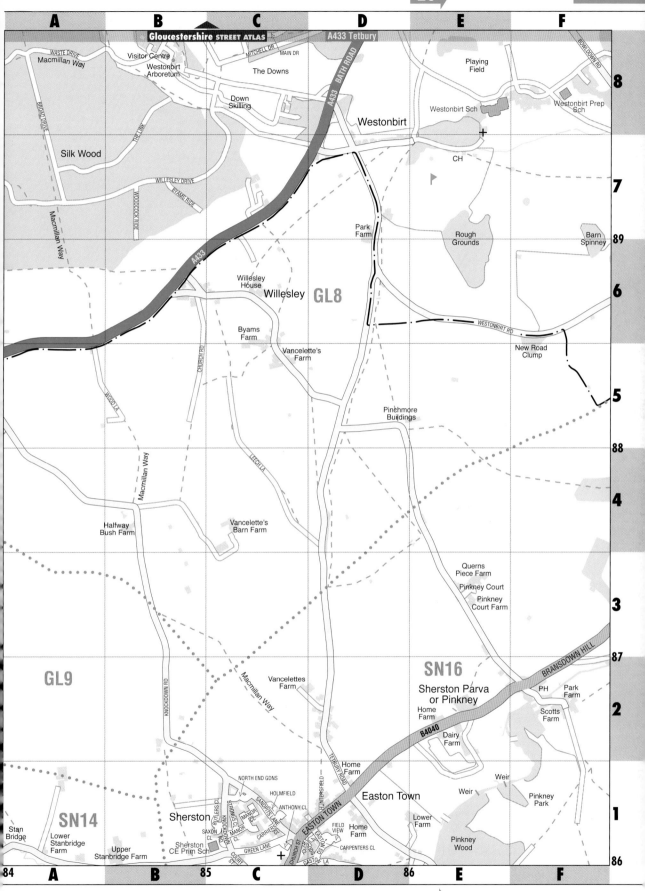

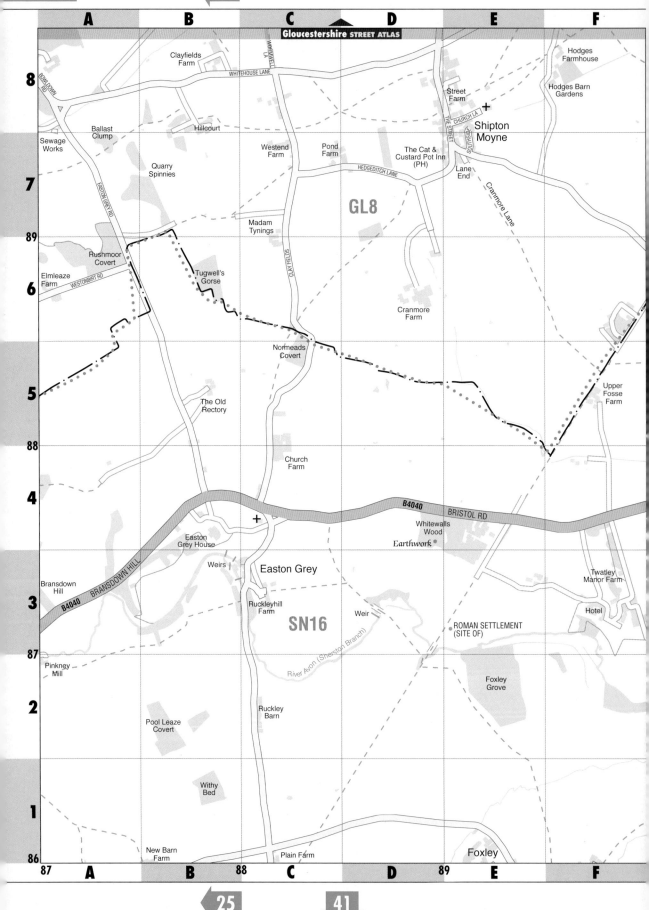

A   B   C   D   E   F

Gloucestershire STREET ATLAS

8

Hodges
Farmhouse

Clayfields
Farm

WHITEHOUSE LANE

Street
Farm

Hodges Barn
Gardens

Shipton
Moyne

Ballast
Clump

Hillcourt

Sewage
Works

Westend
Farm

Pond
Farm

The Cat &
Custard Pot Inn
(PH)

Quarry
Spinnies

7

Lane
End

HEDGEDITCH LANE

GL8

Cranmore Lane

Madam
Tynings

89

Rushmoor
Covert

CLAY FIELDS

Elmleaze
Farm

WESTONBIRT RD

Tugwell's
Gorse

6

Cranmore
Farm

5

Normeads
Covert

Upper
Fosse
Farm

The Old
Rectory

88

Church
Farm

4

B4040   BRISTOL RD

Whitewalls
Wood

Earthwork

Easton
Grey House

Weirs

Easton Grey

Twatley
Manor Farm

Bransdown
Hill

BRANSDOWN HILL

B4040

Ruckleyhill
Farm

SN16

Weir

Hotel

ROMAN SETTLEMENT
(SITE OF)

3

87

Pinkney
Mill

River Avon (Sherston Branch)

Foxley
Grove

2

Pool Leaze
Covert

Ruckley
Barn

1

Withy
Bed

86

New Barn
Farm

Plain Farm

Foxley

87   A   B   88   C   D   89   E   F

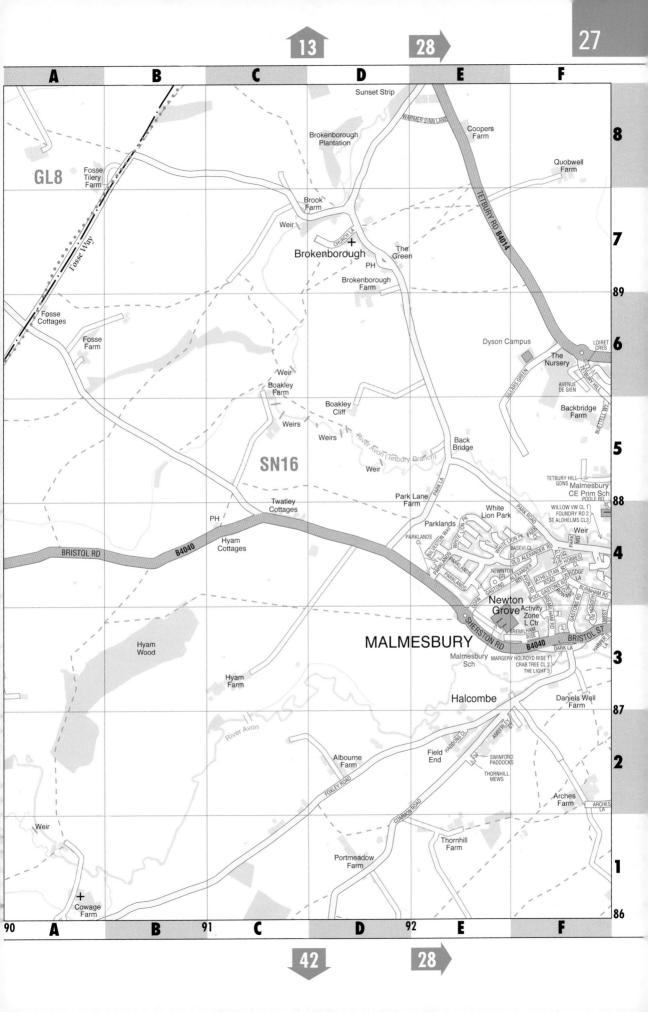

A **B** **C** **D** **E** **F**

8

Sunset Strip

WARMER SINN LANE

Coopers Farm

Brokenborough Plantation

GL8

Fosse Tilery Farm

Quobwell Farm

TETBURY RD B4014

7

Brook Farm

Weir

Church La

Brokenborough

PH

The Green

89

Fosse Cottages

Brokenborough Farm

Fosse Farm

Dyson Campus

LOIRET CRES

The Nursery

6

TETBURY HILL

Weir

Boakley Farm

Boakley Cliff

SILLARS GREEN

AVENUE DE GIEN

BLUETELL WY

Backbridge Farm

SN16

Weirs

Weirs

River Avon (Tetbury Branch)

Back Bridge

5

Weir

Weir

PARK LA

TETBURY HILL GDNS

Malmesbury CE Prim Sch

POOLE RD

88

Twatley Cottages

Park Lane Farm

PARK ROAD

WILLOW VW CL 1
FOUNDRY RD 2
ST ALDHELMS CL3

Parklands

White Lion Park

PARK MD

Weir

PH

Hyam Cottages

PARKLANDS CL

WHITE LION PK

SILVESTON WAY

PARKLANDS

BASEVI CL

OLD ALEXANDER RD

PARK RD

ST ALDHELMS HOBBES CL

HODGE LA

1

4

BRISTOL RD

B4040

PARKLANDS

PARKLANDS

NEWNTON GR

ALEXANDER

ATHELSTAN ROAD

GASTONS RD

AVON RD

BURNHAM RD

BREMILHAM RD

WEST ST

Hyam Wood

GASTONS

Newton Grove

Activity Zone L Ctr

BREMILHAM RISE

HARPER'S LA

3

DOWN

SHERSTON RD

MALMESBURY

Malmesbury Sch

MARGERY HOLROYD RISE 1
CRAB TREE CL 2
THE LIGHT 3

DARK LA

BRISTOL ST

Hyam Farm

Halcombe

Daniels Well Farm

87

Albourne Farm

Field End

AMBERLEY CT

SWINFORD PADDOCKS

HADDONS CL

Arches Farm

ARCHES LA

2

River Avon

FOXLEY ROAD

THORNHILL MEWS

COMMON ROAD

Thornhill Farm

Weir

Portmeadow Farm

1

Cowage Farm

86

90 **A** 91 **B** **C** **D** 92 **E** **F**

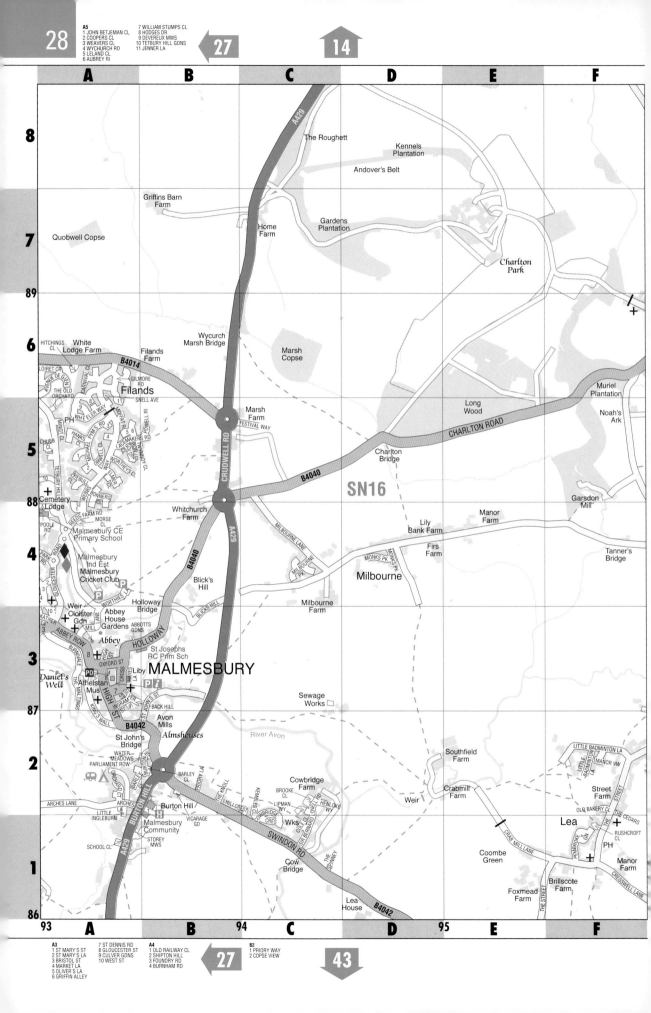

28

A5
1 JOHN BETJEMAN CL
2 COOPERS CL
3 WEAVERS CL
4 WYCHURCH RD
5 LELAND CL
6 AUBREY RI

7 WILLIAM STUMPS CL
8 HODGES DR
9 DEVEREUX MWS
10 TETBURY HILL GDNS
11 JENNER LA

27

14

A B C D E F

8
7
89
6
5
88
4
3
87
2
86

The Roughett
Kennels Plantation
Andover's Belt
Griffins Barn Farm
Home Farm
Gardens Plantation
Charlton Park
Quobwell Copse

Wycurch Marsh Bridge
HITCHINGS CL
White Lodge Farm
Filands Farm
Marsh Copse
Muriel Plantation

LOIRET CR
AVENUE DE GLEN
THE OLD ORCHARD
B4014
GILMORE RD
Filands
SNELL AVE

Long Wood
Noah's Ark

CARNIVAL CL
WHEELER WAY
MOFFATT RD
POWELL RI
Marsh Farm
FESTIVAL WAY
Marsh Farm

PH
CHUBB CL
MINOT CL
HANKS CL
MICHAEL PI
PIM'S RD
ORNELL WAY
ELMER WAY
LACEMAKERS CL
TANNERY CL
WORTHEYS CL
BONNERS CL

CRUDWELL RD
B4040
Charlton Bridge
CHARLTON ROAD
Garsdon Mill

Whitchurch Farm

SN16

MILBOURNE LANE
Lily Bank Farm
Manor Farm

TETBURY HILL RD
Cemetery Lodge
WEBBS CL
REEDS FARM RD
MORSE CL
POOLE RD
Malmesbury CE Primary School

Firs Farm
Tanner's Bridge

PARK RD
GLOUCESTER RD
Malmesbury Ind Est
Malmesbury Cricket Club
P
WORTHIES LA
B4040
A429
Blick's Hill
MONKS PK
MILBOURNE PK
Milbourne

KATIFER LA
Weir
Cloister Gdn
P
Abbey House Gardens
ABBOTTS GDNS
Holloway Bridge
BLICKS HILL
Milbourne Farm

ABBEY ROW
MILL
Abbey
HOLLOWAY
St Josephs RC Prim Sch

Daniel's Well
HIGH ST
OXFORD ST
CROSS HAYES
St Johns St
INGRAM ST
MALMESBURY
Liby
PO
Athelstan Mus
P
KING'S WALL
BACK HILL
Sewage Works

B4042
Avon Mills
St John's Bridge
Almshouses
River Avon

WATER MEADOWS
PARLIAMENT ROW
BARLEY CL
PRIORY LA
Cowbridge Farm
Southfield Farm
LITTLE BADMINTON LA
LITTLE BADMINTON LA
MANOR VW

ARCHES LANE
ORCHARD CL
BARLEY
BURTON HILL
THE KNOLL
KEMBLE DR
BROOKE CL
LIPMAN WY
Weir
Crabmill Farm
Street Farm

LITTLE INGLEBURN
ARCHES LA
VICARAGE GD
HILLCREST
COWBRIDGE CRES
CASTLE CL
ST BERNARD RD
OVETT RD
HEMLOCK WY
Wks
OLD BAKERY CL
THE CEDARS
Lea
RUSHCROFT CL
PH

Burton Hill
H
Malmesbury Community
STOREY MWS
SWINDON RD
THE SPINNEY
CRAB MILL LANE
PENARROW GN
Coombe Green
Manor Farm

SCHOOL CL
A429
Cow Bridge
Lea House
B4042
Foxmead Farm
Brillscote Farm
THE STREET
CRESSWELL LANE

93 A B 94 C D 95 E F

A3
1 ST MARY'S ST
2 ST MARY'S LA
3 BRISTOL ST
4 MARKET LA
5 OLIVER'S LA
6 GRIFFIN ALLEY

7 ST DENNIS RD
8 GLOUCESTER ST
9 CULVER GDNS
10 WEST ST

A4
1 OLD RAILWAY CL
2 SHIPTON HILL
3 FOUNDRY RD
4 BURNHAM RD

B2
1 PRIORY WAY
2 COPSE VIEW

27

43

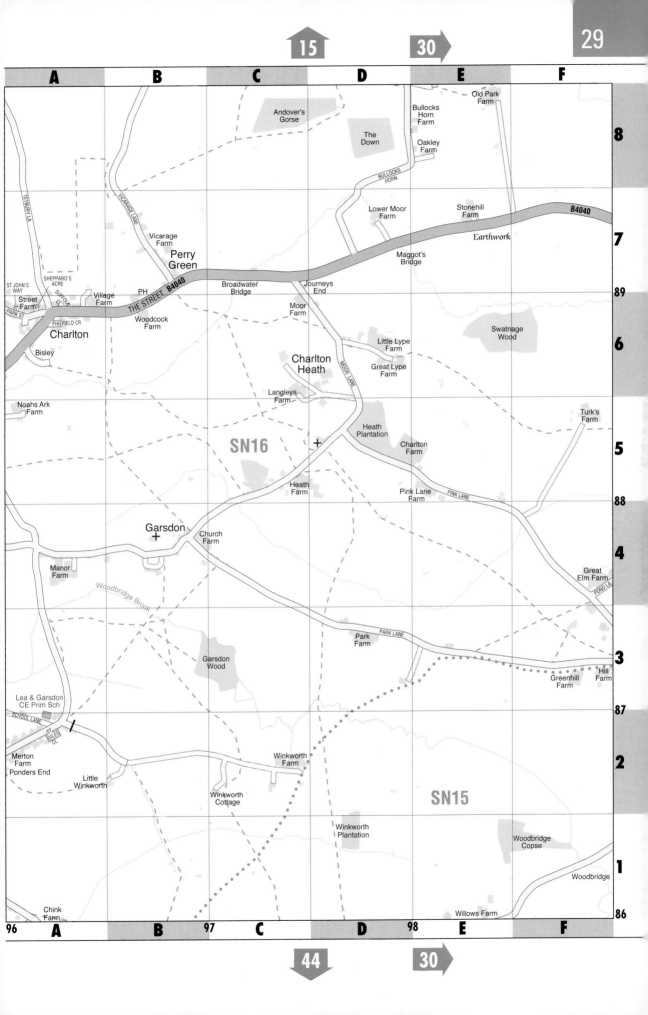

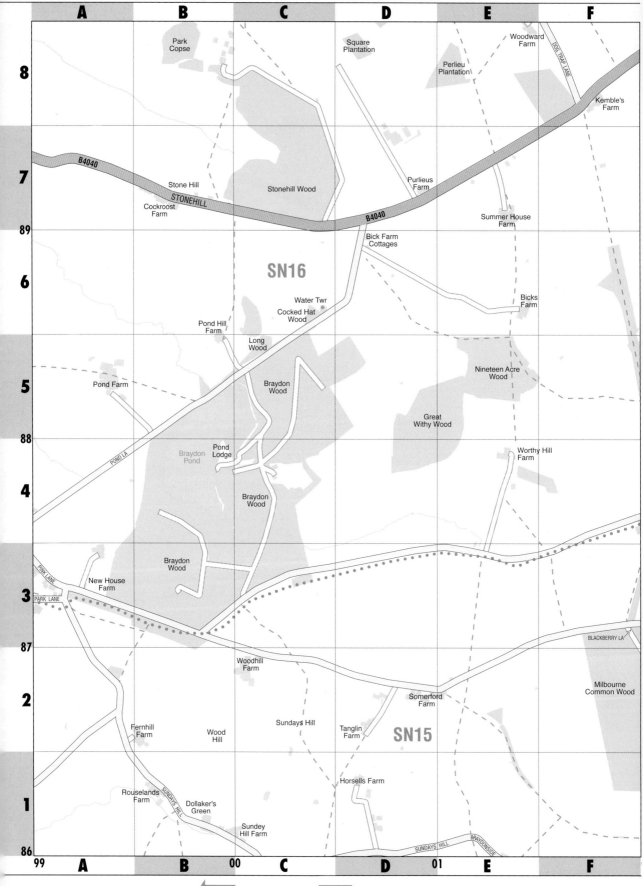

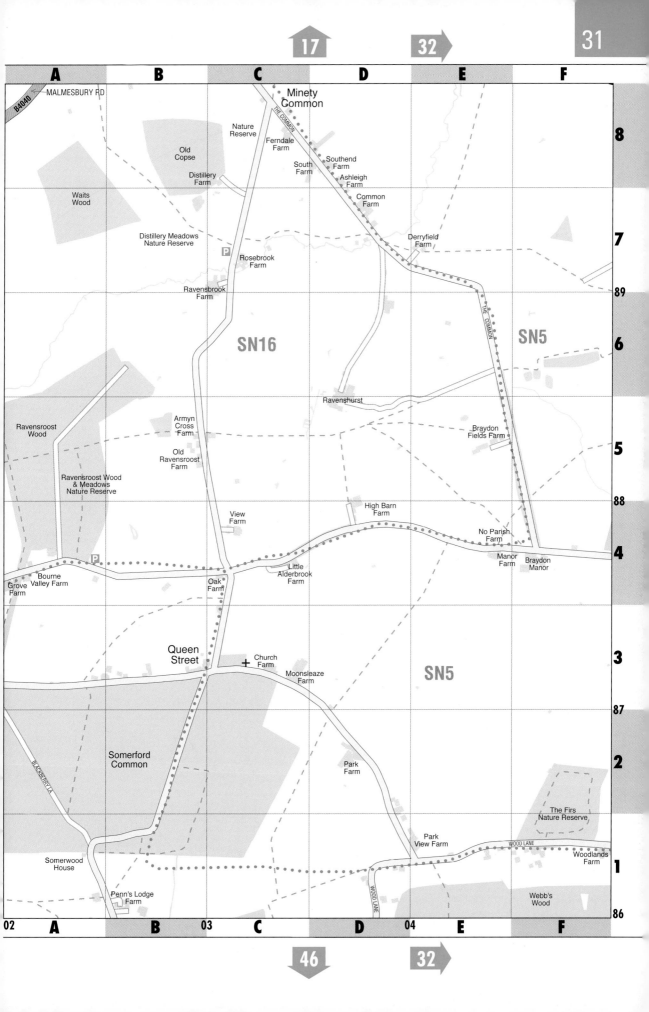

Map content:

Top navigation: 17 ↑ 32 →

Grid columns (top): A B C D E F
Grid rows (right): 8 7 89 6 5 88 4 3 87 2 1 86

B4040

MALMESBURY RD

Minety Common

Nature Reserve

Old Copse

Ferndale Farm

Southend Farm

South Farm

Ashleigh Farm

Distillery Farm

Waits Wood

Common Farm

Distillery Meadows Nature Reserve

Derryfield Farm

Rosebrook Farm

SN5

Ravensbrook Farm

SN16

THE COMMON

Ravenshurst

Ravensroost Wood

Armyn Cross Farm

Braydon Fields Farm

Old Ravensroost Farm

Ravensroost Wood & Meadows Nature Reserve

View Farm

High Barn Farm

No Parish Farm

Little Alderbrook Farm

Manor Farm

Braydon Manor

Bourne Valley Farm

Grove Farm

Oak Farm

Queen Street

Church Farm

Moonsleaze Farm

SN5

BLACKBERRY LA

Somerford Common

Park Farm

The Firs Nature Reserve

Park View Farm

WOOD LANE

Woodlands Farm

Somerwood House

WOOD LANE

Webb's Wood

Penn's Lodge Farm

Grid columns (bottom): 02 A B 03 C D 04 E F

Bottom navigation: 46 ↓ 32 →

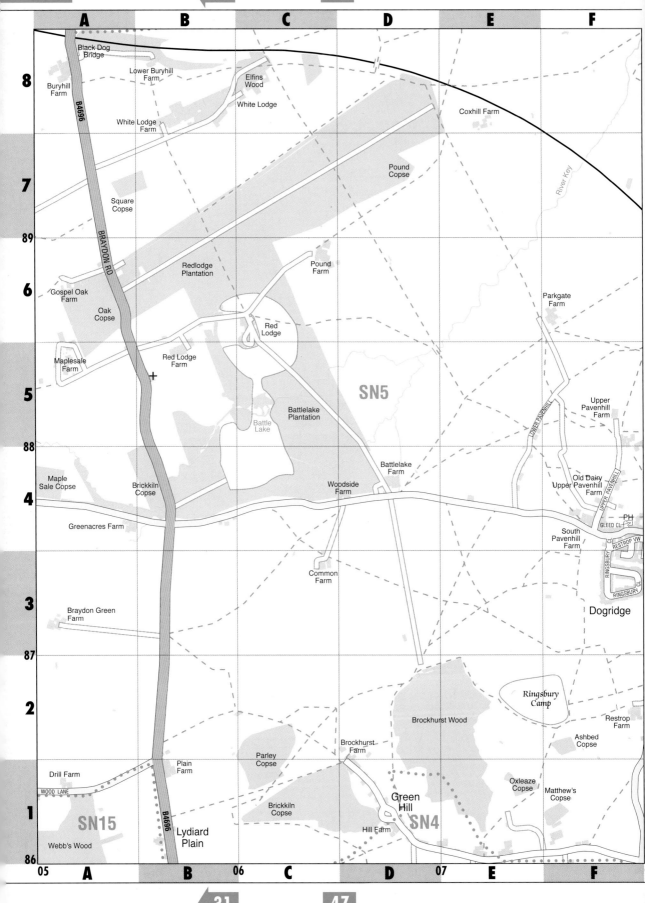

Black Dog Bridge

Lower Buryhill Farm

Elfins Wood

White Lodge

Buryhill Farm

White Lodge Farm

B4696

BRAYDON RD

Square Copse

Coxhill Farm

Pound Copse

River Key

Redlodge Plantation

Pound Farm

Gospel Oak Farm

Oak Copse

Red Lodge

Parkgate Farm

Maplesale Farm

Red Lodge Farm

Battlelake Plantation

Battle Lake

SN5

LOWER PAVENHILL

Upper Pavenhill Farm

Maple Sale Copse

Brickkiln Copse

Battlelake Farm

Woodside Farm

UPPER PAVENHILL

Old Dairy Upper Pavenhill Farm

PH

GLEED CL

Greenacres Farm

South Pavenhill Farm

RESTROP VW

RINGSBURY CL

RINGSBURY CL

Braydon Green Farm

Common Farm

Dogridge

Ringsbury Camp

Restrop Farm

Brockhurst Wood

Ashbed Copse

Drill Farm

Plain Farm

Brockhurst Farm

Parley Copse

Oxleaze Copse

Matthew's Copse

WOOD LANE

SN15

B4696

Brickkiln Copse

Green Hill

SN4

Lydiard Plain

Webb's Wood

Hill Farm

A B C D E F

8

Bentham LA
Swindon & Cricklade Railway
Bentham House Farm
Hurstead Farm
CRICKLADE ROAD
B4553
HAYES KNOLL
Crosslanes Farm
Blunsdon
Bentham Farm
Bentham House
COW STREET
POND LA
Bentham LA
PACKHORSE LANE
CROSSLANES
TADPOLE LA

Old Dairy Farm
PACK HORSE
Woodwards Bridge Farm

New Farm
Park House Farm
Polly Down Farm
Down Farm

7

West Marsh
Sewage Works
MOPES LANE
CRICKLADE ROAD
Downfield Farm
SMITHHEAD LA
B4553

89

Pound Farm
SN5

Hansells Farm
Pry Farm

6

CLARDON LANE
WIDHAM
Pen Farm
PH
NEW ROAD
Widham Bridge
COLLINS LANE
THE PRY

LOCKS LA
Widham Grove
Widham
LC
Diana Lodge

5

Purton Common
WHITFIELD CL
WITT'S LANE
GLEVUM CL
SHAFTSBURY CL
STATION ROAD

HOGGS LA
Malthouse Farm
VASTERNE HILL
VASTERNE CL
JUBILEE EST
SMITH'S CT
THE SIDINGS
BAMFORD CL

88

Paven Hill
VASTERNE
WAITE MEADS CLOSE

WILLOWBROOK
Purton Liby & Museum
PO
HYDE LA
Gallops Farm

4

Purton
HOOKS HL
PH
OLD SURGERY CL
THE HYDE
Quarry Farm

THE MASONS
THOMPSON CT
CEDAR GLEN
HIGH STREET
COLLEGE RD
PLAY CL
Church St
THE HYDE

RESTROP VW
PAVENHILL
LONG ACRE
THE PEAK
St Marys CE Prim Sch
The Fox

DOGRIDGE
HIGHRIDGE CL
RED GABLES CL
REID'S PIECE
THE PEAK
REID'S PIECE
Mill Farm
B4553

3

ORCH WATER GDNS FIELD
RESTROP ROAD
POOR ST
Bradon Forest Sch
CHURCH END
COMMON PLATT

BATTLEWELL
WARD CL
CL FLOUD
KIBBLEWHITE CL
Manor Farm
Manor House
Purton House
Church End
Fox Mill Farm

MUD LA
87

Restrop
Bagbury Lane Farm
PH

2

Common Platt
THE CRESCENT

BAGBURY LANE
Manor Hill Farm
WASHPOOL
RUSSLEY

Bagbury Green Farm
STONE LANE
ROUGHMOOR FARM CL

1

Bagbury Farm
Keycroft Copse
Lydiard Millicent

THE BEECHES
Lydiard House Farm
Manor House
Church Farm
CHESTNUT SPRINGS

LYDIARD GREEN
Manor Farm
CHURCH

86

08 A B 09 C D 10 E F

F1
1 MARDALE CL
2 DALEFOOT CL
3 BERRY COPSE
4 KEYCROFT COPSE

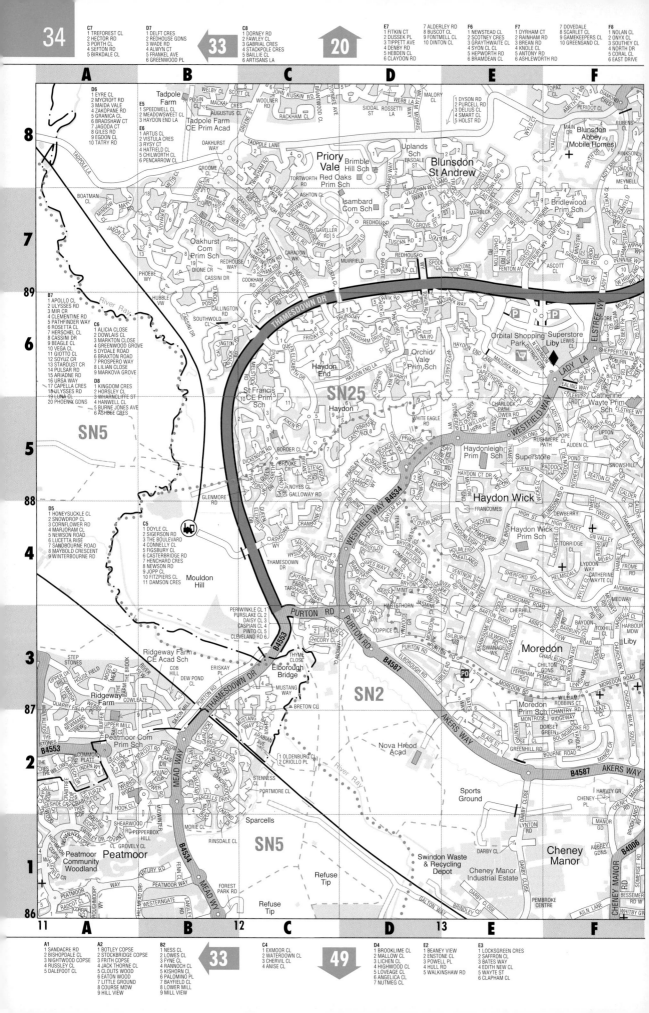

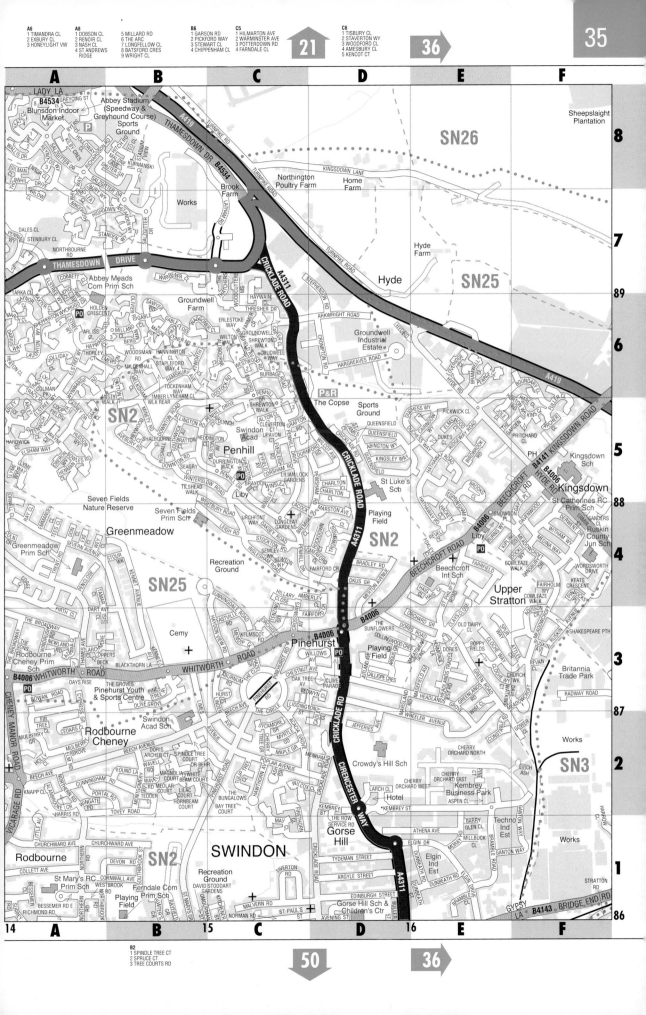

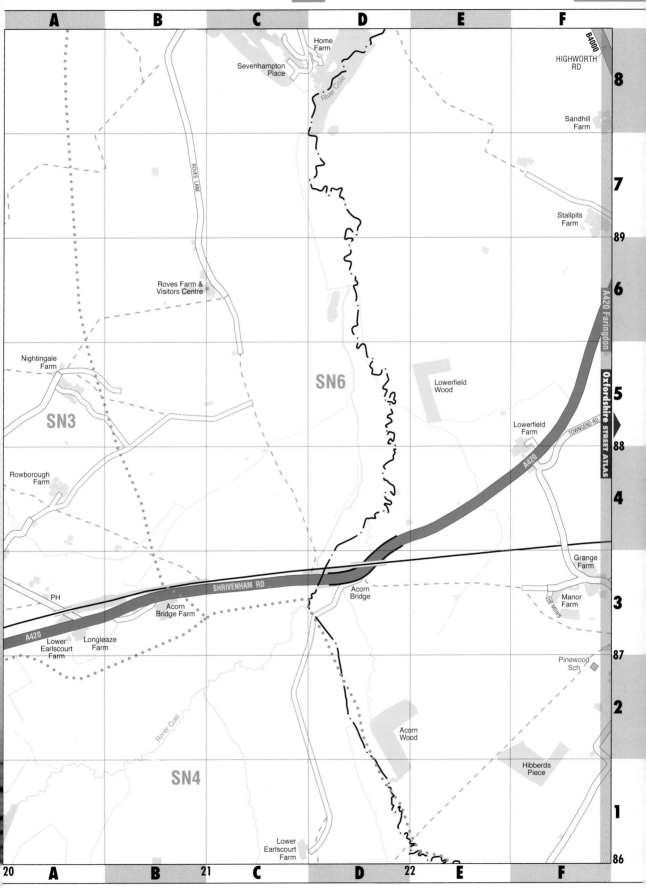

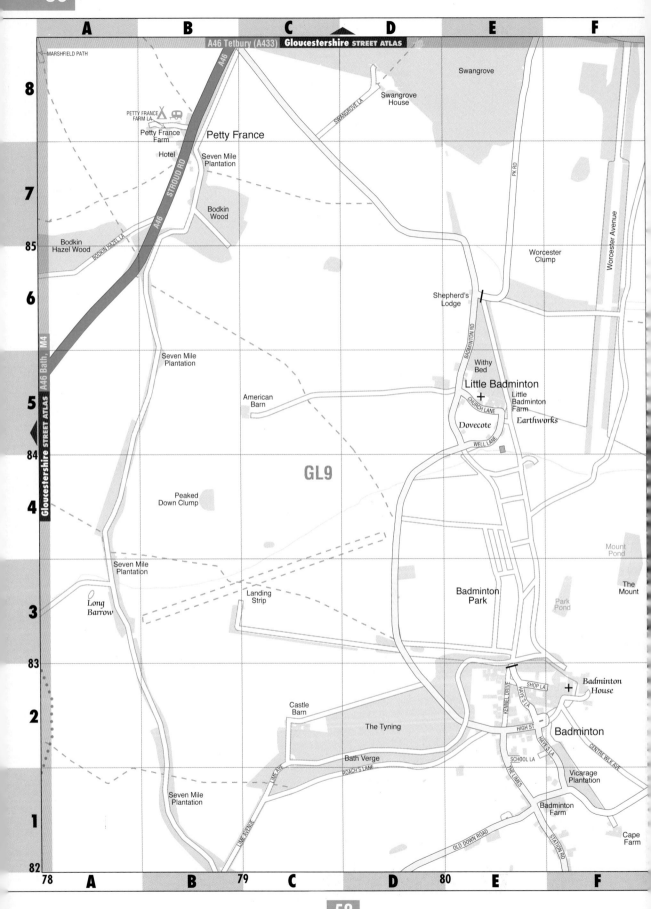

MARSHFIELD PATH

Swangrove

Swangrove House

PETTY FRANCE FARM LA.

Petty France Farm

Petty France

Hotel

Seven Mile Plantation

Bodkin Wood

PK RD

Bodkin Hazel Wood

BODKIN HAZEL LA.

Worcester Avenue

Worcester Clump

A46 Bath, M4

Gloucestershire STREET ATLAS

STROUD RD

A46

Seven Mile Plantation

American Barn

Shepherd's Lodge

BADMINTON RD

Withy Bed

Little Badminton

Little Badminton Farm

Earthworks

Dovecote

CHURCH LANE

WELL LANE

GL9

Peaked Down Clump

Seven Mile Plantation

Long Barrow

Landing Strip

Badminton Park

Mount Pond

Park Pond

The Mount

Badminton House

Castle Barn

The Tyning

KENNEL DRIVE

SHOP LA.

HAYES LA.

HIGH ST

Badminton

CENTRE WLK AVE

Bath Verge

ROACH'S LANE

LIME AVE

SCHOOL LA.

HAYES LA.

THE LIMES

Vicarage Plantation

Seven Mile Plantation

LIME AVENUE

Badminton Farm

STATION RD

OLD DOWN ROAD

Cape Farm

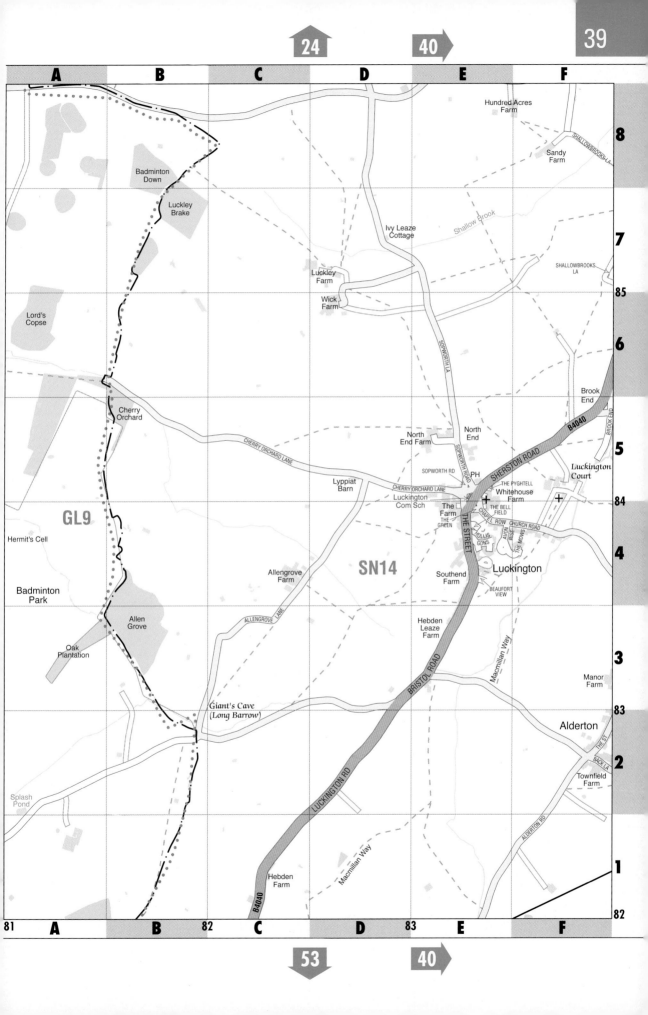

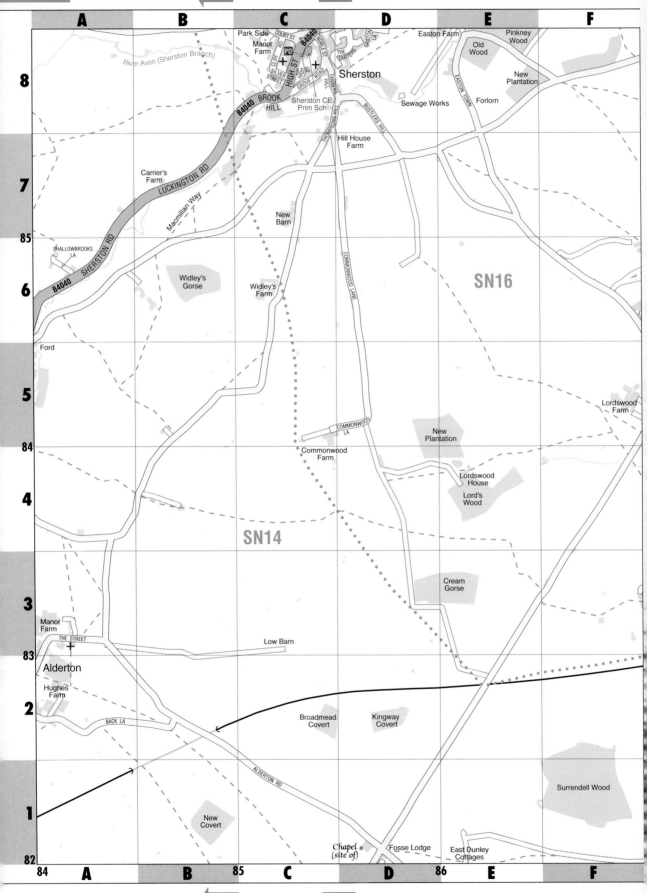

A **B** **C** **D** **E** **F**

River Avon (Sherston Branch)

Park Side
Manor Farm
PO
Sherston
Easton Farm
Old Wood
Pinkney Wood
New Plantation

COURT ST
CLIFF RD
SILVER STREET
HIGH ST
GROVE ROAD
NOBLE ST
THE TARTERS
GASTON LA

B4040
BROOK HILL

Sherston CE Prim Sch
Sewage Works
Forlorn

Carrier's Farm
LUCKINGTON RD
Macmillan Way

New Barn

Hill House Farm
BUSTERS HILL
EASTON TOWN
THOMPSON'S HILL
TANNERS HILL

SHALLOWBROOKS LA
B4040 SHERSTON RD

Widley's Gorse
Widley's Farm
COMMONWOOD LANE

SN16

Ford

Lordswood Farm

COMMONWOOD LA
New Plantation
Lordswood House
Lord's Wood

Commonwood Farm

SN14

Cream Gorse

Manor Farm
THE STREET
Low Barn
Alderton
Hughes Farm
BACK LA

Broadmead Covert
Kingway Covert

ALDERTON RD

Surrendell Wood

New Covert

Chapel (site of)
Fosse Lodge
East Dunley Cottages

84 **A** 85 **B** **C** 86 **D** **E** **F**

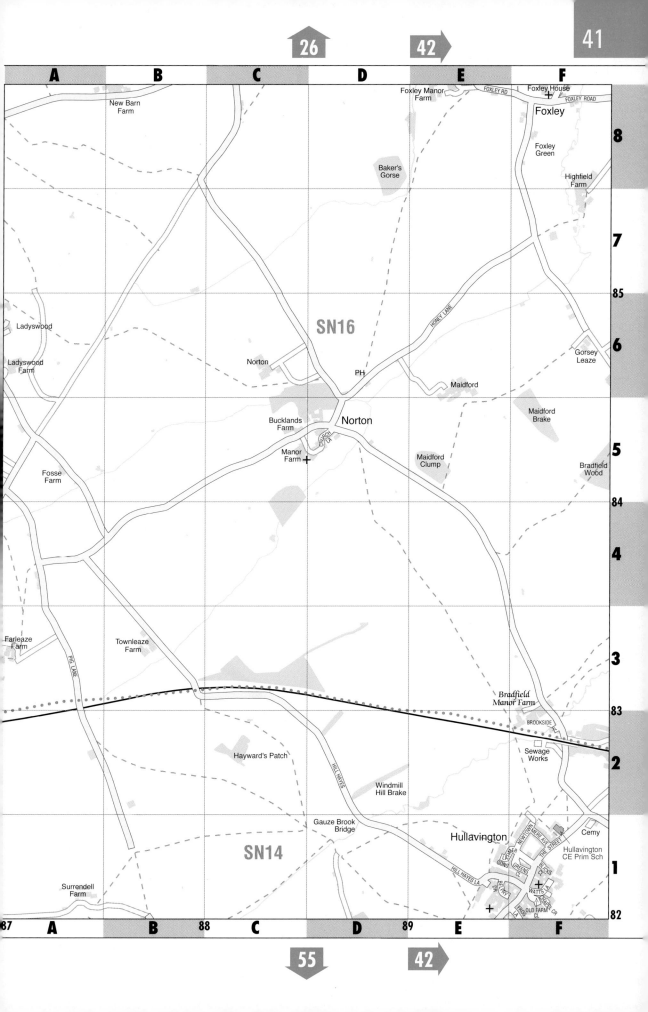

A B C D E F

Foxley Manor Farm
FOXLEY RD
Foxley House
FOXLEY ROAD
Foxley

8

New Barn Farm

Foxley Green

Baker's Gorse

Highfield Farm

7

85

SN16

HONEY LANE

6

Ladyswood

Gorsey Leaze

Ladyswood Farm

Norton

PH

Maidford

Maidford Brake

Norton

5

Bucklands Farm

CHURCH LA

Maidford Clump

Bradfield Wood

Fosse Farm

Manor Farm

84

4

Farleaze Farm

Townleaze Farm

PIG LANE

Bradfield Manor Farm

3

BROOKSIDE

83

Sewage Works

2

Hayward's Patch

HILL HAYES

Windmill Hill Brake

Gauze Brook Bridge

Hullavington

NEWNHAM MERE AV
THE STREET
Cemy

Hullavington CE Prim Sch

SN14

HILL HAYES LA

1

Surrendell Farm

82

A   B   C   D   E   F

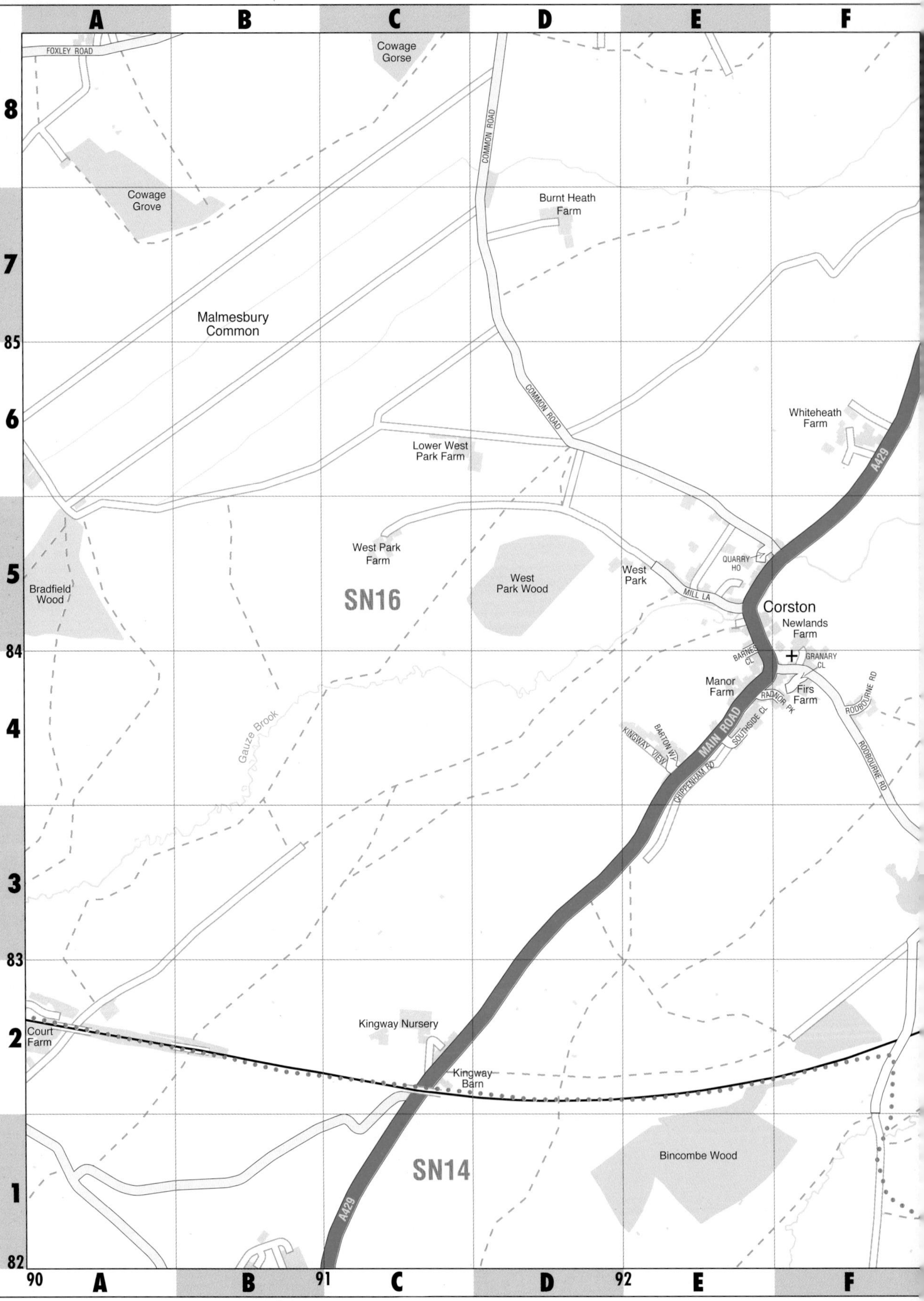

FOXLEY ROAD

Cowage
Gorse

8

Cowage
Grove

Burnt Heath
Farm

7

85

Malmesbury
Common

COMMON ROAD

6

Lower West
Park Farm

Whiteheath
Farm

A429

West Park
Farm

QUARRY
HO

5

Bradfield
Wood

SN16

West
Park Wood

West
Park

MILL LA

Corston

Newlands
Farm

GRANARY
CL

84

Gauze Brook

BARNES
CL

Manor
Farm

Firs
Farm

RADNOR PK

RODBOURNE RD

4

KINGWAY VIEW

BARTON WY

MAIN ROAD

SOUTHSIDE CL

CHIPPENHAM RD

RODBOURNE RD

3

83

2

Court
Farm

Kingway Nursery

Kingway
Barn

A429

SN14

Bincombe Wood

1

A429

82

90   A   B   91   C   D   92   E   F

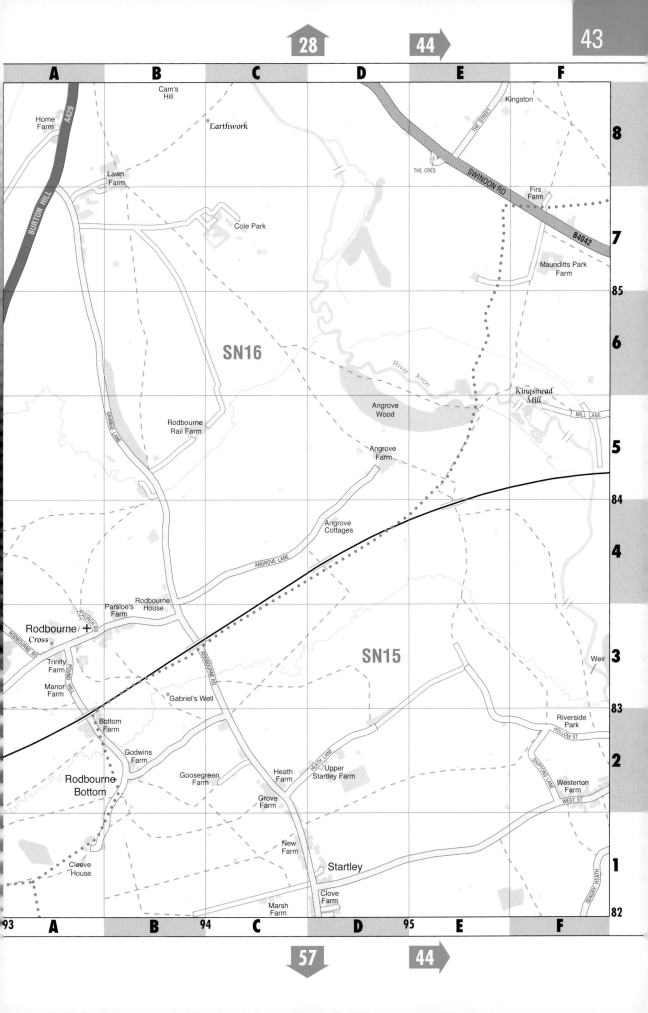

A | B | C | D | E | F

8

SN16

Chink Farm

Cleverton Farm

Manor Farm

Coles Farm

Lea Wood

CRESSWELL LANE

Cleverton

Street Farm

Crows Nest Farm

7

Malthouse Cottage Farm

B4042

Hillview Farm

Lovett Farm

B4042

EAST END LA

Malthouse Farm

85

Coach House Farm

6

THE HILL

CLAY STREET

Field End

East End Farm

Kingsmead House

PH

Forge Mill Farm

THE STREET

LEA LA

Yew Tree Farm

EAST END LANE

5

Church Farm

Manor Farm

Little Somerford

MILL LANE

MEADOW LANE

Cemy

Brinkworth Brook

84

The Council Houses

SN15

DAUNTSEY RD

Somerford Bridge

4

The Withy Bed

Idover Demesne Farm

3

Peter's Wood

River Avon

Home Idover Farm

Motte

Brook Farm

SOMERBROOK

Nannies Belt

Church Farm

FROG LA

THE FOLLY

83

HOLLOW STREET

PARK LANE

Great Somerford

RIVERSIDE PK

TOP STREET

PADDOCK CL

WILKINS LA

Somerfords Walter Powell VA CE Prim Sch

The Lake Covert

Dauntsey Park

2

MANOR PK

WEST STREET

MINTY

Dauntsey House

PH

PO

Broadfield Farm

DAUNTSEY ROAD

Dauntsey End

CHURCH LANE

Idover House

SEAGRY HEATH

Downfield Farm

Dauntsey Church Bridge

Glebe Farm

RIDGEWAY LA

MILE DR

CHURCH LANE

Chestnut Farm

1

82

96 | A | 97 | B | C | 97 | D | 98 | E | F

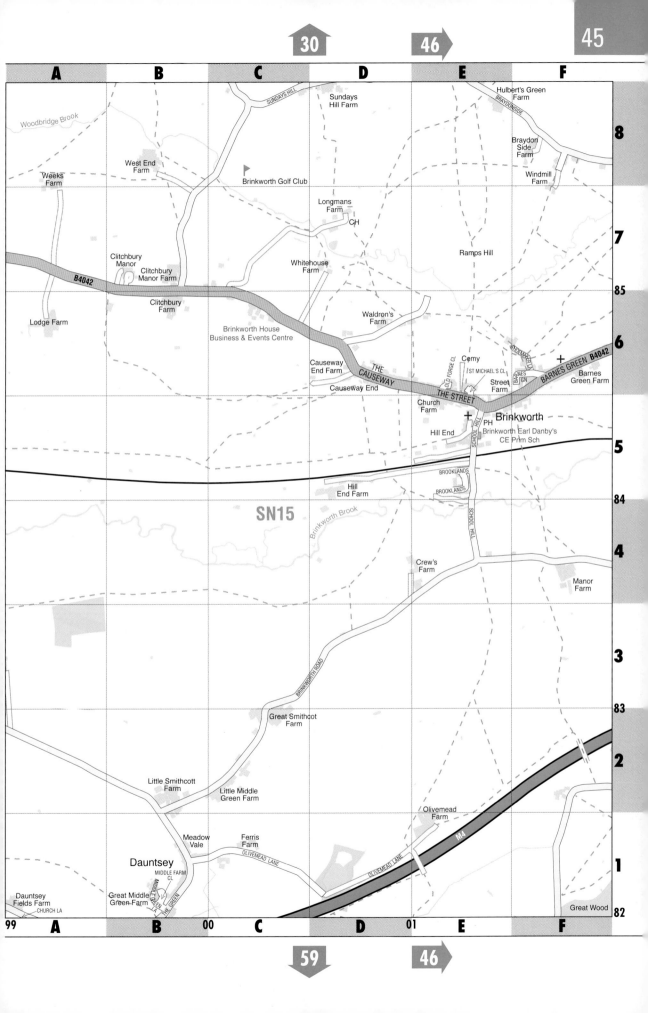

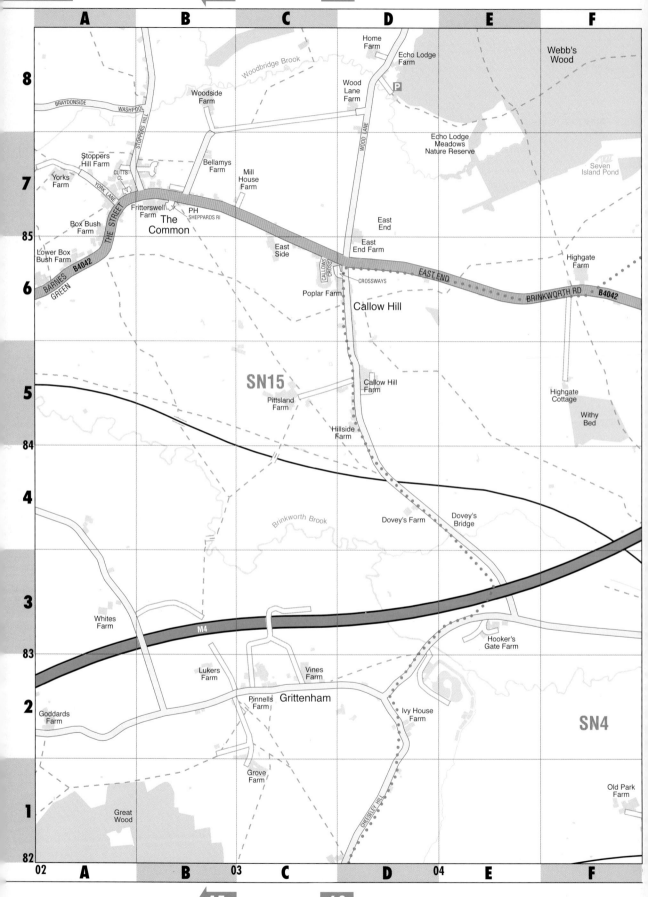

A   B   C   D   E   F

8

Woodbridge Brook

Home
Farm

Echo Lodge
Farm

Webb's
Wood

Braydonside   WASHPOOL

Woodside
Farm

Wood
Lane
Farm

P

Echo Lodge
Meadows
Nature Reserve

Seven
Island Pond

7

Stoppers
Hill Farm

CUTTS
CL

Bellamys
Farm

Mill
House
Farm

Yorks
Farm

STOPPERS HILL

YORK LANE

85

Box Bush
Farm

THE STREET

Fritterswell
Farm

PH
SHEPPARDS RI

The
Common

East
Side

East
End

East
End Farm

Highgate
Farm

Lower Box
Bush Farm

BARNES
GREEN

B4042

CALLOWS CROSS

CROSSWAYS

EAST END

BRINKWORTH RD   B4042

6

Poplar Farm

Callow Hill

SN15

Callow Hill
Farm

Highgate
Cottage

5

Pittsland
Farm

Withy
Bed

84

Hillside
Farm

4

Brinkworth Brook

Dovey's Farm

Dovey's
Bridge

3

Whites
Farm

M4

Hooker's
Gate Farm

83

Lukers
Farm

Vines
Farm

2

Goddards
Farm

Pinnells
Farm

Grittenham

Ivy House
Farm

SN4

Grove
Farm

1

Great
Wood

CHESSLEY HILL

Old Park
Farm

82

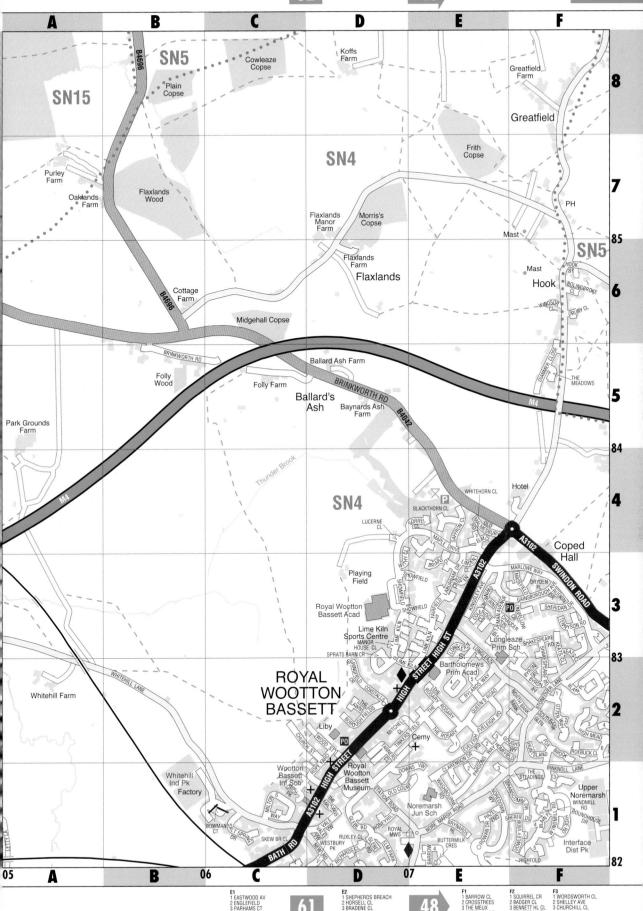

A B C D E F

SN5
SN15
SN5
SN4

Purley Farm
Oaklands Farm
Flaxlands Wood
Cottage Farm
B4696
Cowleaze Copse
Plain Copse
Koffs Farm

Greatfield Farm
Greatfield
Frith Copse
PH
Mast
Hook
Mast
HOOK ST
BOLINGBROKE CL
DRURY CL
WINDSOR CL

Flaxlands Manor Farm
Morris's Copse
Flaxlands Farm
Flaxlands

Midgehall Copse
BRINKWORTH RD
Folly Wood
Folly Farm
Ballard Ash Farm
Ballard's Ash
Baynards Ash Farm
BRINKWORTH RD
B4042
DANNER CLOSE
THE MEADOWS
M4

Park Grounds Farm
M4
Thunder Brook

SN4

Hotel
WHITEHORN CL
BLACKTHORN CL
Coped Hall
A3102
SWINDON ROAD

Playing Field
Royal Wootton Bassett Acad
Lime Kiln Sports Centre
MANOR HOUSE CL
SPRATS BARN CR

LUCERNE CL
SORREL CL
MAPLE DRIVE
SAFFRON CL
ELM CL
OLD MALMESBURY RD
SHOWFIELD
SHOWFIELD
LIME KILN
LIME KILN
LABURNUM
FAIRFIELD
KINGSLEY AVE
BENJAMIN CHASE CL
LONGLEAZE
Longleaze Prim Sch
MARLOWE WAY
DRYDEN CL
MANSFIELD
RUSKIN CL
GAINSBOROUGH RD
SHERIDAN DR
TENNYSON RD
SHAKESPEARE RD
KEATS CL
BYRON
BLAKE

Whitehill Farm
WHITEHILL LANE
ROYAL WOOTTON BASSETT
HIGH STREET HIGH ST
Bartholomews Prim Acad)
RYLANDS WAY
RYLANDS ROAD
QUEEN'S ROAD
EVELEIGH RD
NORTH BANK
STONEACRE
SOUTHBANK
OUTER WAY
HIGH MEAD
FOX BROOK
ROEBUCK CL

Liby
PO
THE LAWS
THE BOROUGH FIELDS
SPRINGFIELD
CONSTABLE
MITCHELL CL
TINKERS FIELD
THE ROSARY
THE ROSARY
EVELEIGH RD
GOUGHS WAY
HAZEL ISLAND
BINKNOLL LANE
THE STEADINGS

Whitehill Ind Pk Factory
Wootton Bassett Inf Sch
Royal Wootton Bassett Museum
CHURCH ST
ROPE ABD
WOOD ST
THE MALWAYS
VALE VW
DOWNS VW
STATION ROAD
OLD COLAR
ROYAL MWS
CLARENDON DR
PARSONS WAY
WASHBOURNE
NORELOWAN
BRANSCOMBE DR
SHERFIELDS
NORWLEY VIEW
HIGHFOLD

BOWMAN CT
MILTON WAY
SALT SPRING DR
SKEW BR CL
A3102
BATH RD
HIGH STREET
NEW RD
WESTBURY PK
RICHARDS CL
RUXLEY CL
GLEBE RD
HONEYHILL
ELM PARK
BARROW
BUTTERMILK CRES
Noremarsh Jun Sch
NORE MARSH ROAD
BAYNARDS
ORCHARD END
HAZEL DR
BARNBY
WINDMILL RD
ROUNDHOUSE DR
BLAIN PL
Upper Noremarsh
Interface Dist Pk

8 7 85 6 5 84 4 3 83 2 82 1

05 06 07

E1
1 EASTWOOD AV
2 ENGLEFIELD
3 PARHAMS CT
4 DAISY BROOK

E2
1 SHEPHERDS BREACH
2 HORSELL CL
3 BRADENE CL
4 BUXTON WAY
5 CRICKETERS CL

F1
1 BARROW CL
2 CROSSTREES
3 THE MEUX
4 POSTMILL DR
5 POTTERS PL

F2
1 SQUIRREL CR
2 BADGER CL
3 BENNETT HL CL
4 SQUIRES HL CL
5 BARDSEY CL
6 GARRAWAYS

F3
1 WORDSWORTH CL
2 SHELLEY AVE
3 CHURCHILL CL

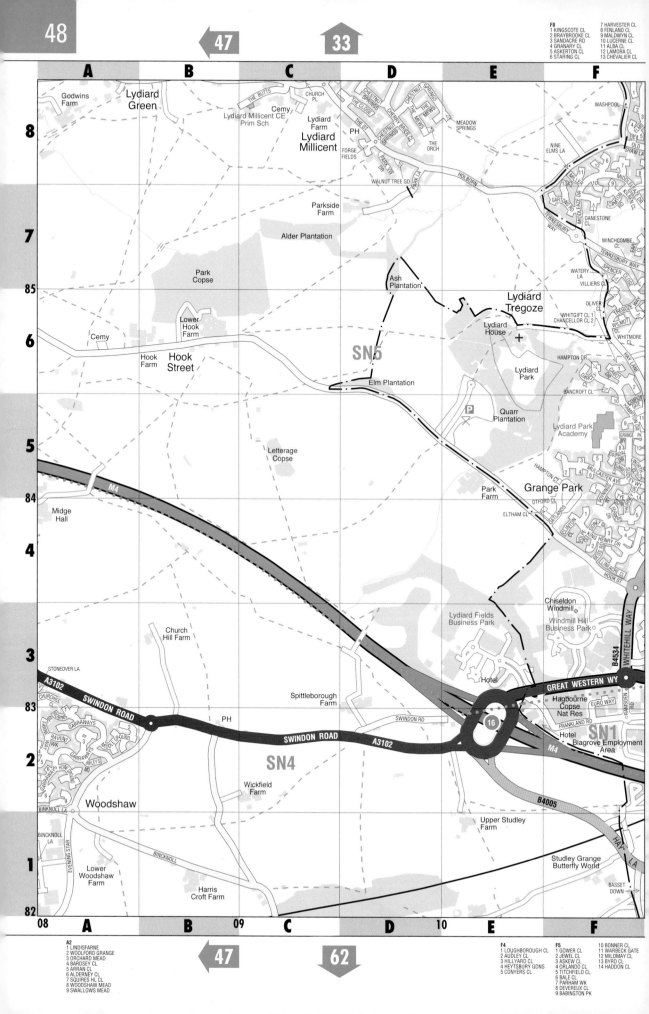

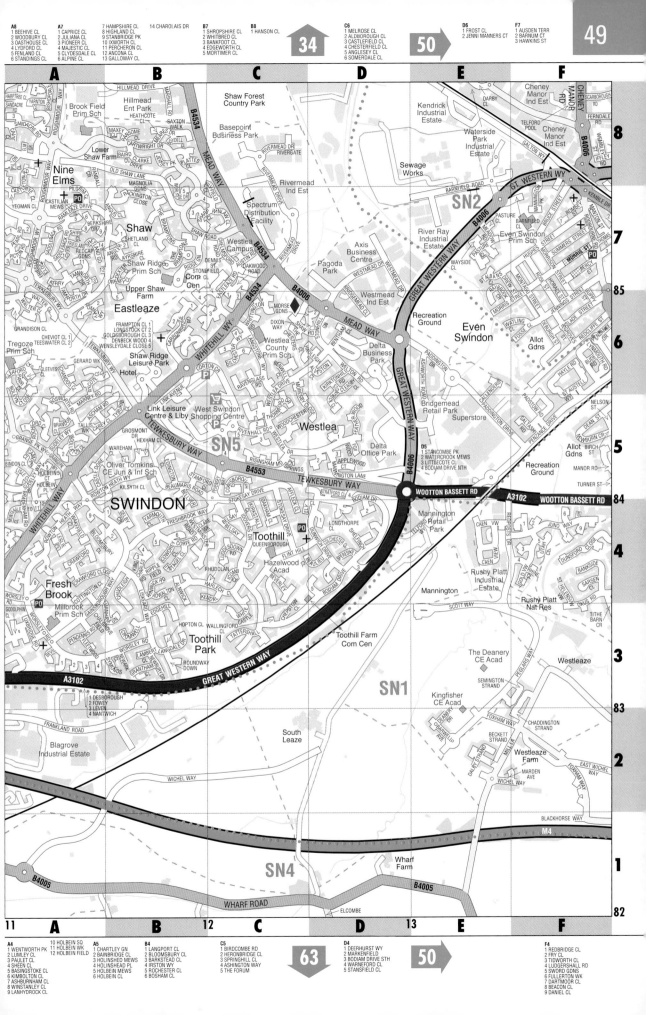

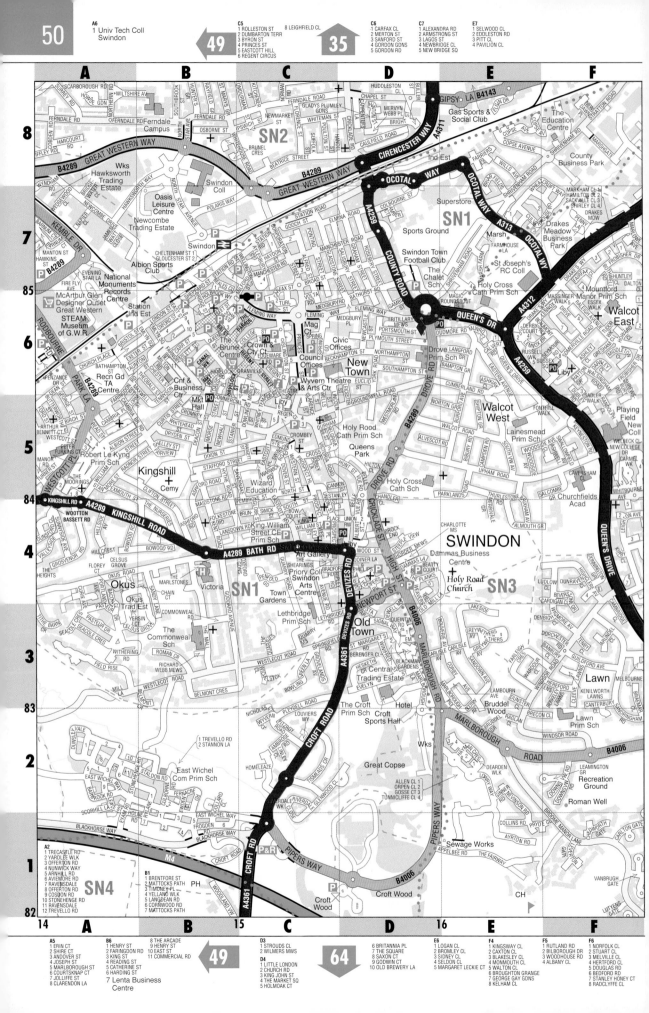

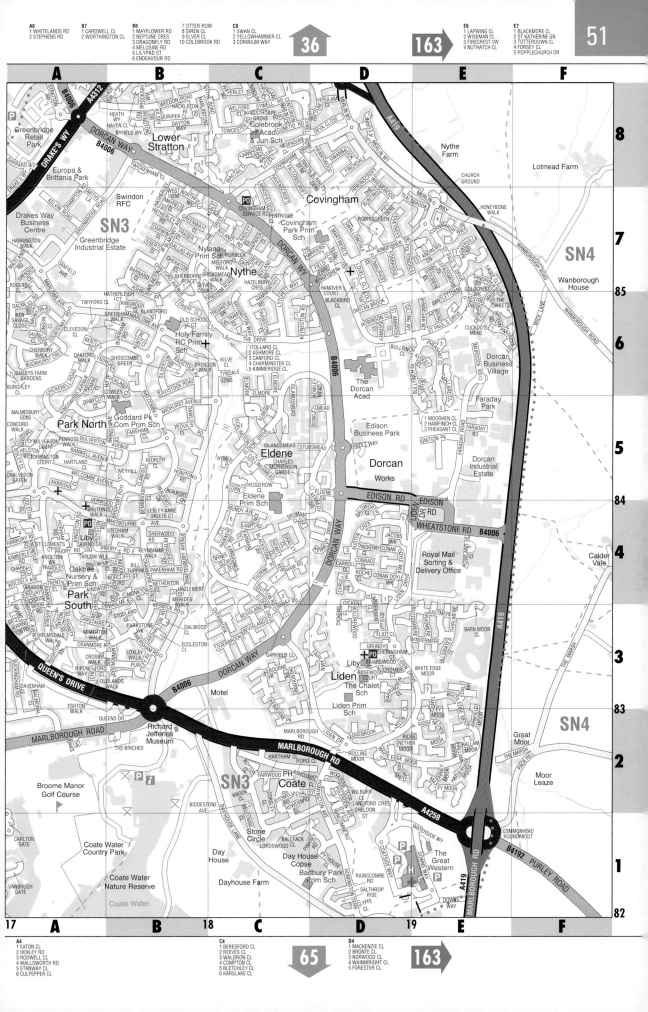

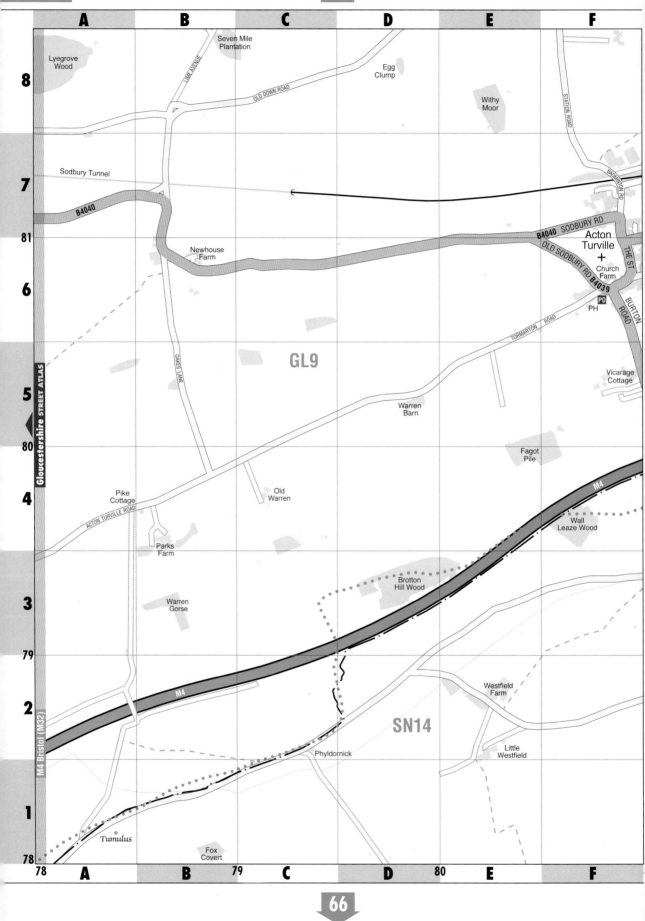

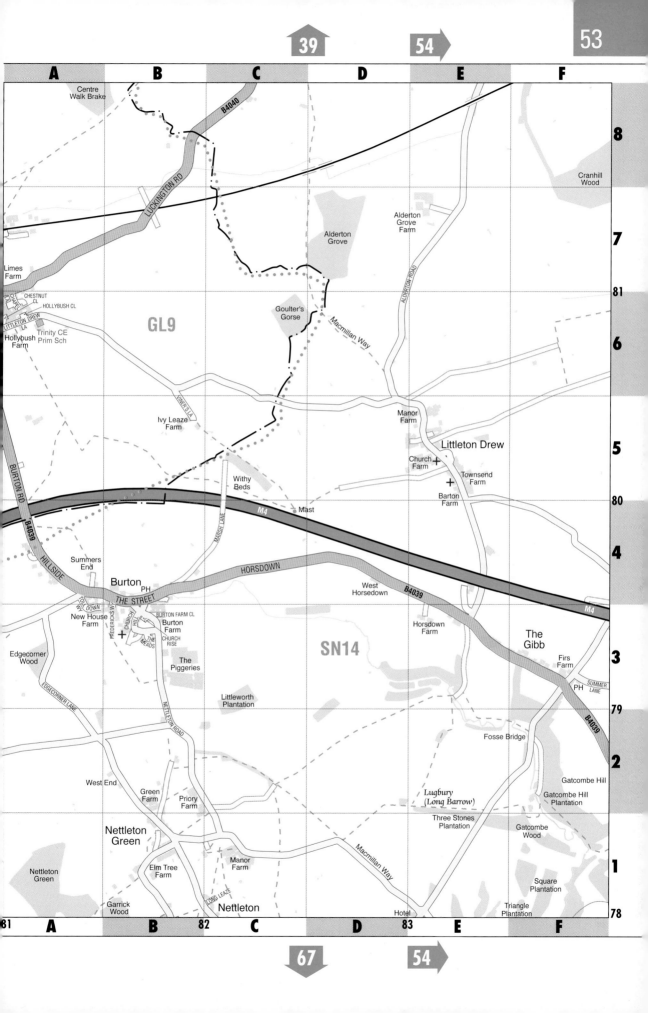

A B C D E F

8

Cranhill
Wood

Dunley
Gorse

East
Dunley
Farm

Little
Worth
Wood

Clapcote
Brake

West
Dunley
Farm

Dunley

Dunley Wood

Dunley Wood

7

81

Brimsol
Spring

Ford

FOSSE WAY

Ash
Bed

Dunley Wood

Newlands
Farm

6

Oldlands Wood

High Elms
Covert

5

80

Grittleton

Manor
Farm

ALDERTON ROAD

SCHOOL LA

THE STREET

PH

Sewage
Works

Limekiln
Cottage

SN14

Grittleton
Stables

4

Fosse
Gate

Old Mead
Covert

Foscote

Ryley's
Farm

M4

M4

3

Fields
Plantation

79

Thorngove
Cottage

West
Foscote
Farm

Lucknow
Plantation

East
Sevington
Farm

2

SUMMER LANE

THE GIBB

Woodbury Hill
Plantation

B4039

Delhi
Plantation

Rathill
Plantation

Rat
Hill

RAT HILL

1

White Gate
Plantation

GIBB RD

West
Sevington
Farm

78

84 A 85 B C 86 D E F

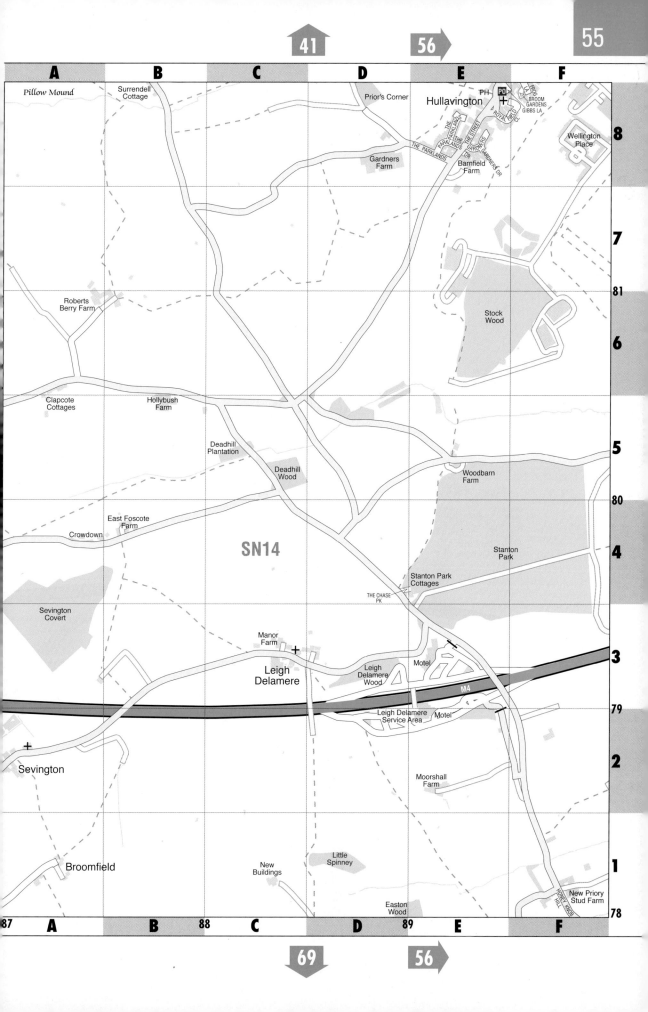

A B C D E F

8
7
81
6
5
80
4
3
79
2
1
78

Pillow Mound

Surrendell Cottage

Prior's Corner

Hullavington

PH PO

THE PARKLAND
THE PARKLANDS
THE STREET
GARDNERS DR
ROYAL MD

FROG LA
BROOM GARDENS
GIBBS LA

Wellington Place

Gardners Farm

Barnfield Farm

Roberts Berry Farm

Stock Wood

Clapcote Cottages

Hollybush Farm

Deadhill Plantation

Deadhill Wood

Woodbarn Farm

East Foscote Farm

Crowdown

SN14

Stanton Park

Sevington Covert

Stanton Park Cottages

THE CHASE PK

Manor Farm

Leigh Delamere

Leigh Delamere Wood

Motel

M4

Motel

Leigh Delamere Service Area

Sevington

Moorshall Farm

Broomfield

New Buildings

Little Spinney

Easton Wood

New Priory Stud Farm

HONEY KNOB HILL

87 88 89

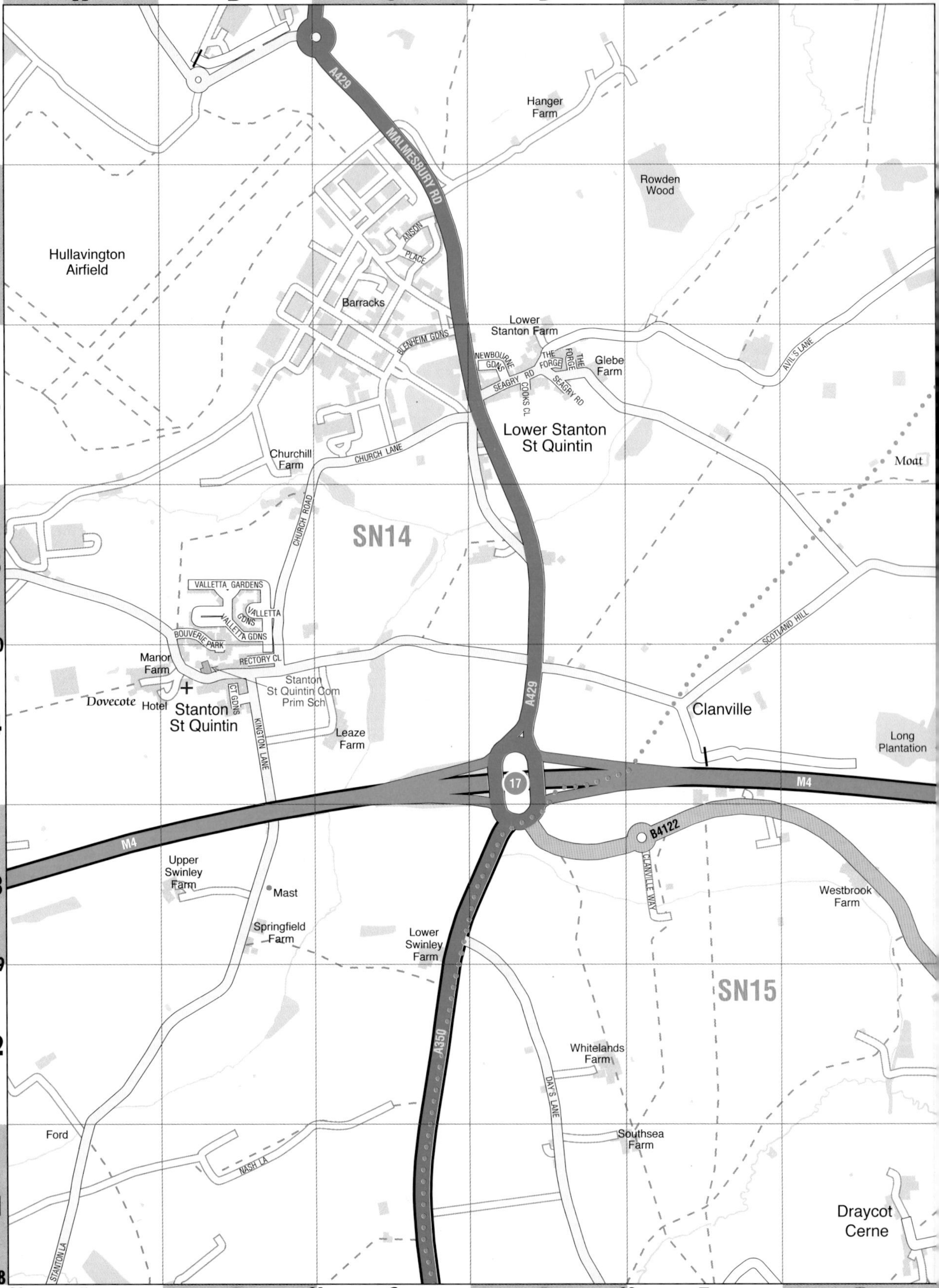

A B C D E F

8

7

81

6

5

80

4

3

79

2

1

78

90 91 92

Hullavington Airfield

Hanger Farm

Rowden Wood

MALMESBURY RD

A429

ANSON PLACE

Barracks

BLENHEIM GDNS

Lower Stanton Farm

NEWBOURNE GDNS

SEAGRY RD

COOKS CL

THE FORGE

SEAGRY RD

Glebe Farm

AVIL'S LANE

Moat

Churchill Farm

CHURCH LANE

CHURCH ROAD

SN14

Lower Stanton St Quintin

VALLETTA GARDENS

VALLETTA GDNS

BOUVERIE PARK

VALLETTA GDNS

RECTORY CL

Manor Farm

Dovecote

Hotel

Stanton St Quintin

CT GDNS

KINGTON LANE

Stanton St Quintin Com Prim Sch

Leaze Farm

A429

SCOTLAND HILL

Clanville

Long Plantation

M4

17

B4122

CLANVILLE WAY

M4

Upper Swinley Farm

Mast

Westbrook Farm

Springfield Farm

Lower Swinley Farm

A350

SN15

Ford

DAY'S LANE

Whitelands Farm

NASH LA

Southsea Farm

STANTON LA

Draycot Cerne

A **B** **C** **D** **E** **F**

8

Weir

RIDGEWAY LANE

MILE DRIVE

7

M4

81

River Avon

The Bourne

MILE DRIVE

6

Dodford Farm

B4069

DODFORD LANE

Dodford Site

Ridgeway Farm

Great Ridgeway Farm

MAIN ROAD

5

SN15

Swallet House

80

M4

Swallett Farm

4

Upper Town

Selstead Farm

Home Farm

Beanhill Farm

Barn Owl

MAIN ROAD

Paradise Farm

Bright's Farm

Mermaid Farm

B4069

3

FRIDAY STREET

Brights Reservoir

PH

WOODLANDS CL

STATION ROAD

ROUNDWOOD VW

Friday Street Farm

79

PO

THE NURSERIES

Recreation Ground

CHURCH RD

THE GREEN

LYE COMM

Melsome Wood

2

Cross

Christian Malford CE Prim Sch

CHURCH RD

STATION RD

LIME TREES

Christian Malford

Thorn End Farm

LIME TREES

PH

Mast

CORONATION CL

FOXHAM RD

Thornend

Charwood Copse

1

78

96 **A** 97 **B** **C** 98 **D** **E** **F**

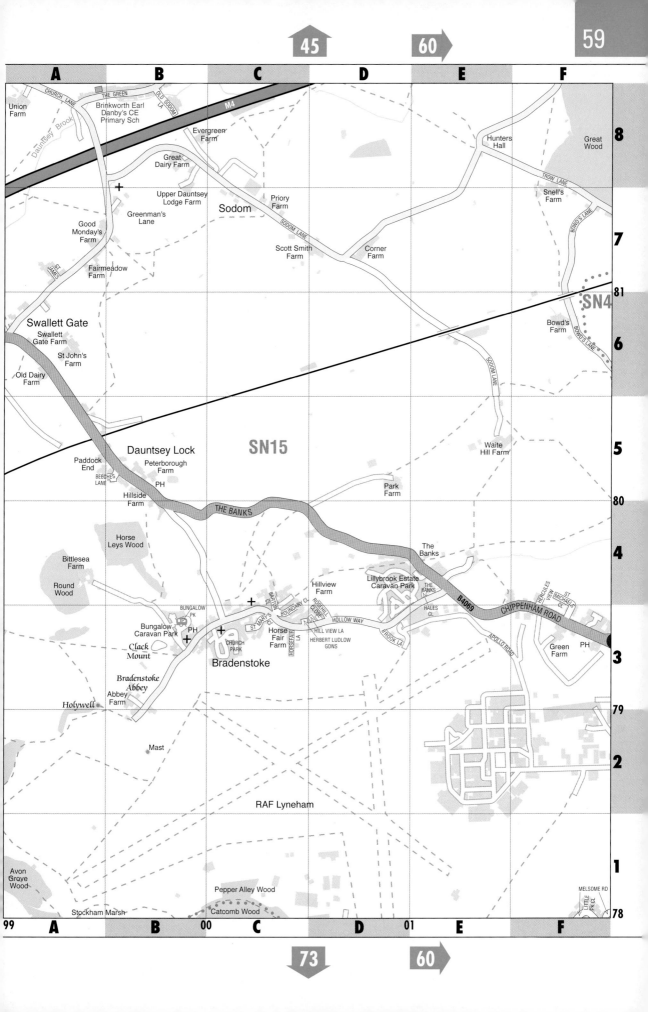

59 46

A B C D E F

SN15

Great Wood

Manor House

Hart Farm

Vastern Wood

Vastern

8

Old Park Farm

Cheeseley Hill Farm

Great Wood Farm

Trow Lane Farm

7

West Close Copse

Manor House

Wiltshire Bassett Golf Club

81

TROW LANE

Tockenham Wick

A3102

Hillocks Wood

Teagles Copse

6

Tockenham Reservoir

BOWD'S LA

Tockenham CORNER

THE HILLOCKS

PRIMROSE HILL

Tockenham Manor Farm

5

A3102

Shaw Farm

SN4

80

SOUTH VIEW

Brickkiln Copse

Rowley Copse

4

THE GREEN

FARTHING LA

SOUTH VEIW

SN15

Beckett's Copse

Shaw Farm

Court Farm

ORCHARD LA

Queen Court Farm

Moat

Tockenham Farm

PO

Cowleaze Copse

Tockenham

3

POUND CL

WEBB'S CT

PH

HOCKETTS

PAPERS

WEBB'S CT

CHURCH FARM MEWS

A3102

CALNE RD

Manorhouse Farm

79

Church End

Liby

CHURCH LA

LANCASTER SQ

Lyneham

HARROW

HASTINGS DRIVE

BELFAST MEAD

Tockenham Court Farm

Greenway Farm

GREENWAY

AF

Lyneham CHURCH END

Lyneham Prim Sch

GROVE

CARAVEN

YORK RD

COMET CL

CROSS

LIME CL

Middlehill Farm

2

REME Mus

EIDER AVE

TEAL AVENUE

SHIELD DR

MUSCOVEY DR

MALLARD AVE

PINTAIL

PAWAN CT

BRITANNIA

ARGOSY CT

ASH CL

VICTORIA DRIVE

ELM CL

SYCAMORE CL

EIDER AV

EIDER AVE

PRESTON LANE

CALNE ROAD

SLESSOR RD

TREVARD

DICKSON RD

PORTAL PL

1

MELSOME RD

Preston End Farm

Preston

Preston East Farm

Thickthorn Farm

78

02 A 03 B C 04 D E F

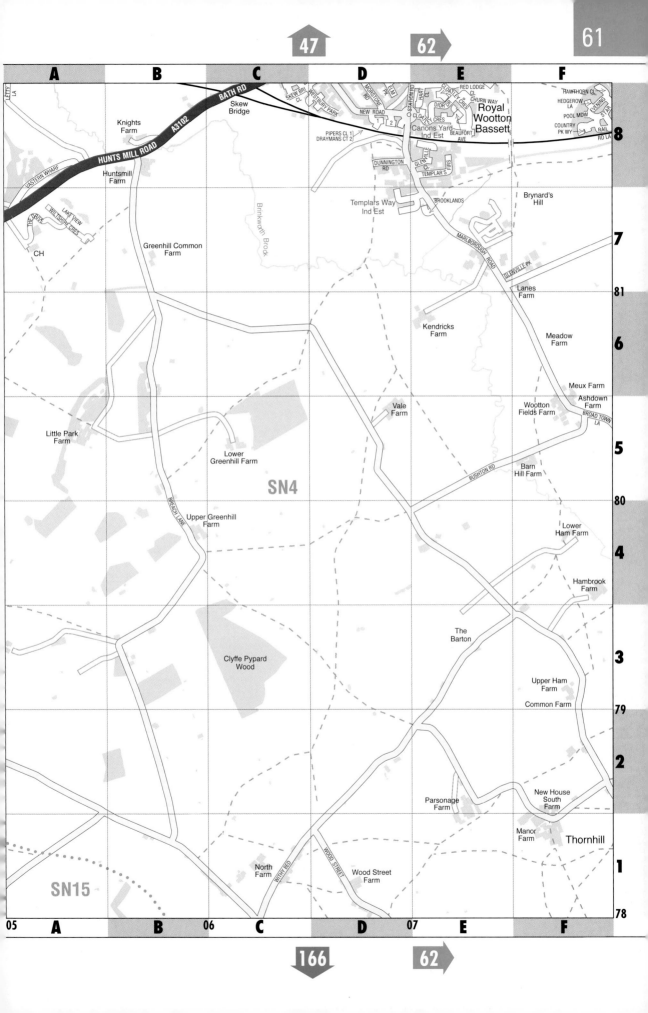

A B C D E F

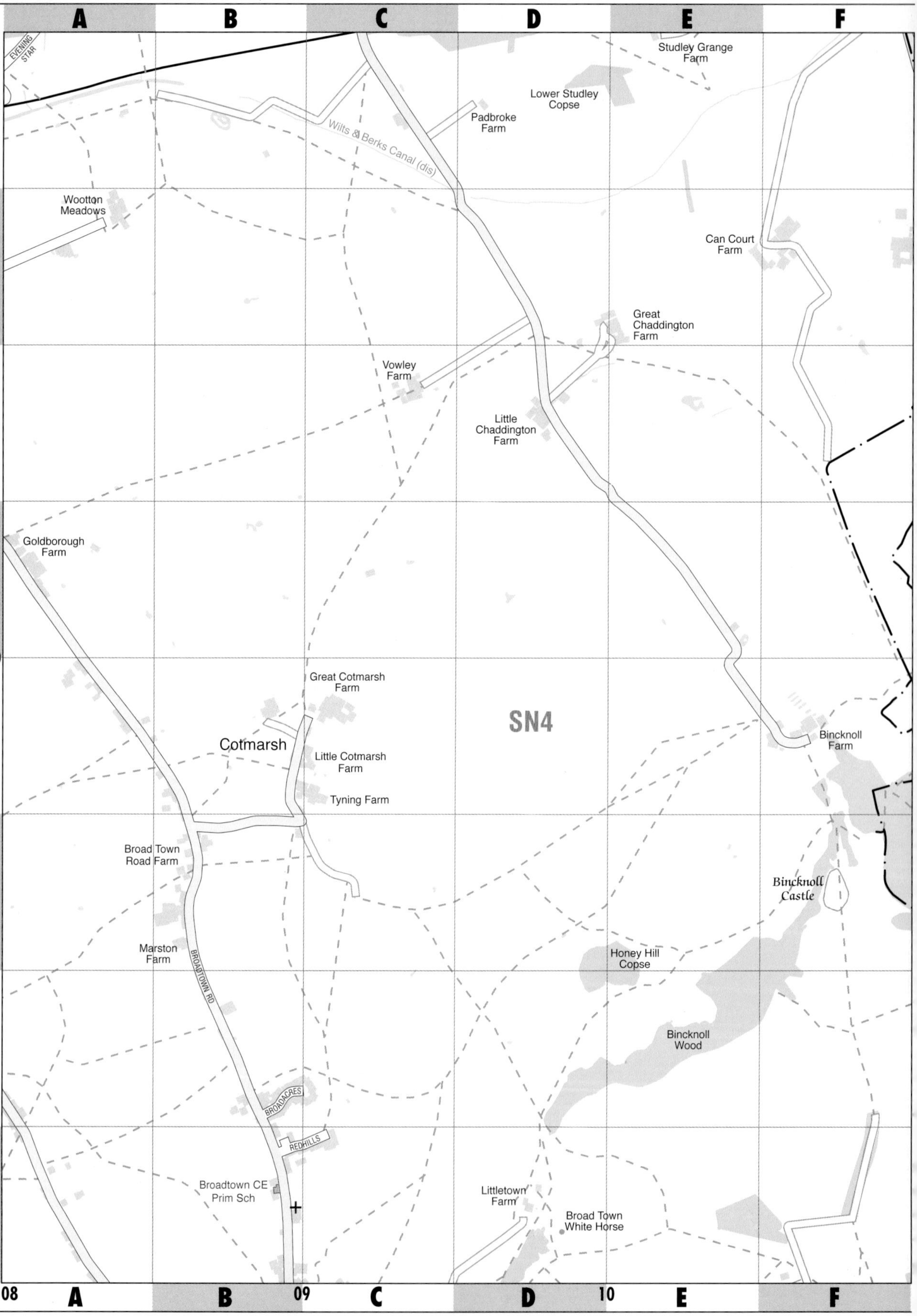

8

7

81

6

5

80

4

3

79

2

1

78

EVENING STAR

Wilts & Berks Canal (dis)

Wootton Meadows

Padbroke Farm

Lower Studley Copse

Studley Grange Farm

Can Court Farm

Great Chaddington Farm

Vowley Farm

Little Chaddington Farm

Goldborough Farm

Great Cotmarsh Farm

SN4

Cotmarsh

Little Cotmarsh Farm

Tyning Farm

Bincknoll Farm

Broad Town Road Farm

Bincknoll Castle

Marston Farm

Honey Hill Copse

BROADTOWN RD

Bincknoll Wood

BROADACRES

REDHILLS

Broadtown CE Prim Sch

Littletown Farm

Broad Town White Horse

08 A B 09 C D 10 E F

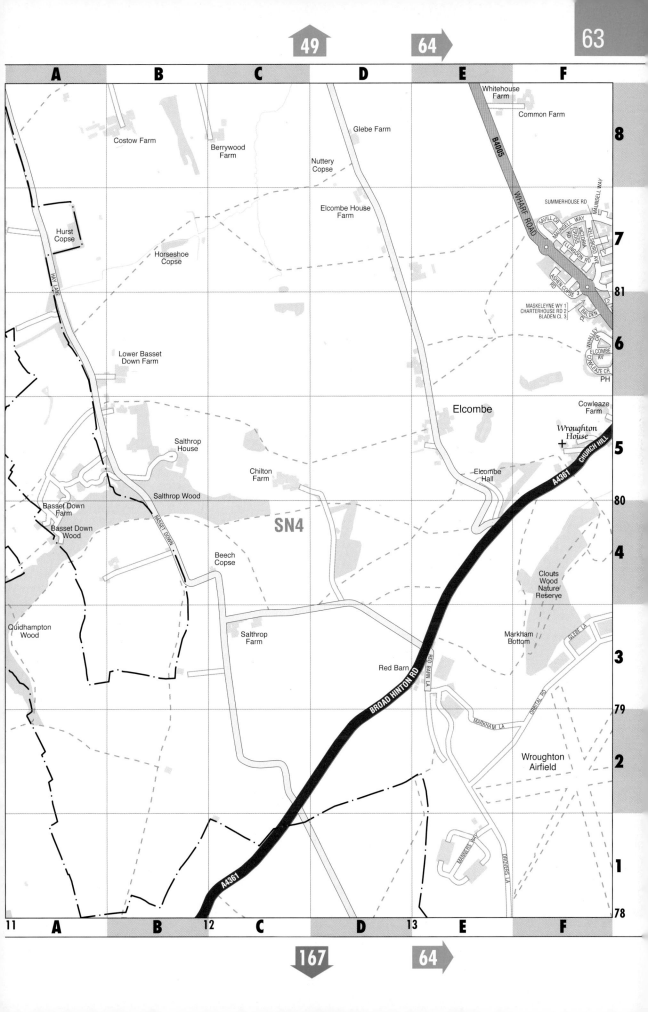

49
64

A B C D E F

8
7
81
6
5
80
4
3
79
2
1
78

Whitehouse Farm
Common Farm
B4005
WHARF ROAD
SUMMERHOUSE RD
MAUNSELL WAY
SAVILL CR
MAUNSELL WAY
VICTORIA CROSS
KELLSBORO RD
ELLINGDON RD
ASTER COPSE RD
BALDEN CL
MASKELEYNE WY 1
CHARTERHOUSE RD 2
BLADEN CL 3
WHALLEY CR
ELCOMBE AV
COWLEAZE CR
PH

Costow Farm
Berrywood Farm
Glebe Farm
Nuttery Copse
Elcombe House Farm

Hurst Copse
HAY LANE

Horseshoe Copse

Lower Basset Down Farm

Salthrop House
Chilton Farm
Elcombe
Cowleaze Farm
Wroughton House
A4361 CHURCH HILL

Salthrop Wood
Elcombe Hall

Basset Down Farm
Basset Down Wood
SN4
BASSET DOWN

Beech Copse
Clouts Wood Nature Reserve

Quidhampton Wood

Salthrop Farm
Markham Bottom
GLEBE LA

Red Barn
RED BARN LA
BROAD HINTON RD
MARKHAM LA
DURSTAL RD
Wroughton Airfield

MARINERS WAY
DROVERS LA

A4361

A B C D E F

11 12 13

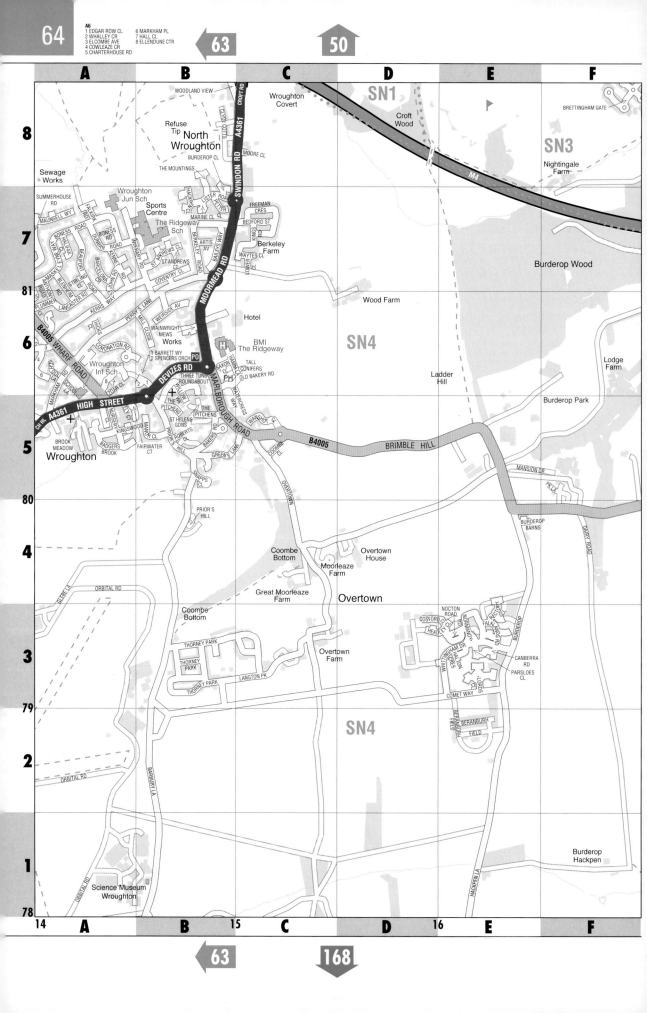

A B C D E F

8

Badbury
Wick

SN3

Burderop
Wood

Badbury
Farm

B4192

PURLEY
RD

SN4

AMFORD
CL

BERRYFIELD
CROFTON RD
ROCKLEY
BUSHTON
CHISBURY RD
BOLEHYDE CL
CLITCHBURY CL
COATLEY CL

A419

HODINGTON AVE

DAY HOUSE LANE

BRICKWORTH PL

LUCKNAM CRES

MARLBOROUGH ROAD

7

M4

Long
Copse

Crook's
Copse

Green
Hill

INTHAM
FLINTHAM

A419

MEADOW WY

Medbourne
Farm

Taylor's Copse

81

15

BERRICOT LA

MEDBOURNE LA

M4

6

A346

MARLBOROUGH ROAD

BERRICOT LANE

PH

Hodson

PH

Pinkcombe
Wood

Sewage Works

PH

West Farm

Badbury

Lansdown

5

B4005

Badbury
House
Farm

80

HODSON ROAD

HONE CL
HOME CLOSE
MANOR VIEW MEWS
MANOR RISE
UPPER LA
STROUD ST HILL
HIGH ST
CHURCH
ST
DEWEY CL
BUTTS ROAD
SAXON
MILL
WINDMILL
PIECE
VIEW ROAD
DOWNS RD
CASTLE
SCHOOL
STATION
CL
THE ORCH
CASTLE VIEW ROAD

Chiseldon
Prim Sch

MARLBOROUGH ROAD

4

SOUTHFIELD

Recreation
Ground

Liby
PO
TURNBALL
BALD
WIN CL
MAY'S LA
THE CURNICKS
TRINDLE
CL
TURNBALL
REAR
OF FOUR CANNEY CLOSE
THE
CANNEY
CHISELDON
B4005

NEW ROAD

Bush
House

CARISBROOK TERR

PH
Chiseldon

P

NORRIS CLOSE

JOHN ALDER CL

New Farm

3

SN4

THE CRES

DRAYCOT ROAD

79

2

THE RIDGEWAY

LADYSMITH ROAD

DRAYCOT LA

SAMBRE ROAD

A346

1

CAMBRAI RD
AISNE RD
SAMBRE ROAD

78

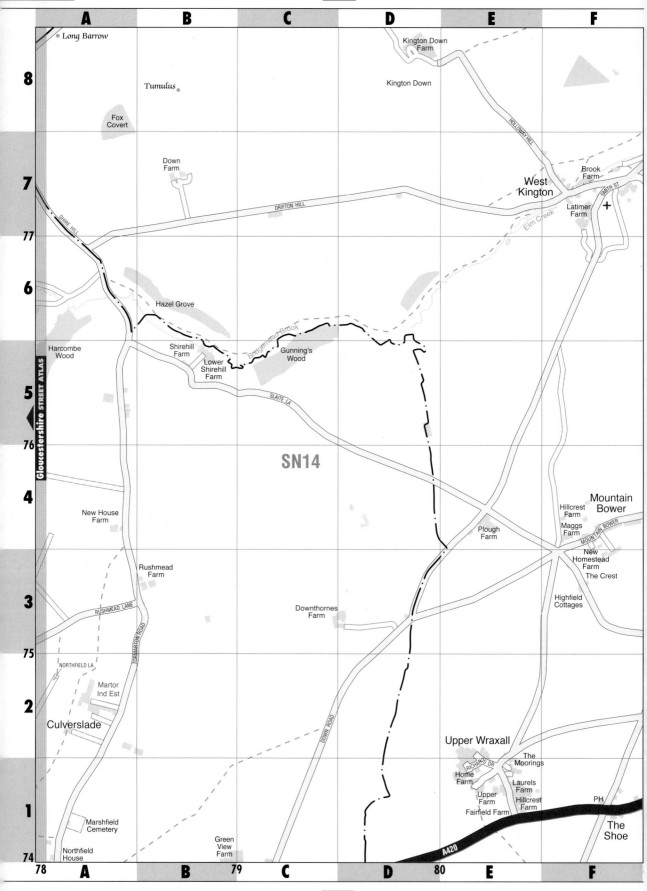

Long Barrow

Tumulus

Fox Covert

Down Farm

Kington Down Farm

Kington Down

HOLLOWAY HILL

West Kington

Brook Farm

SMITH ST

Latimer Farm

DRIFTON HILL

SHIRE HILL

Elm Creek

77

6

Hazel Grove

Bridgemead Brook

Harcombe Wood

Shirehill Farm

Lower Shirehill Farm

Gunning's Wood

SLAITE LA

5

Gloucestershire Street Atlas

76

SN14

4

New House Farm

Rushmead Farm

Hillcrest Farm

Mountain Bower

Maggs Farm

MOUNTAIN BOWER

Plough Farm

New Homestead Farm

The Crest

Highfield Cottages

3

RUSHMEAD LANE

Downthornes Farm

TORMARTON ROAD

75

NORTHFIELD LA

Martor Ind Est

2

DOWN ROAD

Culverslade

Upper Wraxall

The Moorings

RICHARDS DR

Home Farm

Laurels Farm

Upper Farm

Hillcrest Farm

Fairfield Farm

PH

1

Marshfield Cemetery

Green View Farm

A420

The Shoe

Northfield House

74

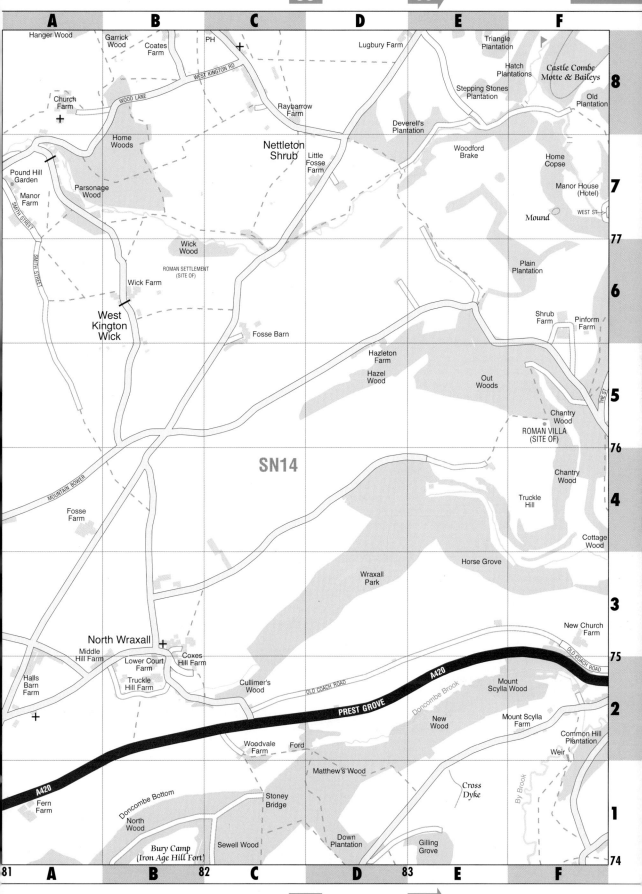

A **B** **C** **D** **E** **F**

Hanger Wood

Garrick Wood

Coates Farm

PH ✛

Lugbury Farm

Triangle Plantation

Hatch Plantations

Castle Combe Motte & Baileys

8

WEST KINGTON RD

WOOD LANE

Church Farm ✛

Stepping Stones Plantation

Old Plantation

Home Woods

Raybarrow Farm

Deverell's Plantation

Woodford Brake

Home Copse

Nettleton Shrub

Little Fosse Farm

Manor House (Hotel)

7

SMITH STREET

Pound Hill Garden

Parsonage Wood

Mound

WEST ST →

Manor Farm

77

SMITH STREET

Wick Wood

Plain Plantation

6

ROMAN SETTLEMENT (SITE OF)

Wick Farm

Shrub Farm

Pinform Farm

West Kington Wick

Fosse Barn

Hazleton Farm

Out Woods

THE ST

Hazel Wood

Chantry Wood

5

Chantry Wood

ROMAN VILLA (SITE OF)

76

MOUNTAIN BOWER

SN14

Truckle Hill

4

Fosse Farm

Cottage Wood

Horse Grove

Wraxall Park

3

New Church Farm

OLD COACH ROAD

North Wraxall ✛

Middle Hill Farm

Lower Court Farm

Coxes Hill Farm

Cullimer's Wood

OLD COACH ROAD

A420

Mount Scylla Wood

75

Halls Barn Farm

Truckle Hill Farm

PREST GROVE

Doncombe Brook

New Wood

Mount Scylla Farm

2

✛

Common Hill Plantation

Woodvale Farm

Ford

Weir

A420

Matthew's Wood

Cross Dyke

By Brook

Fern Farm

Doncombe Bottom

Stoney Bridge

1

North Wood

Down Plantation

Gilling Grove

Bury Camp (Iron Age Hill Fort)

Sewell Wood

74

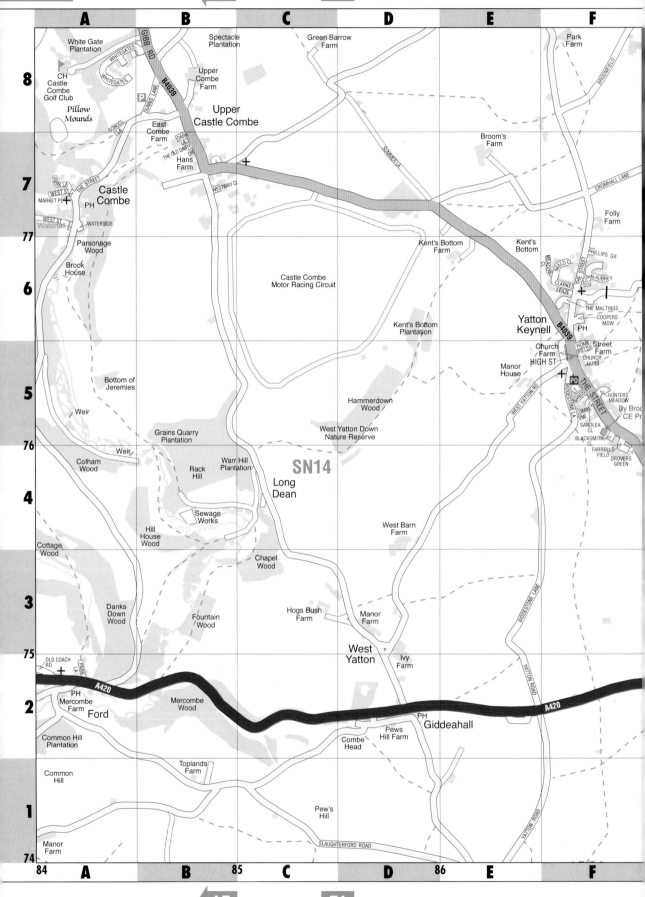

A B C D E F

White Gate
Plantation
CH Castle
Combe
Golf Club

GIBB RD
B4039
WHITEGATES
WHITEGATES

Spectacle
Plantation

Green Barrow
Farm

Park
Farm

BROOMFIELD

8

Pillow
Mounds

P

Upper
Combe
Farm

East
Combe
Farm

SCHOOL LA
DUNNS LANE

DARK LA
THE OLD DAIRY
THE OLD DAIRY DRI

Upper
Castle Combe

Hans
Farm

Broom's
Farm

CROMHALL LANE

Folly
Farm

7

PARK LA
WEST ST
MARKET PL

THE STREET

Castle
Combe

PH

WESTWAY CL

SUMMER LA

Kent's
Bottom

Phillips GR
MEADOW CL
WEOLD CL
CLARKES
LEAZE
THE STREET
JOHN AUBREY
THE MALTINGS
COOPERS
MDW

77

WEST ST
Waterfall
WATERSIDE

Parsonage
Wood

Kent's Bottom
Farm

Yatton
Keynell

B4039

PH

6

Brook
House

Castle Combe
Motor Racing Circuit

Kent's Bottom
Plantation

Church
Farm
HIGH ST

Manor
House

HOME
FIELDS

Street
Farm
CHURCH
FARM

5

Bottom of
Jeremies

Weir

Hammerdown
Wood

West Yatton Down
Nature Reserve

PO
BIDDESTONE LA
SANDS

COMBE
LANN
SANDLEA
CL

HUNTERS
MEADOW

By Broo
CE Pri

76

Colham
Wood

Weir

Grains Quarry
Plantation

Rack
Hill

Warr Hill
Plantation

SN14

Long
Dean

BLACKSMITH
CL
FARRELLS
FIELD

DROVERS
GREEN

4

Cottage
Wood

Danks
Down
Wood

Hill
House
Wood

Sewage
Works

Fountain
Wood

Chapel
Wood

West Barn
Farm

BIDDESTONE LANE

3

Hogs Bush
Farm

Manor
Farm

YATTON ROAD

75

OLD COACH
RD
PARK
LA
A420
PH
Mercombe
Farm
Ford

West
Yatton

Ivy
Farm

A420

2

Mercombe
Wood

Combe
Head

Pews
Hill Farm

PH

Giddeahall

Common Hill
Plantation

Toplands
Farm

YATTON ROAD

1

Common
Hill

Pew's
Hill

Manor
Farm

SLAUGHTERFORD ROAD

74

84 A B 85 C D 86 E F

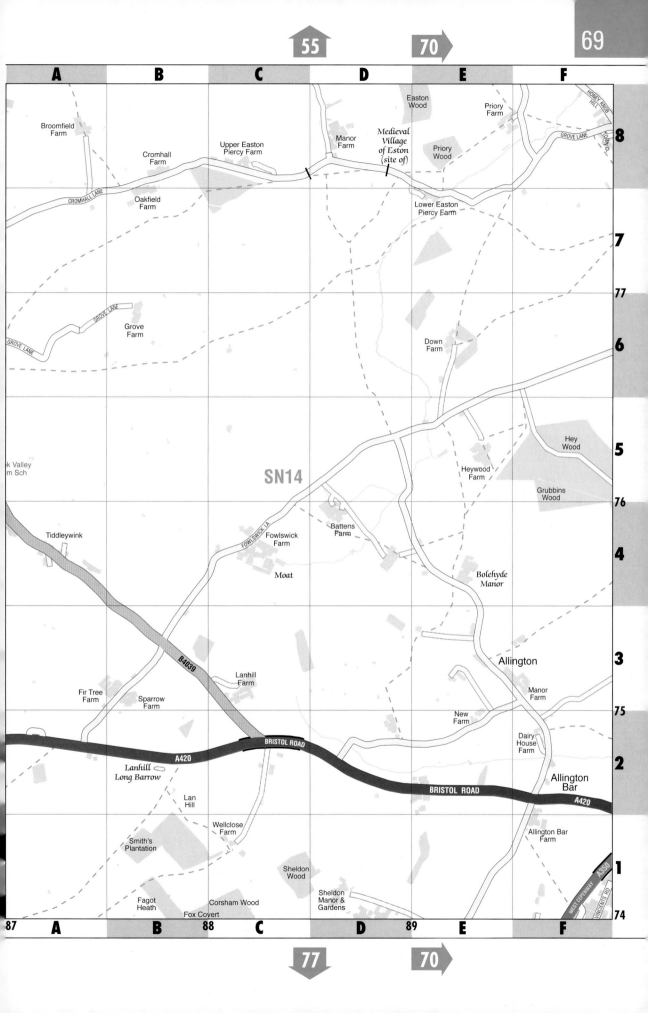

A B C D E F

8 Kington
St Michael

Tradewinds Farm

Hillside
Farm

Lypgate
Farm

Westbrook
Farm

Bowldown

NEWLANDS CL

Kington
St Michael CE
Prim Sch

PADDOCK END

7 Manor
Farm
Almshouses

PH

Courtfield
Farm

WAYSIDE CL

DOVE'S TERRACE

SILVER
ST

FAIRLEIGH
RISE

Kington
Langley
PH

77 Tor
Hill

STUBBS LANE

Bright
Side

Church
Farm

Church Road

LOWER COMMON

6 Tor Farm

PH

The Moors

PLOUGH LANE

Langley
Fitzurse
CE Prim Sch

Limetree
Farm

UPPER COMMON

SWINDON RD

PLOUGH LA

MOORS CNR

PH

Steinbrook
Farm

5 Hey
Wood

Lodge
Farm

P

Nature
Reserve

B4069

SWINDON ROAD

76 White Wood

SN14

A350

JACKSOM'S LANE

Marsh
Farm

SN15

Langley
House

4 Chippenham
Golf Club

CH

PW DR

MALMESBURY ROAD

Jacksom's
Farm

Bird's
Marsh

Dog Kennel
Plantation

CHIPPENHAM RD

3 HONEYSUCKLE CL

Superstore

WEST CEPEN WAY

PH

A350

WEST CEPEN WAY

GANS WY

ARGYLE DRIVE

SCOTT CT

HOLLOWAY GR

CLUTTERBUCK CL

GAINEY GDNS

Barrow
Farm

TYDDYMAN CL

HATHERALL DR

FILBERT ST

THE COMMON

B4069

CAUSEWAY

BUTTERCUP CL 1
SORREL DR 2
BLUEBELL DR 3
PRIMROSE WY 4
HARES PATCH 5
PARTRIDGE CL 6
ROBINS CL 7
WOODPECKER MEWS 8
HARNISH WY 9

TRINITY GDNS

B4158

EDDOLLS LA

HARVEY CT

HAZEL CRES

HICKORY WAY

75 SANDPIPER GDNS

HARDENHUISH LA

Wiltshire Ambulance
Service NHS Trust HQ

VINES CL

BULL LA

SCOTT ASHE

CHIPPENHAM

BRYANT

THE NUT TR

2 HOLLYBUSH CL

STAINERS WY

B4528

CHURCH VW

RIDINGS (LANES HEAD)

LONG RIDINGS

BROOKWELL CL

BELLINGHAM CL

WITTS GR

ST Paul's
Prim Sch

ELMS RD

COUZENS CL

NEATH CT

CLARK DR

HILL CORNER ROAD

HEATHFIELD

PARSONAGE WAY

Hardenhuish
School

MAIDSTONE WY

OAKLAND CT

THE OAKS

GREENWAY LA

Greenway
Park

PEW HILL

MAUD HEATH'S

Parsonage Way
Industrial Estate

BRISTOL RD
A420

A350

BLACKBERRY CL

ACACIA

CWILLOWBANK

FALLOW CT

FOXGROVE

HARDENHUISH LANE

St Nicholas
School

BROOMFIELD

OAKLANDS

GREENWAY LANE

BIRCH GROVE

MURRAYFIELD

B4069

MAUD HEATH'S CW

O'DONNELL CL

FARMER

EASTLANDS

WESTINGHOUSE WY

1 MOUNT
PLEASANT

JASMINE CL

Sheldon
School

Hardenhuish
Park

PORTAL CLOSE

YEWSTOCK CR

ASHE CRESCENT

CEDAR GR

MAPLE GR

GREENWAY GD

LANSDOWN GR

TWICKENHAM WY

Langley
Park

Bumpers Farm
Ind Est

MULBERRY

THE POPLARS

BYTHEBROOK

GREENFIELDS

OLD HARDENHUISH LA

Sports
Ground

WEDMORE AV

PARKLANDS
GDNS

GREENWAY

CLIFT AV

JUBILEE RD

HAWTHORN RD

COWLEAZE

Westpoint
Business
Park

VINCIENTS
RD

KINGTON WAY

HUNGERDOWN

BRISTOL ROAD A420

BRISTOL RD

HARDENHUISH AV

ROWLANDS WAY

TUGELA RD

74

90 A 91 B C 92 D E F

A1
1 LONGSTONE RD
2 ALLINGTON WY
3 THE BATTENS
4 BARKEN RD
5 PIPSMORE RD
6 LOWER FIELD
7 CORNFIELDS
8 MIDDLELEAZE
9 BARLEY LEAZE

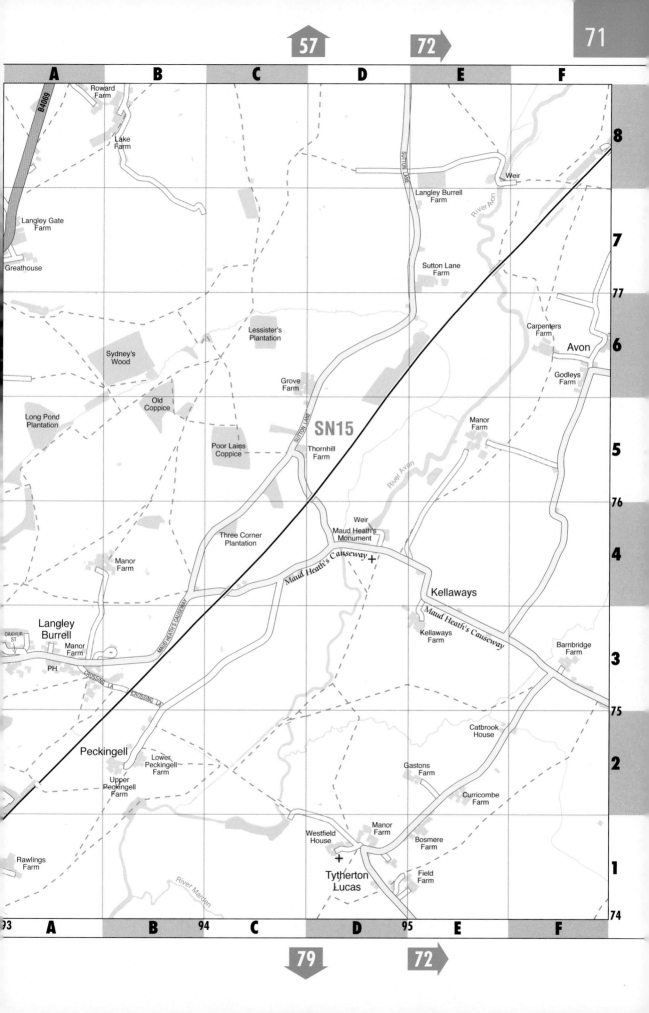

A   B   C   D   E   F

8
7
77
6
5
76
4
75
2
1
74

B4069

Roward
Farm

Lake
Farm

Langley Gate
Farm

Greathouse

Sydney's
Wood

Long Pond
Plantation

Old
Coppice

Lessister's
Plantation

Grove
Farm

SN15

Poor Lains
Coppice

Thornhill
Farm

SUTTON LANE

Three Corner
Plantation

Manor
Farm

Langley
Burrell

OAKHUR
ST

Manor
Farm

PH

CROSSING LA

CROSSING LA

MAUD HEATH'S CAUSEWAY

Maud Heath's Causeway

Maud Heath's
Monument

Weir

Kellaways

Maud Heath's Causeway

Kellaways
Farm

Peckingell

Lower
Peckingell
Farm

Upper
Peckingell
Farm

Rawlings
Farm

River Marden

Westfield
House

Tytherton
Lucas

Manor
Farm

Bosmere
Farm

Field
Farm

Gastons
Farm

Curricombe
Farm

Catbrook
House

Barnbridge
Farm

Manor
Farm

River Avon

River Avon

Sutton Lane
Farm

Langley Burrell
Farm

SUTTON LANE

Weir

Carpenters
Farm

Avon

Godleys
Farm

93   A   B   94   C   D   95   E   F   74

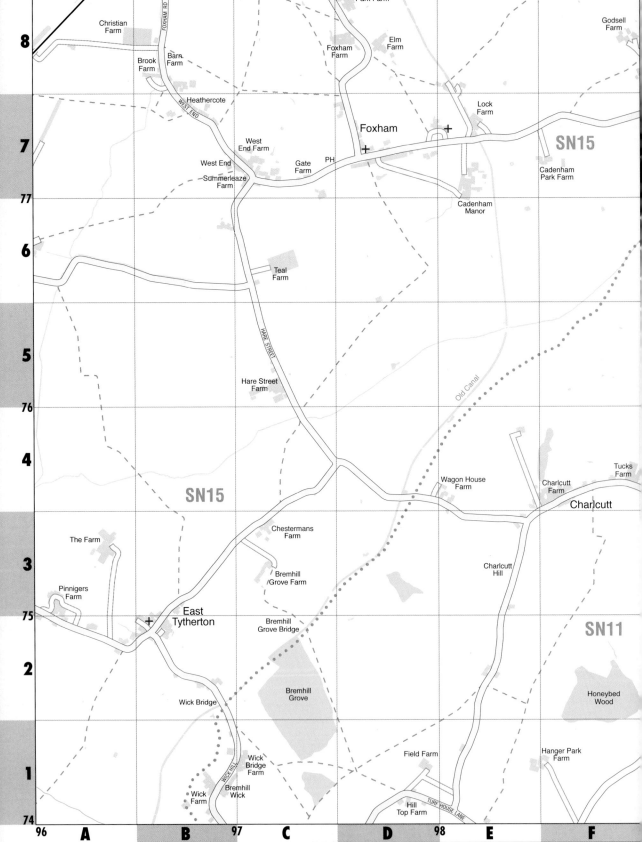

8

Christian Farm

FOXHAM RD

Park Farm

Godsell Farm

Barn Farm

Brook Farm

Foxham Farm

Elm Farm

Heathercote

WEST END

Lock Farm

7

West End Farm

Foxham

SN15

West End

Gate Farm

PH

Cadenham Park Farm

Summerleaze Farm

77

Cadenham Manor

6

Teal Farm

HARE STREET

Old Canal

5

Hare Street Farm

76

Tucks Farm

4

Wagon House Farm

Charlcutt Farm

Charlcutt

SN15

Charlcutt Hill

The Farm

Chestermans Farm

3

Pinnigers Farm

Bremhill /Grove Farm

SN11

75

East Tytherton

Bremhill Grove Bridge

2

Wick Bridge

Bremhill Grove

Honeybed Wood

WICK HILL

Wick Bridge Farm

Field Farm

Hanger Park Farm

1

Wick Farm

Bremhill Wick

Hill Top Farm

TURF HOUSE LANE

74

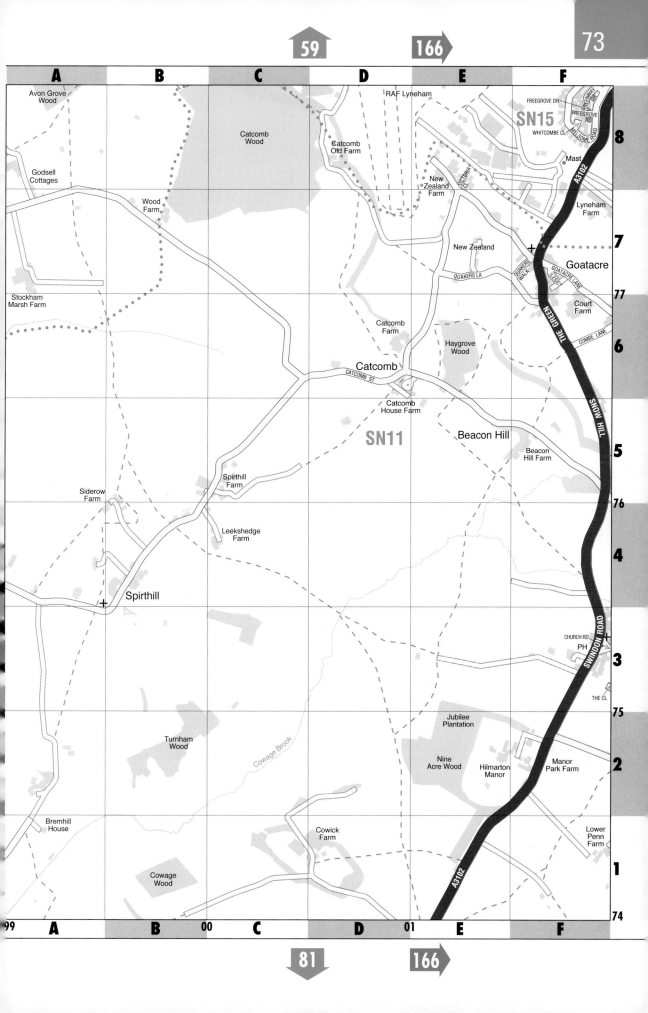

Marshfield

A420 Bristol

CHIPPENHAM RD

A420   CHIPPENHAM RD

A420

8

PO
Hayfield
Bell Sq
HAYFIELD
CHIPPENHAM ROAD
MARKET PL
HAY STREET
FAIRFIELD CL
BACK LA
BARN END
WITHYMEAD
Marshfield
Prim Sch

Garston
Farm

Star
Farm

STAR LA

Bond's
Wood

HIGH ST
CHURCH LA
PLACE
LITTLE END

East End

Newleaze
Wood

Woodlands
Farm

OLD SCHOOL CT

Pitt
Farm

DONCOMBE HILL

Doncombe
Scrubs

PINEWOOD WAY

PINEWOOD WAY

PINEWOOD WAY

Northwood
Farm

7

Ringswell

Sewage
Works

Cloud
Wood

73

Henleyhill
Barn

WALNUT DR
LINDEN CL
HOLT CR
LARCH RD
CYPRESS WLK

6

Henley
Hill

Henleyhill
Plantation

Marshfield
Wood

FOSS WAY

Raizes
Wood

LAUREL DRIVE

ASPEN
CL

OAK
POPLAR
WAY

5

SN14

Raizes
Plantation

The
Raizes

72

ASHWICKE RD

West
Lodge

Barracks

4

Ashwicke
Grange

Grange
Plantation

Centre
Plantation

Colerne
Airfield

DUKWICK LA

Ashwicke
Home Farm

East
Lodge

3

Motcombe
Farm

Clift Wood

ASHWICKE ROAD

Diamond
Wood

Colerne Rugby
Football Club

71

Longley
Wood

Cherry
Wood

BATH ROAD

Ranch
House Farm

Motcombe Wood

OAKFORD LANE

Bandywell
Wood

Lictum
Spring

2

Dicknick
Wood

Rocky
Wood

The
Rocks

Hunters
Hall

Breach
Wood

BA1

Orchard
Wood

Abbotscombe
Wood

Ryder's
Wood

1

Fewells
Wood

Moonshine
Wood

Brokenboro
Wood

RODE HILL

Draught
Wood

Westwood
Farm

West Wood

SN13

ST CATHERINE LA

Oakford
Farm

Rodney
Wood

Three Shire
Stones

70

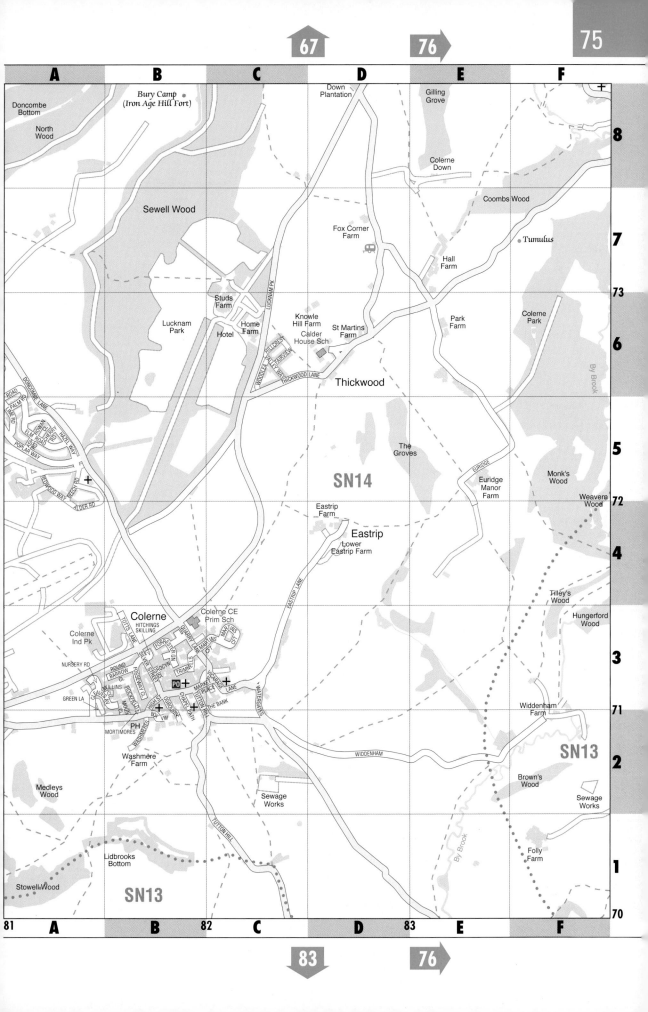

A   B   C   D   E   F

8
7
73
6
5
72
4
3
71
2
1
70

Doncombe
Bottom

North
Wood

Bury Camp
(Iron Age Hill Fort)

Down
Plantation

Gilling
Grove

Colerne
Down

Sewell Wood

Coombs Wood

Fox Corner
Farm

Tumulus

Hall
Farm

Studs
Farm

Lucknam
Park

Home
Farm

Knowle
Hill Farm

Calder
House Sch

St Martins
Farm

Park
Farm

Colerne
Park

Hotel

Thickwood

Thickwood

SN14

The
Groves

Euridge
Manor
Farm

Monk's
Wood

Weavern
Wood

Eastrip
Farm

Eastrip

Lower
Eastrip Farm

Tilley's
Wood

Hungerford
Wood

Colerne

Colerne CE
Prim Sch

Colerne
Ind Pk

HITCHINGS
SKILLING

TOTTS LANE

NURSERY RD

ROUND
BARROW

GREEN LA

MULLINS

FOSSEWAY CL

PO

MARKET
PLACE

WATERGATES

Widdenham
Farm

SN13

PH

MORTIMORES

Washmere
Farm

WIDDENHAM

Brown's
Wood

Sewage
Works

Medleys
Wood

Sewage
Works

TUTTON HILL

Lidbrooks
Bottom

Folly
Farm

Stowell Wood

SN13

By Brook

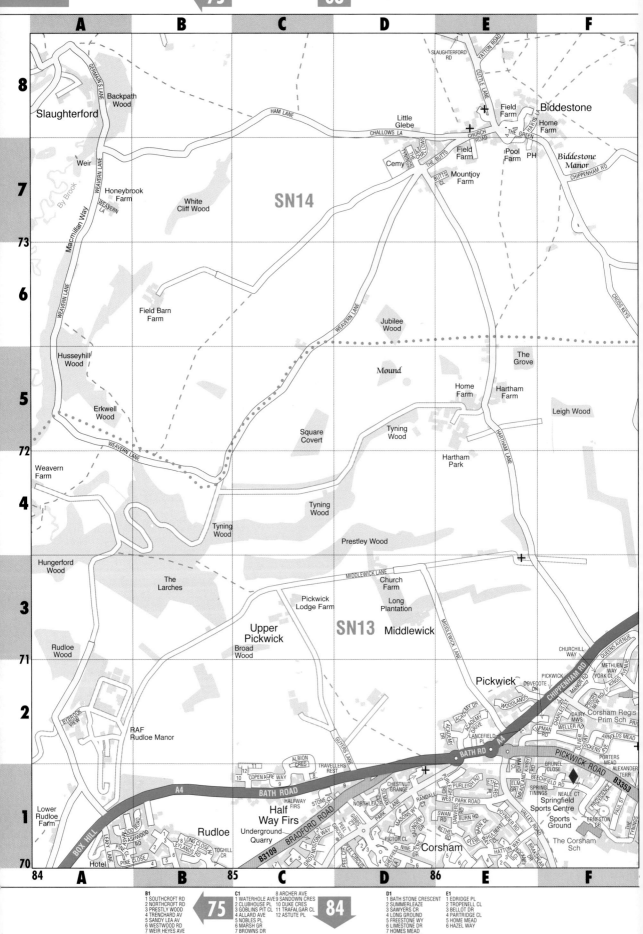

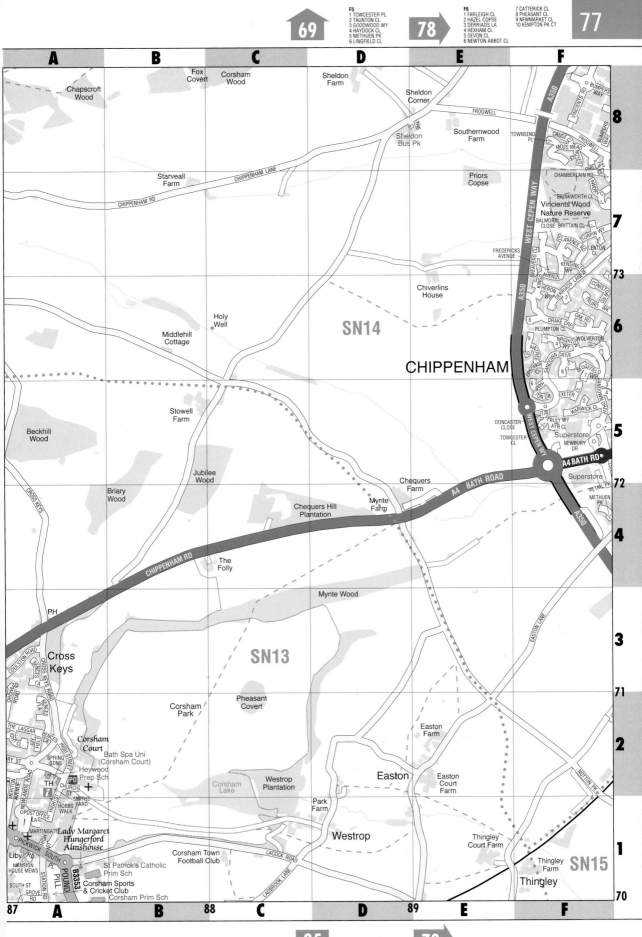

69

78

F5
1 TOWCESTER PL
2 TAUNTON CL
3 GOODWOOD WY
4 HAYDOCK CL
5 METHUEN PK
6 LINGFIELD CL

F6
1 FARLEIGH CL
2 HAZEL COPSE
3 DERRIADS LA
4 HEXHAM CL
5 DEVON CL
6 NEWTON ABBOT CL

7 CATTERICK CL
8 PHEASANT CL
9 NEWMARKET CL
10 KEMPTON PK CT

Chapscroft Wood

Fox Covert

Corsham Wood

Sheldon Farm

Sheldon Corner

Frogwell

BUMPERS WAY

A350

Southernwood Farm

TOWNSEND

CRUSE CL
FROGWELL
PHILLIPS CL
MOSS MEAD

Starveall Farm

CHIPPENHAM LANE

CHIPPENHAM RD

Priors Copse

CHAMBERLAIN RD

Vincients Wood Nature Reserve

BRINKWORTH CL

BALMORAL CLOSE
BRITTAIN CL

WEST CEPEN WAY

Fredericks Avenue

CLARENCE RD
LENTON CL
TURPIN WY

73

KENSINGTON WY

WEAVERS CL
KINGS AVENUE
DERRIADS LANE
CONISTON CL
TRURO WK

SN14

Chiverlins House

A350

HERON WY

DRAKE CRES
OAK RD

6

Holy Well

Middlehill Cottage

PLUMPTON CL

WOLVERTON CL
BRIGHTLY WY
SANDOWN DRIVE

CHIPPENHAM

EPSOM RD

DON DR

EXETER

WARWICK CL

SEDGEFIELD WY

Beckhill Wood

Stowell Farm

WEST CEPEN WAY

DONCASTER CLOSE

TOWCESTER CL

BEVERLEY WY
AYR CL

Superstore

NEWBURY DR

5

A4 BATH RD

Jubilee Wood

Chequers Farm

A4 BATH ROAD

Superstore

RETAIL PK

METHUEN PK

72

Briary Wood

Chequers Hill Plantation

Mynte Farm

A350

4

CHIPPENHAM RD

The Folly

Mynte Wood

EASTON LANE

Cross Keys

PH

SN13

3

CROSS KEYS

COULSTON ROAD

CROSS KEYS ROAD
BENCES LA

Pheasant Covert

71

Corsham Park

Easton Farm

2

Corsham Court

Bath Spa Uni (Corsham Court)
Heywood Prep Sch

Easton

Easton Court Farm

THE LAGGAR
HIGH STREET
SPRING GDNS

HOBBS WALK

Westrop Plantation

Park Farm

Thingley Court Farm

NOTTON PK

PO
TH

SMITHS YARD

Westrop

Thingley Farm

SN15

Martingate
Lady Margaret Hungerford Almshouse

Corsham Town Football Club

LACOCK ROAD

1

Liby

PICKWICK

Mansion House Mews

South St

SOUTH ST
GROVE RD

STATION RD

B3353

POUND PILL

St Patrick's Catholic Prim Sch

Corsham Sports & Cricket Club

Corsham Prim Sch

LADBROOK LANE

Thingley

70

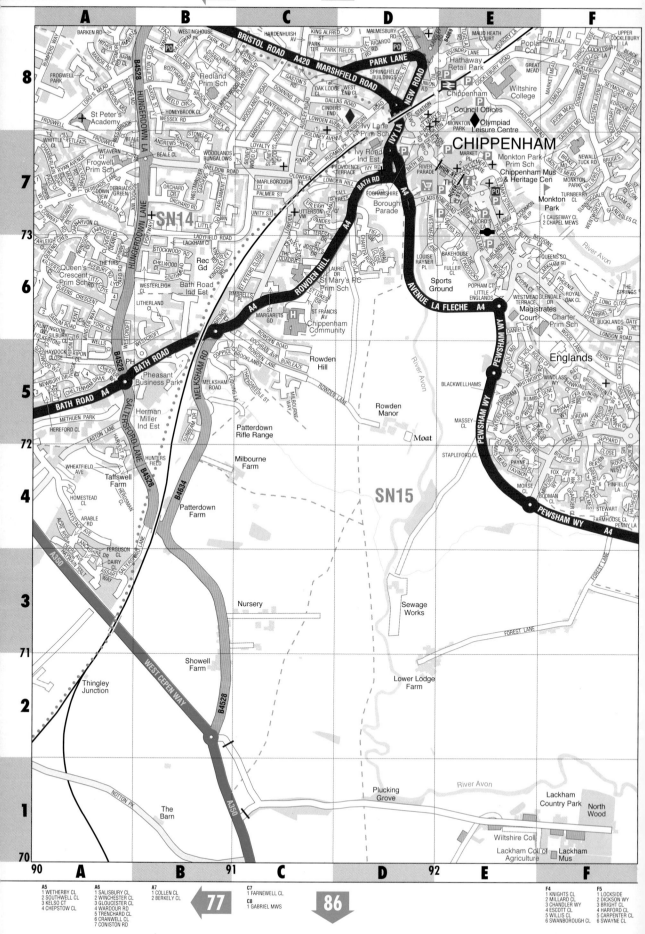

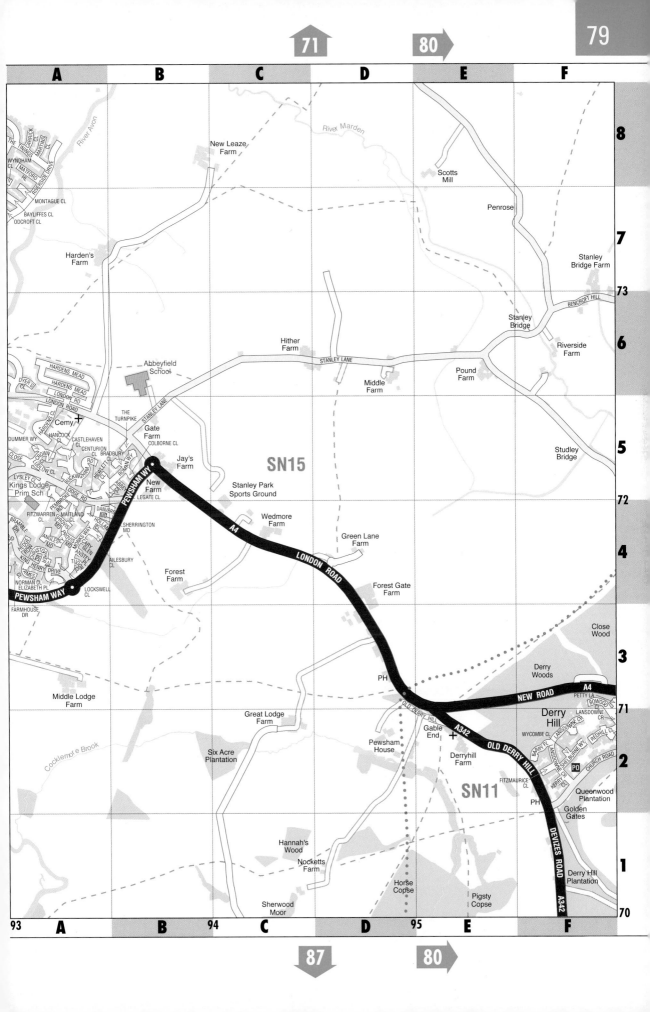

A B C D E F

8

7

73

6

5

72

4

3

71

2

1

70

THE TININGS
CARRICK CL
MARTINS CL
WYNDHAM
HILL
MATFORD
RIVERSIDE DRIVE
MONTAGUE CL
BAYLIFFES CL
ODCROFT CL

River Avon

Harden's Farm

New Leaze Farm

River Marden

Scotts Mill

Penrose

Stanley Bridge Farm

BENCROFT HILL

Stanley Bridge

Riverside Farm

Hither Farm

STANLEY LANE

Middle Farm

Pound Farm

Studley Bridge

Abbeyfield School

HARDENS MEAD
HARDENS MEAD
DYER ST
CL
HARDENS RD
LONDON RD
THE TURNPIKE
STANLEY LANE

Cemy

Gate Farm
COLBORNE CL

SN15

Jay's Farm

New Farm
LEGATE CL

PEWSHAM WY

Stanley Park Sports Ground

Wedmore Farm

Green Lane Farm

A4

LONDON ROAD

Forest Farm

Forest Gate Farm

Kings Lodge Prim Sch

PEWSHAM WAY

LOCKSWELL CL

FARMHOUSE DR

Middle Lodge Farm

Cocklemore Brook

Great Lodge Farm

Six Acre Plantation

Close Wood

Derry Woods

A4
NEW ROAD
PETTY LA
BOWOOD

Derry Hill
LANSDOWNE CR

PH

OLD DERRY HILL

A342

OLD DERRY HILL

WYCOMBE CL
LANSDOWNE CL
SHELBURNE WY
REDHILL CL
CHURCH ROAD
KERRY CL
BARRY PL

Gable End

Pewsham House

Derryhill Farm

FITZMAURICE CL

SN11

PO

PH

Queenwood Plantation

Golden Gates

Hannah's Wood

Nocketts Farm

Horse Copse

Pigsty Copse

Sherwood Moor

DEVIZES ROAD

A342

Derry Hill Plantation

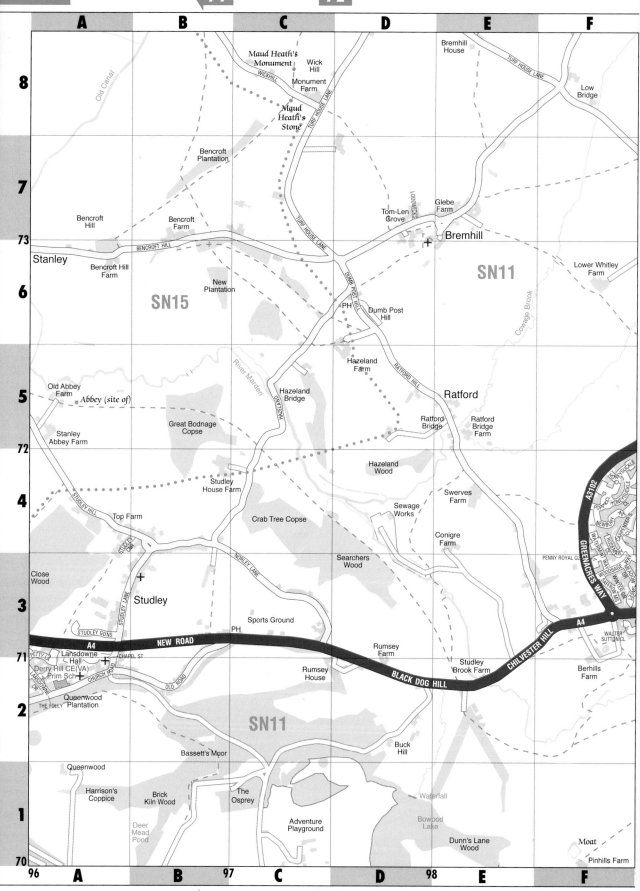

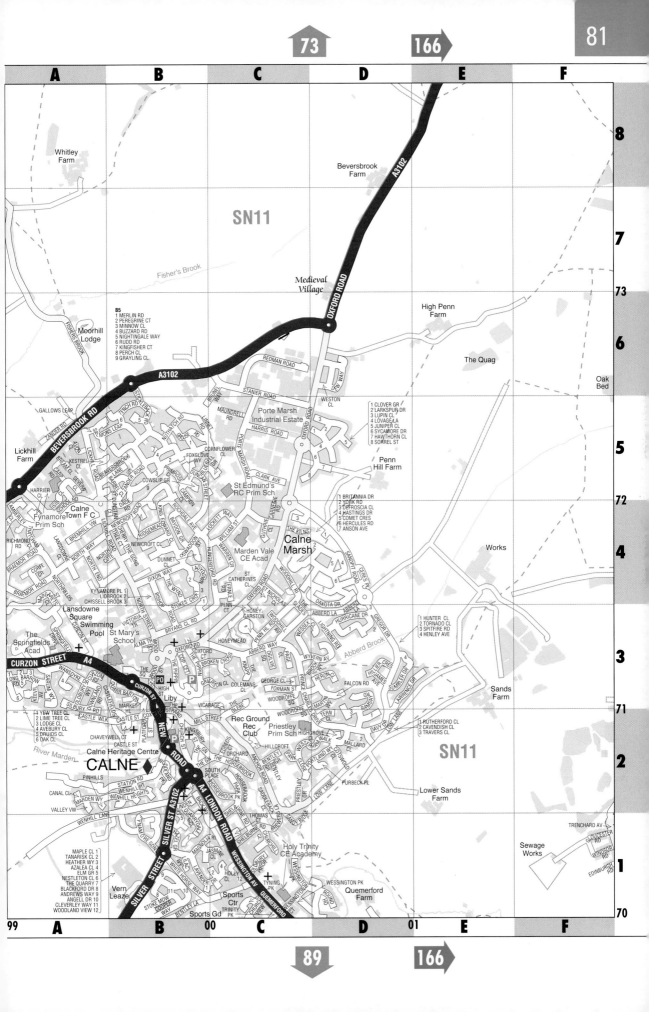

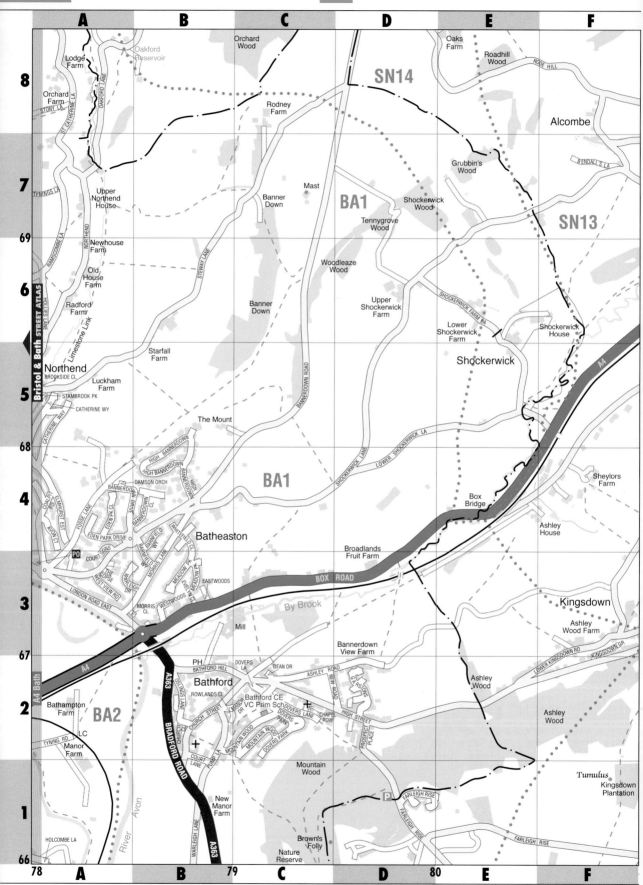

SN14

BA1

SN13

Alcombe

Shockerwick
Wood

Grubbin's
Wood

Tennygrove
Wood

Woodleaze
Wood

Upper
Shockerwick
Farm

Lower
Shockerwick
Farm

Shockerwick
House

Shockerwick

Oaks
Farm

Roadhill
Wood

RODE HILL

BENDALL'S LA

SHOCKERWICK FARM BA

Orchard
Wood

Rodney
Farm

Banner
Down

Mast

Oakford
Reservoir

Lodge
Farm

Orchard
Farm

Upper
Northend
House

Newhouse
Farm

Old
House
Farm

Radford
Farm

Starfall
Farm

Northend

Luckham
Farm

The Mount

Banner
Down

STEWAR LANE

BANNERDOWN ROAD

OAKFORD LANE

ST CATHERINE LA

STONY LA

RAMSCOMBE LA

TYNINGS LA

NORTHEND

CHARLES LANE

Limestone Link

BROOKSIDE CL

STAMBROOK PK

CATHERINE WY

CATHERINE WAY

Bristol & Bath STREET ATLAS

BA1

Batheaston

High Bannerdown
HIGH BANNERDOWN
DAMSON ORCH
BANNERDOWN DRIVE
BANNERDOWN CL
BANNERDOWN
HIGH BANNERDOWN

FOSSE LANE

BANNFIELD
BANWELL CL
MORRIS LANE
WHITEFIELD PL
MEADOW DR
EVELYN CT
MEADOW CL

COAL PIT RD
ELMHURST EST
AVON CL
EDEN PARK DRIVE
COALPIT RD

PO

COURT GDNS
THE COPSE
WAYLEIGH
WEST VIEW RD
LONDON ROAD EAST
MORRIS CL
WESTWOODS

EASTWOODS

Mill

Box
Bridge

Broadlands
Fruit Farm

SHOCKERWICK LANE
LOWER SHOCKERWICK LA

Sheylors
Farm

Ashley
House

BOX ROAD

By Brook

Kingsdown

Ashley
Wood Farm

LOWER KINGSDOWN RD
KINGSDOWN GR

A4

Bannerdown
View Farm

Ashley
Road

Ashley
Wood

PH
BATHFORD HILL

DOVERS
LA
TITAN DR

NEW ROAD

GASTONS

HIGH STREET

PROSPECT PLACE

CHAPEL ROW

Bathford

Bathford CE
VC Prim Sch

DOVERS LANE

DOVERS
PARK

ROWLANDS CL

HASTINGS LANE

CHURCH STREET

PUMP LA

MANOR DR

MOUNTAIN WOOD
MOUNTAIN WOOD
DOVERS PARK

COURT
LANE

A363

BRADFORD ROAD

Bathampton
Farm

BA2

Manor
Farm

TYNING RD

LC

HOLCOMBE LA

River Avon

WARLEIGH LANE

A363

New
Manor
Farm

Brown's
Folly

Nature
Reserve

Mountain
Wood

FARLEIGH RISE
FARLEIGH RISE

P

Ashley
Wood

Tumulus

Kingsdown
Plantation

FARLEIGH RISE

A4 Bath

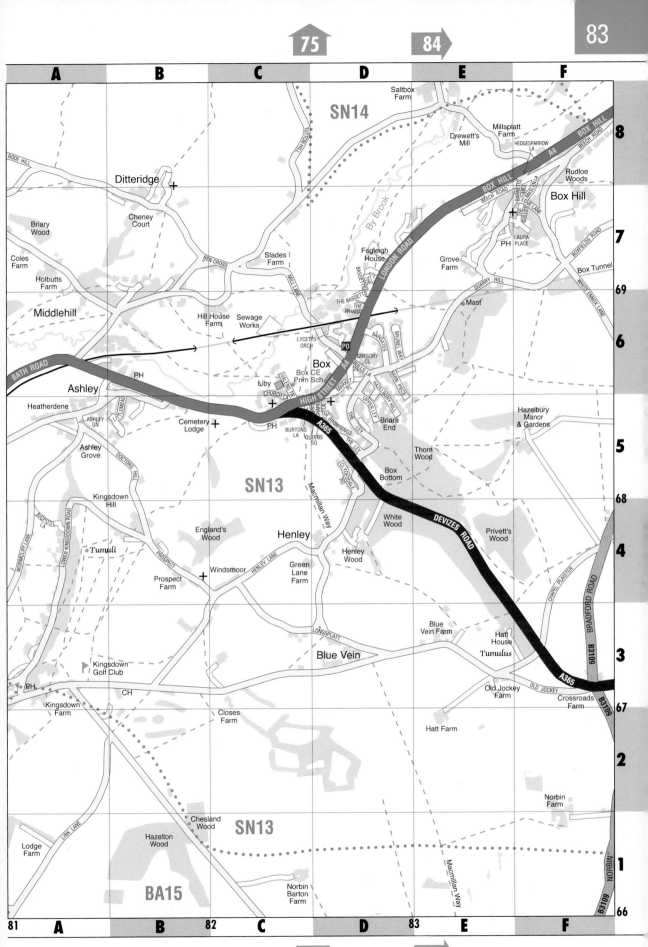

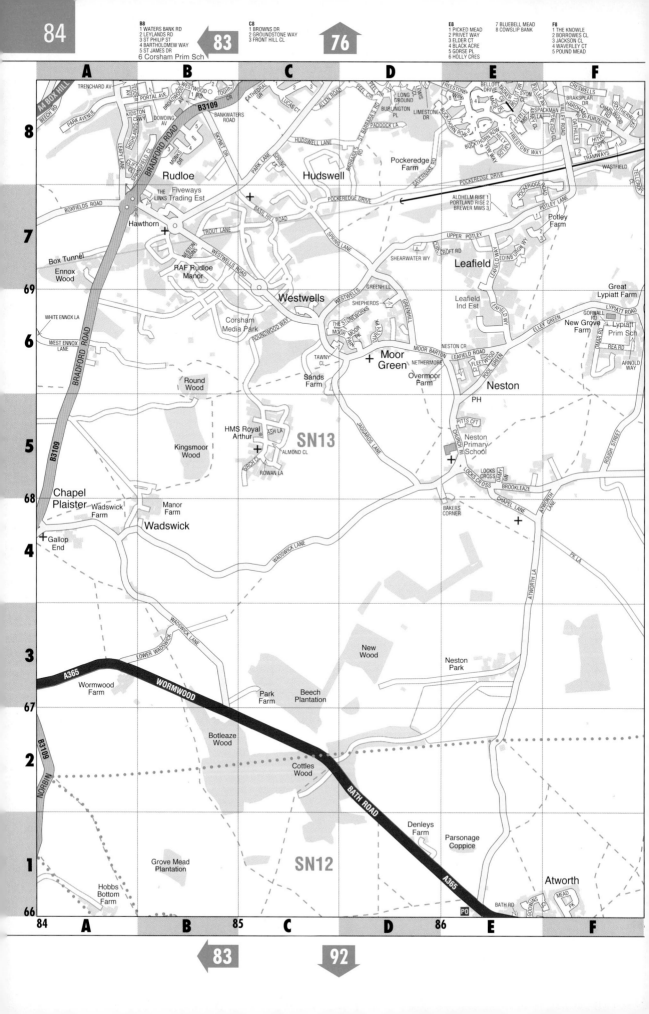

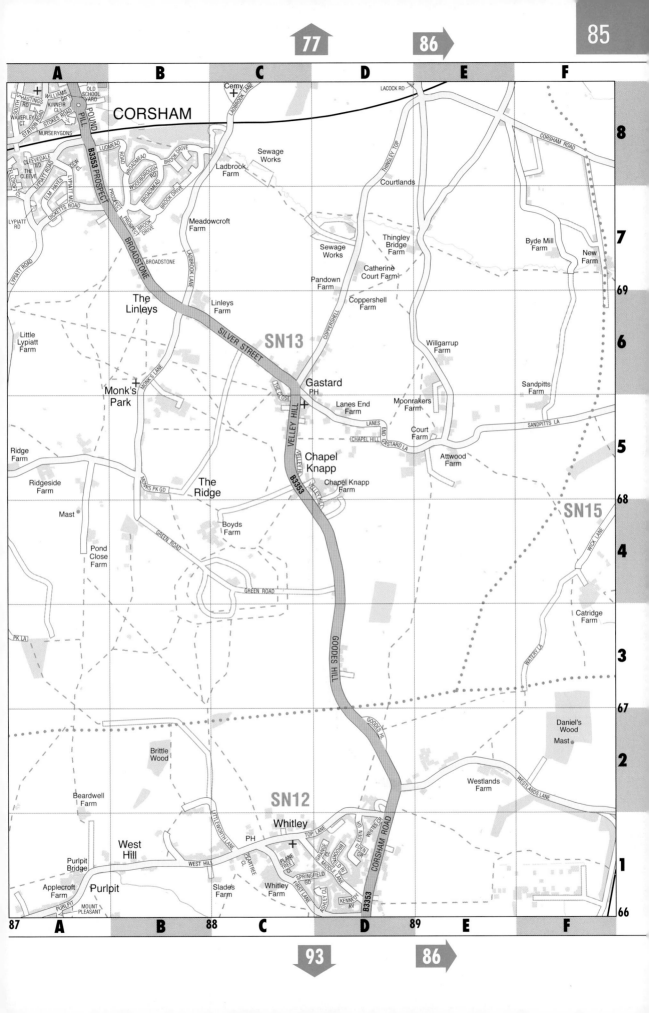

	A	B	C	D	E	F

8

NOTTON PK

Notton House Sch

Great Notton Farm

Home Farm

Lackham Wood

Notton

Larksnest Farm

A350

MONS LANE

Rake Pond Wood

Weir

7

CORSHAM ROAD

Cuckoo Bush Farm

Rey Mill

Naish Hill

ROSEMARY LA

White Hall Farm

Reybridge

MONS LANE

New End Farm

69

CANTAX HILL

NETHEROTT HILL

SN15

BEWLEY LANE

6

CHAPEL HILL

Lacock Pottery

EAST ST

Bewley Court

Mill Farm

CHURCH ST

Lacock Abbey

SANDPITTS LA

WICK LANE

FOLLY LANE

Lacock CE Prim Sch

HIGH ST

Lacock

Fox Talbot Museum

Bewley Common

NT

5

WEST STREET

PO

PH

P

Folly Farm

FOLLY LA

HITHER WAY

BEWLEY LANE

THE WHARF

BOWDEN HILL

MELKSHAM ROAD

Packhorse Bridge

PH

68

Wick Farm

Strode Farm

4

Sewage Works

River Avon

FOREST LANE

3

Earthwork

67

Riverside Farm

FOREST LANE

Halfway Farm

2

Queenfield

LOWER WOODROW

SN12

1

WESTLANDS LANE

THE LAURELS

CHAPEL LA

A350

Upper Beanacre Farm

BEANACRE ROAD

PH

66

90	A		B	91	C		D	92	E		F

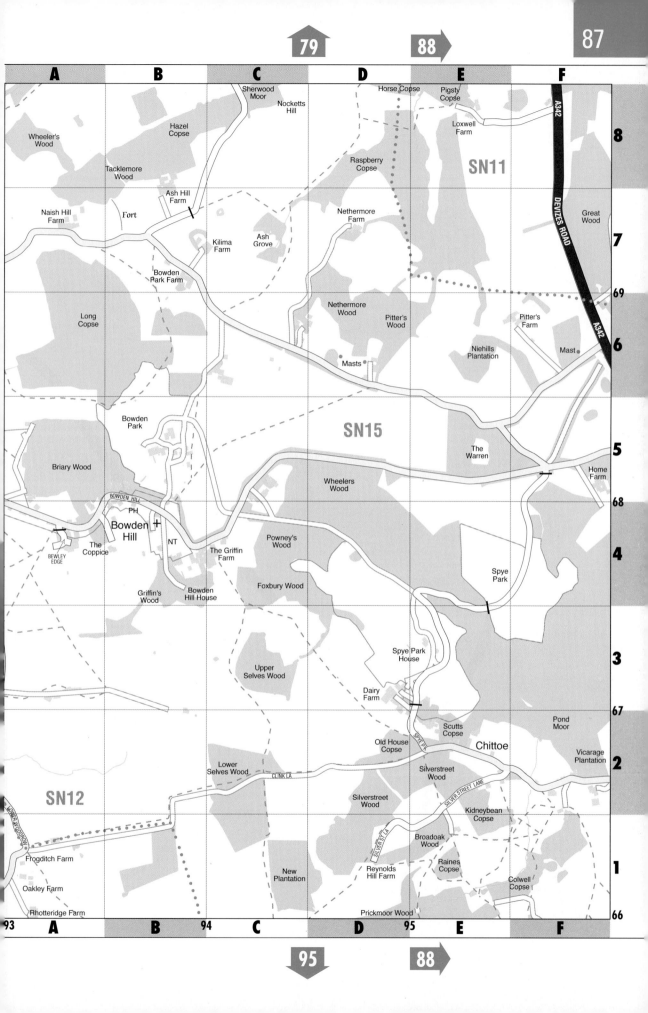

A B C D E F

8

7

69

6

5

68

4

3

67

2

1

66

A342

DEVIZES ROAD

A342

SN11

SN15

SN12

Wheeler's Wood

Sherwood Moor

Nocketts Hill

Hazel Copse

Horse Copse

Pigsty Copse

Loxwell Farm

Great Wood

Tacklemore Wood

Ash Hill Farm

Raspberry Copse

Naish Hill Farm

Fort

Kilima Farm

Ash Grove

Nethermore Farm

Bowden Park Farm

Nethermore Wood

Pitter's Wood

Pitter's Farm

Long Copse

Niehills Plantation

Mast

Masts

Bowden Park

The Warren

Briary Wood

Wheelers Wood

Home Farm

BOWDEN HILL

PH

Bowden Hill

NT

The Coppice

BEWLEY EDGE

The Griffin Farm

Powney's Wood

Spye Park

Griffin's Wood

Bowden Hill House

Foxbury Wood

Upper Selves Wood

Spye Park House

Dairy Farm

Pond Moor

Scutts Copse

Chittoe

Vicarage Plantation

Old House Copse

SPYE PK

Lower Selves Wood

CLINK LA

Silverstreet Wood

SILVER STREET LANE

Silverstreet Wood

Kidneybean Copse

SILVER ST LA

Broadoak Wood

Raines Copse

Colwell Copse

Frogditch Farm

LOWER WOODROW

New Plantation

Reynolds Hill Farm

Oakley Farm

Rhotteridge Farm

Prickmoor Wood

93 A B 94 C D 95 E F

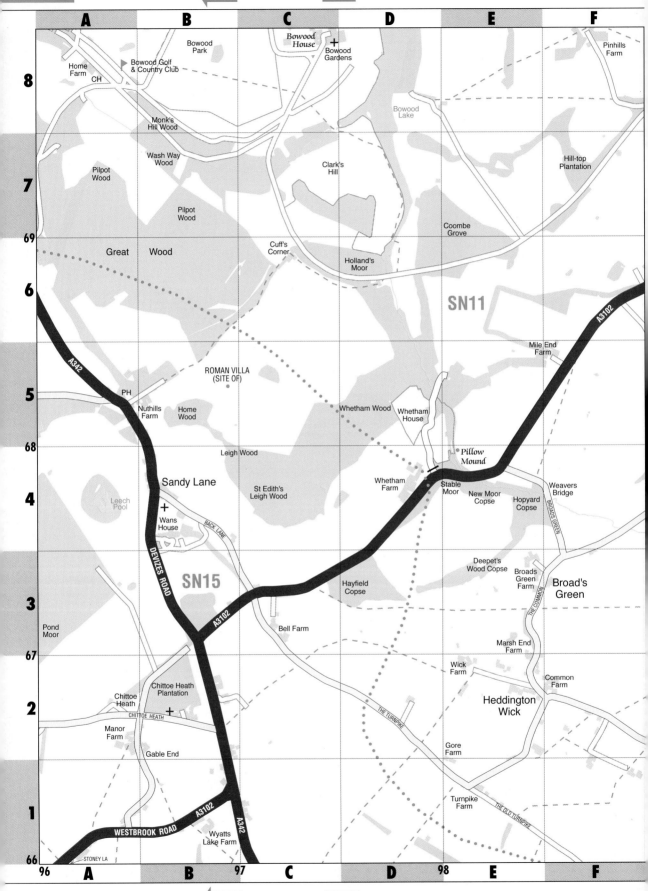

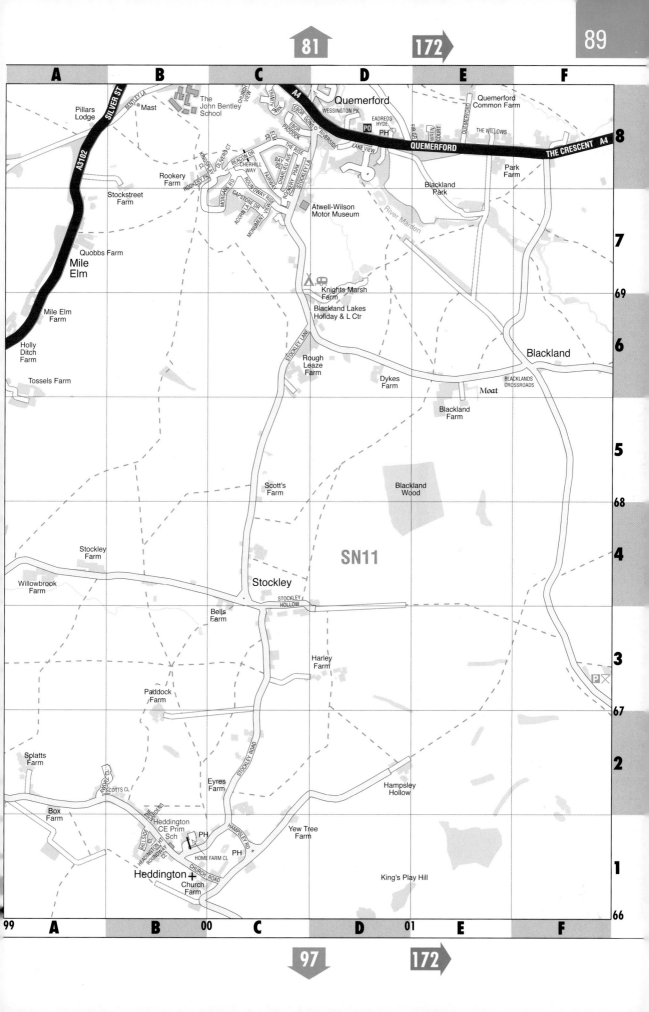

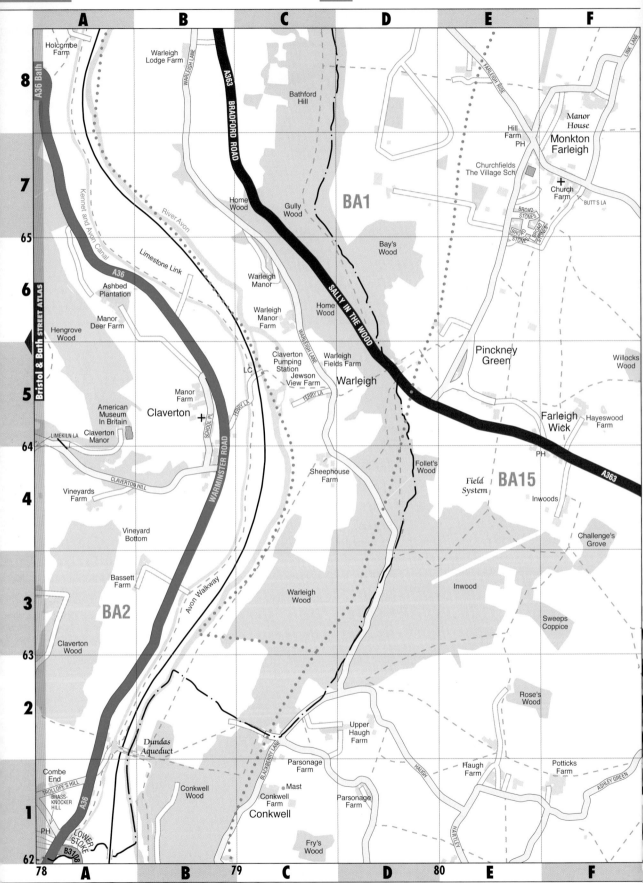

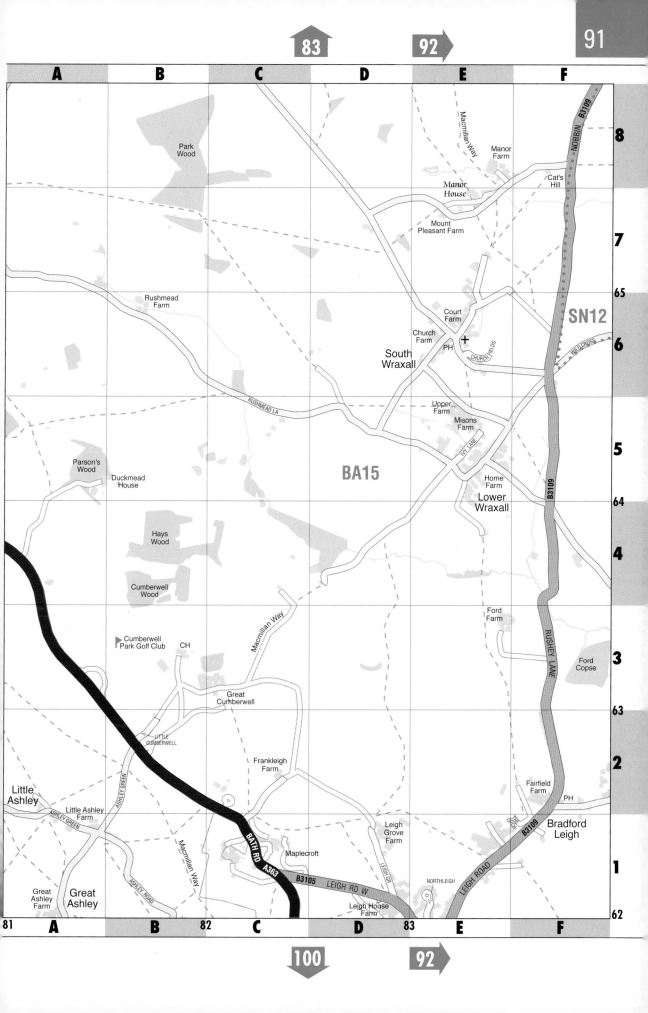

91
84

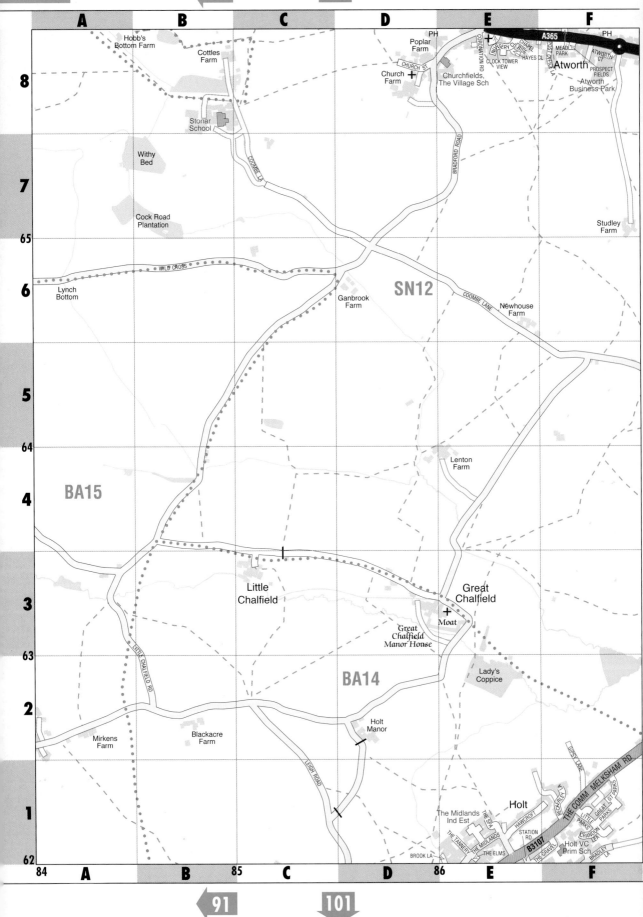

101

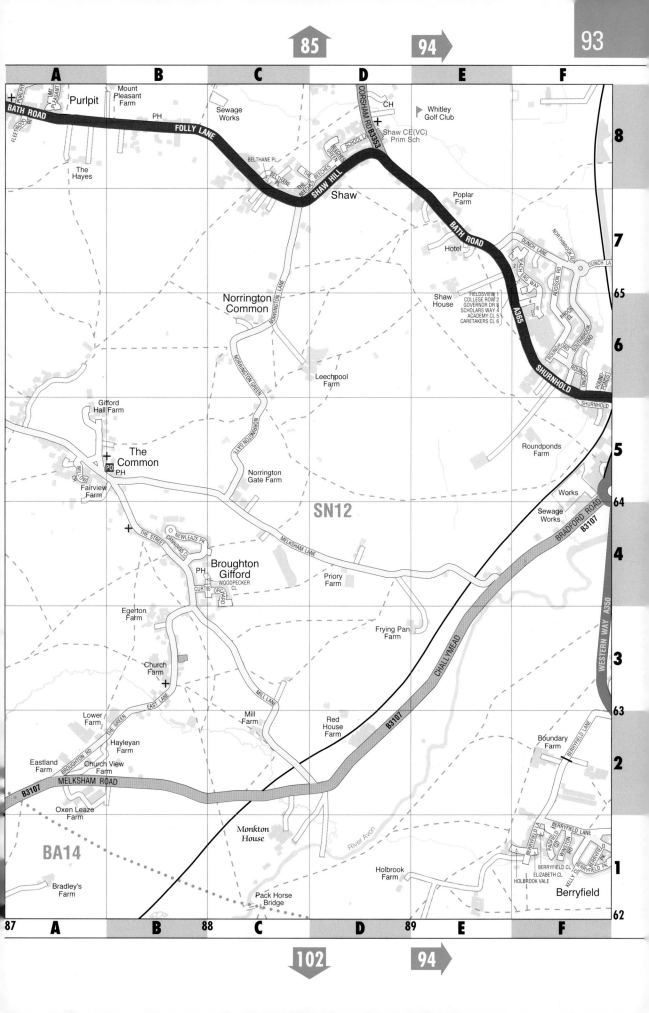

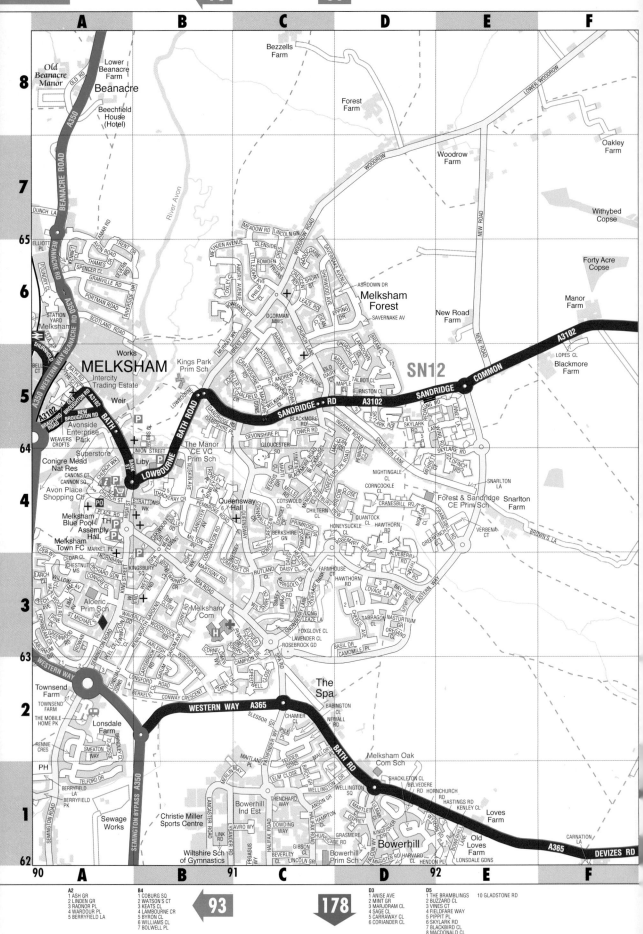

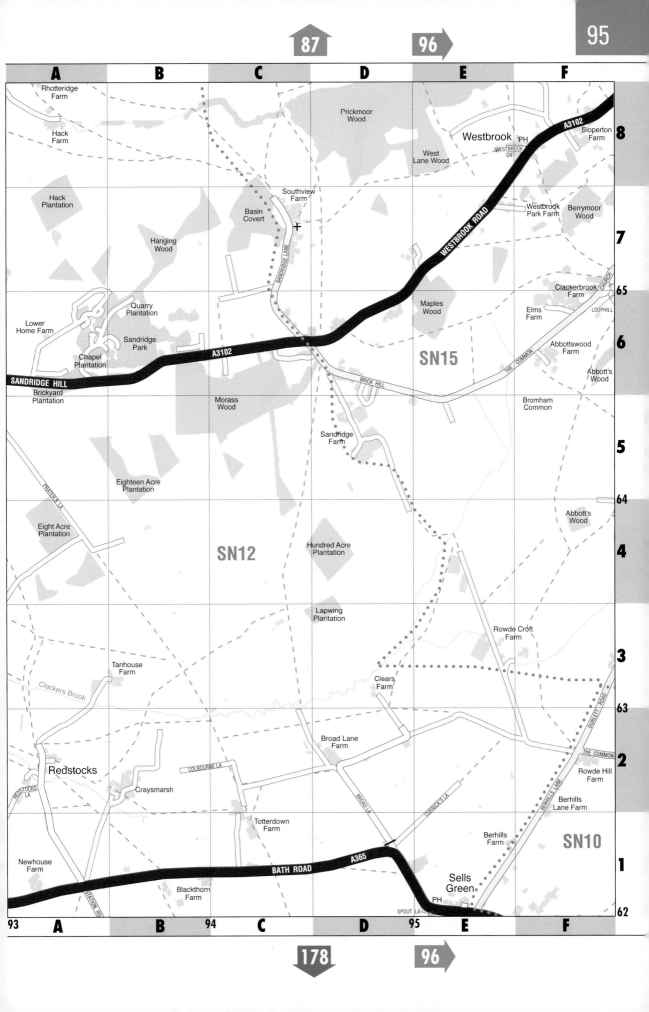

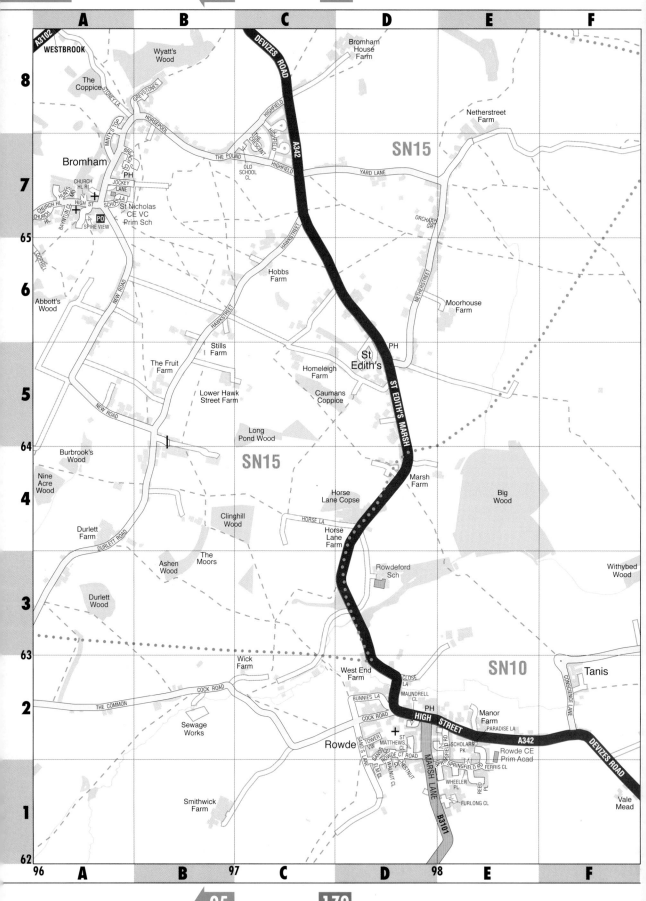

A3102
WESTBROOK

The Coppice

Wyatt's Wood

Bromham

PH

CHURCH HL RI
JOCKEY LANE
HIGH ST
BA WYTUN CL
CHURCH HL
CHURCH HL
HUN'S MD
SPIRE VIEW
PO

St Nicholas CE VC Prim Sch

GREYSTONES

MINTY'S TOP

HORSEPOOL

BRIC CL

THE POUND

OLD SCHOOL CL

LIME CRESCENT
HIGHFIELD
HIGHFIELD
HIGHFIELD

DEVIZES ROAD

Bromham House Farm

Netherstreet Farm

SN15

A342

YARD LANE

ORCHARD GR

NETHERSTREET

8

7

65

6

5

64

4

3

63

2

1

62

LODHILL

Abbott's Wood

NEW ROAD

Burbrook's Wood

Nine Acre Wood

NEW ROAD

Durlett Farm

Durlett Wood

DURLETT ROAD

Hobbs Farm

Stills Farm

The Fruit Farm

Lower Hawk Street Farm

HAWKSTREET

HAWKSTREET

Long Pond Wood

Clinghill Wood

Ashen Wood

The Moors

SN15

Homeleigh Farm

Caumans Coppice

St Edith's

ST EDITH'S MARSH

PH

Moorhouse Farm

Marsh Farm

Horse Lane Copse

HORSE LA

Horse Lane Farm

Rowdeford Sch

Big Wood

Withybed Wood

Wick Farm

THE COMMON

COCK ROAD

Sewage Works

Smithwick Farm

West End Farm

BUNNIES LA

COCK ROAD

Rowde

SAND S LANE

ST
VW
TOWER
MATTHEWS CL
LANDS
ROWDE CT ROAD
WALNUT CL
ELM CL
CHESTNUT
CRES
CLOSE LA
MAUNDRELL CL
PH
HIGH STREET

Manor Farm

PARADISE LA

SCHOLARS PK

Rowde CE Prim Acad

MARSH LANE

SPRINGFIELD RD
FERRIS CL
WHEELER PL
REED PL
FURLONG CL

B3101

SN10

Tanis

CONSCIENCE LANE

A342

DEVIZES ROAD

Vale Mead

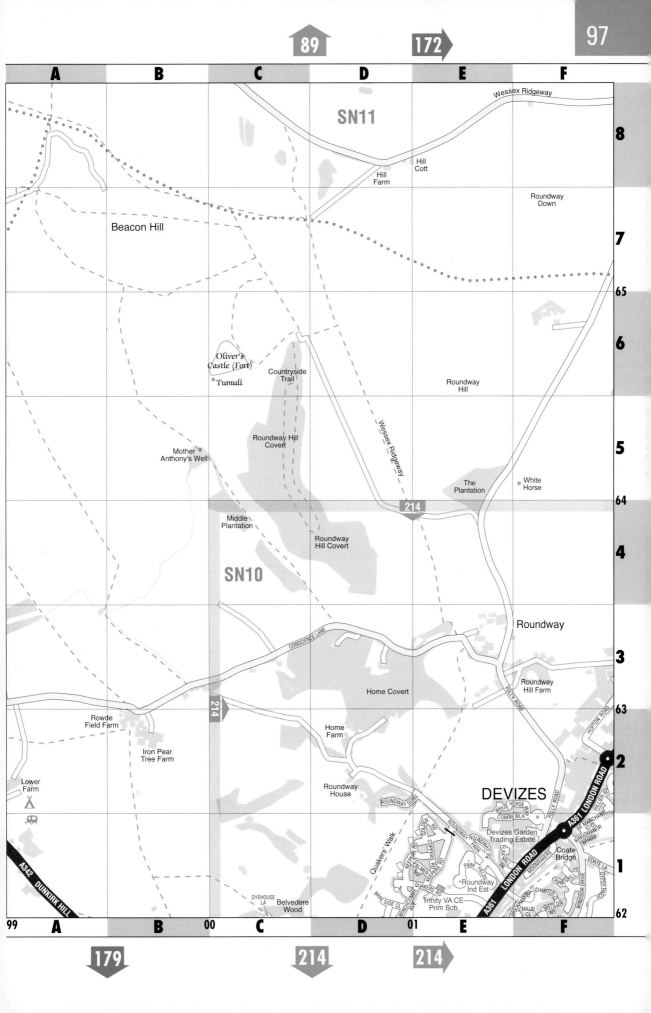

A   B   C   D   E   F

SN11

Wessex Ridgeway

8

Hill Cott

Hill Farm

Roundway Down

7

Beacon Hill

65

Oliver's Castle (Fort)

6

Countryside Trail

Tumuli

Roundway Hill

Roundway Hill Covert

Wessex Ridgeway

5

Mother Anthony's Well

The Plantation

White Horse

64

Middle Plantation

214

SN10

Roundway Hill Covert

4

Roundway

3

Roundway Hill Farm

214

Conscience Lane

Home Covert

63

Rowde Field Farm

Roundway Hill Farm

Folly Road

Home Farm

Iron Pear Tree Farm

2

Lower Farm

Roundway House

DEVIZES

Hopton Road

Hillier Rd

A361 London Road

Kingsmanor

Le Marchant Cl

Roundway Gdns

Roundway Park

White Horse

Combe Wlk

Devizes Garden Trading Estate

Coate Bridge

Coate La

1

Quakers' Walk

Palmers Rd

Coppers Rd

Keepers Rd

Park Fields

Roundway Ind Est

Flax Mill Pk

Folly Pk

Moonrakers

Cranesbill Cl

Charters

Windsor Drive

Dyehouse La

Belvedere Wood

Brae Side Cl

Windsor Cl

Trinity VA CE Prim Sch

Brickmakers Rd

Maud Cl

Matilda Wy

62

A342 Dunkirk Hill

A361 London Road

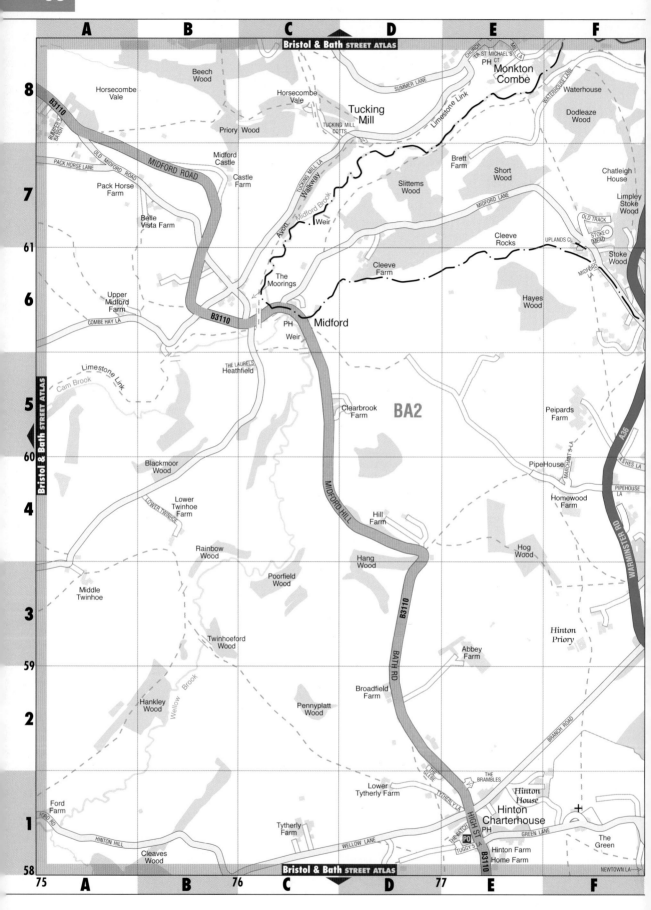

Monkton Combe

Waterhouse

Horsecombe Vale

Beech Wood

Horsecombe Vale

Tucking Mill

Dodleaze Wood

Chatleigh House

Priory Wood

Midford Castle

Castle Farm

Brett Farm

Short Wood

Limpley Stoke Wood

Pack Horse Farm

Belle Vista Farm

Slittems Wood

Midford Lane

OLD TRACK

STOKEO MEAD

Stoke Wood

Cleeve Rocks

UPLANDS CL

Cleeve Farm

The Moorings

Weir

Midford

Cleeve Farm

Hayes Wood

Upper Midford Farm

COMBE HAY LA

B3110

PH

Weir

Limestone Link

THE LAURELS

Heathfield

Cam Brook

BA2

Clearbrook Farm

Peipards Farm

PipeHouse

Homewood Farm

Blackmoor Wood

Lower Twinhoe Farm

LOWER TWINHOE

Hill Farm

Hog Wood

Hinton Priory

Rainbow Wood

Poorfield Wood

Hang Wood

MIDFORD HILL

Middle Twinhoe

Twinhoeford Wood

BATH RD

Abbey Farm

Hankley Wood

Wellow Brook

Pennyplatt Wood

Broadfield Farm

BRANCH ROAD

THE BRAMBLES

Hinton House

Ford Farm

FORD RD

HINTON HILL

Cleaves Wood

Tytherly Farm

Lower Tytherly Farm

TYTHERLY LA

THE GLEBE

HIGH ST

Hinton Charterhouse

PH

Green Lane

The Green

WELLOW LANE

PO

TUGGY'S LA

B3110

Hinton Farm

Home Farm

NEWTOWN LA

WARMINSTER RD

A36

ASHES LA

PIPEHOUSE LA

MARCHANT'S LA

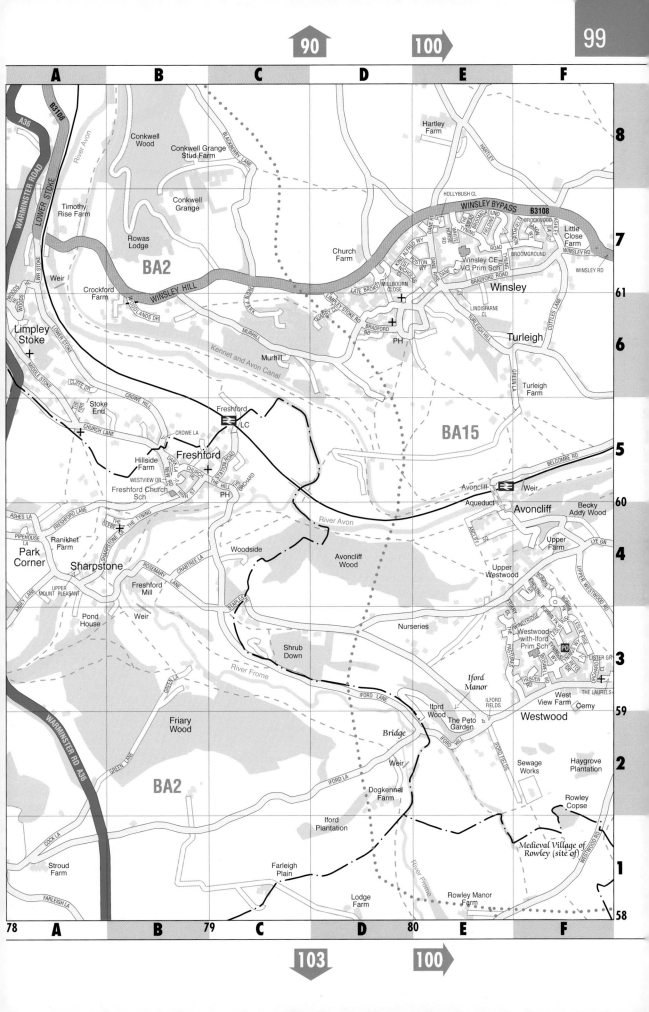

D6
1 ST MARGARET'S HILL
2 ST MARGARET'S PL
3 ST MARGARET'S VILLAS
4 KINGSTON RD
5 THE PADDOCK
6 ORCHARD GDNS
7 LONGS YARD
8 BARTON CL
9 STATION APP
10 BRIDGE YARD
11 GRIST CT
12 NORDEN

A B C D E F

Woolley Green
Woolley Barn Farm

B3105

Lower Bearfield Farm
PH
Macmillan Way
Recreation Ground
Northleigh
Hotel
Sladesbrook
Woolley Grange Farm

Ashley Road
Wiltshire Music Centre
St Laurence Sch
Bearfield Bldgs
Christ Church Prim Sch
Woolley

1 THE OLD ORCH
2 WOOLLEY ORCH
3 NEW RD CT
4 LUCCOMBE QUARRY

B3108
WINSLEY ROAD
MASONS LANE
NEW ROAD
B3109
HOLT RD
Cemy

Belcombe Court
Swimming Pool
Bradford-on-Avon
SILVER STREET
Liby & Mus
BRADFORD-ON-AVON
River Avon
Weir

Barton Packhorse Bridge
Barton Farm
Tithe Barn
Fitzmaurice Prim Sch
Bradford-on-Avon Golf Club
CH

Grip Wood
Grip Wood Farm
Sewage Works

BA15

Becky Addy Wood
Barton Farm Country Park
Lye Green Farm
Mast
Lye Green

Spencers Orchard
Rowden Farm
Widbrook
Old Farm
PH

TROWBRIDGE ROAD
A363

Upper Westwood
The Laurels
Westwood Manor House

Elms Cross
Vineyard
Hudds Farm

FROME ROAD
BRADFORD RD

Hotel

WESTWOOD ROAD

Midway Manor
Oxstall Farm

Trowle Common
Manor Farm
Manor Court Farm
BA14

B3109
Trowle Wood
Kingsley Pl

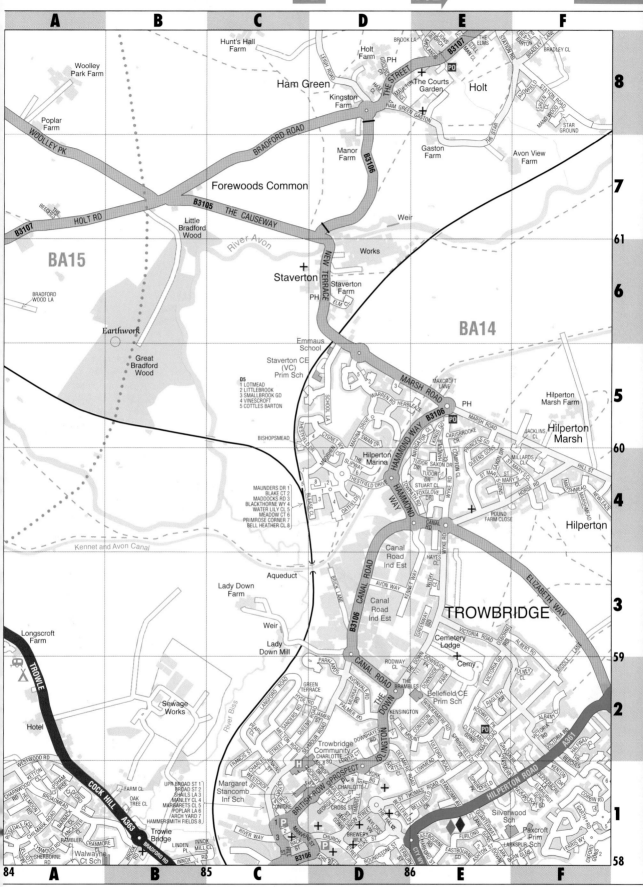

A B C D E F

8
7
61
6
5
60
4
3
59
2
1
58

Woolley Park Farm

Poplar Farm

WOOLLEY PK

THE BEECHES

B3107

BA15

BRADFORD WOOD LA

Earthwork

Great Bradford Wood

Hunt's Hall Farm

BRADFORD ROAD

Forewoods Common

B3105 THE CAUSEWAY

HOLT RD

Little Bradford Wood

River Avon

Ham Green

LEIGH ROAD

Kingston Farm

THE STREET

Manor Farm

B3106

Holt Farm PH

HAM GREEN GASTON

Staverton

Staverton Farm

PH ELM CT

New Terrace

Weir

Works

Emmaus School

Staverton CE (VC) Prim Sch

D5
1 LOTMEAD
2 LITTLEBROOK
3 SMALLBROOK GD
4 VINESCROFT
5 COTTLES BARTON

BISHOPSMEAD

SCHOOL LA

THESTLE DR

CYGNET WAY

WARREN RD

MARINA DRIVE

SWAN DR

THE SLIPWAY

MORVEN

Hilperton Marina

THESTFIELD DRIVE

BLAISE CL

OATLEDS

MAUNDERS DR 1
BLAKE CT 2
MADDOCKS RD 3
BLACKTHORNE WY 4
WATER LILY CL 5
MEADOW CT 6
PRIMROSE CORNER 7
BELL HEATHER CL 8

Aqueduct

Kennet and Avon Canal

BROOK LA

HOLT

The Courts Garden

PO

Gaston Farm

Avon View Farm

THE ELMS

STATION ROAD

BRADLEY LA BRADLEY CL

MAND WOOD

STAR GROUND

THE STAR

BA14

MARSH ROAD

HAMMOND WAY

B3106 PH PO

HERBLEAZE

NAVIGATOR CL

KINGS GD

TUDOR DR

SAXON DR

STUART CL

FOXGLOVE DR

COMPTON CL

CARISBROOKE CR

PRINCESS GD

MARSH ROAD

Hilperton Marsh Farm

Hilperton Marsh

JACKLINS CL

MILLARDS CL

HILL ST

MARSHMEAD

NEWLEAZE

QUEENS GDNS

ST MARYS GDNS

ST MARYS SCH

ST MARY'S ST

HORSE RD

POUND FARM CLOSE

Hilperton

CANAL RD

HAYES CL

WYKE RD

WITHY CL

KENNET WAY

Canal Road Ind Est

AVON WAY

Canal Road Ind Est

ELIZABETH WAY

TROWBRIDGE

Cemetery Lodge

Cemy

VICTORIA ROAD

ALBERT RD

FULNEY CL

MIDDLE LANE

GREENWAY

BRICK LANE

B3106

CANAL ROAD

THE DOWN

Lady Down Farm

Weir

Lady Down Mill

River Biss

Sewage Works

Longscroft Farm

TROWLE

Hotel

WESTWOOD RD

CHARNWOOD

ROSEDALE GDV

CHILMARK RD

KELTON

OSHAM CL

BROADMEAD

BARNACK

ASHTON

KINGSBURY

SHERBORNE RD

RAMBLER CL

CRANMORE

COCK HILL

A363

Walwayne Ct Sch

FARM CL

OAK TREE CL

Trowle Bridge

LINDEN PL

INNOX

BRADFORD RD

BROOK

INNOX MILL CL

UPR BROAD ST 1
BROAD ST 2
SHAILS LA 3
MANLEY CL 4
MARGARETS CL 5
POPLAR LA 6
ARCH YARD 7
HAMMERSMITH FIELDS 8

Margaret Stancomb Inf Sch

LANGFORD ROAD

PARK LANDS

GREEN TERRACE

HYDE RD

AVONVALE RD

THE DOWN

RODWAY CL

FRANCIS ST

WESTCROFT

CONIGRE

River Way

P

PEARL CL

WAVERLEY RD

SEYMOUR RD

SANDERS RD

PALMER RD

JAMES ST

QUEENS RD

CHARLES ST

STREET

MURRAY WALK

BRITISH ROW

PROSPECT

Trowbridge Community

H

CHARLOTTE

PL

YORK BG

CHARLOTTE CT

MANVERS ST

BACK ST

CHURCH ST

BREWERY ST

DUKE ST

ROUNDSTONE ST

UNION ST

GEORGE ST

CROSS ST

ST THOMAS

TIMBRELL ST

ISLINGTON

KENSINGTON

The Brambles

The Mount

CONISTON RD

FULFORD RD

HAYES

DOWN

DELAMERE ROAD

LOWMEAD

Bellefield CE Prim Sch

WINDERMERE RD

VICTORIA GD

OSBORNE RD

RAGLETH RD

CLEVELAND GDNS

RODWELL RD

ALBANY

VICTORIA RD

A361

PO

SPRINGFIELD RD

STANCOMB

CT

BELLEFIELD

HAYDON RD

Silverwood Sch

Paxcroft Prim Sch

HILPERTON ROAD

EASTBOURNE GDNS

ASHTON ST

FURLONG

LARKSPUR GN

CTY WW

THE BEECHES

HALFWAY

KELTON RD

CORBIN RD

GARTH RD

FERRIS WY

OXFORD

BAEN GLEA

DARTERN

CLARENDALE

E1
1 HILPERTON RD
2 HEATHER SHAW

F1
1 WALMESLEY CHASE
2 SUSSEX WLK
3 HEEKS CRES
4 SYLVESTER DR
5 MALWAYN CL
6 HULBERT CL

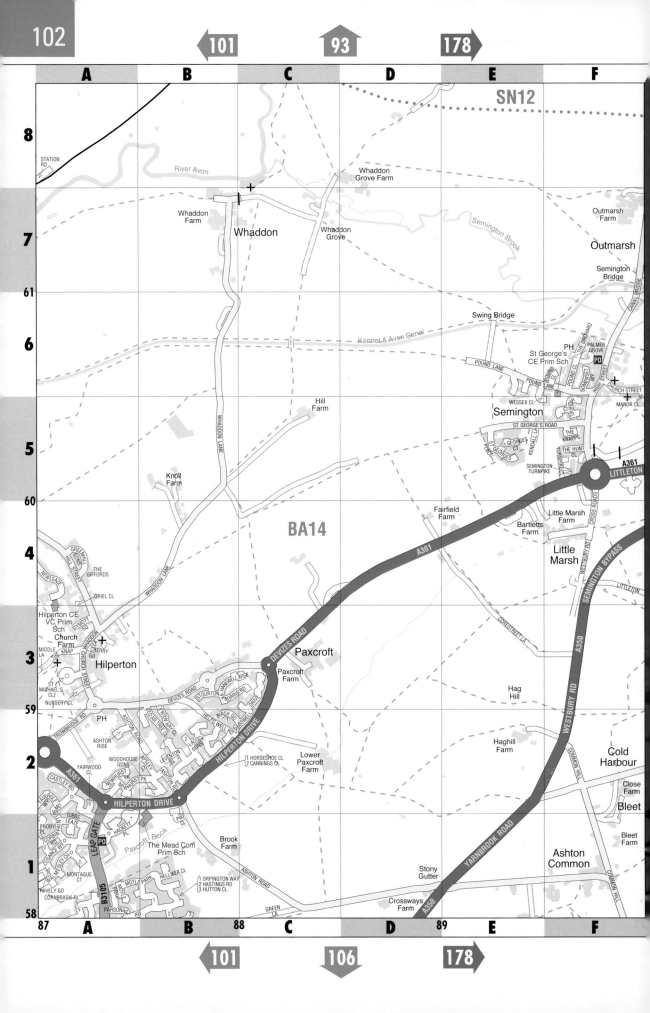

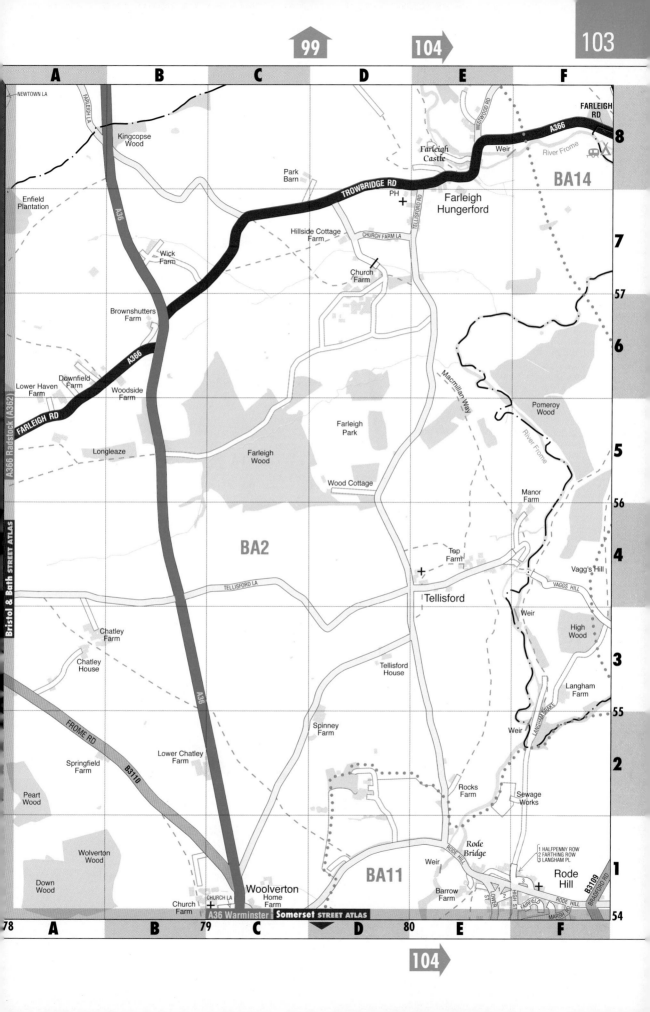

A   B   C   D   E   F

NEWTOWN LA

FARLEIGH LA

FARLEIGH RD

Kingcopse Wood

8

Farleigh Castle

Weir

River Frome

FARLEIGH RD

A366

BA14

Park Barn

TROWBRIDGE RD

PH

Farleigh Hungerford

Enfield Plantation

A36

Wick Farm

Hillside Cottage Farm

CHURCH FARM LA

7

TELLISFORD RD

Church Farm

57

Brownshutters Farm

A366

6

Macmillan Way

Pomeroy Wood

Lower Haven Farm

Downfield Farm

Woodside Farm

River Frome

FARLEIGH RD

Manor Farm

Longleaze

Farleigh Park

5

Farleigh Wood

56

Wood Cottage

BA2

Top Farm

Vagg's Hill

4

VAGGS HILL

Tellisford

Weir

High Wood

TELLISFORD LA

3

Chatley Farm

Chatley House

Tellisford House

Langham Farm

LANGHAM BRAKE

55

FROME RD

Spinney Farm

Weir

2

B3110

Springfield Farm

Lower Chatley Farm

Rocks Farm

Sewage Works

Peart Wood

A36

1 HALFPENNY ROW
2 FARTHING ROW
3 LANGHAM PL

Wolverton Wood

Rode Bridge

RODE HILL

1

Weir

B3109

BRADFORD RD

Down Wood

BA11

Barrow Farm

Rode Hill

Church Farm

CHURCH LA

Woolverton Home Farm

54

LOWER ST

HIGH ST

FAIRFIELD

RODE HILL

MARSH

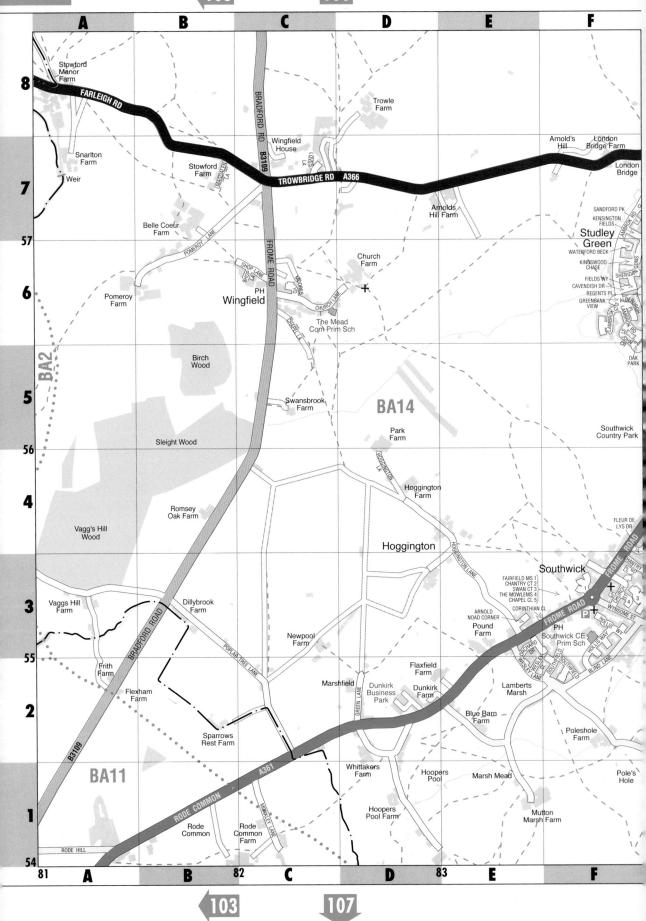

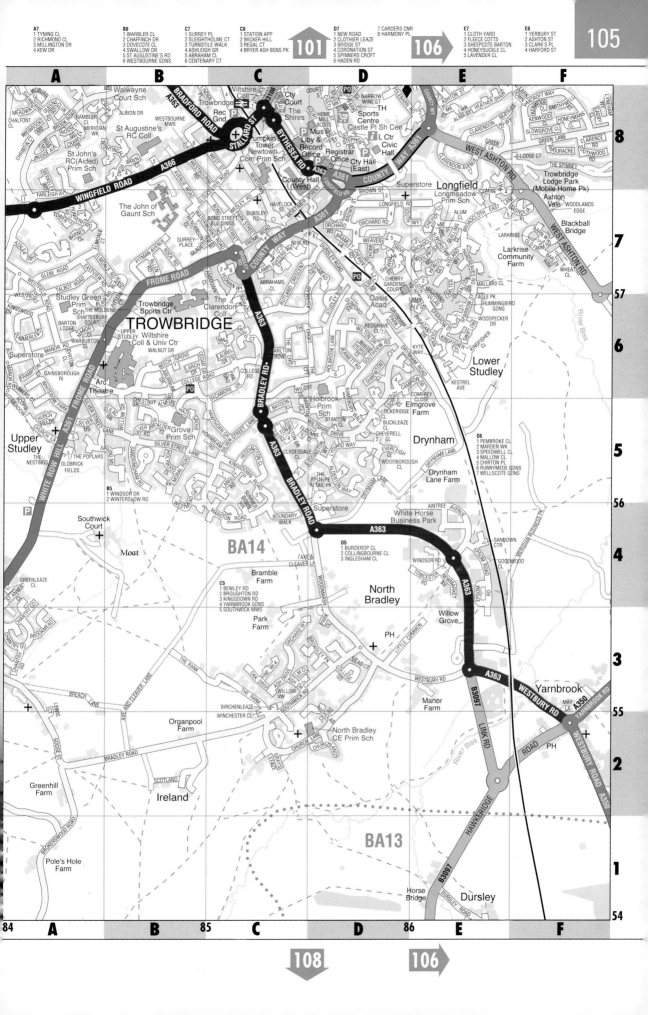

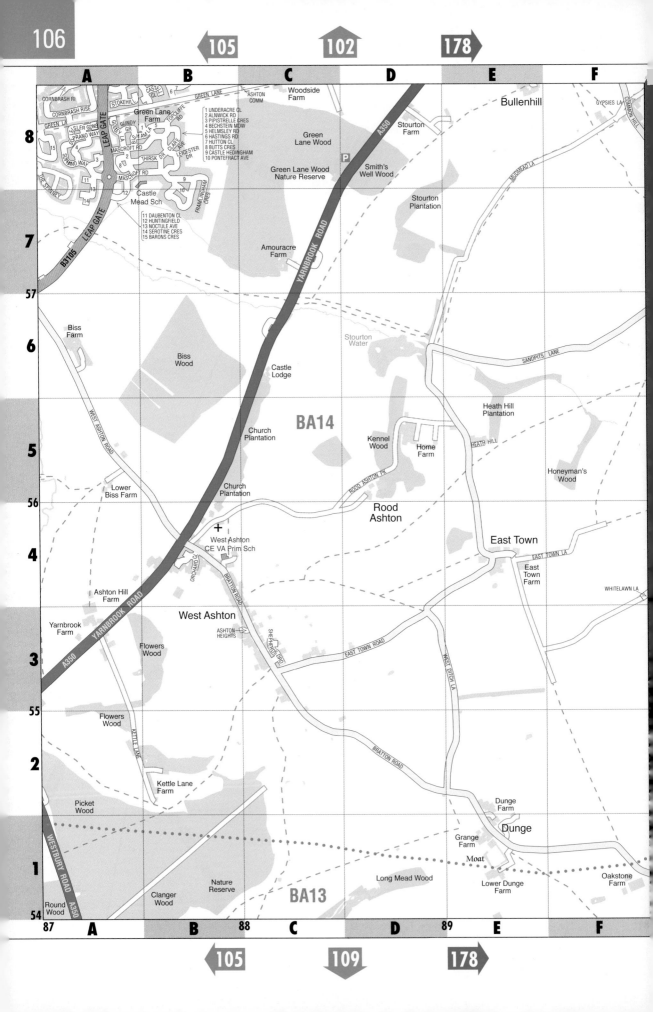

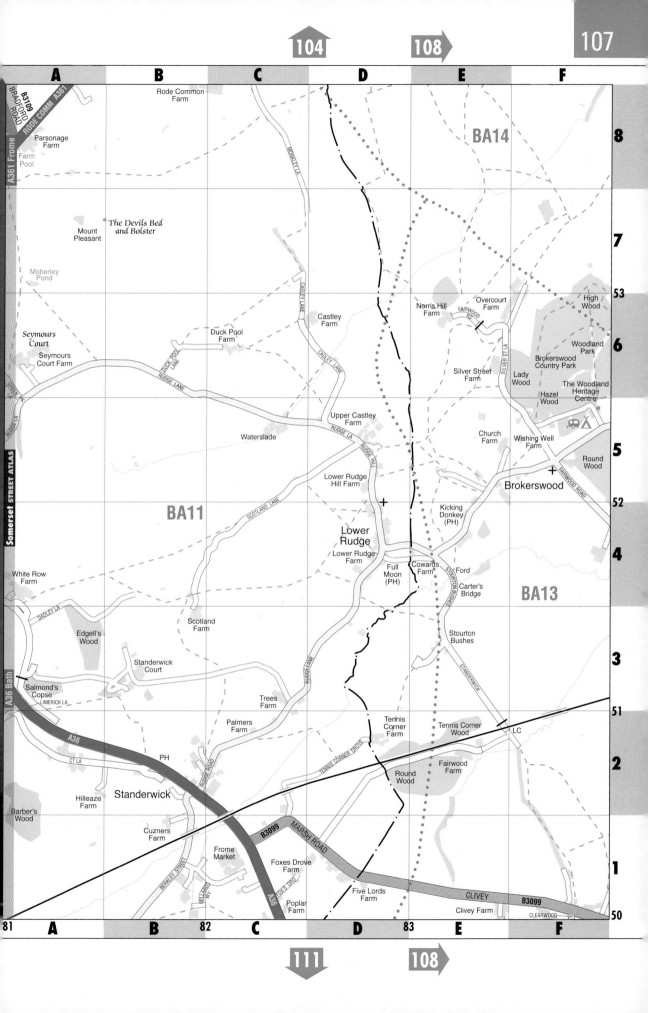

A　B　C　D　E　F

Somerset STREET ATLAS

8

7

53

6

5

52

4

3

51

2

1

50

BA14

BA11

BA13

B3109
BRADFORD
RODE COMM A361
ROAD

A361 Frome

Rode Common
Farm

Parsonage
Farm

Farm
Pool

Mount
Pleasant

The Devils Bed
and Bolster

Moberley
Pond

Seymours
Court

Seymours
Court Farm

GREEN PK

RUDGE LANE

DUCK POOL LANE

RUDGE LANE

Duck Pool
Farm

CASLEY LANE

Castley
Farm

CASLEY LANE

Norris Hill
Farm

FAIRWOOD RD

Overcourt
Farm

High
Wood

SILVER ST LA

Silver Street
Farm

Woodland
Park

Brokerswood
Country Park

Lady
Wood

Hazel
Wood

The Woodland
Heritage
Centre

Waterslade

Upper Castley
Farm

RUDGE LA

RUDGE HILL

Church
Farm

Wishing Well
Farm

Round
Wood

SCOTLAND LANE

Lower Rudge
Hill Farm

Lower
Rudge

Kicking
Donkey
(PH)

Brokerswood

FAIRWOOD ROAD

White Row
Farm

DADLEY LA

Lower Rudge
Farm

Full Moon
(PH)

Cowards
Farm

Ford

Carter's
Bridge

STOURTON BUSHES

Scotland
Farm

Edgell's
Wood

Standerwick
Court

Stourton
Bushes

STANDERWICK

Salmond's
Copse

LIMERICK LA

A36 Bath

Trees
Farm

RUDGE ROAD

Palmers
Farm

Tennis
Corner
Farm

Tennis Corner
Wood

LC

A36

CT LA

PH

Standerwick

Hilleaze
Farm

TENNIS CORNER DROVE

Round
Wood

Fairwood
Farm

STANDERWICK

Barber's
Wood

Cuzners
Farm

BERKLEY STREET

MILLARDS WY

Frome
Market

B3099

FOXES DRO

MARSH ROAD

Foxes Drove
Farm

Five Lords
Farm

CLIVEY

B3099

A36

Poplar
Farm

Clivey Farm

CLEARWOOD

107
105

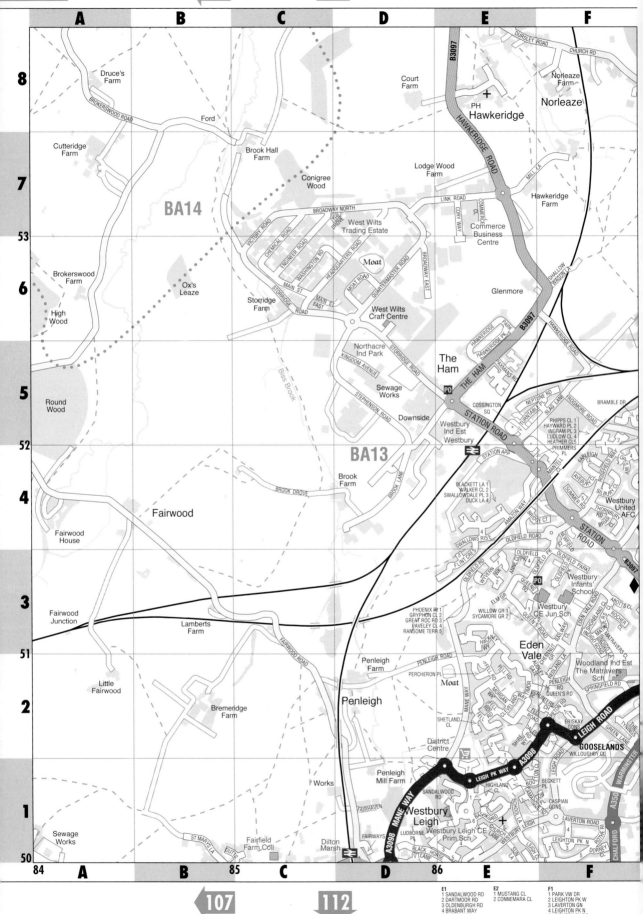

107
112

E1
1 SANDALWOOD RD
2 DARTMOOR RD
3 OLDENBURGH RD
4 BRABANT WAY
5 SUFFOLK RD
6 EXMOOR RD
7 PALOMINO PL
8 SALISBURY CL

E2
1 MUSTANG CL.
2 CONNEMARA CL.

F1
1 PARK VW DR
2 LEIGHTON PK W
3 LAVERTON GN
4 LEIGHTON PK N
5 LEIGHTON PK RD
6 SAND HOLE LA

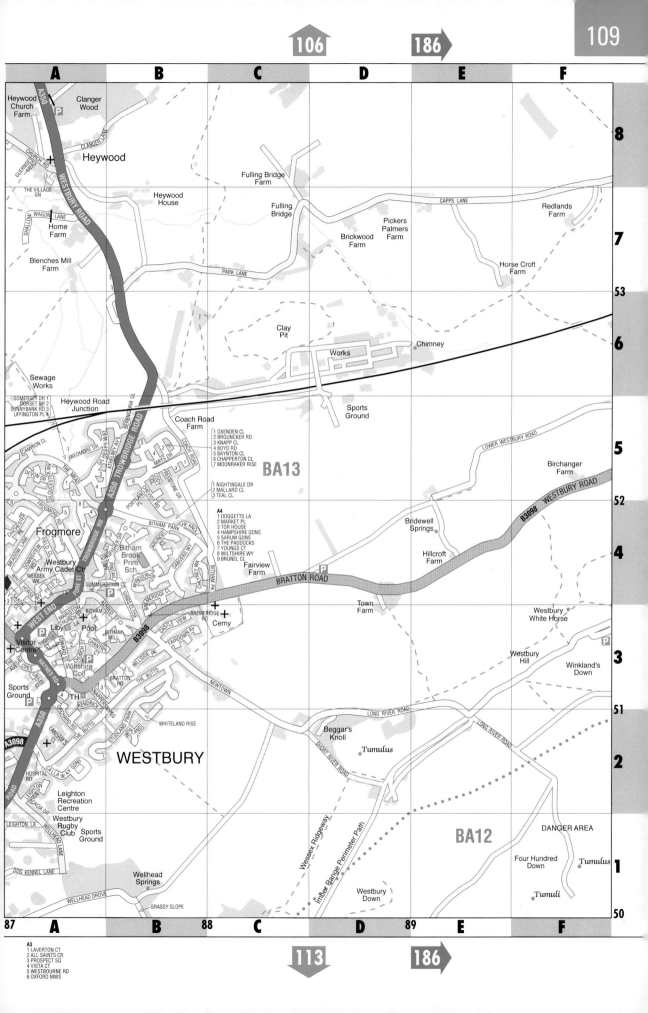

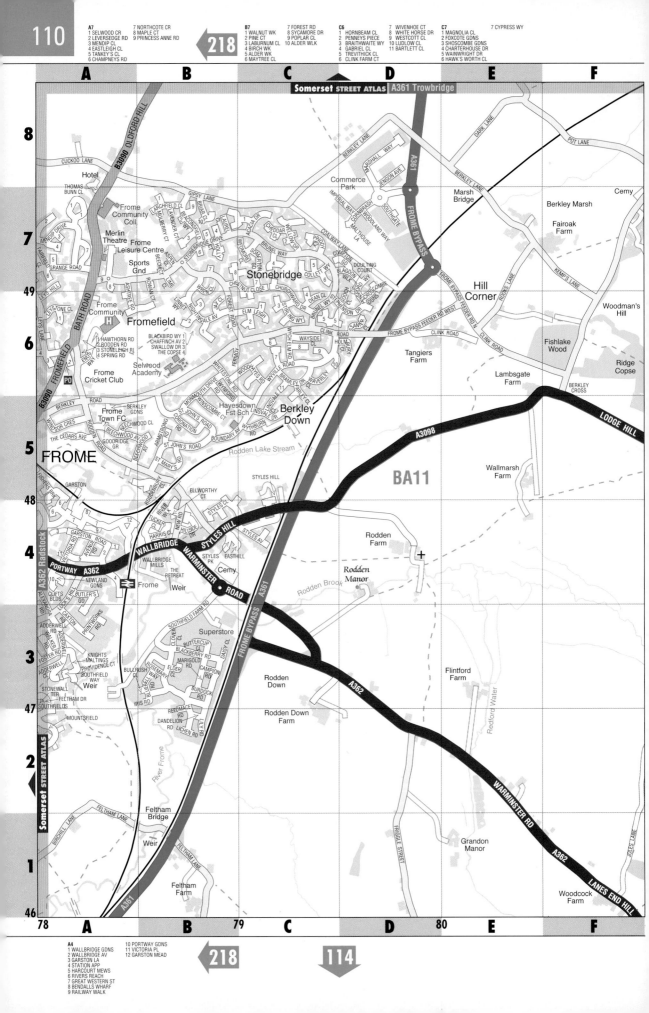

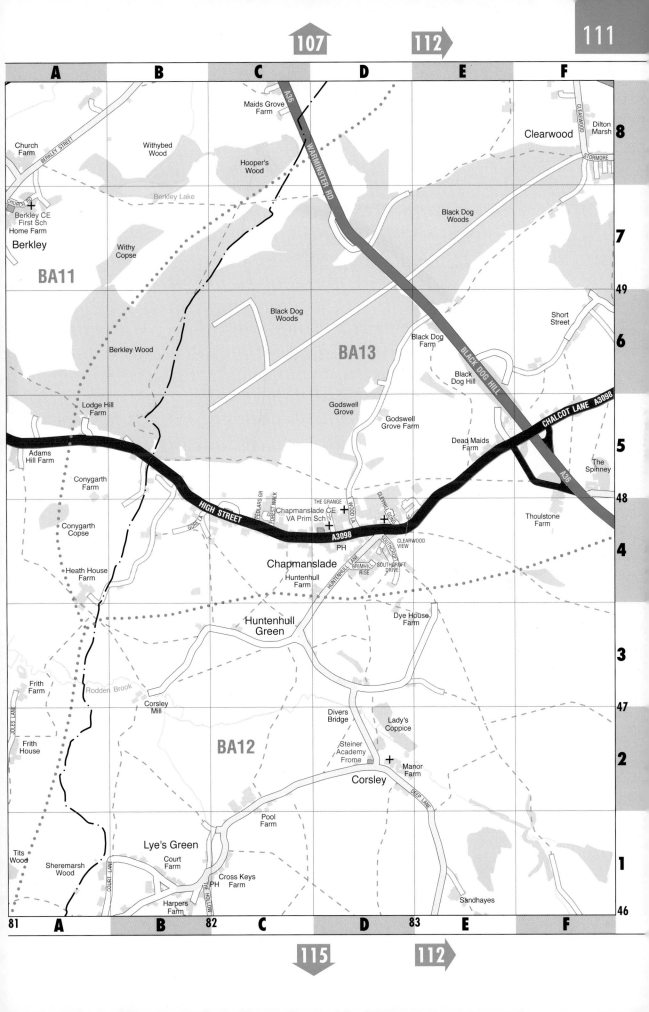

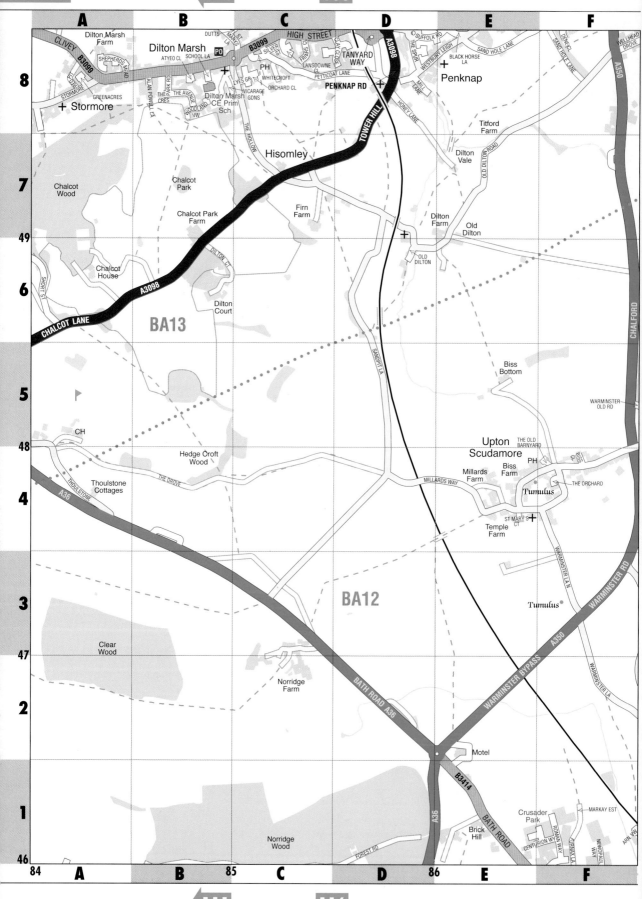

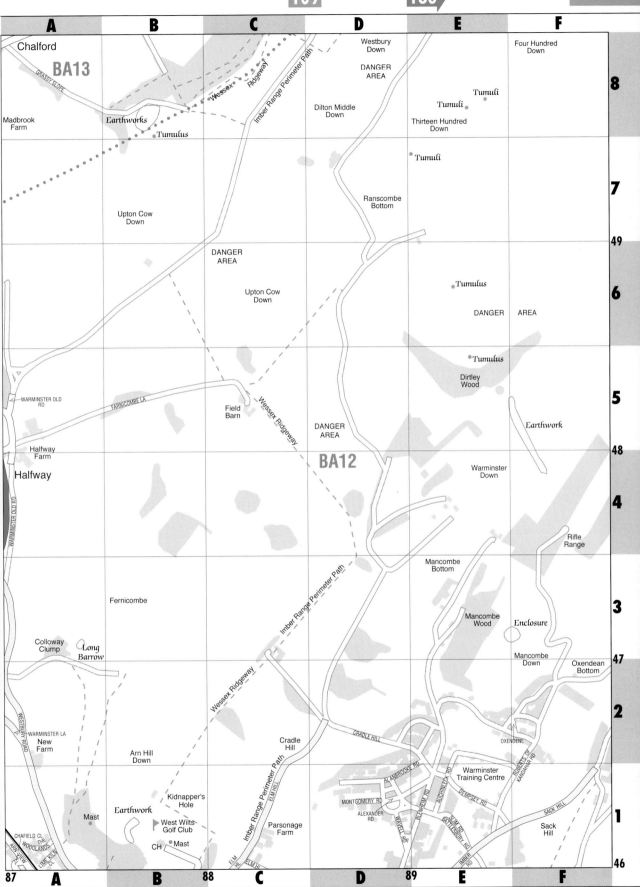

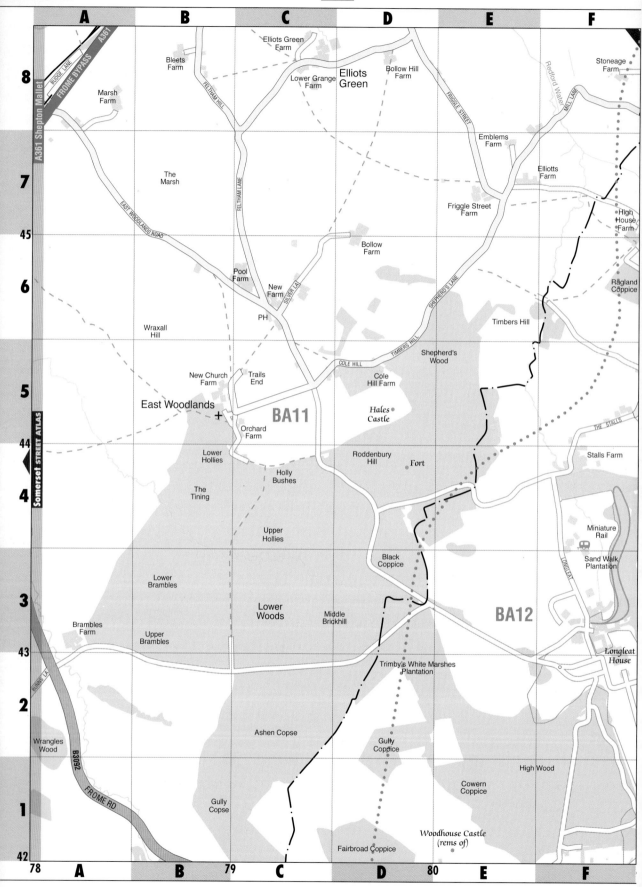

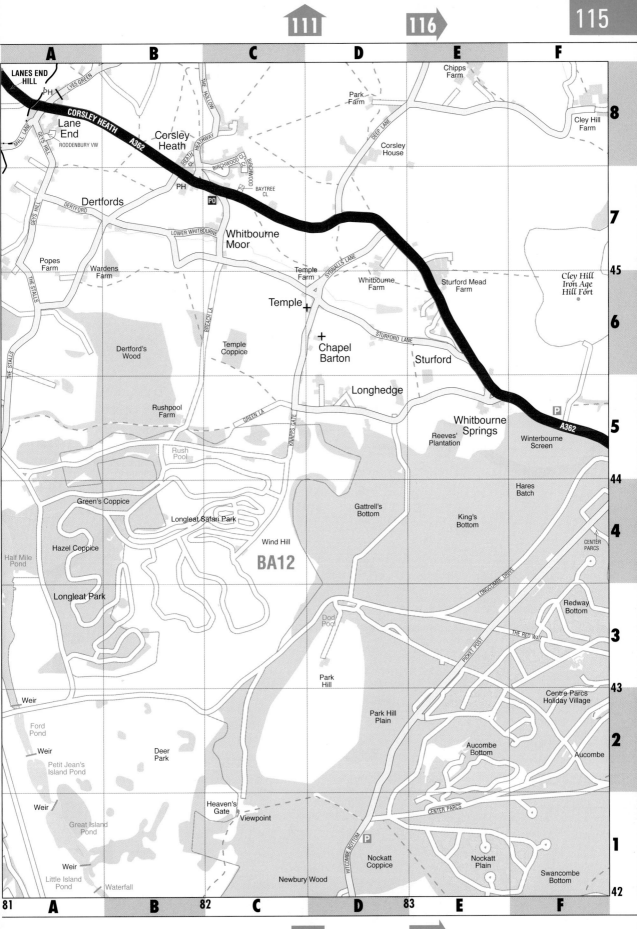

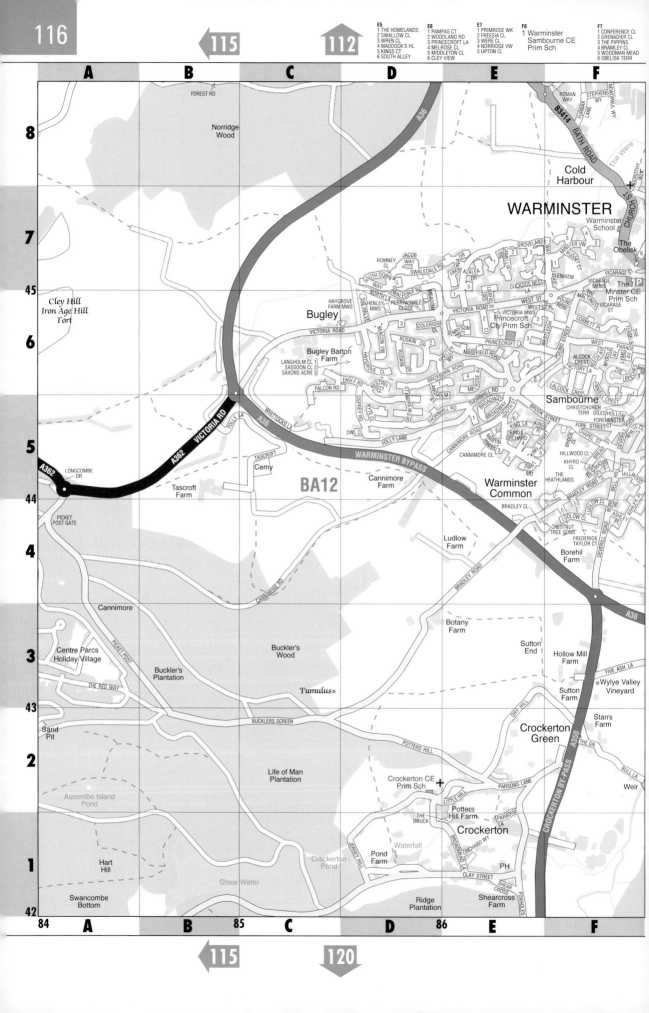

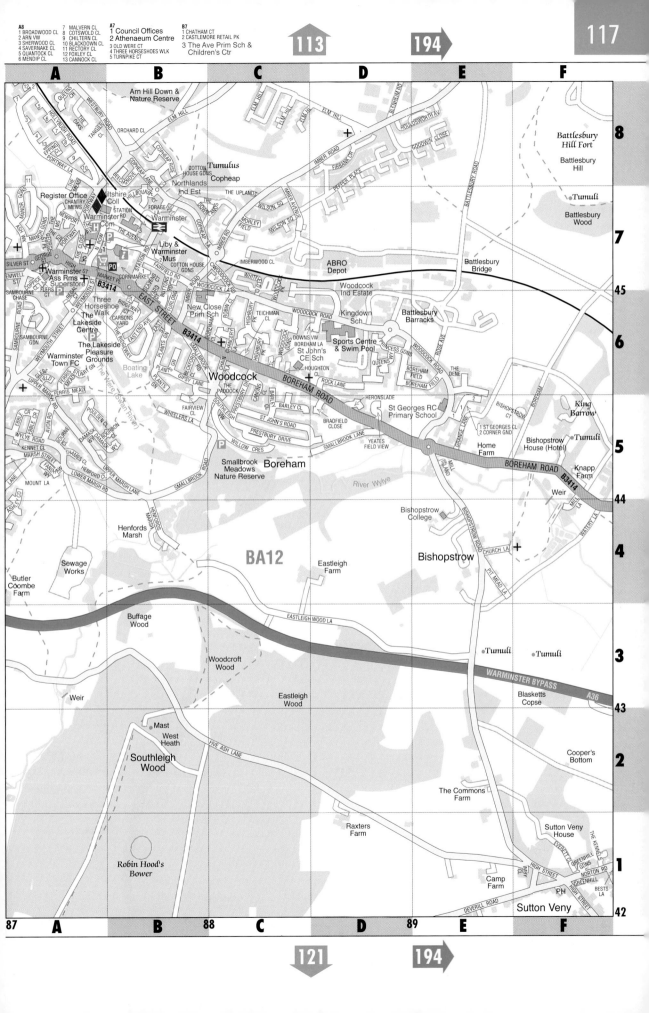

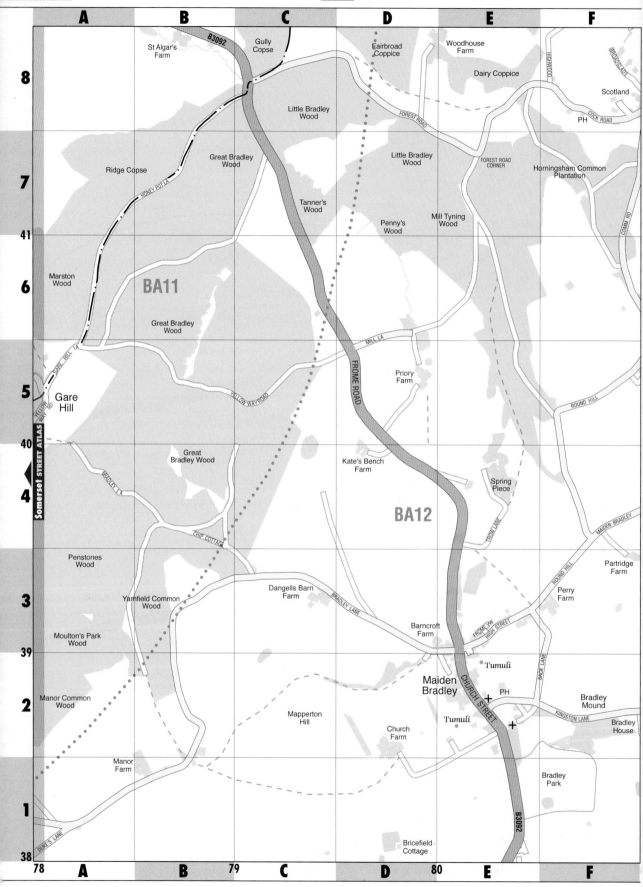

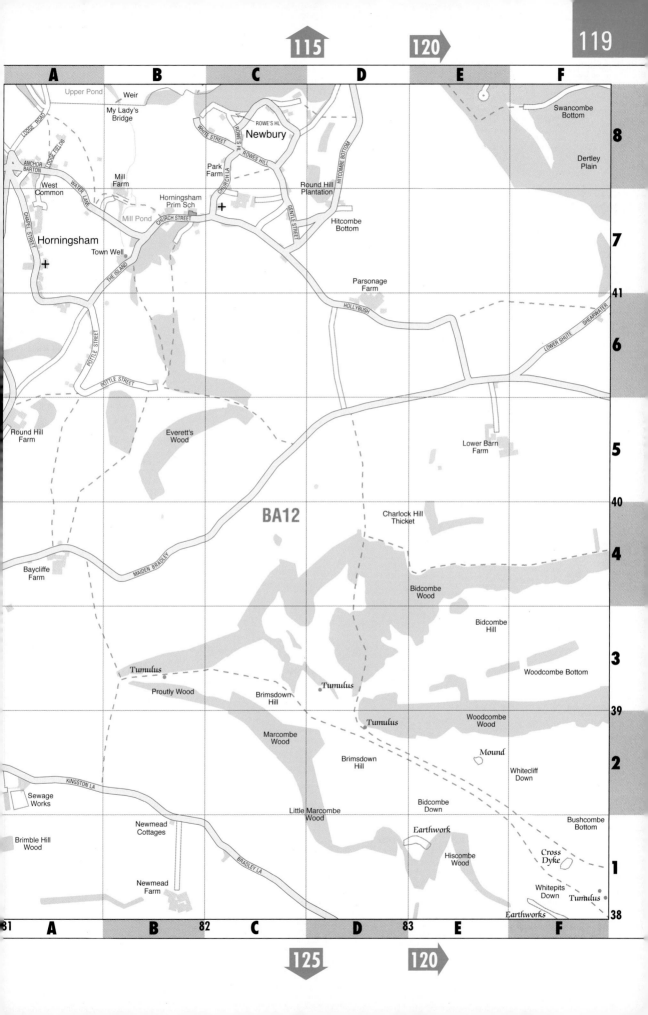

A | B | C | D | E | F

8
7
41
6
5
40
4
3
39
2
1
38

Upper Pond
Weir
My Lady's Bridge
ROWE'S HL
Newbury
WHITE STREET
ROWE'S HL
ROWES HILL
Park Farm
CHURCH LA
Mill Farm
GENTLE STREET
HITCOMBE BOTTOM
Swancombe Bottom
Dertley Plain
LODGE ROAD
LODGE FIELDS
ANCHOR BARTON
West Common
WATER LANE
Horningsham Prim Sch
Round Hill Plantation
CHAPEL STREET
Mill Pond
CHURCH STREET
Hitcombe Bottom
Horningsham
Town Well
THE ISLAND
Parsonage Farm
HOLLYBUSH
SHEARWATER
LOWER SHUTE
POTTLE STREET
POTTLE STREET
Round Hill Farm
Everett's Wood
Lower Barn Farm
BA12
Charlock Hill Thicket
Baycliffe Farm
MAIDEN BRADLEY
Bidcombe Wood
Bidcombe Hill
Woodcombe Bottom
Tumulus
Proutly Wood
Brimsdown Hill
Tumulus
Marcombe Wood
Tumulus
Woodcombe Wood
Brimsdown Hill
Mound
Whitecliff Down
KINGSTON LA
Sewage Works
Little Marcombe Wood
Bidcombe Down
Bushcombe Bottom
Newmead Cottages
BRADLEY LA
Brimble Hill Wood
Earthwork
Hiscombe Wood
Cross Dyke
Newmead Farm
Whitepits Down
Tumulus
Earthworks

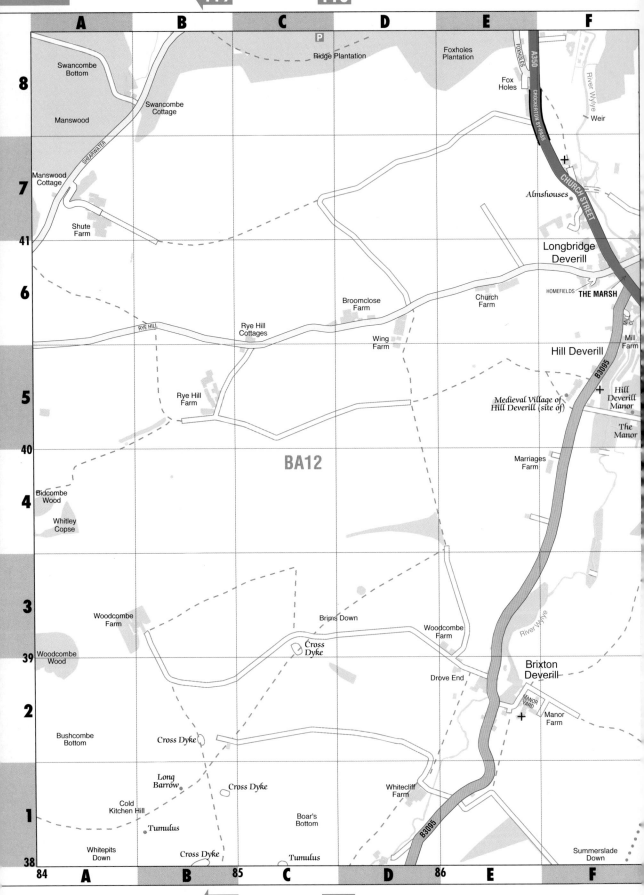

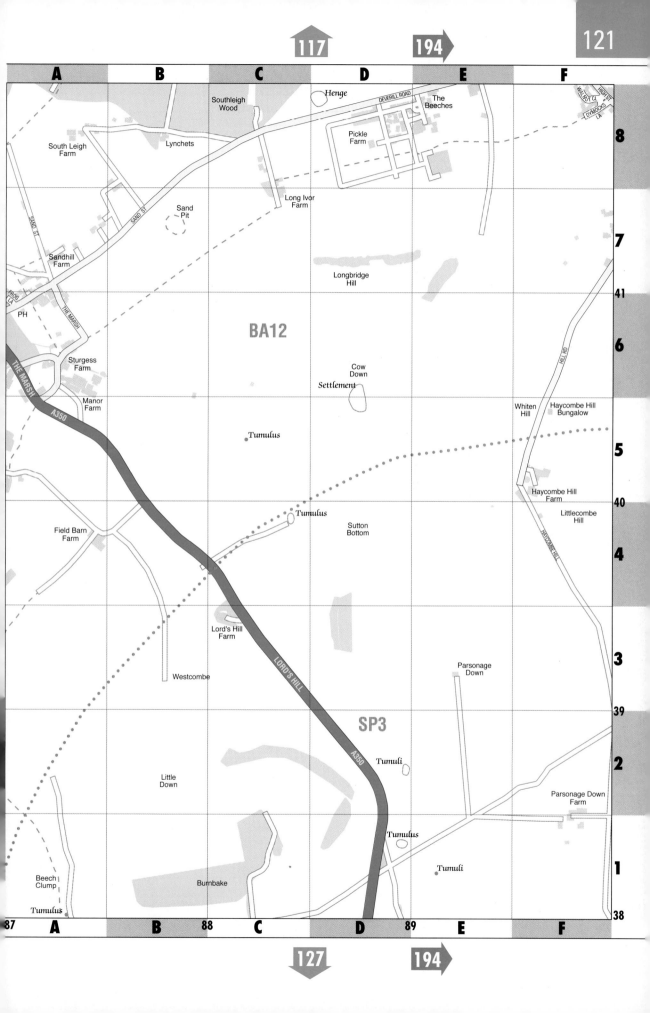

A | B | C | D | E | F

Henge
DEVERILL ROAD
The Beeches
WALNUT CL
DYMOCKS LA
HIGH ST

Southleigh Wood

Pickle Farm

South Leigh Farm

Lynchets

8

Long Ivor Farm

Sand St

Sand Pit

7

Sandhill Farm

41

Longbridge Hill

BA12

HILL RD

6

Cow Down

Settlement

FROG LA

PH

THE MARSH

Sturgess Farm

Whiten Hill

Haycombe Hill Bungalow

Manor Farm

A350

Tumulus

5

Haycombe Hill Farm

40

Field Barn Farm

Tumulus

Sutton Bottom

Littlecombe Hill

HAYCOMBE HILL

4

Lord's Hill Farm

LORD'S HILL

3

Parsonage Down

Westcombe

39

SP3

A350

Tumuli

2

Little Down

Parsonage Down Farm

Tumulus

Beech Clump

Tumulus

Burnbake

Tumuli

1

38

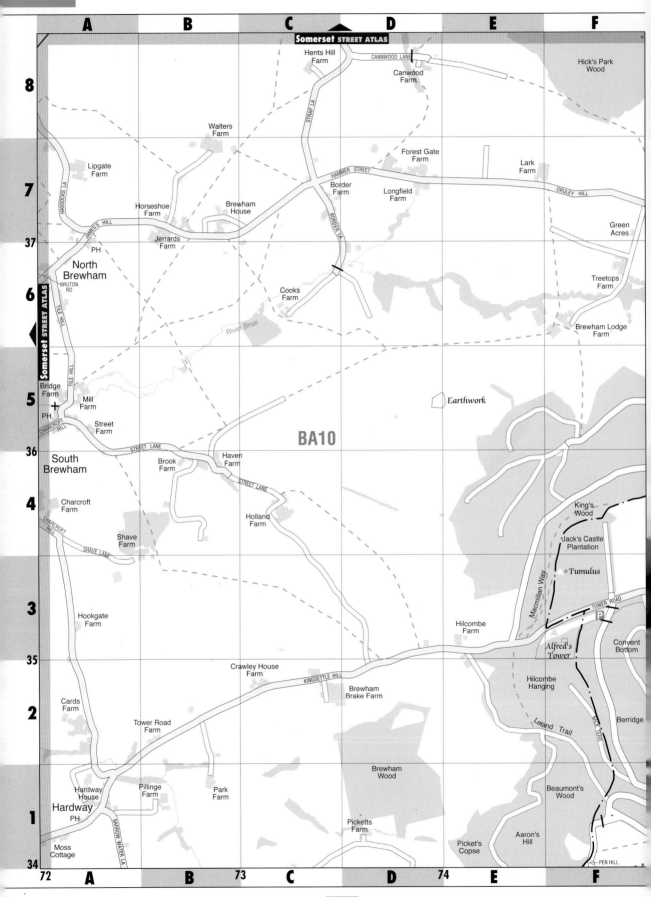

A **B** **C** **D** **E** **F**

8

Hick's Park Wood

Hents Hill Farm

CANNWOOD LANE

Canwood Farm

Walters Farm

STRAP LA

7

Lipgate Farm

HASSOCKS LA

Forest Gate Farm

HAMMER STREET

Lark Farm

DRULEY HILL

Horseshoe Farm

Brewham House

Border Farm

Longfield Farm

JAMES'S HILL

37

Jerrards Farm

BORDER LA

Green Acres

PH

North Brewham

BRUTON RD

Treetops Farm

6

Somerset STREET ATLAS

TILE HILL

Cooks Farm

Brewham Lodge Farm

River Brue

Earthwork

5

Bridge Farm

PH

CHARCROFT HILL

Mill Farm

Street Farm

BA10

36

South Brewham

Brook Farm

STREET LANE

Haven Farm

STREET LANE

4

Charcroft Farm

CHARCROFT HILL

SHAVE LANE

Shave Farm

Holland Farm

King's Wood

Jack's Castle Plantation

Macmillan Way

Tumulus

3

Hookgate Farm

Hilcombe Farm

TOWER ROAD

P

Convent Bottom

Alfred's Tower

35

Crawley House Farm

KINGSETTLE HILL

Hilcombe Hanging

2

Cards Farm

Tower Road Farm

Brewham Brake Farm

Leland Trail

BOW LEAZE

Berridge

Brewham Wood

Beaumont's Wood

1

Hardway House

Pillinge Farm

Park Farm

Picketts Farm

Picket's Copse

Aaron's Hill

Hardway

PH

BARROW WATER LA

Moss Cottage

34

PEN HILL

72 **A** **B** **73** **C** **D** **74** **E** **F**

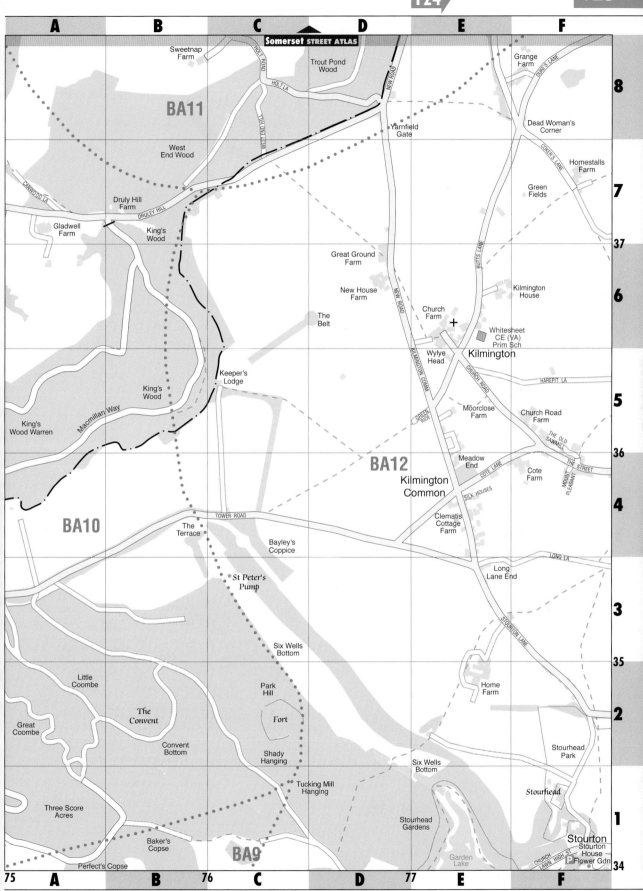

Somerset STREET ATLAS

8

BA11

Sweetnap Farm

Trout Pond Wood

Grange Farm

Dead Woman's Corner

Yarnfield Gate

Homestalls Farm

7

West End Wood

Green Fields

37

Druly Hill Farm

Druley Hill

Great Ground Farm

Kilmington House

6

Gladwell Farm

King's Wood

New House Farm

Church Farm

The Belt

Whitesheet CE (VA) Prim Sch

Kilmington

King's Wood

Keeper's Lodge

Wylye Head

HAREPIT LA

5

King's Wood Warren

Macmillan Way

Moorclose Farm

Church Road Farm

THE OLD SAWMILL

36

BA12

Meadow End

Cote Farm

THE STREET

Kilmington Common

4

BA10

TOWER ROAD

The Terrace

Long Lane End

LONG LA

Bayley's Coppice

St Peter's Pump

Clematis Cottage Farm

SILK HOUSES

3

Little Coombe

Six Wells Bottom

STOURTON LANE

35

Park Hill

Home Farm

The Convent

Fort

2

Great Coombe

Convent Bottom

Shady Hanging

Stourhead Park

Tucking Mill Hanging

Six Wells Bottom

Stourhead

Three Score Acres

Stourhead Gardens

1

Baker's Copse

BA9

Stourton

Stourton House Flower Gdn

Perfect's Copse

Garden Lake

CHURCH

34

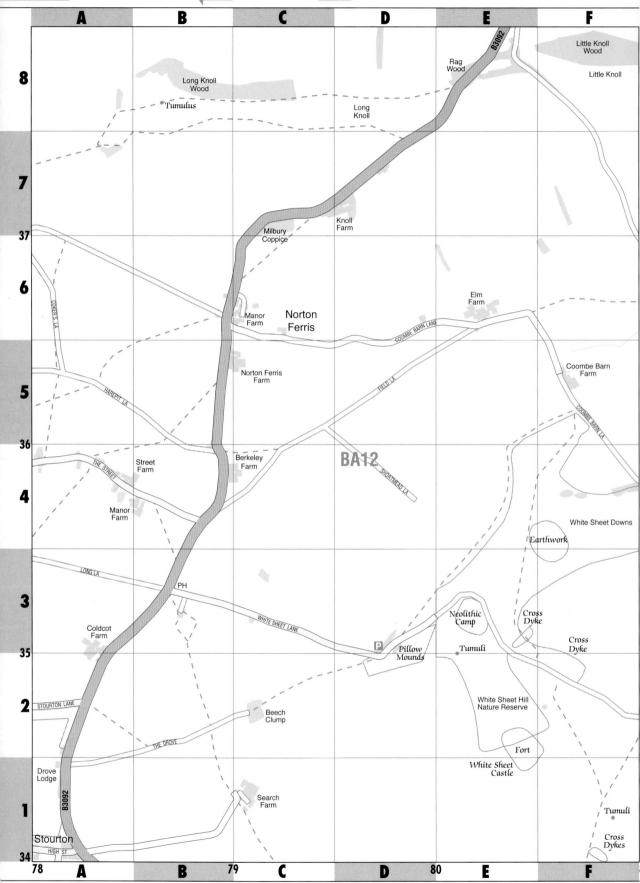

A **B** **C** **D** **E** **F**

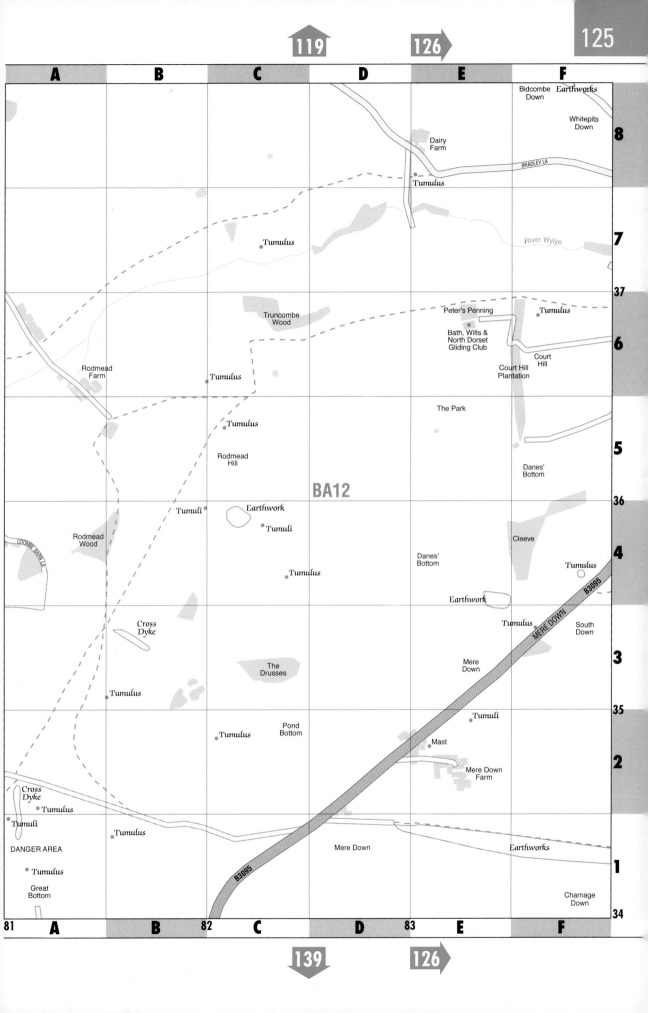

Bidcombe Earthworks
Down

Whitepits
Down

8

Dairy
Farm

BRADLEY LA

Tumulus

River Wylye

7

37

Tumulus

Truncombe
Wood

Peter's Penning

Tumulus

Bath, Wilts &
North Dorset
Gliding Club

6

Court
Hill

Rodmead
Farm

Tumulus

Court Hill
Plantation

The Park

5

Rodmead
Hill

Danes'
Bottom

BA12

36

Tumuli

Earthwork

Cleeve

COOMBE BARN LA

Rodmead
Wood

Tumuli

Tumulus

4

Danes'
Bottom

Tumulus

B3095

Earthwork

Tumulus

Tumulus

MERE DOWN

South
Down

Cross
Dyke

Mere
Down

3

The
Drusses

Tumulus

Tumuli

35

Tumulus

Pond
Bottom

Mast

2

Mere Down
Farm

Cross
Dyke

Tumulus

Tumuli

Tumulus

DANGER AREA

Mere Down

Earthworks

1

B3095

Tumulus

Great
Bottom

Charnage
Down

34

81 **A** **B** **82** **C** **D** **83** **E** **F**

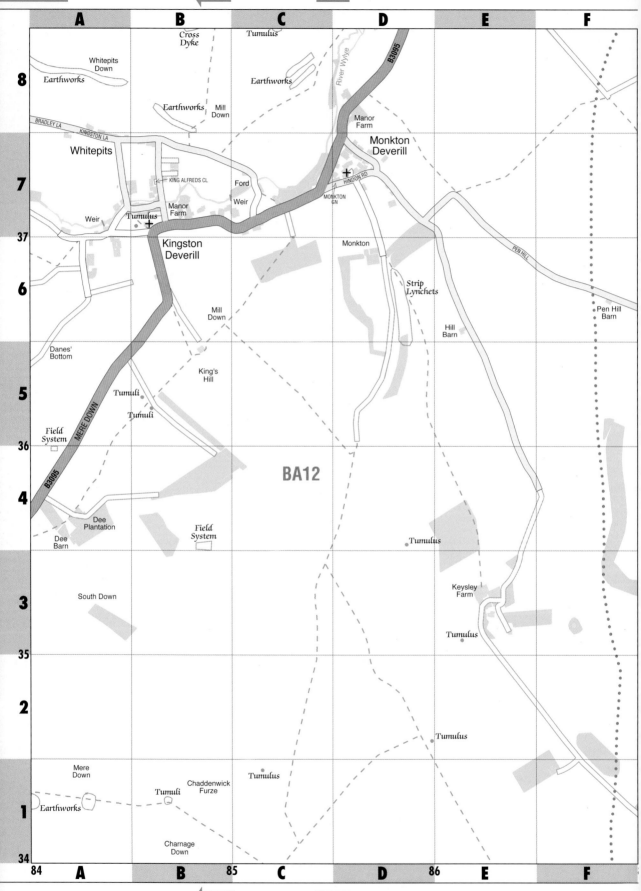

A B C D E F

8

Whitepits
Down
Earthworks

Cross
Dyke

Tumulus

Earthworks

River Wylye

B3095

Earthworks

Mill
Down

Manor
Farm

Monkton
Deverill

BRADLEY LA

KINGSTON LA

Whitepits

7

KING ALFREDS CL

Manor
Farm

Ford

Weir

HINDON RD

MONKTON
GN

Weir

Weir

Tumulus

Kingston
Deverill

37

Monkton

PEN HILL

6

Danes'
Bottom

Mill
Down

King's
Hill

Strip
Lynchets

Hill
Barn

Pen Hill
Barn

MERE DOWN

5

Tumuli

Tumuli

Field
System

36

B3095

BA12

4

Dee
Plantation

Field
System

Tumulus

Dee
Barn

Keysley
Farm

3

South Down

Tumulus

35

Tumulus

2

Tumulus

Mere
Down

Tumulus

Chaddenwick
Furze

1

Tumuli

Earthworks

Charnage
Down

34

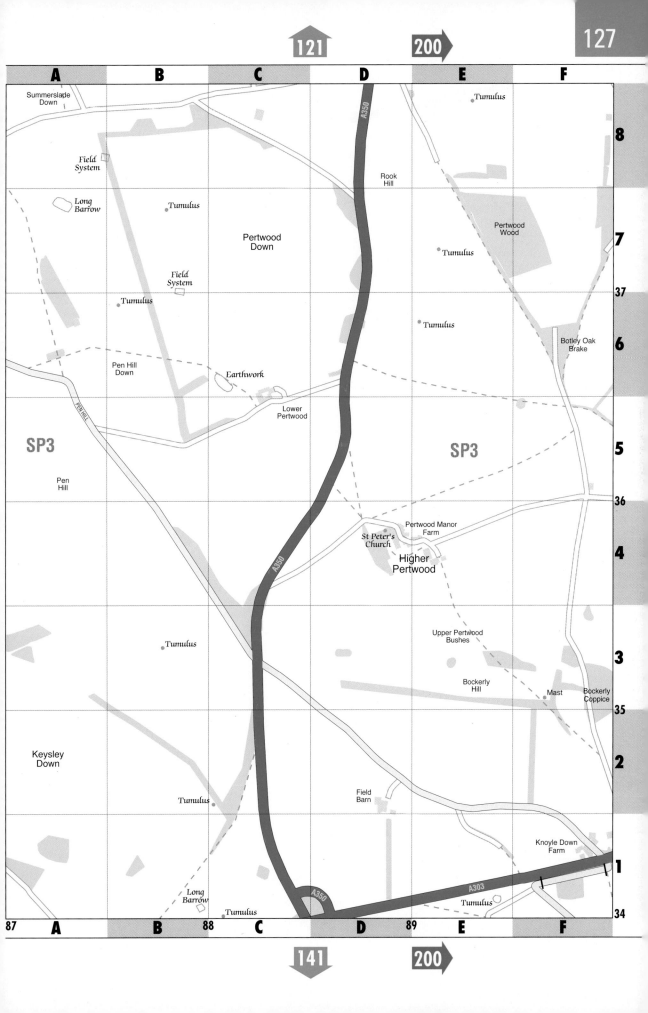

A B C D E F

8

Summerslade
Down

Field
System

Long
Barrow

Tumulus

Pertwood
Down

Rook
Hill

Tumulus

Pertwood
Wood

7

37

Field
System

Tumulus

Tumulus

Tumulus

Botley Oak
Brake

6

Pen Hill
Down

Earthwork

Lower
Pertwood

PEN HILL

SP3

SP3

5

Pen
Hill

36

Pertwood Manor
Farm

*St Peter's
Church*

Higher
Pertwood

4

Upper Pertwood
Bushes

Tumulus

Bockerly
Hill

Mast

Bockerly
Coppice

3

35

Keysley
Down

2

Tumulus

Field
Barn

Tumulus

Knoyle Down
Farm

Long
Barrow

Tumulus

A350

A303

A350

Tumulus

1

34

87 A B 88 C D 89 E F

201
196

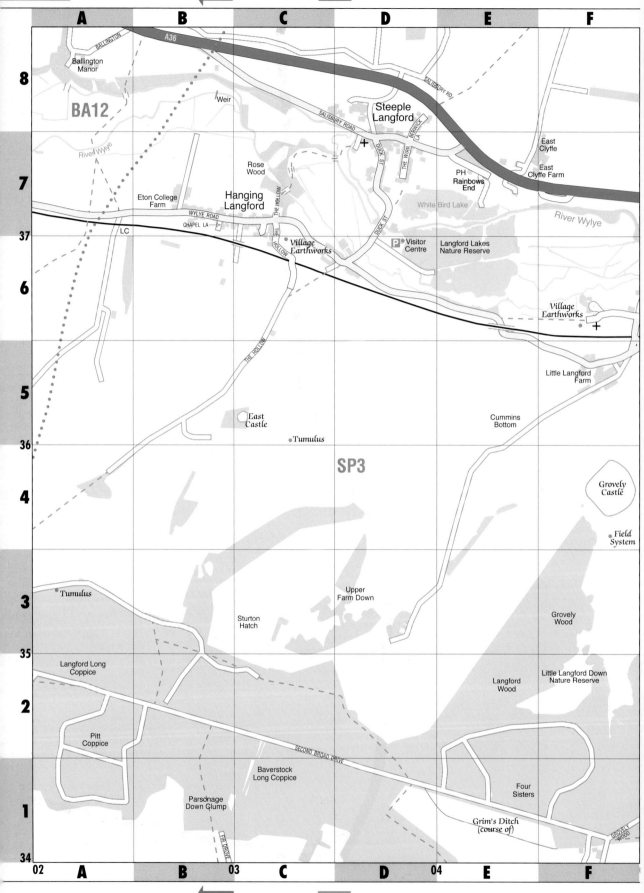

201
142

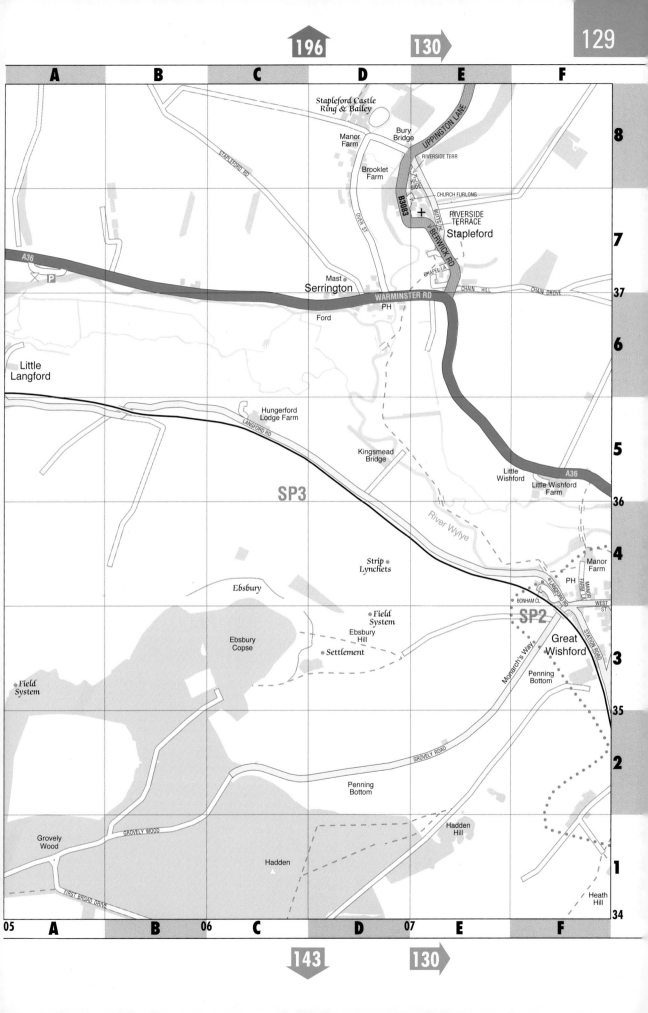

A   B   C   D   E   F

8

Stapleford Castle
Ring & Bailey

Manor
Farm

Bury
Bridge

UPPINGTON LANE

RIVERSIDE TERR

Brooklet
Farm

STAPLEFORD RD

HILL
SIDE

CHURCH FURLONG

DYER ST

B3083

BUTTS TH

RIVERSIDE
TERRACE

Stapleford

7

BERWICK RD

CHAPEL LA

Mast

Serrington

WARMINSTER RD

CHAIN   HILL

CHAIN DROVE

37

PH

Ford

6

A36

P

Little
Langford

Hungerford
Lodge Farm

LANGFORD RD

Kingsmead
Bridge

Little
Wishford

A36

Little Wishford
Farm

5

SP3

36

River Wylye

Strip
Lynchets

Manor
Farm

4

MANOR FARM LA

PH

Ebsbury

Field
System

BONHAM CL

WEST
ST

LANGFORD RD

SP2

Ebsbury
Copse

Ebsbury
Hill

Settlement

Monarch's Way

Great
Wishford

STATION ROAD

3

Penning
Bottom

Field
System

35

GROVELY ROAD

2

Penning
Bottom

Hadden
Hill

Grovely
Wood

GROVELY WOOD

Hadden

1

FIRST BROAD DRIVE

Heath
Hill

34

A   B   C   D   E   F

8

Eighteen Acre Plantation

Stapleford Down

Camp Plantation

SP3

7

Chain Hill

Camp Cottages

Tumulus

37

Monarch's Way

6

CHAIN DROVE

Stoford Hill Buildings

Tumulus

SP4

WISHFORD RD

Monarch's Way

5

36

A36

Stoford Bottom

Enclosure

MOUNT PLEASANT
RIVERSIDE CL
STOFORD BOTTOM

4

Great Wishford C.E. VA Prim Sch

PH

Newton Barrow

Charity Farm

WEST ST

Stoford Bridge

Stoford

Masts

Wishford Farm

Village Earthworks

3

SOUTH ST

Town End

Stoford Farm

SP2

GROVELY COTTS

KINGSMEAD

35

River Wylye

STATION RD

2

HIGHLAND VIEW
VALE VIEW RD
WOODLAND VIEW
JUBILEE TERR
OAK CL RD
ST ANDREW'S
BRIDGE SIDE

South Newton

SUTTON CL

ASHLEIGH CL

South Newton Hospital

PH

WARMINSTER RD

1

WISHFORD RD

Manor Farm

SP3

Mill Farm

A36

34

08   A   B   09   C   D   10   E   F

A360

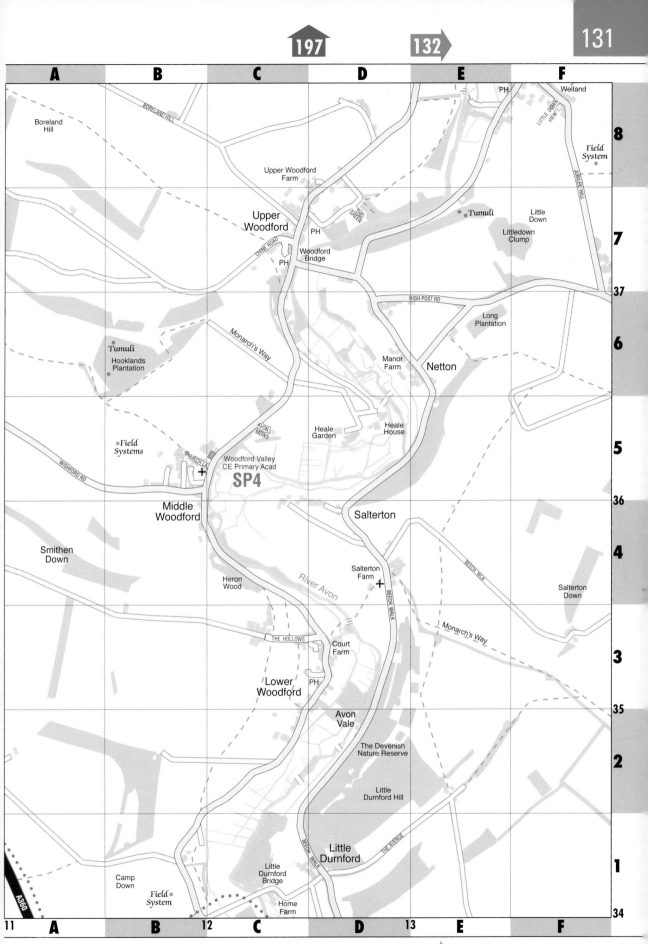

A **B** **C** **D** **E** **F**

Boreland Hill

BORELAND HILL

Upper Woodford Farm

Upper Woodford

PH

THE GREEN

PH

Woodford Bridge

PH

CAINE ROAD

8

PH

Welland

LITTLE DOWN VIEW

Field System

Tumuli

Little Down

Littledown Clump

7

37

HIGH POST RD

Long Plantation

Monarch's Way

Tumuli

Hooklands Plantation

Manor Farm

Netton

6

Field Systems

WISHFORD RD

AVON MDWS

Heale Garden

Heale House

CHURCH LA

Woodford Valley CE Primary Acad

SP4

Middle Woodford

Salterton

5

36

Smithen Down

Heron Wood

River Avon

Salterton Farm

BEECH WALK

Salterton Down

4

THE HOLLOWS

Court Farm

PH

Lower Woodford

BEECH WALK

Monarch's Way

3

35

Avon Vale

The Devenish Nature Reserve

Little Durnford Hill

2

A360

Camp Down

Field System

Little Durnford Bridge

Home Farm

BEECH WALK

Little Durnford

THE AVENUE

1

34

11 **A** **B** **12** **C** **D** **13** **E** **F**

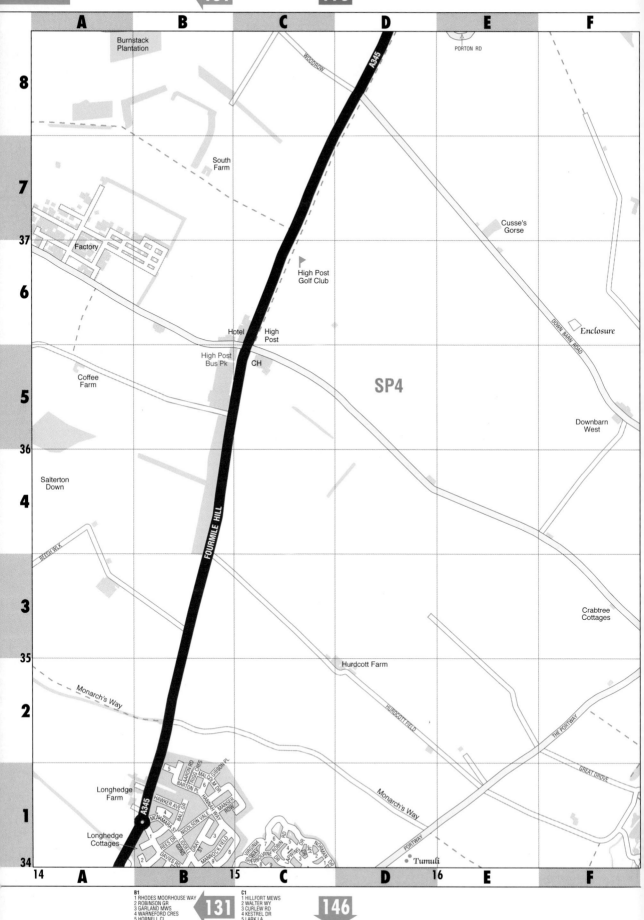

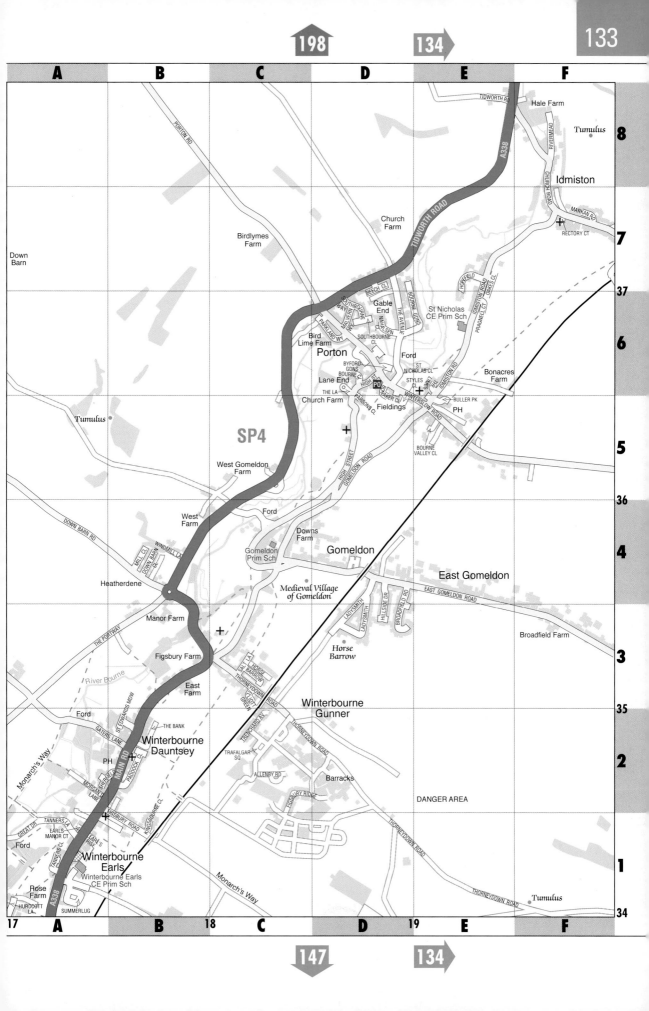

8

Down Barn

Tumulus

PORTON RD

Birdlymes Farm

Church Farm

TIDWORTH ROAD

Hale Farm

Tumulus

RIVERMEAD

CHURCH ROAD

Idmiston

A338

MARKAN RD

RECTORY CT

7

37

BEECH CL

SOUTHBOURNE WAY

WALVERN CL

Gable End

NAHLSEN CL

THE AVENUE

BOURNE GDNS

HOPEFIELD

IDMISTON ROAD

OAKES CL

PIGNELL CT

St Nicholas CE Prim Sch

6

Bird Lime Farm

PARKLAND WAY

Porton

SOUTHBOURNE CL

Ford

St NICHOLAS CL

IDMISTON RD

Bonacres Farm

SP4

BYFORD GDNS

BOURNE

Lane End

THE LA

Church Farm

HIGH ST

PO

STYLES

STYLES LANE

WINTERSLOW ROAD

BULLER PK

PH

Tumulus

PARSONS CL

SHAKER CL

Fieldings

West Gomeldon Farm

HIGH STREET

GOMELDON ROAD

BOURNE VALLEY CL

5

36

West Farm

Ford

Downs Farm

Gomeldon Prim Sch

Gomeldon

East Gomeldon

Broadfield Farm

4

DOWN BARN RD

MILL CL

DOWN BARN CL

WINDMILL LA

Heatherdene

Medieval Village of Gomeldon

LADYSMITH

LADYSMITH

HILLSIDE DR

BROADFIELD RD

EAST GOMELDON ROAD

Manor Farm

THE PORTWAY

Figsbury Farm

River Bourne

East Farm

Ford

ST EDWARDS MDW

CATERS LANE

THE BANK

HORSE BARROW

THORNEYDOWN RD

LIGHT GREEN

THORNEYDOWN ROAD

Horse Barrow

Winterbourne Gunner

3

35

Monarch's Way

PH

MAIN RD

PADDOCK CL

MORGAN'S LANE

SHEPHERDS

Winterbourne Dauntsey

TRENCHARD AV

TRAFALGAR SQ

ALLENBY RD

FISBURY RIDGE

Barracks

DANGER AREA

2

TANNERS LA

GREAT DR

EARLS MANOR CT

EARL'S RISE

FIGSBURY ROAD

KINGSBOURNE CL

Ford

TANNERS CL

Winterbourne Earls

Winterbourne Earls CE Prim Sch

Rose Farm

HURDCOTT LA

A338

SUMMERLUG

Monarch's Way

THORNEYDOWN ROAD

Tumulus

1

34

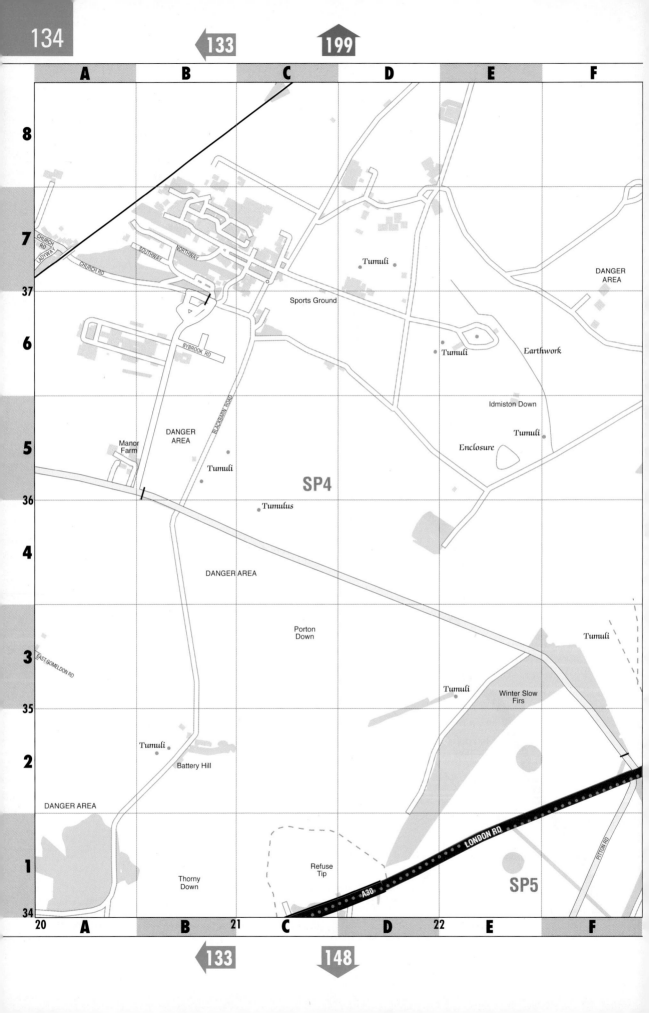

A   B   C   D   E   F

8

7

37

6

5

36

4

3

35

2

1

34

20   A   21   C   22   E   F

CHURCH RD

LADYWAY

CHURCH RD

SOUTHWAY

NORTHWAY

BYBROOK RD

BLACKBARN ROAD

Sports Ground

Tumuli

DANGER
AREA

Earthwork

Idmiston Down

Tumuli

Enclosure

Manor
Farm

DANGER
AREA

Tumuli

Tumulus

SP4

DANGER AREA

Porton
Down

Tumuli

EAST GOMELDON RD

Tumuli

Winter Slow
Firs

Tumuli

Battery Hill

DANGER AREA

Thorny
Down

Refuse
Tip

LONDON RD

A30

PITTON RD

SP5

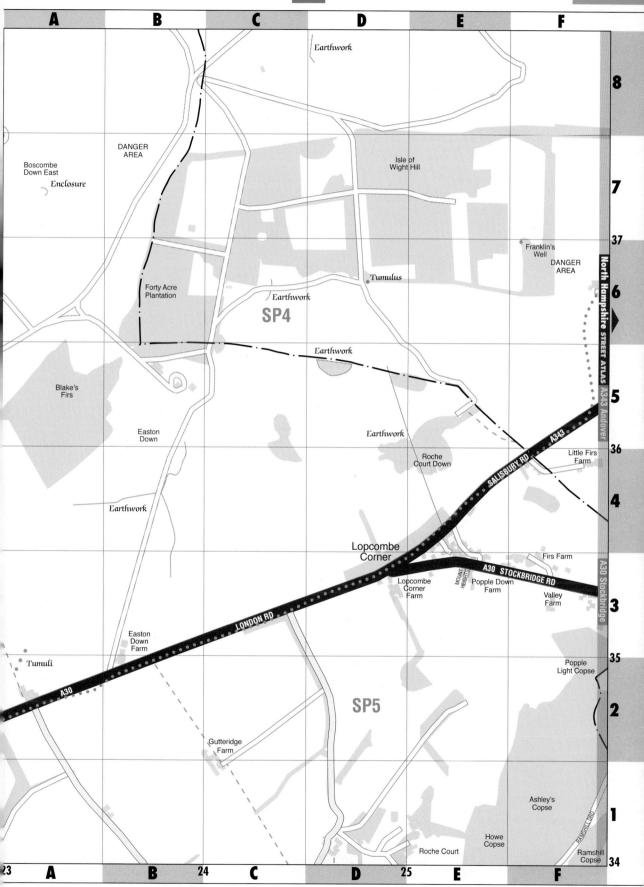

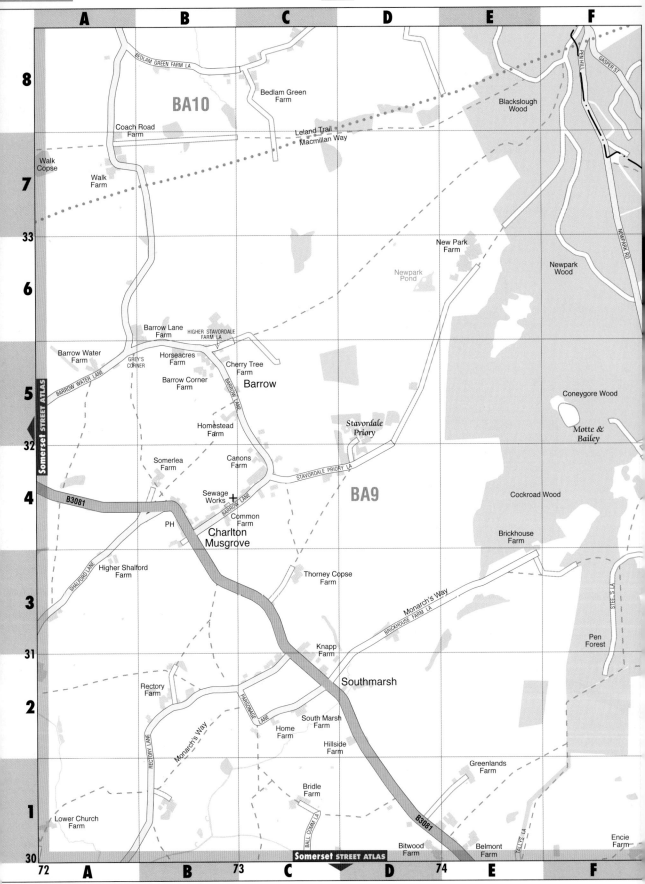

A B C D E F

8

BA10

Bedlam Green Farm La

Bedlam Green Farm

Coach Road Farm

Leland Trail
Macmillan Way

Blackslough Wood

PEN HILL

GASPER ST

Walk Copse

7

Walk Farm

33

New Park Farm

Newpark Pond

Newpark Wood

NEWPARK RD

6

Barrow Lane Farm

HIGHER STAVORDALE FARM LA

Barrow Water Farm

GREY'S CORNER

Horseacres Farm

Cherry Tree Farm

Coneygore Wood

Motte & Bailey

5

BARROW WATER LANE

Barrow Corner Farm

BARROW LANE

Barrow

Homestead Farm

Stavordale Priory

32

Somerlea Farm

Canons Farm

STAVORDALE PRIORY LA

BA9

Cockroad Wood

4

B3081

Sewage Works

BARROW LANE

Common Farm

PH

Charlton Musgrove

Brickhouse Farm

SHALFORD LANE

Higher Shalford Farm

Thorney Copse Farm

Monarch's Way

BRICKHOUSE FARM LA

SITE LA

3

Pen Forest

31

Knapp Farm

Southmarsh

Rectory Farm

PARSONAGE LANE

2

RECTORY LANE

Monarch's Way

South Marsh Farm

Home Farm

Hillside Farm

Greenlands Farm

TALLY'S LA

1

Lower Church Farm

Bridle Farm

BALL COMM LA

B3081

Bitwood Farm

Belmont Farm

Encie Farm

30

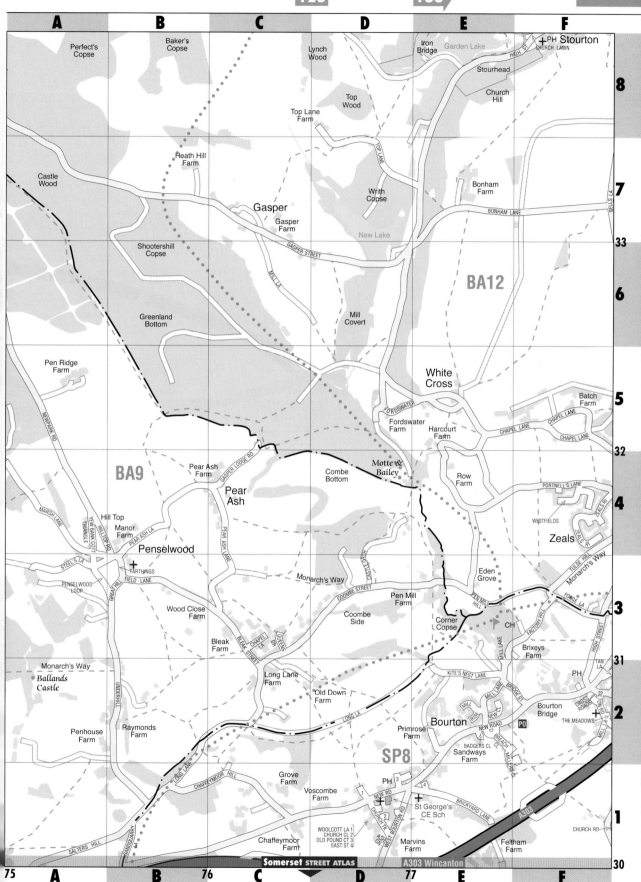

Dorset STREET ATLAS

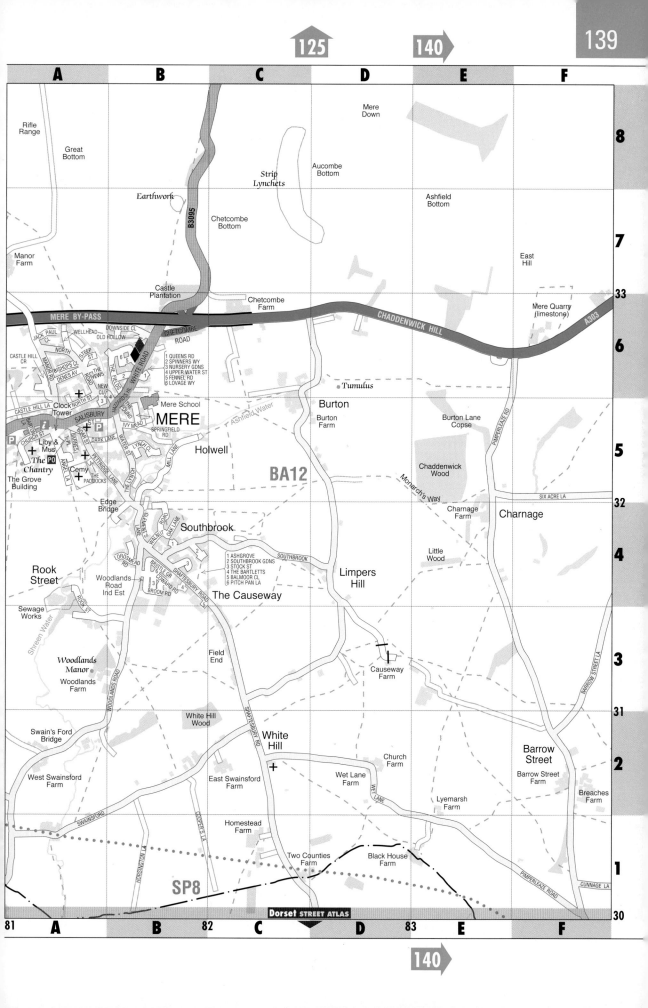

A   **B**   **C**   **D**   **E**   **F**

Rifle
Range

Great
Bottom

Earthwork

Mere
Down

Strip
Lynchets

Aucombe
Bottom

Ashfield
Bottom

8

Manor
Farm

B3095

Chetcombe
Bottom

East
Hill

7

Castle
Plantation

Chetcombe
Farm

MERE BY-PASS

CHADDENWICK HILL

Mere Quarry
(limestone)

A303

33

DOWNSIDE CL

OLD HOLLOW

CHETCOMBE
ROAD

6

JACK PAUL
CL

WELLHEAD

WHITE ROAD

1 QUEENS RD
2 SPINNERS WY
3 NURSERY GDNS
4 UPPER WATER ST
5 FENNEL RD
6 LOVAGE WY

Tumulus

CASTLE HILL
CR

MANOR RD

NORTH
STEEP ST

THE FIELDS

Mere School

Burton

Burton
Farm

Burton Lane
Copse

Chaddenwick
Wood

MERE

Ashfield Water

6

Clock
Tower

SALISBURY
ST

NEW
CUT

Holwell

BA12

Six Acre La

5

Liby & Mus

The
Chantry

The Grove
Building

Cemy

THE
PADDOCKS

Springfield RD

IVY MEAD

MILL LANE

Chaddenwick
Wood

32

Edge
Bridge

Southbrook

SOUTHBROOK

Charnage
Farm

Charnage

Rook
Street

WALNUT
LANE

OAK LANE

SHAFTESBURY ROAD

1 ASHGROVE
2 SOUTHBROOK GDNS
3 STOCK ST
4 THE BARTLETTS
5 BALMOOR CL
6 PITCH PAN LA

Limpers
Hill

Little
Wood

4

LORDSMEAD
RD

BRISTLE GR

CWARD RD

BROOM RD

The Causeway

Monarch's Way

Sewage
Works

Shreen Water

ROOK ST

Woodlands
Road Ind Est

Field
End

BARROW STREET LA

3

Woodlands
Manor

Woodlands
Farm

WOODLANDS ROAD

Causeway
Farm

Swain's Ford
Bridge

SHAFTESBURY RD

White Hill
Wood

31

West Swainsford
Farm

East Swainsford
Farm

White
Hill

Wet Lane
Farm

Church
Farm

Barrow
Street

Barrow Street
Farm

2

Lyemarsh
Farm

WET LANE

Breaches
Farm

SWAINSFORD

COOPER'S LA

HORSINGTON LA

Homestead
Farm

Two Counties
Farm

Black House
Farm

PIMPERLEAZE ROAD

CUNNAGE LA

1

SP8

PIMPERLEAZE RD

30

81   **A**   **B**   **82**   **C**   **D**   **83**   **E**   **F**

A **B** **C** **D** **E** **F**

8

Charnage
Down

Tumulus

CHADDENWICK HILL

A303

7

33

A303

West Hill
Farm

THE CLEEVE

NEW CLOSE

The
Warren

Tumulus

6

Manor
Farm

West
Knoyle

Broadoak
Game Farm

Cleeve
Hill

Pinnock's
Coppice

Longmead
Coppice

Cleeve
Coppice

East Hill
Farm

Monarch's Way

Atkin's
Coppice

Parson's
Coppice

5

THE STREET

STONEY BR

Tumulus

The Middles

Hickmans
Farm

BA12

32

SIX ACRE LANE

BARROW STREET LANE

Broadmead
Farm

Puck Well
Nature Reserve

Hang
Wood

MARTHA'S LANE

4

SAWPIT HILL

Puckwell
Coppice

Skidmarsh
Wood

Oxleaze
Farm

Wood
Farm

Mitchell's
Coppice

Mackintosh
Davidson Wood
Nature Reserve

Great High
Croft Wood

SP3

3

31

Bush Farm
Bison
Centre

Common
Wood

Windmill Hill

Convish
Farm

Underhill

Underhill
Farm

Park Corner
Farm

2

Vernhill
Farm

Windmill
Farm

Brickyard
Farm

Park Pale

Lugmarsh
Farm

CUNNAGE LANE

Knowl

Lugmarsh
Plantation

Moor's
Farm

1

Park Pale

Park
Pale

30

84 **A** **B** 85 **C** **D** 86 **E** **F**

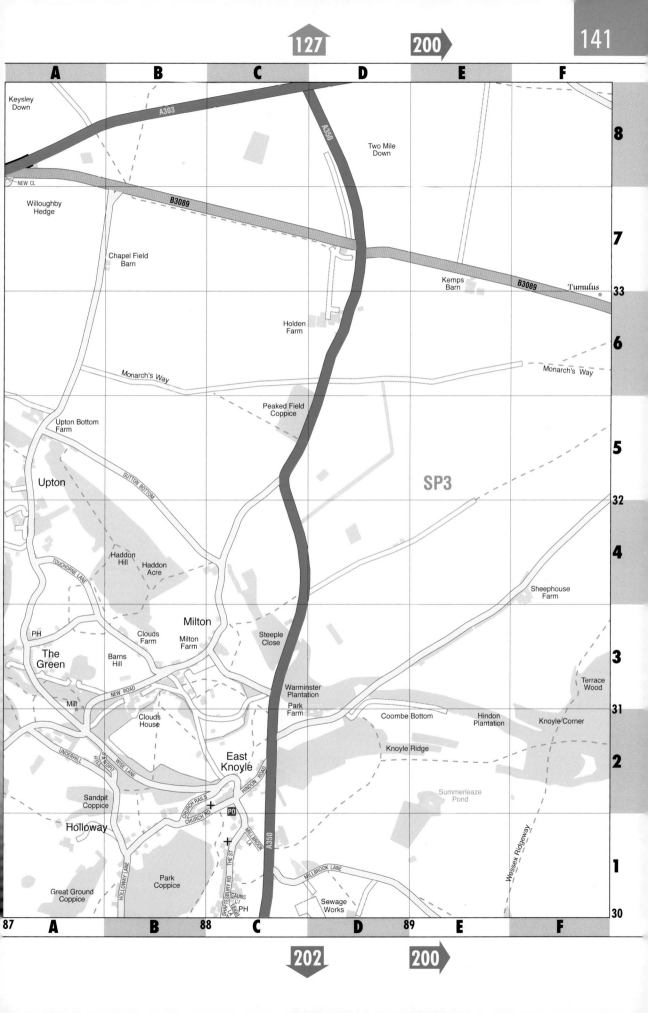

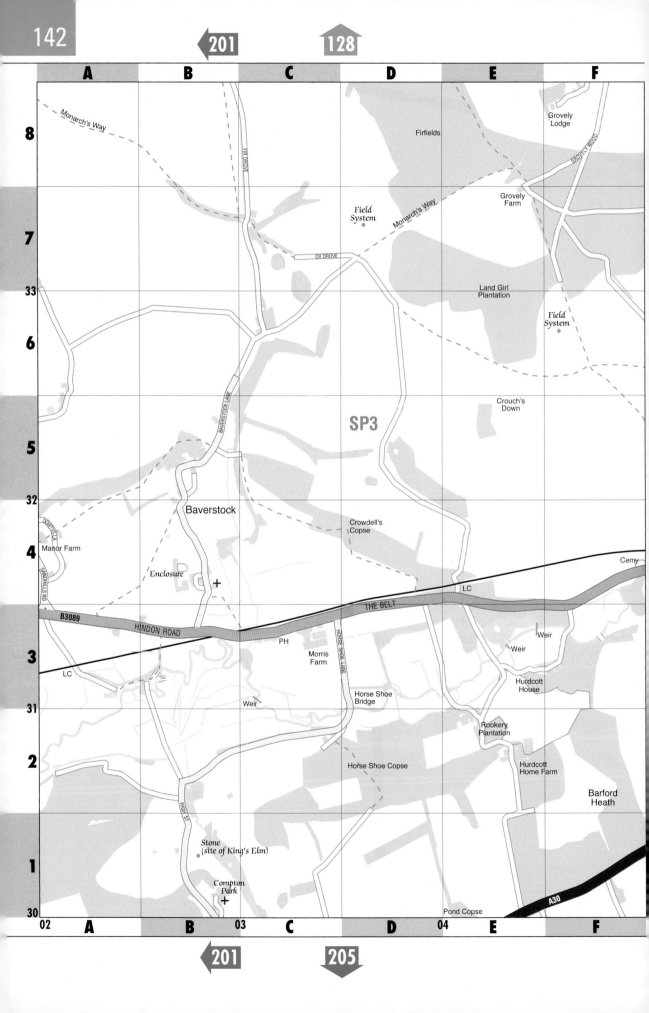

A B C D E F

8

Monarch's Way

Firfields

Grovely
Lodge

GROVELY WOOD

7

Field
System

Monarch's Way

Grovely
Farm

OX DROVE

33

Land Girl
Plantation

6

Field
System

Crouch's
Down

SP3

5

BAVERSTOCK LANE

32

Baverstock

Crowdell's
Copse

DOVDG LA.

Manor Farm

4

SANDHILLS RD

Enclosure

THE BELT

LC

Cemy

B3089

HINDON ROAD

PH

LC

Weir

Weir

3

LC

Morris
Farm

HORSE SHOE LANE

Weir

Hurdcott
House

31

Weir

Horse Shoe
Bridge

Rookery
Plantation

2

Horse Shoe Copse

Hurdcott
Home Farm

Barford
Heath

HIGH ST

1

Stone
(site of King's Elm)

Compton
Park

A30

30

Pond Copse

02 A B 03 C D 04 E F

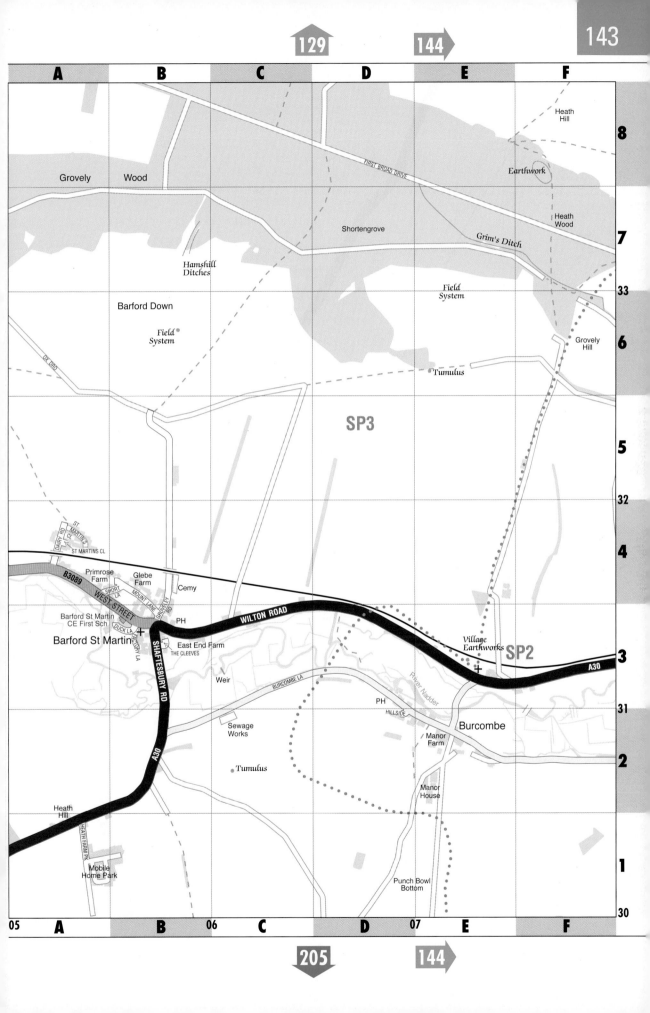

A   B   C   D   E   F

8
Heath Hill
Grovely   Wood
Earthwork
Heath Wood
7
Shortengrove
Grim's Ditch
33
Hamshill Ditches
Field System
Barford Down
6
Field System
Grovely Hill
OX DRO
Tumulus
SP3
5
32
4
ST MARTINS CL
DAIRY RD
ST MARTINS CL
Primrose Farm
Glebe Farm
Cemy
B3089
WEST STREET
SHORT LA
MOUNT LANE
GROVELY RD
PH
WILTON ROAD
Village Earthworks
SP2
Barford St Martin CE First Sch
DUCK LA
FACTORY LA
Barford St Martin
East End Farm
THE CLEEVES
A30
3
SHAFTESBURY RD
Weir
BURCOMBE LA
River Nadder
PH
HILLSIDE
31
A30
Sewage Works
Burcombe
Manor Farm
2
Tumulus
Manor House
Heath Hill
HEATH FARM PK
Punch Bowl Bottom
1
Mobile Home Park
30

05   A   B   06   C   D   07   E   F

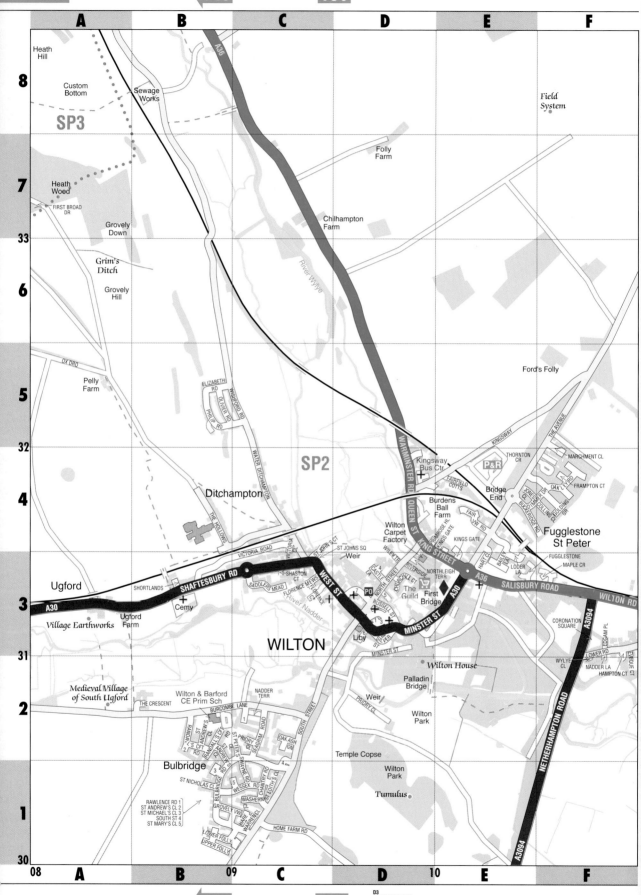

D3
1 GREYHOUND LA
2 PENNY'S LA
3 KINGSBURY SQ
4 CASTLE KEEP
5 ALBANY TERR
6 BELL LA
7 CROW LA

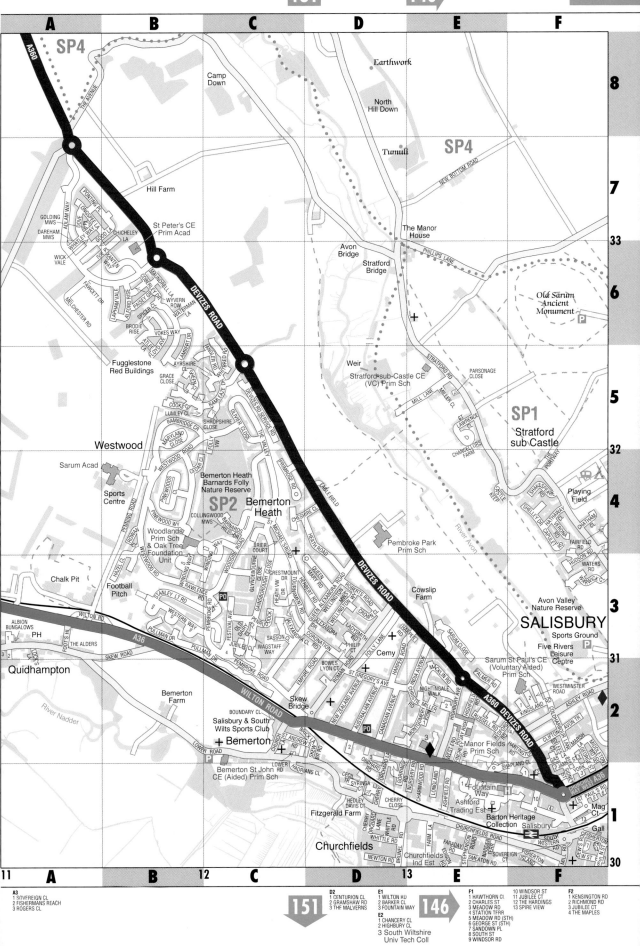

B8
1 ROBINSON GR
2 BAZALGETTE LA
3 THOMPSON CL
4 MCLEOD PL

145

C8
1 DEVONALD WAY
2 HENRY LA
3 BUNTING LA
4 WALTER WAY

132

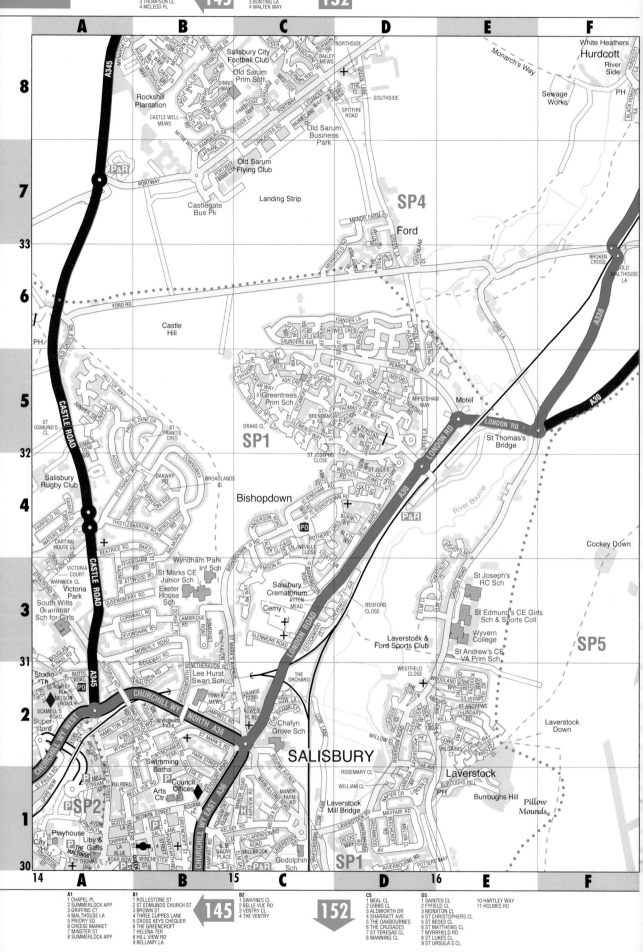

A1
1 CHAPEL PL
2 SUMMERLOCK APP
3 GRIFFINS CT
4 MALTHOUSE LA
5 PRIORY SQ
6 CHEESE MARKET
7 MINSTER ST
8 SUMMERLOCK APP

B1
1 ROLLESTONE ST
2 ST EDMUNDS CHURCH ST
3 BROWN ST
4 THREE CUPPES LANE
5 CROSS KEYS CHEQUER
6 THE GREENCROFT
7 HELENA TER
8 HILL VIEW RD
9 BELLAMY LA

145

B2
1 SWAYNES CL
2 BELLE VUE RD
3 VENTRY CL
4 THE VENTRY

152

C5
1 NEAL CL
2 GIBBS CL
3 ALDWORTH DR
4 SHARRATT AVE
5 THE OAKBOURNES
6 THE CRUSADES
7 ST TERESAS CL
8 MANNING CL

D5
1 SAINTES CL
2 FYFIELD CL
3 MONXTON CL
4 ST CHRISTOPHERS CL
5 ST BEDES CL
6 ST MATTHEWS CL
7 MYRRFIELD RD
8 ST LUKES CL
9 ST URSULA'S CL

10 HARTLEY WAY
11 HOLMES RD

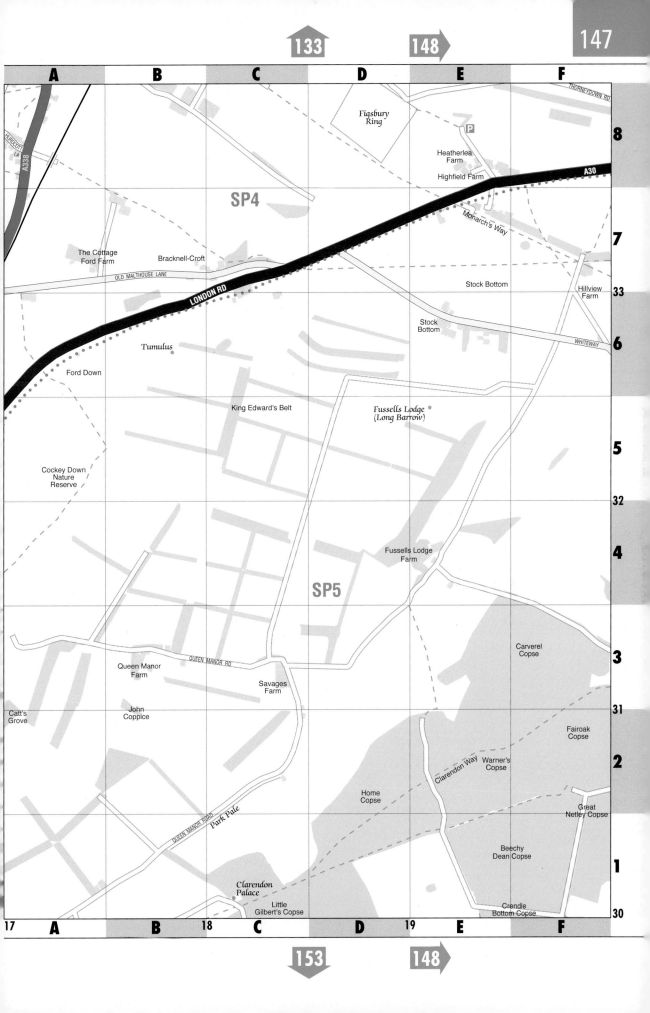

THORNEYDOWN RD

8

Figsbury Ring

P

Heatherlea Farm

Highfield Farm

A30

SP4

Monarch's Way

7

The Cottage Ford Farm

Bracknell-Croft

OLD MALTHOUSE LANE

Stock Bottom

Hillview Farm

33

LONDON RD

Stock Bottom

WHITEWAY

6

Tumulus

Ford Down

King Edward's Belt

Fussells Lodge (Long Barrow)

5

Cockey Down Nature Reserve

32

Fussells Lodge Farm

4

SP5

Carverel Copse

QUEEN MANOR RD

3

Queen Manor Farm

Savages Farm

John Coppice

Catt's Grove

31

Fairoak Copse

Clarendon Way

Warner's Copse

2

Home Copse

Great Netley Copse

QUEEN MANOR ROAD

Park Pale

Beechy Dean Copse

1

Clarendon Palace

Little Gilbert's Copse

Crendle Bottom Copse

30

147
134

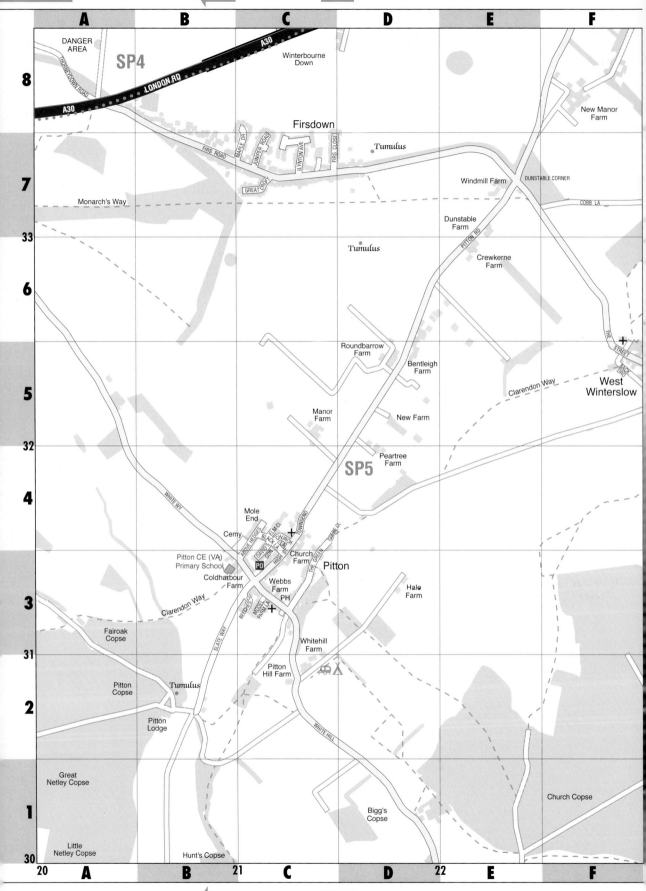

147
154

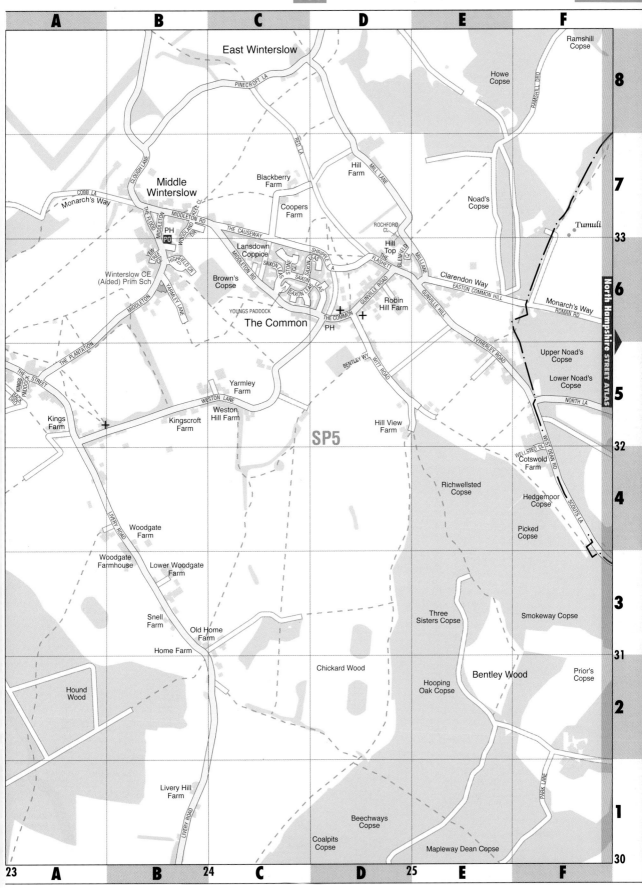

East Winterslow

Middle Winterslow

Monarch's Way

PINECROFT LA

COBB LA

CLOUGH LANE

THE FLOOD

MIDDLETON RD

WOODLAND DR

MIDDLETON RD

THE CAUSEWAY

Blackberry Farm

RED LA

Hill Farm

MILL LANE

Howe Copse

Ramshill Copse

RAMSHILL DRO

Coopers Farm

Noad's Copse

Tumuli

ROCHFORD CL

Hill Top

Clarendon Way

Lansdown Coppice

SHRIPPLE LA

GLENFIELD CL

STONE LEAS

GUNVILLE ROAD

EASTON COMMON HILL

Monarch's Way

ROMAN RD

Brown's Copse

SAXON LEAS

SAXON LEAS

SAXON LEAS

Robin Hill Farm

GUNVILLE HILL

Winterslow CE (Aided) Prim Sch

MIDDLETON

YARMLEY LANE

HIGHFIELD CR

YEW TREE CLOSE

PH

PO

YOUNGS PADDOCK

THE COMMON

The Common

PH

TYTHERLEY ROAD

Upper Noad's Copse

Lower Noad's Copse

NORTH LA

THE PLANTATION

Yarmley Farm

BENTLEY WY

WITT ROAD

KINGS PADDOCK

THE STREET

BACK DRO

Kings Farm

WESTON LANE

Kingscroft Farm

Weston Hill Farm

Hill View Farm

SP5

WELLSTED OL RD

WEST DEAN RD

Cotswold Farm

SCOUTS LA

Richwellsted Copse

Hedgemoor Copse

Picked Copse

LIVERY ROAD

Woodgate Farm

Woodgate Farmhouse

Lower Woodgate Farm

Snell Farm

Old Home Farm

Home Farm

Hound Wood

Chickard Wood

Three Sisters Copse

Hooping Oak Copse

Smokeway Copse

Bentley Wood

Prior's Copse

PARK LANE

Livery Hill Farm

LIVERY ROAD

Coalpits Copse

Beechways Copse

Mapleway Dean Copse

North Hampshire STREET ATLAS

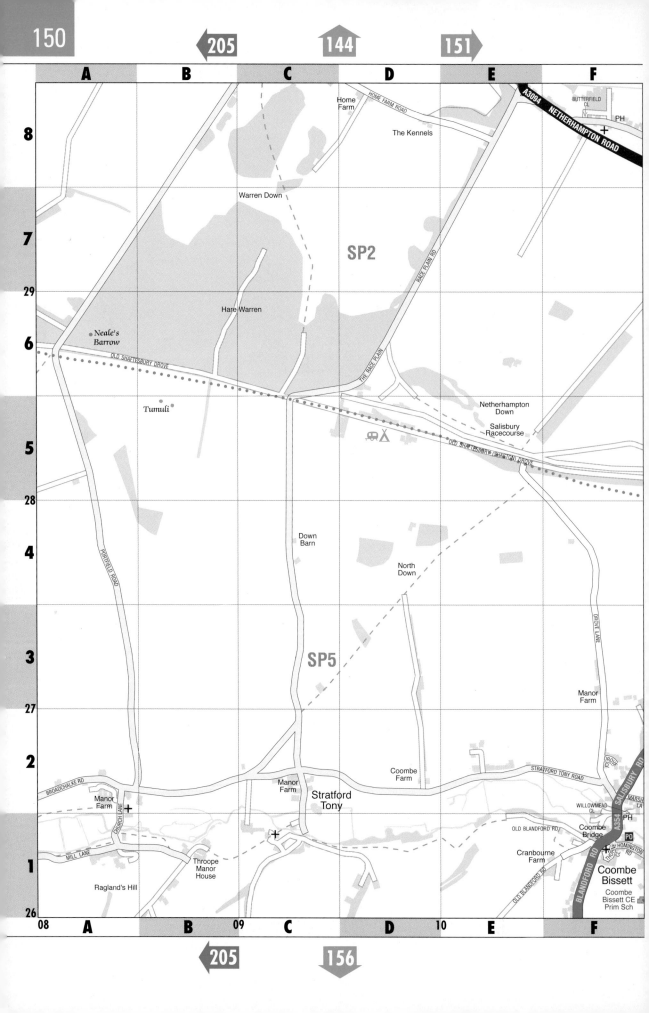

145

E7
1 STEPHENS CL
2 TURNER CL
3 MUNKS CL

152

F5
1 HARVARD CL
2 CHRISTOPHER CL

F6
1 GRASMERE CL

151

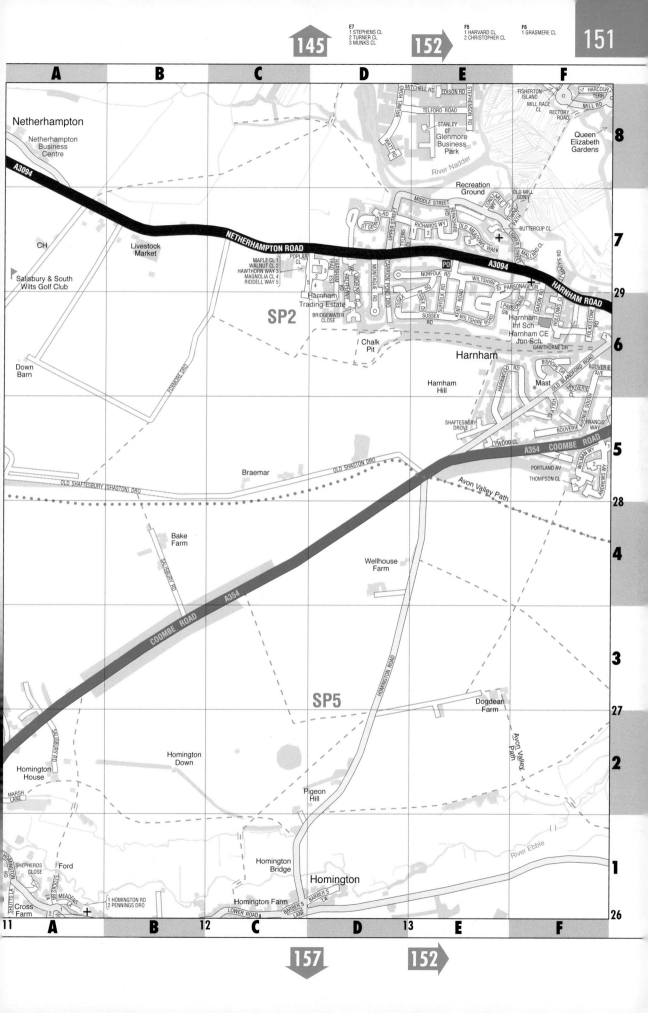

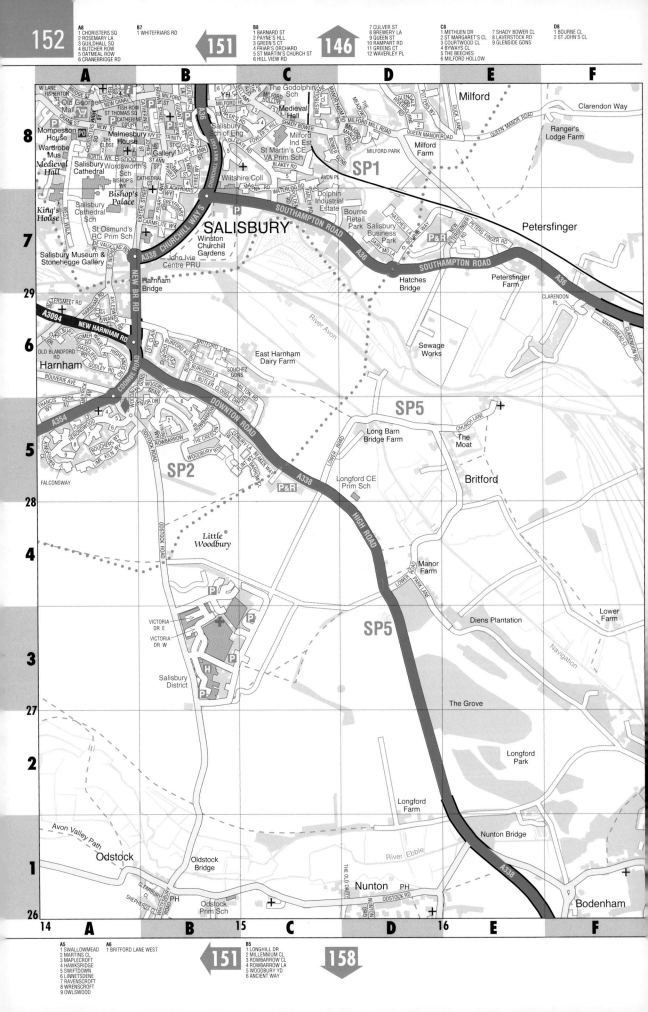

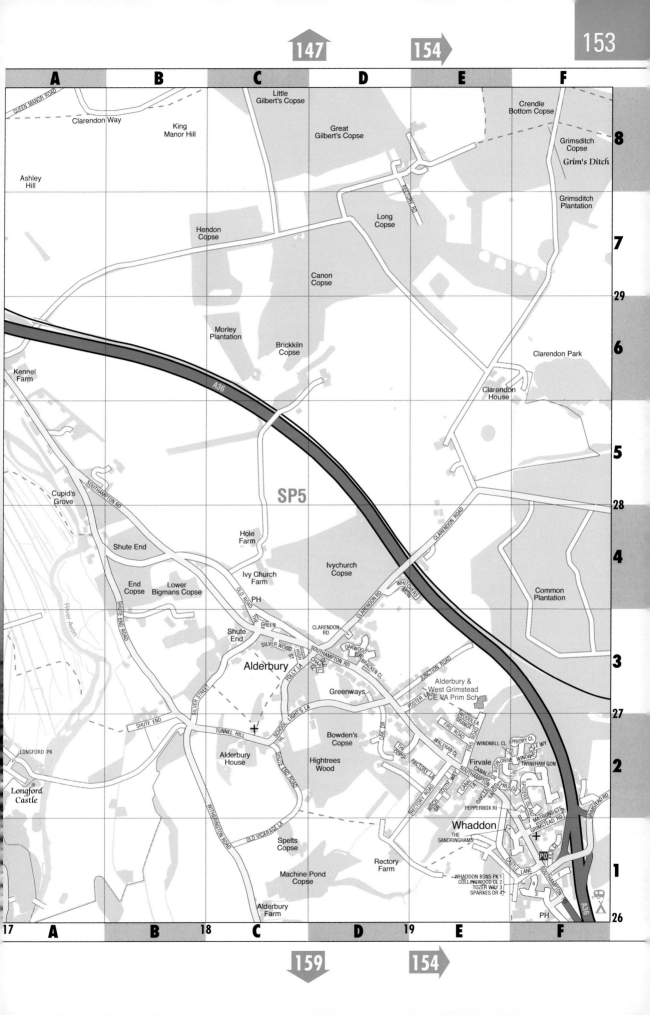

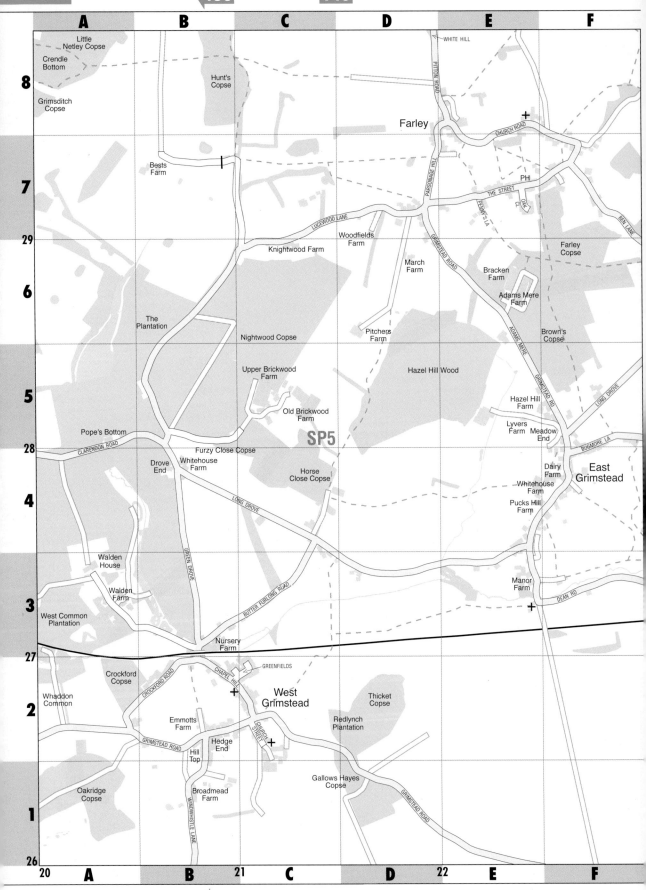

SP5

A B C D E F

8
7
29
6
5
28
4
3
27
2
1
26

Church Rd
Farley Farm
Blackmoor Copse
Blackmoor Copse Nature Reserve
Ben Lane
Long Drove
Lower Highwood Copse
Hawks Grove
Upper Highwood Copse
Churchway Copse

Livery Farm
The Livery
Livery Rd
Bentley Wood
Barnridge Copse
Bentley Woods
Keepers Cott
Howe Farm
Howe Copse West
Pegsbrook Copse
West Dean Farm
Grimstead Rd

Coalpits Copse
Park Lane
Bentley Wood Nature Reserve
Hatchers Farm
Barnridge Farm
Dean View Farm
Hatchers Copse
New Berryfield Copse
Fine Wood

Dean Copse
Redridge Copse
Howe Copse East
Beegarden Copse
Heath Copse
Dean Copse
Donkey Copse
Green Acre
Moody's Hill
Ashmore Lane
Dean La
Dean Hill

Park Copse
Beechwood Copse
Pilgrims Croft
Dean Road
Rookery Cotts
Motte
West Dean
Rectory Hl
Dean
LC
East Dean Rd
Orchard Farm
Hill Side Cl
The Hanging

23 A B 24 C D 25 E F 26

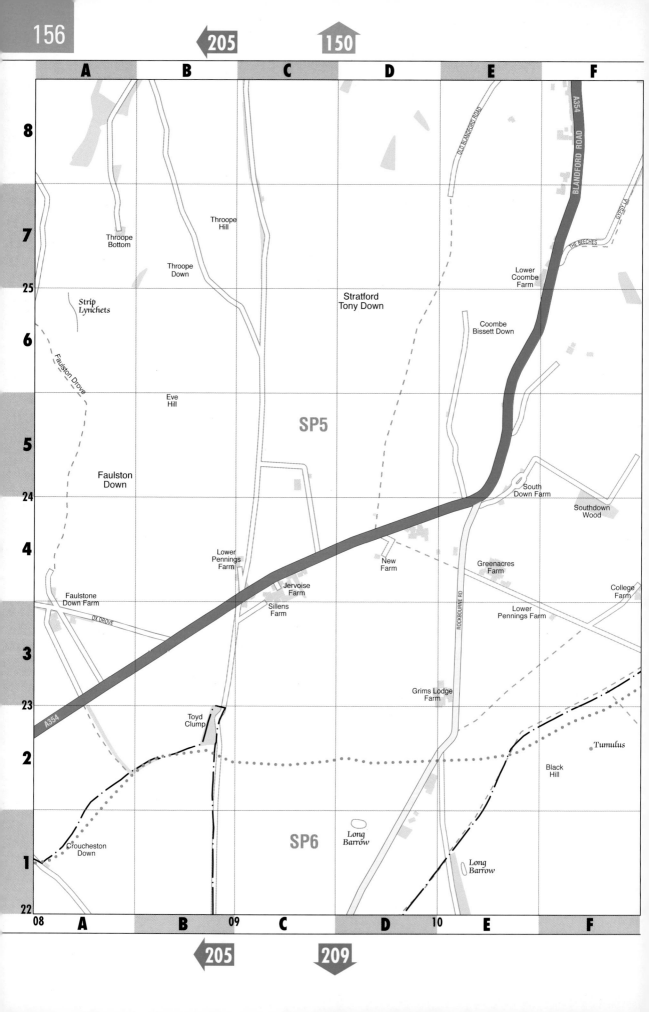

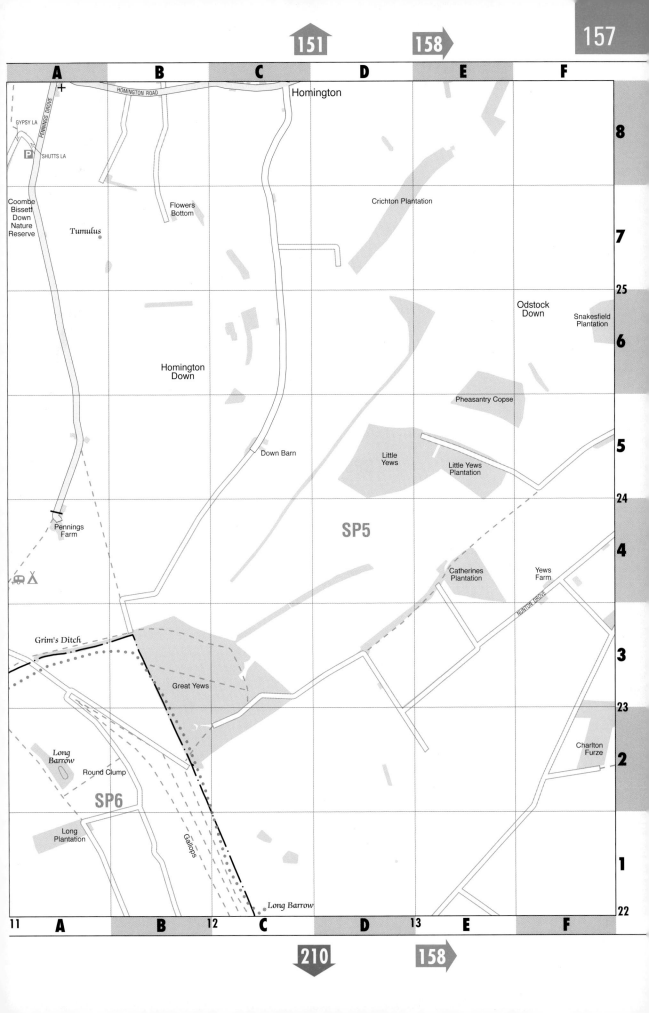

157
152

A **B** **C** **D** **E** **F**

SHEPHERDS
CL

Avon Valley Path

Nunton

H
New Hall

8

Bodenham Hill
Plantation

7

Fir Plantation

Earthworks

WHITSBURY RD

THE AVE

NUNTON DROVE

A338

THE HIGHWAY

Matrimony
Farm

25

Odstock Copse

Nunton
Copse

Charlton
Plantation

6

Clearbury
Plantation

NUNTON DROVE

Clearbury
Ring

Charlton
Manor Farm

5

SP5

THE HIGHWAY

PH

24

Clearbury Down

NUNTON
DROVE

4

North
Field Copse

3

Warren
Plantation

The Giant's Grave
(Long Barrow)

23

Giant's Grave
Plantation

The Giant's
Chair (Tumulus)

2

New Court
Down Barn

New Court
Down

1

22

14 **A** **B** 15 **C** **D** 16 **E** **F**

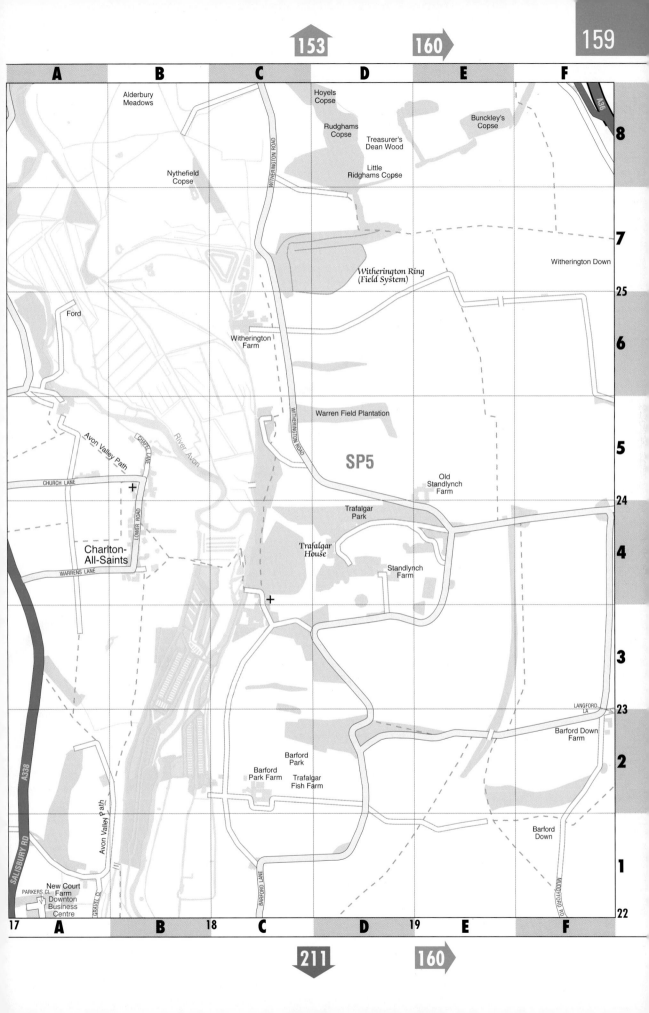

A B C D E F

Alderbury Meadows

Hoyels Copse

Bunckley's Copse

Nythefield Copse

Rudghams Copse

Treasurer's Dean Wood

Little Ridghams Copse

WITHERINGTON ROAD

Witherington Ring (Field System)

Witherington Down

Ford

Witherington Farm

Warren Field Plantation

WITHERINGTON ROAD

SP5

Old Standlynch Farm

River Avon

Avon Valley Path

CHAPEL LANE

CHURCH LANE

LOWER ROAD

Trafalgar Park

Trafalgar House

Standlynch Farm

Charlton-All-Saints

WARRENS LANE

A338

SALISBURY RD

GRAVEL CL.

Avon Valley Path

PARKERS CL.

New Court Farm Downton Business Centre

BARFORD LANE

Barford Park Farm

Barford Park

Trafalgar Fish Farm

Barford Down Farm

LANGFORD LA.

Barford Down

MUDDYFORD RD

8 7 25 6 5 24 4 3 23 2 1 22

17 18 19

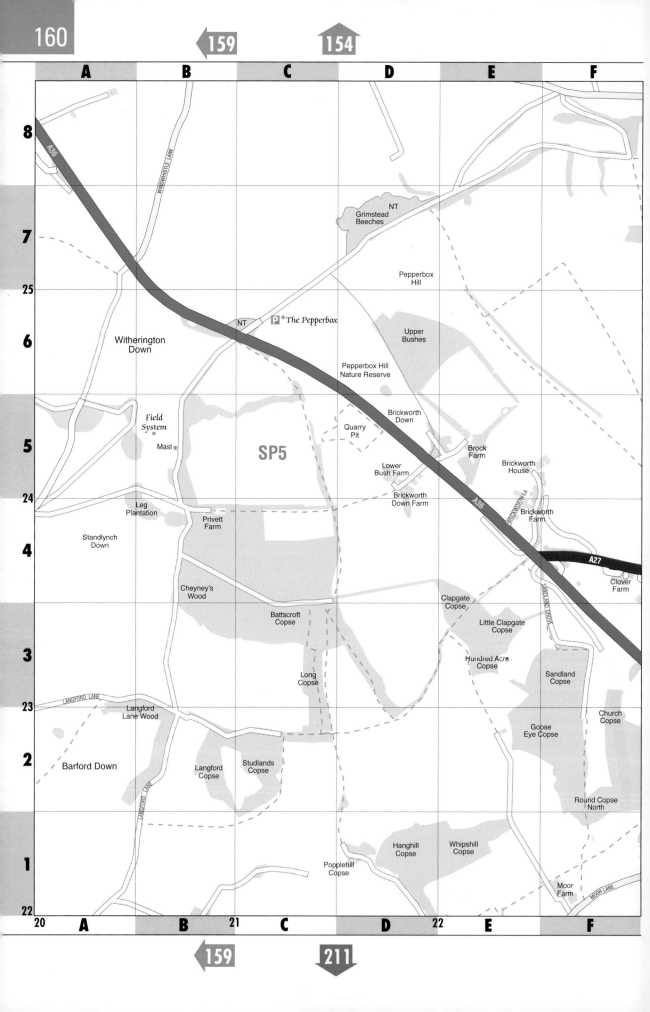

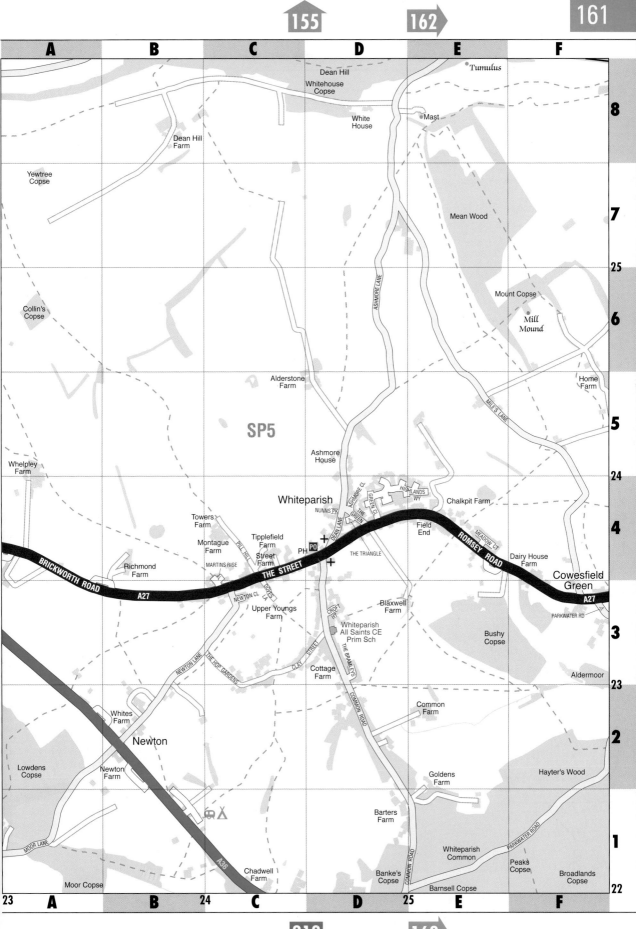

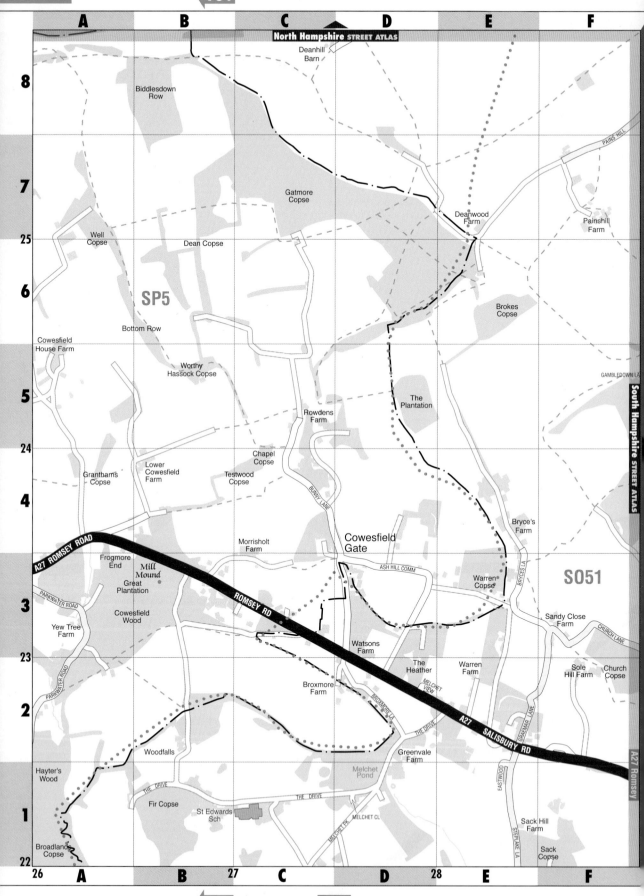

North Hampshire STREET ATLAS

South Hampshire STREET ATLAS

A B C D E F

8

7

25

6

SP5

Deanhill Barn

Biddlesdown Row

Gatmore Copse

Dean Copse

Well Copse

Deanwood Farm

Painshill Farm

PAINS HILL

Brokes Copse

Bottom Row

Cowesfield House Farm

Worthy Hassock Copse

The Plantation

GAMBLEDOWN LA

5

24

Rowdens Farm

Chapel Copse

Granthams Copse

Lower Cowesfield Farm

Testwood Copse

BURNT LANE

Bryce's Farm

4

Morrisholt Farm

Cowesfield Gate

Warren Copse

BRYCE'S LA

SO51

A27 ROMSEY ROAD

Frogmore End

Mill Mound

Great Plantation

ASH HILL COMM

Sandy Close Farm

CHURCH LANE

PARKWATER ROAD

3

ROMSEY RD

Cowesfield Wood

Yew Tree Farm

Watsons Farm

The Heather

Warren Farm

Sole Hill Farm

Church Copse

23

MELCHET VIEW

PARKWATER ROAD

Broxmore Farm

BROXMORE LA

A27 SALISBURY RD

GRAEMAR LANE

2

Woodfalls

Greenvale Farm

THE DRIVE

A27 Romsey

Hayter's Wood

THE DRIVE

Fir Copse

THE DRIVE

Melchet Pond

EASTWOOD

1

St Edwards Sch

MELCHET CL

Sack Hill Farm

STEPLAKE LA

MELCHET PK

Broadlands Copse

Sack Copse

22

26 A B 27 C D 28 E F

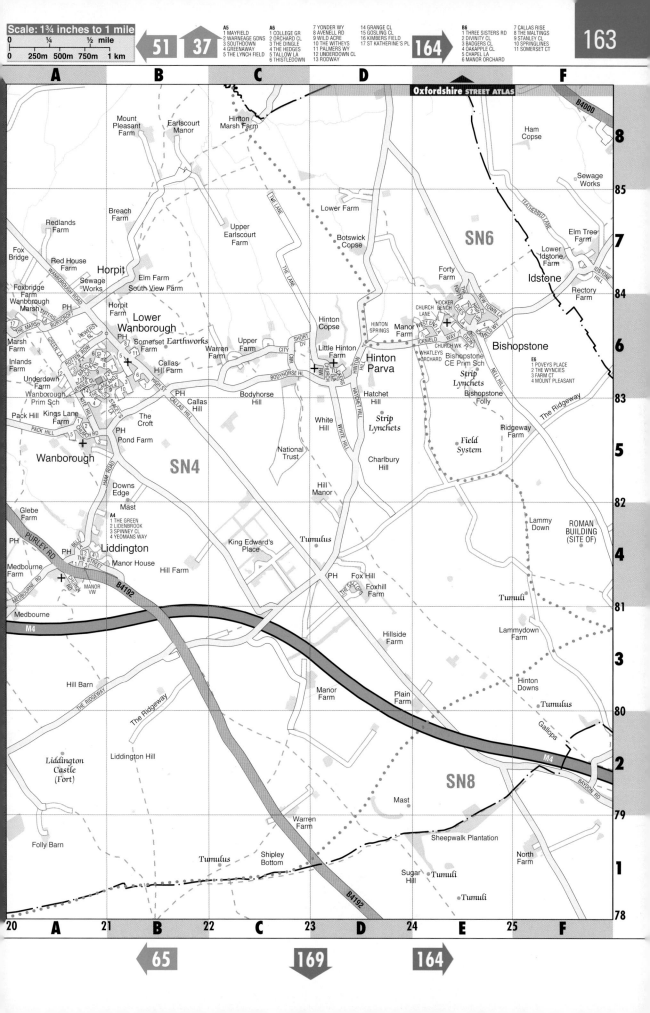

◄ 163

Scale: 1¾ inches to 1 mile

0 ¼ ½ mile

0 250m 500m 750m 1 km

Oxfordshire STREET ATLAS

Kingstone
Winslow

Kingstone
Farm

B4000

STATION RD

B4507

Winslow
Bank

Odstone
Hill

Wayland's Smithy
(Long Barrow)

Ridgeway

Long
Plantation

Uffington
Down

Lambourn Valley Way

The Mnr
Hse

WIXES PIECE

Odstone
Coombes

Knighton
Barn

Ashbury with
Compton Beauchamp
CE (Aided) Prim Sch

PO

Kingstone
Coombes

Pingoose
Covert

Cross
Dyke

Kingstone
Warren

SN7

Idlebush
Barrow

Ashbury

CHURCH LA

Ashbury Hill

ASHBURY HILL

Odstone
Barn

Ashbury
Folly

P

Down
Folly

Settlement

Compton
Bottom

Woolstone
Down

Kingston Warren Down

Gallops

OX12

Idstone
Plantation

Idstone
Hill

Ridgeway

SN6

HONEYBUNCH
CORNER

Tower
Hill

Knighton Down

Tumulus

Settlement

Field System

Gallops

Hailey
Wood

B4000

Odstone
Down

Whit
Coombe

Wellbottom
Down

Gallops

Crowberry
Tump

Knighton Bushes
Plantation

Starveall
Farm

Middle Wood

Kingstone
Down

Weathercock
Hill

Park Down
Farm

Baldback
Covert

Maddle
Farm

Alfred's
Castle

Ashdown
Park

P

Weathercock

Postdown
Border

Swinley
Down

Ashdown
House

Parkfarm Down

Old Warren

Lye
Leaze

Swinley
Copse

Tumuli

Park Pale

Ashdown
Farm

Upper
Wood

Halfmoon
Covert

Tumulus

RG17

MADDLE ROAD

Harley
Bushes

Park Pale

Park
Farm

Hangman's Stone

Tumulus

Three
Barrows

Whiteshere

Park Pale

Lambourn
Corner

Russley Downs

Dean Bottom

Botley
Bottom

Tumulus

Upper
Lambourn

Earthworks

Bishopstone
Downs

Idstone Down

Fognam
Down

Kings Farm

HIGH ST

MADDLE RD

Russley Park

Settlement

Botley
Copse

Fognam
Farm

B4000

Nugent Farm

Cemy

Gallop

SN8

GORE LANE

Gore Lane
Farm

Bailey
Hill

Row
Down

Gallops

PH

MALT SHOVEL LA

Peaks Downs

Hazelbury
Farm

Bailey Hill
Copse

Gallops

White House
Farm

M4

Near Down

Peaks
Wood

Bailey Hill
Farm

Down Farm

FOLLY ROAD

FOLLY ROAD

Baydon

FIVEWAYS
CL

Baydon St Nicholas
CE Prim Sch

Baydon Hole
Farm

Farncombe
Farm

East Leaze
Farm

BAYDON ROAD

DOWNSMEAD

PO

Hedden's
Copse

M4

Thornslait
Plantation

Farncombe Down

Gallops

BAYDON ROAD

◄ 163   170 ▼

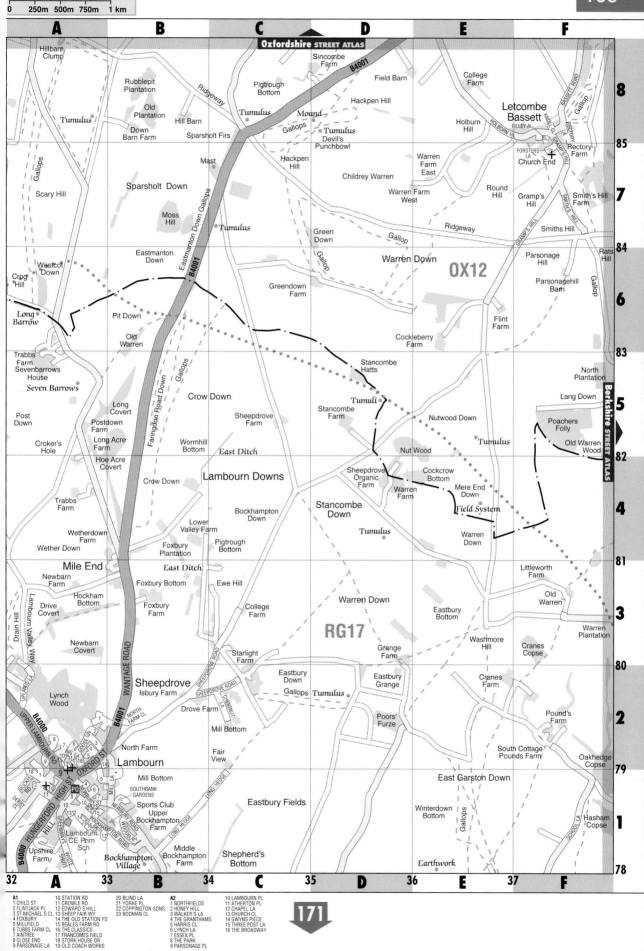

A1
1 CHILD ST
2 FLINTJACK PL
3 ST MICHAEL'S CL
4 FOXBURY
5 MILLFIELD
6 TUBBS FARM CL
7 AINTREE
8 CLOSE END
9 PARSONAGE LA

10 STATION RD
11 CROWLE RD
12 EDWARD'S HILL
13 SHEEP FAIR WY
14 THE OLD STATION YD
15 BEALES FARM RD
16 THE CLASSICS
17 FRANCOMES FIELD
18 STORK HOUSE DR
19 OLD COACH WORKS

20 BLIND LA
21 YORKE PL
22 COPPINGTON GDNS
23 BODMAN CL

A2
1 NORTHFIELDS
2 HONEY HILL
3 WALKER'S LA
4 THE GRANTHAMS
5 HARRIS CL
6 LYNCH LA
7 ESSEX PL
8 THE PARK
9 PARSONAGE PL

10 LAMBOURN PL
11 ATHERTON PL
12 CHAPEL LA
13 CHURCH CL
14 GWYNS PIECE
15 THREE POST LA
16 THE BROADWAY

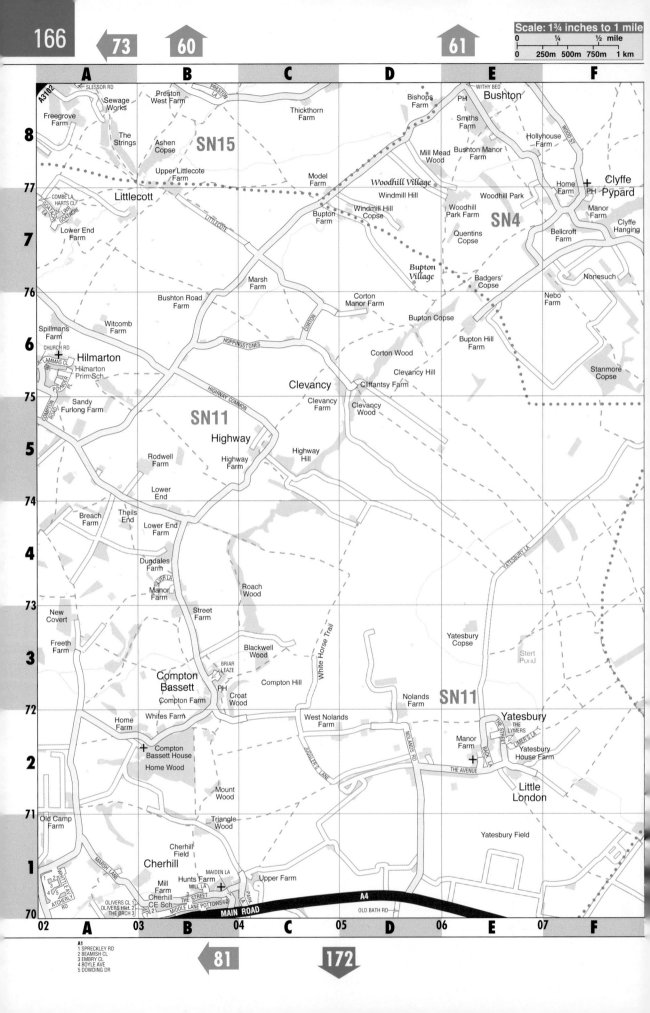

Scale: 1¾ inches to 1 mile

0   ¼   ½   mile
0   250m 500m 750m 1 km

A   B   C   D   E   F

A3102

SLESSOR RD
Freegrove Farm
Sewage Works
The Strings
Preston West Farm
Ashen Copse
PRESTON LA
Thickthorn Farm
Bishops Farm
PH
Withy Bed
Bushton
Smiths Farm
Mill Mead Wood
Bushton Manor Farm
Hollyhouse Farm
WOOD ST

SN15

Upper Littlecote Farm
Model Farm
Woodhill Village
Home Farm
PH
Clyffe Pypard

Littlecott
COMBE LA
HARTS CL
GOATACRE LA
GOATACRE
Lower End Farm
LITTLECOTE
Bupton Farm
Windmill Hill
Windmill Hill Copse
Woodhill Park Farm
Woodhill Park
Quentins Copse
Manor Farm
Clyffe Hanging
SN4

Marsh Farm
Bushton Road Farm
CORTON
Corton Manor Farm
Bupton Copse
Bupton Village
Badgers' Copse
Bellcroft Farm
Nebo Farm
Nonesuch

Spillmans Farm
CHURCH RD
AMMAS CL
Hilmarton
Hilmarton Prim Sch
POWDER PL
Witcomb Farm
HOPPINGSTONES
Bupton Hill Farm
Stanmore Copse

Sandy Furlong Farm
COMPTON ROAD
HIGHWAY COMMON
Corton Wood
Clevancy Hill
Cliffantsy Farm
Clevancy

SN11

Highway
Clevancy Farm
Clevancy Wood

Rodwell Farm
Highway Farm
Highway Hill
Highway Hill

Breach Farm
Theils End
Lower End
Lower End Farm

Dugdales Farm
SILVER LA
Manor Farm
Roach Wood
YATESBURY LA

New Covert
Street Farm

Freeth Farm
Blackwell Wood
BRIAR LEAZE
White Horse Trail
Yatesbury Copse
Stert Pond

Compton Bassett
Compton Farm
PH
Croat Wood
Compton Hill
Compton Hill
Nolands Farm

SN11

Whites Farm
West Nolands Farm
Yatesbury
THE STREET
THE LYMERS

Home Farm
Compton Bassett House
Home Wood
JUGGLER'S LANE
NOLANDS RD
Manor Farm
Yatesbury House Farm
BACK LA
LIMER'S LA
Little London

Mount Wood
THE AVENUE

Old Camp Farm
Triangle Wood
Yatesbury Field

WHITTLE A'LY
ATCHERLY RD
MARSH LANE
Cherhill Field
Cherhill
MAIDEN LA
Hunts Farm
MILL LA
Upper Farm

1 SPRECKLEY RD
2 BEAMISH CL
3 EMBRY CL
4 BOYLE AVE
5 DOWDING DR
Mill Farm
Cherhill CE Sch
THE STREET
PARK LA
A4
OLIVERS CL 1
OLIVERS HILL 1
THE ORCH 3
Middle Lane POTTOWS FO
MAIN ROAD
OLD BATH RD

02   A   03   B   04   C   05   D   06   E   07   F

A1

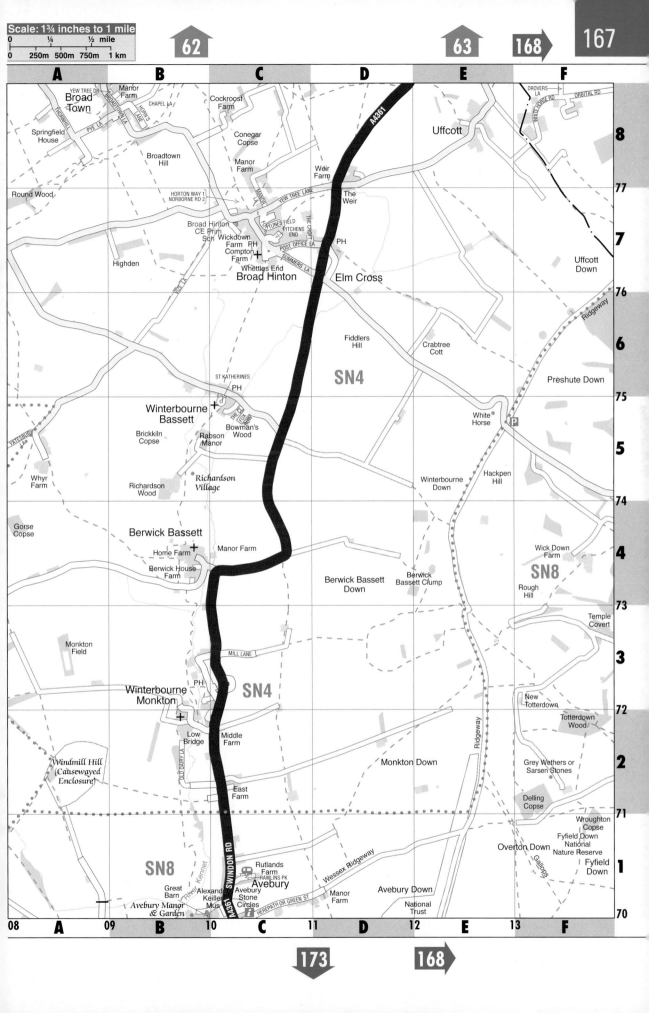

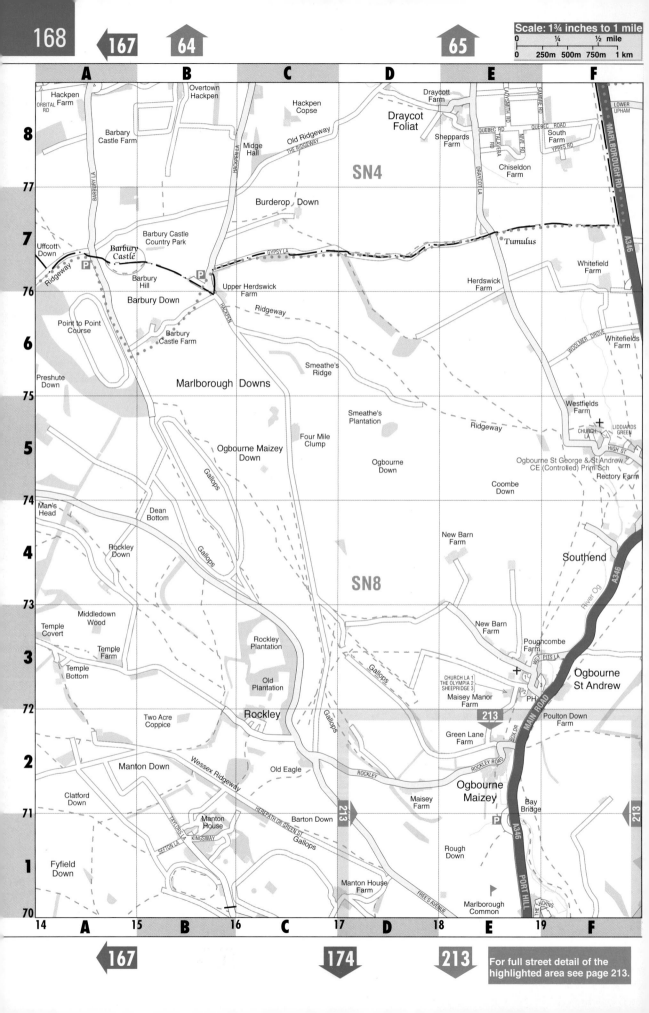

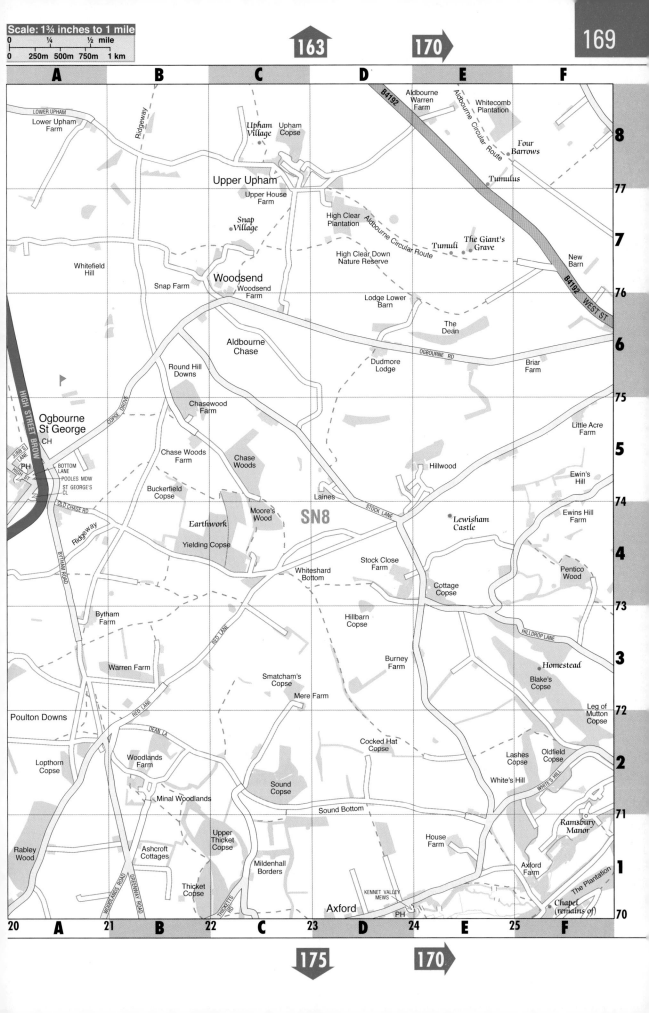

Scale: 1¾ inches to 1 mile

0   ¼   ½ mile
0   250m 500m 750m 1 km

A B C D E F

LOWER UPHAM
Lower Upham Farm
Ridgeway
Upham Village
Upham Copse
B4192
Aldbourne Warren Farm
Aldbourne Circular Route
Whitecomb Plantation
Four Barrows
Tumulus

8

Upper Upham
Upper House Farm
High Clear Plantation
Aldbourne Circular Route
Tumuli
The Giant's Grave

77

Snap Village
High Clear Down Nature Reserve
New Barn

7

Whitefield Hill
Snap Farm
Woodsend
Woodsend Farm
Lodge Lower Barn
The Dean
B4192
WEST ST

76

Aldbourne Chase
Round Hill Downs
Dudmore Lodge
OGBOURNE RD
Briar Farm

6

Chasewood Farm
Hillwood
Little Acre Farm

75

Ogbourne St George
CH
JUBB'S LANE
PH
HIGH ST
BOTTOM LANE
POOLES MDW
ST GEORGE'S CL
Chase Woods Farm
Chase Woods
Laines
Ewin's Hill

5

COPSE DRIVE
HIGH STREET BROW
Buckerfield Copse
Moore's Wood
Laines
STOCK LANE
Lewisham Castle
Ewins Hill Farm

74

OLD CHASE RD
Ridgeway
Earthwork
Yielding Copse
SN8
Whiteshard Bottom
Stock Close Farm
Cottage Copse
Pentico Wood

4

BYTHAM ROAD
Bytham Farm
RED LANE
Hillbarn Copse
HILLDROP LANE

73

Warren Farm
Smatcham's Copse
Mere Farm
Burney Farm
Homestead
Blake's Copse

3

Poulton Downs
RED LANE
DEAN LA
Cocked Hat Copse
Lashes Copse
Oldfield Copse
Leg of Mutton Copse

72

Lopthorn Copse
Woodlands Farm
Minal Woodlands
Sound Copse
Sound Bottom
White's Hill
WHITE'S HILL
Ramsbury Manor

2

Rabley Wood
Ashcroft Cottages
Upper Thicket Copse
Mildenhall Borders
House Farm
Axford Farm
The Plantation

71

WOODLANDS ROAD
GREENWAY ROAD
Thicket Copse
THICKETS RD
KENNET VALLEY MEWS
Axford
PH
Chapel (remains of)

1

20 A 21 B 22 C 23 D 24 E 25 F

A6
1 RECTORY WOOD
2 SOUTHFIELD
3 CLARIDGE CL
4 TURNPIKE
5 MARLBOROUGH RD
6 THE GARLINGS

7 GLEBE CL
8 ST MICHAEL'S CL
9 BACK LA
10 THE PADDOCKS
11 GODDARDS LA
12 THE KNOLL
13 WESTFIELD CHASE

14 WHITELEY RD
15 HILLWOOD RD
16 HAWKINS RD
17 BARNES YD
18 VALLEY VIEW

← 169

↑ 164

Scale: 1¾ inches to 1 mile
0   ¼   ½ mile
0   250m   500m   750m   1 km

A7
1 CHANDLER'S LA
2 LOTTAGE WAY
3 WINDMILL CL
4 ALMA RD
5 COOK RD

B2
1 HILLDROP CL
2 KNOWLEDGE CRES
3 LAWRENCE MD
4 BURDETT ST
5 ORCHARD CL
6 ISLES RD
7 SWAN'S BOTTOM
8 CHAPEL LA
9 SWAN'S CL
10 TOWNFIELD
11 WHITEHILL CL
12 ATHERTON CL
13 GREEN ACRES
14 THE PADDOCKS
15 TANKARD LANE
16 SCHOLARD'S LA
17 BURDETT ST

Grid columns: A 26 B 27 C 28 D 29 E 30 F 31

Grid rows: 8 77 7 76 6 75 5 74 4 73 3 72 2 71 1 70

Place names and features:

North Field Barn
DOWNSMEAD
NEWTONS WK
BARLEY FIELDS
WALRONDS CL
Baydon
Sewage Works
ERMIN ST
FINCHES LA
MANOR LA
ERMIN CL
Farncombe Down
Farn Combe
Windmill Farm
Lodge Farm
Lodge Down
Lodge Copse
Coppington Down
B4000
Greenhills
Aldbourne Road
Midge Copse
Kingwood House
Platt Lane
Great West Wood
Ermin Street
Little West Wood
Holly Farm
LAMBOURN BSNS PK
Lottage Farm
GRASSHILLS LA
LOTTAGE RD
KANDAHAR
OXFORD
Green Hill
Gore's Copse
Baydon Hill Farm
Woodley's Copse
Coneygre Copse
Common Barn Copse
Hadley Farm
Battens Farm
Hurst Farm
PH
Dixon's Farm
St Michael's CE Aided Prim Sch
Aldbourne
Liby
PO
B4192
WEST ST
CASTLE ST
STOCK LANE
HAWKINS RD
THE DOWNS
BUTTS
FARM LA
SOUTHWARD LANE
Ford Farm
Pigs' Hill Wood
Baydon Wood
St Johns Wood
Membury Service Area
Aerial Business Park
RAMSBURY RD
Aerial Farm
Lyedown Copse
Cuckoo Copse
Housedd's Hill
Long Copse
Hillier's Copse
Paxlet Plantation
Membury Castle (site of)
SN8
Woodcock Grove
Hoddes Bridge
Southward Down
Baydon Manor
Marridge Hill
Anchor Copse
Balak Farm
Membury Farm
Lyckweed Farm
Moon's Copse
Leigh Farm
RG17
Preston
Crowood Farm
Shell's Wood
Marridge Hill Wood
Witcha Copse
Ballard's Copse
Long Barrow
Hunt's Copse
Witcha Farm
Tumulus
Ragnal
Love's Copse
Hails Grove
Eastridge House
Raffin Stud
Wiltshire Bottom
Southern Copse
Pond Wood
Crowood House
Woodlands Farm
Whittonside Farm
Bower Wood
Crooked Soley
Hilldrop Farm
HILLDROP LANE
Boltsridge Copse
Bolstridge Farm
Love's Farm
LOVE'S LANE
CROWOOD LA
Little Wood
Whittonditch
Balaam's Wood
Queen's Coppice
Westfield Copse
LANGFIELDS
Ramsbury Prim Sch
ASHLEY PC
OXFORD
UNION ST
WHITTONDITCH ROAD
Oaken Coppice
Foxbury Wood
Fewley Coppice
Princess Copse
Manor Farm
Ramsbury
BACK LA
Liby
HIGH ST
PH
PO
Ambrose Farm
New Town
NEWTOWN ROAD
Knighton
Balaam's Wood
Daffy Copse
King's Copse
WHITE'S HILL
MILL LA
LAMPLANDS
Weir
River Kennet
B4192
Chilton Foliat
Manor Farm
Spring Hill
Atherton Coppice
Whitehill Coppice
ROMAN VILLA
Littlecote
Weir
The Plantation
Bungalow Bridge Farm
Bridge Farm
Park Coppice
Hotel
Great Coppice
Darrell's Farm

← 169

↑ 176

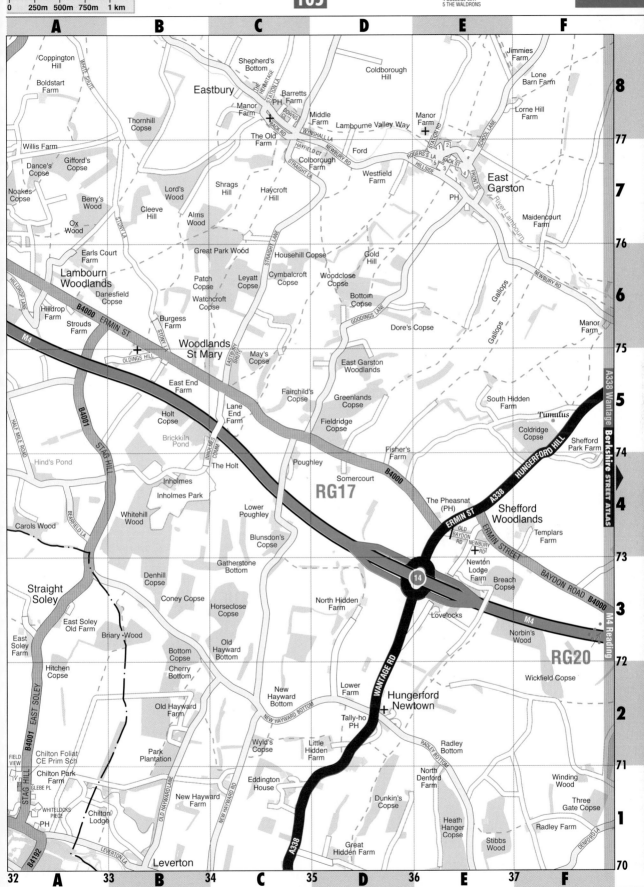

A   B   C   D   E   F

8
77
7
76
6
75
5
74
4
73
3
72
2
71
1
70

Coppington Hill
Boldstart Farm
Willis Farm
Dance's Copse
Gifford's Copse
Noakes Copse
Berry's Wood
Ox Wood
Earls Court Farm
Lambourn Woodlands
Hilldrop Farm
Strouds Farm
Danesfield Copse
Burgess Farm
Woodlands St Mary
Oldings Hill
East End Farm
Holt Copse
Brickkiln Pond
Inholmes Comm
Lane End Farm
The Holt
Hind's Pond
Inholmes
Inholmes Park
Whitehill Wood
Carols Wood
Briary Wood
Straight Soley
East Soley Old Farm
East Soley Farm
Hitchen Copse
Old Hayward Farm
Park Plantation
Chilton Foliat CE Prim Sch
Chilton Park Farm
Chilton Lodge
Leverton
Leverton La

Thornhill Copse
Cleeve Hill
Lord's Wood
Alms Wood
Great Park Wood
Patch Copse
Watchcroft Copse
Leyatt Copse
Shrags Hill
Haycroft Hill
May's Copse
Denhill Copse
Coney Copse
Horseclose Copse
Gatherstone Bottom
Blunsdon's Copse
Lower Poughley
Bottom Copse
Cherry Bottom
New Hayward Bottom
Wyld's Copse
New Hayward Farm
Eddington House

Eastbury
Shepherd's Bottom
Manor Farm
The Old Farm
Colborough Farm
Household Copse
Cymbalcroft Copse
Fairchild's Copse
Greenlands Copse
Fieldridge Copse
Poughley
Somercourt
Lower Poughley
North Hidden Farm
New Hayward Bottom
Little Hidden Farm
Tally-ho PH
Great Hidden Farm

Middle Farm
Ford
Westfield Farm
Gold Hill
Woodclose Copse
Bottom Copse
Dore's Copse
East Garston Woodlands
Fisher's Farm
The Pheasnat (PH)
Lower Farm
Hungerford Newtown
Dunkin's Copse
North Denford Farm

Coldborough Hill
Lambourne Valley Way
Barretts Farm
Manor Farm
East Garston
Maidencourt Farm
Gallops
Manor Farm
South Hidden Farm
Tumulus
Coldridge Copse
Shefford Park Farm
Shefford Woodlands
Templars Farm
Newton Lodge Farm
Breach Copse
Lovelocks
Norbin's Wood
Wickfield Copse
Radley Bottom
Radley Farm
Heath Hanger Copse
Stibbs Wood
Winding Wood
Three Gate Copse

Jimmies Farm
Lone Barn Farm
Lorne Hill Farm

RG17
RG20

M4
B4000 ERMIN ST
B4001
STAG HILL
STONY LA
HALF MILE ROAD
BEARFIELD LA
HILLDROP LANE
EASTBURY SHUTE
STRAIGHT LANE
HAYFIELD CT
STRAIGHT LA
NEWBURY RD
STATION LA
THE HERMITAGE
WYNSHALL LA
DOWNS CL
BEACH RD
INHOLMES COMM
GOODINGS LANE
B4000
ERMIN ST
OLD BAYDON RD
NEWBURY RD
ERMIN STREET
HUNGERFORD HILL
A338
A338 Wantage
Berkshire STREET ATLAS
River Lambourn
NEWBURY RD
BAYDON ROAD
B4000
M4
M4 Reading
WANTAGE RD
NEW HAYWARD BOTTOM
OLD HAYWARD LANE
NEW HAYWARD RD
EAST SOLEY
STAG HILL
GLEBE PL
WHITELOCKS PIECE
FIELD VIEW
B4192
LEVERTON LA
DENFORD LA
RADLEY BOTTOM
ROGERS'S LA
HILLSIDE
BACK ST
FRONT ST
SCHOOL LANE
14
PH
PH

32   33   34   35   36   37

A   B   C   D   E   F

8

LABOUR-IN-VAIN HILL   MAIN RD
A4
Quemerford Gate
P
PH
OLIVERS HILL
Quemerford Gate Farm
Hayle Farm
White Horse Plantation
OLD BATH RD
Wessex Ridgeway   Tumulus
A4
SN8
Cherhill White Horse
Knoll Down
P

Theobald's Green
GREENS LA
Tumulus
Cherhill Down
Gallops

69

MOGGS LA
Sprays Farm
Oldbury Castle (Hillfort)
Witch Plantation
West Down
Harepit Way
Tumuli

7

Manor Farm
East Farm
Ranscombe Bottom
Calstone Down
Gallops   Tumuli

Calstone Wellington
South Farm
Tumulus
North Down
The Firs

68

SN11
Wessex Ridgeway
Tumuli
North Down
Tumuli
A361

6

Horsecombe Bottom
Tumuli
Tumulus
Tumulus
Gallops

Morgan's Hill Nature Reserve
Enclosure
Hemp Knoll

67

Tumuli
Masts
Baltic Farm
Bishop's Canning Down
Gallops
Horton Down

CH
Furze Knoll
Tumuli
Wansdyke
Tumuli
Tumulus
Gallops

5

Long Barrow
Shepherds' Shore
Tumulus
Easton Down Long Barrow

66

Wansdyke Path
Roughridge Hill

4

Easton Hill
Strip Lynchets
Tumulus

65

Roundway Hill
Bourton
Tumuli   Tumuli
Strip Lynchets
Kitchen Barrow

Bishops Cannings
SN10
Earthwork
Tumuli

3

West End Farm
WEST END
BOURTON LA
Easton Farm

Blackwell Farm
THE ESTATE YD
Bishops Cannings CE (Aided) Prim Sch
Bourton Manor Farm
Harepath Farm

PH   CHURCH WLK
Court Farm

64

214
OAK CL
Kennet & Avon Canal
Horton Mill Farm
Townsend Farm

2

Hopton Park Ind Est
A361
Swing-bridge
Horton Chain Bridge
Park Farm

BEECHFIELD RD
CHANDLERS LANE
DAIRY LA
Allington

SERGEANT ROGERS WY
WELLINGTON DR
HORTON ROAD
PH
Horton Bridge
Horton
The Knoll
Manor Farm
Home Farm
Cannings Cross Farm

63

HOPTON RD
214
Laywood Bridge
Little Horton
PIG LANE
Lower Mill Farm
Swing-bridge
Swing-bridge
Woodway Bridge
All Cannings Bridge

LONDON RD
Devizes Marina
Calcote Farm
Manor Farm
SPANIELS BRIDGE RD
Sewage Works
Allington Bridge
MATTHEWS CL 1
WYCOMBE LA 2
GRANGEFIELD 3
THORNYCROFT LA 4

62

COATE LANE

02   A   03   B   04   C   05   D   06   E   07   F

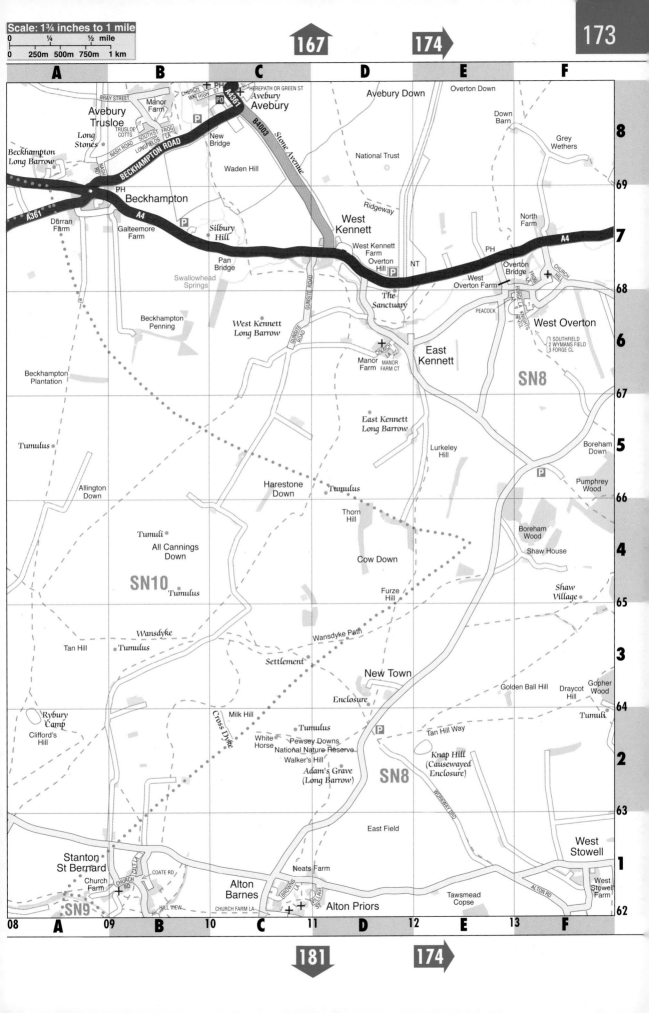

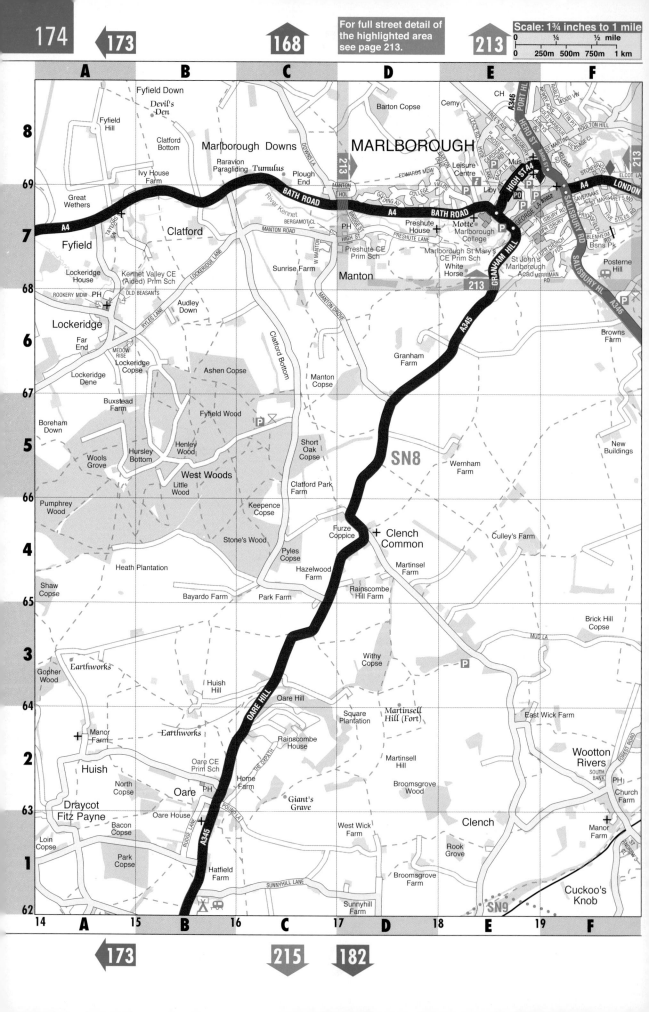

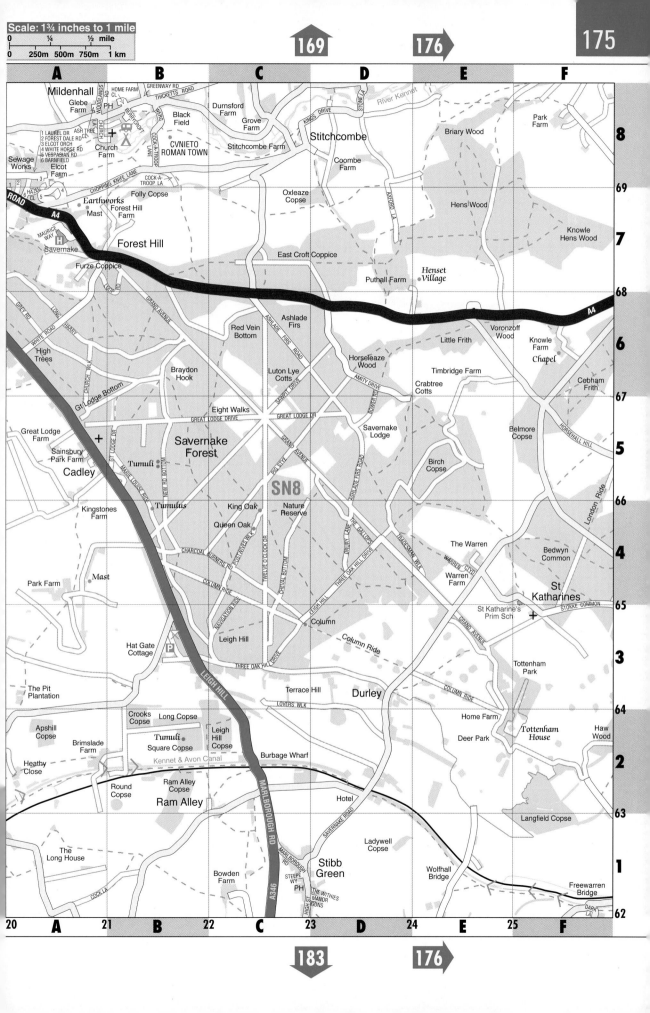

Scale: 1¾ inches to 1 mile

0   ¼   ½   mile
0   250m   500m   750m   1 km

A   B   C   D   E   F

8
The Plantation
Brickkiln Copse
Burnt Wood
Bottom Coppice
Rudge Coppice
Lawn Coppice
Littlecote Park Farm
Cake Wood
Scrope Farm
Little Copse
Rudge
Rudge Manor Farm
Rudge Farm House
69
Highclose Farm
Scrope's Wood
Scrope's Wood
7
Froxfield
BATH ROAD
68
Harrow Farm
A4   BATH ROAD
Green Farm
MANOR PK
CHURCH RD
G FARM RD
LITTLECOTE RD
PH
Lock
BREWHOUSE HILL
MANOR FARM
Sewage Works
RG17
6
Noke Wood
Almshouse Copse
Lock
OAK HILL
Firth Copse
Oak Hill
LOWER OAK HILL
North Standen House
67
Withy Copse
Round Copse
Bushelleys Copse
Lock
FOREBRIDGE
Jugg's Wood
Trindledown Copse
BEECH WLK
LONG WALK
Lady's Wood
Upper Horsehall Hill Farm
Lower Farm
5
Chisbury
CHURCH ST
Fore Bridge
Stype Wood
Catmore Copse
LONDON RIDGE
MONK'S LA
Chisbury Lane Farm
Oldhouse Wood
Strouds Farm
SCHOOL LA
Little Bedwyn
66
CHISBURY LANE
CHISBURY LA
Chisbury Manor Farm
St Martin's Chapel
Lock
HIGH ST
Stype Grange
Cowleaze Coppice
Tumuli
Park Copse
Chisbury Camp
SN8
Little Bonning's Copse
Barn Copse
Furze Copse
Bagshot
4
Faggotty Copse
Chisbury Wood
KELSTON ROAD
PH
Bewley Farm
Brimley Copse
Great Bedwyn CE Sch
WANSDYKE RD
Parlow Bottom
Bonning's Copse
Wentworth's Copse
Hillcroft Copse
Westcott Copse
65
STOKKE COMM
Horse Copse
Lock
Burridge Heath
Eastcourt Farm
Stokke Manor
ROSEMARY CL
PH
WILLIS CL
Sewage Works
Strockeridge Copse
Burridgeheath Plantation
Gully Copse
ANNETS LA
SIX ACRE LA
Polesdon House
3
Stock Common
FOREST HILL HIGH ST
BROWN'S LA
FARM LANE
PH
KNAPP
Bedwyn
GALLEY LANE
Bedwyn Dyke
Foxbury Wood
Baverstock's Copse
A338
Shawgrove Copse
PO
Great Bedwyn
BRACKLA
BROOK STREET
Foxwood Farm
Shalbourne Heath Plantation
64
HATCHET LA
SHAWGROVE
CHURCH STREET
Lock
BOLLAND CL
Mill Bridge
BROOK STREET
Round Copse
Birch Copse
Long Copse
Haw Wood
Bedwyn Stone Museum
MILL CL
Ivy's Copse
Folly Farm
Newtown
Shalbourne CE Prim Sch
MILL LA
Sewage Works
Bloxham Copse
Kennet & Avon Canal
Brail Farm
Shalbourne
2
Bloxham Lodge
LC
Lock
Castle Copse
SHALBOURNE RD
West Farm
Baverstock Farm
PH
Ropewind Farm
63
CROFTON ROAD
Lock
Bedwyn Brail
Harding Copse
CARVERS HILL
PO
COLS LANE
BURR LA
Westcourt Farm
Crofton Farm
Weir
Wilton Brail
Harding Farm
THE CLOSE
KINGSTON RD
LITTLE MEAD
1
Crofton
LC
Dodsdown Farm
Wilton Common
West Farm
A338
RIVER DUN
SANDY LA
THE LYNCH
Lock
Crofton Beam Engines
Wilton Water
Tumulus
Wilton Down
Marlmere Farm

62
26   A   27   B   28   C   29   D   30   E   31   F

B3
1 NAPIERS
2 COPYHOLD
3 CASTLE RD
4 FAIRFIELD
5 COSTER VIEW
6 GRANARY RD
7 MANOR RD

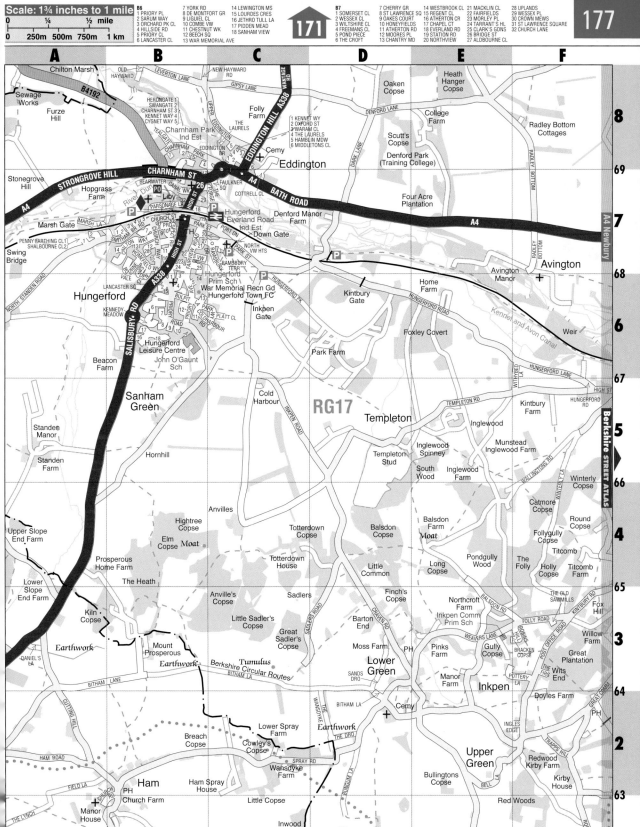

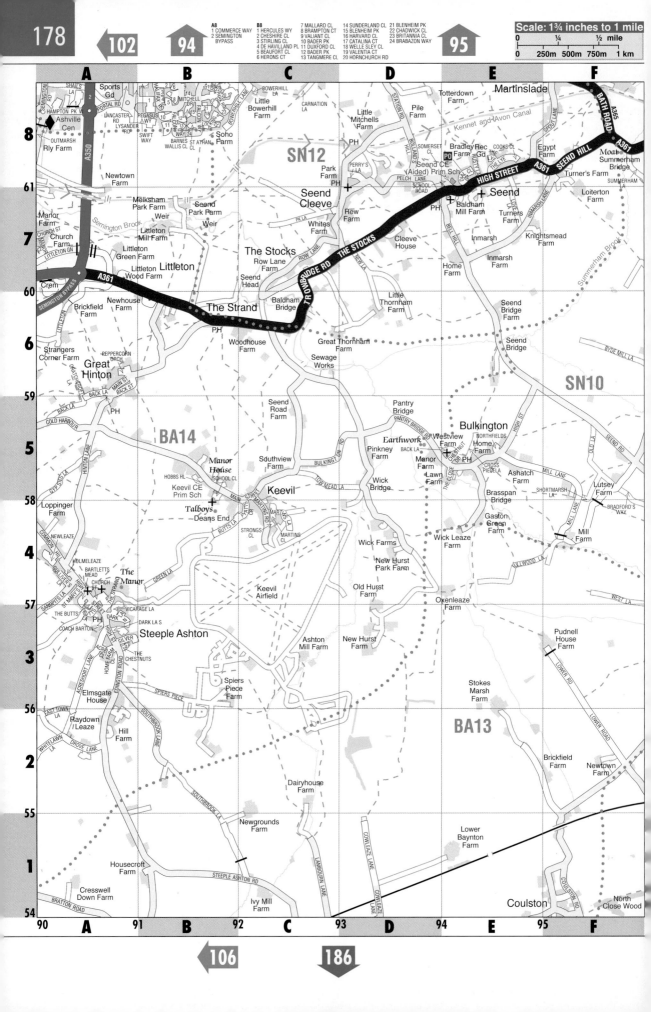

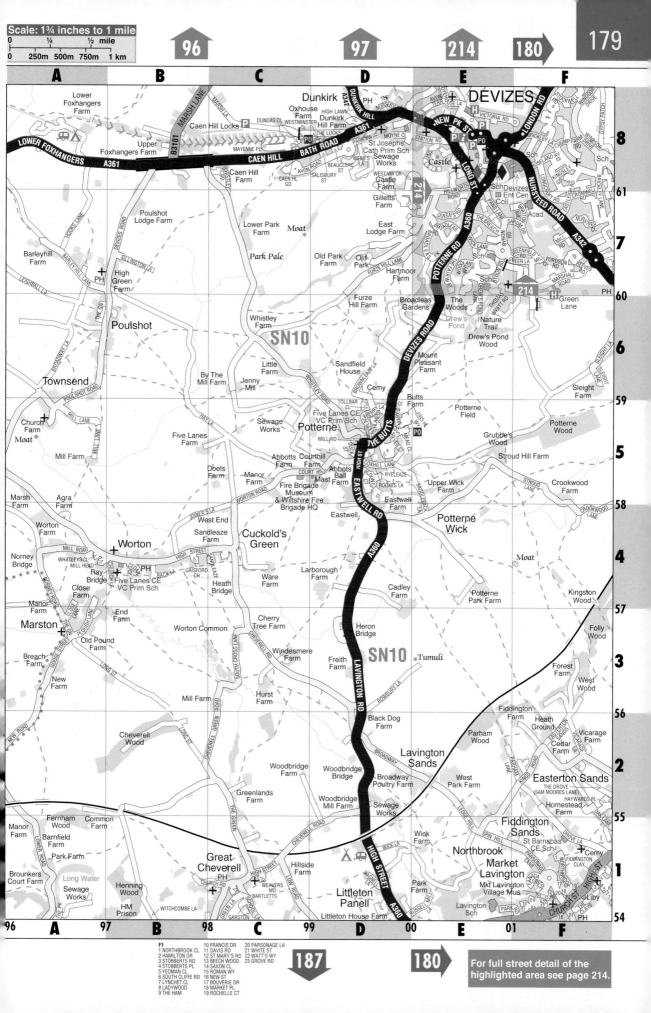

180

For full street detail of the highlighted area see page 214.

214 172

Scale: 1¾ inches to 1 mile
0   ¼   ½ mile
0   250m 500m 750m 1 km

A   B   C   D   E   F

8

PUDDLES LA

Coate

Lowerfields Farm

BYSTONE LA

All Cannings PH

THE STREET

1 GREENHOUSE RD
2 PUB LA
3 THE GLEBE
4 TUMLINS
5 CHANDLERS CL

CHANDLERS LA

LURGATE

DREWITTS LA

SCHOOL LA

All Cannings CE Prim Sch

Wessex Ridgeway

214

PH

61

LITTLE COATE

Nursteed Com Prim Sch

WINDSOR DR

TEASEL CL

LONGLEYS CL

Manor Farm

PATNEY RD

SN10

7

Nursteed Farm

Etchilhampton

Etchilhampton Hill

MIXON CL

CHURCH VIEW

Wayside Farm

Heath Knapp

South Farm

South Farm

Nursteed

BRICKLEY LA

Etchilhampton Water

Manor Farm

60

214

MONUMENT HILL A342

SLEIGHT RD

SLEIGHT LA

STERT VALLEY LA

Manor Farm

Stert

Westfield Farm

Etchilhampton Plantation

Patney Copse

6

Field Head

Wabi Farm

Patney Bridge

PO

Byde Farm

Fullaway Farm

PH

Sunnyside Farm

Hatfield Farm

Patney

59

Marsh Farm

PUCKLANDS

WOODLAND ROAD

MANOR FARM LANE

5

Crookwood Mill Farm

SN10

PATNEY ROAD

Patney

Bridge Farm

Stert Valley Farm

B4
1 PEPPERCOMBE LA
2 CHAPEL LA
3 THE ORCHARD
4 CHURCH VW
5 BOWDENS
6 PEPPERCOMBE CL
7 THE GREEN

CRATE LA

MARSH LA

Sewage Works

58

CROOKWOOD LANE

Franklins Farm

C4
1 CHURCH LA
2 THE HAM
3 FRIARS LA
4 ST MICHAEL S CL
5 WALNUT CL
6 MANOR FARMYARD

Manor Farm

CARTWAY

Chirton CE VC Prim Sch

Heron Nest Wood

Knightleaze Farm

Peppercombe Wood Nature Reserve

UPHILL

S GATE RD

HIGH ST

Wedhampton

The Manor

Chirton

CHERRINGTON FIELD

MILLER CL

4

Wickham Green Farm

Cuckoo's Corner

PO

Urchfont

Foxley Fields

PLUM LA

THE ORCHARD

YEW TREE CL

SMALL ST

Kingston Wood

Oakfrith Wood

PH

CROSS LA

ROOKERY VIEW

B3098

A342

Manor Farm

Conock

THE HOLLOW

FUSSELL CL

57

The Three Graves

Urchfont CE Prim Sch

BLACKBOARD LA

WYNCHILL LA

Foxley Corner

PH

Goosehole Farm

Townsend

THE CROFT

Cemy

BULLDOG LA

3

B3
1 MANOR CL
2 THE PADDOCK
3 STONE PIT LA

Redhorn Plantation

56

BRACKLAND

Eastcott

EASTCOTT COMMON

Goosehole Plantation

Dogtail Plantation

Redhorn Hill

2

KINGS RD

B3098

Eastcott Manor

New Plantation

P

Urchfont Hill

Chirton Bottom

Chirton Maggot

Easterton

A2
1 STRAWBERRY FIELDS
2 THE DROVE (SAM MOORES LA)

Tumulus

Tumulus

P

Tumulus

55

PH

WHITE ST

Penning Down

DANGER AREA

HIGH ST

THE CLAY

Westdown Artillery Range

1

STIRLING RD

FIDDINGTON HL

MELROSE CL

FIDDINGTON CLAY

Wessex Ridgeway

DANGER AREA

Tumulus

Chirton Down

THE PADDOCK

SOUTH CLIFFE RD

DANGER AREA

Tumuli

Old Plantation

54

Great Fore Down

02   A   03   B   04   C   05   D   06   E   07   F

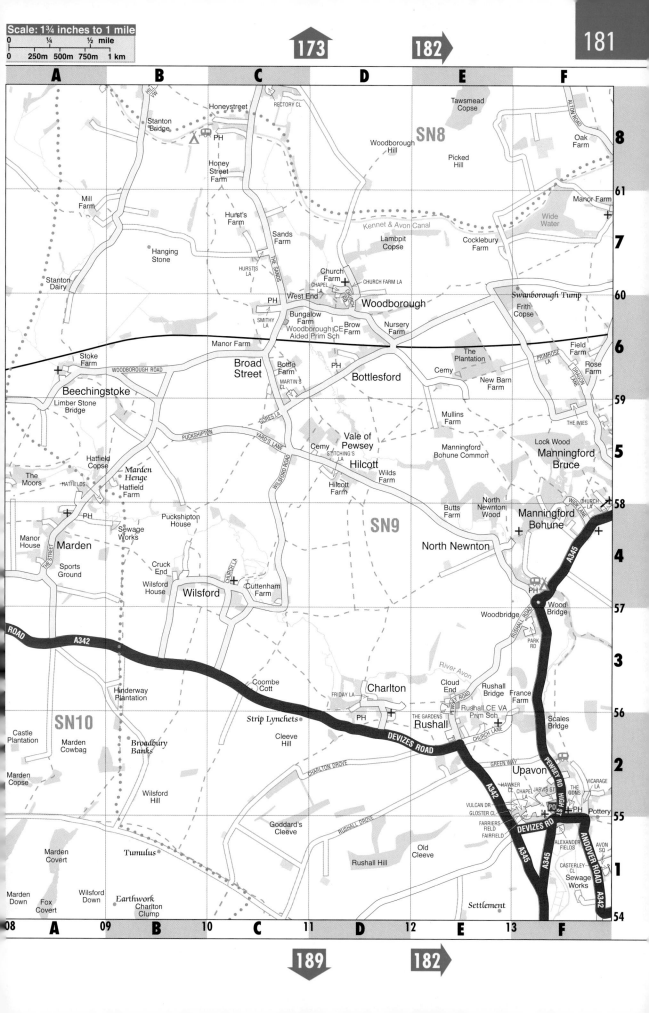

182
181
For full street detail of the highlighted area see page 215.
174
Scale: 1¾ inches to 1 mile
0   ¼   ½   mile
0   250m   500m   750m   1 km

A **B** **C** **D** **E** **F**

Round Copse
Stowell Park
Canal Cl
Bristow Bridge
MARLBOROUGH ROAD
SN8
Pewsey Wharf
215
Inlands Farm
HOLLYBUSH LA
Anvill's Farm
New Mill
Milkhouse Water
Totteridge Farm
Deane Water

8

THE OLD DAIRY
PH
VALTON RD
Wilcot
A345
St Francis Sch
OLD HOSPITAL RD
Fairfield Farm
B3087
BURBAGE ROAD
Littleworth
CROSS ROADS
PH

61

Sharcott Pennings Farm
SMITHS CL
WILCOT ROAD
Pewsey
Knowle
BUCKLEAZE LA
BROADCROFT
HOLLYBUSH LA
DURSEGAT LANE
Little Ann Copse
MILTON ROAD
Fyfield
FORGE CL
PH
THE NEW SEVERALLS
Little Salisbury
LAWN FARM CL
Milton Lilbourne
THE STREET
The Manor House

7

Woodborough Road
Cemy
Pewsey Prim Sch
Pewsey Vale Sch
ASTON CL CRES
TH CL
Liby
P
P
PO
HIGH ST
Pewsey
BALL RD
EASTERTON LA
Kepnal
PH
Vale View
THE OLD SEVERALLS
HAVERING LA
HAVERING LA
Lower Farm

60

215
SHARCOTT DRO
Ayrshire Farm
BROADFIELDS
Bouverie Hall
SWAN ROAD
RAFFIN LA
Wits End
TINKERS MEAD
SOUTHCOTT ROAD
Mills Farm
CLAY LA

Manor Farm
Sewage Works
New Farm
River Avon
EVERLEIGH ROAD
SWAN
GREEN DROVE
WOODLANDS RD
Southcott
Green Drove Farm
Strip Lynchets

6

Sharcott
Hill View
SN9

59

Manningford Abbots
A345
215
Pewsey White Horse
WINTERS DROVE
SOUTHCOTT RD
Strip Lynchets
Fyfield Down
Giant's Grave (Long Barrow)
Milton Hill Clump
Milton Hill
Milton Hill Field System

5

Drove Farm
Denny Sutton Hipend
Settlement
Pewsey Hill
Winter's Penning
Tumuli

58

Pewsey Hill Farm
Field System
Settlements
Pewsey Down
Milton Hill Farm

4

Tumulus

Bruce Field Barn
Chalk Pit
Bruce Down
Abbots Down
Tumulus
Grant's Firs
Bruce Down
Abbots Down
Everleigh Barrows
Down Farm
Tumuli
Everleigh Ashes
Milton Wood
Cow Down

57

3

COMET AV 1
HASTINGS AV 2
HASTINGS CL 3
PEMBROKE RD 4
OXFORD RD 5
BEVERLEY CR 6
DEVON RD 7
Earthwork
West Everleigh Down

56

Strip Lynchets
Upavon Hill
Earthwork
BRITANNIA WAY
ARMADA WAY
Bohune Down
Tumulus
Round Down

2

Chisman's Cleeve
Upavon Golf Club
CH
YORKS RD
PO
WATER LA
Tumuli
Windward Ball Plantation
West Everleigh Down
A342

55

Rowden's Cleeve
WATSON CL
Upavon Down
Tumuli
Lower Everleigh
West Everleigh Down

1

A342
Upavon Airfield
SN8
A342

54

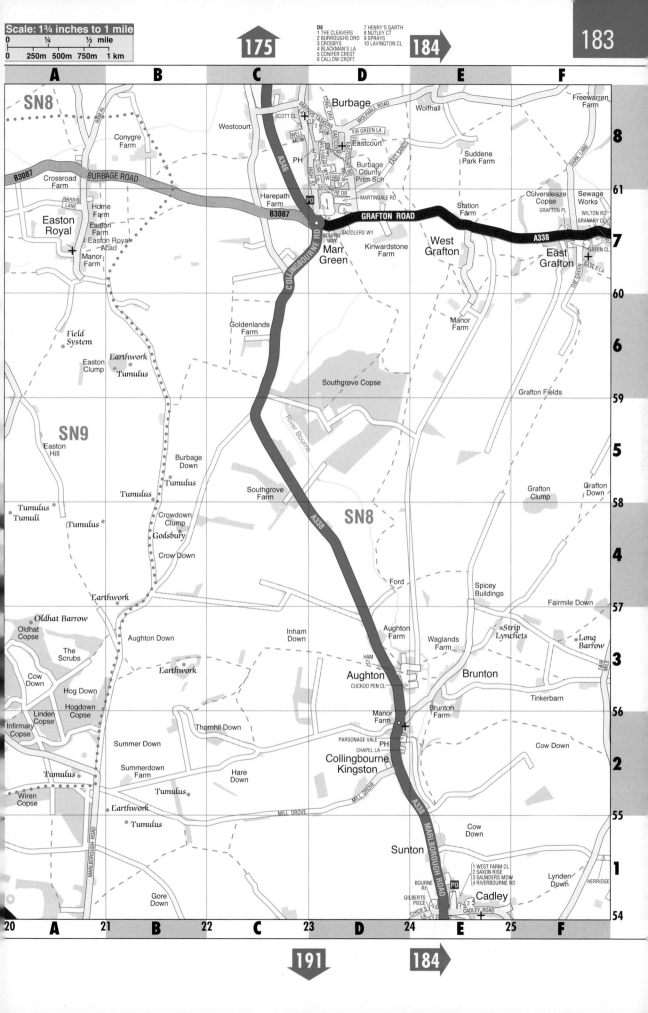

Scale: 1¾ inches to 1 mile

0   ¼   ½ mile
0 250m 500m 750m 1 km

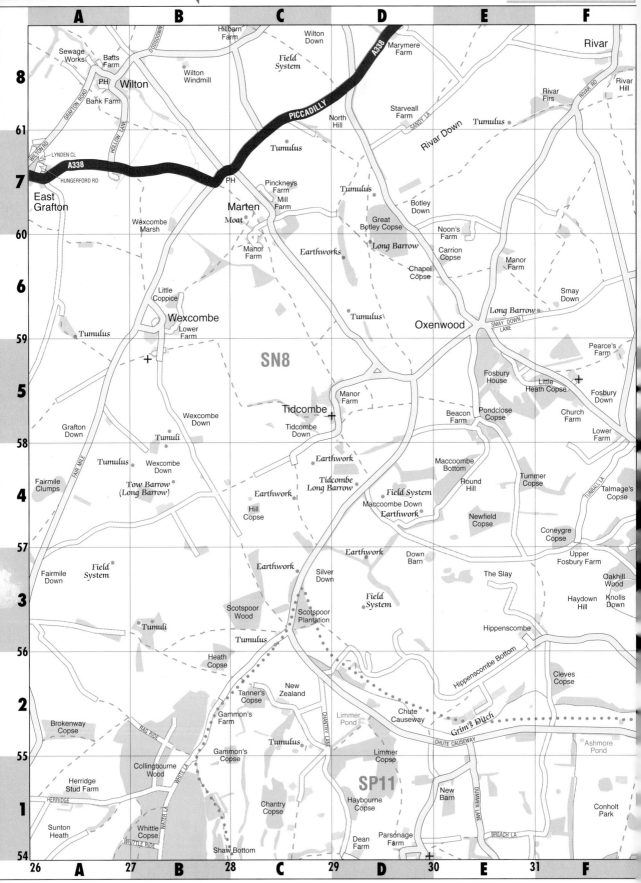

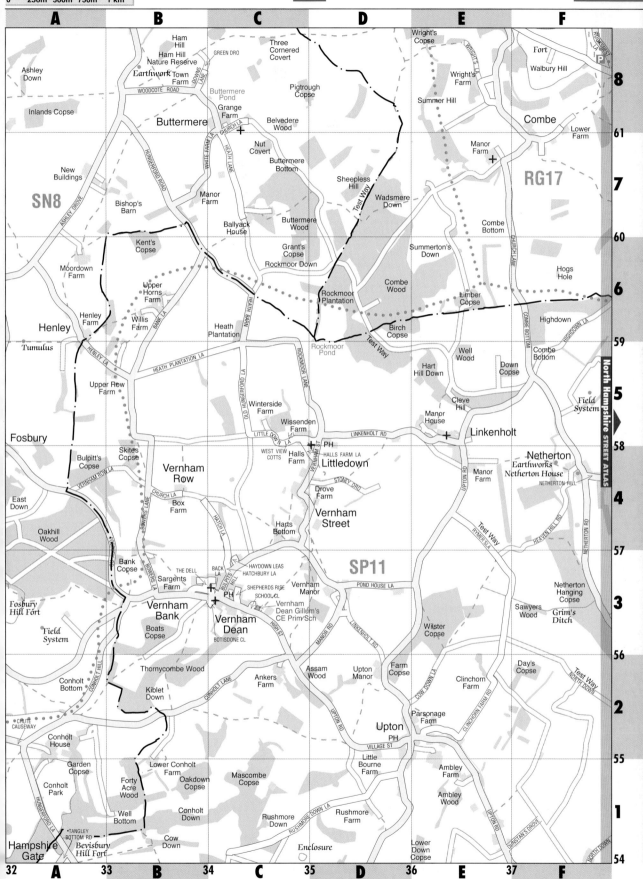

B7
1 ROSENHEIM RISE
2 PEAR TREE ORCH
3 REDLANDS
4 CARPENTERS LA
5 MANOR FIELDS
6 FLOWERS MEAD
7 HOLME LA
8 UPPER GARSTON LA
9 TYNING LA
10 EMMS
11 ETHENDUN
12 THE PICQUET
13 CHESTNUT CNR
14 REEVES PIECE
15 MILLDITCH
16 CHURCH LA
17 ORCHARD CT
18 BLATCHS ORCH

◄ 109

178

Scale: 1¾ inches to 1 mile

0 ¼ ½ mile
0 250m 500m 750m 1 km

A B C D E F

Bratton Rd
Capps Lane
Penn Farm
Crossroads Farm
Woodbridge Rd
Hudds Mill La
Trowbridge Road
Bonnie Farm
Bridge Farm
BA13
Wood Bridge
Fish Pond
Edington Station Yard
Steeple Ashton Rd
Tinhead Rd
Inmead
Lower Greatwoods
Greater La
Greenhills
The Weir
Edington Priory
PH
PO
Cowleaze Lane
Berry Rd
Little Ct La
Sunnycroft Farm
Charlton La
Charlton Hl
Coach Hollow
Upper Baynton Farm
Moat
The Dro
Earthworks
Spicers Close Farm
Erlestoke Sands Golf Club
CH
Coulston Rd
Edington
Ashton Coombe
Longlands Close
Greatwoods
Downsview
The City
Salisbury Hollow
B3098
Baynton Hillside Wood
Coulston Hillside Wood
Bitham Wood
Hill Wood
Moat
Court House
Flowers Farm
Lower Road
Bratton Prim Sch
Westbury Road
Greater Lane Farm
Edington Hill
Long Hollow
Long Barrow
Tottenham Wood
Coulston Hill
Stoke Hill
Lower Westbury Rd
LWR Westbury Rd
Tiswell Spring
The Hollow
B3098
Court La
Melbourne St
Sandy Lane
Tumuli
Long Barrow
Mast
Stokehill Farm
Westbury Road
Hitchfield Farm
Burr
Butts
PO
Traub Rd
Bratton
Pillow Mound
Luccombe Bottom
Mounds
Tinhead Hill
Tinhead Hill Farm
Castle Rd
Coombe Farm
Church Rd
Church Springs
Luccombe Springs
Port Way
Bratton Camp
Long Barrow
Combe Bottom
White Cliff
Patcombe Hill
Strip Lynchets
Barn Bottom
Combe Hill
Field System
Strip Lynchets
Imber Road
Tumulus
Tumuli
Longcombe Bottom
Wessex Ridgeway
Quarry Rd
Imber Range Perimeter Path
Brouncker's Down
Earthworks
Warden's Down
Tenantry Down
Tumulus
Baynton Down
Coulston Down
Brouncker's Well
Dilton Down
Tumulus
Tumulus
Knapp Plantation
Middle Ridge Plantation
Summer Down
BA12
Tumulus
Wadman's Coppice
Earthworks
Tumulus
Knapp Down
Middle Ridge Down
Tumuli
Tumulus
Tumuli
Summer Down
Tumuli
Tumulus
Warminster Rd
Tumulus
Tumulus
Earthwork
Tumuli
Tumulus
Tumulus
Warminster Down
South Down Sleight
Tumulus
DANGER AREA
Oxendean Bottom
Tumuli
Earthwork
Rifle Range
Long Barrow
Boreham Down
Bishopstrow Down
Earthwork
Tumulus
Bowls Barrow (Long Barrow)
Sack Hl
Middleton Down
Strip Lynchets
Norton Down

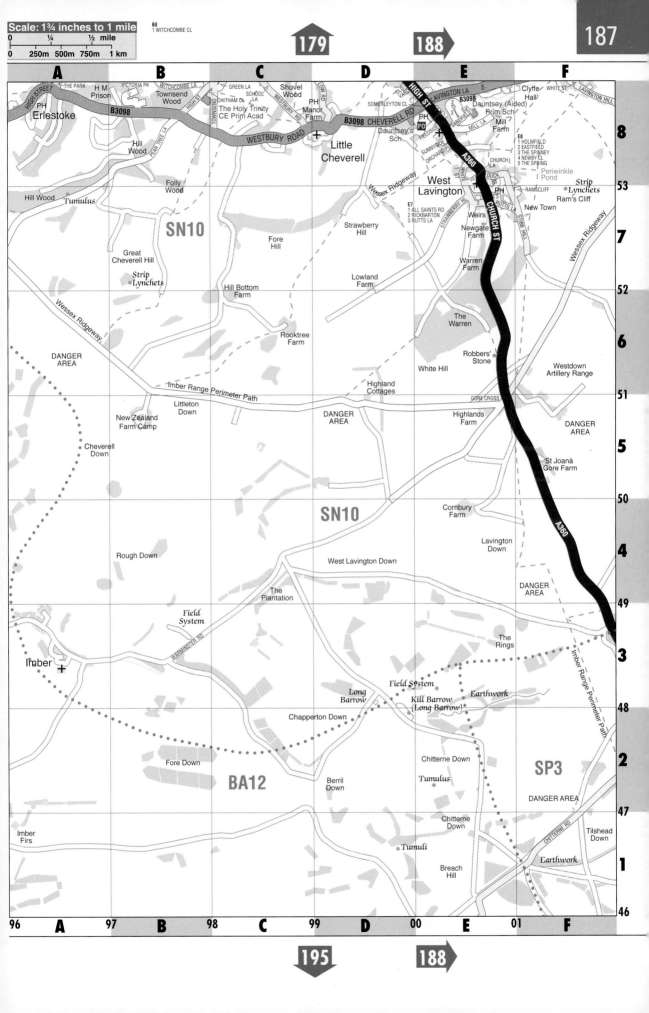

187
180

A   B   C   D   E   F

8

Long Ditch

Wessex Ridgeway   THE CLAY

Earthwork

Gibbet Knoll

Great Fore Down

53

Westdown Artillery Range

Little Hill

Wilsford Down

7

Church Hill

Urchfont Down

Field System

52

DANGER AREA

SN10

6

Warren Down

Tumulus

Westdown Artillery Range

Black Heath

Ell Barrow (Long Barrow)

51

Earthwork

Ball Down

Tumulus

New Copse Down

Grove Down

Summer Down

SP4

5

Westdown Artillery Range

Candown Copse

Can Down

Enclosure

New Copse

Rushall Down

Enclosure

50

Barrow Plantation

Long Barrow

East Down

Honeydown Bottom

4

DANGER AREA

West Down Plantation

East Down Plantation

49

Westdown Artillery Range

Earthwork

Field System

Westdown Artillery Range

3

DANGER AREA

St Thomas A Becket CE Aided Prim Sch

NORTH CROFT

Tilshead

Earthwork

West Down

Orcheston Down

BACK LA

IMBER PL

CANDOWN LA RD

Horse Down

Long Barrow

Imber Range Perimeter Path

CHITTERNE RD

PH   CHAPTER RISE

LODGE VIEW

West End

MARVINS CL

Pembroke Farm

Westdown Camp

SP3

Nut Park

Long Plantation

Earthwork

Halfmoon Copse

2

HIGH STREET

Sewage Works

Earthwork

Silver Barrow

Tilshead Down

47

White Barrow (Long Barrow)

NT

Orcheston Down

Tumulus

Long Barrow

1

Copehill Down

Imber Range Perimeter Path

Copehill Plantation

A360

DANGER AREA

DANGER AREA

Gallops

46

187
196

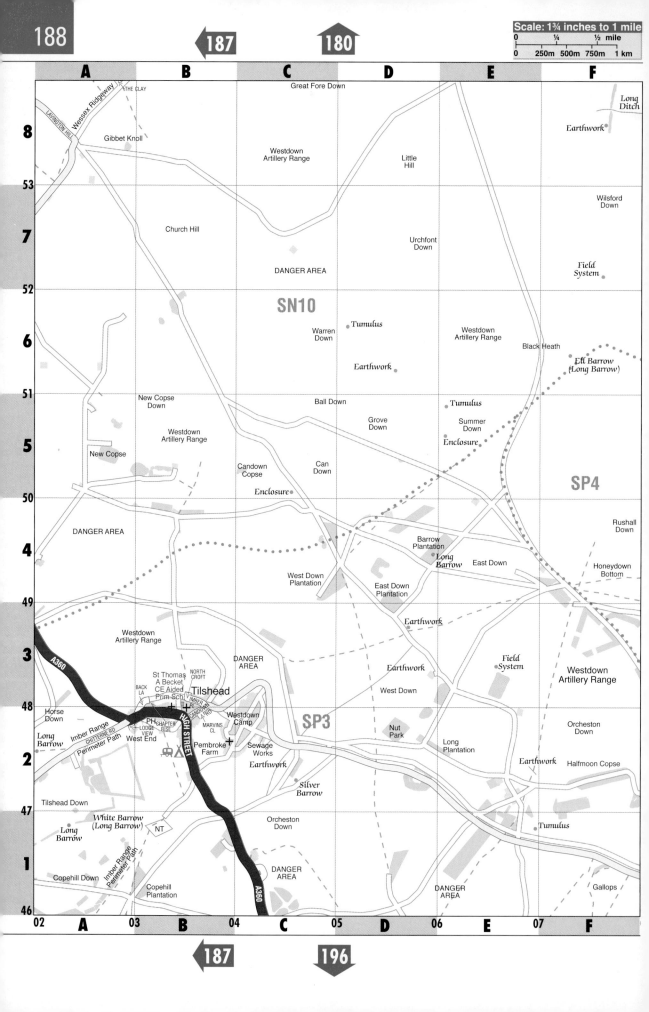

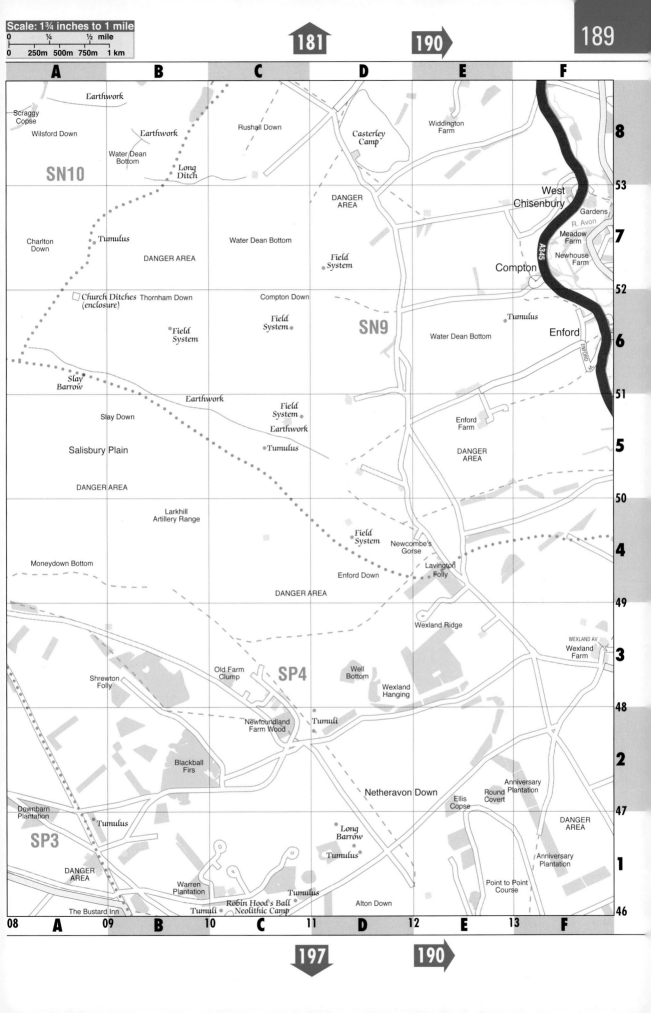

0   ¼   ½   mile
0   250m   500m   750m   1 km

A   B   C   D   E   F

8

Scraggy Copse
Earthwork
Wilsford Down
Earthwork
Rushall Down
Casterley Camp
Widdington Farm

53

SN10
Water Dean Bottom
Long Ditch
DANGER AREA
West Chisenbury

Gardens
R. Avon

7

Charlton Down
Tumulus
Water Dean Bottom
Field System
Meadow Farm
A345
Newhouse Farm

DANGER AREA
Compton

52

Church Ditches (enclosure)
Thornham Down
Compton Down
SN9
Enford

6

Field System
Field System
Water Dean Bottom
Tumulus
ENFORD AV

Slay Barrow
Earthwork

51

Slay Down
Field System
Earthwork
Enford Farm

Salisbury Plain
Tumulus
DANGER AREA

5

DANGER AREA

50

Larkhill Artillery Range
Field System
Newcombe's Gorse

4

Moneydown Bottom
Enford Down
Lavington Folly
Wexland Ridge

DANGER AREA
WEXLAND AV
Wexland Farm

3

Old Farm Clump
SP4
Well Bottom
Wexland Hanging
Shrewton Folly

48

Newfoundland Farm Wood
Tumuli
Netheravon Down

2

Blackball Firs
Anniversary Plantation
Ellis Copse
Round Covert

47

Downbarn Plantation
Tumulus
DANGER AREA

SP3
Long Barrow
Anniversary Plantation

1

DANGER AREA
Tumulus
Warren Plantation
Tumulus
Point to Point Course

The Bustard Inn
Tumuli
Robin Hood's Ball Neolithic Camp
Tumulus
Alton Down

46

08   A   09   B   10   C   11   D   12   E   13   F

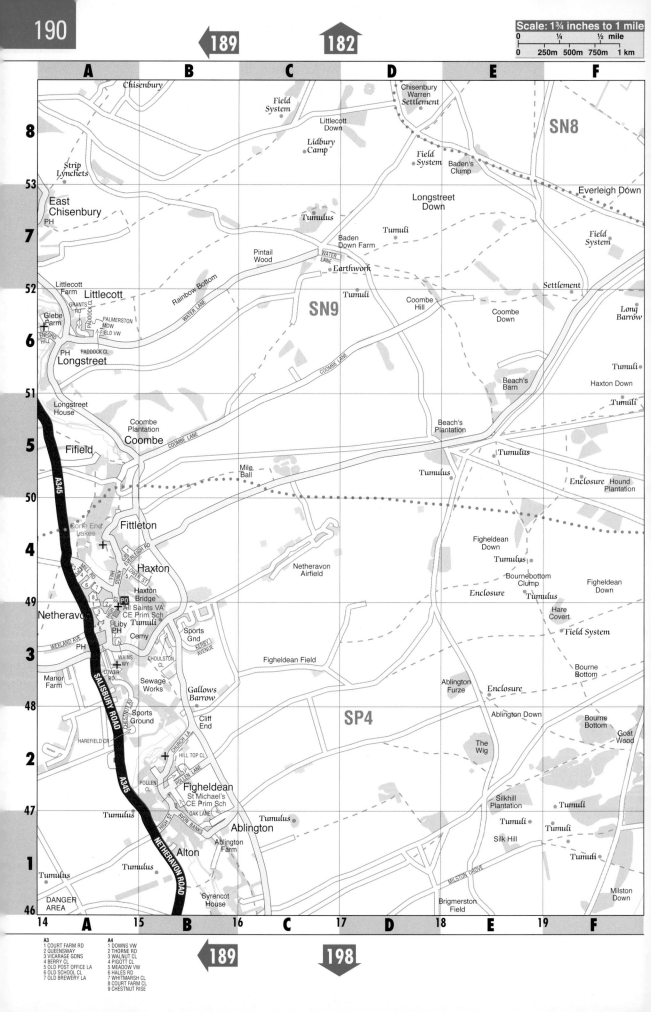

A3
1 COURT FARM RD
2 QUEENSWAY
3 VICARAGE GDNS
4 BERRY CL
5 OLD POST OFFICE LA
6 OLD SCHOOL CL
7 OLD BREWERY LA

A4
1 DOWNS VW
2 THORNE RD
3 WALNUT CL
4 PIGOTT CL
5 MEADOW VW
6 HALES RD
7 WHITMARSH CL
8 COURT FARM CL
9 CHESTNUT RISE

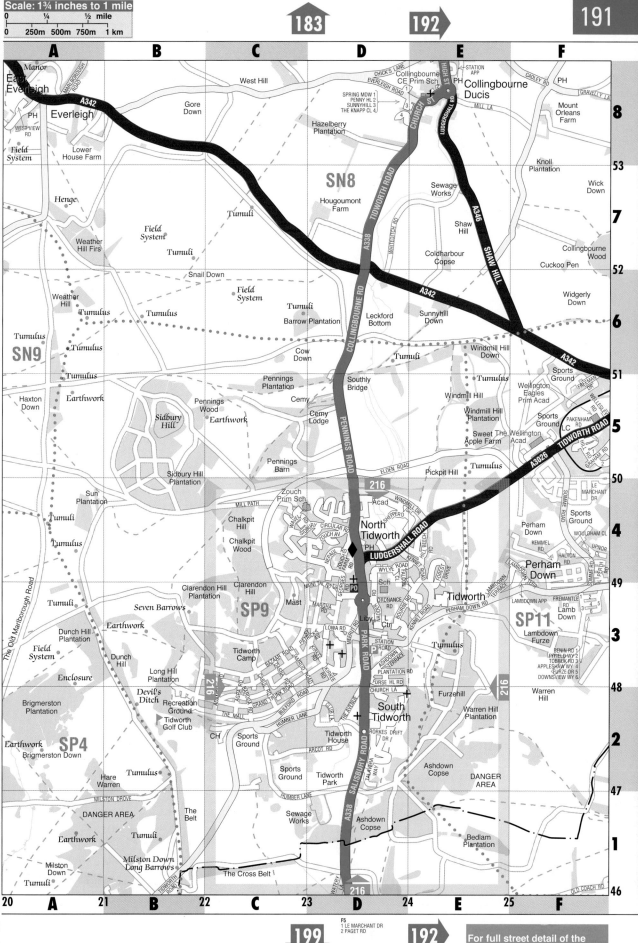

Scale: 1¾ inches to 1 mile

For full street detail of the highlighted area see page 216.

F5
1 LE MARCHANT DR
2 PAGET RD

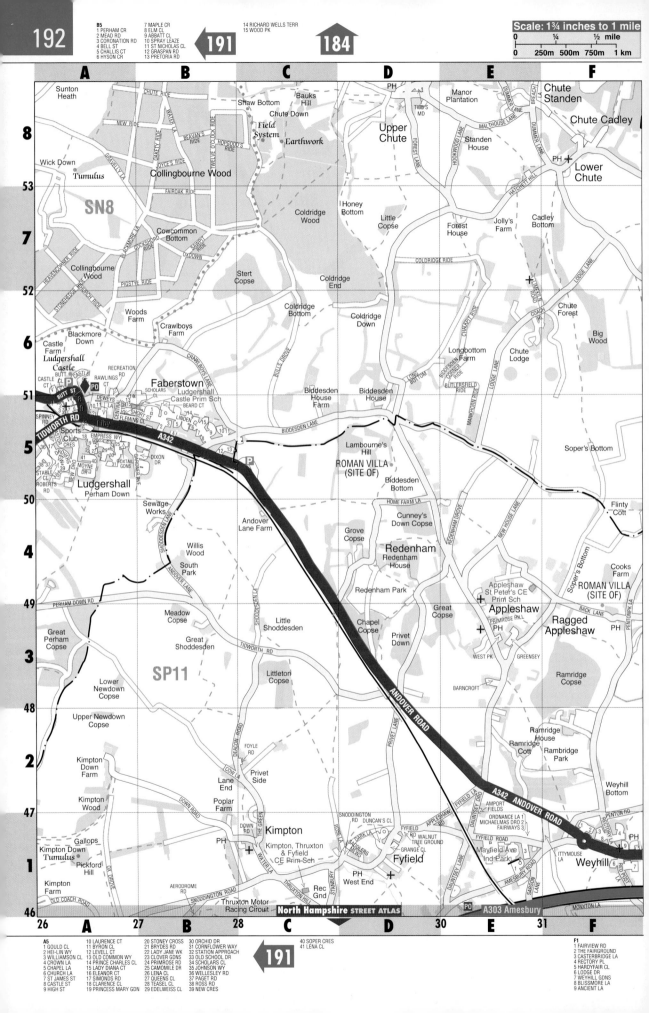

Scale: 1¾ inches to 1 mile
0 ¼ ½ mile
0 250m 500m 750m 1 km

E2
1 LILLYWHITE CR
2 COLE CL
3 GAWAINE CL
4 CAERLEON DR
5 LOVERIDGE CL
6 EDGAR CL
7 MOOT CL
8 WITAN CL
9 DANEGELD CL
10 OLAF CL
11 RYON CL
12 MELIOT RISE
13 LIVIA CL
14 CORINTHIAN CL
15 CLAUDIUS CL
16 GENOA CT
17 TURIN CT
18 TINTAGEL CL
19 VESPASIAN RD
20 HADRIAN RD
21 FLORENCE CT
22 LAUNCELOT CL
23 YORK CT
24 TIBERIUS RD
25 GALAHAD CL
26 ATHOLL CT
27 AGRAVAINE CL
28 CAMELOT CL
29 CONSTANTINE SQ
30 OLYMPIC PARK RD
31 HAMPTON RD
32 BURKAL DR
33 Shepherds Spring Jun & Inf Sch

185

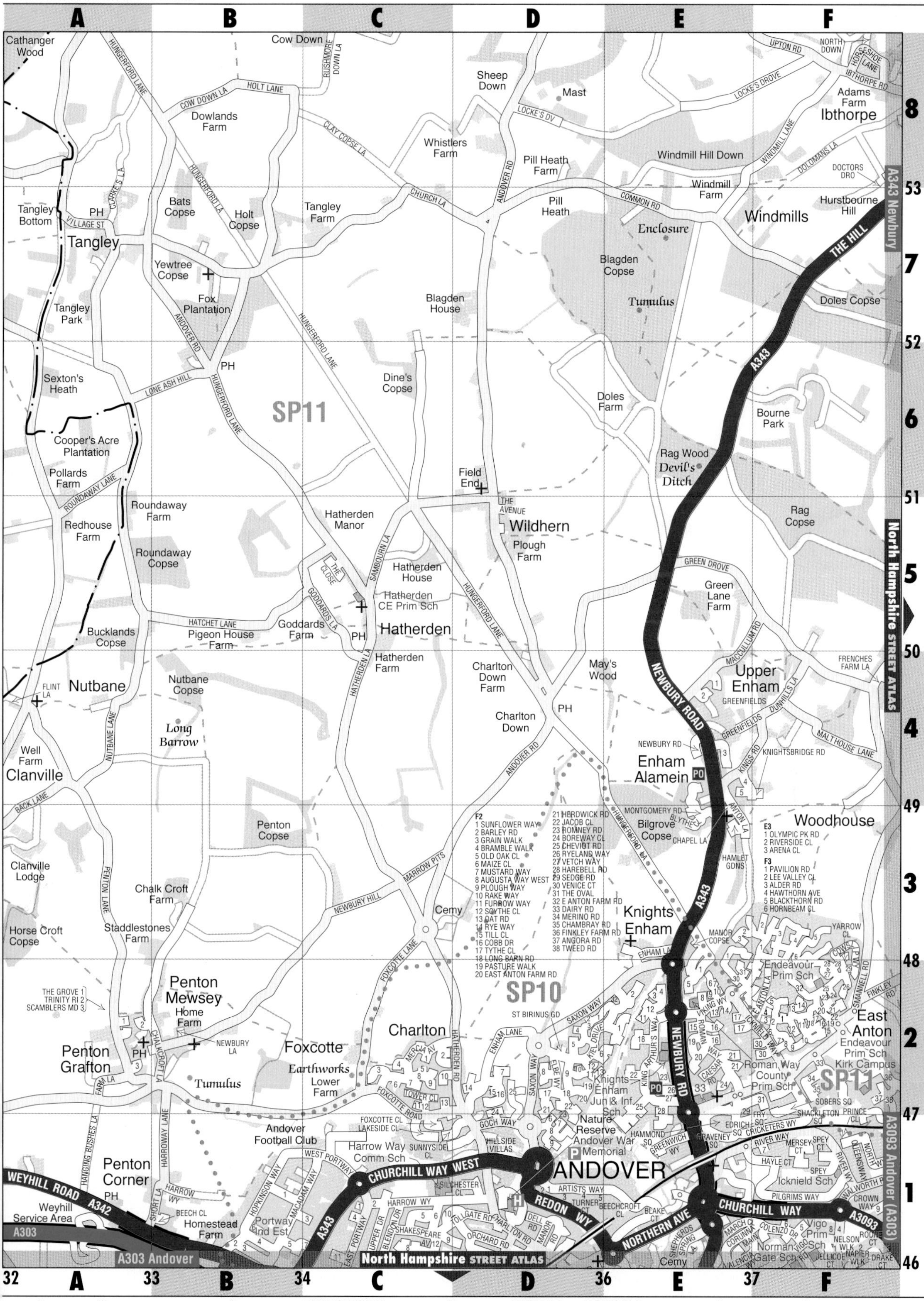
A
B
C
D
E
F
Cathanger Wood
Cow Down
Sheep Down
Mast
Dowlands Farm
Whistlers Farm
Pill Heath Farm
Adams Farm
Ibthorpe
Windmill Hill Down
Windmill Farm
Hurstbourne Hill
Windmills
Tangley Bottom
Tangley
Bats Copse
Holt Copse
Tangley Farm
Pill Heath
Enclosure
Blagden Copse
Yewtree Copse
Fox Plantation
Tangley Park
Blagden House
Tumulus
Doles Copse
Sexton's Heath
Dine's Copse
SP11
Doles Farm
Bourne Park
Cooper's Acre Plantation
Pollards Farm
Rag Wood
Devil's Ditch
Field End
Roundaway Farm
Redhouse Farm
Hatherden Manor
Wildhern
Plough Farm
Rag Copse
Roundaway Copse
Hatherden House
Hatherden CE Prim Sch
Green Lane Farm
Bucklands Copse
Pigeon House Farm
Goddards Farm
Hatherden
Hatherden Farm
Charlton Down Farm
May's Wood
Upper Enham
Nutbane
Nutbane Copse
Charlton Down
Long Barrow
Well Farm
Clanville
Enham Alamein
Woodhouse
Penton Copse
Bilgrove Copse
Clanville Lodge
Chalk Croft Farm
Cemy
Knights Enham
Horse Croft Copse
Staddlestones Farm
Endeavour Prim Sch
Penton Mewsey
Home Farm
SP10
East Anton
Endeavour Prim Sch Kirk Campus
Penton Grafton
Charlton
Foxcotte
Earthworks
Lower Farm
Tumulus
Roman Way County Prim Sch
Knights Enham Jun & Inf Sch
Nature Reserve
Andover War Memorial
Andover Football Club
Harrow Way Comm Sch
Penton Corner
ANDOVER
Icknield Sch
Weyhill Service Area
Homestead Farm
Portway Ind Est
Vigo Prim Sch
Norman Gate Sch
CHURCHILL WAY WEST
CHURCHILL WAY
NEWBURY ROAD
NORTHERN AVE
WEYHILL ROAD
A342
A343
A3093
A303
A343 Newbury
A3093 Andover (A303)
A303 Andover
North Hampshire STREET ATLAS
THE HILL
F2
1 SUNFLOWER WAY
2 BARLEY RD
3 GRAIN WALK
4 BRAMBLE WALK
5 OLD OAK CL
6 MAIZE CL
7 MUSTARD WAY
8 AUGUSTA WAY WEST
9 PLOUGH WAY
10 RAKE WAY
11 FURROW WAY
12 SCYTHE CL
13 OAT RD
14 RYE WAY
15 TILL CL
16 COBB DR
17 TYTHE CL
18 LONG BARN RD
19 PASTURE WALK
20 EAST ANTON FARM RD
21 HERDWICK RD
22 JACOB CL
23 ROMNEY RD
24 BOREWAY CL
25 CHEVIOT RD
26 RYELAND WAY
27 VETCH WAY
28 HAREBELL RD
29 SEDGE RD
30 VENICE CT
31 THE OVAL
32 E ANTON FARM RD
33 DAIRY RD
34 MERINO RD
35 CHAMBRAY RD
36 FINKLEY FARM RD
37 ANGORA RD
38 TWEED RD
E3
1 OLYMPIC PK RD
2 RIVERSIDE CL
3 ARENA CL
F3
1 PAVILION RD
2 LEE VALLEY CL
3 ALDER RD
4 HAWTHORN AVE
5 BLACKTHORN RD
6 HORNBEAM CL
THE GROVE 1
TRINITY RI 2
SCAMBLERS MD 3
8
53
7
52
6
51
5
50
4
49
3
48
2
47
1
46
32
33
34
36
37

B1
1 SMEATON RD
2 REITH WY
3 JOULE RD
4 WHITTLE RD
5 ROYCE CL
6 TELFORD GATE

C1
1 STERLING PK
2 CAXTON CL
3 MITCHELL CL
4 WATT CL
5 CHAUCER AV
6 MILTON AV
7 SOPWITH PK
8 LAWNS CL
9 MAY TREE RD
10 APPLE TREE GR
11 STEPHENSON CL
12 THE DROVE

C2
1 BRANCASTER AV
2 BRADWELL CL
3 RICHBOROUGH DR
4 ETHELBERT DR
5 HENGEST CL
6 RECULVER WY
7 BEDE DR
8 PORCHESTER CL
9 AUGUSTINE WY
10 HOME FARM GDNS
11 LITCHFIELD CL
12 BARTON CL
13 DACRE CL

D1
1 GAINSBOROUGH CT
2 MUNNINGS CT
3 STUBBS CT
4 REYNOLDS CT
5 SUTHERLAND CT
6 ALFRED GDNS
7 ST ALPHEGE GDNS
8 ST SWITHIN WY
9 ST BIRSTAN GDNS

D2
1 MARSUM CL
2 OLD ENGLISH DR
3 JUTLAND CR
4 RUNE DR
5 MONEYER RD
6 ANDEFERAS RD
7 ALDRIN CL
8 BORKUM CL
9 CUXHAVEN WAY
10 HAMBURG CL
11 HOLLAND DR
12 LINGEN CL
13 MINDEN CL
14 ST THOMAS CL
15 COLLINS CL
16 ARMSTRONG RISE
17 ALTONA GDNS
18 EMDEN RD
19 VERDEN WY
20 FLENSBURG CL
21 BREMEN GDNS
22 LUBECK DR
23 HATTEM PLACE
24 WETHERBY GDNS
25 PEAKE WAY

218

E4
1 WESTON CT
2 ATHLONE CL
3 LANDALE CL
4 ALAMEIN RD
5 TOBRUK CL

F1
1 JERVIS CT
2 SOMERVILLE CT
3 TOVEY CT
4 LONDON RD
5 MADRID RD
6 TOLEDO GROVE
7 BEAULIEU CT
8 GRANADA PL
9 WEST WAY

117
C5
1 GREENLANDS
2 WESTLANDS
3 GLEBELANDS
4 COTLEY PL
186

Scale: 1¾ inches to 1 mile
0   ¼   ½ mile
0   250m   500m   750m   1 km

A   B   C   D   E   F

DANGER AREA

Strip Lynchets

Long Barrow   Long Barrow
Norton Down

8

Wessex Ridgeway

Battlesbury Wood   Strip Lynchets

Rifle Range

45

Tumulus   Earthworks
Middle Hill   Pillow Mound
Strip Lynchets   Tumulus   Enclosure   Earthworks   Knook Barrow (Long Barrow)
Medieval Village of Middleton   North Farm   West Hill Farm   West Hill   Tumulus
7
Middleton Farm   Scratchbury Hill   Scratchbury Camp   Knook Down
Yew Tree Farm   Tumuli   The Copse   Long Barrow   WEST HILL   East Hill Farm
44
B3414   Norton Plantation   Quebec Farm
WARMINSTER RD   BA12   Triangle Bungalow   Willis's Field Barn
6   Tumuli   New Copse   Heytesbury Plantation   Flower's Field Barn
Pit Meads   Cotley Hill Woods   Dunscombe Bottom   ANSTY HILL
Tumulus   South Farm   Cotley Hill   Imber Range Perimeter Path   Strip Lynchets   Ansty Hill
43
A36   Norton Bavant   Tumulus   HEYTESBURY PK   Heytesbury House   Tumulus
Tumulus   Hazel Copse   Dairy Plantation   Weir   HOSPITAL OF ST JOHN   Pound Copse   B390   CAMP RD
WARMINSTER BYPASS   HEYTESBURY RD   LONDON   Knook Camp   Upton Great Barrow
5   Heytesbury CE Prim Sch   HIGH ST   CHAPEL RD   NEWTOWN   OLD FORGE CL
Heytesbury   PO   MILL ST   PH   PARK ST   West Farm
SANDFIELD   Slaters Farm   MANTLES LA   CHITTERNE ANSTEY
BEST'S LA   North End Farm   TYTHERINGTON RD   MILL LA   Knook
42   Knook Manor   Manor Farm   Well Bottom
Sutton Veny CE Sch   STATION RD   East Farm   Knook Horse Hill
Old Manor House   The Knoll   Manor Farm   Wessex Ridgeway   Ridgeway   Well Bottom Plantation
4   Tumulus   A36   River   Tumulus
St Leonard's Church   Glebe Farm   Tumulus   Wylye   ASH WALK   UP ST   UPTON FOLLY   Well Bottom Belt
Hayden Farm   Tytherington   Wylye   PH   Upton Lovell
HAYCOMBE HILL   CHURCH RD   New Rise Farm   SALISBURY RD
41   CORTON RD   Sundial Farm   LC
Haycombe Bottom   Downlands   Church Farm   Model Farm   Corton   COOMBE VIEW   WATER ST
3   TYTHERINGTON RD   Burial Ground   PH
Tytherington Hill   Corton   Long Barrow   Suffers Bridge   Weir   Wylye Valley
40   Barrow Hill   LC
Littlecombe Bottom   Boyton
2   Corton Hill   Vineyard Wood   Boyton Manor
Bottom Barn   Boyton Bottom   Motte
HAYCOMBE HILL   Whatcomb Bottom   Boyton Wood
Settlement   Sherrington
39   Grenadier Wood   Tumuli
SP3   Earthwork   North Soupir   Tumulus
1   South Soupir   Long Barrow   Sherrington Dairy
Corton Down   Boyton Down
Long Bottom   Birch Copse   Larch Copse
38
90   A   91   B   92   C   93   D   94   E   95   F

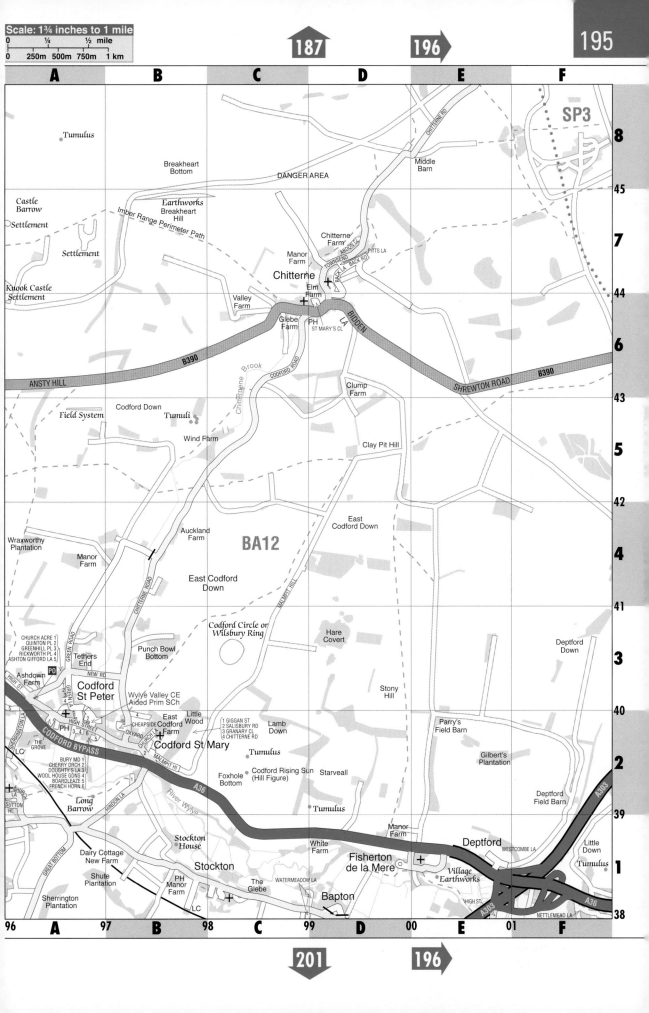

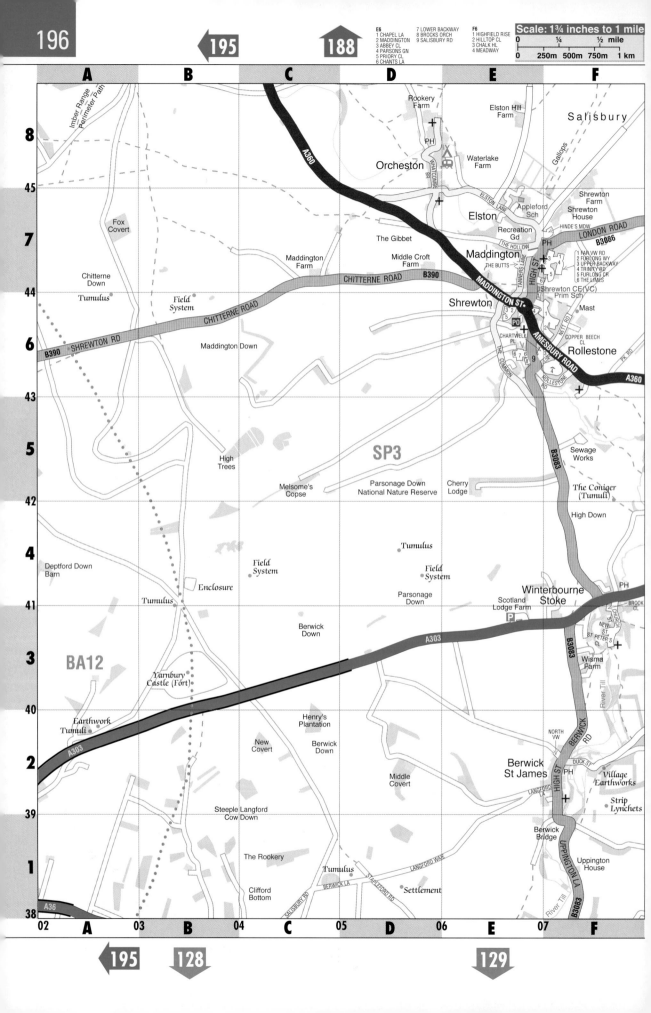

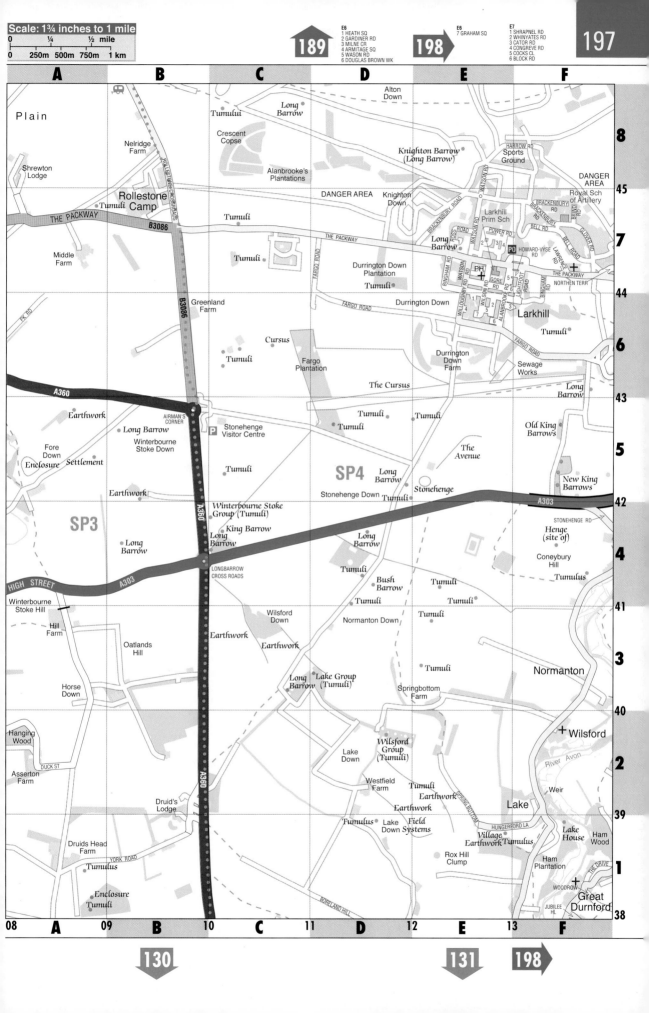

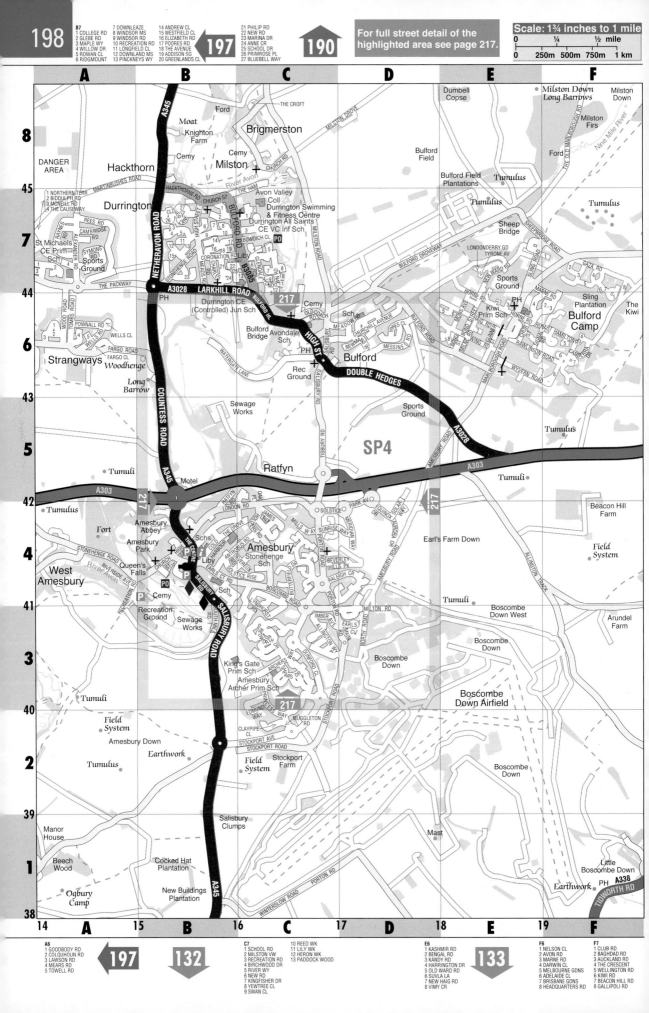

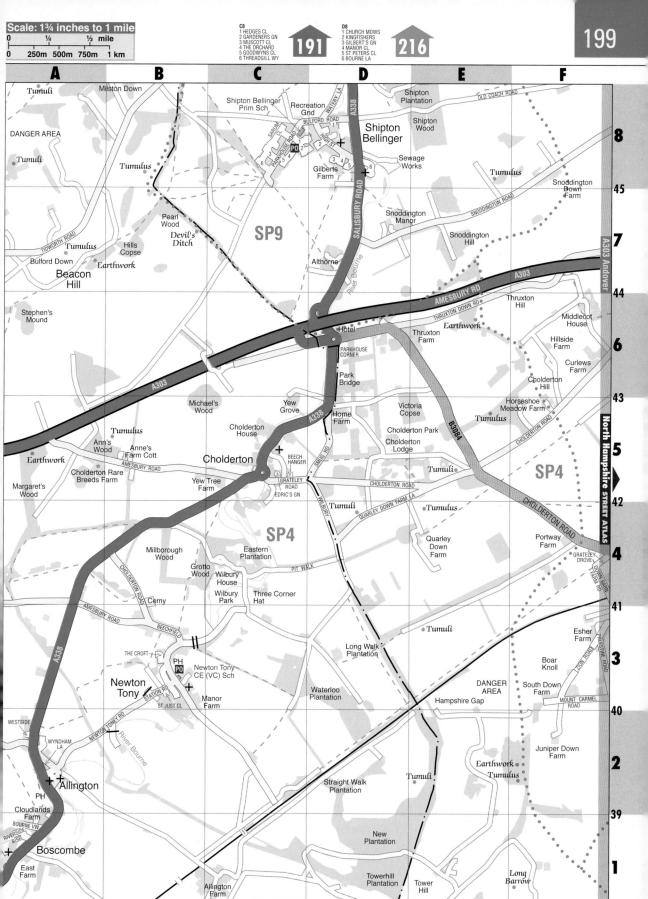

Scale: 1¾ inches to 1 mile

0   ¼   ½   mile
0 250m 500m 750m 1 km

C8
1 HEDGES CL
2 GARDENERS GN
3 MUSCOTT CL
4 THE ORCHARD
5 GOODWYNS CL
6 THREADGILL WY

191

D8
1 CHURCH MDWS
2 KINGFISHERS
3 GILBERT'S GN
4 MANOR CL
5 ST PETERS CL
6 BOURNE LA

216

A   B   C   D   E   F

North Hampshire STREET ATLAS

DANGER AREA

Tumuli
Milston Down
Tumuli
Tumulus
Pearl Wood
Devil's Ditch
Hills Copse
Tumulus
Bulford Down
Earthwork
Beacon Hill
Stephen's Mound

Shipton Bellinger Prim Sch
Recreation Gnd
Bulford Road
High St
Shipton Bellinger
Shipton Plantation
Shipton Wood
Old Coach Road
Sewage Works
Tumulus
Snoddington Down Farm
PO
Gilberts Farm
Snoddington Manor
Snoddington Road
Snoddington Hill

SP9

Althorne
River Bourne
Hotel
AMESBURY RD
Thruxton Down Rd
Thruxton Hill
Middlecot House
Hillside Farm
Curlews Farm
Parkhouse Corner
Park Bridge
Thruxton Farm
Earthwork
Cholderton Hill
Horseshoe Meadow Farm

SALISBURY ROAD
A338
A303 Andover

A303
Michael's Wood
Yew Grove
Home Farm
Victoria Copse
Cholderton House
Cholderton Park
Cholderton Lodge
Tumuli
Tumulus
SP4
Ann's Wood
Anne's Farm Cott
Cholderton
BEECH HANGER
Earthwork
Tumulus
Amesbury Road
Cholderton Rare Breeds Farm
Yew Tree Farm
GRATELEY ROAD
EDRIC'S GN
Cholderton Road
Margaret's Wood
A338
B3084
CHOLDERTON ROAD
SMITS RD
WILBURY
Tumuli
Quarley Down Farm La
Tumulus
Portway Farm
Grateley Drove
CORN BARN FARM RD
PALESTINE ROAD
PIT WALK
Quarley Down Farm
Esher Farm
Millborough Wood
Eastern Plantation
SP4
Grotto Wood
Wilbury House
Wilbury Park
Three Corner Hat
Cholderton Road
AMESBURY ROAD
BEECHFIELD
Cemy
Tumuli
Long Walk Plantation
Boar Knoll
South Down Farm
MOUNT CARMEL ROAD
THE CROFT
PH PO
Newton Tony CE (VC) Sch
Waterloo Plantation
DANGER AREA
Hampshire Gap
Newton Tony
STATION RD
Manor Farm
ST JUST CL
WESTSIDE
NEWTON TONEY RD
WYNDHAM LA
River Bourne
Allington
PH
Cloudlands Farm
BOURNE VW
RIVERSIDE
RISE
East Farm
Boscombe
Allington Farm
Straight Walk Plantation
Tumuli
Earthwork
Tumulus
Juniper Down Farm
New Plantation
Towerhill Plantation
Tower Hill
Long Barrow
DANGER AREA

8
45
7
44
6
43
5
42
4
41
3
40
2
39
1
38

20   A   21   B   22   C   23   D   24   E   25   F

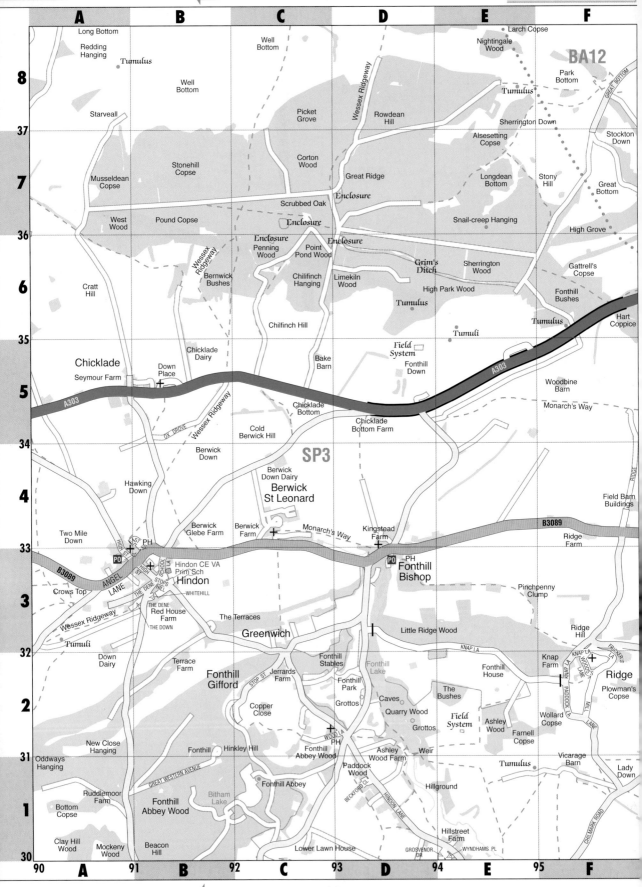

Scale: 1¾ inches to 1 mile

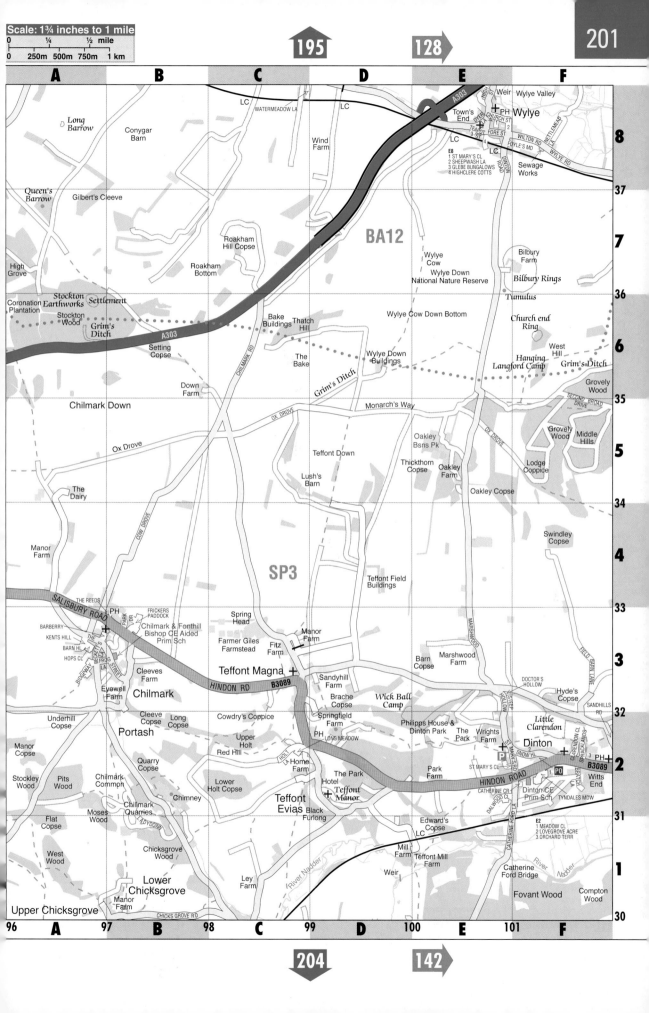

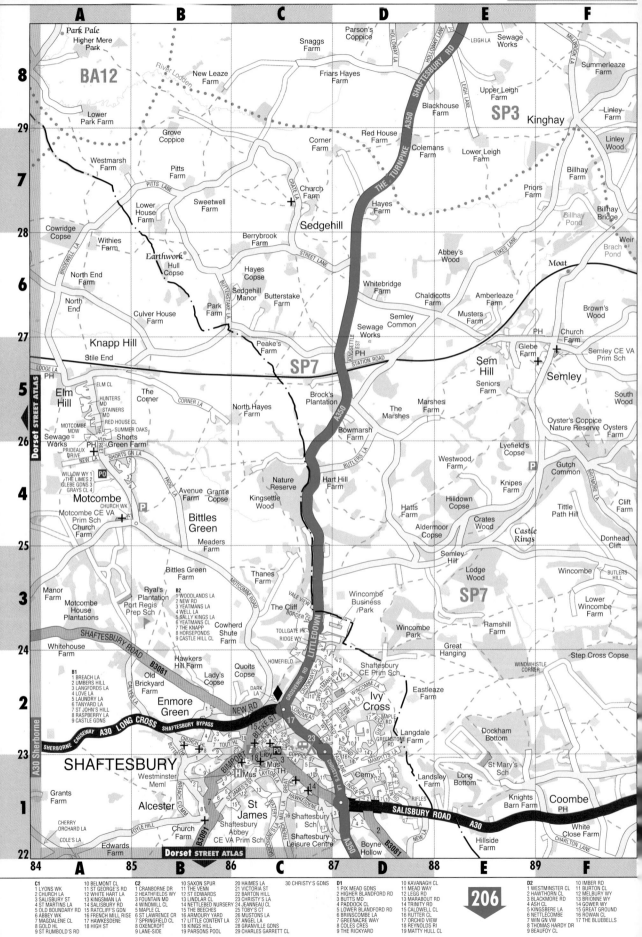

C1
1 LYONS WK
2 CHURCH LA
3 SALISBURY ST
4 ST MARTINS LA
5 OLD BOUNDARY RD
6 ABBEY WK
7 MAGDALENE CL
8 GOLD HL
9 ST RUMBOLD'S RD
10 BELMONT CL
11 ST GEORGE'S RD
12 WHITE HART LA
13 KINGSMAN LA
14 SALISBURY RD
15 RATCLIFF'S GDN
16 FRENCH MILL RISE
17 HAWKESDENE
18 HIGH ST

C2
1 CRANBORNE DR
2 HEATHFIELDS WY
3 FOUNTAIN MD
4 WINDMILL CL
5 MAPLE CL
6 ST LAWRENCE CR
7 SPRINGFIELD CL
8 OXENCROFT
9 LANE-SIDE
10 SAXON SPUR
11 THE VENN
12 ST EDWARDS
13 LINDLA CL
14 NETTLEBED NURSERY
15 THE BEECHES
16 ARMOURY YARD
17 LITTLE CONTENT LA
18 KINGS HILL
19 PARSONS POOL
20 HAIMES LA
21 VICTORIA ST
22 BARTON HILL
23 CHRISTY'S LA
24 JEANNEAU CL
25 TOBY'S CT
26 MUSTONS LA
27 ANGEL LA
28 GRANVILLE GDNS
29 CHARLES GARRETT CL
30 CHRISTY'S GDNS

D1
1 PIX MEAD GDNS
2 HIGHER BLANDFORD RD
3 BUTTS MD
4 PADDOCK CL
5 LOWER BLANDFORD RD
6 BRINSCOMBE LA
7 GREENACRE WAY
8 COLES CRES
9 THE RICKYARD
10 KAVANAGH CL
11 MEAD WAY
12 LEGG RD
13 MARABOUT RD
14 TRINITY RD
15 CALDWELL CL
16 RUTTER CL
17 ORCHID VIEW
18 REYNOLDS RI
19 MATTY HULL CL

D2
1 WESTMINSTER CL
2 HAWTHORN CL
3 BLACKMORE RD
4 ASH CL
5 KINGSBERE LA
6 NETTLECOMBE
7 WIN GN VW
8 THOMAS HARDY DR
9 BEAUFOY CL
10 IMBER RD
11 BURTON CL
12 MELBURY WY
13 BRIONNE WY
14 LOWER WY
15 GREAT GROUND
16 ROWAN CL
17 THE BLUEBELLS

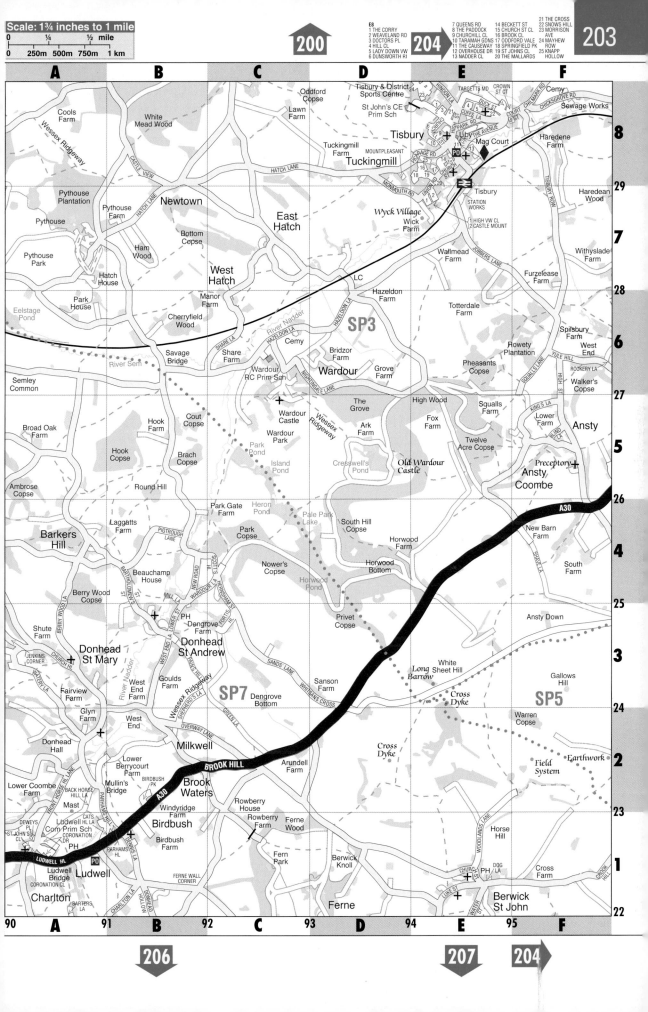

Scale: 1¾ inches to 1 mile

0   ¼   ½   mile
0   250m   500m   750m   1 km

A   B   C   D   E   F

8

CHICKSGROVE ROAD
Quarry Farm
LC
Colemans Farm
Apshill Copse
PH
Chicksgrove
Thorny Bottom
CHICKSGROVE RD
Ham Cross Farm
Mill Farm
Daslett Farm
Panters
Longs Farm
THE POPLARS
Great Ground Hill
MOOR HILL
HOME CL
PH
Gerrards Farm
THE ELMS
Fovant Wood
Fovant Wood
Compton Wood
Fir Hill Plantation
Fir Hill
MARY BARTERS LA
Fovant
Woodcock Corner Copse
Little Wurs Copse
Greystones
A30 SHAFTESBURY RD

29

Haredene Wood
Sutton Row
Whitmarsh Wood
Common Hill Wood
Swell Hill Wood
Mast
LAGPOND LA
Sutton Mandeville
Larkhams Farm
Townsend Wood
Church Farm
Townsend Copse
SUTTON HILL
RECTORY RD
SUTTON RD
GLASS'S LANE
Dean End
Dean Copse
DEAN LANE
Dean Lane Farm
Ings Farm
PH
Pembroke Farm
PO
Hotel
East Farm
Fovant Regimental Badges
Chiselbury

7

Castle Ditches (Fort)
Chestnut Tree Farm
Manor Farm
SP3
West Farm

28

Swallowcliffe Wood
PH
Buxbury Farm
Greenlands Farm
Fovant Down
Chalk Pit
Gurston Holes

6

ROOKERY LA
GIGANT ST
Parsonage Farm
PH
Poles Farm
LODERS LANE
Swallowcliffe
BUXBURY HOLLOW
Red House Farm
Tumulus
Sheep Well
Fovant Down Poultry Farm
Fovant Hut
Gurston Knowle

27

5

A30
Long Barrow
Swallowcliffe Down
Sutton Down
Fifield Down

26

Swallowcliffe Down

4

Cross Dyke
Field System
Middle Down
Cross Dyke
Ebbesborne Down
North Hill Farm
Prescombe Down National Nature Reserve
Church Bottom
Enclosure
North Barn
Tumulus
Fifield Bavant
HIGH LANE

25

Field System
Long Bottom
Stowford Bridge
Messcombe Wood

3

West End Farm
WEST END
TOP RD
Prescombe Farm
HIGH LANE

Norrington Manor
THE STREET
Brooklands Farm
DUCK ST
West End
DUCK ST
HILLVIEW
MAY LA
HANDLEY ST
POUND ST
THE CROSS
PH
Chalkway Head
SP5

24

Church Farm
ELCOMBE LA
Alvediston
Manor Farm
PH
Samways Farm
EBBESBORNE HOLLOW
Ebbesbourne Wake
Barrow Hill
Hill Farm
Rookhay Farm
HOLLY CL

2

Windmill Hill
CROOK HILL
Trow Farm
Elcombe Farm
Cleeves Farm
QUIDHAM ST
CHURCH ST
SHEPHERDS CROFT
Hedge End
Misselfore

23

1

SP7
Pincombe Down
Trow Down
Field System
Elcombe Hollow
East Combe Wood
Tumuli
Woodminton Field System
Woodminton Farm
Targetts Farm

22

Lower Bridmore Farm
Goscombe Copse

96   A   97   B   98   C   99   D   00   E   01   F

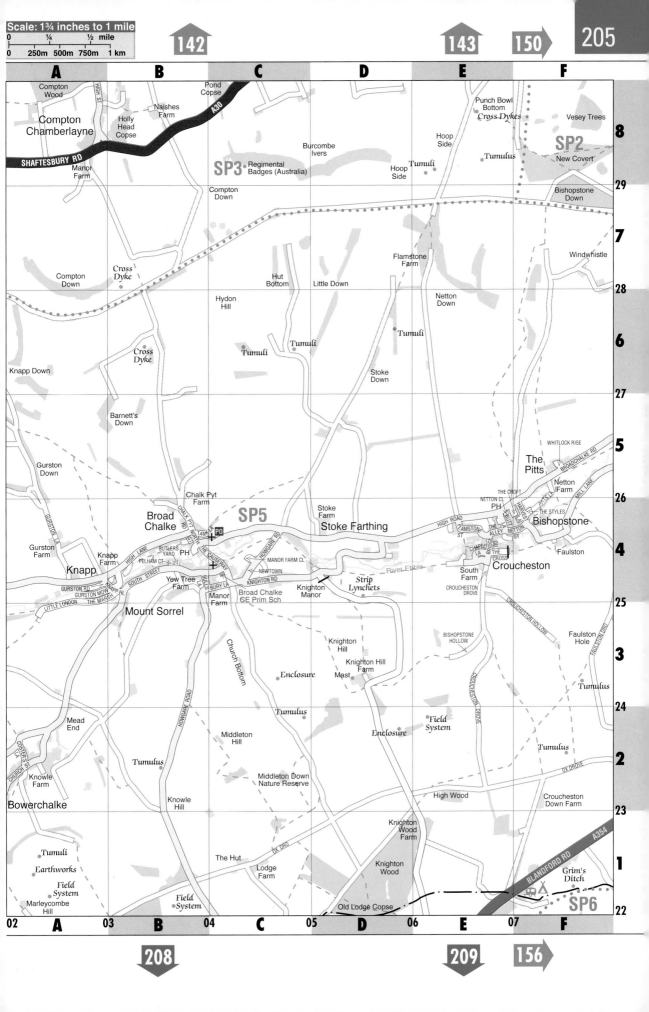

Compton Wood
Compton Chamberlayne
HIGH ST
Holly Head Copse
Naishes Farm
A30
Pond Copse
SHAFTESBURY RD
Manor Farm
SP3   Regimental Badges (Australia)
Burcombe Ivers
Hoop Side
Hoop Side
Tumuli
Punch Bowl Bottom
Cross Dykes
Tumulus
Vesey Trees
SP2
New Covert

8

Compton Down
Bishopstone Down

29

Compton Down
Cross Dyke
Flamstone Farm
Windwhistle

7

Cross Dyke
Hydon Hill
Hut Bottom
Little Down
Netton Down

28

Knapp Down
Tumuli
Tumuli
Tumuli
Stoke Down

6

Barnett's Down

27

Gurston Down
WHITLOCK RISE
The Pitts
BROADCHALKE RD

5

Chalk Pyt Farm
SP5
Stoke Farm
THE CROFT
Netton CL
THE STYLES
Netton Farm
MILL LANE
PITS CL

26

Gurston Farm
Broad Chalke
CHALK PYT RD NORTH
PO
Stoke Farthing
HIGH ROAD
FLAMSTONE ST
PH
BUTTS
NETTON ST
HARVESTS
Bishopstone

Gurston Down
GURSTON LA
Gurston Farm
Knapp Farm
HIGH LANE
TANS
PH
THE CAUSEWAY
MANOR FARM CL
CHAPEL
BRIDGE
THE CROSS
South Farm
Faulston
Croucheston

4

Knapp
BUTLERS YARD
PELHAM CT
NEWTOWN
Manor Farm
KNIGHTON RD
River Ebble
CROUCHESTON DROVE

GURSTON RD
SOUTH STREET
Yew Tree Farm
Knighton Manor
Strip Lynchets
Faulston Hole
FAULSTON DRO

GURSTON MDW
LITTLE LONDON
THE MARSH
Mount Sorrel
Broad Chalke CE Prim Sch
BISHOPSTONE HOLLOW
CROUCHESTON HOLLOW

25

COSTER'S LA
Church Bottom
Knighton Hill
Knighton Hill Farm
Mast
CROUCHESTON DROVE
Tumulus

3

Mead End
Enclosure
OX DROVE

24

Knowle Farm
Tumulus
Middleton Hill
Enclosure
Field System
Tumulus

2

Bowerchalke
CHURCH ST
Tumulus
Knowle Hill
Middleton Down Nature Reserve
High Wood
Croucheston Down Farm

23

Knighton Wood Farm
BLANDFORD RD
A354

Tumuli
Earthworks
Field System
The Hut
Lodge Farm
OX DRO
Knighton Wood
Grim's Ditch

1

Marleycombe Hill
Field System
Old Lodge Copse
SP6

22

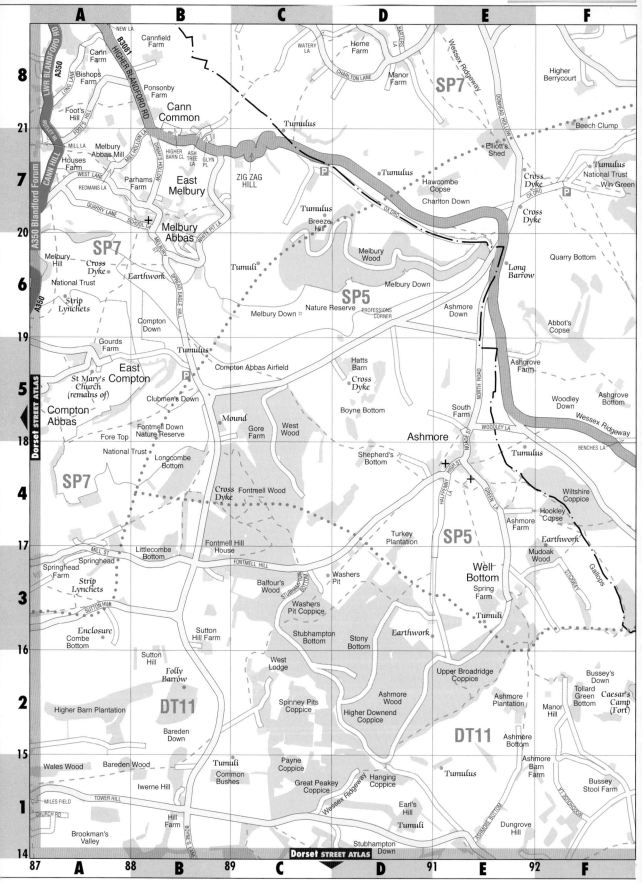

Scale: 1¾ inches to 1 mile

0   ¼   ½   mile
0   250m 500m 750m 1 km

A B C D E F

8

LWR BLANDFORD RD
A350
B3061
HIGHER BLANDFORD RD
New La
Cannfield Farm
Cann Farm
Bishops Farm
Foot's Hill
Foot's Hill
Houses Farm
Cann Hill
A350 Blandford Forum
Mill La
Melbury Abbas Mill
West Lane
Parhams Farm
Redmans La
Quarry Lane
School La
Ponsonby Farm
Cann Common
Hill Hollow La
Dinah's Hollow
Higher Barn Cl
Ash Tree La
Glyn Pl
East Melbury
White Pit La
Melbury Abbas
Zig Zag Hill
Tumulus
Watery La
Charlton Lane
Home Farm
Manor Farm
Barters La
SP7
Wessex Ridgeway
Donhead Hollow
Higher Berrycourt
Beech Clump
Elliott's Shed
Cross Dyke
Tumulus
National Trust
Win Green
Cross Dyke
P
P
P
Ox Dro
Ox Dro
Hawcombe Copse
Charlton Down
Tumulus
Breeze Hill
Tumulus

21

7

20

6

Melbury Hill
Cross Dyke
National Trust
Strip Lynchets
A350
SP7
Earthwork
Spread Eagle Hill
Melbury La
Compton Down
Tumuli
Melbury Down
Nature Reserve
Professors Corner
Melbury Wood
Melbury Down
Long Barrow
Quarry Bottom
Ashmore Down
Abbot's Copse
Ashgrove Farm
Ashgrove Bottom
Woodley Down
Wessex Ridgeway
North Road
SP5

19

5

Gourds Farm
Tumulus
East Compton
St Mary's Church (remains of)
Compton Abbas
P
Compton Abbas Airfield
Clubmen's Down
Hatts Barn
Cross Dyke
Boyne Bottom
South Farm
Ashmore
Woodley La
High St
Noade St
Benches La
Tumulus

18

4

Fore Top
National Trust
Fontmell Down Nature Reserve
Longcombe Bottom
Cross Dyke
Fontmell Wood
Mound
Gore Farm
West Wood
Shepherd's Bottom
Halfpenny La
Green La
Ashmore Farm
Hookley Copse
Wiltshire Coppice
Earthwork
Gallops
SP7
SP5

17

3

Springhead Farm
Springhead
Mill St
Strip Lynchets
Sutton Hill
Littlecombe Bottom
Fontmell Hill House
Fontmell Hill
Balfour's Wood
Stubhampton Bottom
Washers Pit
Washers Pit Coppice
Stubhampton Bottom
Stony Bottom
Turkey Plantation
Earthwork
Well Bottom
Spring Farm
Tumuli
Mudoak Wood
Stickway

16

2

Enclosure Combe Bottom
Sutton Hill Farm
Sutton Hill
Folly Barrow
DT11
Higher Barn Plantation
Bareden Down
West Lodge
Spinney Pits Coppice
Ashmore Wood
Higher Downend Coppice
Upper Broadridge Coppice
Ashmore Plantation
Manor Hill
DT11
Ashmore Bottom
Bussey's Down
Tollard Green Bottom
Caesar's Camp (Fort)

15

1

Miles Field
Church Rd
Wales Wood
Tower Hill
Bareden Wood
Iwerne Hill
Hill Farm
Boyne's Lane
Tumuli
Common Bushes
Payne Coppice
Great Peakey Coppice
Wessex Ridgeway
Hanging Coppice
Earl's Hill
Stubhampton Down
Tumuli
Tumulus
Ashmore Barn Farm
Ashmore Bottom
Woodcutts La
Dungrove Hill
Bussey Stool Farm

14

Brookman's Valley

Dorset STREET ATLAS

87 A 88 B 89 C 90 D 91 E 92 F

Dorset STREET ATLAS

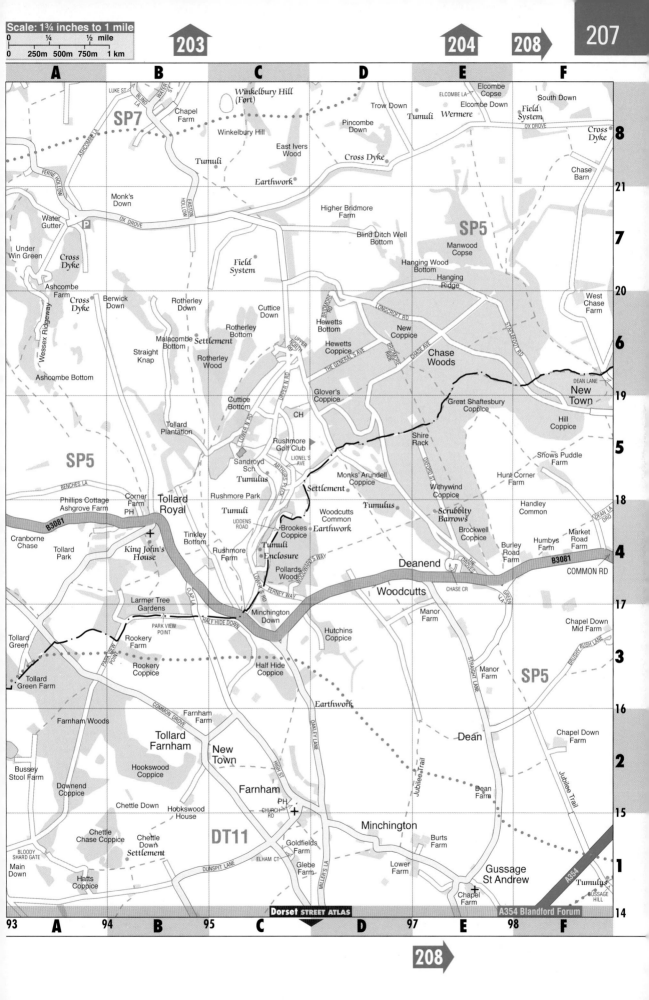

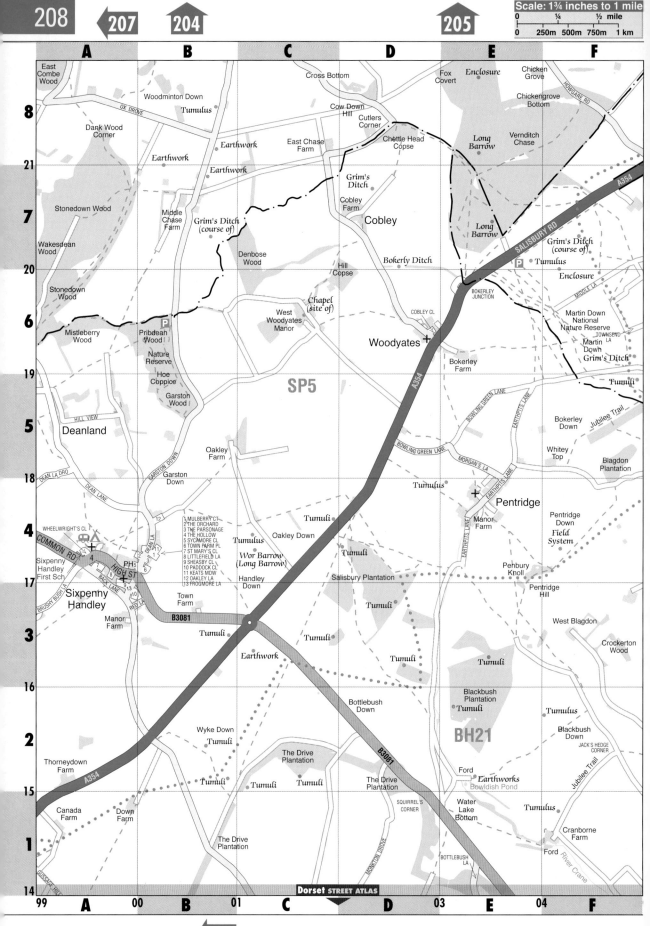

A   B   C   D   E   F

East Combe Wood

Woodminton Down

Tumulus

Cross Bottom

Fox Covert

Enclosure

Chicken Grove

Chickengrove Bottom

OX DROVE

Dank Wood Corner

Earthwork

Earthwork

Earthwork

East Chase Farm

Cow Down Hill

Cutlers Corner

Chettle Head Copse

Long Barrow

Vernditch Chase

HOWGARE RD

A354

8

21

Stonedown Wood

Middle Chase Farm

Grim's Ditch (course of)

Grim's Ditch

Cobley Farm

Cobley

Long Barrow

SALISBURY RD

Grim's Ditch (course of)

7

Wakesdean Wood

Denbose Wood

Hill Copse

Bokerly Ditch

P

Tumulus

Enclosure

MIDDLE LA

20

Stonedown Wood

Pribdean Wood

P

West Woodyates Manor

Chapel (site of)

COBLEY CL

Bokerley Junction

Martin Down National Nature Reserve

TOWNSEND

Martin Down

6

Mistleberry Wood

Nature Reserve

Hoe Coppice

Woodyates

Bokerley Farm

Grim's Ditch

Tumuli

19

Garston Wood

SP5

A354

BOWLING GREEN LANE

Bokerley Down

Jubilee Trail

Deanland

HILL VIEW

Garston Down

Oakley Farm

Bowling Green Lane

MORGAN'S LA

EARTHPITS LANE

Whitey Top

Blagdon Plantation

5

18

DEAN LA DRO

DEAN LANE

Garston Down

Tumulus

Manor Farm

Pentridge

Pentridge Down Field System

WHEELWRIGHT'S CL

COMMON RD

DEAN LA

T2

1 MULBERRY CT
2 THE ORCHARD
3 THE PARSONAGE
4 THE HOLLOW
5 SYCAMORE CL
6 TOWN FARM PL
7 ST MARY'S CL
8 LITTLEFIELD LA
9 SHEASBY CL
10 PADDOCK CL
11 KEATS MDW
12 OAKLEY LA
13 FROGMORE LA

Tumulus

Oakley Down

Tumuli

Tumuli

Manor Farm

Pentridge Hill

4

17

Sixpenny Handley First Sch

PH

HIGH ST

BACK LANE

RED LA

Wor Barrow (Long Barrow)

Handley Down

Salisbury Plantation

EARTHPITS LANE

Pehbury Knoll

Penbury Knoll

Pentridge Hill

West Blagdon

Crockerton Wood

Sixpenny Handley

BRUSHY BUSH LA

Manor Farm

Town Farm

B3081

Tumuli

Tumuli

Tumuli

Blackbush Plantation

Tumulus

3

16

Earthwork

Tumuli

Bottlebush Down

Blackbush Down

Tumulus

Blackbush Down

JACK'S HEDGE CORNER

2

A354

Wyke Down

Tumuli

The Drive Plantation

B3081

BH21

Ford

Earthworks

Bowldish Pond

Jubilee Trail

15

Canada Farm

Down Farm

Tumuli

Tumuli

Tumuli

The Drive Plantation

SQUIRREL'S CORNER

Water Lake Bottom

Tumulus

Cranborne Farm

1

The Drive Plantation

MONKTON DROVE

BOTTLEBUSH LA

Ford

River Crane

GUSSAGE HILL

14

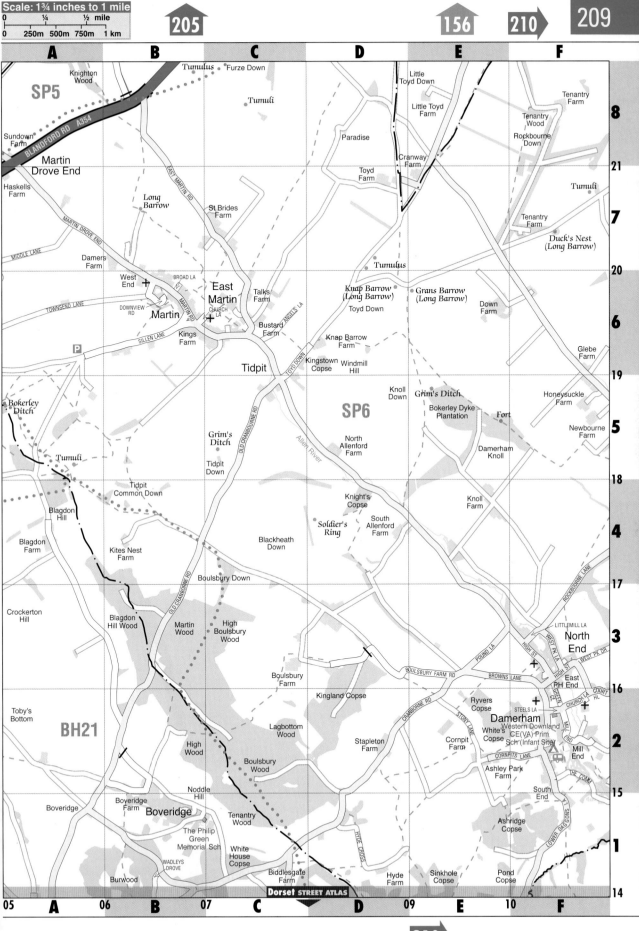

Scale: 1¾ inches to 1 mile

0   ¼   ½ mile
0 250m 500m 750m 1 km

SP5

Knighton Wood
Tumulus
Furze Down
Tumuli
Little Toyd Down
Little Toyd Farm
Tenantry Farm
Tenantry Wood
Rockbourne Down
Sundown Farm
BLANDFORD RD   A354
Paradise
Cranway Farm
Martin Drove End
EAST MARTIN RD
Toyd Farm
Tenantry Farm
Tumuli
Haskells Farm
Long Barrow
St Brides Farm
Tenantry Farm
Duck's Nest (Long Barrow)
MARTIN DROVE END
Damers Farm
MIDDLE LANE
BROAD LA
West End
DOWNVIEW RD
East Martin
Talks Farm
Tumulus
Knap Barrow (Long Barrow)
Grans Barrow (Long Barrow)
Down Farm
TOWNSEND LANE
Martin
CHURCH LA
Bustard Farm
Toyd Down
Knap Barrow Farm
P
SILLEN LANE
Kings Farm
Tidpit
TOYD DOWN
Kingstown Copse
Windmill Hill
Glebe Farm
Bokerley Ditch
Grim's Ditch
OLD CRANBOURNE RD
Allen River
SP6
Knoll Down
Grim's Ditch
Bokerley Dyke Plantation
Fort
Honeysuckle Farm
Tumuli
Tidpit Down
North Allenford Farm
Damerham Knoll
Newbourne Farm
Tidpit Common Down
Knight's Copse
Knoll Farm
Blagdon Hill
Blagdon Farm
Kites Nest Farm
Blackheath Down
Soldier's Ring
South Allenford Farm
Boulsbury Down
Crockerton Hill
Blagdon Hill Wood
Martin Wood
High Boulsbury Wood
LITTLEMILL LA
North End
WEST PK LA
WEST PK DR
ROCKBOURNE LANE
HIGH ST
Boulsbury Farm
Kingland Copse
BOULSBURY FARM RD
POUND LA
BROWNS LANE
East End
PH End
CHURCH LA
COURT HL
GREEN LA
Toby's Bottom
BH21
Lagbottom Wood
CRANBORNE RD
Stapleton Farm
Ryvers Copse
STONY LANE
STEELS LA
Damerham
Western Downland CE(VA) Prim Sch (Infant Site)
MILL END
Mill End
High Wood
Boulsbury Wood
Cornpit Farm
White's Copse
CORNPITS LANE
THE COM
Noddle Hill
Ashley Park Farm
South End
Boveridge
Boveridge Farm
Boveridge
Tenantry Wood
HYDE CROSS
Ashridge Copse
LOWER DASONS LA
The Philip Green Memorial Sch
WADLEYS DROVE
White House Copse
Hyde Farm
Sinkhole Copse
Pond Copse
Burwood
Biddlesgate Farm

Dorset STREET ATLAS

05   06   07   08(C)   09   10

210

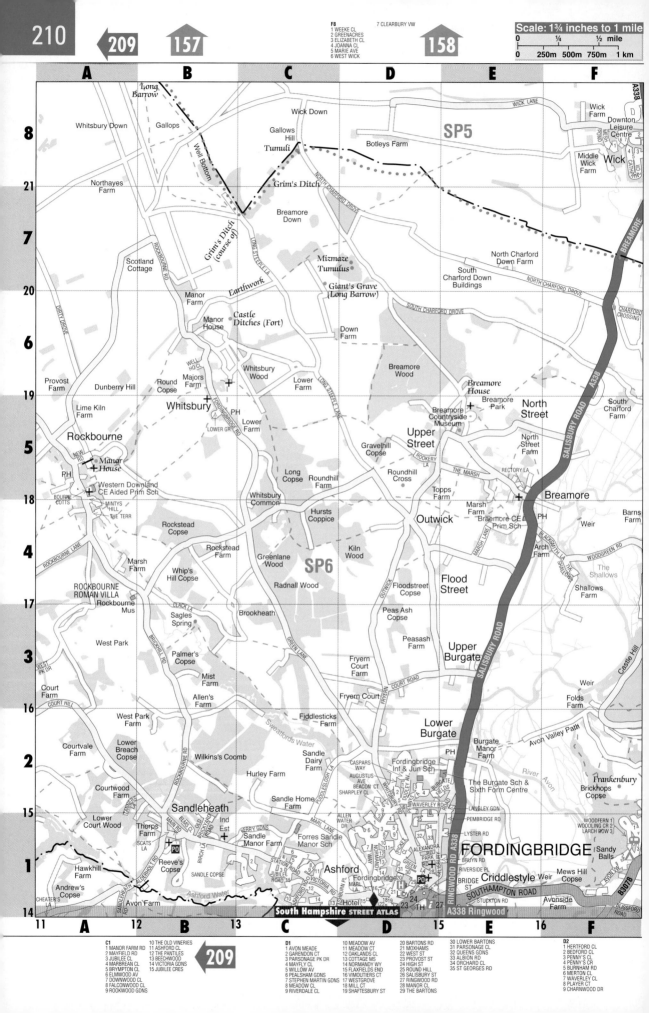

209 157 158

Scale: 1¾ inches to 1 mile
0   ¼   ½ mile
0 250m 500m 750m 1 km

F8
1 WEEKE CL
2 GREENACRES
3 ELIZABETH CL
4 JOANNA CL
5 MARIE AVE
6 WEST WICK

7 CLEARBURY VW

South Hampshire STREET ATLAS

C1
1 MANOR FARM RD
2 MAYFIELD RD
3 JUBILEE CL
4 MARBREAN CL
5 BRYMPTON CL
6 ELMWOOD AV
7 DOWNWOOD CL
8 FALCONWOOD CL
9 ROOKWOOD GDNS
10 THE OLD VINERIES
11 ASHFORD CL
12 THE PANTILES
13 BEECHWOOD
14 VICTORIA GDNS
15 JUBILEE CRES

D1
1 AVON MEADE
2 GARENDON CT
3 PARSONAGE PK DR
4 MAYFLY CL
5 WILLOW AV
6 PEALSHAM GDNS
7 STEPHEN MARTIN GDNS
8 MEADOW CL
9 RIVERDALE CL
10 MEADOW AV
11 MEADOW CT
12 OAKLANDS CL
13 COTTAGE MS
14 NORMANDY WY
15 FLAXFIELDS END
16 VIMOUTIERS CT
17 WESTGROVE
18 MILL CT
19 SHAFTESBURY ST
20 BARTONS RD
21 MOXHAMS
22 WEST ST
23 PROVOST ST
24 HIGH ST
25 ROUND HILL
26 SALISBURY ST
27 RINGWOOD RD
28 MANOR CL
29 THE BARTONS
30 LOWER BARTONS
31 PARSONAGE CL
32 QUEENS GDNS
33 ALBION RD
34 ORCHARD CL
35 ST GEORGES RD

D2
1 HERTFORD CL
2 BEDFORD CL
3 PENNY'S CL
4 PENNY'S CR
5 BURNHAM RD
6 MERTON CL
7 WAVERLEY CL
8 PLAYER CT
9 CHARNWOOD DR

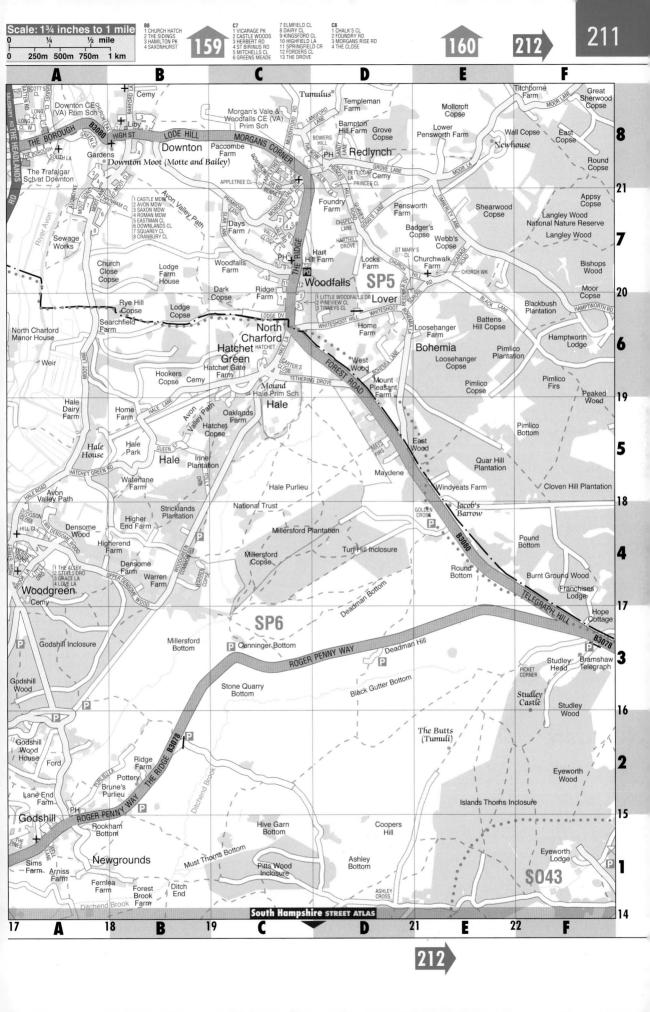

A B C D E F

8
Moor Copse
Ivory Copse
Sunt Copse
Glazier's Copse
Earldoms Lodge
Earldoms Farm
Earthwork
Barnsell Copse
Peaks Copse
Bush Farm
Landfordwood
Landsbrook Farm
Melchet Park
Melchet Park Farm
Melchetcourt Farm
White House Farm
Plaittford Wood
Boulder Wood
Plaittford Wood Farm
Pilgrims La
Hazel Wood
Hazelwood Farm
Short's Farm
Plaitford Green

21
Bagfield Copse
Out Wood
Homan's Copse
Northlands
North Common La
North Common Farm
Wickets Green Farm
Stock Lane Farm
Landfordwood Farm
Landford
Brooklyn Wood Farm
Bracken Farm
Plaittford Copse
Yewtree Farm
Bowles Farm
Gardiner's Farm

7
Whitterns Hill Farm
Coles's La
Landford Lodge
North Common Farm
Barrows Lane
Southampton Rd
Stock Lane
Sandown Farm
Manor Farm
Compton's Dr
Gauntletts Farm
Bowers Farm
Bourne Farm
Spoults La

20
Hamptworth Farm
CH
Elmtree Farm
King's Copse
River Blackwater
Whitehouse Farm
Highfield Farm
Pound Hill
B3079
PH
Glebe Farm
Brookside
Southampton Rd
Landford Manor
Elm Farm
Home Farm
Nelson Farm
Moat
Ford
Church La
Bridgefoot Farm
River Blackwater
Powell's Farm
Lukes Copse
Pembroke Farm

6
Bath Hole Plantation
Cuckoo Farm
PH
Manor Farm
Ford
Hamptworth Rd
Heath Copse
Lyndhurst Rd
Landford
Captain's Copse
Cherry Tree Farm
Giles Lane Ind Est
Furze Farm
PH
NT
Salisbury Road
A36 Southampton

19
Home Farm
Pond Wood
Hamptworth
SP5
Latchmoor Dro
Lane End Farm
PO
Beech Grange
Pine Cl
Landford Common Farm
Partridge Hill Farm
Plaitford
Heatherlands
Partridge Hill

5
Woodcock Copse
Lyburn Birches
Broomhill
Landford Bog Nature Reserve
Tumuli
Landford Common
New Road
Newlands Farm
Plaitford Common
National Trust
Tumulus
West Wellow Common
Sunny Side

18
Horse Common
Lyburn Farm
Tumuli
Hamptworth Common
Lyburn Road
Risbury Hill Farm
Cloven Hill Plantation
Pear Tree Dri
Whitehorse La
Oak Drv
Woodside Plantation
Greenhill Farm
Sturtmoor Common
S051
Heathlands
Canada
Plantation Rd
Kingston Pk

4
Browse Green Wood
Franchises Wood
Tinney's Plantation
Telegraph
Broom Hill Wood
Mire Wood
Shorthill Farm
The New Forest CE Prim Sch
Lyburn House
York Drv
Forest Rd
North La
South La
PH
Woodside Bottom Rd
Oak Plantation
Deazle Wood
Dazelwood
Dazel Cnr
Closed Copse
Penn Common
Canada Common
Sedgemore Farm
Canada Comm Rd

17
Burnt Tree Copse
Lyburn Park Farm
Chapel La
Forest Rd
Nomansland
Barford Farms
Lower Barford Farm
Penn Common Hungerford Farm
Lampards Farm
Moorbridge Farm
Furzley
South View Farm
Penn Comm Rd
NT

3
B3078
Firs Hill Copse
Crow's Nest Copse
Appsey Copse
Pipers Wait
Two Beeches Bottom
Bramshaw Wood
Forest Road
Lyndhurst Rd
Parsonage Farm
Wych Gn
Bloodoaks Farm
Harley La
Linhay Farm
Penn Farm
Fry's Copse
Penn Vale
Oak Copse
Furzley Comm Rd
Blackhill

16
Dark Hat Wood
SP6
Crow's Nest Bottom
Tumuli
Black Bush Plain
Bramble Hill Hotel
Margaret's Bottom
Bramble Hill
Morgans Vale
Bramshaw
Porters Farm
Penn Copse
Furzley Common
Tumuli
Stagbury Hill
National Trust
Mount Pleasant Copse

2
Howen Bottom
Longcross Plain Rd
Longcross Pond
Roger Penny Way
Great Wood
Bramshaw Hill Rd
Long Cross
Stock's Cross
Merry Orch
Upper Rowhill Farm
Vice La
Reservoir Copse
Burnside Farm
Rowhill
Blenman's Farm
Pit Copse
Cadnam Common
Tumuli

15
Longcross Plain
Jamesmoor Plain Rd
Coppice of Linwood
S043
Shepherds Copse
Court Farm
B3079
Warren's House
Warren's Park
Black Close Copse
Poplars Marsh
Kewlake Wood
Rings Copse

1
Fritham Lodge
Coppice of Linwood
Salisbury Trench
Broom Hill
Brook Wood
Brook Hill
Brook Gn
Bramshaw Golf Club
Brook Hill Farm
Bell Inn
Warren's Farm
Kewlake La
Furze Copse
Lewlake La
Manor Farm
Wittensford La

14
Fritham
PH
Whitesides Farm
Heatherdean
Fritham House
Gibbet Wood
Round Hill
Lyndhurst Rd
B3078
CH
Brook

F6
1 BOTTOM LA
2 ITCHEN CL
3 BOURNE CL
4 THE BEECHES
5 STOUR CL
6 ARUN WY
7 PEARTREE CL
8 NIGHTINGALE CL
9 SPUR OFF MAURY'S LA

168
168
169

A **B** **C** **D** **E** **F**

8

MAIN ROAD

Poulton Down
Farm

Tumulus

Green Lane
Farm

ROCKLEY ROAD

BOX RD

A346

Ogbourne
Maizey

7

Maisey Farm

Bay
Bridge

71

P

6

Barton
Down

Barton
Down
Gallop

Wessex Ridgeway

HEREPATH OR GREEN ST

Rough
Down

Rabley
Wood

River Og

5

Manton House
Farm

FREE'S AVENUE

Tumuli

Marlborough
Common

PORT HILL

SN8

70

CH

Marlborough
Golf Club

The Thorns
The Rogers
Newby Acre
RABLEY WOOD TW

4

Barton
Copse

Cemy

D3
1 HUGHENDEN YD
2 RUSSELL SQ
3 NEATES YD
4 CHANDLERS YD
5 IRONMONGER LA
6 RIDING SCHOOL YARD

CHIMINAGE
CL

Earthwork

HERD STREET

A346

PORT FIELD
PUBLIN
ACRE

NORTH VIEW
LAINES RD

COLD HARBOUR LANE
BLOMFORD
SOUTH VIEW

POULTON
CRES

TIN PIT

POULTON HILL

Marlborough Downs

River Kennet

LEAZE ROAD
HYDE LANE
CROSS LA
ST JO
CL
KINGSBURY ST
ST DAVID'S WAY

CARDIGAN RD
CLARENDON
CT
ST MARTINS
OXFORD ST

ALEC TCE
THE GREEN
KENNET PL

VICARAGE

MARLBOROUGH

BARROW CL
BARROW RD

3

B2
1 AUBREY CL
2 TENNYSON CL
3 SASSOON WK
4 BENSON CL

Summerfield
Sports Ground

HYDE LANE

The
Merchant's
House

OXFORD ST
KENNET
MEWS

TH

BRIDEWELL ST

PLUME OF
FEATHERS LA

Marlborough
Town FC

GALES
GROUND
STONE RD
ELCOT LANE
ELCOT
NURSERIES

A4

MACNEICE DR

DANDO
DR

BARTON DENE

WROBLYNES WAY
JEFFERIES CL
COLLEGE FIELDS

L Ctr

P

Barton
Farm

P
CHANTRY LA

HIGH ST

P

A4
HILLIERS YD
FIGGINS LA

TOWN MILL

P

P
OXFORD ST

P
CLUTCH
CT

PELHAM CT

SAVERNAKE
CT

SAVERNAKE
CT

ST MARGARET'S

LONDON RD

LAUREL DR

69

MANTON
HOLLOW

FARRAR DR
BETJEMAN RD
DAVIES CL
GOLDING AVE
HUGHES CL

MORRIS ROAD
SMILEY CL
THOMSON
WAY
SHAKESPEARE
DR

HAWKINS
MDW
TALKER CL

i
Liby

River
Pk

RIVER PARK

PRIORY CT

P

PRIORSFIELD

ST MARGARET'S MEAD

QUEENS WY
SOUTHERN RD
FIVE STILES RD
SAVERNAKE CR

Priory &
Gdns

The Old
Ropeworks

Katherine Ho
Gallery
Rec
Ground

2

MANTON
MANTON

BRIDGE STREET

River Kennet

A4 **BATH ROAD**

BATH RD

Marlborough
College

PEWSEY RD

FIGGINS LA

B3052
LOWER
CHURCH FIELDS

GEORGE LA

Marlborough
St Mary's CE
Prim Sch

DUCKS MEAD
UPPER CHURCH FIELDS

ISBURY RD
ORCHARD RD

SALISBURY ROAD

CHERRY
ORCHARD

ERIC
LEADER CL

PRIORY CT
WOODS
CL

BLENHEIM RD

Earthwork

1

SCHOOL LA
PH
MANTON CL
HIGH ST

Preshute CE
Prim Sch

Manton

PRESHUTE LANE

Preshute
House

Marlborough
College

Sports Ground

White Horse

Preshute
Marlborough
College

GRANHAM HILL

A345

St John's
Marlborough
Acad

CHARLES
WOOD CL

WILLIAM
MERRIMAN
RD
JENNINGS CL
ROBERT TISHER DR

A346

SALISBURY HILL

Marlborough
Business
Park

HERTFORD
CL

Postern
Hill

E1
1 GARSIDE WAY
2 ELSIE KNOCKER GRO

LONG HARRY

68

17 **A** **B** **18** **C** **D** **19** **E** **F**

174
174
175

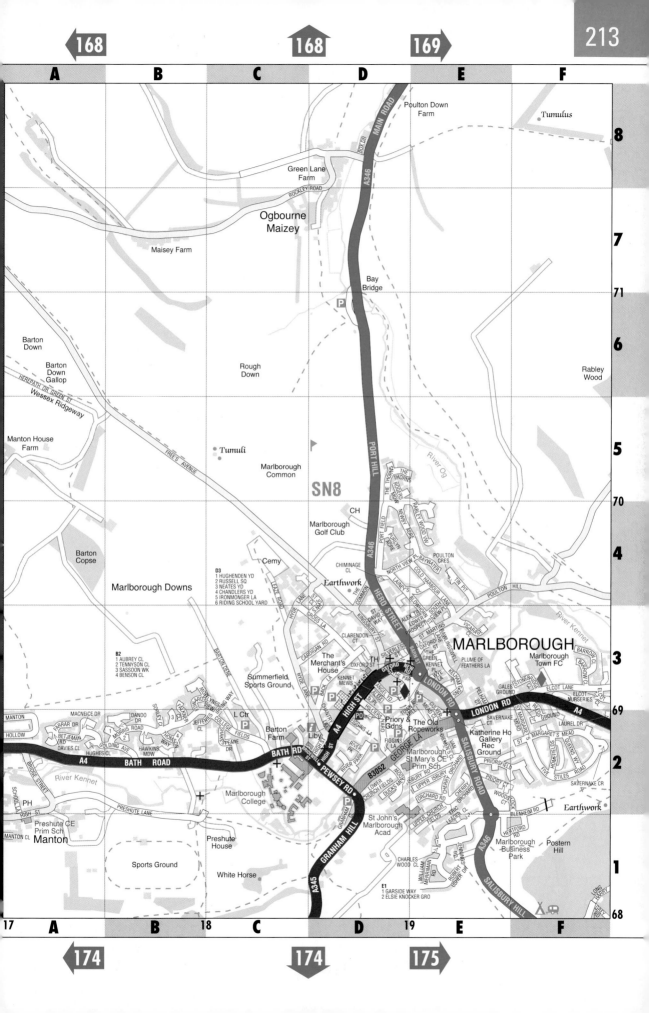

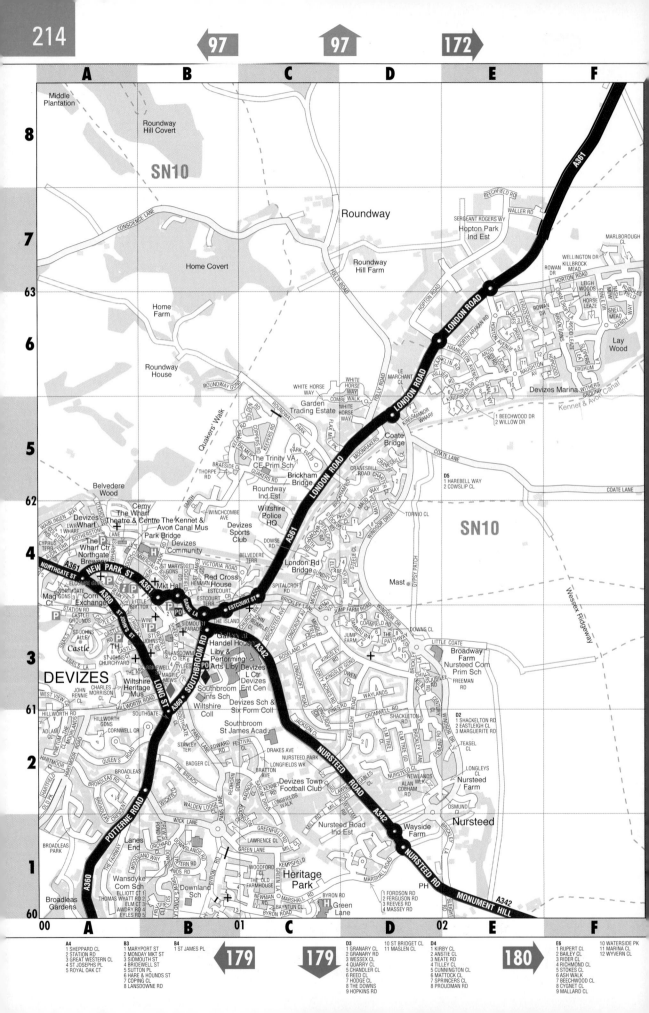

A4	B3	B4	D3	D ST BRIDGET CL	D4	E6	10 WATERSIDE PK
1 SHEPPARD CL	1 MARYPORT ST	1 ST JAMES PL	1 GRANARY CL	11 MASLEN CL	1 KIRBY CL	1 RUPERT CL	11 MARINA CL
2 STATION RD	2 MONDAY MKT ST		2 GRANARY RD		2 ANSTIE CL	2 BAILEY CL	12 WYVERN CL
3 GREAT WESTERN CL	3 SIDMOUTH ST		3 WESSEX CL		3 NEATE RD	3 RIDER CL	
4 ST JOSEPHS PL	4 BRIDEWELL ST		4 QUARRY CL		4 TILLEY CL	4 RICHMOND CL	
5 ROYAL OAK CT	5 SUTTON PL		5 CHANDLER CL		5 CUNNINGTON CL	5 STOKES CL	
	6 HARE & HOUNDS ST		6 REED CL		6 MATTOCK CL	6 ASH WALK	
	7 COPING CL		7 HODGE CL		7 SPRINCERS CL	7 BEECHWOOD CL	
	8 LANSDOWNE RD		8 THE DOWNS		8 PROUDMAN RD	8 CYGNET CL	
			9 HOPKINS RD			9 MALLARD CL	

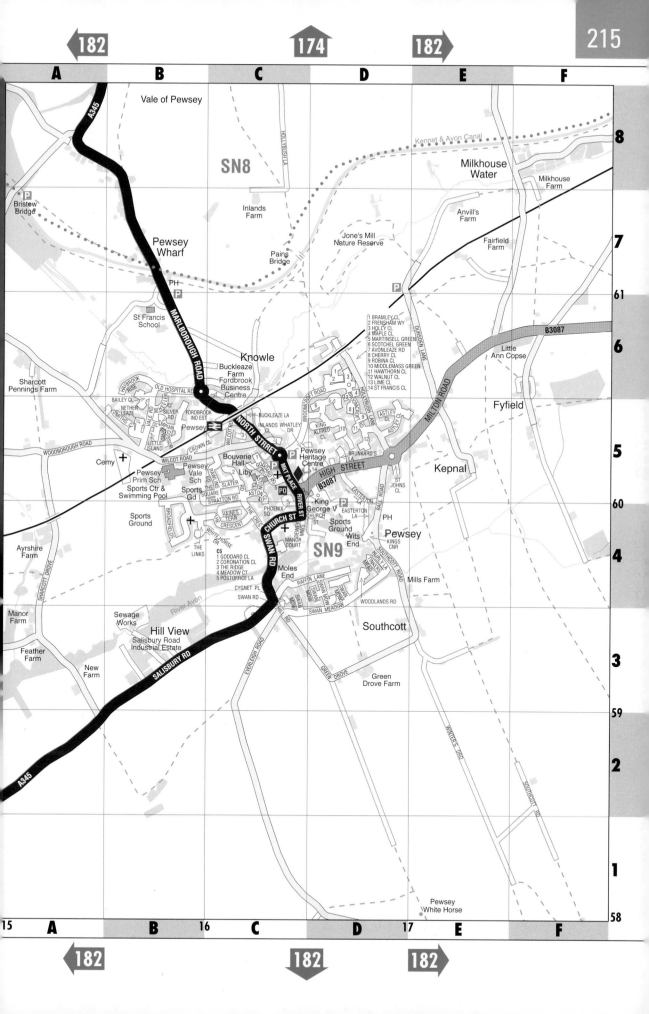

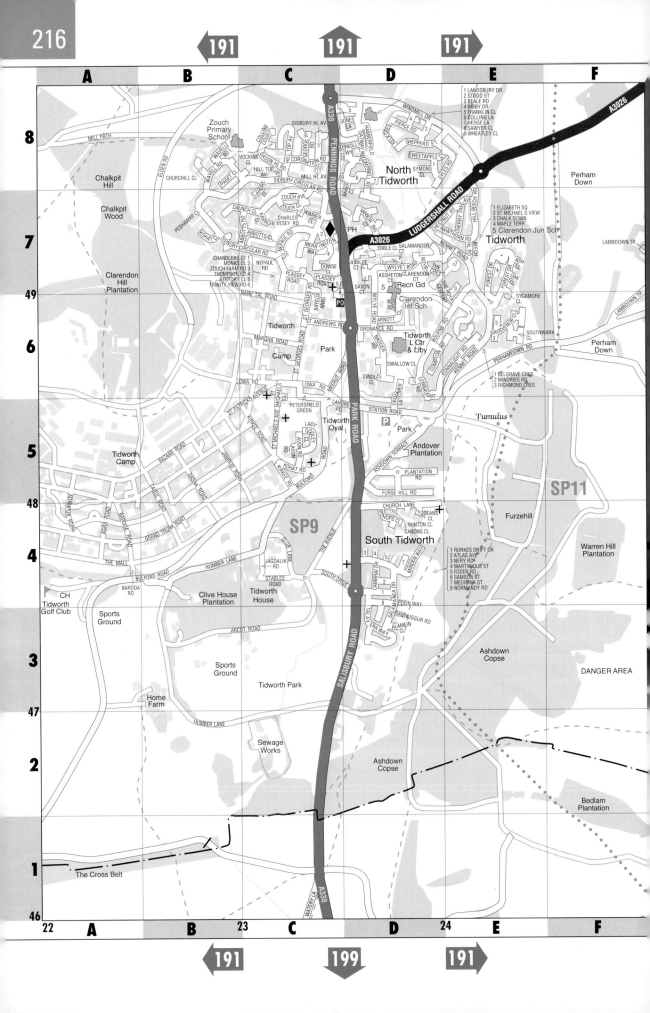

Chalkpit Hill

Chalkpit Wood

Clarendon Hill Plantation

Zouch Primary School

North Tidworth

Perham Down

1 Landsbury Dr
2 Studd St
3 Beale Rd
4 Bibby Dr
5 Franklin Cl
6 Colling La
7 Hedge La
8 Sawyer Cl
9 Wheatley Cl

1 Elizabeth Sq
2 St Michael's View
3 Chalk Down
4 Maple Terr
5 Clarendon Jun Schl

Tidworth

LAMBDOWN TR

LAMBDOWN TR

CHANDLERS CT 1
MONKS CL 2
ZOUCH FARM RD 3
THOMPSON RD 4
RECTORY CL 5
TRINITY VIEW RD 6

Tidworth Park

Camp

Tidworth Oval

Tidworth L Ctr & Liby

Recn Gd

Clarendon Inf Sch

Tumulus

Perham Down

1 Belgrave Cres
2 Minories Rd
3 Richmond Cres

SP11

Petersfield Green

Tidworth Camp

Andover Plantation

Furzehill

Warren Hill Plantation

SP9

Clive House Plantation

Tidworth House

South Tidworth

1 Rorkes Drift Dr
2 Atlas Ave
3 Nery Rd
4 Martinique St
5 Foden Rd
6 Samson St
7 Mediuna St
8 Normandy Rd

CH Tidworth Golf Club

Sports Ground

Ashdown Copse

DANGER AREA

Sports Ground

Tidworth Park

Home Farm

Sewage Works

Ashdown Copse

Bedlam Plantation

The Cross Belt

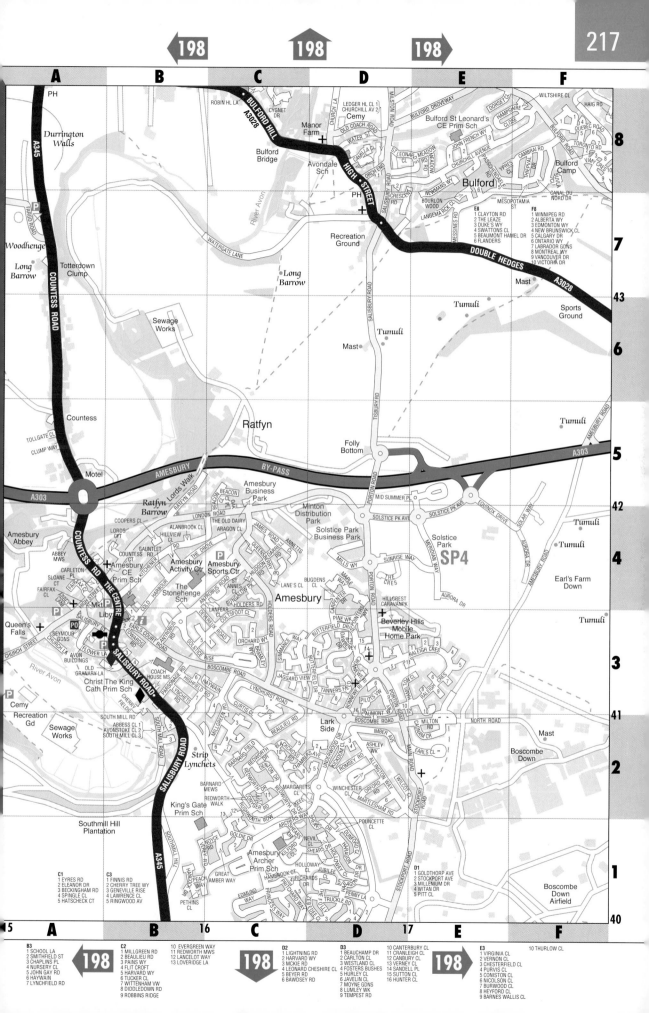

A   B   C   D   E   F

PH
Durrington
Walls

Woodhenge

Long
Barrow

Totterdown
Clump

ROBIN HL LA
BULFORD HILL
A3028
CYGNET DR

Manor
Farm

Bulford
Bridge

Avondale
Sch

River Avon

WATERGATE LANE

Long
Barrow

Sewage
Works

LEDGER HL CL 1
CHURCHILL AV 2
CHURCH LA
Cemy

OLD COACH ROAD
WATER ST
CAMILLA CL
ORCHARD END

HIGH · STREET
PH

Recreation
Ground

SALISBURY ROAD

BOURLON
WOOD
LANGEMA RCK CL

MESSINES RD

Mast

Tumuli

Mast

Tumuli

Ratfyn

Folly
Bottom

BULFORD DROVEWAY
MILSTON ROAD
Bulford St Leonard's
CE Prim Sch
ST LEONARD
MEADOW MEADOW RD
JOHN FRENCH WY
CHURCHILL AVENUE
YPRES CL
NEWMANS WY
CRESC RD
THEPVAL
LANGEMA RCK CL

WILTSHIRE CL
DORSET CL
HAMPSHIRE CLOSE
BULFORD ROAD
HAIG RD
QUEBEC RD
TORONTO RD
VIMY CRES
Bulford
Camp
CAMBRAI RD
CANAL DU NORD DR

MESOPOTAMIA ST
Bulford

DOUBLE HEDGES   A3028

Sports
Ground

Tumuli

E8
1 CLAYTON RD
2 THE LEAZE
3 DUKE'S WY
4 SWATTONS CL
5 BEAUMONT HAMEL DR
6 FLANDERS

F8
1 WINNIPEG RD
2 ALBERTA WY
3 EDMONTON WY
4 NEW BRUNSWICK CL
5 CALGARY DR
6 ONTARIO WY
7 LABRADOR GDNS
8 MONTREAL WY
9 VANCOUVER DR
10 VICTORIA DR

TOLLGATE CL
CLUMP WAY

Countess

COUNTESS ROAD
A345

Motel
A303

AMESBURY   BY-PASS

Ratfyn
Barrow
LORDS WALK
RATFYN ROAD
LONDON ROAD

Amesbury
Business
Park
BEACON
The Old Dairy
ARAGON CL

Minton
Distribution
Park
JAMES ROAD
ANNETTS CL

MID SUMMER PL
SOLSTICE PK AVE

Amesbury
Abbey

Queen's
Falls

River Avon

Cemy

Recreation
Gd

Sewage
Works

ABBEY
MWS
CARLETON
PL
SLOANE
PL
FAIRFAX
CL
SEYMOUR
GDNS
CHURCH STREET
CHURCH LA
FLOWER LA

COOPERS CL
LORDS
CFT
GAUNTLET
RD
COUNTESS
CT
ABBESS ST
KITCHENERS

Amesbury
CE
Prim Sch
COUNTESS RD
THE CENTRE
Mkt
Lib

SALISBURY ROAD
A345

ALANBROOK CL
HILLVIEW
THE DROVE
OLD HARBOUR

Amesbury
Activity Ctr

The
Stonehenge
Sch
ANTROBUS ROAD
ANTROBUS ST
ST ANNES
BUNGALOW
COLTSFOOT CL
HOLDERS RD
DEVEREUX ROAD
SOLSTICE RISE
EARLS COURT ROAD
BOSCOMBE ROAD
COACH
HOUSE MS
HIGHFIELD
RD
LYNCHES
RD
HAYWAIN

Amesbury
Sports Ctr
HUDSON RD
QUEENSBOROUGH
LANE'S CL
BUGDENS CL
MAPLE WY
PINE WK

Amesbury
MILLS WY
PORTON ROAD

Solstice Park
Business Park
SUNRISE WAY
MERIDIAN WAY

SOLSTICE PK AVE
EQUINOX DRIVE

Solstice
Park
SP4

AURORA DR
HILLCREST

Beverley Hills
Mobile
Home Park
RALEIGH CRES
RALEIGH CRES

THE CRES
AURORA DR
SOLAR WAY

Earl's Farm
Down

Tumuli

Tumuli

Tumuli

CARTERTON

Christ The King
Cath Prim Sch
OLD
GRANARY LA
AVON
BUILDINGS
CHERRY
FIELDS
SOUTH MILL RD
SOUTHMILL HILL
A345
ABBESS CL 1
AVONSTOKE CL 2
SOUTH MILL CL 3

Strip
Lynchets

Southmill Hill
Plantation

King's Gate
Prim Sch

BARNARD
MEWS
REDWORTH
WALK
BARNARD FIELD
REDWORTH
DENZIN DR
RUSWORTH ROW
ARCHERS WAY

Amesbury
Archer
Prim Sch
PETHINS
CL
HAMPEACH WAY
HANDEL
NOYCE CL
VERE RD
GOLDIE DR
EDMUND WAY
GREAT
AMBER WAY
PRINCESS WAY
KILFORD CL
SAGE CL

BLACKCROSS
CHAMBERS AVE
MARGARETS CL
WINCHESTER CL
GINGER RD
KEEFE
REDWORTH DR

LYNDHURST ROAD
CURTIS CL
BRAMLEY
JAGGARD VIEW
Tanners FC
BUTTERFIELD DRIVE
BUTTERFIELD
SIMMANCE WAY

Lark
Side

BEAUCHAMP DR
MILLGREEN RD
BEAULIEU RD
MILLGREEN RD

ROMSEY RD
UNDERWOOD DR
ALLINGTON WAY
ASHLEY
WK
WINCHESTER CL
ORFORD RD
MARTLESHAM RD
POUNCETTE
CL
DURFORD CL
ARAGON CL
JUBILEE
HOLLOWAY DR
RICHARDS CL
PENNY LA
THE FOLLY
THE TRUCKLE WAY
EYRE CL
SHEARS CL

BEAUMONT WY
PILOT'S VW
ROMNEY WY
IMBER AVE
BOSCOMBE ROAD
CADNAM CR
MILTON

North Road
STOCKPORT ROAD
EARLS CL
WILCOT RD
MAIN ROAD

Mast

Boscombe
Down

Tumuli

41

D1
1 GOLDTHORP AVE
2 STOCKPORT AVE
3 MILLENIUM DR
4 WITAN DR
5 PITT CL

Boscombe
Down
Airfield

8
7
43
6
5
42
4
3
41
2
1
40

C1
1 EYRES RD
2 ELEANOR DR
3 BECKINGHAM RD
4 NURSERY CL
5 HATSCHECK CT

C3
1 FINNIS RD
2 CHERRY TREE WY
3 GENEVILLE RISE
4 LAWRENCE CL
5 RINGWOOD AV

A   B   C   D   E   F

B3
1 SCHOOL LA
2 SMITHFIELD ST
3 CHAPLINS PL
4 NURSERY CL
5 JOHN GAY RD
6 HAYWAIN
7 LYNCHFIELD RD

C2
1 MILLGREEN RD
2 BEAULIEU RD
3 PAINS WY
4 FLIT CROFT
5 HARVARD WY
6 TUCKER CL
7 WITTENHAM VW
8 DIDDLEDOWN RD
9 ROBBINS RIDGE

10 EVERGREEN WAY
11 REDWORTH MWS
12 LANCELOT WAY
13 LOVERIDGE LA

D2
1 LIGHTNING RD
2 HARVARD WY
3 MCKIE RD
4 LEONARD CHESHIRE CL
5 BEYER RD
6 BAWDSEY RD

D3
1 BEAUCHAMP DR
2 CARLTON CL
3 WESTLAND CL
4 FOSTERS BUSHES
5 HURLEY CL
6 JAVELIN CL
7 MOYNE GDNS
8 LUMLEY WK
9 TEMPEST RD

10 CANTERBURY CL
11 CRANLEIGH CL
12 CANBURY CL
13 VERNEY CL
14 SANDELL PL
15 SUTTON CL
16 HUNTER CL

E3
1 VIRGINIA CL
2 VERNON CL
3 CHESTERFIELD CL
4 PURVIS CL
5 CONISTON CL
6 NICOLSON CL
7 BURWOOD CL
8 HEYFORD CL
9 BARNES WALLIS CL

10 THURLOW CL

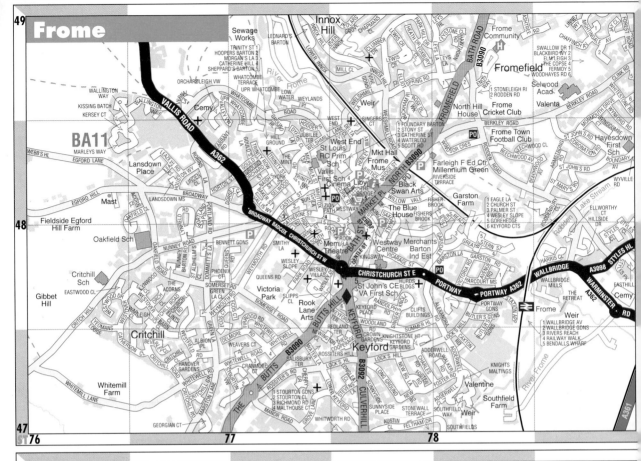

Frome

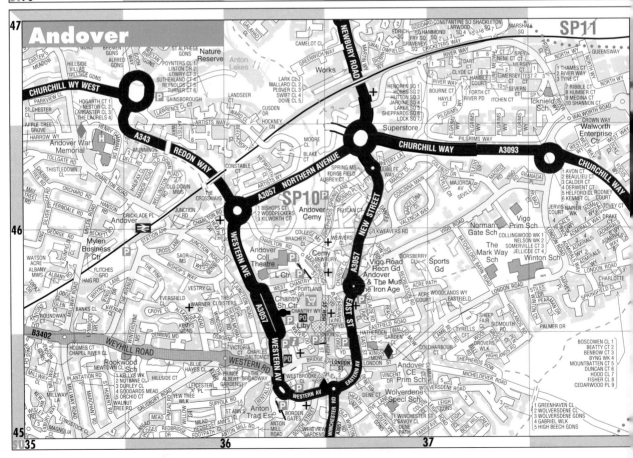

Andover

Index

Place name May be abbreviated on the map

Location number Present when a number indicates the place's position in a crowded area of mapping

Locality, town or village Shown when more than one place has the same name

Postcode district District for the indexed place

Page and grid square Page number and grid reference for the standard mapping

→ **Church Rd 6** Beckenham BR2..........**53** C6

Cities, towns and villages are listed in CAPITAL LETTERS

Public and commercial buildings are highlighted in **magenta**   **Places of interest** are highlighted in blue with a star*

Abbreviations used in the index

Acad	**Academy**	Comm	**Common**	Gd	**Ground**	L	**Leisure**	Prom	**Promenade**
App	**Approach**	Cott	**Cottage**	Gdn	**Garden**	La	**Lane**	Rd	**Road**
Arc	**Arcade**	Cres	**Crescent**	Gn	**Green**	Liby	**Library**	Recn	**Recreation**
Ave	**Avenue**	Cswy	**Causeway**	Gr	**Grove**	Mdw	**Meadow**	Ret	**Retail**
Bglw	**Bungalow**	Ct	**Court**	H	**Hall**	Meml	**Memorial**	Sh	**Shopping**
Bldg	**Building**	Ctr	**Centre**	Ho	**House**	Mkt	**Market**	Sq	**Square**
Bsns, Bus	**Business**	Ctry	**Country**	Hospl	**Hospital**	Mus	**Museum**	St	**Street**
Bvd	**Boulevard**	Cty	**County**	HQ	**Headquarters**	Orch	**Orchard**	Sta	**Station**
Cath	**Cathedral**	Dr	**Drive**	Hts	**Heights**	Pal	**Palace**	Terr	**Terrace**
Cir	**Circus**	Dro	**Drove**	Ind	**Industrial**	Par	**Parade**	TH	**Town Hall**
Cl	**Close**	Ed	**Education**	Inst	**Institute**	Pas	**Passage**	Univ	**University**
Cnr	**Corner**	Emb	**Embankment**	Int	**International**	Pk	**Park**	Wk, Wlk	**Walk**
Coll	**College**	Est	**Estate**	Intc	**Interchange**	Pl	**Place**	Wr	**Water**
Com	**Community**	Ex	**Exhibition**	Junc	**Junction**	Prec	**Precinct**	Yd	**Yard**

Index of towns, villages, streets, hospitals, industrial estates, railway stations, schools, shopping centres, universities and places of interest

A

Aaron Rd SP4 . . . . . . 132 B1
Abberd La SN11 . . . . . . 81 D3
Abberd Way SN11 . . . . .81 C3
Abbess Cl SP4 . . . . . . 217 B2
Abbey CE VA Prim Sch
The SP3 . . . . 202 B1
Abbey Cl
Chippenham SN15 . . . . 79 B5
3 Shrewton SP3 . . . . 196 E6
Abbey Farm Prim Sch
SN26 . . . . .20 F1
Abbeyfield Sch SN15 . .79 B6
Abbey House Gdns*
SN16 . . . . .28 C3
Abbey La
Amesbury SP4 . . . . . 217 A4
Hinton Charterhouse
BA2 . . . . 99 A3
Swindon SN1 . . . . . . .50 C5
Abbey Meads Com Prim
Sch SN25 . . . . .35 A7
Abbey Row SN16 . . . . . 28 A3
Abbey Stadium SN25 . .35 A8
Abbey View Rd SN25 . .34 E3
Abbey Wlk 6 SP7 . . 202 C1
Abbot Rd SP1 . . . . . . 146 C4
Abbotsbury Way SN25 .35 A8
Abbots Way GL7 . . . . . .4 F7
Abbots Wlk GL7 . . . . . .2 D1
Abbots Cl SP9 . . . . . 216 C7
Abbotts Gdn SN16 . . .28 A3
Abbotts Rd SP9 . . . . 216 C7
Abdon Cl BA12 . . . . . 195 D7
Abingdon Ct La SN6 . . .19 E8
Abington Way SN2 . . . 35 D5
ABLINGTON 190 B1
Abney Moor SN3 . . . . .51 E2
Abotts Cl BA13 . . . . . 108 F3
Above Hedges SP5 . . . 148 C3
Abraham Cl 5 BA14 . 105 C7
Abrahams Cl BA14 . . 105 C7
Acacia Cl SN14 . . . . . .70 A1
Acacia Cres BA14 . . . 105 A8
Acacia Dr
Frome BA11 . . . . 110 C7
Westbury BA13 . . . . . 109 A2
Acacia Gr SN2 . . . . . . .35 C2
Academy Cl SN12 . . . . .93 F6
Academy Dr SN13 . . . .76 E2
Acorn Cl SN3 . . . . .51 C5

Acorn La SN11 . . . . . . .89 C7
Acorn Meadow BA14. 105 A5
Acre Cl BA14 . . . . 178 A3
Acre Rise SN14 . . . . . . .78 A4
Acreshort La BA14 . . 178 A3
Acres Rd SN14 . . . . . 214 C3
Activity Zone Leisure Ctr
SN16 . . . . .27 F3
ACTON TURVILLE 52 F6
Acton Turville Rd GL9. .52 A4
Adampur Rd SP9 . . . . 216 A4
Adam's Grave (Long
Barrow)* SN8 . . . . 173 D2
Adams Mere SP5 . . . . 154 E6
Adcroft Dr BA14 . . . . 101 D1
Adcroft St BA14 . . . . . 101 C1
Adderwell BA11 . . . . . 110 A3
Adderwell Cl BA11 . . . 110 A3
Adderwell Rd BA11 . . 110 A3
Addinsell Rd SN25 . . . .34 E8
Addison Cres SN25 . . . .35 F3
Addison Rd SN12 . . . . .93 F6
Addison Sq 19 SP4. . . 198 B7
Adelaide Cl 6 SP4. . . 198 F6
Adlam Cl SN10. . . . . . 214 A2
Adwalton Cl SN5. . . . . .49 B4
Aerial Bsns Pk RG17 . . 170 E6
Affleck Cl SN5 . . . . . . .49 C5
Agra Rd SP9. . . . . 216 A4
Agravaine Cl 27 SP10 193 E2
Aiken Rd SN25 . . . . . . .34 C5
Ailesbury Cl SN15 . . . .79 A4
Ailesbury Way SN8 . . 183 D8
Ainsworth Rd SN3 . . . .51 A4
Aintree 7 RG17 . . . . 165 A1
Aintree Ave BA14 . . . 105 E4
Aintree Dr SN14 . . . . . .77 F6
Airman's Cnr SP3 . . . . 197 B5
Aisne Rd SN4 . . . . 65 D1
Akenfield Cl SN25 . . . .34 F5
Akers Ct SN26 . . . . . . .21 C2
Akers Way SN2 . . . . . .34 E2
Aki Ct SN26. . . . . .21 C2
Alamein Cl SN9 . . . . . 216 D3
Alamein Rd 4 SP11. . 193 E4
Alanbrook Cl SP4. . . . 217 B4
Alanbrooke Rd
Durrington SP4 . . . . . 197 E6
Warminster BA12 . . . 113 D1
Alan Cobham Rd
SN10. . . . . 214 D2

Alan Powell La BA14 . 112 B8
Alba Cl 11 SN5. . . . . . . .48 F8
Albany Cl BA14 . . . . . 101 F2
Albany Rd SP1. . . . . . 146 B1
Albany Terr 5 SP2 . . 144 D3
Alberta Way 2 SP4. . 217 F8
Albert Rd BA14 . . . . . 101 F3
Albert St SN1. . . . . 50 D4
Albion Bglws SP2. . . . 145 A3
Albion Cres SN13 . . . . .76 C1
Albion Dr BA14 . . . . . 105 B8
Albion Rd 33 SP6 . . . 210 D1
Albion St SN1 . . . . . . .50 A5
ALCESTER 202 B1
Alcock Crest BA12 . . . 116 F6
ALCOMBE. 82 F8
Aldborough Cl 2
SN5. . . . . .49 C6
ALDBOURNE 170 A6
Aldbourne Cl
Blunsdon St Andrew
SN2 . . . . 35 C6
27 Hungerford RG17. . 177 B7
Aldbourne Four
Barrows* SN8 . . . . 169 E8
Aldbourne Rd SN8. . . 170 B7
Aldeburgh Pl BA14 . . 104 F6
ALDERBURY 153 C3
Alderbury & West
Grimstead CE VA Prim
Sch SP5. . . . . 153 E3
Alder Cl
Swindon SN2 . . . . . . 34 D4
Trowbridge BA14. . . . 105 B8
Alderholt Rd SP6 . . . 210 B1
Alderley Rd 7 SN25 . . .34 E7
Alderney Cl 8 SN4 . . .48 A2
Alder Rd SN14 . . . . . . .75 A4
Alders The SP2 . . . . . 145 A3
ALDERTON. 39 F2
Alderton Rd
Alderton SN14 . . . . . . .39 F1
Alderton SN14 . . . . . 40 C1
Grittleton SN14 . . . . 54 D5
Luckington SN14 . . . . 53 D6
Alderton Way BA14 . . 105 D5
Alder Way SN12 . . . . . .94 A4
Alder Wlk 5 BA11. . . 110 B7
Aldhelm Rise SN13 . . . .84 E7
Aldrin Cl 7 SP10 . . . 193 D2
Aldworth Dr 3 SP1. . 146 C5
Alexander Fields
SN9. . . . . 181 F1

Alexander Keiller Mus*
SN8. . . . . 167 B1
Alexander Rd
Malmesbury SN16 . . . .27 F4
Warminster BA12 . . . 113 D1
Alexander Terr SN13. .77 A1
Alexandra Cl SP2 . . . 145 C3
Alexandra Rd
Fordingbridge SP6. . . 210 D1
Frome BA11. . . . . . . 110 A4
1 Swindon SN1 . . . . 50 C7
Alexandra Terr SN8. . 213 D3
Alfred Gdns 6 SP10 . 193 D1
Alfred's Castle*
RG17. . . . . 164 B5
Alfred St
Swindon SN1 . . . . . . 50 C7
Westbury BA13 . . . . . 109 A4
Alfred's Twr* BA10. . 122 F3
Alicia Cl 1 SN25. . . . .34 C6
Allard Ave 4 SN13. . .76 C1
ALL CANNINGS. 180 E8
All Cannings CE Prim Sch
SN10. . . . . 180 F8
Allenby Rd SP4 . . . . 133 C2
Allen Cl SN3. . . . . . . .50 E2
Allengrove La SN14. . .39 C3
Allen Rd
Corsham SN13. . . . . . 84 C8
Shaftesbury SP7 . . . . 202 D1
Trowbridge BA14. . . . 105 B7
Allen Water Dr SP6 . . 210 D2
Alley The
Bishopstone SP5 . . . . 205 E4
Woodgreen SP6. . . . . 211 A4
ALLINGTON
All Cannings. 172 E2
Amesbury. 199 A2
Chippenham Without. . . 69 E3
ALLINGTON BAR. 69 E3
Allington Rd SN2 . . . . 35 B5
Allington Tk SP4. . . . 198 E4
Allington Way
Amesbury SP4 . . . . . 217 D2
2 Chippenham SN14 . . 70 A1
All Saints Cres 9
BA13. . . . . 109 A3
All Saints Rd 1
SN10. . . . . 187 E7
All Saints VA CE Prim Sch
SP4. . . . . 190 A3
Alma Pl SN8. . . . . . . 213 D3
Alma Rd SN8 . . . . . . 170 A7

Alma St BA14 . . . . . . 105 E8
Alma Terr SN11. . . . . .81 B3
Almond Cl SN13 . . . . .84 C5
Almond Gr BA14 . . . . 105 B5
Alnwick SN5. . . . . 49 B4
Alnwick Rd 2 BA14 . . 106 A8
Aloeric Prim Sch
SN12. . . . . .94 A3
Alpine Cl 6 SN5. . . . .49 A7
ALTON. 190 B1
Altona Gdns 17 SP10 . 193 D2
ALTON BARNES 173 C1
Alton Barnes White
Horse* SN8 . . . . . 173 C1
Alton Cl SN2. . . . . 35 C5
ALTON PRIORS 173 D1
Alton Rd
Avebury SN8. . . . . . . 173 B8
Wilcot SN8. . . . . 181 F8
Alum Cl BA14. . . . . . 105 E7
ALVEDISTON 204 B2
Alvescot Rd SN3. . . . . 50 D5
Alveston Cl SN5 . . . . . 49 D6
Alwyn Ct 4 SN25 . . . .34 D7
Amazon Way BA13. . . 108 E4
Amber Ct SN1 . . . . . . 50 D7
Amberley Cl
Calne SN11 . . . . 81 A4
Swindon SN25 . . . . . 35 C4
Amberley Ct SN16 . . . .27 E2
Ambrose House Business
Ctr SN1 . . . . .50 B6
Ambrose Rd SN1 . . . . .50 C2
American Museum in
Britain* BA2. . . . . . .90 A5
Amersham Rd SN3. . . . 51 B3
AMESBURY 217 C4
Amesbury Archer Prim
Sch SP4. . . . . 217 C1
Amesbury Bsns Pk
SP4. . . . . 217 C5
Amesbury Bypass
SP4. . . . . 217 B5
Amesbury CE VC Prim
Sch SP4. . . . . 217 C3
Amesbury Cl 4 SN2 . . .35 C6
Amesbury Rd
Amesbury SP4 . . . . . 217 F4
Amport SP11 . . . . . . 192 C1
Newton Tony SP4 . . . 199 A3
Shrewton SP3 . . . . . 196 E6
Amesbury Sports Ctr
SP4. . . . . 217 C4

Aar–Ans

Amethyst Rd SN25 . . . .34 F8
Amity Dr SN8. . . . . . . 175 D6
Amouracre BA14 . . . . 105 F8
Ancaster Cl BA14 . . . 101 A1
Anchor Barton BA12 . 119 A8
Anchor Rd SN11 . . . . .81 C2
Ancliff Sq BA15. . . . . . 99 E4
Ancona Cl 12 SN5. . . .49 A7
Andeferas Rd 6
SP10. . . . . 193 D2
Anderson Cl SN3 . . . . 51 D3
Anderson Rd SP1. . . . 146 C4
Andover La SP11 . . . 192 B4
Andover Rd
Amport SP11 . . . . . . 192 E2
Chirton SN10. . . . . . . 180 F3
Fyfield SP11. . . . . . . 192 D3
Upavon SN9 . . . . 181 F1
Andover St 3 SN1. . . .50 A5
Andover Cl 14 SP4. . . 198 B7
Andrew Cl SN14 . . . . .78 B7
Andrews Way
Calne SN11 . . . . 81 B1
Salisbury SP2. . . . . . 151 F5
Angelica Cl 6 SN2 . . 34 D4
Angel La
Hindon SP3 . . . . 200 A3
Mere BA12. . . . . 139 A5
27 Shaftesbury SP7.. 202 C2
Angell Dr SN11 . . . . . .81 B1
Angels' La SP6 . . . . . 209 C6
Angel Yd SN8. . . . . . . 213 D3
Angler Rd
Salisbury SP2. . . . . . 145 C5
Swindon SN5 . . . . . . 49 B7
Anglesey Cl 5 SN5 . . .49 C6
Anglesey Mead SN15 . .79 A4
Angrove Cotts SN16 . . 43 C4
Angrove La SN16 . . . . 43 C4
Angus Cl SN5. . . . . . . .49 B7
Anise Cl 4 SN2. . . . . .34 C4
Anne Cl BA13. . . . . . 108 E3
Anne Cres 24 SP4. . . 198 B7
Annetts Cl SP4 . . . . . 217 C4
Annett's La RG17 . . . 176 F4
Anson Ave
Calne SN11 . . . . 81 D4
Upavon Down SN9. . . 182 B3
Anson Gr SN12 . . . . . .94 C1
Anson Pl SN14. . . . . . .56 C7

Anstey Pl SN15 . . . . . . .79 A4
ANSTY. 203 F5
ANSTY COOMBE. . . . 203 F5
Ansty Hill BA12 . . . . . 195 A6
Ansty Wlk SN2. . . . . . . .35 B6
Anthony Cl SN16. . . . . . .25 C1
Anthony Rd SN4 . . . . . . .64 A7
Anton La SP11. . . . . . . 193 E4
Antony Rd **5** SN25. . . .34 F7
Antrobus Rd SP4 . . . . . 217 B3
Anvil St SN26. . . . . .21 C1
Anzio Rd SN10. . . . . . . 214 E6
Apollo Cl **1** SN25. . . . . .34 B7
Apollo Rd SN15. . . . . . . .59 E3
Apostle Way SP1 . . . . 146 C5
Appleford Sch SP3. . . . 196 F2
APPLESHAW 192 E3
Appleshaw Way
 Perham Down SP11. . . 191 F3
 Salisbury SP1. . . . . . . 146 D5
Appletree Cl SP5 . . . . 211 C8
Apple Tree Gr **10**
 SP10. . . . . 193 C1
Appletree Rd SP5 . . . . 211 C8
Applewood Cl SN14. . . .78 B8
Applewood Cl SN5. . . . 49 D5
Applin Rd SP1. . . . . . . 146 D5
Apsley Cl BA14 . . . . . . 102 B2
Arabian Ave SN5. . . . . .34 C2
Arable Rd SN4 . . . . .78 A4
Aragon Cl SP4 . . . . . . 217 C4
Aragon Ct SN3. . . . . . . .51 A4
Arcade The **8** SN1 . . . .50 B6
Archer Ave **8** SN13. . . .76 C1
Archer Cl SN2 . . . . .35 F5
Archers Ct SP2 . . . . . . 146 A2
Archers The SN6 . . . . . .22 F5
Archers Way SP4 . . . . 217 C1
Arches La SN16. . . . . . . .27 F2
Arch Yard BA14. . . . . . 101 C1
Arcot Rd SP9 . . . . 216 B3
Arc Theatre BA14 . . . . 105 A6
Arden Cl SN12. . . . . . . .94 C5
Argosy Rd SN15 . . . . . . .60 B1
Argus Gn SN25 . . . . . . .35 D3
Argyle Dr SN14 . . . . . . .70 C3
Argyle St SN2 . . . . .35 D1
Ariadne Rd **15** SN25. . .34 B7
Ark The SN10. . . . . . . 214 A3
Arkwright Rd SN25 . . . . 35 D6
Arley Cl SN25. . . . . .35 A5
Arlingdon Fields
 Somerford Keynes GL7 . .5 F3
 Somerford Keynes GL7 . .6 A3
Arlington Cl SN3. . . . . . .51 B7
Arliss Cl SN25 . . . . .35 B6
Armfield Rd SN25. . . . . .20 C1
Armitage Sq **4** SP4 . . . 197 E6
Armoury Yd **16** SP7 . . 202 C2
Arms Gdns SN15. . . . . . .57 C1
Armstrong Rd BA11. . . .10 B3
Armstrong Rise **16**
 SP10. . . . . 193 D2
Armstrong St **2** SN1. . .50 C7
Arney Cl SN13 . . . . .84 E8
Arnfield Moor SN3. . . . .51 E2
Arnhem Cross SN15. . . .60 B2
Arn Hill Down & Nature
 Reserve★ BA12 . . . . . 117 B8
Arnhill Rd **5** SN1. . . . .50 A2
Arnold Noad Corner
 BA14. . . . . 104 E3
Arnolds Mead SN13. . . .76 F2
Arnold St SN25. . . . . . . .34 E7
Arnold Way SN13. . . . . .84 F6
Arnott Cl SP9 . . . . 216 D6
Arn View
 Cold Harbour BA12 . . . 112 F1
 2 Warminster BA12. . . 117 A8
Arran Cl **5** SN4. . . . . . .48 A2
Arran Way SN6 . . . . . . .22 F7
Arras Cl BA14. . . . . . . 105 C6
Arthur Bennett Ct
 SN1. . . . . .50 A5
Arthurs Pleck SP5 . . . . 207 C5
Artisans La
 Swindon SN25 . . . . . . .20 C1
 6 Swindon SN25 . . . . 34 C8
Artis Ave SN4. . . . . . . .64 B7
Artus Cl **1** SN25. . . . . .34 E6
Arundel Cl
 Chippenham SN14 . . . . 78 A7
 Swindon SN3 . . . . .50 F3
Arundell Cl BA13 . . . . . 109 B4
Arun Rd SN25 . . . . .34 F3
Arun Way **6** SO51 . . . 212 F6
Ascot Cl SN14 . . . . .78 A5
Ascott Cl SN25. . . . . . . .34 F7
Ashanti Way SN26 . . . . 21 E8
Ashbee Cres **6** SN25 . 34 D8
Ashburnham Cl **7**
 SN5. . . . . .49 A4
Ashburn Pl SP6. . . . . . 210 D1
ASHBURY. 164 A7
Ashbury Ave SN3 . . . . . .51 B7
Ashbury Hill SN6 . . . . . 164 A7
Ashbury with Compton
 Beauchamp CE Prim
 Sch SN6. . . . . 164 A8
Ash Cl
 Lyneham SN15. . . . . . . 60 B2
 4 Shaftesbury SP7. . . 202 D2
 Swindon SN5 . . . . 34 A2
 Tidworth SP9. . . . . . . 216 E7

Ashcombe La SP5 . . . . 207 A8
Ash Cres SP1 . . . . 146 C5
Ashcroft Cotts SN8 . . . 169 B1
Ashdown Dr SN12 . . . . 94 D6
Ashdown Pk★ RG17 . 164 C5
Ashdown Terr SP9 . . . . 216 B5
Ashdown Way SN2. . . . .34 C4
Ash Dr BA14. . . . . 105 C3
Ashe Cl SN15 . . . . 70 D1
Ashe Cres SN15. . . . . . . 70 D1
Ashen Copse Rd SN4. . .63 F7
Ashes La
 Freshford BA2. . . . . . . .99 A4
 Kington Langley SN15 . . 70 E7
 Sharpstone BA2. . . . . . 99 A4
Ashfield SN6 . . . . .7 A1
Ashfield Rd
 Chippenham SN15 . . . . 70 D1
 Salisbury SP2. . . . . . . 145 E1
ASHFORD 210 C1
Ashford Cl **11** SP6 . . . 210 C1
Ashford Rd
 Fordingbridge SP6. . . . 210 C1
 Swindon SN1 . . . . 50 B4
Ashford Trad Est
 SP2. . . . . 145 E1
Ash Gdns SN3 . . . . .36 E4
Ash Gn SP8. . . . . 137 D1
Ash Gr
 1 Melksham SN12 . . . .94 A2
 Swindon SN2 . . . . 35 C2
Ashgrove BA12 . . . . . . 139 B4
Ash Hill Comm SP5 . . 162 D3
Ashie Cl SN5 . . . . .34 B2
Ashington Way **4**
 SN5. . . . . .49 C5
Ashkirk Cl SN3. . . . . . . .50 E6
Ash La SN13 . . . . .84 C8
Ashlade Firs Rd SN8 . . 175 C6
Ashlands SN4. . . . . 146 D6
Ashleigh Cl SP2 . . . . . . 130 B2
Ashleigh Gr **4** BA14 . 105 C7
Ashleworth Rd **6**
 SN25. . . . . .34 F7
ASHLEY
 Ashley. 3 A2
 Box. 83 A6
Ashley Cl
 Atworth/Whitley SN12 . .85 D1
 Bradford-on-Avon
  BA15 . . . . 100 B8
 Swindon SN3 . . . . 50 F6
Ashley Coombe
 BA12. . . . . 117 A4
Ashleycross SP6. . . . . . 211 D1
Ashley Dro SN8. . . . . . 185 A7
Ashley Gn SN13. . . . . . .83 A5
Ashley Green
 Little Ashley BA15 . . . . 91 A1
 Little Ashley BA15 . . . . 91 B2
 Winsley BA15. . . . . . . .90 F1
Ashley La BA15. . . . . . . .99 F7
Ashley Piece SN8. . . . . 170 C2
Ashley Pl BA12 . . . . . . 116 F4
Ashley Rd
 Bath BA1 . . . . 82 C2
 Bradford-on-Avon BA15. 91 B1
 Salisbury SP2. . . . . . . 145 F2
Ashley Wlk SP4. . . . . . 217 D2
Ashmead BA14 . . . . . . 105 D6
Ashmead Ct BA14. . . . 105 D7
ASHMORE 206 D5
Ashmore Bottom
 DT11. . . . . 206 E1
Ashmore Cl
 Swindon SN3 . . . . 51 C6
 Whiteparish SP5 . . . . . 161 D4
Ashmore La
 West Dean SP5 . . . . . . 155 E2
 Whiteparish SP5 . . . . . 161 D6
Ash Rd SN14. . . . . .75 A5
Ashton Cl SN25 . . . . . . .34 C7
Ashton Comm BA14. . . 106 C8
ASHTON COMMON. . . 102 F1
Ashton Coombe
 BA13. . . . . 186 B7
Ashton Gifford La
 BA12. . . . . 195 A3
Ashton Heights BA14 . 106 B3
ASHTON KEYNES. 6 F1
Ashton Keynes CE Prim
 Sch
 Ashton Keynes SN6. . . . .6 E1
 Ashton Keynes SN6 . . . 17 E8
Ashton Rd
 Ashton Keynes SN16 . . . 17 E7
 Siddington GL7. . . . . . . 6 D8
 Trowbridge BA14. . . . . 102 A2
Ashton Rise BA14. . . . . 102 A2
Ashton Road SN16. . . . . 17 E6
Ashton St **2** BA14 . . . 105 E8
Ash Tree Cl SN8 . . . . . 175 A8
Ash Tree La SP7 . . . . . 206 B7
Ashtree Rd BA11. . . . . 110 A4
Ashville Ctr SN12 . . . . 178 A8
Ashwell Cl SN3 . . . . . . .50 F5
Ashwicke Rd
 Marshfield SN14 . . . . . 74 A4
 Marshfield SN14 . . . . . 74 B3
Ash Wlk
 Upton Lovell BA12. . . . 194 E4
 Warminster BA12 . . . . 117 A7
Ashwood Rd SN13. . . . . 76 A1
Ashworth Rd SN5. . . . . .49 E6
Askerton Cl SN5 . . . . . .48 F8
Askew Cl **3** SN5. . . . . 48 F5
Aspen Cl
 Colerne SN14. . . . . . . .74 F6

Aspen Cl continued
 Frome BA11. . . . . 110 B7
 Royal Wootton Bassett
  SN4. . . . . 47 E3
 Swindon SN25 . . . . . . 35 E2
Assart Way SN14. . . . . .78 A3
Assheton Ct SP9 . . . . . 216 D7
Assisi Rd SP1. . . . . 146 A4
Astley Cl SN9 . . . . 215 D5
Aston Cl SN9 . . . . 215 C5
Aston Mead SP1. . . . . . 146 C3
Astor Cres SP11 . . . . . 192 A5
Astute Pl **12** SN13. . . . 76 C1
Atbara Cl SN25 . . . . . . .35 A3
Atcherly Rd SN1. . . . . . 166 A1
Athelney Ave BA13. . . . 109 B5
Athelstan Mus★ SN16 .28 A3
Athelstan Rd SN16. . . . . 27 F4
Athena Ave SN2. . . . . . . 35 E1
Athenaeum Ctr **2**
 BA12. . . . . 117 A7
Atherton Cl **12** SN8 . . 170 B2
Atherton Cres **16**
 RG17. . . . . 177 B7
Atherton Pl **11** RG17 . 165 A2
Atherton Rd **11** RG17. 77 B7
Athlone Cl **2** SP11. . . 193 E4
Atholl Ct **28** SP10 . . . 193 E2
Atlas Ave SP9. . . . . . . 216 D4
Attlee Cres SN2. . . . . . . 35 E3
Attwood Rd **1** SN4 . . 146 A3
Atwell-Wilson Motor
 Mus★ SN11. . . . . 89 D7
ATWORTH 92 F8
Atworth Bsns Pk SN12 .92 F8
Atworth Cl SN12. . . . . . .35 B6
Atworth Ct SN12. . . . . . .92 F8
Atworth La
 Corsham SN13. . . . . . . 84 E4
 Neston SN13 . . . . 84 E4
Atyeo Cl BA13 . . . . 112 B8
Aubrey Gdns SN2. . . . . . 34 F1
Aubrey Rise **6** SN16. . 28 A5
Auchinleck Rd BA12 . . 113 E1
Auckland Rd **3** SP4 . . 198 F7
Auden Cl SN25. . . . . . . .34 F5
Audley Cl **2** SN5 . . . . .48 F4
Audley Gate BA13. . . . 108 E2
Audley Rd SN14 . . . . . . .78 C8
AUGHTON 183 D3
Augusta Cl SN25. . . . . . 34 C7
Augusta Way W **8**
 SP11. . . . . 193 F2
Augustine Way **9**
 SP10. . . . . 193 C2
Augustus Cl SN25. . . . . 34 B8
Ausden Terr **1** SN1. . . 49 F7
Austen Cres SN3. . . . . . 51 D4
Austin Rd SN5. . . . . . . .49 C7
Australian Ave SP2 . . . 145 D2
AVEBURY 173 C8
Avebury Cl
 Calne SN11 . . . . .81 A3
 Westbury BA13 . . . . . . 108 F4
Avebury Manor & Gdns★
 SN8. . . . . 167 B1
Avebury Mus★ SN8. . . 167 B1
Avebury Rd
 Chippenham SN14 . . . . 78 A6
 Swindon SN2 . . . . 35 B5
Avebury Stone Circles★
 SN8. . . . . 167 C1
AVEBURY TRUSLOE . 173 B8
Avenell Rd **8** SN4 . . . 163 A6
Avening St SN2. . . . . . . 35 D1
Avens Cl SN2. . . . . 34 D4
Avenue De Gien
 Malmesbury SN16. . . . . 27 F6
 Malmesbury SN16 . . . . 28 A6
Avenue La Fleche
 SN15. . . . . 78 D6
Avenue Prim Sch &
 Children's Ctr The
 BA12. . . . . 117 B7
Avenue The
 Chertill SN11. . . . . 166 E2
 Claverton BA2. . . . . . . 90 A4
 Durnford SP4. . . . . . . 131 D1
 18 Durrington/Bulford
  SP4. . . . . 198 B7
 Porton SP4. . . . . 133 D6
 Salisbury SP1. . . . . . . 146 C1
 South Tedworth SP9. . . 216 C4
 Stanton Fitzwarren SN6 22 B1
 Tangley SP11 . . . . 193 D5
 Tisbury SP3 . . . . 203 E8
 Warminster BA12 . . . . 117 A7
 Westbury BA13 . . . . . . 109 A3
 Wilton SP2. . . . . 144 F5
 Woodford SP2. . . . . . . 145 A8
Aviemore Rd **6** SN1. . . 50 A2
Avil's La SN14. . . . . . . .56 F6
Avington SP4 . . . . 177 F7
Avocet Cl SN3 . . . . .51 E6
AVON. 71 F6
Avon App SP2 . . . . 146 A1
Avon Bldgs SP4. . . . . . 217 A3
Avon Cl
 Bradford-on-Avon
  BA15 . . . . 100 E5
 Calne SN11 . . . . 81 A5
AVONCLIFF. 99 F4
Avoncliff Sta BA15. . . . . 99 E5

Avon Ct BA1. . . . . .82 A4
Avondale Prep Sch
 SP4. . . . . 217 D8
Avondown Rd SP4 . . . . 198 C7
Avon Dr SP5. . . . . 153 E2
Avondyke SP5. . . . . . . 211 A7
Avonfield BA14 . . . . . . 101 F8
Avonfield Ave BA15. . . 100 E5
Avonleaze Rd SN9 . . . . 215 D5
Avonmead SN25. . . . . . .34 F4
Avon Mead SN15. . . . . . .78 F8
Avon Meade **1** SP6. . 210 D1
Avon Meadow SP5. . . . 211 A8
Avon Meadows SP4. . . 131 C5
Avon Mills SN15 . . . . . . .28 B2
Avon Park BA2. . . . . . . .99 C7
Avon Pl **1** SP1 . . . . . 152 C8
Avon Pl Sh Ctr SN12 . . .94 A4
Avon Rd
 Devizes SN10. . . . . . . 179 C8
 2 Durrington/Bulford
  SP4. . . . . 198 F6
 Malmesbury SN16. . . . . 27 F4
 Melksham SN12. . . . . . 94 A6
 Tidworth SP9. . . . . . . 216 C5
 Warminster BA12 . . . . 117 A5
Avon Reach SN15. . . . . .78 D7
Avon Rise SN14. . . . . . . 39 E4
Avonside Enterprise Pk
 SN12. . . . . .94 A5
Avon Sq SN9 . . . . 181 F1
Avonstoke Cl SP4. . . . . 217 B2
Avon Terr
 Devizes SN10. . . . . . . 214 A4
 Salisbury SP2. . . . . . . 145 F2
Avonvale Rd BA14 . . . . 101 D2
Avon Valley College
 SP4. . . . . 198 C2
Avon Valley Nature
 Reserve★ SP1. . . . . . 145 F3
Avon View SP6 . . . . . . 210 F1
Avon Way
 Chippenham SN15 . . . . 70 F1
 Trowbridge BA14. . . . . 101 D3
Avonweir La SN15 . . . . 57 F3
Avro Way SN12 . . . . . . .94 C1
Awdry Ave SN12 . . . . . .94 C6
Awdry Cl
 Chippenham SN15 . . . . 77 F7
 Heddington SN11. . . . . 89 A2
Awdry Rd SN10. . . . . . 214 B1
Axbridge Cl SN3. . . . . . .51 A5
Axe & Cleaver La
 BA14. . . . . 105 C4
AXFORD 169 D1
Axis Bsns Ctr SN5. . . . 49 D7
Aylesbury Cl GL7 . . . . . 7 A6
Aylesbury St SN1 . . . . . .50 C7
Ayleswade Rd SP2. . . . 152 A6
Aymer Pl SN3. . . . . .51 C5
Ayr Cl SN14. . . . . .77 F5
Ayrshire Cl
 Salisbury SP2. . . . . . . 145 B5
 Swindon SN5 . . . . 49 B7
Ayrton Cl BA14 . . . . . . 105 A6
Azalea Cl SN11 . . . . . . .81 C1
Azalea Dr
 Trowbridge BA14. . . . . 105 A7
 Warminster BA12 . . . . 116 F2
Azelin Ct SN3. . . . . 36 B3

B

Babington Pk **9** SN5 . .48 F5
Back Dro
 West Winterslow SP5 . . 148 F5
 West Winterslow SP5 . . 149 A5
Back Hill SN16. . . . . 28 A3
Back Horse Hill La
 SP7. . . . . 203 A2
Back La
 9 Aldbourne SN8. . . . 170 A6
 Alderton SN14 . . . . 39 F2
 Alderton SN14 . . . . 40 A2
 Blunsdon St Andrew
  SN26 . . . . 21 B3
 Calne Without SN15. . . 88 B4
 Cerney Wick GL7 . . . . . .7 F4
 Cherhill SN11. . . . . . . 166 E2
 Chitterne BA12 . . . . . . 195 D7
 Great Bedwyn SN8 . . . 176 B3
 Great Hinton BA14. . . . 178 A5
 Maiden Bradley with
  Yarnfield BA12. . . . . . 118 F2
 Marlborough SN8. . . . . 213 D3
 Marshfield SN14 . . . . . 74 A8
 Penton Grafton SP11. . 193 A3
 Ramsbury SN8. . . . . . 170 B2
 Sixpenny Handley SP5. 208 A4
 Tilshead SP3 . . . . 188 B3
 Vernhams Dean SP11 . 185 C3
Back Rd
 Calne SN11 . . . . .81 B2
 Chitterne BA12 . . . . . . 195 D7
 Down Ampney GL7. . . . . .8 E7
Back St
 Ashton Keynes SN6 . . . . .6 F1
 East Garston RG17 . . . 171 E7
 Great Hinton BA14. . . . 178 A6
 Trowbridge BA14. . . . . 101 C1
Back Terr BA10. . . . . . 122 F2
Bacon Cl SN1. . . . . .50 A4
BADBURY. 65 F5
BADBURY WICK 65 D8
Bader Pk **10** SN12. . . . 178 B8
Badger Cl
 Devizes SN10. . . . . . . 214 D2

Badger Cl continued
 2 Royal Wootton Bassett
  SN4 . . . . .47 F2
Badgers Brook SN4. . . . .64 C5
Badgers Cl
 Bourton SP8. . . . . 137 E2
 3 Wanborough SN4. . 163 B6
BADMINTON 38 F2
Badminton House★
 GL9. . . . . .38 F2
Badminton Pk★ GL9. . .38 F3
Badminton Rd
 Acton Turville GL9 . . . . 52 F7
 Little Badminton GL9. . . 38 E6
Bagbury La SN5. . . . . . . 33 B1
Bagbury Rd BA12 . . . . 194 F4
Baghdad Rd **2** SP4. . . 198 F7
BAGSHOT. 176 F4
Bailey Cl SN9 . . . . 215 B5
Bailey La SP2. . . . . 144 E3
Bailey Mews SP4 . . . . . 146 C8
Baileys Barn BA15. . . . 100 D5
Baileys Farm Gdns
 SN3. . . . . .51 A6
Baileys La SN6. . . . . 11 A3
Bailey's Mead SN4. . . . . 48 A2
Baileys Way SN4. . . . . . .64 B7
Bailiffe Piece SN6 . . . . .8 D1
Baillie Cl **5** SN25. . . . . 34 C8
Bainbridge Cl **2** SN5 . 49 A5
Bainton Cl BA15. . . . . . 100 D7
Baird Cl SN5. . . . . .49 B8
Bakehouse Cl SN15 . . . .78 E6
Baker Cl SP9 . . . . 216 D8
Bakers Cnr SN13. . . . . . .84 E4
Bakers Ct SN3. . . . . 36 B2
Bakers Field SN15 . . . . . 60 A3
Bakers Rd SN4 . . . . .64 B5
Balden Cl SN4. . . . . .63 F6
Baldwin Cl SN4. . . . . . . 65 D4
Bale Cl **6** SN5. . . . . . . 48 F5
Ballands Castle★
 BA9. . . . . 137 A2
BALLARD'S ASH 47 D5
Ball Comm La BA9 . . . 136 C1
Ball Gr SP4. . . . . 132 B1
Ballie Cl SN25. . . . . .20 C1
Ballington BA12 . . . . . . 128 A8
Ball Rd SN9 . . . . 215 D4
Balmoor Cl BA12 . . . . . 139 B3
Balmoral Cl
 Chippenham SN14 . . . . .77 F7
 Swindon SN3 . . . . .51 A3
Balmoral Rd
 Salisbury SP1. . . . . . . 146 B4
 Trowbridge BA14. . . . . 105 B5
Bamford Cl SN5. . . . . . . 33 C5
Bampton Gr SN3. . . . . . .50 E6
Banbury Cl SN3. . . . . . . .50 F3
Bancroft BA15. . . . . . . 100 D7
Bancroft Cl SN15 . . . . . .48 F6
Bankfoot Cl **3** SN5. . . . 49 B7
Bank La SP11. . . . . 185 B6
Bankside SN1 . . . . .49 F4
Bank St SN12. . . . . .94 A4
Banks The SN15 . . . . . . .59 E4
Bank The SN14 . . . . . . .75 C3
Bankwaters Rd SN13. . .84 B8
Bannerdown Cl BA1 . . . .82 B4
Bannerdown Dr BA1. . . .82 A4
Bannerdown Rd BA1. . . .82 C5
Banwell Ave SN3 . . . . . .51 A5
BAPTON 195 D1
Barbel Cl SN11. . . . . . . .81 B5
Barberry SP3. . . . . 201 A3
Barbers La SP3. . . . . . . 204 A5
Barber's La SP5 . . . . . . 151 C1
Barbrook Rd SN1. . . . . . .50 A2
Barbury Castle★
 SN4. . . . . 168 A7
Barbury Castle Ctry Pk★
 SN4. . . . . 168 B7
Barbury Cl
 Swindon SN3 . . . . 34 F3
 Swindon SN25 . . . . . . 34 F3
Barbury La SN4. . . . . . 168 A7
Barcelona Cres SN4 . . . .64 A7
Barcete Cl SN25. . . . . . . 34 D7
Bardsey Cl **5** SN4 . . . . 47 F2
Barford La SP5 . . . . . . 159 C1
BARFORD ST
 MARTIN 143 A3
Barford St Martin CE Fst
 Sch SP3. . . . . 143 A3
Bargates SN13. . . . . 83 D6
Barken Rd
 4 Chippenham SN14. . 70 A1
 Chippenham SN14 . . . . 78 A8
Barker Cl **9** SP4 . . . . 132 B1
BARKERS HILL 203 A4
Barkstead Cl **3** SN5 . . 49 B4
Barley Cl
 Malmesbury SN16. . . . . 28 A2
 Warminster BA12 . . . . 117 C5
Barley Fields SN8. . . . . 170 B8
Barley Hill La SN10 . . . 179 B7
Barley Rd **2** SP11 . . . 193 F2
Barley Rise BA14 . . . . . 105 F7
Barlow Cl SN25. . . . . . . .35 A4
Barnack Cl BA14. . . . . . 101 A1
Barnard Cl SN3. . . . . . . .51 B7
Barnard Field SP4 . . . . 217 C2
Barnard Mews SP4 . . . 217 C2
Barnards Hill Dr SP2. . 145 C4
Barnard St **1** SP1 . . . 152 B8
Barn Cl
 Chippenham SN14 . . . . 78 A8
 Corsham SN13. . . . . . . 76 E1

Barncroft SP11. . . . . . 192 E3
Barn End SN14. . . . . . . .74 A8
Barnes Cl
 Corston SN16. . . . . 42 E4
 Trowbridge BA14. . . . . 105 A7
Barnes Gn SN15 . . . . . . .45 F6
Barnes Pl BA12. . . . . . 139 A5
Barnes Rd
 Chippenham SN14 . . . . 70 B2
 Swindon SN3 . . . . 36 B6
Barnes Wallis Cl
 9 Amesbury SP4 . . . 217 C3
 Melksham Without
  BA14 . . . . 178 B8
Barnes Yd **17** SN8. . . 170 A6
Barnetts Hill SN13. . . . .83 F7
Barnfield Cl SN2. . . . . . .49 F7
Barnfield Rd SN2. . . . . . .49 E7
Barnfield Way BA1. . . . .82 B4
Barn Glebe BA14 . . . . . 101 E1
Barn Hill SP3 . . . . 201 A3
Barn Moor Cl SN3 . . . . .51 E3
Barn Owl Rd SN14 . . . . .70 B2
Barn Piece
 Box SN13 . . . . 83 D6
 Bradford-on-Avon
  BA15 . . . . 100 D4
Barnsley Cl SN25 . . . . . .20 B1
Barn St SN8 . . . . 213 D3
Barnstaple Cl SN3 . . . . .51 B5
Barnum Ct
 2 Swindon SN1. . . . . 49 F7
 Swindon SN2 . . . . 50 A7
Barn Way BA14 . . . . . . 105 F7
Baroda Rd SP9 . . . . . . 216 A4
Baron Cl
 Lyneham SN15. . . . . . . 59 C4
 4 Swindon SN3 . . . . 36 B3
Barons Cres BA14. . . . 106 A8
Barons Mead SN14 . . . .78 A8
Barracks SN14. . . . . 74 F4
Barra Cl SN6 . . . . 22 E6
Barrett La SN15. . . . . . . 57 D2
Barrett Way SN4. . . . . . .64 B6
Barrington Cl SN3 . . . . .51 D3
Barrington La SN15. . . .57 C2
Barrington Rd SP1. . . . 146 C3
BARROW 136 C5
Barrowby Gate SN3. . . .36 A4
Barrow Cl
 Marlborough SN8. . . . . 213 D3
 Royal Wootton Bassett
  SN4 . . . . .47 B1
 Salisbury SP5. . . . . . . 152 C5
Barrow Gn SN15. . . . . . .70 E2
Barrow La BA9 . . . . . . 136 B5
Barrow St La
 Mere BA12. . . . . 139 F3
 West Knoyle BA12 . . . . 140 A4
Barrows La SP5. . . . . . 212 B7
BARROW STREET. . . . 139 F2
Barrow Water La
 Charlton Musgrove
  BA9 . . . . 136 A5
 Hardway BA10. . . . . . . 122 A1
Barry Glen Cl SN2 . . . . .35 E1
Barry Pl SN11. . . . . .79 F7
Barters La SP7. . . . . . . 206 D8
Bartholomew Way **4**
 SN13. . . . . .84 B8
Bartlett Cl **1** BA11. . . 110 C6
Bartlett Rd SP1. . . . . . 146 B4
Bartletts SN10. . . . . . . 179 C1
Bartletts Mead SN14 . . 178 A4
Bartletts The BA12. . . . 139 B4
Barton Cl
 12 Andover SP10. . . . 193 C2
 8 Bradford-on-Avon
  BA15 . . . . 100 C6
Barton Farm Ctry Pk★
 BA15. . . . . 100 A5
Barton Hill **22** SP7 . . 202 C2
Barton La BA12 . . . . . . 139 A5
Barton Lodge BA14 . . . 105 A6
Barton Orch BA15 . . . . 100 C6
Barton Pl SP4 . . . . 132 B1
Barton Rd SN25. . . . . . . 34 E3
Bartons Rd **20** SP6. . . 210 D1
Bartons The **29** SP6 . . 210 D1
Barton Way SN16. . . . . .42 E4
Barwell Ave SN1. . . . . . .49 E2
Basepoint Bsns Ctr
 SN5. . . . . .49 C8
Basevi Cl SN16. . . . . . . .27 F4
Bashkir Cl SN5 . . . . .34 C2
Bashkir Rd BA13. . . . . . 108 E1
Basil Cl SN2 . . . . 34 D4
Basil Hill Rd SN13. . . . . .84 C7
Basingstoke Cl **5**
 SN5. . . . . .49 A4
Baskerville Rd SN3 . . . .51 E7
Bassett Rd OX12 . . . . . 165 F8
Bassetts Pasture
 BA15. . . . . 100 C6
Bassetts The SN13. . . . .83 D6
Batch The BA12. . . . . . . .98 F1
Bates Way SN25 . . . . . . 34 E3
Bathampton St SN1. . . .50 B6
BATHEASTON. 82 B4
BATHFORD 82 C2
Bathford CE VC Prim Sch
 BA1. . . . . .82 C2
Bathford Hill BA1. . . . . .82 B2
Bath Rd
 Atworth SN12 . . . . 84 D1
 Atworth SN12 . . . . 84 E1
 Atworth/Whitley SN12 . .93 A3
 Box SN13 . . . . 83 A6

Bath Rd *continued*
Bradford-on-Avon BA15. **91** C1
Chippenham Without
SN14 . . . . **77** F5
Colerne SN14. . . . . **74** F3
Corsham SN13 . . . . **77** B4
Cricklade SN6 . . . . **19** D8
Devizes SN10. . . . . . **179** C8
Frome BA11. . . . . **110** A6
Hinton Charterhouse
BA2 . . . . **98** D3
Hungerford RG17. . . . **176** F7
Marlborough SN8. . . . **213** D8
Melksham SN12. . . . . . **94** A5
Melksham Without SN12 **93** F2
Preshute SN8. . . . . . . **174** C7
Royal Wootton Bassett
SN4 . . . . **47** C1
Seend SN12 . . . . **95** C1
Swindon SN1 . . . . **50** C4
Upton Scudamore
BA12 . . . . **112** D2
Warminster BA12 . . . **112** E1
Westonbirt with Lasborough
GL8. . . . . **25** D8
Bath Rd Ind Est SN14. .**78** B6
Bath Road
Chippenham SN14 . . . . . **77** E5
Knockdown GL8. . . . . . .**24** F5
Bath Road Retail Pk
SN14. . . . . **77** F4
Bath Spa University
(Corsham Court)
SN13. . . . . **77** A2
Bath Stone Cres [1]
SN13. . . . .**76** D1
Bathurst Rd SN1. . . . . **50** D6
Batsford Cres [8] SN25 .**35** B8
Batten Rd SP5. . . . . . **211** A8
Battens The [3] SN14. . .**70** A1
Battlesbury Barracks
BA12. . . . . **117** E6
Battlesbury Hill Fort ★
BA12. . . . . **117** F8
Battlesbury Rd
Warminster BA12 . . . . **113** E1
Warminster BA12 . . . . **117** E2
Battlewell SN5. . . . . . .**33** A3
Batt's La SN8. . . . . . **183** F7
BAVERSTOCK **142** B4
Baverstock La SP3. . . **142** B5
Bawdsey Rd [6] SP4 . . **217** D2
Baxter Cl SN25. . . . . . .**35** A7
Bay Cl SN11 . . . .**89** C8
BAYDON **170** C8
Baydon Cl
Swindon SN25 . . . .**34** F3
Trowbridge BA14. . . . **105** C5
Baydon Gr SN11. . . . . .**81** B4
Baydon Rd
Aldbourne SN8. . . . . . **164** B1
Great Shefford RG17. . **171** F3
Baydon St Nicholas CE
Prim Sch SN8 . . . . . **164** C1
Baydons La SN15. . . . . **78** E6
Bayes Cl SN25 . . . .**20** C1
Bayfield SN5. . . . . **34** B2
Bayleaf Ave SN2. . . . . . **34** D4
Bayliffes Cl SN15. . . . . .**79** A7
Baynton Cl BA13. . . . **109** B5
Baynton Way BA13. . **186** D8
Bayntun Cl
Bromham SN15. . . . . . . **96** A7
Devizes SN10. . . . . . . **214** C1
Baytree Cl BA12. . . . . **115** C7
Bay Tree Cl SN2. . . . . . **35** C2
Baywater SN8. . . . . . . **213** E4
Bazaar Rd SP9. . . . . . **216** B5
Beacon Cl
Amesbury SP4. . . . . . **217** C4
[8] Swindon SN1 . . . . . .**49** F4
Beacon Ct SP6. . . . . . **210** D2
Beacon Dr SN11. . . . . .**89** C8
BEACON HILL
Bromham **97** B7
Bulford **199** A7
Hilmarton **73** E5
Beacon Hill Rd [7]
SP4. . . . . **198** F7
Beaconsfield Way
BA11. . . . . **110** B7
Beacon View BA12. . . **116** D6
Beale Cl SN14. . . . .**78** B7
Beale Ct SN14. . . . . **78** A7
Beale Rd SP9 . . . . **216** D8
Beale's Barton BA14. . **101** F8
Beales Cl SN1. . . . .**50** B7
Beales Farm Rd [15]
RG17. . . . . **165** A1
Beamish Cl [2] SN11. . **166** A1
BEANACRE **94** A8
Beanacre Old Manor ★
SN12. . . . . **94** A8
Beanacre Rd
Melksham SN12. . . . . . . **94** A7
Melksham Without SN12 **86** A1
Beaney Vw [1] SN2 . . . . **34** E2
Beanlands The SN4 . . **163** A6
Bear Cl BA15 . . . . **100** B7
Beard Ct SP11. . . . . . **192** B5
Beardsley La SN26. . . . **20** D1
Bearfield Bldgs BA15 **100** C8
Bearfield La RG17 . . . **171** A4
Bearwater RG17 . . . . **177** B7
Beatrice Rd SP1. . . . . **146** A4
Beatrice St SN2. . . . . . .**50** C8
Beatrice Way BA14 . . **105** E8

Beatty Ct SN3 . . . . **50** D4
Beauchamp Dr [1]
SP4 . . . . **217** D3
Beauchamp-Proctor Rise
[8] SP4 . . . . **132** B1
Beauclerc St SN10. . . **179** D8
Beaufort Ave SN4. . . . .**61** E8
Beaufort Cl [5] SN12 . **178** B8
Beaufort Rd SN4. . . . . .**64** A7
Beaufort Vw SN14. . . . **39** E4
Beaufoy [1] SP7 . . . . . **202** D2
Beaulieu Cl SN5. . . . . . **49** C4
Beaulieu Rd [2] SP4. . **217** C2
Beaumaris Rd SN5. . . . **49** B5
Beaumont Rd SN3. . . . **50** E6
Beaumont Way SP4. . **217** D2
Beaven Cl SN15. . . . . . .**78** F4
Beavens Ct BA14. . . . . **117** B7
Bechstein Mdw BA14 **106** A8
Beck Cl SN25. . . . . **35** A3
Beckerley La BA14. . . . .**92** F1
Beckett Pl BA13. . . . . **108** F1
Beckett's La SP3. . . . . . **50** C5
Beckett St [14] SP3. . . **203** E8
Beckett Strand SN1. . . **49** E2
Becket Way SP1. . . . . **146** D1
Beckford Cl
Tisbury SP3 . . . . **200** D1
Warminster BA12 . . . **117** B6
BECKHAMPTON **173** B7
Beckhampton (Long
Barrow) ★ SN8 . . . . **173** A8
Beckhampton Rd
SN8. . . . . **173** B8
Beckhampton St SN1 . .**50** C6
Beddington Ct SN2 . . . .**36** A5
Beddoe Cl BA15 . . . . . **100** E4
Bede Dr [7] SP10. . . . . **193** C2
Bedford Cl [2] SP6 . . . **210** D2
Bedford Rd
Salisbury SP2. . . . . . . **145** E2
[9] Swindon SN3 . . . . . .**50** F6
Bedlam Green Farm La
BA10. . . . . **136** B8
Bedlam La SN6. . . . . . . **22** D8
Bedwin St SN1. . . . . . **146** B1
Bedwyn Cl SN2. . . . . . . **35** C3
Bedwyn Dyke ★ SN8 . **176** C3
Bedwyn Sta SN8. . . . . **176** B3
Bedwyn Stone Mus ★
SN8. . . . . **176** B2
Beech Ave
Melksham SN12. . . . . . . **94** A3
Swindon SN2 . . . .**35** A2
Warminster BA12. . . . **116** F6
Beech Cl
Andover SP11 . . . . **193** B1
Porton SP4. . . . . **133** D6
Beechcroft Cl SP10 . . . **193** B1
Beechcroft Inf Sch
SN25. . . . . **35** E4
Beechcroft Rd
Salisbury SP1. . . . . . . **146** B1
Swindon SN2 . . . .**35** E4
Beech Ct BA11. . . . . . . **110** B7
Beech Dr SN5. . . . .**34** A2
Beeches Cl SP5. . . . . . **148** C3
Beeches Gn SN12. . . . . **93** D8
Beeches La SN15 . . . . . .**59** A5
Beeches The
Bradford-on-Avon
BA15 . . . . **101** A7
Coombe Bissett SP5. . **156** F7
Lydiard Millicent SN5. . **48** F7
Melksham Without SN12 **93** C7
[5] Salisbury SP1 . . . . **152** C8
[15] Shaftesbury SP7 . . **202** C2
Trowbridge BA14. . . . **101** F2
Warminster BA12 . . . **116** F6
[4] West Wellow SO51 .**212** F6
Beechfield SN1. . . . . . **101** A7
Beechfield Dr SN10. . . **214** E5
Beechfield Rd
Corsham SN13. . . . . **76** E1
Roundway SN10. . . . . . **214** E7
Beech Gr
Highworth SN6. . . . .**22** F5
Trowbridge BA14. . . . **105** B6
Beech Grange SP5. . . **212** C5
Beechgrove BA12. . . . **117** B8
Beech Hanger SP4. . . **199** C5
Beech Hill Rd SP9 . . . **216** E7
BEECHINGSTOKE . . . **181** A6
Beech Lea
Broad Blunsdon SN26 . . **21** C1
Meysey Hampton GL7 . . **1** A4
Beech Rd
Box SN13. . . . . **84** A8
Colerne SN14. . . . .**75** A5
Corsham SN13 . . . . **83** E7
Beech Sq [12] RG17 . . . **177** B6
Beech Wlk
Durnford SP4. . . . . . . **131** C1
Salterton SP4. . . . . . . **131** E4
Salterton SP4. . . . . . . **132** A4
Beechwood [13] SP6 . . **210** C1
Beech Wood [8] SN10 **179** F1
Beechwood Ave
BA11. . . . . **110** A5
Beechwood Cl
Frome BA11. . . . . **110** A5
Roundway SN10. . . . . . **214** E6
Beechwood Rd SN14. . .**78** B8
Beehive Cl [1] SN5 . . . . .**49** A8
Begle Cl [9] SN25 . . . . . .**34** F7
Belcombe Ct ★ BA15. . **100** B6
Belcombe Pl BA15. . . . **100** C6

Belcombe Rd
Avoncliff BA15 . . . .**99** F5
Bradford-on-Avon
BA15 . . . . **100** B6
Belfast Mead SN15. . . . **60** C2
Belfry Dr SN14. . . . .**41** E1
Belgrave Cres SP9. . . **216** E6
Belgrave St SN1. . . . . . **50** C5
Bellamy La SP1. . . . . . **152** B8
Bell Cl BA12 . . . . **117** B6
Bellefield CE Prim Sch
BA14. . . . . **101** E2
Bellefield Cres BA14. . **101** D1
Belle Vue Rd
Salisbury SP1. . . . . . . **146** A1
Swindon SN1 . . . .**50** D4
Bell Field The SN14 . . . **39** E4
Bell Gdns SN3. . . . . **36** E4
Bell Hill
Seend SN12 . . . . **178** E7
Warminster BA12 . . . **116** F5
Bellinger Cl SN15. . . . . **70** C3
Bellingham La SN6 . . . . **23** A2
Bell La
Inkpen RG17 . . . . **177** E2
Lechlade GL7 . . . .**2** C3
Liddington SN4. . . . . . **163** A4
Sutton Benger SN15. . . **57** D2
[6] Wilton SP2 . . . . . . **144** D3
Bellot Dr
[3] Corsham SN13. . . . . **76** E1
Corsham SN13 . . . . **84** E8
Bellott Dr SN13. . . . . . . **84** E8
Bell Piece SN15. . . . . . . **57** D2
Bell Rd SP4. . . . . **197** F7
Bells La BA12. . . . . . . **137** F7
Bell Sq SN14. . . . . **74** A8
Bell St
[4] Ludgershall SP11 . . **192** B5
Shaftesbury SP7 . . . . . **202** C2
Bellver SN5. . . . .**49** B5
Belmont Cl
[10] Shaftesbury SP7. . **202** C1
Swindon SN3 . . . . **36** A4
Belmont Cres SN1 . . . . **50** A3
Belsay SN5. . . . . **49** C4
Belthane Pl SN12. . . . . **93** C8
Belvedere Rd
Bowerhill SN12 . . . . **94** D1
Swindon SN3 . . . . **51** A3
Belvedere Terr SN10. . **214** C4
Bembridge Cl SN3 . . . . **51** B4
BEMERTON **145** C2
BEMERTON HEATH . . **145** C4
Bemerton St John CE
Aided Prim Sch
SP2. . . . . **145** C2
Bences La SN13. . . . . . . **77** A2
Benches La
Ashmore SP5. . . . . . . **206** F4
Tollard Royal SP5. . . . **207** B4
Bencroft Hill
Bremhill SN15. . . . . **80** B6
Stanley SN15. . . . . **79** F6
Ben Cross SN13. . . . . . . **83** B7
Bendall's La SN13. . . . . **82** F7
Bendy Bow SN16. . . . . . **15** F7
Benin Rd SP11. . . . . . . **191** F3
Benjamin St BA15. . . . **100** E6
Ben La SP5. . . . . **154** F7
Ben Lane SP5 . . . . **155** A6
Bennett Cl SN5 . . . . . . **211** C7
Bennett Hill Cl [3] SN4 . **47** F2
Bentham Cl SN5 . . . . . . **49** D6
Bentham La SN5. . . . . . **33** A8
Bentley Cl SN3 . . . . **51** A4
Bentley Gr SN11 . . . . . . **81** C2
Bentley La
Calne SN11 . . . . **81** B1
Quemerford SN11 . . . . . **89** B8
Bentley Way SP5 . . . . **149** D5
Bentley Woods SP5. . . **155** C6
Benwell Cl SN5. . . . . . . **49** C6
Beranburh Field SN4 . . **64** E2
Berengaria Cl BA13 . . **109** B5
Berenger Cl SN3 . . . . . . **50** D3
Beresford Cl [1] SN3 . . **51** C4
Bergamot St SN4 . . . . **174** C7
Bergman Cl SN25 . . . . . **35** B6
Berhills La SN10 . . . . . . **95** F2
Bericot La SN4 . . . . **65** E6
Berkeley Cl
Melksham SN12. . . . . . . **94** A2
South Cerney SN5. . . . . . .**6** F6
Berkeley Lawns SN3 . . **50** F3
Berkeley Rd
Trowbridge BA14. . . . **105** A8
Wroughton SN4. . . . . . **64** B7
Berkely Cl [2] SN14. . . . **78** A7
BERKLEY **111** A7
Berkley CE Fst Sch
BA11. . . . . **111** A7
Berkley Cross BA11. . . **110** F6
BERKLEY DOWN. **110** D8
Berkley La BA11. . . . . **110** D8
Berkley Rd BA11. . . . . **107** B1
Berkshire Dr SN5. . . . . **49** D7
Berkshire Rd SP2. . . . **151** E7
Bermerton Heath &
Barnards Folly Nature
Reserve ★ SN2 . . . . . **145** C4
Berrington Rd SN3. . . . **51** A3
Berry Cl [4] SP4. . . . . . **190** A3
Berrycroft
Ashbury SN6. . . . . **164** A7

Berrycroft *continued*
Mildenhall SN8. . . . . . **175** B8
BERRYFIELD **93** F1
Berryfield Cl SN12. . . . **93** F1
Berryfield La SN12. . . . **93** F1
Berryfield Pk SN12. . . . **93** F1
Berryfield Rd BA15 . . . **100** D8
Berry Rd BA13 . . . . . . **186** D8
Berry Wood La SP7. . . **203** A3
Bertha's Field GL9 . . . . **24** B4
Berton Cl SN2. . . . .**21** C2
BERWICK BASSETT . . **167** B4
Berwick La
Steeple Langford SP3 . **128** D7
Steeple Langford SP3 . **196** C1
Berwick Rd
Berwick St James
SP3. . . . . **196** E2
Stapleford SP3. . . . . . **129** E2
BERWICK ST JAMES . **196** E2
BERWICK ST JOHN . . **203** E1
BERWICK ST
LEONARD **200** C4
Besomer Dro SP5. . . . **211** D6
Bessemer Cl SN2. . . . . . **35** A1
Bessemer Rd E SN2. . . . **35** A1
Bessemer Rd W SN2. . . **34** F1
Bess Rd SN5. . . . . **48** F4
Bests La BA12 . . . . **117** F1
Best's La BA12. . . . . . **194** A5
Bethel Rd SN13. . . . . . . **76** E1
Betjeman Ave SN4. . . . . **47** E3
Betjeman Rd SN8. . . . . **213** A2
Betony Cl SN25. . . . . . . **34** E5
Bettertons Cl GL7. . . . . . .**1** F7
Bevan Cl SN2. . . . . **35** F3
Beverley SN5. . . . . **49** C4
Beverley Cl SN12. . . . . . **94** C1
Beverley Cres SN9. . . . **182** B2
Beverley Hills Mobile
Home Pk SN4 . . . . . . **217** D3
Beverley Way SN14 . . . . **77** F5
Beversbrook La SN11. . . **81** A5
Beversbrook Rd SN11. . **81** A5
Beverstone Cl SP2. . . . . . .**6** F6
Beverstone Gr SN3 . . . . **50** F4
Beverstone Rd ★ SN6 . . .**6** F5
Bevil SN5. . . . . **49** A3
Bevisbury Hill Fort ★
SP11. . . . . **185** A1
Bevisland SN3. . . . . **51** C3
Bewick Cl GL7. . . . .**7** A6
BEWLEY COMMON. . . . **86** E5
Bewley Ct ★ SN15. . . . . . **86** F6
Bewley Edge SN15. . . . . **87** A4
Bewley Rd SN15. . . . . . . **86** F5
Beyer Rd [5] SP4. . . . . **217** D2
Bibby Dr SP9 . . . . **216** D8
Bibury Rd SN3. . . . . **50** E5
Bicton Rd SN5. . . . . **34** F6
Biddel La BA12. . . . . . **195** D6
Biddesden La SP11 . . . **192** C5
BIDDESTONE **76** F7
Biddestone La SN14. . . . **68** C3
Biddestone Manor ★
SN14. . . . . **76** F7
Biddulph Rd SP4. . . . . **198** A4
Bideford Cl SN3 . . . . . . **51** A5
Big La RG17 . . . . **165** A2
Bigpool La SN13. . . . . . **83** A4
Bilborough Dr [2] SN3 . .**50** F5
Bill Turpin Ct SN3 . . . . **51** B4
Bimport SP7. . . . . **202** B1
Bincknoll Cl SN5. . . . . . **48** B1
Bincknoll La SN5. . . . . . **48** A1
Bindon Cl SN5. . . . . **49** A5
Bingham Rd
Durrington SN4. . . . . . **197** E7
Salisbury SP1. . . . . . . **146** C4
Binknoll La SN4 . . . . . . **47** F1
Birch Ash SN2. . . . . **35** F2
Birch Cl SN13. . . . . **84** C5
Birchenleaze BA14. . . **105** C3
Birches The SN3. . . . . . **51** B2
Birch Gdns BA14. . . . **102** B2
Birch Glade SN6. . . . . . . **17** F8
Birch Gr
Bower Hill SN12. . . . . . . **94** C1
Chippenham SN15 . . . . **70** E1
Whaddon SP5. . . . . . . **153** E2
Birchill La BA11 . . . . . **110** A1
Birch St SN1. . . . . **49** F5
Birch Wlk [4] BA11 . . . **110** B7
Birchwood Cl BA12 . . . **115** C7
Birchwood Dr [4]
SP4. . . . . **198** C2
Birchwood Rd SN3. . . . . **36** B2
Birdbrook Rd SN2. . . . . **35** E5
BIRDBUSH **203** B1
Birdcombe Rd [1] SN5. **49** C5
Birds Marsh View
SN15. . . . . **70** E2
Birkdale Cl [5] SN25. . . **34** C7
Bisham La BA14 . . . . . **106** A8
Bishopdale Cl [2] SN5. . **34** A1
BISHOPDOWN **146** C4
Bishopdown Rd SP1 . . **146** B3
Bishop Rd SN11. . . . . . . **81** B4
BISHOPS
CANNINGS. **172** B3
Bishops Cannings CE
(Aided) Prim Sch
SN10. . . . . **172** B3

Bishops Cannings CE Pri
Sch SN10. . . . . **172** B3
Bishops Cl
Chippenham SN15 . . . . **78** F4
Mere BA12. . . . . **139** A6
Tidworth SP9 . . . . **216** D4
Bishops Dr SP2. . . . . . **151** F6
Bishopsfield [6] SN6 . . **19** D8
Bishopsmead SN4. . . . **101** C5
Bishops Mead SP1. . . **146** E4
Bishop's Palace ★
SP1. . . . . **152** A7
BISHOPSTONE
Shaftesbury **205** F4
Swindon **163** E6
Bishopstone CE Prim Sch
SN6. . . . . **163** E6
Bishopstone Hollow
SN6. . . . . **205** E3
BISHOPSTROW. **117** E4
Bishopstrow Coll
BA12. . . . . **117** E4
Bishopstrow Ct BA12 **117** E5
Bishopstrow Rd
BA12. . . . . **117** E4
Bishop's Wlk SP1. . . . **152** A8
Bishop Wordsworth's
Gram Sch SP1. . . . . **152** A8
Bisley SN16. . . . . **29** A6
Bisley Cl SN3. . . . . **51** A5
Biss Cl BA12 . . . . **117** B6
Biss Meadow BA14 . . . **105** A8
Bitham Brook Prim Sch
BA13. . . . . **109** B4
Bitham La
Ham RG17 . . . . **177** A3
Westbury BA13 . . . . . **109** A3
Bitham Mill BA13 . . . . **109** B3
Bitham Pk BA13 . . . . . **109** B4
Bittern Cl GL7. . . . .**7** A6
Bittern Rd SN3. . . . . **51** E6
BITTLES GREEN **202** B4
Black Acre [4] SN13. . . **84** E8
Blackbarn Rd SP4 . . . . **134** B5
Blackberry Cl SN14. . . . **70** A2
Blackberry La
Brinkworth SN16. . . . . . **30** F3
Brinkworth SN16. . . . . . **31** A2
Potterne SN10. . . . . . . **179** D5
Winsley BA15. . . . . **90** C1
Blackbird Cl
[7] Melksham SN12. . . **94** D5
Swindon SN3 . . . . **51** D7
Blackbird Way BA11 . . **110** B6
Blackboard La SN10 . . **180** B4
Black Bridge Rd SN15 . **78** F8
Blackcross SN15. . . . . . . **78** F6
Blackcross Rd SP4. . . . **217** C2
Black Dog Hill
Calne Without SN11. . . .**80** D2
Chapmanslade BA13 . . **111** E6
Blackdown Cl [10]
BA12. . . . . **117** A8
Blackford Dr SN11. . . . . **81** B4
Blackford La SN6. . . . . . **18** C4
Blackfriars Way SP1 . . **152** B8
Blackhill Rd SO51. . . . **212** F3
Black Horse La
Westbury BA13 . . . . . **108** D1
Westbury BA13 . . . . . **112** E8
Winterbourne SP4. . . . **146** F4
Blackhorse Way
Swindon SN1 . . . . **49** F1
Swindon SN1 . . . . **50** A1
Black La
Pitton & Farley SP5. . . **148** C4
Redlynch SP5. . . . . . . **211** E6
BLACKLAND **89** C6
Blacklands Crossroads
SN11. . . . . **89** C6
Blackman Gdns SN1 . . **50** D3
Blackman's La [4]
SN8. . . . . **183** D8
Blackmoor Copse Nature
Reserve ★ SP5. . . . . **155** A7
Blackmore Cl [1] SN3 . **51** C4
Blackmore La SN8 . . . **192** A7
Blackmore Rd
Melksham SN12. . . . . . . **94** C4
[3] Shaftesbury SP7. . **202** D2
Blacksmith Cl SN14 . . . **68** F5
Blackstone Ave SN3 . . **51** C4
Blackthorn Cl SN14 . . . **47** E4
Blackthorn La SN25. . . **35** A3
Blackthorn Mews
SN15. . . . . **78** F5
Blackthorn Way
BA14. . . . . **101** D4
Blackwell Cl SN25. . . . . **20** B1
Blackworth SN6. . . . . . . **22** F8
Bladen Cl SN4. . . . . **63** F7
Blagdon Wlk BA11. . . . **110** C7
Blagrove Ind Est SN1. . **49** A2
Blain Pl
Royal Wootton Bassett
SN4 . . . . **47** F1
Royal Wootton Bassett
SN4 . . . . **47** F2
Blair Rd BA14. . . . . . . **105** B7
Blake Cres SN3. . . . . . . **36** C2
Blake Ct BA14. . . . . . . **101** D4
Blakehill Farm Nature
Reserve ★ SN6 . . . . . . **19** A3
Blakeney Ave SN3. . . . . **51** B7
Blakesley Cl [3] SN3. . . **50** F4
Blakey Rd SP1. . . . . . . **152** C8
Blanchard Rd SN26. . . . **20** B1

Blandford Alley SN6 . . **23** A5
Blandford Ct SN3 . . . . . **51** B6
Blandford Rd
Bishopstone SP5 . . . . **205** F1
Coombe Bissett SP5 . . **150** F1
Martin Drove End SP6 . **209** A8
Blatchs Orch [18]
BA13. . . . . **186** B7
Blaygrove Ind Est SN1 **49** A2
Bleak St BA9 . . . . **137** C3
Blease Cl BA14. . . . . . **101** D4
BLEET **102** F2
Bleke St SP7. . . . . **202** C2
Blendon Dr SN11 . . . . . **80** F3
Blenheim Gdns SN14. . **56** C6
Blenheim Pk [21]
SN12. . . . . **178** B8
Blenheim Rd
Marlborough SN8. . . . **213** F2
Warminster BA12 . . . . **113** E1
Warminster BA12 . . . . **117** D8
Wroughton SN4. . . . . . **64** A7
Blenhiem Cl BA12 . . . . **117** A8
Bletchley Cl [5] SN3. . . **51** C4
Blicks Cl SN14. . . . . **41** F1
Blicks Hill SN16. . . . . . . **28** B3
Blick's Hill SN16. . . . . . **28** B4
Blind La
Ansty SP3. . . . . **203** F5
Berwick St John SP7 . . **207** B8
Southwick BA14. . . . . **104** F2
Blissford Rd SP6. . . . . **210** F1
Blissmore La [8] SP11 **192** F1
Block Rd [6] SP4 . . . . . **197** E7
Bloody Shard Gate
DT11. . . . . **207** A1
Bloomsbury Ct [2] SN4 **59** B4
Blossom Dr [9] SN13 . . **76** D1
Blounts Ct SN10 . . . . . **179** D5
Blowhorn St SN8. . . . . **213** D4
Bluebell Dr SN14. . . . . . **70** B3
Bluebell Gr SN11 . . . . . . **81** B5
Bluebell Mead [7]
SN13. . . . . **84** E8
Bluebell Way [27] SP4 . **198** D5
Blueberry Rd SN12. . . . . **94** D3
Blue Boar Row SP1. . . **146** A1
BLUE VEIN **83** D3
Blunsdon Abbey SN25 .**34** F8
Blunsdon Hill SN26. . . . **20** F3
BLUNSDON ST
ANDREW **34** E8
Blunsdon Sta SN5 . . . . . **33** F8
Blunt Rise SN26. . . . . . . **21** D2
Blythe Cl
[10] Cricklade SN6. . . . . **19** D8
Enham Alamein SP11. . **193** C3
Blyth Way SP1. . . . . . . **146** D1
BMI The Ridgeway Hospl
SN4. . . . . **64** C6
Boardleaze BA12 . . . . **195** A2
Boar St BA12 . . . . **139** A5
Boatman Cl SN25. . . . . . **34** A7
Bobbin La BA15. . . . . . . **99** F4
Bobbin Pk BA15. . . . . . . **99** F3
Bockhampton Rd
RG17. . . . . **165** A1
Bockhampton Village ★
RG17. . . . . **165** B1
BODENHAM **152** F1
Bodiam Dr SN5. . . . . . . **49** D4
Bodiam Dr N [4] SN5 . . **49** D4
Bodiam Dr S [3] SN5 . . **49** D4
Bodkin Hazel La GL9. . .**38** A6
Bodman Cl SN15. . . . . . **78** F4
Bodmin Cl SN1. . . . . **51** A6
Bodyhorse Hill SN4 . . . **163** C6
BOHEMIA **211** E6
Bohemia La SP5. . . . . . **211** D6
Bokerley Ditch ★
SP5. . . . . **209** A5
Bokerley Junc SP5. . . . **208** E6
Boldrewood SN3. . . . . . **51** D3
Bolehyde Manor ★
SN14. . . . . **69** C4
Boleyn Cl SN5. . . . . **49** A6
Bolingbroke Cl SN5. . . . **47** F6
Bolingbroke Rd SN2 . . . **34** F2
Bolland Cl SN8 . . . . . . **176** B2
Bolland's Hill SN12. . . **178** D8
Bonaker Cl SP4. . . . . . **133** D6
Bond St Bldgs BA14. . **105** C7
Bond St
Durrington/Bulford
SN4 . . . . **198** E6
Trowbridge BA14. . . . **105** C7
Boness Rd SN4 . . . . **64** A7
Bonham Cl SP2. . . . . . **129** F4
Bonham La BA12 . . . . . **137** E7
Bonner Cl [10] SN5. . . . **48** F5
Bonners Cl SN16. . . . . . **28** A5
Bonnewe Rise SP4. . . . **217** D3
Bonnie Pk BA13 . . . . . **186** B8
Boothmead SN14. . . . . . **78** B8
Borage Cl SN2. . . . . **34** D5
Border Cl SN25. . . . . . . **34** C5
Border La BA10. . . . . . **122** C7
BOREHAM **117** C5
Boreham Field BA12. . **117** D6
Boreham Rd
Warminster BA12 . . . . **117** C5
Warminster BA12 . . . . **117** E5
Warminster BA12 . . . . **117** F5

Bore Hill BA12 . . . . . . 116 F4
Boreland Hill
  Great Durnford SP4 . . 197 D1
  Upper Woodford SP4 . . 131 B8
Boreway Cl SN4 . . . . 50 B4
Borkum Cl 8 SP10 . . 193 D2
Borough Fields SN4 . . 47 D2
Borough Parade Sh Ctr
  SN15 . . . . 78 D7
Borough The SP5 . . . . 211 A8
Borrowes Cl 2 SN13. . . . 84 F8
BOSCOMBE 199 A1
Boscombe Down Airfield
  SP4 . . . . 198 E3
Boscombe Rd
  Amesbury SP4 . . . . . 217 C3
  Swindon SN25 . . . . 34 E4
Bosham Cl 6 SN5 . . . . . 49 B4
Boswell Rd BA15 . . . . . . 99 F3
Bosworth Rd SN5 . . . . . 49 A5
Botany SN6 . . . . 22 E5
Bothwell Rd SN3 . . . . . . 50 F7
Botisdone Cl SP11 . . . 185 C3
Botley Copse 1 SN5 . . . 34 A2
Bottlebush La BH21 . . . 208 E1
BOTTLESFORD 181 D6
Bottom La
  Ogbourne St George
    SN8 . . . . 169 A5
  1 Swindon SN1 . . . . . 50 C3
Bouchers Way SP2 . . . 152 A5
Boulevard The 8
  SN25 . . . . 34 C5
Boulsbury Farm Rd
  SP6 . . . . 209 E3
Boulton Cl BA13 . . . . . 108 E1
Boundary Ave BA11 . . . 110 B5
Boundary Cl
  Lyneham SN15 . . . . 59 C3
  Swindon SN2 . . . . 35 F6
Boundary Rd
  Chippenham SN15 . . . . . 78 F8
  Salisbury SP1 . . . . 146 E2
Boundary Wlk BA14 . . . 105 C4
Bourbon Cl BA12 . . . . . 117 B5
Bourne Ave SP1 . . . . . . 146 C2
Bourne Cl
  Porton SP4 . . . . 133 D6
  1 Salisbury SP1 . . . . . 152 B8
  Warminster BA12 . . . . . 117 A5
  3 West Wellow SO51. . 212 F6
Bourne Gdns SP4 . . . . . 133 D6
Bourne Hill SP1 . . . . . . 146 B1
Bourne La 6 SP9 . . . . . 199 D8
Bourne Lake Pk SN6 . . . . 18 E6
Bourne Pk★ SP11 . . . . 193 F6
Bourne Rd
  Swindon SN2 . . . . 34 F2
  Tidworth SP9 . . . . 216 D6
Bourne Ret Pk SP1 . . . . 152 D7
Bourne Rise SN8 . . . . . 183 E1
Bourne Vale RG17 . . . . 177 B7
Bourne Valley Cl
  SP4 . . . . 133 E5
Bourne View SP4 . . . . . 199 A1
Bourne Way SP1 . . . . . . 152 D7
BOURTON
  Bishops Cannings 172 C3
  Bourton 137 E2
Bourton Ave SN3 . . . . . . 36 B2
Bourton La SN10 . . . . . 172 C3
Bouverie Ave
  Harnham SP2 . . . . 151 F6
  Salisbury SP2 . . . . 152 A6
  Swindon SN3 . . . . 50 B7
Bouverie Ave S SP2 . . . 151 F5
Bouverie Cl SP2 . . . . . . 151 F6
Bouverie Dr 17 SN10 . . 179 F1
Bouverie Pk SN14 . . . . . 56 B5
BOVERIDGE 209 B1
Bow Ct SN1 . . . . 50 C4
Bowden Cres SN12 . . . . 94 C6
BOWDEN HILL 87 B4
Bowden Hill
  Bewley Common SN15. . . 86 F5
  Bowden Hill SN15 . . . . . 87 B5
Bowden Pk★ SN15 . . . . 87 B5
Bowdich Cl SP4 . . . . . . 198 C7
Bowd's La SN15 . . . . 60 A6
BOWERCHALKE 205 A2
Bower Gdns SP1 . . . . . . 152 C8
BOWERHILL 94 D1
Bowerhill Ind Est
  SN12 . . . . 94 C1
Bowerhill La SN12 . . . . . 94 E1
Bowerhill Prim Sch
  SN12 . . . . 94 C1
Bower Hill Rd SP1 . . . . . 146 C2
Bower Rd SN8 . . . . 175 D5
Bowers Hill SP5 . . . . . . 211 D8
Bowers La SP11 . . . . . . 185 B4
Bowes Lyon Ct SP2 . . . . 145 D3
BOWLDOWN 70 E8
Bowldown Rd GL8 . . . . . 25 F8
Bowles Rd SN25 . . . . . . 35 A5
Bowleymead SN3 . . . . . . 51 D5
Bowling Gn La
  Pentridge SP5 . . . . . . 208 D5
  Swindon SN1 . . . . 50 C3
Bowls Barrow (Long
  Barrow)★ BA12 . . . . . 186 E1
Bowman Cl 5 SN3 . . . . . 36 B3
Bowman Ct SN4 . . . . 47 C1
Bowmans Ct SN12 . . . . . 94 C6
Bowood Cl SN11 . . . . . . 79 F3

Bowood House & Gdns★
  SN11 . . . . 88 C8
Bowood Rd SN11 . . . . . . 50 B4
Bow Wow GL7 . . . . 7 A7
BOX 83 D6
Boxbush Cl GL7 . . . . 7 A7
Boxbush Rd GL7 . . . . 7 A7
Box CE Prim Sch
  SN13 . . . . 83 C6
Box Dr SN8 . . . . 213 D8
Boxfields Rd SN13 . . . . . 83 F7
BOX HILL 83 F7
Box Hill
  Box SN13 . . . . 76 A1
  Corsham SN13 . . . . 83 E7
Box Rd BA1 . . . . 82 C3
Box View SN14 . . . . 75 B2
Boydell Cl SN5 . . . . 49 B8
Boyd Rd BA13 . . . . 109 B5
Boyle Ave 4 SN13 . . . . 166 A1
Boyne's La DT11 . . . . . 206 B1
BOYTON 194 E2
Bozley Hill SP7 . . . . . . 206 A8
Brabant Way 4
  BA13 . . . . 108 E1
Brackenbury 8
  SP10 . . . . 193 C1
Brackenbury Rd SP4 . . . 197 E7
Bracken Cl SP5 . . . . . . 153 D3
Brackland SN10 . . . . . . 180 A2
Bradbury Cl SN5 . . . . . . 49 A5
Bradene Cl 3 SN4 . . . . . 47 C1
Bradenham Rd SN5 . . . . 49 A5
BRADENSTOKE 59 C3
Bradenstoke Abbey★
  SN15 . . . . 59 B3
Bradfield Cl BA12 . . . . . 117 D5
BRADFORD LEIGH 91 F1
BRADFORD-ON-
  AVON 100 E6
Bradford-on-Avon Mus★
  BA15 . . . . 100 C6
Bradford-on-Avon Sta
  BA15 . . . . 100 C6
Bradford-on-Avon
  Swimming Pool
    BA15 . . . . 100 C6
Bradford Rd
  Atworth SN12 . . . . 92 E7
  Bathford BA1 . . . . 82 B2
  Box SN13 . . . . 83 F3
  Broughton Gifford SN12 . 93 F4
  Corsham SN13 . . . . 76 C1
  Melksham SN12 . . . . . . 94 A5
  Rode BA11 . . . . 103 F1
  Swindon SN1 . . . . 50 C4
  Wingfield BA14 . . . . . . 104 C8
  Wingfield BA15 . . . . . . 100 C2
  Winsley BA15 . . . . 99 D6
Bradford Wood La
  BA15 . . . . 100 C6
Bradford-on-Avon
  BA15 . . . . 101 A6
Bradley Cl
  Holt BA14 . . . . 101 F8
  Warminster BA12 . . . . . 116 E4
Bradley La
  Holt BA14 . . . . 92 F1
  Kingston Deverill BA12 125 A8
  Kingston Deverill BA12 125 F8
  Maiden Bradley BA11 . 118 A4
  Maiden Bradley BA12 . 119 C1
  Maiden Bradley with
    Yarnfield BA12 . . . . 118 C3
Bradley Mound★
  BA12 . . . . 118 F2
Bradley Pk★ BA12 . . . . 118 F1
Bradley Rd
  Southwick BA14 . . . . . 105 B2
  Swindon SN2 . . . . 35 D4
  Trowbridge BA14 . . . . . 105 C5
  Warminster BA12 . . . . . 116 E4
Bradon Forest Sch
  SN5 . . . . 33 B3
Bradshaw Ct 6 SN25 . . . 34 D6
Bradwell Cl 2 SP10 . . . 193 C2
Bradwell Moor SN3 . . . . 51 D2
Braemar Cl SN3 . . . . 50 F3
Braemar Rise SP1 . . . . . 146 B4
Braemore CE Prim Sch
  SP6 . . . . 210 E4
Braemor Rd SN11 . . . . . 81 A4
Braeside Cl SN10 . . . . . . 97 D1
Braithwaite Way 3
  BA11 . . . . 110 C6
Brake Mead SN15 . . . . . 78 F7
Brakspear Dr SN13 . . . . . 76 E1
Bramble Cl SN2 . . . . 35 F3
Bramble Cl 7 SN6. . . . . . 19 D8
Bramble Dr
  Chippenham SN15 . . . . . 79 A4
  Westbury BA13 . . . . . . 108 F5
Bramble Hill SO43 . . . . 212 D2
Bramble Rd SN2 . . . . . . 35 E1
Brambles The
  Hinton Charterhouse
    BA2 . . . . 98 E1
  Salisbury SP1 . . . . 146 C2
  Trowbridge BA14 . . . . . 101 D2
Bramble Wlk 4
  SP11 . . . . 193 F2
Brambling Mews GL7 . . . 7 A6
Bramblings The 1
  SN12 . . . . 94 D5
Bramdean Cl 6 SN25 . . . 34 F6

Bramley Cl
  Pewsey SN9 . . . . 215 D6
  4 Warminster BA12 . . 116 F7
Bramley Dr BA11 . . . . . 110 C6
Bramley Hill BA14 . . . . . 138 F5
Bramley La BA14 . . . . . 105 D7
Bramleys The SP5 . . . . 161 D3
Bramley Way SN4 . . . . . 217 C3
Brampton Ct 8
  SN12 . . . . 178 B8
Bramptons The SN5 . . . . 49 B7
BRAMSHAW 212 E3
Bramshaw Hill Rd
  SO43 . . . . 212 C2
Bramshaw Telegraph★
  SP6 . . . . 211 F3
Bramwell Cl SN2 . . . . . . 35 E6
Brancaster Ave 1
  SP10 . . . . 193 C2
Branch Rd BA2 . . . . 98 F2
Branders 4 SN6 . . . . . . 19 D8
Brandon Cl SN5 . . . . 34 A3
Branksome Rd SN25 . . . . 34 E3
Branscombe Dr SN4 . . . . 47 E1
Bransdown Hill
  Easton Grey SN16 . . . . . 26 A3
  Sherston SN16 . . . . 25 F2
Brantwood Cl
  Swindon SN25 . . . . 20 D1
  Swindon SN25 . . . . 34 C8
Brassknocker Hill BA2 . 90 A1
Bratch La SP3 . . . . 201 F2
BRATTON 186 B7
Bratton Ave SN10 . . . . . 214 C2
Bratton Cl SN2 . . . . 35 B5
Bratton Prim Sch
  BA13 . . . . 186 A6
Bratton Rd
  Edington BA13 . . . . . . 186 A8
  West Ashton BA14 . . . . 106 B4
  Westbury BA13 . . . . . . 109 B3
  Westbury BA13 . . . . . . 109 C4
Braxton Rd 6 SN25 . . . . 34 C6
Braybrooke 2 SN5 . . . . . 48 F8
Braydon Cl SN2 . . . . 35 C5
Braydon La SN6 . . . . 18 F4
Braydonside
  Leigh SN5 . . . . 17 F3
  Leigh SN6 . . . . 18 A2
  Purton SN5 . . . . 32 A6
Bray St SN8 . . . . 173 A8
Breach Cl
  Bourton SP8 . . . . 137 E2
  Bromham SN15 . . . . 96 A4
Breach La
  Chute SP11 . . . . 184 E1
  Chute SP11 . . . . 192 E8
  Longhedge BA12 . . . . . 115 C6
  Royal Wootton Bassett
    SN4 . . . . 61 B5
  1 Shaftesbury SP7. . . 202 B1
  Southwick BA14 . . . . . 105 A3
Breach The SN10 . . . . . 214 B2
Bread St BA12 . . . . 116 F5
Bream Cl
  Calne SN11 . . . . 81 A5
  Melksham SN12 . . . . . . 94 D6
BREAMORE 210 F5
Breamore Countryside
  Mus★ SP6 . . . . 210 E5
Breamore House★
  SP6 . . . . 210 E6
Breamore Rd SP5 . . . . . 210 F7
Brean Rd 8 SN25 . . . . . 34 F7
Brecon Cl
  Melksham SN12 . . . . . . 94 D4
  Swindon SN3 . . . . 50 E2
Bremen Gdns 21
  SP10 . . . . 193 D2
Bremeridge Cl BA13 . . . 109 B3
Bremeridge Rd BA13 . . 109 B3
BREMHILL 80 E7
Bremhill Cl SN2 . . . . 35 C4
Bremhill View SN11 . . . . 81 A4
Bremilham Rd SN16 . . . . 27 F4
Bremilham Rise SN16 . . . 27 E3
Brendon Wlk SN3 . . . . . . 51 B6
Brentfore St 1 SN1. . . . . 50 B1
Breton Cl SN5 . . . . 34 C2
Breton Rd BA13 . . . . . . 108 F2
Brettingham Gate
  SN3 . . . . 64 F8
Brewer Mead SN15 . . . . 78 F4
Brewer Mws SN13 . . . . . 84 E7
Brewers La SN11 . . . . . . 81 C1
Brewery Rd 8 SP1 . . . . 152 B8
Brewery St SN6 . . . . 23 A5
Brewery Wlk BA14 . . . . 101 D1
Brewhouse Hill SN8 . . . 176 D6
Briar Cl
  Frome BA11 . . . . 110 B7
  Westbury BA13 . . . . . . 108 F4
Briar Fields SN1 . . . . . . 50 F7
Briar Leaze SN11 . . . . . 166 B3
Briars Cl SN5 . . . . 47 E3
Briarswood Ct SN3 . . . . 51 D3
Briary Rd GL7 . . . . 2 C6
Brickham Rd
  Devizes SN10 . . . . 97 F1
  1 Devizes SN10 . . . . 214 D5
Brick Hill SN15 . . . . 95 D6
Brickhouse Farm La
  BA9 . . . . 136 D3

Brick La
  Salisbury SP2 . . . . 145 C2
  Trowbridge BA14 . . . . . 101 D3
Bricklia La SN10 . . . . . . 214 D2
Bricksteed Ave SN10 . . 214 C3
Brickworth La SP5 . . . . 160 E4
Brickyard La SP8 . . . . . 137 E1
Bridewell La SP7 . . . . . 202 A6
Bridewell Sq SN10 . . . . 214 B3
Bridewell St SN8 . . . . . 213 C2
Bridge Ave SN10 . . . . . 105 A8
Bridge Cl GL7 . . . . 2 E3
Bridge Ct BA13 . . . . . . 108 E4
Bridge End Rd
  Swindon SN3 . . . . 35 F1
  Swindon SN3 . . . . 36 A1
Bridgeman Cl SN3 . . . . . 36 B2
Bridgemead Cl SN5 . . . . 49 D7
Bridgemead Ret Pk
  SN5 . . . . 49 E5
Bridge Rd SP5 . . . . 205 E4
Bridge St
  Bourton SP8 . . . . 137 E2
BRIDGWATER Cl
  Harnham SP2 . . . . 151 D6
  Swindon SN2 . . . . 50 A7
Bridge Yard 10 BA15 . . 100 D6
Bridlewood Prim Sch
  SN25 . . . . 34 F7
Bridmore Rd SP5 . . . . . 207 D6
Bridmore Ride SP5 . . . . 207 D6
Bridport Rd SN3 . . . . . . 51 B4
Brier Ct SP2 . . . . 145 C4
Briery Cl SN3 . . . . 36 A4
Bright Cl 3 SN15 . . . . . . 78 F5
Brighton Way SN14 . . . . 77 F6
Bright St SN2 . . . . 50 B8
BRIGMERSTON 198 C8
Brimble Hill SN4 . . . . . . 64 D5
Brimble Hill Sch
  SN25 . . . . 34 D8
Brimhill Rise BA13 . . . . 111 D4
Brind Cl SN3 . . . . 51 E6
Brindley Cl SN3 . . . . 34 E1
Brind Rd SP4 . . . . 197 F7
Brington Rd SN3 . . . . . . 51 B8
BRINKWORTH 45 E5
Brinkworth Cl SN14 . . . . 45 E5
Brinkworth Earl Danby's
  CE Primary Sch SN15 . 45 E5
Brinkworth Earl Danby's
  CE Prim Sch SN15 . . . . 45 E5
Brinkworth House Bsns &
  Events Ctr SN15. . . . . . 45 C6
Brinkworth Rd SN15 . . . . 45 C3
Brinscombe La 6
  SP7 . . . . 202 D1
Brionne Way 13 SP7 . . . 202 D2
Brisbane Gdns 7
  SP4 . . . . 198 F6
Bristle Gr BA12 . . . . . . 139 B4
Bristol Rd
  Chippenham SN14 . . . . . 78 C8
  Chippenham Without
    SN14 . . . . 69 E2
  Easton Grey SN16 . . . . . 26 E4
  Luckington SN14 . . . . . . 39 D3
  Malmesbury SN16 . . . . . 27 A4
Bristol St
  3 Malmesbury SN16 . . 28 A3
  Swindon SN1 . . . . 50 A6
Britannia Ave SN9 . . . . 182 B2
Britannia Cres SN15 . . . 60 B8
Britannia Dr SN11 . . . . . 81 D4
Britannia Pl 6 SN1 . . . . . 50 D4
Britannia Trade Pk
  SN3 . . . . 35 F3
BRITFORD 152 E5
Britford La SP2 . . . . 152 B6
Britford La W 1 SP2. . . 152 A6
Britmore La SP7 . . . . . . 202 F4
Brittain Cl SN14 . . . . . . 77 F7
Britten Rd SN25 . . . . 34 E2
Brittox The SN10 . . . . . 214 B3
Brixham Ave SN10 . . . . . 50 E5
BRIXTON DEVERILL . . . 120 E2
Broadacres SN4 . . . . 62 B2
BROAD BLUNSDON 21 C2
Broadbury Banks★
  SN9 . . . . 181 B2
BROADBUSH 21 D1
Broad Bush SN26 . . . . . . 21 D1
BROAD CHALKE 205 B4
Broad Chalke CE Prim
  Sch SP5 . . . . 205 C4
Broadchalke Rd
  Bishopstone SP5 . . . . . 150 A2
  Bishopstone SP5 . . . . . 205 F5
Broadcloth E La
  BA14 . . . . 105 E7
Broadcloth La BA14 . . . 105 E7
Broad Dr GL8 . . . . 25 A8
Broadfield Rd SP4 . . . . 133 D3
Broadfields SN9 . . . . . . 215 B4
BROAD HINTON 167 C7
Broad Hinton CE Prim
  Sch SN4 . . . . 167 C7

Broad Hinton (Hackpen)
  White Horse★ SN4 . . 167 E5
Broad Hinton Rd SN4 . . 63 D3
Broad La SP6 . . . . 209 B6
Broadlands Cl SP1 . . . . 146 B4
Broadleas Cl SN10 . . . . 214 A2
Broadleas Cres SN10 . . 214 A2
Broadleas Gdns★
  SN10 . . . . 214 A1
Broadleas Pk SN10 . . . 214 A1
Broadleas Rd SN10 . . . 214 A2
Broadleaze
  Down Ampney GL7 . . . . . 8 E8
  Seagry SN15 . . . . 57 D6
Broadley Pk BA14 . . . . 105 D3
Broadmead
  Corsham SN13 . . . . 85 B7
  Trowbridge BA14 . . . . . 101 A1
Broadmead La BA14 . . . . 85 B7
Broadmead Wlk SN3 . . . 51 B7
Broadmoor Rd SN3 . . . . 36 D7
Broads Green SN11 . . . . 88 F4
Broad's GREEN 88 F3
Broadslade BA12 . . . . . 118 F8
Broad St
  Swindon SN1 . . . . 50 C7
  Trowbridge BA14 . . . . . 101 C1
Broadstone SN13 . . . . . . 85 B7
Broad Stones BA15 . . . . 90 E7
BROAD STREET 181 C6
BROAD TOWN 167 A8
Broad Town CE Prim Sch
  SN4 . . . . 62 B1
Broadtown La SN4 . . . . . 61 F5
Broadtown Rd SN4 . . . . . 62 B3
Broad Town Rd SN4 . . . . 62 B2
Broad Town White
  Horse★ SN4 . . . . . . 62 D1
Broadway
  Market Lavington
    SN10 . . . . 179 D2
  Warminster BA12 . . . . . 116 E5
Broadway Cl GL7 . . . . . . 10 D7
Broadway E BA13 . . . . . 108 D6
Broadway GL7 . . . . 7 A5
Broadway Lane GL7. . . . . . 6 F6
Broadway N BA13 . . . . . 108 C7
Broadway The SN25 . . . . 35 A3
Broadwood Ave SN13 . . . 84 B8
Broadwood Cl 1
  BA12 . . . . 117 A8
Brockley Rise SN2 . . . . . 36 A5
Brocks Orch 8 SP3 . . . 196 E6
Brockwood Cl SP5 . . . . . 99 F7
Broken Cross
  Calne SN11 . . . . 81 B3
Broken Cross
  Calne SN11 . . . . 81 B3
BROKENBOROUGH 27 D7
Brokerswood 107 F5
Brokerswood Ctry Pk★
  BA13 . . . . 107 F6
Brokerswood Rd
  BA14 . . . . 105 A1
BROMHAM 96 A7
Bromley Cl 2 SN3 . . . . . 50 E6
Bronte Cl 2 SN3 . . . . . . 51 D4
BROOK 212 E1
Brook Cl
  Melksham SN12 . . . . 93 F6
  16 Tisbury SP3 . . . . . 203 E8
  Warminster BA12 . . . . . 116 E5
  Winterbourne Stoke
    SP3 . . . . 196 F3
Brookdene SN25 . . . . . . 34 E4
Brook Dr SN13 . . . . 85 D7
Brook Dro BA13 . . . . . . 108 C4
Brooke Cl SN16 . . . . 28 C2
Brooke Cres SN2 . . . . . . 34 C5
Brook End SN14 . . . . 39 F5
Brookfield SN6 . . . . 22 F7
Brook Field Prim Sch
  SN5 . . . . 49 A8
Brookfield Rise SN12 . 85 D1
Brookfields SO51 . . . . . 212 F6
Brook Gdns SN10 . . . . . 214 F6
Brook Gn SO43 . . . . . . 212 D1
BROOK HILL 212 D1
Brook Hill
  Donhead St Andrew
    SP7 . . . . 203 B2
  Sherston SN16 . . . . 40 C8
Brook La
  Bradenstoke SN15 . . . . . 59 D3
  Holt BA14 . . . . 92 D1
  Holt BA14 . . . . 101 E8
  Westbury BA13 . . . . . . 108 D4
  Woodgreen SP6 . . . . . 211 A4
Brooksby Way
  Swindon SN3 . . . . 36 B1
  Swindon SN3 . . . . 51 B8
Brooks Cl SN5 . . . . 35 E5
Brookside
  Crudwell SN16 . . . . 14 E6
  Hullavington SN14 . . . . 41 F7

Brookside continued
  Landford SP5 . . . . 212 C6
Brookside Cl BA1 . . . . . . 82 A5
Brook St
  Chippenham SN14 . . . . . 78 B8
  Fovant SP3 . . . . 204 E7
  Great Bedwyn SN8 . . . 176 C3
  Warminster BA12 . . . . . 116 E5
BROOK WATERS 203 D8
Brook Way SN11 . . . . . . 81 C3
Brookwell Cl SN14 . . . . . 70 C2
Broomcroft Rd SN9 . . . . 215 C3
Broome Manor La
  SN3 . . . . 50 F2
BROOMFIELD 55 A1
Broomfield
  Chippenham SN15 . . . . . 70 D2
  Yatton Keynell SN14 . . . 68 E8
Broom Gdns SN14 . . . . . 55 F8
Broomground BA15 . . . . 99 E7
Broomhill SP5 . . . . 212 C5
Broom Rd BA12 . . . . . . 139 B4
Brotherton Cl SN15 . . . . 78 F5
BROUGHTON
  GIFFORD 93 C4
Broughton Gifford
  SN12 . . . . 93 C4
Broughton Grange 6
  SN3 . . . . 50 F4
Broughton Rd
  Broughton Gifford
    SN12 . . . . 93 A2
  2 Trowbridge BA14 . . 105 C5
Brouncker Rd BA13 . . . 109 B5
Brouncker's Well★
  BA12 . . . . 186 F5
Browning Cl 1 SN3. . . . . 36 B3
Brownings The SN13 . . . 83 D5
Brownleaze La SN10 . . . 179 D6
Browns Dr
  7 Corsham SN13 . . . . . 76 C1
  1 Corsham SN13 . . . . . 84 C8
Brown's Folly★ BA1 . . . . 82 C1
Browns La
  Alton SN8 . . . . 173 C1
  Damerham SP6 . . . . . . 209 E3
  Brown's La SN8. . . . . . 176 B3
Brown St
  3 Salisbury SP1. . . . . 146 B1
  Salisbury SP1 . . . . 152 B8
  Trowbridge BA14 . . . . . 105 D4
Brow The SN25 . . . . 34 E4
Broxburn Rd BA12 . . . . 116 D6
Broxmore La SO51 . . . . 162 D2
Bruce St SN2 . . . . 49 F7
Bruddel Gr SN3 . . . . 50 E2
Bruges Cl SN15 . . . . 78 F7
Brunel Cl
  Corsham SN13 . . . . 76 F1
  Westbury BA13 . . . . . . 109 A4
Brunel Cres SN2 . . . . . . 50 B8
Brunel Ct SN15 . . . . 78 B6
Brunel Ctr The SN1 . . . . 50 B6
Brunel Rd SP2 . . . . 145 D1
Brunel Way
  Box SN13 . . . . 83 D6
  Calne SN11 . . . . 81 C6
  Frome BA11 . . . . 110 C7
Brunkard's La SN9 . . . . 215 D5
Brunswick St SN1 . . . . . 50 C4
BRUNTON 183 F3
Brushy Bush La SP5. . . 207 F3
Bruton Rd BA10 . . . . . . 122 A6
Bruton Wlk SN3 . . . . 51 A4
Bruyn Rd SP6 . . . . 210 E1
Bryans Cl Rd SN11 . . . . . 81 B3
Bryanston Way SN3 . . . . 51 C6
Bryant Rd SN25 . . . . 34 C5
Bryces La SP5 . . . . 162 E3
Brydes Rd 2 SP11 . . . . 192 A5
Bryer Ash Bsns Pk 4
  BA14 . . . . 105 C8
Brympton Cl 5 SP6 . . . 210 C2
Brynards Hill SN4 . . . . . 47 C1
Bryony Way SN2 . . . . 34 D4
Bryworth La GL7 . . . . 2 A6
Buckeridge Rd SP2 . . . 144 E4
Buckhurst Cres SN3 . . . . 51 A6
Buckingham Rd
  Chippenham SN15 . . . . . 79 A5
  Swindon SN3 . . . . 51 A3
Buckland Cl SN3 . . . . . . 51 A6
Bucklands Gr SN14 . . . . 78 F6
Buckleaze Cl BA14 . . . . 105 D5
Buckleaze La SN9 . . . . . 215 C5
Bucklebury Cl SN3. . . . . 36 A1
Buckler Cl GL7 . . . . 1 F6
Bucklers Screen
  BA12 . . . . 116 C2
Buckthorn Dr SN2 . . . . . 34 D4
Buckthorn Row SN13 . . . 84 E8
Budbury Circ BA15 . . . . 100 C7
Budbury Cl BA15 . . . . . 100 C7
Budbury Pl BA15 . . . . . 100 C7
Budbury Ridge BA15 . . 100 C7
Budbury Tyning
  BA15 . . . . 100 C7
Bude Rd SN5 . . . . 49 F6
Budge La BA11 . . . . 114 A8
Buettell Way SN16 . . . . . 27 F5
Bugdens Cl SP4 . . . . . . 217 D4
BUGLEY 116 C6
Bugmore La SP5 . . . . . 154 F4
Buie Cl SN5 . . . . 34 B2
BULBRIDGE 144 B1
Bulbridge Rd SP2 . . . . . 144 B1
BULFORD 217 D4
BULFORD CAMP. 198 F6

Bulford Droveway
SP4................198 D7
Bulford Hill SP4....217 C8
Bulford Rd
 Bulford SP4.........217 F8
 Durrington/Bulford
 SP4................198 B7
 Shipton Bellinger SP9..199 C8
 South Tedworth SP9...216 A4
Bulford St Leonard's CE
 Prim Sch SP4.......217 E6
BULKINGTON.........178 E5
Bulldog La SN10.....180 C3
BULLENHILL..........106 E8
Buller Pk SP4........133 E5
Buller St SN2.........35 C1
Bullfinch Cl SN3.....51 D6
Bull La BA12.........116 F2
BULLOCK'S HORN......15 E1
Bullock's Horn La
 Charlton SN16.......29 D7
 Hankerton SN16......15 D1
Bull Pit BA15........100 D6
Bulls La
 Box SN13...........83 D6
 Broad Chalke SP5...205 B4
Bulpit La RG17.......177 B6
Bulpits Hill SP11....185 C3
Bumper's Batch BA2...98 A8
Bumpers Fram Ind Est
 SN14...............70 A1
Bumpers Way SN1....70 A1
Bunce Rd SN3.........36 A2
Bungalow Pk SN15....59 B3
Bunnies La SN10......96 D2
Bunns La BA11.......114 A2
Bunny La SP5.........162 C4
Buntings The SN3.....51 D7
Bupton Village*
 SN11..............166 D7
BURBAGE............183 D8
Burbage Prim Sch
 SN8...............183 D8
Burbage Rd
 Easton SN9.........183 A8
 Milton Lilbourne SN9..182 F7
 Swindon SN2........35 C6
Burbage Wharf*
 SN8...............175 C2
BURCOMBE...........143 E2
Burcombe La
 Barford St Martin
 SP3...............143 C3
 Wilton SP2..........144 B2
Burcot Cl SN25.......34 C7
Burden Cl SN3........36 C1
Burden Rd SN26......20 D1
Burderop Barns SN4...64 E4
Burderop Cl
 🌢 Trowbridge BA14..105 D5
 Wroughton SN4......64 B8
Burdett St 🌢 SN8...170 B2
Burford Ave
 Salisbury SP2.......152 B6
 Swindon SN3........50 E5
Burford La SP2.......152 B6
Burford Rd
 Little Faringdon GL7...2 E7
 Salisbury SP2.......152 B6
Burford's 🌢 RG17...171 E7
Burford St GL7........2 C4
Burford Stone La
 Hannington SN6......11 B1
 Hannington SN6......11 B1
 Hannington SN6......22 C8
Burgate Fields SN6...210 D2
Burgess Cl SN3.......36 A1
Burgess Gn SP1......146 C4
Burghley Cl SN3.......51 A6
Burkal Dr 🌢 SP10...193 E2
Burlands Rd SN15....78 E6
Burleaze SN15........78 C5
Burlington Pl SN13...84 D8
Burne Jones Ave
 Swindon SN25.......34 D8
 Swindon SN26........20 D1
Burnet Cl
 Melksham SN12......94 B2
 Swindon SN2........34 D5
Burnett Rd BA14.....105 D6
Burnet Way SP1.....146 D4
Burnham Rd
 🌢 Fordingbridge
 SP6...............210 D2
 🌢 Malmesbury SN16..28 A4
 Swindon SN3........51 B6
Burnhams Cl 🌢
 SP10..............193 E2
Burnivale SN16......28 A3
Burn Rd SN13........76 E1
Burnston Cl SN12....94 B8
Burns Way SN2.......35 E4
Burr La SN8.........176 F1
Burroughs Cl SP1....146 E2
Burroughs Dro 🌢
 SN8...............183 D8
BURTON
 Mere..............139 D5
 Nettleton..........53 B4
Burton Cl 🌢 SP7....202 D2
Burton Farm Cl SN14..53 B3
Burton Hill
 Corston SN16........43 A7
 Malmesbury SN16....28 B2

Burton Rd
 Acton Turville GL9....52 F6
 Acton Turville GL9....53 A6
 Burtons La SN13......83 C5
 Burwood Cl 🌢 SP4..217 E3
Burycroft SN4........163 A6
Bury Fields SN5......33 D1
Bury Hill (Settlement)*
 SN6................18 B1
Bury La
 Bratton BA13.......186 B7
 Broad Chalke SP5...205 C4
Bury Mead BA2......195 A2
Burytown La SN26....21 C2
Buscot Cl SN25.......34 E7
Buscot Old Parsonage*
 SN7................7 F4
BUSCOT WICK........12 D8
Bush Barrow* SP4...197 D4
Bush Farm Bison Ctr*
 BA12.............140 B3
BUSHTON............60 E8
Bustlers Hill SN16....40 D8
Bute Cl SN6.........212 C7
Butleigh Rd SN25....34 C7
Butler Cl SP2........152 B6
Butlers Cl SN16......25 C1
Butlers Ct La GL7.....2 B4
Butler's Field GL7.....2 C5
Butler's Gdns BA11...110 A3
Butlers Yard SP5....205 B4
Butt St SP11.........192 A6
Buttercup Cl
 Chippenham SN14....70 B3
 Harnham SP2.......151 F7
Butterfield Cl SP2...150 F8
Butterfield Dr SP4...217 D3
Butterfly World* SN1..48 F1
Butter Furlong Rd
 SP5...............154 C3
BUTTERMERE.........185 B8
Buttermere SN3......51 E3
Butterstake La 🌢 SP2..86 B6
Butterworth St SN1...50 A5
Butt La SP5..........205 E4
Buttons Yd BA12.....117 B7
Butts Cl SN14........76 E7
Butts Cres BA14.....106 A8
Butts Hill SP3........129 E7
Butts La
 Kilmington BA12.....123 E6
 Steeple Ashton BA14..178 A3
Butts Mead 🌢 SP7..202 D1
Butts Rd
 Chiseldown SN4......65 D5
 Salisbury SP1.......146 A2
Butt St SP11.........192 A5
Butts Terr SP2.......146 A2
Butts The
 Aldbourne SN8......170 A6
 Biddestone SN14.....76 D7
 Bratton BA13.......186 B7
 Chippenham SN15....78 E7
 Crudwell SN16.......14 E6
 Lydiard Millicent SN5...48 D7
 Potterne SN10......179 D5
 Shaftesbury SP7....202 B2
 Shrewton SP3......196 F7
 Steeple Ashton BA14..178 A3
 Westbury BA13.....109 A2
Butts (Tumuli) The*
 SP6...............211 E2
Buxbury Hollow SP3..204 B6
Buzzard Cl 🌢 SN12..94 D5
Buzzard Rd
 🌢 Calne SN11.......81 B5
 🌢 Winterbourne SP4..132 C1
Byams Ride GL8......25 B7
By Brook Valley CE Prim
 Sch SN14............68 F5
Bybrook View SN13...76 A2
Bydemill Gdns SN6...22 E5
Byers Cl SN25........35 A8
Byfield Way SN3......51 B8
Byford Gdns SP4.....133 D6
Byrd Cl 🌢 SN5.......48 F5
Byre Cl SN6..........19 D7
Byron Ave SN4........47 F2
Byron Cl
 🌢 Ludgershall SP11..192 A5
 🌢 Melksham SN12....94 B8
Byron Ct SN3.........36 E5
Byron Rd SN10......214 B1
Byron St 🌢 SN1.....50 C5
Bytham Rd SN8......169 A4
Bythebrook SN14.....70 B1
Bythesea Rd BA14...105 C8
Byways Cl 🌢 SP1...152 C8

C

Cabot Dr SN5.........48 F6
Cabul Rd SP9........216 B5
Cadby Cl BA14.......105 F8
Caddy La BA12.......138 F5
Cadley Cl SN2........35 D2
Cadley Clay Shooting Gd
 SN8...............175 A4
Cadley Rd SN8.......183 E1
Cadnam Cres SP4....137 B3
Cadnam La SO51....212 F1
Caen Hill SN10......179 C8
Caen Hill Gdns SN10..179 C8

Caen Hill Locks*
 SN10..............179 C8
Caen View SN1........49 E4
Caerleon Dr 🌢 SP10..193 E2
Caesar Rd SP10......193 E2
Caesar's Camp (Fort)*
 DT11..............206 F2
Cagney Dr SN25.......35 A5
Caird Lawns SN10....214 C2
Cairndow Way SN2....35 E5
CALCUTT............20 A7
Calcutt St SN6.......19 E8
Calder Cl SN25........34 F5
Calder House Sch
 SN14..............75 D6
Caldwell Cl 🌢 SP7..202 D1
Calf La SN8.........173 B1
Calgary Dr 🌢 SP4...217 F8
Callaghan Cl 🌢 SN3..36 B2
Callas Hill SN4.......163 B5
Callas Rise 🌢 SN4...163 B6
Callaway Gdns BA13..109 A2
Callenders SN5........49 E5
Callington Rd SN25...34 B6
Calliope Cres SN25...35 D3
Callow Croft 🌢 SN8..183 D8
CALLOW HILL.........46 D6
Callows Cross SN15...46 C6
CALNE...............81 B2
Calne Heritage Ctr*
 SN11..............81 B2
CALNE MARSH........81 C4
Calne Rd SN15........60 A1
Calstock Rd SN25....34 B6
CALSTONE
 WELLINGTON.......172 A7
Calvert Rd SN3.......50 E6
Calves La SP7........202 A2
Camargue Rd BA13..108 E1
Cambrai Rd SN4......65 D1
Cambria Bridge Rd
 SN1...............50 A5
Cambria Pl SN1.......50 A5
Cambridge Cl SN3....50 F4
Cambridge Rd SP1...146 B3
Camden Cl SN5.......49 A5
Camellia Dr BA12.....116 E7
Camelot St 🌢 SP10..193 E2
Cameron Cl SN3.......36 A1
Camilla Cl SP4.......217 D8
Camomile Dr 🌢
 SP11..............192 A5
Campbell Rd SP1.....146 B2
Campbell Vale 🌢
 SP4...............132 B1
Campden Rd SN3......50 E5
Campion Cl
 Calne SN11..........81 B5
 Westbury BA13.....109 A5
Campion Dr
 Melksham SN12......94 C2
 Trowbridge BA14....105 D6
Campion Gate SN5....48 F5
Camp Rd BA12.......194 E5
Camton Rd SN5.......48 F7
CANADA.............212 F4
Canada Comm Rd
 SO51..............212 F4
Canada Rd SO51.....212 F5
Canada Rise SN10...179 F1
Canadian Ave SP4...145 D2
Canal Bridge BA14...102 F6
Canal Cl
 Calne SN11..........81 A2
 Wilcot SN8.........182 A8
Canal La SP5.........153 E2
Canal Rd
 Chippenham SN15....78 E5
 Trowbridge BA14....101 D3
Canal Rd Ind Est
 BA14..............101 D3
Canalside SP5........153 E2
Canal Way SN10.....214 C6
Canal Wlk
 Hungerford RG17....177 B7
 Swindon SN1........50 B6
Canberra Dr SP4....198 F6
Canberra Rd SN4.....64 E3
Candown Rd SP3....188 B2
Canford Cl SN3.......51 C6
Canney Cl SN4........65 D4
Canney The SN4......65 D4
Cann Hill SP7.......206 A7
Cannimore Cl BA12..116 C5
Cannimore Rd
 Warminster BA12....116 C4
 Warminster BA12....116 D5
Cannings Cl
 Broughton Gifford
 SN12..............93 C4
 🌢 Hilperton BA14....102 B2
Cannock Rd 🌢 BA12..117 A8
Cannon Sq SN14......94 A4
Cannon St SN1.......50 C5
Cannwood La BA10..122 D8
Canon Dr GL7.........2 E3
Canons Cl
 Tidworth SP9.......216 D4
 Warminster BA12....117 C5
Canons Ct SN12.......94 A4
Canons Yard Ind Est
 SN4................61 E8
Cantax Hill SN15......86 C6
Cantelo Cl SN25.......34 F7
Canterbury Cl
 🌢 Amesbury SP4....217 D3
 Swindon SN3........50 F3

Canterbury St SN14...78 C8
Cantors Way SN16....17 C2
Canwood La BA10...123 A7
Capella Cres 🌢 SN25..34 B7
Capesthorne Dr SN25..34 E6
Capitol Cl SN3........36 D1
Capps La BA13......109 E7
Caprice Cl 🌢 SN5....49 A7
Caradon Way SN3....34 C7
Caraway Dr SN2......34 C4
Carders Cnr 🌢 BA14..105 D7
Cardigan Cl SN3.....50 E4
Cardigan Rd SN8....213 C3
Cardwell Cl 🌢 SN3..51 B7
Caretakers Cl SN12...93 F6
Carey Cl SN5.........49 A5
Carfax Cl 🌢 SN1.....50 C5
Carfax St SN1........50 C6
Cargill Pl SN16.......15 F8
Carisbrooke Cres
 BA14..............101 E5
Carisbrook Rd SN12..94 B2
Carisbrook Terr SN4...65 C3
Carleton Pl SP4.....217 A4
Carlisle Ave SN3......50 D3
Carlton Cl 🌢 SP4...217 D3
Carlton Gate SN3....50 F1
Carlton Row BA14...105 C6
Carman Cl SN3.......36 A3
Carmelite Way SP1..152 B7
Carmel Wlk SN3......50 F5
Carnarvon Cl SN14...78 A7
Carnation La SN12...178 C8
Carnegie Rd SN11....81 C4
Carnival SN16.........28 A6
Carpenter Cl 🌢 SN15..78 F5
Carpenter Dr SP4...217 D4
Carpenters Cl BA14..106 B8
Carpenters Cl SN16...25 C1
Carpenter's Cl SN11..80 F1
Carpenters La
 🌢 Bratton BA13.....186 B7
 Swindon SN2........50 D8
Carp Rd SN11.........81 A5
Carrick Cl SN15.......79 A8
Carriers Cl SN16......25 C1
Carrion Pond Dro
 SP2...............151 D7
Carroll Cl SN3........51 D4
Carronbridge Rd SN5..49 B6
Carr St SN1...........50 B6
Carshalton Rd SN3...51 B3
Carsons Yd SP4......132 B1
Carstairs Ave SN3....51 A3
Carter Cl SN25........35 C6
Carter's Cl SP6.......211 C6
Cartway SN10........180 E4
Cartwright Dr SN5....49 B8
Carver Cl SN3.........36 C2
Carvers Hill SN8.....176 E1
Cary Glen SN5.........79 A4
Casley La BA11......107 C7
Caspian Cl SN2........34 C3
Caspian Gdns BA13..108 F1
Cassini Dr
 Swindon SN25.......34 B6
 🌢 Swindon SN25.....34 B7
Casson Rd SN3.......36 A2
Castell Cl BA14......106 B8
Casterbridge La 🌢
 SP11..............192 F1
Casterbridge Rd
 Swindon SN3........34 C5
 🌢 Swindon SN3.....34 C5
Castilian Mews SN5...49 A7
Castle Barrow*
 BA12..............195 A7
CASTLE COMBE.......68 A7
Castle Combe Motor
 Racing Circuit*
 SN14..............68 C6
Castle Combe Motte &
 Baileys* SN14......67 F8
Castle Ct SP3........204 A7
Castle Ditches Hill Fort*
 SP3...............204 A7
Castle Dore SN5......49 A5
CASTLE EATON.......10 B4
Castlefield Cl 🌢 SN5..49 C6
Castlefields SN11.....81 A3
Castlegate Bsns Pk
 SP4...............146 B7
Castle Grounds
 SN10..............214 A4
Castlehaven Cl SN15..79 A4
Castle Hedingham
 BA14..............106 B8
Castle Hill Cl 🌢 SP7..202 D1
Castle Hill Cres BA12..139 A6
Castle Hill (Fort)*
 SN26..............21 D3
Castle Hill La BA12..139 A5
Castle Keep
 Salisbury SP1......145 E4
 🌢 Salisbury SP2....144 D3
Castle La
 Alderbury SP5......153 E1
 Devizes SN10......214 A3
 Wilton SP2.........144 D2
Castle Meadow SP5..211 A8
Castle Mead School
 BA14..............106 B8
Castle Orch BA9....137 D3
Castle Pl Sh Ctr
 BA14..............105 D7

Castle Prim Sch
 SP11..............192 B5
Castle Rd
 Bratton BA13.......186 A6
 Devizes SN10......214 A3
 🌢 Great Bedwyn SN8..176 B3
 Salisbury SP1......146 A3
Castle St
 Aldbourne SN8.....170 A6
 Calne SN11..........81 B2
 🌢 Ludgershall SP11..192 A5
 Mere BA12.........138 F5
 Salisbury SP2......146 A2
 Trowbridge BA14....105 D8
Castleton Rd SN5.....49 A7
Castle View
 Westbury BA13.....109 B3
 West Tisbury SP3...203 B8
Castle View Rd
 Chiseldown SN4......65 E4
 Swindon SN3........36 C1
Castle Well Dr SP4..146 B8
Castle Well Mews
 SP4...............146 B8
Castle Wlk SN11......81 A2
Castle Woods 🌢 SP5..211 C7
Castley Rd BA14.....102 A2
Catalina Ct 🌢 SN12..178 B8
CATCOMB...........73 D6
Catcomb St SN11.....73 D6
Cathedral Ct SP1....152 B8
Catherine Cres
 Dinton SP3.........201 E2
 Downton SP5.......210 F8
Catherine Ford La
 Dinton SP3.........201 E1
 Fovant SP3.........204 E8
Catherine St
 Salisbury SP1......152 B8
 🌢 Swindon SN1.....50 B6
Catherine Way BA1...82 A5
Catherine Wayte Cl
 SN25..............34 F4
Catherine Wayte Prim
 Sch SN25...........34 F4
Catmint Cl SN3......34 D4
Cator Rd 🌢 SP4....197 E7
Cats Hill La SP7.....203 A1
Catterick Cl 🌢 SN14..77 F6
Caulfield Rd SN2.....50 D8
CAUSEWAY THE.....139 C4
Causeway The
 Brinkworth SN15....45 D6
 Broad Chalke SP5...205 B4
 Chippenham SN15....78 E7
 The Common SP5...149 C7
 🌢 Tisbury SP3.......203 E8
Cavell Ct BA14......105 C6
Cavendish Cl SN11...81 D3
Cavendish Dr BA14..104 F6
Cavendish Sq SN3....51 A4
Caversham Cl SN3....50 F5
Cavie Cl SN5.........49 A8
Cawte Mews SN3....36 A4
Caxton Cl
 🌢 Andover SP10....193 C1
 🌢 Swindon SN3.....50 F4
Caxton Rd BA11......110 A3
Cayenne Pk SN2......34 C4
Cecil Ave SP2.......152 A5
Cecil Rd SN3.........51 A6
Cecil Terr SP2.......145 D1
Cedar Cl
 Melksham SN12......94 A3
 Salisbury SP2......145 B4
 Worton SN10.......179 B4
Cedar Glen SN5.......33 B4
Cedar Gr
 Chippenham SN15....70 E1
 Trowbridge BA14....105 B6
Cedars Cl SN2........35 A2
Cedars The SN15......28 F2
Cedar Tree Cl BA12..102 B3
Celandine Way BA14..70 B2
Celsus Gr SN1........50 A3
Cemetery La BA15...100 F7
Centenary Cl BA14..102 B2
Centenary Ct 🌢
 BA14..............105 C7
Center Parcs
 Longhedge BA12....115 E1
 Longhedge BA14....115 F4
Central St SP11.....192 A5
Central Trad Est SN3..50 D3
Centre The SP4.....217 A4
Centre Wlk Ave GL9...38 C7
Centurion Cl
 Chippenham SN15....79 A5
 🌢 Salisbury SP2....145 D2
Centurion Way
 Swindon SN3........51 C8
 Warminster BA12....112 E1
Century Rd SN5.......34 B1
Ceres Pl SN11........81 D4
Ceres Rd SN26.......21 A1
CERNEY WICK.........7 D5
Cerney Wick La GL7...7 D5
Chaddenwick Hill
 Mere BA12.........139 D6
 West Knoyle BA12...140 D7
Chaddington Strand
 SN1...............49 F2
Chadwick Cl 🌢 SN12..178 B8
Chaffeymoor Hill
 SP8...............137 B1
Chaffinch Ave BA11..110 B6

Chaffinch Dr 🌢
 BA14..............105 B8
Chafield Cl BA12.....113 A1
Chafyn Gr Sch SP1...146 C2
Chain Dro
 South Newton SP3...130 B6
 Stapleford SP3......129 F7
Chain Hill SP3........129 E7
Chain La BA12.......117 C6
Chalcot La
 Chapmanslade BA13..111 F5
Upton Scudamore
 BA13..............112 A6
Chalfield Cres SN1...53 C4
Chalfield Glebe BA15..100 F6
Chalfont Cl BA14....105 A8
CHALFORD...........113 A8
Chalford
 Westbury BA12.....112 F6
 Westbury BA13.....108 F1
Chalford Ave SN3....50 E5
Chalgrove Field SN5...49 A3
Chalkcroft La SP11...193 E2
Chalk Hill 🌢 SP3...196 F6
Chalk Pyt Rd SP5....205 B4
Chalk's Cl 🌢 SP5...211 C8
Challis Ct 🌢 SP11...192 A5
Challows La SN14.....76 D8
Challymead SN12....93 E3
Chalvedon Gn SN3....51 A5
Chamberlain Rd
 Chippenham Without
 SN14..............77 F7
 Swindon SN3........50 C6
Chambers Ave SP4..217 C2
Chambon Cl SN11....17 A2
Champneys Rd 🌢
 BA11..............110 A7
Chancellor Cl SN5....48 F5
Chancel Way GL7.....2 C4
Chancery Cl 🌢 SP2..145 C2
Chancery La SN11...117 C6
Chandler Cl SN3......50 D5
Chandlers Cl SN10...180 F8
Chandlers Ct
 North Tidworth SP9..216 C7
 Tidworth SP9.......216 C7
Chandlers La
 All Cannings SN10...180 F8
 Bishops Cannings
 SN10..............172 B2
Chandler's La 🌢 SN8..170 A7
Chandlers Tynings
 BA15..............100 E7
Chandler Way 🌢 SN15..78 F7
Chandos Cl SN5.......49 A6
Chanterelle Pk BA15..100 D5
Chantry Ct
 Southwick BA14....104 F3
 Westbury BA13.....109 A3
Chantry Gdns BA14..104 F3
Chantry La
 Chute SP11.........184 C2
 Marlborough SN8...213 D2
Chantry Mead 🌢
 RG17..............177 B7
Chantry Mews BA12..117 A7
Chantry Rd
 Swindon SN3........34 F2
 Wilton SP2.........144 C1
Chantry The* BA12..139 A5
Chants 🌢 SP3......196 E6
CHAPEL BARTON....115 D5
Chapel Cl
 Kempsford GL7......10 D6
 Southwick BA14....104 F3
Chapel Cnr SN14.....41 F1
Chapel Ct 🌢 RG17..177 B7
Chapel Hill
 Broad Blunsdon SN26..21 B2
 Gastard SN13.......85 E5
 Grimstead SP5......154 B2
 Lacock SN15........86 C6
CHAPEL KNAPP.......85 D5
Chapel La
 Acton Turville GL9....53 A6
 Andover SP11......193 E3
 Bishopstone SP5...205 E4
 Box SN13...........83 D5
 Broad Town SN4....167 B8
 Chippenham SN15....78 E7
 Collingbourne Kingston
 SN8...............183 D2
 Corsham SN13......84 E4
 Downton SP5.......159 B5
 Hanging Langford SP3..128 B7
 Hankerton SN16.....15 C2
 🌢 Lambourn RG17...165 A2
 🌢 Ludgershall SP11..192 A5
 Melksham Without SN12..86 A1
 Minety SN16.........17 A2
 Nomansland SP5....212 C4
 Pen Selwood BA9...137 C3
 🌢 Ramsbury SN8....170 B2
 Redlynch SP5.......211 D7
 🌢 South Marston SN3..36 E5
 Stapleford SP3......129 E7
 Upavon SN9.........181 F2
 🌢 Wanborough SN4..163 B6
 Wingfield BA14.....104 C6
 Woodborough SN9...181 D7
 Zennor BA12.......137 E5
Chapel Mews SN15...78 E7

Chapel Orch **6** SN4 . . 163 B6
Chapel Path SN14 . . . . .75 B3
Chapel Pl **1** SP2 . . . . 146 A1
CHAPEL PLAISTER. . . .84 A5
Chapel Plaister SN13 . .83 F4
Chapel Rd
　2 Ashbury SN6 . . . . . 164 A8
　Heytesbury BA12 . . . . 194 C5
　Kempsford SL7 . . . . 10 D7
Chapel Rise SN12. . . . . .92 E8
Chapel Row
　Bathford BA1 . . . . .82 C2
　Luckington SN14 . . . . . 39 E4
Chapel St
　Horningsham BA12 . . 119 A4
　Studley SN11 . . . . .80 A2
　Swindon SN2 . . . . .50 D8
　Warminster BA12 . . . 116 F5
Chapel Way SN16. . . . . 14 D6
Chapel Wlk GL9 . . . . . .24 B3
Chaplins Pl **3** SP4. . . 217 B3
CHAPMANSLADE 111 C4
Chapmanslade CE Prim
　Sch BA13. . . . . 111 C4
Chapperton Cl BA13 . 109 B5
Chapter Rise SP3 . . . . 188 B2
Charcoal Burners Rd
　SN8. . . . . 175 B4
Charcroft Hill BA10 . . 122 A5
Charfield Cl SN3. . . . . .51 A4
Charlbury Cl SN25 . . . .34 E3
CHARLCUTT 72 F4
Charles Garrett Cl **39**
　SP7. . . . . 202 C2
Charles McPherson Gdns
　SN3. . . . . .51 C5
Charles Morrison Cl
　SN10. . . . . 214 A3
Charles Rd SP4. . . . . . 198 B7
Charles St
　Corsham SN13. . . . . . .76 F2
　2 Salisbury SP2. . . . 145 F1
　Trowbridge BA14. . . . 101 C1
Charles Vesey Rd
　SP9. . . . . 216 C7
Charlham La CL7. . . . . . .8 D7
Charlieu Ave SN11. . . . .89 C8
Charlock Path SN25 . . .34 E5
Charlotte Ct BA14. . . . 101 D1
Charlotte Mews SN3. . .50 D4
Charlotte Sq BA14 . . . 101 D1
Charlotte St BA14. . . . 101 D1
CHARLTON
　Andover 193 C2
　Donhead St Mary. . . . 203 A1
　Malmesbury. 29 A6
　Pewsey. 181 D3
CHARLTON-ALL-
　SAINTS 159 A4
Charlton Cl SN2 . . . . . .35 D5
Charlton Dro SN9. . . . 181 D2
CHARLTON HEATH . . . 29 D6
Charlton Hill BA13 . . 186 D8
Charlton La SP7 . . . . . 202 F1
CHARLTON
　MUSGROVE. 136 B4
Charlton Pk **7** SN6. . . 14 D1
Charlton Pk **8** SN6. . . .28 E7
Charlton Rd SN16. . . . .28 E5
Charlwood Rd SN13. . .84 F8
Charminster Cl SN3. . . .51 C6
CHARNAGE 139 E4
Charnham La RG17 . . 177 B8
Charnham Pk RG17 . . 177 B8
Charnham Pk Ind Est
　RG17. . . . . 177 B8
Charnwood Dr **9**
　SP6. . . . . 210 D2
Charnwood Rd
　Salisbury SP2. . . . . . 145 E1
　Trowbridge BA14. . . . 101 A1
Charolais Dr **14** SN1 . .49 A2
Charter Cl **3** SN10. . . 214 D5
Charterhouse Dr **4**
　BA11. . . . . 110 C7
Charterhouse Rd
　Wroughton SN4. . . . . .63 F6
　5 Wroughton SN4 . . 64 A6
Charter Prim Sch
　SN15. . . . . .78 F6
Charter Rd SN15. . . . . .78 D7
Chartley Gn **1** SN5. . .49 A5
Chartwell Pl SP3 . . . . 196 E6
Chartwell Rd SN25. . . .34 F7
Chase Ave SP5 . . . . . . 207 E6
Chase Cres SP5. . . . . . 207 E4
Chase Wood SN5 . . . . .34 A2
Chastleton Rd SN25. . .34 E7
Chatfield SN25 . . . . . . 20 D1
Chatham Cl SP1 . . . . . 145 F4
Chatham Ct **1** BA12. . 117 B7
Chatsworth Rd SN25. . .34 F7
Chaucer Ave **5** SP10 193 C1
Chaucer Cl SN4. . . . . . .47 E3
Chaveywell Ct SN11. . .81 B2
Cheapside BA12 . . . . . 195 A2
Cheater's La SP6 . . . . . 210 A1
Cheddar Cl BA11. . . . . 110 C7
Cheddar Rd SN25. . . . .34 E3
CHEDGLOW. 14 C7
Chedworth Gate SN3 . .50 F7
Cheese Mkt **1** SP1 . . 146 A1
Cheese Wharf ★ SN7. . . .2 F1
Chelmsford Rd SN5. . . .48 F4
Cheltenham Dr SN14. . .78 A5

Cheltenham St SN1. . . .50 B7
Chelwood Cl SN14. . . . .78 B6
CHELWORTH. 4 C1
Chelworth House SN16 . .4 B1
Chelworth Ind Est
　SN6. . . . . 19 A5
CHELWORTH LOWER
　GREEN. 19 A5
Chelworth Rd SN6. . . . .19 B6
Chelworth Road
　Chelworth Upper Green
　SN6. . . . . .19 A5
　Chelworth Upper Green
　SN6. . . . . .19 A4
CHELWORTH UPPER
　GREEN. 19 A6
Chemical Rd BA13 . . . 108 C6
CHENEY MANOR. 34 F1
Cheney Manor Ind Est
　SN2. . . . . .34 E1
Cheney Manor Rd SN2 .34 F2
Cheney Pl SN2. . . . . . . .34 F2
Chepston Pl BA14. . . . 100 F1
Chepstow Cl
　4 Chippenham SN14 . .78 A5
　Swindon SN5 . . . . . . .49 C3
Cheraton Cl SN3. . . . . .51 B7
Cherbury Wlk SN3 . . . .51 A6
CHERHILL. 166 B1
Cherhill CE Sch SN11 166 B1
Cherhill Ct SN25. . . . . .34 E3
Cherhill Way SN11. . . . .89 C8
Cherhill White Horse ★
　SN11. . . . . 172 C8
Cherrington Field
　SN10. . . . . 180 F4
Cherry Cl
　Pewsey SN9. . . . . 215 D5
　Salisbury SP2. . . . . . 145 D1
Cherry Gdns BA14 . . . 102 A3
Cherry Gdns Ct BA14. 105 D7
Cherry Gr **7** RG17 . . 177 B7
Cherry Orch
　Codford St Peter
　BA12. . . . . 195 A2
　Highworth SN6. . . . . . 23 A5
　Marlborough SN8. . . . 213 D2
Cherry Orch E SN2. . . .35 E2
Cherry Orch La
　Cann SP2. . . . . 202 A1
　Luckington SN14 . . . . .39 C5
　Salisbury SP2. . . . . . 145 D1
Cherry Orch N SN2 . . . .35 E2
Cherry Orch W SN2 . . . .35 D2
Cherry Rd SN14. . . . . . .75 A5
Cherry Tree Ave SP9. . 216 E7
Cherry Tree Ct SN11. . .81 B4
Cherry Tree Gr SN2 . . . .35 C2
Cherry Tree Rd SN6. . . 19 D8
Cherry Tree Way **2**
　SP4. . . . . 217 C3
Chervil Cl **3** SN2 . . . .34 C4
Cherwell SN26. . . . . . . 20 D1
Chesford Cl SN3. . . . . .51 A4
Cheshire Cl
　2 Bower Hill SN12. . 178 B8
　Salisbury SP2. . . . . . 145 C4
Chesterfield Cl
　3 Amesbury SP4. . . 217 E3
　4 Swindon SN5 . . . .49 C6
Chester St SN1 . . . . . . .50 B6
Chesters The SN5. . . . .49 C6
Chester Way SN14 . . . .78 A5
Chestnut Ave
　Netheravon SP4. . . . . 190 A2
　Swindon SN2 . . . . 35 C3
　Tidworth SP9 . . . . . . 216 D7
Chestnut Cl
　Acton Turville GL9 . . . 53 A6
　Down Ampney GL7. . . . .8 D7
　Frome BA11. . . . . 110 B7
　Rowde SN10 . . . . .96 D2
　Salisbury SP1. . . . . . 146 D3
Chestnut Cnr **13**
　BA13. . . . . 186 B7
Chestnut Dr SN10. . . . 178 E5
Chestnut Gr
　Sutton Benger SN15 . .57 C2
　Trowbridge BA14. . . . 105 B5
　Westbury BA13 . . . . . 108 F3
　Westwood BA15 . . . . . .99 F4
Chestnut Grange
　SN13. . . . . 76 D1
Chestnut Mews SN12 . .94 A3
Chestnut Rd
　Chippenham SN14 . . . .78 B8
　Sutton Benger SN15 . .57 C2
Chestnut Springs SN5 33 D1
Chestnut Tree Gdns
　BA12. . . . . 116 F4
Chestnut Wlk **11**
　RG17. . . . . 177 B6
Chetcombe Rd BA12 . 139 B6
Chevalier Cl **13** SN5. . .48 F8
Cheverell Ave SP1. . . . 146 C3
Cheverell Cl BA14. . . . 105 D5
Cheverell Gn Rd
　SN10. . . . . 179 C2
Cheverell Rd
　Cheverell Parva SN10 179 C1
　West Lavington SN10 187 D8
Cheviot Cl
　Swindon SN5. . . . . . . .49 A6
　Trowbridge BA14. . . . 105 F2
Cheviot Rd **25** SP11. . 193 F2
Chevral Cl SN14 . . . . . .70 B2
Cheyney Wlk BA13. . . 109 B4

Chichester Cl SP2 . . . 152 B6
Chichester Pk BA13. . 109 A4
Chickerell Rd SN3 . . . .51 A4
CHICKLADE 200 A5
CHICKSGROVE 204 B8
Chicks Grove Rd SP3. 201 B1
Chick's La SN8 . . . . . . 183 E1
Chicory Cl SN2 . . . . . . .34 C3
Chiffchaff Cl GL7 . . . . . .7 A6
Child St **1** RG17. . . . 165 A1
CHILMARK 201 B3
Chilmark & Fonthill
　Bishop CE Aided Prim
　Sch SP3. . . . . 201 B3
Chilmark Rd
　Stockton SP3 . . . . . . 201 C6
　Tisbury SP3 . . . . 200 F1
　Trowbridge BA14. . . . 100 F1
　Trowbridge BA14. . . . 101 A1
Chiltern Cl
　Melksham SN12. . . . . .94 C4
　9 Warminster BA12. . 117 A8
CHILTON FOLIAT 170 F1
Chilton Foliat CE Prim
　Sch RG17. . . . . 171 A2
Chilton Gdns SN25. . . .34 F3
Chilton Way RG17 . . . 171 A2
Chilvester Hill SN11. . .80 C2
Chilworth Cl **5** SN25 .34 E6
Chine Rd SP4. . . . . 131 C7
Chip Cottage BA11. . . 118 B4
CHIPPENHAM. 78 E7
Chippenham Cl **4**
　SN25. . . . . .35 B6
Chippenham Com Hospl
　SN15. . . . . .78 C6
Chippenham La SN14 . .77 B7
Chippenham Lane
　SN14. . . . . .77 C7
Chippenham Mus &
　Heritage Ctr ★ SN15 .78 E7
Chippenham Rd
　Biddestone SN14 . . . . .76 F7
　Chippenham SN14 . . . .77 B7
　Corsham SN13. . . . . . .76 F2
　Corsham SN13. . . . . . 77 B4
　Corston SN16. . . . . . . 42 E4
　Lyneham & Bradenstoke
　SN15. . . . . 59 E3
　Marshfield SN14 . . . . .74 A8
　Marshfield SN14 . . . . .74 C8
　Chippenham Sta SN15 .78 E8
Chipper La SP1. . . . . . 146 A1
CHIRTON 180 F4
Chirton CE Prim Sch
　SN10. . . . . 180 F4
Chirton Pl **5** BA14. . . 105 D6
CHISBURY 176 B5
Chisbury Camp ★
　SN8. . . . . 176 C4
Chisbury La SN8. . . . . 176 C5
Chiselbury Gr SP2 . . . 152 A6
CHISELDON 65 D3
Chiseldon Ct SN4. . . . .65 C4
Chiseldon Prim Sch
　SN4. . . . . .65 E4
Chissell Brook SN11. . .81 B4
Chitham Cl SN10. . . . . 187 C8
CHITTERNE 195 C7
Chitterne Anstey
　BA12. . . . . 194 E5
Chitterne Rd
　Chitterne BA12 . . . . . 195 E8
　Codford BA12. . . . . . . 195 B3
　Codford St Mary BA12. 195 B2
　Shrewton SP3 . . . . . . 196 B6
　Tilshead SP3 . . . . 187 F1
　Tilshead SP3 . . . . 188 A2
CHITTOE. 87 E2
Chittoe Heath SN15. . . .88 A2
Chivers Rd
　Chippenham SN15. . . .78 E5
　Devizes SN10. . . . . . . 214 D3
Chives Way SN2 . . . . . .34 D4
Chobham Cl SN2 . . . . .36 A5
CHOLDERTON 199 C5
Cholderton Rare Breeds
　Farm ★ SP4 . . . . 199 A5
Cholderton Rd
　Amport SP4 . . . . 199 D5
　Quarley SP4. . . . . 199 F5
Chopping Knife La
　SN8. . . . . 175 A7
Choristers Sq **1** SP1. 152 A8
Choulston Cr SN4. . . . 190 B3
Christ Church Prim Sch
　BA15. . . . . 100 E8
Christchurch Rd
　BA15. . . . . 100 D8
Christchurch Terr
　BA12. . . . . 116 F5
CHRISTIAN
　MALFORD. 58 B2
Christian Malford CE
　Prim Sch SN15 . . . . .58 A2
Christie Cl SN3 . . . . . . 51 D4
Christie Miller Rd
　SP2. . . . . 145 B4
Christie Miller Sports Ctr
　SN12. . . . . .94 B1
Christin Ct BA14. . . . . 105 A8
Christopher Cl **2**
　SP2. . . . . 151 F5
Christopher Dr SN15. . .79 A4

Christ the King RC Prim
　Sch SP4. . . . . 217 B3
Christy's Gdns **30**
　SP7. . . . . 202 C2
Christy's La **23** SP7 . . 202 C2
Chubb Cl SN16 . . . . . . .28 A5
Chudleigh SN5. . . . . . .49 B4
Church Acre
　Bradford-on-Avon
　BA15. . . . . 100 C7
　Codford BA12. . . . . . . 195 A3
　Seagry SN15 . . . . .57 F6
Church Cl
　Bath BA1 . . . . 82 B2
　Bourton SP8. . . . . 137 D1
　13 Lambourn RG17. . 165 A2
Church End SN5 . . . . . .33 D3
Church End Cl SN15 . . .60 A2
Churches BA15 . . . . . . 100 C7
Church Farm
　9 Swindon SN3 . . . .36 B3
　Vernhams Dean SP11 . 185 B4
　Yatton Keynell SN14 . .68 F5
Church Farm La
　Alton Barnes SN8 . . . 173 C1
　Farleigh Hungerford
　BA2 . . . . 120 A5
　South Marston SN3 . . .36 A4
　Woodborough SN9. . . 181 D7
Church Farm Mews
　SN15. . . . . .60 A2
Church Farm Rd SN6 . .8 D4
Churchfield SN25. . . . .34 F4
CHURCHFIELDS 145 D1
Churchfields BA15. . . .91 E6
Church Fields BA14. . 105 A5
Churchfields Academy
　SN3. . . . . .50 F5
Churchfields Ind Est
　SP2. . . . . 145 E1
Churchfields Rd SP2. 145 E1
Churchfields the Village
　Sch BA15. . . . . .90 E2
Churchfields, the Village
　School SN12 . . . . . . .92 E8
Church Furlong SP3. . 129 E2
Church Ground SN3 . . .36 F4
Church Hatch **1** SP5 211 B8
Church Hill
　Bromham SN15. . . . . .95 F7
　Donhead St Mary SP7. 203 A3
　Limpley Stoke BA2. . . . 99 B5
　Nettleton SN14 . . . . . .53 B3
　Redlynch SP5. . . . . . . 211 D7
　Shaftesbury SP7 . . . . 202 B2
　West Overton SN8. . . 173 F7
　Wroughton SN4. . . . . .63 F5
Church Hill Rise SN15. .96 A7
Churchill Ave
　Broad Blunsdon SN26 . 21 C2
　Durrington/Bulford
　SP4. . . . . 217 D8
　Melksham SN12. . . . . .94 D5
Churchill Cl
　Calne SN11 . . . . .81 C1
　North Tidworth SP9. . 216 B8
　3 Royal Wootton Bassett
　SN4 . . . . .47 F3
Churchill Ct SP2. . . . . 144 D3
Churchill Est SP3 . . . . 203 E8
Churchill Way SN13. . .76 F3
Churchill Way E SP1. . 146 B1
Churchill Way N SP1 . 146 A2
Churchill Way S SP1. . 152 B7
Churchill Way W
　Charlton SP10. . . . . . 193 C1
　Salisbury SP2. . . . . . 146 A1
Church La
　Amesbury SP4 . . . . . . 217 A3
　Ashbury SN6 . . . . 164 A7
　Ashton Keynes SN6. . . .6 E1
　Bishopstone SN6 . . . . 163 E6
　Bishopstone SP5 . . . . 150 A1
　Bishopstrow BA12. . . 117 E4
　Box SN13. . . . . 83 C5
　16 Bratton BA13. . . 186 B7
　Britford SP5. . . . . 152 E5
　Brokenborough SN16 . .27 D7
　Buttermere SN8. . . . . 185 C7
　Codford St Peter BA12 195 B2
　5 Cricklade SN6. . . 19 D8
　Damerham SP6 . . . . . 209 F2
　Dauntsey SN15 . . . . . .44 E1
　Dauntsey SN15 . . . . . .45 A1
　Down Ampney GL7. . . .8 D6
　Downton SP5 . . . . 159 A5
　Durrington/Bulford
　SP4. . . . . 217 D8
　East Kennet SN8 . . . . 173 D6
　Fovant SP3 . . . . 204 D8
　Great Somerton SN15. .44 E1
　Hankerton SN16 . . . . . 15 C2
　Hawkesbury GL9 . . . . .38 E5
　32 Hungerford RG17. 177 B7
　Inglesham GL7. . . . . . . .2 B1
　Kington Langley SN15. .70 E6
　Limpley Stoke BA2. . . . 99 A5
　6 Ludgershall SP11. 192 A5
　Lyneham SN15. . . . . . .60 A2
　Marshfield SN14 . . . . .74 A8
　Martin SP6. . . . . 209 B6
　Melchet Park & Plaitford
　SO51. . . . . 212 E7
　Melksham SN12. . . . . .94 C6
　Middle Woodford SP4 . 131 B6
　Mildenhall SN8. . . . . . 175 A8
　Monkton Combe BA2. . .98 E8
　Newbury BA12 . . . . . . 119 C8

Church La continued
　Norton SN16 . . . . 41 D5
　Ogbourne St Andrew
　SN8 . . . . 168 E3
　Ogbourne St George
　SN8 . . . . 168 F5
　Pitton & Farley SP5. . 148 C4
　Rushall SN9 . . . . 181 E2
　Salisbury SP2. . . . . . 145 C2
　2 Shaftesbury SP7 . 202 C1
　Sherfield English SO51 162 F3
　Sherrington BA12 . . . 194 F2
　Shipton Moyne GL8. . . 26 E3
　Sopworth SN14 . . . . . .24 D1
　South Cerney GL7. . . . . .6 F7
　Stanton Fitzwarren SN6 .22 B1
　Stanton St Quintin SN14 56 E3
　Stanton St Quintin SN14 56 C6
　Tidworth SP9 . . . . 216 D4
　Trowbridge BA14. . . . 105 A5
　Vernhams Dean SP11. . 185 B4
　Westbury BA13 . . . . . 108 E1
　West Lavington SN10 187 E8
　Wingfield BA14 . . . . . 104 C6
　Woolverton BA2. . . . . 103 C1
Churchlands BA14. . . 105 D2
Church Lawn
　Stourton BA12. . . . . . 123 F1
　Stourton BA12. . . . . . 137 F8
Church Leat SP5. . . . . 211 A8
Church Mdws **1**
　SP9. . . . . 199 D8
Church Piece SN5 . . . .57 D2
Church Pk SN15 . . . . . .59 C3
Church Pl
　Lydiard Millicent SN5. .33 C1
　Lydiard Millicent SN5. .48 C8
　1 Swindon SN1 . . . .50 A6
Church Rails SP3 . . . . 141 B1
Church Rd
　Biddestone SN14. . . . .76 E7
　Bourton SP8. . . . . 137 F1
　Bratton BA13. . . . . . . 186 B6
　Calne Without SN11. . . .80 A2
　Cheverell Magna SN10 179 B1
　Christian Malford SN15. .58 A2
　Derry Hill/Studley SN11 .79 F2
　East Knoyle SP3. . . . . 141 B1
　Farley SP5 . . . . 155 A8
　Farnham DT11. . . . . . 207 C2
　Froxfield SN8 . . . . 176 D7
　Ham SN8 . . . . 177 A1
　Heddington SN13. . . . . 89 B1
　Hilmarton SN11 . . . . . .73 F3
　Idmiston SP4 . . . . 133 F8
　Iwerne Minster DT11. . 206 A1
　Kemble GL7 . . . . .4 F7
　Kempsford GL7 . . . . . . 10 E6
　Kilmington BA12 . . . . 123 E5
　Kington Langley SN15. .70 E6
　Lechlade-on-Thames GL7 . 2 D4
　Liddington SN4. . . . . . 163 A4
　Luckington SN14 . . . . .39 E4
　Milston SP4 . . . . 198 C8
　Norleaze BA13. . . . . . 108 F8
　Pitton & Farley SP5. . 154 E7
　St Paul Malmesbury Without
　SN16. . . . . 43 A3
　Salisbury SP1. . . . . . 146 E3
　Sherston GL8. . . . . 25 B5
　Silton SP8. . . . . 138 A1
　Stanton St Bernard
　SN8 . . . . 173 B1
　Stanton St Quintin SN14 56 E3
　2 Swindon SN1 . . . .50 D4
　Tytherington BA12. . . 194 B4
　Wanborough SN4. . . . 163 A5
　Woodborough SN9. . . 181 D2
Church Ri SN14. . . . . . .53 B3
Church Ride SP1 . . . . . 192 A6
Church Rise SN13. . . . .84 E5
Church Row SN14 . . . . 163 D6
Church St Cl **15** SP3. . 203 E8
Church St
　Amesbury SP4 . . . . . . 217 A3
　Atworth SN12 . . . . . . .92 D8
　Bath BA1 . . . . 82 B2
　Berwick St John SP7. . 203 E1
　Bowerchalke SP5. . . . 204 F1
　Bower Chalke SP5 . . . 205 A2
　Bradford-on-Avon
　BA15. . . . . 100 C6
　Calne SN11 . . . . .81 B2
　Chiseldown SN4 . . . . . 65 D4
　Collingbourne Ducis
　SN8 . . . . 191 E8
　Corsham SN13. . . . . . 77 A2
　Durrington/Bulford
　SP4. . . . . 198 B7
　Great Bedwyn SN8 . . 176 B2
　Grimstead SP5. . . . . . 154 C2
　Horningsham BA12 . . 119 B7
　Hungerford RG17. . . . 177 B7
　Keevil BA14 . . . . 178 A4
　Lacock SN15 . . . . .86 D6
　Little Bedwyn SN8 . . . 176 D5
　Longbridge Deverill
　BA12. . . . . 120 F7
　Maiden Bradley with
　Yarnfield BA12. . . . . 118 E2
　Market Lavington SN10 179 F1
　Melksham SN12. . . . . .94 A4
　Mere BA12. . . . . 139 A5
　Pewsey SN9. . . . . 215 D4
　Purton SN5. . . . . 33 C4
　Royal Wootton Bassett
　SN4 . . . . .47 C2
　Semington BA14 . . . . 102 F6

Church St continued
　Sherston SN16. . . . . . .25 C1
　Southwick BA14. . . . . 104 F3
　Swindon SN3. . . . . 36 B3
　Tisbury SP3 . . . . 203 E8
　Trowbridge BA14. . . . 101 D1
　Warminster BA12 . . . 116 F7
　Westbury BA13 . . . . . 109 A4
　West Lavington SN10 187 E8
　Winterbourne Stoke
　SP3. . . . . 196 F3
　Wylye BA12 . . . . 201 E8
Church Tk SP8 . . . . . . 137 D1
Church View
　Calne SN11 . . . . .81 C1
　Castle Eaton SN6. . . . . 10 B4
　Chippenham SN14 . . . .70 C2
　Quemerford SN11. . . . .89 C8
　Sutton Benger SN15 . .57 E2
Churchward Ave SN2. . .35 A1
Churchward Dr BA11 . 110 C7
Churchward Sch SN26 .20 E7
Churchway SN26. . . . . .21 C2
Church Way
　Hungerford RG17. . . . 177 B7
　7 Swindon SN3 . . . .36 B3
Church Wlk
　Ashton Keynes SN6. . . .6 E1
　Avebury SN8. . . . . 173 B8
　Bishops Cannings
　SN10 . . . . 172 B3
　Bishopstone SN6 . . . . 163 E6
　Devizes SN10. . . . . . . 214 C3
　Melksham SN12. . . . . .94 A4
　Motcombe SP7. . . . . . 202 A4
　Redlynch SP5. . . . . . . 211 E7
　Swindon SN2 . . . . .35 C1
Church Wlk N SN25. . . .34 F3
Church Wlk S SN2 . . . .34 F3
Churn Cl GL7. . . . . .6 F7
Chur St SP4 . . . . 198 E6
CHUTE CADLEY 192 F8
Chute Causeway
　SP11. . . . . 185 A2
Chute Cswy SP11. . . . 184 E2
CHUTE STANDEN . . . 192 F8
Cinders End SN14. . . . .78 D8
Circle The SN2 . . . . . . .35 C2
Cirencester Rd
　Fairford GL7. . . . . .1 C1
　Latton GL7. . . . . .7 E3
　South Cerney GL7. . . . . .6 F8
Cirencester Way
　Swindon SN2 . . . . .50 D8
　Swindon SN25. . . . . . .35 D2
Citrine Cl SN25 . . . . . . 20 F1
City Cnr SN4. . . . . 163 C6
City The SN12 . . . . .94 A5
Clack La SP6 . . . . 210 B3
Clanfield Rd SN3 . . . . .51 B5
Clanger La BA13. . . . . 109 A8
CLANVILLE
　Penton Grafton 193 A4
　Stanton St Quintin . . . 56 E4
Clanville Way SN15. . . .56 E3
Clapham Cl **6** SN25 . .34 E3
Clap La SP5 . . . . 207 B4
Clardon La SN5. . . . . . .33 C6
Clare Ave BA14 . . . . . . 106 B4
Clarence Cl **18** SP11 . 192 A5
Clarence Rd
　Chippenham SN14 . . . .77 F7
　Trowbridge BA14. . . . 105 F8
Clarence St SN1 . . . . . .50 C6
Clarendon Ave BA14 . 105 E8
Clarendon Cl SP3. . . . 201 F2
Clarendon Coll The
　BA14. . . . . 105 C4
Clarendon Ct
　Marlborough SN8. . . . 213 D3
　Tidworth SP9 . . . . 216 D7
Clarendon Dr SN4 . . . .47 E1
Clarendon Infs Sch
　SP9. . . . . 216 D7
Clarendon Jun Sch
　SP9. . . . . 216 D7
Clarendon Pal ★ SP5. 147 C1
Clarendon Rd
　Alderbury SP5 . . . . . . 153 D3
　Clarendon Park SP5. . 152 F6
　Grimstead SP5. . . . . . 154 A4
　Salisbury SP1. . . . . . 146 C1
　Trowbridge BA14. . . . 105 E8
Clare Wlk SN5. . . . . . . .49 B4
Claridge Cl **3** SN8. . . 170 A2
Clark Ave SN11 . . . . . . .81 C5
Clarkes Field SN6. . . . . 17 B1
Clarke Dr SN5 . . . . .49 B8
Clarke's La SP11. . . . . 193 A7
Clarkes Leaze SN14. . . .68 F5
Clark's Gdns **25** RG17 177 B7
Clarks Hay GL7 . . . . .6 F7
Clark's Pl **3** BA14 . . . 105 E8
Classics The **16** RG17 165 A1
CLATFORD. 174 B7
Clattinger Farm Nature
　Reserve ★ SN16 . . . . .16 C7
Claudius Cl **15** SP10. . 193 E2
CLAVERTON. 90 B5
Claverton Hill BA2. . . .90 A4
Claverton Pumping Sta ★
　BA1. . . . . .90 C5
Clay Cl BA13. . . . . 112 C8
Claydon Rd **6** SN25. . .34 E7
Clay Fields **6** GL8. . . . .26 C6
Clayfurlong Gr GL7 . . . .4 F8
Clayhill Copse SN5 . . . .34 A2

Clays Cl SN2. . . . . .35 E3
Clay St
  Little Somerford SN15. . 44 C6
  Longbridge Deverill
  BA12. . . . . 116 E1
  Whiteparish SP5. . . . . . 161 C3
Clays The SN10. . . . . . 179 F1
Clay The SN10. . . . . . . 180 A1
Clayton Rd SP4. . . . . . . 217 E8
Clearbury Ring★
  SP5. . . . . 158 C5
Clearbury Vw 7 SP5. . 210 F8
CLEARWOOD. 111 F8
Clearwood
  Dilton Marsh BA13. . . . 107 F1
  Westbury BA13. . . . . . 111 F8
Clearwood View
  BA13. . . . . 111 D4
Cleasby Cl SN5 . . . . 49 D6
Cleavers The 1 SN8. . 183 D8
Cleaves Ave SN14. . . . . .75 A3
Cleevedale Rd SN13 . . .85 A8
Cleeve Lawns SN3. . . . . 50 F3
Cleeves Cl SN5. . . . . . . 49 A6
Cleeves The SP3. . . . . . 143 B3
Cleeve The
  Corsham SN13. . . . . . . 85 A8
  West Knoyle BA12. . . . 140 A6
Clementine Rd 4
  SN25. . . . . .34 B7
Clement's La BA12. . . 139 B4
CLENCH. 174 E1
CLENCH COMMON. . . 174 D4
CLEVANCY. 166 C6
Clevedon Cl SN3. . . . . . 51 A6
Cleveland Gdns BA14 101 E2
Cleveland Rd SN2. . . . . 34 C3
Cleveland Way BA13. . 108 E2
Cleverley Way SN11. . . .81 B1
CLEVERTON. 44 D8
Cleverton Ct SN2 . . . . . 35 C5
Cleves Cl SN5 . . . . 49 A6
Cleyhill Gdns BA13. . . 111 D5
Cley Hill (Hill Fort)★
  BA12. . . . . 116 A6
Cley View 6 BA12. . . 116 E6
Cliffe Dr BA2. . . . . 99 A6
Cliffords SN6. . . . . .19 C8
Cliff Rd SN16. . . . . 40 C8
Cliff Ave SN15 . . . . 70 E1
Clift Cl SN13. . . . . 84 A8
Clifton Cl SN14 . . . . . . .78 B8
Clifton Rd SP2. . . . . . . 145 F2
Clifton St SN11. . . . . . . 50 B5
Clifts Bldgs BA11. . . . . 110 A4
Clinchorn Farm Rd
  SP11. . . . . 185 E2
Clink Farm Ct 6
  BA11. . . . . 110 C6
Clink La SN12. . . . . 87 C2
Clink Rd BA11. . . . . 110 E6
Clinton Cl SN5. . . . . . . .48 F4
Clipsham Rise BA14. . 101 A3
Clive Parade SN2. . . . . 35 D3
Clivey BA13. . . . . 107 E1
CLOATLEY. 15 E2
Cloatley Cres SN4 . . . . 61 E8
CLOATLEY END. 16 B1
Cloatley Manor★
  SN16. . . . . .15 D2
Cloatley Mdws Nature
  Reserve★ SN16. . . . . . 15 E2
Cloatley Rd SN16 . . . . .15 C2
Cloche Way SN2. . . . . . 35 E3
Clock Tower Vw SN12. .92 E8
Cloford Cl BA14 . . . . . 101 A1
Cloister Gdn★ SN16. . 28 A3
Close End 8 RG17. . . 165 A1
Close La
  Marston SN10. . . . . . . 179 A3
  Rowde SN10 . . . . 96 D2
Close The
  Bulkington SN10. . . . . 178 E5
  Chippenham SN14. . . . 77 E8
  Corsham SN13. . . . . . . 85 C6
  Kington St Michael SN14 70 A8
  Laverstock SP4 . . . . . 146 D8
  Lydiard Millicent SN5. . 48 B8
  Melksham SN12. . . . . . 94 B3
  4 Redlynch SP5. . . . . 211 C8
  Salisbury SP1. . . . . . . 152 A8
  Tangley SP11. . . . . . . 193 C5
  Warminster BA12. . . . 117 A7
Clothier Leaze 2
  BA14. . . . . 105 D7
Cloth Yd 1 BA14. . . . . 105 E7
Cloudberry Rd SN25 . .34 B5
Clough La SN5 . . . . 149 B7
Clouts Wood 5 SN5. .34 A2
Clouts Wood Nature
  Reserve★ SN4. . . . . . .63 F4
Clover Cl SN12. . . . . . . .94 C3
Clover Dean SN14. . . . .78 A6
Clover Gdns 25 SP11. 192 A5
Clover Gr SN11 . . . . . . 81 D5
Clover La
  8 Cricklade SN6. . . . . 19 D8
  Durrington/Bulford
  SP4. . . . . 198 B7
Cloverlands SN25. . . . 34 D4
Clover Pk SN12. . . . . . . 94 C3
Clubhouse Pl 2 SN13. 76 C1
Club La SP9 . . . . 216 C4
Club Rd SP4 . . . . 198 F7
Clump Way SP4 . . . . . . 217 A5
Clydesdale Cl
  5 Swindon SN5 . . . . . 49 A7

Clydesdale Cl continued
  Trowbridge BA14. . . . . 105 C5
Clydesdale Rd SN13. . 83 D5
CLYFFE PYPARD. 166 F8
Coach Barton BA14. . 178 A3
Coach Hill SP11. . . . . . 192 E6
Coach Hollow BA13. . 186 D8
Coach Ho Mews SP4. . 217 B3
Coach Rd
  Bradford-on-Avon
  BA15. . . . . 100 C6
  Westbury BA13. . . . . . 109 B5
Coalpit Rd BA1. . . . . . . .82 A4
Coalway La BA11. . . . . 110 C7
COATE
  Bishops Cannings. . . 180 C8
  Chiseldon. 51 C2
Coate La
  Devizes SN10. . . . . . . .97 F1
  Devizes SN10. . . . . . . 214 E5
Coate Rd SN8. . . . . 173 B1
Coate Water Ctry Pk★
  SN3. . . . . .51 A1
Coate Water Nature
  Reserve★ SN3. . . . . . .51 B1
Coatside Way SN3 . . . 51 F1
Cobb Dr 16 SP11. . . . . 193 F2
Cobbett Cl SN25. . . . . 35 A7
Cobbett Pl BA12. . . . . 116 F6
Cobb La
  Middle Winterslow
  SP5. . . . . 149 A7
  Winterslow SP5. . . . . 148 F7
Cobden Rd SN25. . . . . 50 A8
Cob Hill SN25. . . . . .34 B3
COBLEY. 208 D7
Cobley Cl SP5 . . . . 208 D6
Cob Pl BA13. . . . . 108 E2
Coburg Sq 1 SN12. . . 94 B4
Cochran Ave SN14. . . .78 C5
Cock-a-Troop La
  SN8. . . . . 175 B8
Cock Hill BA14. . . . . . . 101 A1
Cock La BA2. . . . . .99 A1
Cocklebury La SN15 . .70 F1
Cocklebury Rd SN15 . .78 E8
Cock Rd
  Horningsham BA12. . . 118 F8
  Rowde SN10 . . . . 95 F2
Cocks Cl 5 SP4 . . . . . 197 E7
Codford Bypass
  BA12. . . . . 195 A2
Codford Circ or Wilsbury
  Ring★ BA12. . . . . . . 195 C3
Codford Rd BA12. . . . 195 C6
Codford Rising Sun (Hill
  Figure)★ BA12. . . . . 195 C2
CODFORD ST MARY. . 195 B2
CODFORD ST
  PETER. 195 A3
Cody Cl BA13. . . . . 109 B5
Coffin Cl SN6. . . . . .23 A6
Coker's La
  Kilmington BA12. . . . . 123 F7
  Kilmington BA12. . . . . 124 A6
Colbert Pk SN25. . . . . 34 F6
Colborne Cl SN15. . . . .79 B5
Colbourne St SN1. . . . 50 D7
Colchester Cl SN5 . . . 49 D4
COLD HARBOUR
  Great Hinton. 102 F2
  Warminster 116 F8
Cold Harbour SP4. . . 217 B3
Coldharbour La SP2. . 145 F2
Cold Harbour La SN8 213 E4
Coldharbour Rd
  RG17. . . . . 177 B6
Colebrook Inf Acad
  SN3. . . . . .51 C8
Colebrook Rd SN3. . . 36 B1
Cole Cl
  2 Andover SP10. . . . 193 E2
  Malmesbury SN16. . . . 28 C1
  Swindon SN3. . . . . . . 51 D6
Cole Hill BA12. . . . . . . 114 D5
Colemans Cl SN11. . . .81 C3
Coleridge Cl
  Royal Wootton Bassett
  SN4 . . . . 47 E3
  Warminster BA12. . . . 116 D6
Coleridge Rd SN25. . . .34 F6
COLERNE. 75 B3
Colerne Airfield SN14. .74 E3
Colerne CE Prim Sch
  SN14. . . . . .75 B3
Colerne Industrial Pk
  SN14. . . . . .75 A3
Colerne Pk★ SN14. . 75 F6
Coles Cres 8 SP7. . . 202 D1
Cole's La SP7. . . . . . . 202 A1
Coles's La SP5. . . . . . 212 A7
Collard Cl SN1. . . . . . . .50 B2
College Cl SN15 . . . . . .78 F8
College Farm La 5
  SN6. . . . . 164 A8
College Fields SN8 . . 213 C4
College Gdns BA14 . . 105 D3
College Gr 1 SN4 . . . 163 A6
College Rd
  1 Durrington/Bulford
  SP4. . . . . 198 B7
  Purton SN5. . . . . 33 C4
  Trowbridge BA14. . . . . 105 B6
  Trowbridge BA14. . . . . 105 D5
College Row SN12. . . .93 F7
College Rd
  Salisbury SP1. . . . . . . 146 B1
  Swindon SN1 . . . . 50 C6

College Way 4 RG17. 171 E7
Collen Cl 1 SN14. . . . .78 A7
Collett Ave SN2. . . . . . 35 A1
Collett Pl SN6. . . . . . . .8 C3
Collett Way BA11. . . . 110 C7
Collingbourne CE Prim
  Sch SN8. . . . . 191 E8
Collingbourne Cl 2
  BA14. . . . . 105 D5
COLLINGBOURNE
  DUCIS. 191 E8
COLLINGBOURNE
  KINGSTON. 183 D2
Colling La SP9. . . . . . . 216 D8
Collingsmead SN3. . . .51 C5
Collingwood Cl SP5. . 153 F1
Collingwood Cres
  SN25. . . . . .35 D3
Collingwood Wlk 4
  SP10. . . . . 193 F1
Collins Cl 5 SP10 . . . 193 D2
Collins Ct SP9 . . . . . . 216 C8
Collins La SN5. . . . . . . .33 E5
Colman Pk SN25. . . . . 35 A6
Coln Cres SN25. . . . . . 35 A4
Coln House Sch GL7. .1 F6
Colquhoun Rd 2
  SP4. . . . . 198 A6
Colston Cl SN3 . . . . . . 51 A4
Colston Rd SN10. . . . . 214 A4
Coltsfoot Cl SP4. . . . . 217 C3
Column Rd SN8. . . . . . 175 E3
COMBE. 185 F8
Combe Bottom SP11. 185 F5
Combe Hay La BA2. . .98 A6
Combe La
  Bratton BA13. . . . . . . 186 B7
  Hilmarton SN11. . . . . . .73 F6
Combe View
  10 Hungerford RG17. 177 B6
  Yatton Keynell SN14. .68 F5
Combe Wlk
  Devizes SN10. . . . . . . 97 E1
  Devizes SN10. . . . . . . 214 D5
Comet Ave SN9. . . . . . 182 B2
Comet Cl SN15. . . . . . 60 B2
Comet Cres SN11. . . . 81 D4
Comfrey Cl
  Swindon SN2. . . . . . . 34 D4
  Trowbridge BA14. . . . . 105 E6
Commerce Bsns Ctr
  BA13. . . . . 108 E7
Commerce Cl BA13 . . 108 E7
Commerce Park
  BA11. . . . . 110 D8
Commercial Rd
  Devizes SN10. . . . . . . 214 A4
  Swindon SN1 . . . . 50 B5
Common Dro DT11. . . 207 B3
Common Hill
  Cricklade SN6. . . . . . . 19 B7
  Great Hinton BA14. . . 102 F2
  Steeple Ashton BA14. 106 F8
COMMON PLATT. 33 F2
Common Platt
  Peatmoor SN5 . . . . . . 34 A2
  Purton SN5. . . . . 33 F2
Common Rd
  St Paul Malmesbury Without
  SN16. . . . . 27 D1
  Sixpenny Handley SP5. 207 F4
  Whiteparish SP5. . . . . 161 E1
Common Slip SN15 . . .78 E7
COMMON THE
  Brinkworth. 46 B7
  Broughton Gifford. . . . 93 B5
  Winterslow. 149 C6
Common The
  Bromham SN15. . . . . . 95 E6
  Holt BA14. . . . . 92 F1
  Kington Langley SN15. 70 E6
  Marlborough SN8. . . . 213 D4
  Minety SN16. . . . . 17 C1
  Shrewton SP3 . . . . . . 196 E6
  The Common SN5. . . . 149 D6
Commonweal Rd SN1. 50 B3
Commonweal Sch The
  SN1. . . . . 50 B3
Commonwood La
  SN16. . . . . 40 D5
Comm Rd BA12. . . . . . 118 F7
COMPTON. 189 F7
COMPTON ABBAS. . . 206 A5
Compton Abbas Airfield
  SP5. . . . . 206 C5
COMPTON BASSETT. 166 B3
COMPTON
  CHAMBERLAYNE. . . 205 A8
Compton Cl
  4 Swindon SN3. . . . . 51 C4
  Trowbridge BA14. . . . . 105 D5
Compton Gdns BA11. 110 C7
Compton Rd SP9 . . . . 216 D6
Compton's Dr SO51. . 212 E7
Conan Doyle Wlk SN3. 51 D4
Concorde Cres GL7. . . 1 F6
Concord Wlk SN3. . . . . 51 A5
Conference Cl 1
  BA12. . . . . 116 F7
Congreve Rd 4 SP4. . 197 E7
Conholt Hill SP11. . . . 185 A2
Conholt La SP11. . . . . 185 B2
Conholt Pk★ SP11. . 184 F1
Conifer Crest 5 SN8. 183 D8
Conifers The SN16. . . .17 A2
Coniger the (Tumuli)★
  SP3. . . . . 196 F5

Conigre BA14. . . . . 101 C1
Conigre Cl SN12. . . . . .94 A3
Conigre Hill BA15. . . . 100 C7
Conigre Mead Nature
  Reserve★ SN12. . . . . 94 A4
Conisborough SN5. . . .49 C5
Coniston Cl 5 SP4 . . . 217 E3
Coniston Rd
  Chippenham SN14. . . . .77 F6
  7 Chippenham SN14 . .78 A6
  Trowbridge BA14. . . . . 101 E2
CONKWELL
  90 C1
Conkwell BA15. . . . . . . 90 C2
Connaught Rd SP9. . . 216 D6
Connelly Cl 4 SN25 . . .34 C5
Connemara Cl 2
  BA13. . . . . 108 E2
Connolly Way SP9 . . . 216 D8
CONOCK. 180 C4
Conrad Cl SN3. . . . . . . 51 D4
Conscience La SN10. . 214 A1
Constable Rd SN2. . . . 35 E2
Constable Way SP2. . 151 E7
Constantine Sq 29
  SP10. . . . . 193 E2
Convent The★ BA10. 123 B2
Conway Cres SN12. . . .94 B2
Conway Rd
  Chippenham SN14. . . . .78 A7
  Swindon SN3 . . . . 51 C3
Conyers Cl 6 SN5. . . .48 F4
Conyger Rd SP4. . . . . 217 C2
Cookham Rd SN25. . . .34 C7
Cook Rd 6 SN8. . . . . . 170 A7
Cooks Cl
  Hullavington SN14. . . . 56 C1
  Salisbury SP2. . . . . . . 145 B5
  Seend SN12. . . . . 178 E8
COOMBE
  Donhead St Mary. . . . 202 F1
  Enford. 190 B5
Coombe Barn La
  Kilmington BA12. . . . . 124 D5
  Kilmington BA12. . . . . 125 A4
COOMBE BISSETT. . . 150 F1
Coombe Bissett CE Prim
  Sch SP5. . . . . 150 F1
Coombe Cl SN4. . . . . . .64 C5
Coombe La
  Atworth SN12. . . . . . . 92 C7
  Enford SN9. . . . . 190 C6
Coombe Rd
  Salisbury SP2. . . . . . . 151 F5
  Swindon SN25. . . . . . .34 F3
Coombe Road SP5. . . 151 B3
Coombe St BA9. . . . . . 137 D3
Coombe View BA12. . 194 D3
Cooper Cl SN26. . . . . . 20 B1
Cooper Fields SN25. . 35 A5
Coopers Cl
  Amesbury SP4. . . . . . 217 C1
  2 Malmesbury SN16. 28 A5
Cooper's La BA13. . . . 139 B1
Coopers Mdw SN14. . .68 F6
Cooper Way SN11. . . . .81 B1
Cop Croft SN11. . . . . . .81 B3
Copenacre SN16. . . . . 16 D2
Copenacre Way SN13. 76 C1
Copheap La BA12. . . . 117 B7
Copheap Rise BA12. . 117 B8
Copper Beech Cl SP3 196 F6
Copper Beeches SN6. .22 F5
Coppershell SN13. . . . 85 D6
Coppers Rd SN10. . . . 214 C5
Coppice Cl
  Chippenham SN14. . . . .78 B5
  Swindon SN2 . . . . 34 D3
  Warminster BA12. . . . 117 A7
Coppice Hill BA15. . . . 100 D7
Coppice La SN16. . . . . .15 E8
Coppice St SP7. . . . . . 202 C1
Copse Ave SN1. . . . . . 50 E8
Copse Dro SN8. . . . . . 169 B5
Copse The
  Alderbury SP5 . . . . . . 153 D2
  Frome BA11. . . . . 110 B6
Copse View 2 SN16. . .28 B2
Copyhold 2 SN8. . . . . 176 B3
Coral Cl 5 SN25. . . . . .34 F8
Corbin Rd BA14. . . . . . 101 F1
Corby Ave SN3. . . . . . . 50 E3
Corestreet La BA14 . . 102 E3
Corfe Cl SN25 . . . . 35 A4
Corfe Cres SN11. . . . . .81 A4
Corfe Rd
  Melksham SN12. . . . . . 94 B3
  Swindon SN5. . . . . . . 49 B4
Coriander Way SN2. . .34 D5
Corinium Way SN3. . . .36 C1
Corinthian Cl
  14 Andover SP10. . . . 193 E2
  Southwick BA14. . . . . 104 F3
Cornbrash BA11. . . . . 110 D7
Cornbrash Rise BA14 102 A1
Corncockle Cl SN12. . 94 D4
Corner Gd BA12. . . . . . 117 C5
Corner La SP7. . . . . . . 202 B5
Cornfield Rd SN10. . . 214 D3
Cornflower Cl SN25. . .81 C5
Cornflower Rd 3
  SN25. . . . . .34 D5
Cornflower Way
  31 Ludgershall SP11. 192 A5
  Melksham SN12. . . . . . 94 A3
Corn Gastons SN16. . .27 E3

Cornmarket BA12. . . . 117 B7
Cornmarsh Way SN3. . .51 E2
Cornpits La SP6. . . . . . 209 E2
Cornwall Ave SN2 . . . . 35 A1
Cornwall Cres SN12. . .94 C4
Cornwall Rd SP1. . . . . 146 A3
Cornwell Cres SN10. . 214 A2
Cornwood Rd 6 SN1. . 50 A1
Coronation Ave BA15 100 E7
Coronation Cl
  Christian Malford
  SN15. . . . . 58 A1
  Donhead St Mary SP7. 203 A1
  2 Pewsey SN9. . . . . . 215 C5
  Sutton Benger SN15. . 57 F1
Coronation Dr SP7. . . 203 A1
Coronation Rd
  Atworth/Whitley SN12. 92 C8
  Durrington/Bulford
  SP4. . . . . 198 B7
  Frome BA11. . . . . 110 B5
  3 Ludgershall SP11. . 192 B5
  Melksham SN12. . . . . . 94 B3
  Salisbury SP2. . . . . . . 145 D3
  Tidworth SP9. . . . . . . 216 C8
  Wroughton SN4. . . . . . 64 A6
Coronation Sq SP2. . . 144 F3
Coronation St
  Fairford GL7. . . . . 1 F1
  4 Trowbridge BA14. . 105 D7
Coronel Cl SN2. . . . . . . 36 A4
Corporation St SN2. . 50 C7
Corral Cl SN5. . . . . .34 A1
Corry The 1 SP3. . . . . 203 E8
Corsham Ct★ SN13. . .77 A2
Corsham Media Pk
  SN13. . . . . 84 C6
Corsham Pk★ SN13. . .77 B2
Corsham Prim Sch
  Corsham SN13. . . . . . . 77 B1
  Corsham SN13. . . . . . . 85 B8
  6 Rudloe SN13. . . . . . 84 B8
Corsham Rd
  Atworth/Whitley SN12. 85 D1
  Lacock SN13. . . . . 85 C6
  Swindon SN2. . . . . . . 35 C5
Corsham Regis Prim Sch
  SN13. . . . . .76 F2
Corsham Sch The
  SN13. . . . . .76 F1
Corsham Sports Club
  SN13. . . . . .77 A1
CORSLEY. 111 D2
CORSLEY HEATH. . . . 115 B8
Corsley Heath BA12. . 115 A8
CORSTON. 42 F5
CORTON. 194 D3
Corton SN11. . . . . 166 C6
Corton Cres SN5. . . . . .49 B6
Corton (Long Barrow)★
  BA12. . . . . 194 D3
Corton Rd BA12. . . . . 194 C3
Cory Way SN3. . . . . . . 108 E2
Cosford Cl SN4. . . . . . . 64 D3
Cossington Sq BA13. 108 E5
Cossor Rd SN9. . . . . . 215 B5
Coster's La SN4. . . . . . 205 A2
Coster View 6 SN8. . 176 B3
Cosway Ct SN3. . . . . . .36 C1
Cote La BA12. . . . . 123 C4
Cotley Pl 4 BA12. . . . 194 C5
COTMARSH. 62 B4
Cotswold Cl
  Calne SN11. . . . . 81 D2
  Melksham SN12. . . . . . 94 C4
  8 Warminster BA12. . 117 A8
COTSWOLD
  COMMUNITY. 6 D4
Cotswold Community The
  / Old Farmhouse SN6. 6 C4
Cotswold Water Pk★
  SN6. . . . . 6 F4
Cotswold Water Pk
  Gateway Ctr★ GL7. . 7 E6
Cottage Mews 13
  SP6. . . . . 210 D1
Cottars Cl 3 SN3. . . . 36 C1
Cotterell St BA15. . . . 100 E6
Cottington Cl SN5. . . . .49 A4
Cottle Ave BA15. . . . . 100 D8
Cottle Mead SN13. . . . 84 E8
Cottles Barton 5
  BA14. . . . . 101 D5
Cottles La BA15. . . . . . .99 C6
Cotton House Gdns
  Warminster BA12. . . . 117 B8
  Warminster BA12. . . . 117 B8
Cottrell Cl RG17. . . . . 177 C7
Couch La SN10. . . . . . 214 A4
COULSTON. 178 E1
Coulston Hollow
  BA13. . . . . 186 F8
Coulston Rd
  Corsham SN13. . . . . . . 77 A3
  Coulston BA13. . . . . . 186 F8
Council Houses The
  SN15. . . . . .44 A8
Countess Rd SP4 . . . . 217 A4
Country Park Way
  SN4. . . . . .61 F8
County Bsns Pk SN1. . 50 D7
County Rd SN1. . . . . . . 50 D7
County Way BA14. . . . 101 C1
Course Mdw SN25. . . .34 A2
Courtenay Rd SN3. . . . 51 A6
Court Farm Cl 8
  SP4. . . . . 190 A4

Cla-Cri 225

Court Farm Rd 1
  SP4. . . . . 190 A3
Courtfields SN6. . . . . . .8 C4
Court Gdns
  Bath BA1. . . . . 82 A3
  Stanton St Quintin SN14 56 B4
Court Hill
  Damerham SP6. . . . . . 209 F2
  Potterne SN10. . . . . . 179 C5
Court La
  Bathford BA1. . . . . 82 B1
  Bratton BA13. . . . . . . 186 B7
  Corsley BA12. . . . . . . 111 B1
  Edington BA13. . . . . . 186 B8
Court St Cl SP3. . . . . . 203 E8
Courts Gdns The★
  BA14. . . . . 101 E8
Courtsknap Ct 6 SN1. 50 A5
Court St
  Sherston SN16. . . . . . 25 C1
  Tisbury SP3. . . . . 203 E8
  Trowbridge BA14. . . . . 105 D8
Courtwood Cl 3
  SP1. . . . . 152 C8
Cove House Gdns SN6 . 6 F1
Coventry Cl SN4 . . . . . .64 B7
COVINGHAM. 51 D7
Covingham Dr SN3. . . 51 C8
Covingham Pk Prim Sch
  SN3. . . . . .51 C7
Covingham Sq SN3 . . 51 C7
Coward Rd BA12. . . . . 139 B4
Cowbridge Cres SN16. 28 C1
Cowdrey Cl SN5 . . . . . 49 B4
Cow Dro SP3. . . . . 201 B4
COWESFIELD
  GREEN. 161 F4
Cow La
  Kimpton SP11. . . . . . . 192 B2
  Laverstock SP1 . . . . . 146 C1
Cowleaze
  Chippenham SN14. . . . .78 F8
  Swindon SN25 . . . . . . 34 A3
Cowleaze Cres SN4. . .63 F6
Cowleaze La BA13. . . 186 D8
Cowleaze Wlk SN2. . . .35 F4
Cowley Way SN15. . . . 57 D1
Cowley Wlk SN3. . . . . 51 B6
Cowslip Bank 8 SN13 84 E8
Cowslip Gr SN11. . . . . .81 B5
Cowslip Way
  Chippenham SN14. . . . 70 B3
  East Anton SP11. . . . . 193 C5
Cow St SN5. . . . . .19 B1
Coxhill La SN10. . . . . . 179 D5
Cox's Hill
  Ashton Keynes SN6. . .6 E2
  Calne SN11. . . . . 81 B2
Cox's La SN8 . . . . 176 F1
Coxstalls SN4. . . . . 47 D2
Crab La BA12. . . . . 138 A7
Crab Mill La SN16. . . . 28 C1
Crab Tree Cl SN16. . . . 27 F3
Crabtree Copse SN5. . 34 A2
Crabtree La BA2. . . . . .99 B4
Cradle Hill BA14. . . . . 113 D2
Crampton Rd SN3. . . . 51 A7
Cranborne Chase SN2. 34 C4
Cranborne Dr 7 SP7 202 C2
Cranborne Rd SP6. . . 209 E2
Cranbury Cl SP5. . . . . 211 A7
Crandon Lea BA14. . . .92 F1
Cranebridge Rd SP2. 152 A8
Crane Furlong SN6. . . .23 A7
Cranesbill Cl SN10. . . 214 D5
Cranesbill Rd
  Devizes SN10. . . . . . . 214 D5
  Melksham SN12. . . . . . 94 A4
Crane St SP1 . . . . 152 A8
Cranmore Ave SN3. . . .51 A3
Cranmore Cl BA14. . . 101 A1
Cranwell Cl 6 SN14. . .78 A6
Cratchcroft La BA14. . 178 A6
Crate La SP7. . . . . 202 C7
Craven Rd RG17 . . . . . 177 D3
Crawford Cl SN5. . . . . .49 A4
Crawlboys La SP11 . . 192 B6
Crawley Ave SN3. . . . . .36 B1
Crawley Cres BA14. . . 105 A8
Craybourne Rd SN12. .94 C5
Crays The SN12. . . . . . .94 C5
Crench Comm Airfield
  SN8. . . . . 174 E4
Crescent Rd
  Durrington/Bulford
  SP4. . . . . 217 D7
  Melksham SN12. . . . . . 94 C6
Crescent The
  Bromham SN15. . . . . . 96 C7
  Calne SN11. . . . . 89 F8
  Chiseldown SN4. . . . . 65 C3
  4 Durrington/Bulford
  SP4. . . . . 198 F7
  Pewsey SN9 . . . . 215 B4
  Swindon SN5. . . . . . . 33 F2
  Westbury BA13. . . . . . 109 A3
  Wilton SP2. . . . . 144 B2
Cresswell Dr BA14. . . 102 B2
Cresswell La SN15. . . .44 B8
Cres The SP2. . . . . 152 B5
Crestmount Dr SP2. . 145 C3
Creswells SN13. . . . . . .84 F8
Creswick SN25 . . . . . . 20 D1
Cricketts La SN15. . . . .78 F5

CRICKLADE 19 E7
Cricklade Leisure Ctr SN6 19 C8
Cricklade Manor Prep SN6 19 E7
Cricklade Mus★ SN6 19 E8
Cricklade Rd
  Highworth SN6 22 F5
  Purton SN5 19 C2
  Swindon SN25 35 D1
Cricklade St SN1 50 D5
CRIDDLESTYLE 210 E1
Crieff Cl SN3 51 B6
Crispin Cl 6 SN3 36 B3
CROCKERTON 116 E1
Crockerton By-Pass
  Crockerton Green BA12 116 F2
  Longbridge Deverill BA12 120 F7
Crockerton CE Prim Sch BA12 116 D2
CROCKERTON GREEN 116 F2
Crockford Rd SP5 154 B2
Croft Cl SN6 8 C4
Croft Hts SP5 161 D3
Croft La SN6 8 C4
CROFTON 176 A1
Crofton Beam Engines★ SN8 176 A1
Crofton Rd SN8 176 A1
Croft Prim Sch The SN1 50 D3
Croft Rd
  6 Hungerford RG17 177 B7
  Swindon SN1 50 C1
Croft Sports Hall SN1 50 D3
Croft The
  Bishopstone SP5 205 E5
  Broad Hinton SN4 167 D7
  Milston SP4 198 C8
  Newton Tony SP4 199 B3
  Trowbridge BA14 105 C6
  Urchfont SN10 180 C3
Crombey St SN1 50 B5
Cromer Ct SN3 51 D3
Cromhall La SN14 69 A7
Cromhall Lane SN14 68 F7
Crompton Rd SN25 35 D6
Cromwell SN5 49 B3
Cromwell Rd SN10 214 D2
Crooked Cnr SN8 170 A6
CROOKED SOLEY 170 F3
Crookhays SP7 202 C2
Crook Hill SP5 204 A1
Crooks La SN10 180 C4
Crookwood La SN10 179 F4
Croome Cl SN25 34 B8
Crosbys 3 SN8 183 D8
Crosby Wlk SN3 51 A3
Croscombe Gdns BA11 110 D6
Cross Hayes La SN16 28 A3
Crossing La SN15 71 B3
CROSS KEYS 77 A3
Cross Keys
  Biddestone SN14 76 F6
  Corsham SN14 77 A4
Cross Keys Chequer 5 SP1 146 B1
Cross Keys Rd SN13 77 A3
Cross La SN8 213 D3
Crosslanes SN5 33 F8
Crossling La SN16 16 E3
Cross Roads
  Bourton BA12 137 F2
  Latton GL7 8 B6
  Semington BA14 102 F4
Cross St
  Swindon SN1 50 C5
  Trowbridge BA14 101 D1
Cross The
  Bishopstone SP5 205 E4
  Ebbesbourne Wake SP5 204 D3
  21 Tisbury SP3 203 E8
Cross Tree Cres GL7 10 C7
Crossways SN4 46 D6
Crossways Ave SN25 35 C3
Crosswood Rd SN3 51 A3
CROUCHESTON 205 F4
Croucheston Dro SP5 205 E3
Croucheston Hollow SP5 205 E4
Crowdy's Hill Sch SN2 35 D2
Crowe Hill BA2 99 B6
Crowe La BA2 99 B5
Crow La 7 SP2 144 D3
Crowle Rd 11 RG17 165 A1
Crown Cl
  Chippenham SN15 79 A5
  Pewsey SN9 215 B5
  Salisbury SP2 145 D3
Crown La 4 SP11 192 A5
Crown Mews 30 RG17 177 B7
Crown Way SP10 193 F1
Crowood La SN8 170 B2
CRUDWELL 14 E6
Crudwell CE Prim Sch SN16 14 F6
Crudwell La
  Crudwell SN16 14 B6
  Long Newnton GL8 13 D6
Crudwell Rd
  Malmesbury SN16 28 B5
  Murcott SN16 14 D3
Crudwell Way SN25 35 C6
Crusader Pk BA12 112 F1
Crusades The 6 SP1 146 C5
Cruse Cl SN14 77 F8
Ct La BA11 107 A2
CUCKOLD'S GREEN 179 C4
Cuckoo La BA11 110 A8
Cuckoo Pen Cl SN8 183 D3
CUCKOO'S CORNER 180 B4
CUCKOO'S KNOB 174 F1
Cuckoo's Mead SN3 51 E6
Cuckoos Nest La BA12 116 E7
Cues La SN6 163 E7
Cuffs La SP3 203 E8
Culborne Rd SN1 50 B2
CULKERTON 3 A5
Cullerne Rd SN3 36 C1
Cullerns The SN6 23 A6
Culpepper Cl 6 SN3 51 A4
Culver Gdns 9 SN16 28 A3
Culverhouse Rd SN1 50 E7
Culvermead Cl SN8 213 E3
Culver Rd BA15 100 E5
CULVERSLADE 66 A2
Culver St 7 SP1 152 B8
Culverwell Rd SN14 78 A7
Cumberland Rd SN3 50 E6
Cunetio Rd SN3 51 C8
Cunnage La BA12 139 F1
Cunningham Rd SN2 35 A2
Curie Ave SN1 50 A4
Curlcroft Rd SN13 84 D7
Curlew Dr SN14 70 A2
Curlew Rd 3 SP4 132 C1
Curnicks The SN4 65 C4
Cursus The★ SP4 197 D6
Cursus The GL7 2 C5
Curtis Orch SN12 93 B4
Curtis St SN1 50 B5
Curzon Cl SN11 81 A3
Curzon St SN11 81 A3
Cusance Way BA14 102 A1
Cuthwine Pl GL7 2 C5
Cutting Hill RG17 177 A2
Cuttle La SN14 76 E8
Cutts Cl SN15 46 A7
Cvnieto Roman Town★ SN8 175 B8
Cygnet Dr SP4 217 C8
Cygnet Pl SN9 215 C4
Cygnet Way BA14 101 D5
Cygney Way RG17 177 B8
Cyppa Ct SN15 78 E6
Cypress Gr SN2 35 A3
Cypress Way 7 BA11 110 C7
Cypress Wlk SN14 74 F6
Cyprus Terr SN10 214 A4

D

Dace Rd SN11 81 B4
Dacre Cl 13 SP10 193 C2
Dacre Rd SN3 51 A6
Dadley La BA11 107 A3
Dairy Cl
  Chippenham SN14 78 A3
  8 Redlynch SP5 211 C7
Dairy La SN10 172 D2
Dairy Mdw La SP1 152 D7
Dairy Mws SN13 76 F2
Dairy Rd
  Barford St Martin SP3 143 A4
  Chiseldon SN4 64 F4
Daisy Cl
  Melksham SN12 94 C3
  Swindon SN2 34 C3
Dakota Dr SN11 81 D4
Dalby Strand SN11 49 E2
Dalefoot Cl SN5 34 A1
Dales Cl SN25 35 A7
Dales Rd BA13 108 E2
Dalewood Rise SP1 146 E2
Dallas Ave SN3 51 B7
Dallas Rd SN14 78 C8
Dalton Cl SN3 50 F7
Dalwood Cl
  Dinton SP3 201 E2
  Swindon SN3 51 B3
Damask Way BA12 117 A5
DAMERHAM 209 F2
Dammas Bsns Ctr SN1 50 D4
Dammas La SN3 50 D4
Damson Cres 11 SN25 34 C5
Damson Orch BA1 82 A4
Damy Gn SN13 84 E5
Dance Ct 6 SN6 19 D7
Dando Dr SN8 213 B2
Dane Cl BA15 99 E7
Danegeld Cl 9 SP10 193 E2
Dane Rise BA15 99 E7
Danes Cl SN15 78 F5
Danestone Cl SN5 48 F7
Daneway SN25 20 B1
Daniel Cl 9 SN1 49 F4
Daniell Crest BA12 116 F6
Daniel's Well★ SN16 28 A3
Danvers Mead SN15 79 A4
Danvers Rd SN13 76 E1
Danvers Way BA13 109 B4
Darby Cl SN2 34 E1
Darcey Cl SN5 48 F6
Darcy Cl SN15 78 F8
Darius Way SN25 35 A6
Dark La
  Berkley BA11 110 E8
  Castle Combe SN14 68 B7
  Grafton SN8 175 F1
  Kintbury RG17 177 D8
  Limpley Stoke BA2 99 B5
  Malmesbury SN16 27 F3
  Mere BA12 139 A5
Dark La N BA14 178 A3
Dark La S BA14 178 A3
Darling Cl SN3 36 A1
Darnley Cl SN3 50 F6
Darrell Rd SP4 217 C4
Dart Ave SN25 35 A3
Dartmoor Cl 7 SN1 49 F4
Dartmoor Rd 2 BA13 108 E1
Darwin Cl
  4 Durrington/Bulford SP4 198 F6
  Swindon SN3 51 B7
Dasna Rd SP9 216 B5
Daubenton Cl BA14 106 A8
Daunch Cl SP9 216 B7
DAUNTSEY 45 B1
Dauntsey Acad Prim Sch SN10 187 E8
Dauntsey Dro SP11 192 E1
Dauntsey La SP11 192 E1
DAUNTSEY LOCK 59 B5
Dauntsey Pk★ SN15 44 E2
Dauntsey Rd
  Great Somerford SN15 44 C2
  Little Somerford SN15 44 D4
Dauntsey's (Aided) Prim Sch BA13 187 E8
Dauntsey's Sch
  West Lavington BA13 187 D8
  West Lavington SN10 187 D8
Davenham Cl SN3 51 A3
Davenwood SN2 35 F4
Dave Watkins Ct SN2 35 F3
David's Gdn SP5 148 C3
David Stoddart Gdns SN2 35 B1
Davies Cl SN8 213 A2
Davies Dr SN10 214 E6
Davies Rd SP4 132 B1
Davis Pl SN1 50 B6
Davis Rd 11 SN10 179 F1
Davy Dr SN11 81 D3
Dawbeney Dr SP4 217 D3
Dawes Cl GL7 1 A5
Dawlish Rd SN3 51 B5
Dawneys The SN16 14 E6
Day Ho La SN3 51 C2
Day's Cl SN3 36 A1
Days Ct SN16 14 E6
Day's La SN15 56 D2
Days Rise SN25 35 A3
Dazel Cnr SO51 212 D4
Deacon Rd SP11 192 B2
Deacon St SN1 50 B5
DEAN 207 E2
Dean Cl
  Frome BA11 110 C6
  Melksham SN12 94 C6
DEANEND 207 E4
Deanery Dr SN1 49 E2
Dean La
  Fovant SP3 204 D7
  Mildenhall SN8 169 B2
  Sixpenny Handley SP5 207 F6
  West Dean SP5 155 E2
  Whiteparish SP5 161 D4
Dean La Dro SP5 207 E4
DEANLAND 208 A5
Dean Rd
  East Grimstead SP5 154 F3
  West Dean SP5 155 B3
Deans Cl SP9 216 D4
Deansfield SN6 19 D7
Dean St SN1 49 F5
Dean Sta SP5 155 F3
Deansway SN15 70 D2
Dearle Rd SN26 20 D1
Deben Cres SN25 34 F5
Deburgh St SN2 49 F6
Deep La BA12 111 D2
Deere Ave SN14 78 A3
Deerhurst Way 1 SN5 49 D4
Deer Pk★ SN8 175 E2
Defrosica Cl SN11 81 D4
De Havilland Pl 4 SN12 178 B8
Delamere Dr SN3 36 A4
Delamere Rd BA14 101 D2
Delft Cres 1 SN25 34 D7
Delius Cl SN25 34 E8
Dell The SP11 185 B3
Delta Bsns Pk SN5 49 D6
Delta Office Pk SN5 49 D5
De Montfort Gr 8 RG17 177 B6
Demorgancres SN26 20 D1
Dempsey Rd BA12 113 E1
Denbeck Wood SN5 49 B6
Denbigh Cl SN3 50 E3
Denby Rd 4 SN25 34 E7
Deneb Dr SN25 34 B7
Dene Cl BA13 112 F8
Denes Ave BA12 139 A6
Dene The
  Hindon SP3 200 B3
Dene The *continued*
  Warminster BA12 117 E6
Denford La RG17 177 D8
Denholme Rd SN3 51 A3
Denison Rise SP1 146 C3
Dennis La SP7 203 B1
Dennis St SN5 49 C7
Denton Dr SP4 217 C2
DEPTFORD 195 E1
Derby Cl
  Chippenham SN15 78 F5
  Lambourn RG17 165 A1
Derby Ct SN3 50 E6
Derriads Gn SN14 78 A7
Derriads La 3 SN14 77 F6
Derryfields SN16 17 E8
DERRY FIELDS 17 F8
DERRY HILL 79 F2
Derry Hill CE (VA) Prim Sch SN11 80 A2
Derry Pk SN16 17 C2
Derry The SN6 17 F8
Dertford BA12 115 A7
DERTFORDS 115 B7
Derwent Dr SN2 35 F4
Desborough SN5 49 A3
Deva Cl SN3 51 D8
De Vaux Pl SP1 152 A7
Devenish Nature Reserve★ SP4 131 D2
Deverell Cl BA15 100 E4
Devereux Cl 8 SN5 48 F5
Devereux Mws 9 SN16 28 A5
Devereux Rd SP4 217 B3
Deverill Rd
  Sutton Veny BA12 117 E1
  Warminster BA12 116 F4
Devils Bed & Bolster The★ BA11 107 A8
DEVIZES 214 A3
Devizes Castle★ SN10 214 A3
Devizes Com Hospl SN10 214 B4
Devizes Enterprise Cen SN10 214 C3
Devizes Leisure Ctr SN10 214 B3
Devizes Rd
  Box SN13 83 E4
  Bromham SN15 88 B4
  Calne Without SN11 87 F7
  Charlton SN9 181 D2
  Derry Hill/Studley SN11 79 F1
  Hilperton BA14 102 C3
  Potterne SN10 179 D6
  Poulshot SN10 179 B7
  Rowde SN10 96 F2
  Salisbury SP2 145 E2
  Swindon SN1 50 D4
  Trowbridge BA14 102 B3
  Wroughton SN4 64 B6
Devizes Sports Club SN10 214 C4
Devizes White Horse★ SN10 97 F5
Devon Cl 5 SN14 77 F6
Devon Dr BA13 109 A5
Devon Rd
  Swindon SN2 35 B1
  Upavon Down SN9 182 B2
Devonshire Pl SN12 94 C5
Devonshire Rd SP1 146 A3
Dewberry Cl SN2 34 F4
Dew Cl SN13 85 A8
Dewell Mews SN1 50 D3
Dewey Cl SN4 65 D4
Dewey Mws SN9 215 C4
Deweys La SP11 192 A5
Dew Pond Cl SN25 34 B3
Dew's Rd SP2 145 F1
Dew Way SN11 81 D6
Dexter Cl SN5 49 B7
Dial Cl SN12 178 E8
Diamond Cres
  Swindon SN25 20 F1
  Swindon SN25 34 F8
Dianmer Cl SN4 47 F5
Dickens Ave SN13 76 F2
Dickens Cl SN3 51 D3
Dickenson Rd SN25 34 C5
Dicketts Rd SN13 85 A7
Dickson Rd SN15 60 A1
Dickson Way 2 SN15 78 F5
Diddledown Rd 8 SP4 217 C2
DIDMARTON 24 C3
Didmarton Rd GL9 24 A3
Dilton Cl BA14 105 C5
Dilton Ct BA13 112 B6
DILTON MARSH 112 B8
Dilton Marsh CE Prim Sch BA13 112 B8
Dilton Marsh Sta BA13 108 C1
Dimmer Dr SP2 144 F4
Dinah's Hollow SP7 206 B7
Dingle The 3 SN4 163 A6
Dinmore Rd SN25 34 F6
Dinnis Way SP4 146 B8
DINTON 201 F2
Dinton CE Prim Sch SP3 201 F2
Dinton Cl 10 SN25 34 E7
Dinton Rd
  Fovant SP3 204 E8
  Wylye BA12 201 E8
Dione Cres SN25 34 B7
Dior Dr SN4 61 E8
Discover Salisbury (Medieval Hall)★ SP1 152 A8
Distillery Mdws Nature Reserve★ SN16 31 B7
DITCHAMPTON 144 C4
DITTERIDGE 83 B8
Divinity Cl 2 SN4 163 B6
Dixon St SN1 50 B5
Dixon Way
  Calne SN11 81 B4
  Swindon SN5 49 C6
Dobbin Cl SN3 51 E7
Dobson Cl 1 SN25 35 A8
Dockle Way SN2 35 F4
Doctors Hill SN13 83 B5
Doctor's Hollow SP3 201 F2
Doctors Pl 3 SP3 203 E8
Dodford La SN15 58 D6
Dodgson Cl SP6 211 A4
Dodsdown SN8 184 B8
Doggetts La BA13 109 A4
Dog Kennel La BA13 109 A1
Dog La SP7 203 E1
DOGRIDGE 32 F3
Dogridge SN5 33 A3
Dog Trap La SN16 16 E1
Dolina Rd SN25 34 D6
Dolphin Ind Est SP1 152 D7
Dolphin St SP1 152 B8
Donaldson Rd SP1 146 A2
Doncaster Cl SN14 77 F5
Don Cl SN25 35 A4
Doncombe Hill SN14 74 E7
Doncombe La SN14 75 A6
Donhead Hollow SP7 206 E8
DONHEAD ST ANDREW 203 B3
DONHEAD ST MARY 203 A3
Donnington Gr SN3 50 F4
DORCAN 51 D5
Dorcan Acad The SN3 51 D6
Dorcan Bsns Village SN3 51 E6
Dorcan Ind Est SN3 51 E5
Dorcan Way SN3 51 A8
Dorchester Rd SN3 50 F3
Dores Ct SN2 35 E3
Dores Rd SN2 35 D3
Doris Archer Ct SN2 35 B2
Dormers The SN6 23 A6
Dorney Cl BA13 108 F1
Dorney Rd SN25 34 C8
Dorothy Wlk BA12 116 F8
Dorset Cl SP4 217 E8
Dorset Cres SN12 94 C3
Dorset Dr BA13 109 A5
Dorset Gn SN2 34 F2
Dorset Rd SP1 146 B3
Doubledays SN6 19 D8
Double Hedges SP4 217 E7
Doughty's La BA12 195 A2
Douglas Brown's Wlk 6 SP4 197 E6
Douglas Haig Rd SP1 146 A3
Douglas Rd 5 SN3 50 F6
Doulting Ct BA11 110 D7
Doulton Cl SN25 34 D7
Dovecote Cl 3 BA14 105 B8
Dovecote Dr SN13 76 F2
Dovedale 7 SN25 34 F7
Dovers La BA1 82 C2
Dovers Pk BA1 82 C2
Dover St
  Chippenham SN14 78 C7
  Swindon SN1 50 C5
Doves La SP5 161 C3
Dovetrees SN3 51 D7
Doveys Terr SN15 70 E7
Dowding Ave SN13 84 B8
Dowding Dr 5 SN11 166 A1
Dowding Way SN12 94 C1
Dowlais Cl 2 SN25 34 C6
Dowland Cl SN25 34 E8
Dowling St SN1 50 C5
DOWN AMPNEY 8 D7
Down Ampney House★ GL7 8 D6
Down Ampney Rd GL7 8 D6
Downavon BA15 100 D5
Down Barn Cl SP4 133 B4
Down Barn Rd
  Winterbourne SP4 132 F6
  Winterbourne Gunner SP4 133 A4
Downham Mead SN15 78 F8
Downhayes Rd BA14 101 D2
Downing St SN14 78 C8
Downland Rd
  Calne SN11 81 A2
  Swindon SN2 34 D4
Downlands 1 RG17 171 E7
Downlands Cl SP5 211 A7
Downlands The BA12 117 B7
Downland Way 12 SP4 198 B7
Downleaze 7 SP4 198 B7
Down Rd
  Kimpton SP11 192 B2
  Marshfield SN14 66 C2
Downs Cl
  Bradford-on-Avon BA15 100 B7
  Devizes SN10 214 D3
  Lambourn RG17 171 C8
Downside Cl BA12 139 A6
Downside Pk BA14 101 E2
Downs La SN8 185 D8
Downslands Rd SN10 214 B1
Downsmead SN8 164 B1
Downs Rd SN4 65 E4
Downs The SN8 170 A5
Downsview BA13 186 C7
Downs View
  Bradford-on-Avon BA15 100 B7
  Highworth SN6 23 A6
  1 Netheravon SP4 190 A4
  Royal Wootton Bassett SN4 47 D1
  Warminster BA12 117 C6
Downsview Rd BA13 109 A4
Downs View Rd SN3 50 F2
Downsview Way SP11 191 F3
Downsway SP1 146 B4
Downs Way SN3 51 E1
Down The
  Hindon SP3 200 B3
  Trowbridge BA14 101 D2
DOWNTON 211 B8
Downton Bus Ctr SP5 159 A1
Downton CE Prim Sch SP5 211 A8
Downton Hill SP5 211 C8
Downton L Ctr SP5 210 F8
Downton Meml Gdns★ SP5 211 A8
Downton Rd
  Salisbury SP2 152 B5
  Swindon SN2 35 B5
Down View SN14 78 A7
Downview Rd SP6 209 B6
Down View Rd SP1 146 E2
Downwood Cl 7 SP6 210 C1
Dowse Cl SP9 216 C7
Dowse Rd SN10 214 C4
Dowtys La SP3 142 A4
Doyle Cl 1 SN25 34 C5
Dragonfly Rd 3 SN3 51 B8
Dragon La SN9 181 F6
Drain Hill RG17 165 A2
Drake Cl SP1 146 C5
Drake Cres SN14 77 F6
Drake Ct SP10 193 F1
Drakes Ave SN10 214 C2
Drakes Mdw SN3 50 F7
Drakes Mdw Bsns Pk SN3 50 F7
Drake's Way SN3 50 E6
Drakes Way Bsns Ctr SN3 51 A7
DRAYCOT CERNE 56 F1
DRAYCOT FITZ PAYNE 174 A2
DRAYCOT FOLIAT 168 D8
Draycot La SN4 168 E8
Draycot Rd SN4 65 C3
Draycott Cl SN3 51 A5
Draymans Ct SN4 61 D8
Dr Behr Ct SN2 35 B2
Dresser Cl SN26 20 D2
Drewitts La SN10 180 E8
Drew's Pond La SN10 214 B1
Drew St SN2 49 E7
Drifton Hill SN14 66 E7
Drive The
  Durnford SP4 197 F1
  Melchet Park & Plaitford SO51 162 C1
  Swindon SN3 51 B7
Drove Cl SP5 150 F2
Drove La
  Coombe Bissett SP5 150 F3
  Market Lavington SN10 179 F1
  Steeple Ashton BA14 178 A2
Drove Prim Sch SN1 50 D6
Drove Rd SN1 50 D5
Drovers Green SN14 68 F4
Drovers La
  Wroughton SN4 63 E1
  Wroughton SN4 167 F8
Drovers Vw SP11 192 A5
Droves The SP5 207 E4
Drove The
  Amesbury SP4 217 B4
  Hawkeridge BA13 108 D7
  13 Redlynch SP5 211 C7
Dr The SN4 61 A7
Druces Hill BA15 100 C7
Druids Cl SN11 81 A3
Druley Hill
  North Brewham BA10 122 F7
  Witham Friary BA10 123 B7
Drummer La SP9 216 D5
Drury Cl SN5 47 F6
Drury La SN8 175 D4
Dryden Cl SP2 152 B5
Dryden St SN1 50 B5
Dry Hill BA12 116 E2
DRYNHAM 105 E5
Drynham La BA14 105 D5
Drynham Pk BA14 105 D6
Drynham Rd BA14 105 D6
Duchess Way SN2 35 D5
Duck La
  Barford St Martin SP3 143 B3
  Laverstock SP1 152 E8
  Salisbury SP1 146 D2
Duck Pool La BA11 107 B6

Ducks Meadow SN8 . 213 D2
Duck's Nest (Long Barrow)★ SP6 . 209 F7
Duck St
Berwick St James SP3 . 196 F2
Berwick St James SP3 . 197 A2
Ebbesborne Wake SP5 . 204 C3
Potterne SN10 . 179 D5
Steeple Langford SP3 . 128 D7
Sutton Veny BA12 . 194 A4
Tisbury SP3 . 203 E8
West Lavington SN10 . 187 E8
Dudley Ave SP6 . 210 D2
Dudley Rd SN3 . 50 F6
Dudmore Rd SN3 . 50 D6
Duffield La BA15 . 100 E6
Duke Cres 10 SN13 . 76 C1
Dukes Cl SN2 . 35 E5
Dukes Field GL7 . 8 D7
Duke's La BA12 . 118 A1
Duke St BA14 . 101 D1
Duke's Way SP4 . 217 E8
Dukwick La SN14 . 74 A3
Dulverton Ave SN3 . 51 A5
Dumbarton Terr 2 SN1 . 50 C5
Dumb Post Hill SN11 . 80 D6
Dummer La SP11 . 184 E1
Dummer Way SN15 . 79 A5
Dunbar Rd SN4 . 64 A7
Dunbeath Ct SN2 . 35 E1
Dunbeath Rd SN2 . 35 E1
Duncan's Cl SP11 . 192 D1
Duncan St SN11 . 81 B5
Dunch La SN12 . 93 F7
Dundas Aqueduct★ BA2 . 90 B2
Dundas Cl SN10 . 179 C8
DUNFIELD . 10 A8
Dunfield Loop GL7 . 10 B8
Dunford Cl
Amesbury SP4 . 217 D1
Trowbridge BA14 . 105 D6
DUNGE . 106 E1
Dunhills La SP11 . 193 F4
DUNKIRK . 179 D8
Dunkirk Bsns Pk BA14 . 104 D2
Dunkirk Hill
Devizes SN10 . 179 D8
Rowde SN10 . 97 A1
Dunley Cl SN25 . 34 D7
Dunley Way SP1 . 146 C5
Dunnet Cl SN11 . 81 B4
Dunnington Rd SN4 . 61 D8
Dunns La SN14 . 68 B8
Dunn's La SP8 . 138 A1
Dunraven Cl SN3 . 50 F4
Dunsford Cl SN1 . 49 F4
Dunsley Vale SN1 . 50 A4
Dunspit La DT11 . 207 B1
Dunstable Cnr SP5 . 148 E7
Dunstan's Dro SP11 . 185 E1
Dunster Cl SN3 . 50 E3
Dunvant Rd SN25 . 34 C7
Dunwich Dr SN5 . 49 D4
Dunworth Rise 6 SP3 . 203 E8
Durham St SN1 . 50 C5
Durlett Rd SN10 . 95 F2
DURLEY . 175 D3
Durley Pk SN13 . 84 D6
Durnford Rd SN2 . 35 C5
DURRINGTON . 198 B7
Durrington bAll Saints CE VC Infs Sch SP4 . 198 C7
Durrington CE (Controlled) Jun Sch SP4 . 198 B6
Durrington Swimming & Fitness Ctr SP4 . 198 C7
Durrington Walls★ SP4 . 217 A8
Durrington Wlk SN2 . 35 C5
Dursden La SN9 . 215 E6
DURSLEY . 105 E1
Dursley Rd
Heywood BA13 . 108 F8
North Bradley BA13 . 105 E1
Dussek Pl 2 SN25 . 34 E7
Dutts
Dilton Marsh BA13 . 112 B8
Westbury BA13 . 108 B1
Duxford Cl 11 SN12 . 178 B8
Dydale Rd SN25 . 34 C6
Dyehouse La SN10 . 214 A4
Dyer La BA12 . 201 E8
Dyer's Cl SN15 . 79 A6
Dyke Mews SN4 . 65 D4
Dymocks La BA12 . 121 F8
Dymott Sq BA14 . 102 A3
Dyrham Ct 1 SN25 . 34 F7
Dyson Campus SN16 . 27 F6
Dyson Rd SN25 . 34 F8

E

Eadreds Hyde SN11 . 89 D8
Eagle Cl SN3 . 51 E7
Eagle Field SP2 . 145 D4
Eagle Pk BA14 . 105 E6
Eagle Rd BA12 . 116 D6
Ealing Way SN2 . 34 F6
Earl Cl SN5 . 48 F7
Earls Cl SP4 . 217 E2
Earls Cnr SN16 . 15 E8
Earls Ct Rd SP4 . 217 B3
Earls Manor Ct SP4 . 133 A1
Earl's Rise SP4 . 133 A1
Earthpits La SP5 . 208 E4
Easdale St SN25 . 34 D8
East Allcourt GL7 . 2 C4
EAST ANTON . 193 F2
East Anton Farm Rd 20 SP11 . 193 F2
Eastbourne Gdns BA14 . 101 E1
Eastbourne Rd BA14 . 101 E1
EASTBURY . 171 C8
Eastbury Shute RG17 . 171 C5
Eastbury Way SN25 . 34 E7
EAST CHISENBURY . 190 A7
EAST COMPTON . 206 A5
EASTCOTT . 180 A2
Eastcott Comm SN10 . 180 A2
Eastcott Hill 5 SN1 . 50 C5
Eastcott Rd SN1 . 50 C5
EASTCOURT . 15 D6
Eastcourt SN8 . 183 D8
Eastcourt Rd SN8 . 183 D8
Eastdean Rd SP5 . 155 F2
East Dr 6 SN25 . 34 F8
East Dunley Cotts SN14 . 40 E1
EAST END . 74 A8
East End Ave BA12 . 117 B6
East End La
Cleverton SN15 . 44 D7
Little Somerford SN15 . 44 D5
Eastern Ave
Chippenham SN15 . 78 F8
Swindon SN3 . 50 E6
EASTERTON . 180 A2
Easterton La SN9 . 215 D4
EASTERTON SANDS . 179 F2
EAST EVERLEIGH . 191 A8
Eastfield
Ashton Keynes SN6 . 6 F1
2 Littleton Panell SN10 . 187 E8
EAST GARSTON . 171 E7
EAST GOMELDON . 133 E4
East Gomeldon Rd SP4 . 133 E4
EAST GRAFTON . 183 F7
EAST GRIMSTEAD . 154 F4
EAST HATCH . 203 C7
Easthill BA11 . 110 B4
East Hill BA12 . 194 C6
East Hill Rd BA12 . 194 C5
EAST KENNETT . 173 E6
East Kennett (Long Barrow)★ SN8 . 173 D5
EAST KNOYLE . 141 C2
East La SN12 . 93 B3
Eastlake SN25 . 20 C1
Eastlands Way SN15 . 70 E1
EASTLEAZE . 49 B6
Eastleaze Rd SN5 . 49 C6
Eastleigh Cl 4 BA11 . 110 A7
Eastleigh Rd SN10 . 214 D2
Eastleigh Wood La BA12 . 117 D3
Eastman Cl SP5 . 211 B7
EAST MARTIN . 209 C6
East Martin Rd SP6 . 209 B7
EAST MELBURY . 206 B7
Eastmere SN3 . 51 E3
EASTON . 77 D2
Easton Comm Hill SP5 . 149 E6
EASTON GREY . 26 C3
Easton Grey Rd GL8 . 26 A7
Easton Hollow SP5 . 207 B7
Easton La SN14 . 77 F3
EASTON ROYAL . 183 A7
Easton Royal Academy SN9 . 183 A7
Easton Sq SN16 . 25 D1
EASTON TOWN . 25 D1
Easton Town
Sherston SN16 . 25 C1
Sherston SN16 . 40 E8
East Portway SP10 . 193 C1
EASTRIP . 75 D4
Eastrip La SN14 . 75 C3
Eastrop SN6 . 23 B5
Eastrop Inf Sch SN6 . 23 A5
East Sands SN8 . 183 D8
East St
Bourton SP8 . 137 E1
Hindon SP3 . 200 A4
Lacock SN15 . 86 D6
Salisbury SP2 . 145 F1
10 Swindon SN1 . 50 B6
Warminster BA12 . 117 B6
EAST TOWN . 106 E4
East Town La BA14 . 106 E4
East Town Rd BA14 . 106 D3
EAST TYTHERTON . 72 B2
Eastview Rd BA14 . 105 A7
Eastville Rd SN25 . 35 C3
Eastwell Rd SN10 . 179 D5
East Wichel Prim Sch SN1 . 50 B2
East Wichel Way
Swindon SN1 . 49 F2
Swindon SN1 . 50 A2
Swindon SN1 . 50 B1
EAST WINTERSLOW . 149 C8
Eastwood SO51 . 162 E1
Eastwood Ave SN4 . 47 E1
EAST WOODLANDS . 114 B5
East Woodlands Rd BA11 . 114 A7
Eastwoods BA1 . 82 B3
East Yewstock Cres SN15 . 70 C1
Eaton Cl 1 SN3 . 51 A4
Eaton Wood 6 SN5 . 34 A2
Ebbesborne Hollow SP5 . 204 D2
EBBESBOURNE WAKE . 204 C2
Ebble Cl SP9 . 216 D7
Ebble Cres BA12 . 117 A5
Ebor Cl SN25 . 34 F7
Ebor Gdns SN11 . 89 C8
Ebor Paddock SN11 . 89 C8
Eccleston Cl SN3 . 51 B3
Echo Lodge Mdws Nature Reserve★ SN15 . 46 E7
Ecklington SN3 . 51 C5
Edale Moor SN3 . 51 E3
EDDINGTON . 177 C8
Eddington Hill RG17 . 177 C8
Eddleston Rd 2 SN1 . 50 E7
Edelweiss Cl 29 SP11 . 192 A5
Edencroft SN6 . 23 B8
Eden Gr SN12 . 85 D1
Eden Pk Cl BA1 . 82 A4
Eden Pk Dr BA1 . 82 A4
EDEN VALE . 108 E3
Eden Vale Rd BA13 . 108 F3
Edgam Pl SP2 . 144 F3
Edgar Cl 6 SP10 . 193 E2
Edgar Row Cl 1 SN4 . 64 A6
Edgecorner La SN14 . 53 A3
Edgehill SN5 . 49 B3
Edgeware Rd SN1 . 50 C6
Edgeworth Cl 4 SN5 . 49 B7
Edinburgh Rd SN11 . 81 F1
Edinburgh St SN2 . 35 D1
Edinburgh Way SN13 . 84 E7
EDINGTON . 186 C8
Edington Cl SN5 . 49 B5
Edington Dr BA14 . 105 C5
Edington Priory★ BA13 . 186 C8
Edington Rd BA14 . 178 A3
Edington Station Yard BA13 . 186 C8
Edison Bsns Pk SN3 . 51 D5
Edison Rd
Salisbury SP2 . 151 E8
Swindon SN3 . 51 D5
Edith New Cl 4 SN25 . 34 E3
Edmonton Way 3 SP4 . 217 F8
Edmund St SN1 . 50 C5
Edreds Ct SN11 . 81 C2
Edrich Sq SP10 . 193 E1
Edric's Gn SP4 . 199 C5
Edridge Cl SN15 . 78 F8
Edridge Pl 1 SN13 . 76 E1
Education Cen The SN1 . 50 F8
Education La
Great Cheverell SN10 . 187 C8
Westbury BA13 . 112 B8
Education Pl BA2 . 90 B5
Edward Rd SN10 . 214 B2
Edward Richardson & Phyllis Amey Nature Reserve★ GL6 . 2 C6
Edwards Hill 12 RG17 . 165 A1
Edwards Meadow SN8 . 213 B3
Edwards Rd SP4 . 217 B3
Edward St BA13 . 109 A3
Egdon Cl 9 SN25 . 34 D6
Egerton Cl SN3 . 51 B7
Eglantyne Ave SN26 . 20 D1
Eider Ave SN15 . 60 A1
Elbe Way SP10 . 193 D2
Elborough Rd SN2 . 34 D3
ELCOMBE . 63 E5
Elcombe SN1 . 49 D1
Elcombe Ave 3 SN4 . 64 A6
Elcombe Cl BA14 . 105 C5
Elcombe Gdns SN10 . 214 A4
Elcombe La
Alvediston SP5 . 204 B2
Alvediston SP5 . 207 E8
Elcot Cl SN8 . 213 F3
Elcot La SN8 . 213 F3
Elcot Orch SN8 . 175 A8
ELDENE . 51 C5
Eldene Dr SN3 . 51 C4
Eldene Prim Sch SN3 . 51 C5
Elden Rd
North Tidworth SP9 . 191 D5
Tidworth SP9 . 216 B8
Elder Cl SN2 . 34 C3
Elder Ct 3 SN13 . 84 E8
Eleanor Ct 16 SP11 . 192 A5
Elgar Cl SN25 . 34 E7
Elgin Dr SN2 . 35 E1
Elgin Ind Est SN2 . 35 E1
Elham Ct DT11 . 207 C1
Eliot Cl SN3 . 51 D3
Elizabeth Cl
3 Downton SP5 . 210 F8
Melksham Without SN12 . 93 F1
Elizabeth Dr SN10 . 214 C4
Elizabeth Gdns GL7 . 1 A5
Elizabeth Pl SN15 . 79 A4
Elizabeth Rd
16 Durrington/Bulford SP4 . 198 B7
Elizabeth Rd *continued*
Wilton SP2 . 144 B5
Elizabeth Sq SP9 . 216 E7
Elizabeth Way BA14 . 101 F3
Elley Gn SN13 . 84 E6
Ellingdon Rd SN4 . 63 F7
ELLIOTS GREEN . 114 D8
Elliott Ct SN10 . 214 B1
Elliott Gn SP4 . 133 C3
Elliott Pl BA14 . 101 A1
Ellworthy Ct BA11 . 110 B4
Elm Cl
Bower Hill SN12 . 94 C1
Calne SN11 . 89 C8
8 Ludgershall SP11 . 192 B5
Lyneham SN15 . 60 B2
Motcombe SP7 . 202 A5
Pitton & Farley SP5 . 148 C4
Rowde SN10 . 96 D1
Royal Wootton Bassett SN4 . 47 E4
Salisbury SP1 . 146 D3
Staverton BA14 . 101 D6
Trowbridge BA14 . 105 C3
ELM CROSS . 167 D7
Elm Ct SN10 . 214 B1
Elmdale Ct BA14 . 105 A7
Elmdale Rd BA14 . 105 A7
Elmer Cl SN16 . 28 A5
Elm Farm Cl SN16 . 16 D2
Elmfield BA15 . 100 C7
Elmfield Cl 7 SP5 . 211 C7
Elm Gr
Calne SN11 . 81 B1
Corsham SN13 . 76 E1
Salisbury SP1 . 146 C1
Swindon SN5 . 49 A8
Westbury BA13 . 108 E3
Elm Gr Pl SP1 . 146 B1
Elm Gr Rd SP1 . 146 B1
Elm Hayes SN13 . 85 A7
ELM HILL . 202 A5
Elm Hill BA12 . 113 C1
Elmhurst Est BA1 . 82 A4
Elmhurst Gdns BA14 . 101 F1
Elmina Rd SN1 . 50 C7
Elm Leigh BA11 . 110 C6
Elmore SN3 . 51 C5
Elm Pk SN4 . 47 D1
Elm Rd
Colerne SN14 . 75 A5
Swindon SN2 . 35 A2
Elms Cl SP6 . 210 B1
Elms Cross BA15 . 100 C3
Elms Cross Dr BA15 . 100 C5
Elms The
Bradford-on-Avon BA15 . 100 B8
Highworth SN6 . 22 F5
Holt BA14 . 92 E1
Swindon SN5 . 48 F8
Elmswood Cl SN2 . 35 E5
Elm Tree Cl SN10 . 214 D2
Elm Tree Gdns SN10 . 214 D2
Elm View GL7 . 5 F4
Elmwood SN15 . 70 E2
Elmwood Ave 6 SP6 . 210 C1
Elsham Way SN25 . 35 A5
ELSTON . 196 E7
Elston La SP3 . 196 E7
Elstree Way
Haydon Wick SN25 . 34 F6
Swindon SN25 . 35 A7
Eltham Cl SN5 . 48 F4
Elver Cl 9 SN3 . 51 B8
Ely Cl SN5 . 49 C4
Ely Ct SN4 . 64 A5
Embankment SN1 . 50 D3
Embry Cl 3 SN11 . 166 A1
Emden Rd 18 SP10 . 193 D2
Emerald Cres SN26 . 21 A1
Emerson Cl SN25 . 35 A6
Emery Gate SN15 . 78 F8
Emlyn Sq SN1 . 50 B6
Emmanuel Cl SN25 . 35 A4
Emmaus Sch BA14 . 101 D5
Emmet Hill SN16 . 16 D2
Emmett Hill Mdws Nature Reserve★ SN16 . 16 D1
Emms La 10 BA13 . 186 B7
Empire Rd SP2 . 145 C2
Empress Way SP11 . 192 A5
Emwell St BA12 . 117 A7
Endeavour Prim Sch SP11 . 193 F2
Endeavour Rd 6 SN3 . 51 B8
Endless St SP1 . 146 A1
ENFORD . 189 F6
Enford Ave SN2 . 35 C6
Enford Hill SN9 . 189 F6
Engineer Rd BA13 . 108 C6
ENGLANDS . 78 F5
Englefield SN4 . 47 E1
ENHAM ALAMEIN . 193 E4
Enham La SP10 . 193 E3
ENMORE GREEN . 202 B2
Enos Way BA11 . 110 A6
Ensor Cl SN25 . 35 A8
Enstone Cl 2 SN2 . 34 E2
Epping Cl BA12 . 117 A8
Epping Dr SN12 . 94 C6
Epsom Cl SN14 . 77 F6
Epsom Rd BA14 . 105 E4
Equinox Dr SP4 . 217 E4
Erin Ct 1 SN1 . 50 A5
Eriskay Gdns BA13 . 108 F2
Eriskay Pl SN5 . 34 B3
Erleigh Dr SN15 . 78 C7
ERLESTOKE . 187 A8
Erlestoke Way SN25 . 35 C6
Ermin Cl SN8 . 170 C8
Ermine St RG17 . 171 A6
Ermin St
1 Baydon SN8 . 164 C1
Baydon SN8 . 170 C8
Blunsdon St Andrew SN26 . 20 F2
Swindon SN2 . 35 F4
Erneston Cres SN13 . 76 F1
Ernle Rd SN11 . 81 C4
Erskine Barracks SP2 . 144 F4
Escott Cl 4 SN15 . 78 F4
Eshton Wlk SN3 . 51 A3
Esmead SN15 . 78 F8
Espringham Pl SN2 . 35 E4
Essex Pl 7 RG17 . 165 A2
Essex Sq SP2 . 151 D6
Essex Wlk SN3 . 50 F6
Estate Yd The SN10 . 172 B3
Estcourt Cres SN10 . 214 B4
Estcourt Rd SP1 . 146 B1
Estcourt St SN10 . 214 B3
Estcourt Terr SN10 . 214 B5
Estella Cl SN25 . 34 D6
Eston Medieval Village of★ SN14 . 69 D8
ETCHILHAMPTON . 180 C7
Ethelbert Dr 4 SP10 . 193 C2
Ethelred Pl SN13 . 76 E1
Ethendun 11 BA13 . 186 B7
Euclid St SN1 . 50 C6
Euridge SN14 . 75 E5
Europa & Brittania Pk SN3 . 51 A8
Euro Way SN1 . 48 F3
Evans Cl SN15 . 70 E1
Eveleigh Rd SN4 . 47 E2
Evelyn Cl BA1 . 82 B3
Evelyn St SN1 . 50 D3
Evening Star
Royal Wootton Bassett SN4 . 61 F8
Royal Wootton Bassett SN5 . 48 A1
EVEN SWINDON . 49 E6
Even Swindon Prim Sch SN2 . 49 F7
Eveque Ct SP2 . 144 F3
Everett Cl BA12 . 117 F1
Evergreen Ind Pk GL7 . 6 F5
Evergreens Cl SN3 . 36 C1
Evergreen Way 10 SP4 . 217 C2
Everland Rd 18 RG17 . 177 B7
Everland Rd Ind Est RG17 . 177 C7
EVERLEIGH . 191 A8
Everleigh Barrows★ SN9 . 182 E3
Everleigh Cl BA14 . 105 D5
Everleigh Rd
Collingbourne Ducis SN8 . 191 D8
Pewsey SN9 . 215 C3
Swindon SN2 . 35 C5
Ewden Cl SN1 . 50 B2
EWEN . 5 C8
Ewen Rd
Ewen GL7 . 5 E6
Siddington GL7 . 6 C7
Eworth Cl SN5 . 48 F5
Exbury Cl 2 SN25 . 35 A6
Exe Cl SN25 . 35 A4
Exeter Cl SN14 . 77 F5
Exeter House Specl Sch SP1 . 146 B3
Exeter St
Salisbury SP1 . 152 B7
Swindon SN1 . 50 A6
Exmoor Cl 1 SN2 . 34 C4
Exmoor Rd 6 BA13 . 108 E1
Exmouth St SN1 . 50 A5
Eyam Rd SN1 . 50 A1
Eyles Rd
Devizes SN10 . 214 B1
North Tidworth SP9 . 216 D8
Eyre Cl 1 SN25 . 34 D6
Eyres Dr SP5 . 153 E2
Eyres Way SP1 . 152 B8
Eysey SN6 . 9 A2

F

FABERSTOWN . 192 B6
Factory Hill SP8 . 137 F3
Factory La
Barford St Martin SP3 . 143 B3
Warminster BA12 . 116 F6
Fairdown Ave BA13 . 109 B3
Fairfax Cl
Amesbury SP4 . 217 A4
Swindon SN3 . 50 F7
Fairfield
1 Cricklade SN6 . 19 D8
4 Great Bedwyn SN8 . 176 B3
Minety SN16 . 17 B1
Rode BA11 . 103 F1
Royal Wootton Bassett SN4 . 47 E3
Fairfield Cl
Frome BA11 . 110 A7
Marshfield SN14 . 74 A8
Fairfield Cotts SP2 . 144 E4
Fairfield Farm Coll BA13 . 108 C1
Fairfield Meadows BA14 . 104 F3
Fairfield Rd
Salisbury SP1 . 146 A4
Warminster BA12 . 117 B7
Fairfields 22 RG17 . 177 B7
Fairfoot Cl SN14 . 78 A7
FAIRFORD . 1 E7
Fairford Airfield GL7 . 1 E1
Fairford Cres SN25 . 35 C3
Fairford Rd GL7 . 2 B4
Fairground The 2 SP11 . 192 F1
Fairhaven BA13 . 108 D1
Fairholme Way SN2 . 35 F4
Fairlane SP7 . 202 C1
Fairlawn SN3 . 51 D3
Fairleigh Rise SN15 . 70 F7
Fair Mile
Collingbourne Kingston SN8 . 183 F3
Grafton SN8 . 184 A4
Fairview
Colerne SN14 . 75 C6
Swindon SN1 . 50 B5
Fairview Cl BA12 . 117 B5
Fairview Rd
1 Andover SP11 . 192 F1
Hungerford RG17 . 177 B7
Salisbury SP1 . 146 C1
Fair View Rd SP2 . 144 E4
Fairwater Ct SN4 . 64 A5
Fairway
Calne SN11 . 89 C8
Melksham SN12 . 94 C5
Fairways
Amport SP11 . 192 E1
Dilton Marsh BA13 . 108 D1
Fairway The SN10 . 214 A1
FAIRWOOD . 108 B4
Fairwood Cl BA14 . 102 A2
Fairwood Rd
Dilton Marsh BA13 . 108 C3
North Bradley BA13 . 107 F5
Falcon Dr BA14 . 105 E7
Falconer Mews SN25 . 35 B6
Falcon Rd
Calne SN11 . 81 D3
Warminster BA12 . 116 C6
Falconscroft SN3 . 51 C8
Falconsway SP2 . 152 A5
Falcon Way SN12 . 94 D1
Falconwood Cl 8 SP6 . 210 C1
Falkirk Rd SN4 . 64 A7
Falklands Rd SN4 . 64 E3
Falkner Cl SN8 . 213 B3
Fallow Field Cl SN14 . 70 B2
Falmouth Gr SN3 . 50 E4
Fanshaw Way BA12 . 117 A5
Fanstones Rd SN3 . 51 C4
Fantley La SP8 . 138 B1
Faraday Pk SN3 . 51 E5
Faraday Rd
Salisbury SP2 . 145 E1
Swindon SN3 . 51 E5
Fareham Cl SN3 . 51 B5
Farfield La SN6 . 19 E4
Fargo Cl SP4 . 198 A6
Fargo Rd SP4 . 217 A7
Faringdon Rd
Lechlade-on-Thames GL7 . 2 E3
2 Swindon SN1 . 50 B6
Farleigh Ave
Melksham SN12 . 94 B3
Trowbridge BA14 . 105 A7
Farleigh Castle★ BA2 . 103 E8
Farleigh Cl
1 Chippenham SN14 . 77 F6
Westbury BA13 . 108 F4
Farleigh Cres SN3 . 50 E3
FARLEIGH HUNGERFORD . 103 E7
Farleigh La
Hinton Charterhouse BA2 . 99 A1
Hinton Charterhouse BA2 . 103 A8
Farleigh Pk★ BA2 . 103 D5
Farleigh Rd
Farleigh Hungerford BA14 . 103 F8
Norton St Philip BA2 . 103 A5
Wingfield BA14 . 104 A8
Farleigh Rise
Bath BA1 . 82 C2
Monkton Farleigh BA1 . 82 D1
FARLEIGH WICK . 90 F5
FARLEY . 154 D8
Farley Cl BA11 . 110 C6
Farley Rd SP1 . 152 C7
Farman Cl SN3 . 51 C4
Farm Cl BA14 . 101 A1
Farm Ct 3 SN6 . 163 E6
Farmer Cl SN15 . 70 E1
Farmer Cres SN25 . 35 C6
Farmer Giles Farmstead★ SP3 . 201 C3
Farmhouse Cl SN15 . 78 F4
Farmhouse Dr SN15 . 78 A4

Farm La
Aldbourne SN8......170 A6
Great Bedwyn SN8...176 B3
Salisbury SP2.......145 E1
Farnborough Rd SN3..51 B3
Farndale Cl 4 SN2.....35 C5
Farne Way SN4.......48 A2
Farnewell Cl 1 SN14..78 C7
FARNHAM.........207 C2
Farnicombe La BA12..113 B5
Farnsby St SN1......50 B6
Farrar Dr SN8......213 A2
Farrells Field SN14...68 F4
Farrfield SN2.........35 E4
Farriers Cl SN1......50 E8
Farriers Field SN9...181 F2
Farthing La SN15.....60 A4
Farthing Row BA11...103 E1
Farthings BA9.......137 B3
Far View Rd SP3.....196 F7
Faulkner Rd SN3.....20 C1
Faulkner Sq RG17....177 C7
Faulston Dro SP5....205 F3
Faverole Way BA14...102 A2
Fawley Cl 2 SN25....34 C8
Fayre Gdns GL7......1 F6
Featherbed La SN6...163 F7
Feather Wood SN5...49 D5
Fell Rd BA13.......108 E2
Felstead SN26.......20 D1
Feltham Dr BA11....110 A3
Feltham Hill BA11...114 B8
Feltham La BA11....110 A2
Fenland Cl
  8 Swindon SN5....48 F8
  5 Swindon SN5....49 A8
Fenn Cl SN5.........34 B1
Fennel Cl SN2.......34 D4
Fennel Rd BA12.....139 B6
Fenton Ave SN25....34 E7
Ferguson Cl SN14...78 A3
Ferguson Rd SN10..214 D1
Fermoy BA11.......110 B6
Fernacre Rd SN1....50 B2
Ferndale Comm Prim Sch
  SN25............35 B1
Ferndale Prim Sch
  SN2.............50 B8
Ferndale Rd SN2....49 F8
FERNE.............203 D1
Ferne Hollow SP5...207 A8
Ferne Wall Cnr SP7..203 B1
Ferney Way SP5.....207 C4
Fernham Rd SN25...34 E3
Ferozeshah Rd SN10.214 E6
Ferrers Dr SN5......48 F4
Ferrers Way GL7......2 E3
Ferris Cl SN10......96 E1
Ferris Gr SN12......94 C4
Ferris Mead BA12...117 A6
Ferris Way BA14....101 F1
Ferry La
  Bathford BA1......90 C5
  Claverton BA2.....90 B5
Festival Ave SN26...145 C3
Festival Way SN16...28 C5
Feversham Rd SP1..146 B3
Fiddington Clay
  SN10............179 F1
Fiddington Hill SN10.180 A1
FIDDINGTON
  SANDS..........179 F1
Fiddle The SN6......19 C7
Field Barn La SP3...201 F3
Field Cl
  South Cerney GL7....7 A7
  Westbury BA13....109 A4
Fieldfare SN3........51 D7
Fieldfare Way 4
  SN12............94 D5
Fieldins BA15.......99 E7
Field La
  Norton Ferris BA12...124 D5
  Pen Selwood BA9...137 B3
Field Rise SN1.......50 A3
Fieldside SN10......187 E8
Fields The
  Mere BA12........139 B6
  Swindon SN3......36 A1
Fieldsview SN12.....93 F7
Field View
  Chippenham SN15...78 D7
  Enford SN9.......190 A6
  Sherston SN16.....25 D1
Field Way BA14.....104 F6
FIFIELD...........190 A5
FIFIELD BAVANT....204 F4
Figgins La SN8.....213 D2
FIGHELDEAN.......190 B2
Figsbury Cl 5 SN25..34 C5
Figsbury Rd SP4....133 B1
Figsbury Ridge SP4..133 C2
Figsbury Ring★ SP4.147 D8
FILANDS...........28 A6
Filsham Rd SN25....34 C7
Finchdale SN3.......51 D8
Finches La
  2 Baydon SN8....164 C1
  Baydon SN8.......170 C8
Finchley Rd SP2....145 E2
Finkley Rd SP11....193 F2
Finnis Rd 4 SN1....217 C3
Firbank Cres BA12..117 D8
Fir Drove
  Dinton SP3.......128 B1

Fir Drove *continued*
  Dinton SP3.......142 C8
Fire Brigade Mus★
  SN10............179 C5
Firecrest View 3 SN3.51 E6
Fire Fly Ave SN2.....50 A7
Firethorn Cl SN25...35 C1
Fir Gn La SN8.......183 D8
Fir Gr SN11.........89 D8
Fir Rd SN14.........74 F6
Firs Cl SP5.........148 C7
FIRSDOWN.........148 C8
Firs Hill Way SN10..179 E5
Firs Rd
  Alderbury SP5.....153 E2
  Firsdown SP5.....148 B7
First Broad Dr
  Barford St Martin
    SP3...........129 A1
  Wilton SP2.......144 A7
Firs The
  Chippenham SN14...78 A6
  Inkpen RG17......177 F3
  Limpley Stoke BA2...99 A5
First La SN12........85 C1
Firth Cl SN25.......35 A3
Fir Tree Cl SN2......35 A2
Fishers Brook
  Calne SN11.......81 A6
  Frome BA11.......110 A5
FISHERTON DE LA
  MERE...........195 D1
Fisherton Island
  Salisbury SP2.....145 F1
  Salisbury SP2.....151 F8
Fisherton St SP2....145 F1
Fish Row SP1.......152 A8
Fison Wlk SP1......146 D4
Fitkin Ct 1 SN25....34 E7
FITTLETON........190 A4
Fitwell Rd SN25.....34 C7
Fitzgerald Ave SN6..22 F7
Fitzmaurice Cl
  Bradford-on-Avon
    BA15..........100 E4
  Calne Without SN11..79 F2
  Swindon SN3......51 D7
Fitzmaurice Pl BA15.100 D5
Fitzmaurice Prim Sch
  BA15............100 D5
Fitzpiers Cl 10 SN25.34 C5
Fitzroy Rd SN1......50 D2
Fitzwarren Cl SN15..79 A4
Five Ash La
  Sutton End BA12...116 F3
  Sutton Veny BA12...117 C2
Five Lanes Prim Sch
  SN10............179 D5
Five Rivers Leisure Ctr
  SP1.............145 F3
Five Stiles Rd SN8..213 F2
Five Thorn La SN15..57 D6
Fiveways Cl SN8....164 B1
Fiveways Trading Est
  SN13............84 B7
Flagstaff Ave SN26...21 D2
Flamstone St SP5...205 E4
Flashett The SP5....149 D6
Flaxfields End 19
  SP6.............210 D1
FLAXLANDS........47 D6
Flax Mill Pk SN10...214 C5
Flayburn Rd SN25...34 F4
Fleece Cotts 2 BA14.105 E7
Fleet Cl SN15.......78 D8
Fleet St SN1........50 B6
Fleetwood Cl SN13..84 E6
Fleetwood Ct SN1...49 A3
Fleetwood Rise SN12.93 A8
Fleming Cl SP11....192 A5
Fleming Way SN1...50 C6
Flensburg Cl 20
  SP10............193 D2
Flers Ct BA12.......117 A6
Fleur De Lys Dr BA14.105 A4
Flint Cres BA13.....108 E3
Flint Hill SN5........49 C4
Flintjack Pl 2 RG17.165 A1
Flint La SP11.......193 A4
Flint Way SP5.......152 C5
Flisteridge Rd
  Hankerton SN16...15 E4
  Minety SN16......16 C3
Flit Croft 4 SP4....217 C2
FLOOD STREET....210 E4
Flood The SP5......149 B7
Flora Cl SN26.......21 A1
Florence Ct
  21 Andover SP10..193 E2
  Wilton SP2.......144 C3
Florence Mews SP2..144 C3
Florence St SN2.....50 C8
Flower La
  Amesbury SP4....217 A3
  Melchet Park & Plaitford
    SO51..........212 F7
Flowers Mead 6
  BA13............186 B7
Flowers Yd SN15....78 E7
Foden Rd SP9......216 D4
Foghamshire SN15..78 D7
Folkestone Cl SN14..78 A6
Folkestone Rd
  Salisbury SP2.....151 F6
  Swindon SN1......49 C6
Folly Barrow★ DT11.206 B2
Folly Cl
  Highworth SN6....23 A7

Folly Cl *continued*
  Salisbury SP2.....151 F5
Folly Cres SN6......23 A7
Folly Dr SN6........23 A7
Follyfield
  Bradford-on-Avon
    BA15..........100 D4
  Hankerton SN16...15 B2
Folly La
  Alderbury SP5.....153 C3
  Melksham Without SN12 93 B8
  Salisbury SP2.....145 D3
  Warminster BA12..116 B5
Folly La E SN15.....86 C5
Folly La W SN15....86 B5
Folly Rd
  Inkpen RG17......177 F3
  Lambourn SN8....164 F1
  Roundway SN10...214 C2
Folly The SN15......44 A2
Folly View SP2......145 C5
Folly Way SN6......23 A7
FONTHILL BISHOP..200 D3
FONTHILL GIFFORD.200 D3
Fonthill Wlk SN3....50 E5
Fontmell Cl 9 SN25.34 E7
Fontmell Hill DT11..206 C3
Foot's Hill
  Cann SP7........206 A4
  Salisbury SP2.....145 A3
Forage La BA12.....117 B7
FORD
  Biddestone......68 A2
  Laverstock.......146 D7
Fordbrook Bsns Ctr
  SN9.............215 C6
Fordbrook Ind Est
  SN9.............215 E2
Forders Cl 12 SP5...211 C2
FORDINGBRIDGE...210 E1
Fordingbridge Hospl
  SP6.............210 D1
Fordingbridge Inf Sch
  SP6.............210 D2
Ford Rd BA2........98 A1
Fordson Rd SN10...214 D1
Ford St SN1........50 A5
Fordswater BA12...137 E5
Foreminster Ct BA12.116 F5
Fore St
  Ashton Keynes SN6..6 F1
  Trowbridge BA14..101 D1
  Warminster BA12..116 F5
  Westbury BA13....109 A4
  Wylye BA12.......201 E8
Forest Dale Rd SN8.175 A8
Forester Cl 5 SN3...51 D4
Foresters Pk Rd SN12.94 C4
FOREST HILL......175 B7
Forest Hill SN8.....176 B3
Forest La
  Chippenham SN15...78 E3
  Chute SP11.......192 D8
  Melksham Without SN12 86 F2
Forest Park Rd SN5..34 B1
Forest Rd
  Bramshaw SP5....212 B3
  Corsley BA12......116 B8
  7 Frome BA11....110 B7
  Horningsham BA12..118 D8
  Melksham SN12....94 B5
  Redlynch SP5.....211 D6
  Warminster BA12..112 D1
  Wooton Rivers SN8..174 F2
Forest Rd Cnr BA12..118 E7
Forest & Sandridge CE
  Prim Sch SN12....94 D4
Forest Wlk BA13....111 C4
FOREWOODS
  COMMON........101 C7
Forge Cl
  Milton Lilbourne SN9..182 E7
  South Newton SP2..130 B1
  West Overton SN8..173 F6
Forge Fields SN5....48 D8
Forge La
  West Overton SN8..173 F7
  Zennor BA12......137 F3
Forge Rd SN26......21 B1
Forge The
  Hungerford RG17...177 C7
  Lower Stanton St Quinton
    SN14..........56 D6
Forman St SN11.....81 C3
Forres Sandle Manor Sch
  SP6.............210 C1
Forrester Gn SN14..75 B3
Forsey Cl 4 SN3....51 E7
Forsters La OX12....165 F7
Fortis Hill SP7......203 C3
Fortuna Rd SN26....21 A2
Fortunes Field SN4..167 C7
Fortune Way SN11..78 F5
Forty Acres Rd SN10.214 C3
Forty The
  Bishopstone SN6..163 E7
  Cricklade SN6.....19 D7
Forum Cl SN3.......51 C8
FOSBURY..........185 A5
Fosbury Hill Fort★
  SN8.............185 A3
Fosbury Rd SN8....185 B4
FOSCOTE..........54 E3
Fosse Cl SN2.......49 F6
Fosse Cotts SN16...27 A6
Fosse La BA1.......82 A4
Fosseway GL7.......4 B8

Fosseway Cl SN14...75 B3
Foss Way SN14.....74 E5
Foster La SP5.......153 E3
Foster Rd BA11.....110 A3
Fosters Bushes 4
  SP4.............217 D3
Fotherby Cres SP1..146 C4
Foundry Cl SN12....94 A6
Foundry La SN15....70 E1
Foundry Rd 2 SP5..211 C8
Fountain Mead
  SP7.............202 C2
Fountain Way Hospl
  SP2.............145 E1
Four Acre Cl SN6....18 A8
Fourmile Hill SP4...132 B3
FOVANT...........204 E8
Fovant Cl SN5......34 A1
Fovant Regimental
  Badges★ SP3....204 F7
Fowey SN5.........49 A3
Fowler's Hill SP1...152 C8
Fowler's Rd SP1....152 B8
Fowlswick La SN14..69 C4
Foxbridge SN3......51 D7
Fox Brook SN4......47 F2
Foxbury 4 RG17....165 A1
Fox Cl SN14........70 B1
Foxcote Gdns 2
  BA11............110 C7
Foxcott SN6........8 C4
FOXCOTTE.........193 C2
Foxcotte Cl SP10...193 C1
Foxcotte La SP11...193 C2
Foxcotte Rd SP10..193 C2
Fox Croft Wlk SN15..78 F4
Foxglove Cl SN12...94 C3
Foxglove Dr BA14..101 E4
Foxglove Rd SN25...34 D5
Foxglove Way SN11..81 B5
Foxgrove SN14......70 A2
FOXHAM...........72 D7
Foxham Rd
  Christian Malford SN15. 58 B1
  Foxham SN15.....72 B8
Foxham Way SN1....49 F2
Foxhill Cl SN25.....34 F3
Foxholes
  Crockerton BA12...116 E1
  Longbridge Deverill
    BA12..........120 E8
Foxleaze SN6.......8 C1
FOXLEY...........41 F8
Foxley Cl
  Swindon SN2......35 E4
  12 Warminster BA12..117 A8
Foxley Cnr SN10....180 D4
Foxley Fields SN10..180 C4
Foxley Rd
  Foxley SN16......26 D1
  Norton SN16......41 E8
  St Paul Malmesbury Without
    SN16..........27 D2
Foxmore Dro SP2...151 B6
Fox Row SN4.......167 C5
Fox's Dro BA11.....107 C1
Foxtail Gdns SP11..192 A5
Fox Wood SN5......49 D5
FOX THE..........33 F3
Foyle Hill SP7......202 B1
Foyle Rd SP11......192 C2
Foyle's Mead BA12..201 E8
Framlingham Cres
  BA14............106 B8
Frampton Cl SN5....49 B6
Frampton Ct
  Trowbridge BA14..105 A6
  Wilton SP2.......144 F4
Francis Rd 10 SN10.179 F1
Francis St BA14....101 C1
Francis Way
  Harnham SP2.....151 F5
  Salisbury SP2.....152 A5
Francomes SN25....34 E4
Francomes Field 17
  RG17............165 A1
Frankel Ave 5 SN25.34 D7
Frankenbury★ SP6..210 F2
Frankland Rd SN1...48 E3
Franklin Cl SP9.....216 D8
Franklin Rd SN10...214 D6
Frankton Gdns 2 SN3.36 B2
Frank Warman Ct 8
  SN3.............36 B3
Fraser Cl SN3.......51 B7
Frederick Ave SN14..77 F7
Fredericks Way SN14.53 B3
Frederick Taylor Ct
  BA12............116 F4
Freegrove Dr SN15..73 F8
Freegrove Rd SN15..73 F8
Freemans Cl 4 RG17.177 B7
Free's Ave SN8.....213 B5
Freesia Cl 2 BA12..116 E7
Freestone Gr BA13..109 B5
Freestone Way
  5 Corsham SN13..76 D1
  Leafield SN13.....84 E8
Fremantle Rd SP11..191 F4
French Mill La SP7..202 C1
French Mill Rise 16
  SP7.............202 C1
Frensham Way SN9.215 D6
Fresden Village★ SN6.23 E4
FRESH BROOK.....49 A4
Freshbrook Way SN5.49 B4

FRESHFORD........99 B5
Freshford Church Sch
  BA2.............99 B5
Freshford I a RA2...99 A4
Freshford Sta BA2..99 C5
Friars Cl BA13......112 C8
Friar's Orch 4 SP1..152 B8
Friars The SN12.....94 C6
Friary Cl BA15......99 E4
Friary La SP1.......152 B7
Friary The SP1......152 B8
Fricker's La SP3....200 F3
Frickers Paddock
  SP3.............201 B3
Friday La SN9......181 D3
Fridays Ham La SN6...7 B3
Friday St
  Christian Malford
    SN15..........58 C3
  Swindon SN6.....34 C6
Friesian Cl SN5.....49 A7
Friesland Cl SN5....49 A7
Friggle St BA11....110 D1
Frilford Dr SN3.....36 A1
FRITHAM.........212 A1
Frith Copse 3 SN5..34 A2
Fritillary Mews SN1..50 D6
Frobisher Dr SN3...50 F6
Frogden Rd SN1....50 B1
Frog La
  Avebury SN8......173 B8
  Chilmark SP3.....201 B3
  Great Bedwyn SN8.176 C3
  Great Somerford SN15.44 B3
  Hullavington SN14..41 F1
  Longbridge Deverill
    BA12..........121 A6
  Motcombe SP7....202 B4
  West Overton SN8..173 F7
FROGMORE.......109 A4
Frogmore La SN5...208 B3
Frogmore Rd BA13..108 F5
Frogwell SN14......77 F8
Frogwell Pk SN14...78 A8
Frogwell Prim Sch
  SN14............78 A7
FROME...........110 A5
Frome Com Coll
  BA11............110 A7
Frome Com Hospl
  BA11............110 A6
FROMEFIELD......110 A6
Frome Leisure Ctr
  BA11............110 A7
Frome Rd
  Bradford-on-Avon
    BA15..........100 C5
  Maiden Bradley with
    Yarnfield BA12..118 D5
  Southwick BA14..104 F3
  Trowbridge BA14..105 C7
  Westbury BA15...100 C3
  West Woodlands BA12 114 A1
  Wingfield BA14...104 C6
  Woolverton BA2...103 A2
Frome Sta BA11....110 B4
Frome View BA12...118 E3
Front Hill Cl 3 BA13..84 E3
Front Horse Hill La
  SP7.............203 A1
Front La SN26......21 A4
Front St RG17......171 E7
Frost Cl 1 SN5......49 D6
FROXFIELD.......176 D7
Fruitfields Cl SN10..214 B1
Fry Cl 2 SN1.......49 F4
Fryern Ct Rd SP6...210 D3
Fry Sq SP10........193 F1
Fugglestone Sq 2 SP2.144 F3
FUGGLESTONE ST
  PETER..........144 F4
Fulford Rd BA14....101 E2
Fuller Ave SN13....84 E4
Fuller Cl
  Chippenham SN14..78 E6
  Swindon SN25.....35 F5
Fuller Gdns SN3....36 E3
Fullers Ave SN6.....19 D8
Fuller's Cl SN12....94 B5
Fullerton Wlk 6 SN1.49 F4
Fulmar Cl SN12.....94 D1
Fulney Cl BA14.....101 F2
Furlong Cl
  Rowde SN10......96 E1
  Swindon SN25.....34 E5
Furlong Cres SP3...196 F7
Furlong Gdns BA14.101 E1
Furlong Way SP3...196 F7
Furnax La BA12....112 F1
Furrow Way 11 SP11.193 F2
Furse Hill Rd SP9..216 D5
Furze Cl SN5.......34 A2
Furze Dr SP11......191 F3
Furzehill SN13......84 F8
Furze Hill La SN10..179 D7
FURZLEY.........212 F3
Furzley Comm Rd
  SO51............212 F2
Furzley La SO51....212 F3
Furzley Rd SO51...212 F2

Fyfield Cl 2 SP1....146 D5
Fyfield Down National
  Nature Reserve★
  SN6.............167 F1
Fyfield La SP11.....192 D1
Fyfield Rd SP11....192 E1
Fyfield Way SP11...191 F3
Fynamore Gdns SN11.81 B1
Fynamore Pl SN11...81 B4
Fynamore Prim Sch
  SN11............81 A4
Fyne Cl 3 SN5......34 B2

G

Gable Cl SN2.......35 B6
Gables Cl SN10....214 D2
Gabrial Cres 3 SN25.34 C8
Gabriel Cl 4 BA11..110 C6
Gabriel Mws 1 SN14.78 C8
Gadwall Cl GL7......7 A6
Gainsborough Ave
  SN4.............47 F3
Gainsborough Cl
  SP2.............145 C3
Gainsborough Ct 1
  SP10............193 D1
Gainsborough Rise
  BA14............105 A6
Gainsborough Way
  SN5.............49 A3
Gains La SN10.....214 B4
Gairlock Cl SN5.....34 B2
Gaisford Chase SN10.179 B4
Galahad Cl 25 SP10.193 E2
Gales Cl SN15......78 F8
Gales Gd SN8......213 E3
Galileo Dr SN15.....70 E1
Gallery at Handel
  House★ SN10...214 B3
Galley La SN8......176 C3
Gallipoli Rd 8 SP4.198 F7
Gallops The SN4...163 D4
Galloway Cl 13 SN5.49 A7
Galloway Dr SN2....34 C5
Galloway Rd SN25..34 C5
Gallows Barrow★
  SP4.............190 B3
Gallows Leap SN1..81 A5
Galsworthy Cl SN3..51 D4
Galton Way
  Swindon SN2.....34 D1
  Swindon SN2.....49 F8
Gambia St SN1.....50 D6
Gamekeepers Cl 9
  SN25............34 F7
Gantlettdene SN3...51 E6
Ganton Way SN3....35 E1
Gardeners Gn 2
  SP9.............199 C3
Gardens The
  Heddington SN11..89 B1
  Rushall SN9......181 E3
  Swindon SN25....35 A3
  Upavon SN9......181 F2
Garden The SN2....35 E5
Garden Trading Est
  SN10............214 C5
Gardiner Rd 2 SP4..197 E6
Gardners Dr SN14..55 E8
GARE HILL........118 A5
Gare Hill La BA11...118 F5
Garendon Ct SP6...210 D1
Garfield Cl SN3.....51 C3
Garland Mws 3 SP4.132 B1
Garlings The 6 SN8.170 A6
Garnet Cres SN26...21 A1
Garrard Way SN3...51 A4
Garraways 6 SN4...47 F2
GARSDON.........29 B4
Garsdon Mill SN16..28 F5
Garsington Dr SN25.34 C7
Garson Rd 1 SN25..35 B6
Garston BA11......110 A4
Garston La 3 BA11..110 A4
Garston Rd BA11...110 A4
Garstons BA1.......82 D2
Garstons The BA1...82 D2
Garth Cl SN14......70 B1
Garth Rd BA14.....101 F1
Gartons Rd SN5....48 F7
Gascelyn Cl SN14...78 C8
Gascoigne's La SP7.202 C1
Gas La
  Cricklade SN6.....19 D7
  Salisbury SP2.....145 F1
Gason Hill Rd SP9..216 C8
GASPER..........137 C7
Gasper Lodge Rd
  BA9.............137 C4
Gasper St
  Gasper BA10.....136 F8
  Stourton with Gasper
    BA12..........137 C6
Gassons Rd GL7.....2 C5
Gassons Way GL7....2 C4
GASTARD.........85 D6
Gastard La SN13....85 E5
Gaston La SN16.....40 C8
Gastons Rd SN16...27 F3
Gaston's Rd SN14...78 C8
Gaters La SP4......133 C4
Gauns Ct SP3......141 C1
Gauntlet Rd SP4...217 B4
Gaveller Rd SN25...34 C7
Gawaine Cl 3 SP10.193 E2

Gawthorne Dr SP2 ... 151 F6
Gaynor Cl SN25 ... 35 A6
Gay's Pl SN2 ... 35 F4
Gayton Way SN3 ... 51 B8
Gaza Rd SP4 ... 198 F7
Geneville Rise 3
SP4 ... 217 C3
Genoa Ct 16 SP10 ... 193 E2
Gentle St BA12 ... 119 C7
George Cl SN11 ... 81 C3
George Gay Gdns 7
SN3 ... 50 F4
George La SN8 ... 213 D2
George St Pl BA12 ... 117 A7
George St (South) 6
SP2 ... 145 F1
George St
Salisbury SP2 ... 145 F1
Swindon SN1 ... 50 A6
Trowbridge BA14 ... 101 D1
Warminster BA12 ... 117 A7
George VI Rd SP9 ... 216 C8
Gerard Wlk SN5 ... 49 A6
Germain's La SN14 ... 76 A8
Geys Hill BA12 ... 115 A7
Giant's Cave (Long Barrow)* SN14 ... 39 C2
Giant's Chair The (Tumulus)* SP5 ... 158 E2
Gibb Rd
Castle Combe SN14 ... 54 A1
Castle Combe SN14 ... 68 B8
Gibbs Cl
2 Salisbury SP1 ... 146 C5
Swindon SN3 ... 51 E7
Westbury BA13 ... 109 B4
Gibbs Ct SN13 ... 76 D1
Gibbs La SN14 ... 55 F8
Gibbs Leaze BA14 ... 102 A1
GIBB THE ... 53 F3
Gibson Cl SN12 ... 94 C1
Gibson Pl SP4 ... 132 B1
GIDDEAHALL ... 68 D2
Gifford Rd SN3 ... 36 B3
Giffords The BA14 ... 102 A4
Gigant St
Salisbury SP1 ... 152 B8
Swallowcliffe SP3 ... 204 A6
Giggan St BA12 ... 195 B2
Gilbert's Gn 3 SP9 ... 199 D8
Gilberts La SN6 ... 23 A5
Gilberts Piece SN8 ... 183 E1
Gilbert Way SP1 ... 146 C4
Giles Ave 1 SN6 ... 19 D7
Giles La SO51 ... 212 F7
Giles La Ind Est SP5 ... 212 E6
Giles Rd 8 SN25 ... 34 D6
Gilhespy Way BA13 ... 109 A5
Gillingham Rd
Mere BA12 ... 138 E4
Silton SP8 ... 138 A1
Gilling Way SN3 ... 51 D6
Gilman Cl SN25 ... 35 A8
Gilmore Ct SN6 ... 23 A5
Gilmore Rd SN16 ... 28 A6
Gimson Cres SN25 ... 20 C1
Giotto Cl 11 SN25 ... 34 B7
Gipsy La
Chippenham SN15 ... 78 D6
Frome BA11 ... 110 B7
Holt BA14 ... 92 F2
Hungerford RG17 ... 177 C8
Swindon SN2 ... 50 E8
Warminster BA12 ... 117 B5
Gladstone Rd
Chippenham SN15 ... 78 D7
Trowbridge BA14 ... 105 B7
Gladstone St SN1 ... 50 C7
Gladys Plumley Gdns
SN2 ... 50 C8
Glass's La SP3 ... 204 D7
Glebe Bglws 3 BA12 ... 201 E8
Glebe Cl
7 Aldbourne SN8 ... 170 A6
Pitton & Farley SP5 ... 148 C4
Glebe Field BA12 ... 117 A6
Glebe Gdns SP7 ... 202 A4
Glebe La
Kemble GL7 ... 4 F7
Landford SP5 ... 212 C6
Wroughton SN4 ... 63 F3
Glebelands 3 BA12 ... 194 C5
Glebe Pl
Chilton Foliat RG17 ... 171 A1
Highworth SN6 ... 23 A6
Glebe Rd
2 Durrington/Bulford
SP4 ... 198 B7
Royal Wootton Bassett
SN4 ... 47 D1
Trowbridge BA14 ... 105 A7
Glebe The
All Cannings SN10 ... 180 F8
Calne SN11 ... 81 C3
Freshford BA2 ... 99 B4
Hinton Charterhouse
BA2 ... 98 D2
Glebe Way SN13 ... 76 E1
Gleed Cl SN5 ... 32 F4
Glendale Cres SP1 ... 152 D8
Glendale Dr SN14 ... 78 E6
Glendale Rd SP4 ... 198 C7
Gleneagles Cl SN15 ... 78 F7
Glenfield Cl SP5 ... 149 D6
Glenmore Bsns Pk
SP2 ... 151 E8
Glenmore Rd
Haydon Wick SN25 ... 34 C5
Glenmore Rd *continued*
Salisbury SP1 ... 146 C3
Glenside SN12 ... 94 C6
Glenville Cl SN4 ... 61 E8
Glenwood Cl SN1 ... 50 C2
Glevum Cl SN5 ... 33 C5
Glevum Rd SN3 ... 36 C1
Globe St SN1 ... 50 C4
Gloucester Cl 3 SN14 ... 78 A6
Gloucester Rd
Calne Without SN11 ... 81 F1
Trowbridge BA14 ... 105 B7
Gloucester Sq SN12 ... 94 C4
Gloucester St
8 Malmesbury SN16 ... 28 A3
Swindon SN1 ... 50 B7
Gloucester Wlk BA13 ... 109 A4
Glover Rd SP4 ... 197 F7
Glyndebourne Cl
SP2 ... 145 C3
Glyn Pl SP7 ... 206 B7
GOATACRE ... 73 F7
Goatacre La SN11 ... 73 F7
Goblins Pit Cl 3 SN13 ... 76 C1
Goddard Ave SN1 ... 50 B4
Goddard Cl 1 SN9 ... 215 C5
Goddard Pk Com Prim
Sch SN3 ... 51 B5
Goddard Rd SN9 ... 215 C5
Goddards La 11 SN8 ... 170 A6
Godley La BA14 ... 106 A8
Godley Rd SP2 ... 152 A6
Godolphin Cl SN5 ... 49 A3
Godolphin Prep Sch
SP1 ... 146 C1
Godolphin Sch The
SP1 ... 152 C8
GODSHILL ... 211 A1
Godwin Ct 9 SN1 ... 50 D4
Godwin Rd SN3 ... 36 B3
Godwins Cl SN12 ... 84 E1
Gogg's La SP5 ... 211 D7
Goldcrest Wlk SN3 ... 51 E7
Golden Cross SP6 ... 211 E4
Golden Rd SN10 ... 214 C5
Goldfinch Rd SN12 ... 94 E1
Gold Hill 8 SP7 ... 202 C1
Golding Ave SN8 ... 213 A2
Golding Gr SP2 ... 144 F4
Goldney Ave SN14 ... 78 C7
Goldsborough Cl SN5 ... 49 B6
Gold View SN1 ... 49 F4
GOMELDON ... 133 D4
Gomeldon Medieval Village of* SP4 ... 133 C4
Gomeldon Prim Sch
SP4 ... 133 C4
Gomeldon Rd SP4 ... 133 D5
Gooch Cl BA11 ... 110 D6
Gooch St SN1 ... 50 C7
Goodbody Rd 1
SP4 ... 198 A6
Goodes Hill SN13 ... 85 D3
Goodings La RG17 ... 171 D6
Goodwin Cl BA12 ... 117 E8
Goodwood Cl BA14 ... 105 E4
Goodwood Way 3
SN14 ... 77 F5
Goodwyns Cl 5 SP9 ... 199 C8
Goor La SN8 ... 164 B2
Goose Gn RG17 ... 165 A2
Gooselands
Crudwell SN16 ... 14 D5
Westbury BA13 ... 108 F2
Goose St
Marston SN10 ... 179 A3
Southwick BA14 ... 105 A2
Gordon Gdns 4 SN1 ... 50 C6
Gordon Rd 5 SN1 ... 50 C6
Gore Cl SN25 ... 34 F6
Gore Cross SN10 ... 187 E5
Gore La BA13 ... 111 B4
Gore Rd SP4 ... 197 E7
Gores La SN9 ... 181 C5
Gornall Rd SN13 ... 84 F6
Gorringe Rd SP2 ... 145 D1
GORSE HILL ... 35 D1
Gorse Hill Sch & Children's Centre
SN2 ... 35 D1
Gorse Pl 5 SN13 ... 84 E8
Gosditch
Ashton Keynes SN6 ... 6 F1
Ashton Keynes SN6 ... 17 E8
Latton SN6 ... 8 C4
Gosling Cl 15 SN4 ... 163 A6
Gosse Ct SN3 ... 50 E2
Goughs Way SN4 ... 47 E2
Gould Cl 1 SP11 ... 192 A5
Goulding Cl 3 SN3 ... 36 B2
Governor Dr SN12 ... 93 F7
Gower Cl
Swindon SN2 ... 35 F2
1 Swindon SN5 ... 48 F5
Gower Rd 14 SP7 ... 202 D2
Grace Cl SP2 ... 145 B5
Grace La SP6 ... 211 A4
Grafton Pl SN8 ... 183 F7
Grafton Rd
Burbage SN8 ... 183 D7
Swindon SN2 ... 35 C5
Graham Sq 7 SP4 ... 197 E6
Graham St SN1 ... 50 D7
Grailey Cl SN3 ... 51 C4
Grain Wlk 3 SP11 ... 193 F2
Gramp's Hill OX12 ... 165 F7
Gramshaw Rd 2
SP2 ... 145 D2
Granary Cl
Codford St Mary
BA12 ... 195 B2
Corston SN16 ... 42 F4
East Grafton SN8 ... 183 F7
4 Swindon SN5 ... 48 F8
Granary Rd 6 SN8 ... 176 B3
Grand Ave SN8 ... 175 E3
Grandison Cl SN5 ... 49 A6
Grand Trunk Rd SP9 ... 216 B4
Grange Cl
Atworth/Whitley SN12 ... 85 D1
Fyfield SP11 ... 192 D1
Highworth SN6 ... 23 A5
14 Wanborough SN4 ... 163 A6
Grange Dr SN3 ... 36 B1
Grangefield SN10 ... 172 F1
Grange Gdns SP1 ... 146 C2
Grange Inf Sch SN3 ... 36 B3
Grange Jun Sch SN3 ... 36 B2
Grange La
St Paul Malmesbury Without
SN16 ... 43 B5
Warminster BA12 ... 117 E5
GRANGE PARK ... 48 F5
Grange Pk Way SN5 ... 48 F5
Granger Cl SN15 ... 78 F4
Grange Rd BA11 ... 110 A7
Grange View BA15 ... 100 E7
Granham Cl SN8 ... 213 D1
Granham Hill SN8 ... 213 D1
Granica Cl 5 SN25 ... 34 D6
Grans Barrow (Long Barrow)* SP6 ... 209 E6
Grantham Cl SN5 ... 49 B3
Granthams The 4
RG17 ... 165 A2
Grantley Cl SN3 ... 51 A3
Grants Rd SN9 ... 190 A6
Granville Gdns 28
SP7 ... 202 C2
Granville Rd SN12 ... 94 A6
Granville St SN1 ... 50 C6
Grasmere
Bower Hill SN12 ... 94 D1
Swindon SN3 ... 51 E3
Trowbridge BA14 ... 101 E2
Grasmere Cl 1 SP2 ... 151 F6
Graspan Rd 12 SP11 ... 192 B5
Grassy Slope
Westbury BA13 ... 109 B1
Westbury BA13 ... 113 A8
Grateley Rd SP4 ... 199 C5
Gravel Cl SP5 ... 211 A8
Gravel The BA14 ... 92 E1
Graveney Sq SP10 ... 193 E1
Grayling Cl 9 SN11 ... 81 B5
Grays Cl SP7 ... 202 A4
Grays Leaze BA14 ... 105 C2
Gray St SP4 ... 132 B1
Graythwaite Cl 3
SN25 ... 34 F6
GREAT ASHLEY ... 91 A1
Great Barn* SN8 ... 167 B1
GREAT BEDWYN ... 176 B3
Great Bedwyn CE Prim
Sch SN8 ... 176 B4
Great Bottom
Sherrington BA12 ... 200 F8
Stockton BA12 ... 195 A1
GREAT CHALFIELD ... 92 E3
Great Chalfield Manor*
BA14 ... 92 D3
GREAT CHEVERELL ... 179 C1
Great Croft SP5 ... 148 C7
Great Dro SP4 ... 132 F1
Great Drove SP4 ... 132 F1
GREAT DURNFORD ... 197 F1
Greater La BA13 ... 186 C8
GREATFIELD ... 47 F8
Great Ground 15 SP7 ... 202 D2
Great Hill BA9 ... 137 B3
GREAT HINTON ... 178 A6
Great La SP7 ... 202 C1
Great Lodge Dr SN8 ... 175 B5
Great Mead SN14 ... 78 F8
Great Parks BA14 ... 92 F1
Great Roc Rd BA13 ... 108 E3
Great Rose La
Broad Blunsdon SN26 ... 21 A6
Swindon SN6 ... 20 F6
GREAT SOMERFORD ... 44 B2
Great Western Acad
SN26 ... 20 E2
Great Western Ave
SP3 ... 200 B1
Great Western Hospl The
SN3 ... 51 D1
Great Western St 7
BA11 ... 110 A4
Great Western Way
SN5 ... 48 F3
Great Wethers*
SN8 ... 174 A7
GREAT WISHFORD ... 129 F3
Great Wishford CE VA Fst
Sch SP2 ... 130 A4
Greatwoods BA13 ... 186 C8
Grebe Cl GL7 ... 7 A6
Greenacres
Dilton Marsh BA13 ... 112 A8
2 Downton SP5 ... 210 F8
Green Acres 13 SN8 ... 170 B2
Greenacres Way SN11 ... 80 F4
Greenacre Way 7
SP7 ... 202 D1
Greenaway 4 SN4 ... 163 A5
Greenbank Vw BA14 ... 104 F6
Greenbridge Ind Est
SN3 ... 51 A7
Greenbridge Rd SN3 ... 51 A7
Greenbridge Retail Pk
SN3 ... 36 A1
Greenbridge Ret Pk
SN3 ... 51 A8
Green Cl
Damerham SP6 ... 209 F2
East Grafton SN8 ... 183 F7
Holt BA14 ... 101 F8
Whiteparish SP5 ... 161 D4
Greencroft St SP1 ... 146 B1
Greencroft The 6
SP1 ... 146 B1
Green Dro
Buttermere SN8 ... 185 C8
Fovant SP3 ... 204 E8
Grimstead SP5 ... 154 B4
Pewsey SN9 ... 215 D3
Smannell SP11 ... 193 E5
Greene St
Swindon SN25 ... 20 C1
Swindon SN25 ... 34 C8
Green Farm Rise
SN8 ... 176 D7
Greenfield Rd SN10 ... 214 C1
Greenfields
Grimstead SP5 ... 154 C2
Smannell SP11 ... 193 F4
South Marston SN3 ... 36 E5
Greenfield Vw SN6 ... 18 F6
Greenfinch Cl SN12 ... 94 D4
Green Gate Rd SN10 ... 180 D4
Greenham Wlk SN3 ... 51 B6
Greenhill
Neston SN13 ... 84 D6
Sutton Veny BA12 ... 117 F1
Westwells SN13 ... 84 D7
GREEN HILL ... 32 D1
Greenhill Gdns
Sutton Veny BA12 ... 117 F1
Trowbridge BA14 ... 102 A4
Greenhill Pl BA12 ... 195 A3
Greenhill Rd SN2 ... 34 E2
Greenhills BA13 ... 186 C8
Greenhouse Rd SN10 ... 180 F8
Green La
Ashmore SP5 ... 206 E4
Cheverell Magna SN10 ... 179 C1
Codford BA12 ... 195 A3
Colerne SN14 ... 75 A3
Deanend SP5 ... 207 E4
Devizes SN10 ... 214 B1
Downton SP5 ... 211 A8
Fordingbridge SP6 ... 210 D1
Hinton Charterhouse
BA2 ... 98 E1
Laverstock SP4 ... 146 D8
Longhedge BA12 ... 115 C5
Rockbourne SP6 ... 210 C3
Salisbury SP1 ... 146 D6
Sherston SN16 ... 25 C1
Southwick BA14 ... 104 D2
Steeple Ashton BA14 ... 102 C1
Trowbridge BA14 ... 105 E8
Westbury BA13 ... 108 F2
Winsley BA15 ... 99 E6
Green La Hospl SN10 ... 214 C1
Greenland Cl SN12 ... 92 E8
Greenland Mills
BA15 ... 100 D6
Greenlands 1 BA12 ... 194 C5
Greenlands Cl 20
SP4 ... 198 B7
Greenlands Rd SN2 ... 35 E3
Greenland View
BA15 ... 100 D6
Greenlane Cl SP4 ... 146 D6
Green La Wood Nature Reserve* BA14 ... 106 C8
Greenleaze Cl BA14 ... 105 A4
Green Mdw Ave SN25 ... 34 F4
GREENMEADOW ... 35 B4
Greenmeadow Prim Sch
SN25 ... 35 A4
Green Pk La BA11 ... 107 A6
Green Rd
Codford BA12 ... 195 A3
Corsham SN13 ... 85 B4
Swindon SN2 ... 35 E3
Green Ride BA12 ... 123 E5
Greensand Cl 10 SN25 ... 34 F7
Greens Cl SN14 ... 41 F1
Green's Ct 3 SP1 ... 152 B8
Greensey SP11 ... 192 E3
Greens La SN11 ... 172 A8
Green's La SN4 ... 64 B5
Greens Meade 6
SP5 ... 211 C7
Green St SN8 ... 167 C1
Greenstone Rd SP7 ... 202 D1
Green Terr BA14 ... 101 C2
GREEN THE ... 141 A3
Green The
Alderbury SP5 ... 153 C3
Biddestone SN14 ... 76 E8
Brokenborough SN16 ... 27 D7
Calne SN11 ... 81 B2
Cheverell Magna SN10 ... 179 C2
Dauntsey SN15 ... 59 A8
Fairford GL7 ... 1 F7
Highworth SN6 ... 22 F5
1 Liddington SN4 ... 163 A4
Lyneham & Bradenstoke
SN15 ... 60 A4
Marlborough SN8 ... 213 E3
Oaksey SN16 ... 15 F7
Green The *continued*
Pitton & Farley SP5 ... 148 C3
Salisbury SP1 ... 146 D2
Upper Woodford SP4 ... 131 D7
Whiteparish SP5 ... 161 D4
Greentrees Prim Sch
SP1 ... 146 C5
Green Valley Ave
SN25 ... 34 F4
Greenway SN4 ... 60 F2
Greenway Ave SN15 ... 70 D1
Greenway Cl SN3 ... 51 B7
Greenway Ct SN15 ... 70 D2
Greenway Dr SN15 ... 73 F8
Greenway Gdns
Chippenham SN15 ... 70 D1
Trowbridge BA14 ... 101 E3
Greenway La SN15 ... 70 D2
Greenway Pk SN15 ... 70 D1
Greenway Rd SN8 ... 169 B1
Greenways RG17 ... 165 A1
GREENWICH ... 200 C3
Greenwich Cl SN25 ... 35 A5
Greenwood Ave SP1 ... 146 D1
Greenwood Gr 4
SN25 ... 34 C6
Greenwood Pl 6
SN25 ... 34 D7
Greenwood Rd SN12 ... 94 A3
Gregor Dr SN11 ... 81 D3
Gregory Cl
Box SN13 ... 83 D6
Sutton Benger SN15 ... 57 C1
Grenadier Cl 2 BA12 ... 116 F7
Gresham Cl SN3 ... 50 F6
Greyfriars Cl SP1 ... 152 B7
Greyhound La 1
SP2 ... 144 D3
Grey's Cnr BA9 ... 136 A5
Greystones SN15 ... 96 B8
Greywethers Ave SN3 ... 50 E3
Grey Wethers or Sarsen Stones* SN8 ... 167 F2
Grierson Cl SN11 ... 81 B3
Griffin Alley 6 SN16 ... 28 A3
Griffins Ct 3 SP2 ... 146 A1
Griffiths Cl SN3 ... 36 B1
Grimstead Beeches*
SP5 ... 160 D7
Grimstead Rd
Alderbury SP5 ... 153 F1
East Grimstead SP5 ... 154 E5
West Dean SP5 ... 155 C2
Grimstead Road SP5 ... 154 D6
Grindal Dr SN5 ... 48 F5
Grist Ct 11 BA15 ... 100 D6
GRITTENHAM ... 46 C2
GRITTLETON ... 54 D5
Grocyn Cl SN14 ... 75 B3
Grosmont Dr SN5 ... 49 B5
Grosvenor close SP9 ... 216 E6
Grosvenor Dr SP3 ... 200 E1
Grosvenor Rd
Shaftesbury SP7 ... 202 C2
Swindon SN1 ... 50 A4
Ground Cnr BA14 ... 101 D8
Groundstone Way
Corsham SN13 ... 76 C1
2 Corsham SN13 ... 84 C8
Groundwell SN25 ... 35 C6
Groundwell Ind Est
SN25 ... 35 D6
Groundwell Rd SN1 ... 50 D5
Grouse Rd
Calne SN11 ... 81 B5
Old Sarum SP4 ... 146 B8
Grove Hill SN6 ... 23 A7
Grove La
Kington St Michael
SN14 ... 69 F8
Redlynch SP5 ... 211 D8
Yatton Keynell SN14 ... 69 A6
Grovelands Ave SN1 ... 50 C3
Grovelands Way
BA12 ... 116 E7
Grove Leaze BA15 ... 100 B6
Groveley Rd SP3 ... 143 B3
Grovely Castle* SP3 ... 128 F4
Grovely Cl SN5 ... 34 A1
Grovely Cotts SP2 ... 130 A3
Grovely Rd SP3 ... 129 E2
Grovely View SP2 ... 144 B1
Grovely Wood
Barford St Martin SP3 ... 128 F1
Barford St Martin SP3 ... 142 F8
Barford St. Martin SP3 ... 129 B1
Grove Orch SN6 ... 22 F7
Grove Prim Sch
BA14 ... 105 B5
Grove Rd
Corsham SN13 ... 77 A1
23 Market Lavington
SN10 ... 179 F1
Sherston SN16 ... 40 C8
Groves St SN2 ... 49 F6
Groves The SN25 ... 35 B3
Grove The
Codford St Peter
BA12 ... 195 A2
Crudwell SN16 ... 4 C1
Penton Mewsey SP11 ... 193 A2
Warminster BA12 ... 117 A7
Grundys SN3 ... 51 D3
Gryphon Cl BA13 ... 108 E3
Guernsey La SN25 ... 34 D6
Guernsey Mead
BA13 ... 109 A8
Guilder La SP1 ... 152 B8
Guildford Ave SN3 ... 50 F3
Guildhall Sq 3 SP1 ... 152 A8
Guild The (Wilton)
SP2 ... 144 E3
Gullet The SN13 ... 83 F7
Gulliver's La BA14 ... 178 A4
Gundry Cl
Chippenham SN15 ... 78 F5
Devizes SN10 ... 214 C4
Gundy Gr BA14 ... 106 A8
Gunner St SP4 ... 198 E6
Gunsite Rd SN8 ... 173 C6
Gunville Hill SP5 ... 149 E6
Gunville Rd SP5 ... 149 D6
Guppy St SN2 ... 49 F7
Gurston La SP5 ... 205 A4
Gurston Meadow
SP5 ... 205 A4
Gurston Rd SP5 ... 205 A4
Gussage Hill
Gussage St Andrew
BH21 ... 208 A1
Gussage St Andrew
SP5 ... 207 F1
GUSSAGE ST
ANDREW ... 207 E1
Guthrie Cl SN11 ... 81 C4
Guyers La SN13 ... 76 D2
Gwyns Piece 14
RG17 ... 165 A2
Gypsies La BA14 ... 106 F8
Gypsy La
Coombe Bissett SP5 ... 156 F7
Coombe Bissett SP5 ... 157 A8
Draycot Foliat SN4 ... 168 C7
Swindon SN25 ... 35 E1
Gypsy Patch SN10 ... 97 F1

H

Habberfield SP9 ... 216 D8
Habrel's Cl SN15 ... 78 F6
Hackett Cl SN2 ... 35 E4
Hackleton Rise SN3 ... 51 B8
Hackney Way BA13 ... 108 E3
Hackpen SN8 ... 168 B6
Hackpen Cl SN4 ... 64 B7
Hackpen La SN4 ... 168 B8
HACKTHORN ... 198 A8
Hackthorne Rd SP4 ... 198 B7
Haddon Cl 14 SN5 ... 48 F5
Haddons Cl SN16 ... 27 E2
Haden Rd 6 BA14 ... 105 D7
Hadleigh Cl SN5 ... 49 C6
Hadleigh Rise SN2 ... 36 A5
Hadrian Rd 20 SP10 ... 193 E2
Hadrians Cl
Salisbury SP2 ... 145 C1
Swindon SN3 ... 36 C1
Swindon SN3 ... 51 C8
Haig Cl SN2 ... 35 E4
Haig Rd SP4 ... 217 F8
HAILSTONE HILL ... 8 A1
Haimes La 20 SP7 ... 202 C2
Haines Terr SN9 ... 215 C4
HALCOMBE ... 27 E3
HALE ... 211 C5
Hale House* SP6 ... 211 A5
Hale La SP6 ... 211 B5
Hale Prim Sch SP6 ... 211 C6
Hale Rd SP6 ... 211 A5
Hales Castle* BA11 ... 114 D5
Hales Cl SN15 ... 59 E4
Hales Rd 6 SP4 ... 190 A4
Half Hide Down SP5 ... 207 B3
Half Mile Rd RG17 ... 171 A5
Halfpenny La SP5 ... 206 E4
Halfpenny Rd SP2 ... 151 D7
Halfpenny Row BA11 ... 103 E1
HALFWAY ... 113 A4
Halfway Cl BA14 ... 101 F2
Halfway Firs SN13 ... 76 C1
HALF WAY FIRS ... 76 C1
Halfway La SN8 ... 170 C2
Halifax Cl SN4 ... 64 A7
Halifax Rd SN12 ... 94 C1
Hallam Moor SN3 ... 51 E2
Hall Cl SN4 ... 64 A6
Halls Farm La SP11 ... 185 D4
Hallsfield SN6 ... 8 D1
Hallum Cl SP1 ... 146 D4
Halton Cres SN4 ... 64 E3
Halton Rd SP11 ... 191 F4
Halve The BA14 ... 101 D1
HAM ... 177 B2
Hambidge La GL7 ... 2 C5
Hamble Ct SP10 ... 193 F1
Hamble Rd SN25 ... 34 F4
Hambleton Ave SN10 ... 214 E6
Hamblin Meadow
RG17 ... 177 C8
Hamburg Cl 10 SP10 ... 193 D2
Ham Cl
Collingbourne Kingston
SN8 ... 183 D3
Holt BA14 ... 101 D8
Trowbridge BA14 ... 101 B1
HAM GREEN ... 101 C8
Ham Green Gaston
BA14 ... 101 E8
Ham Hill Nature Reserve* SN8 ... 185 B8
Hamilton Cl
Amesbury SP4 ... 217 E3

Hamilton Cl *continued*
Swindon SN3 . . . .**50** F7
Hamilton Dr
Chippenham SN14 . . . . . .**77** F5
2 Market Lavington
SN10 . . . . **179** F1
Hamilton Pk 3 SP5. . .**211** B8
Hamilton Rd SP1 . . . .**146** A2
Ham La
Biddestone SN14 . . . . . .**76** C8
Kempsford GL7 . . . .**10** E6
South Cerney GL7 . . . .**6** F5
South Cerney GL7 . . . .**7** A6
Hamlet Ct SN15. . . . . .**70** D1
Hamlet Gdns SP11. . . **193** E3
Hamlet The SN15. . . . .**70** E1
Hammersmith Fields
BA14. . . . . **101** C1
Hammer St BA10 . . . .**122** C7
Hammonds SN6 . . . . . .**19** E8
Hammond Way BA14. **101** D4
Hampshire Cl
Durrington/Bulford
SP4. . . . . **217** D2
7 Swindon SN5 . . . . . .**49** A7
HAMPSHIRE GATE . . **185** A1
Hampshire Gdns
BA13. . . . . **109** A4
Hampshire Pl SN12 . . .**94** B5
Hampsley Rd SN13. . . .**89** C1
Hampstead Way SN25. .**34** F7
HAMPTON **22** D5
Hampton Cl SN12. . . . .**94** C1
Hampton Ct
Quidhampton SP2 . . . .**144** F2
Swindon SN5 . . . .**48** F5
Hampton Dr SN5 . . . . .**48** F5
HAMPTON HILL **22** E5
Hampton Rd 31 SP11. **193** E2
HAMPTWORTH **212** B6
Hamptworth Rd SP5 . .**211** F6
Ham Rd
Ham RG17 . . . .**177** A2
Liddington SN4. . . . . . .**163** A5
Hamshill Ditches *
SP3. . . . . **143** B7
HAM THE **108** E5
Ham The
Durrington/Bulford
SP4. . . . . **198** C4
Kington St Michael SN14 **70** A8
9 Market Lavington
SN10 . . . . **179** F1
Westbury BA13 . . . . . . **108** E5
Hamworthy Rd SN3. . . .**51** C6
Hanbury Rd SN3. . . . . .**51** A4
Hancock Cl SN15 . . . . .**79** A5
Handel St SN2. . . . .**50** C8
Handley St SP5 . . . . . **204** D3
Hanewell Rise BA14 . **102** B2
Hanging Bushes La
SP11. . . . . **193** A1
**HANGING
LANGFORD** **128** C7
Hanging Langford
Camp * BA12. . . . . . **201** F6
Hanging Stone *
SN9. . . . . **181** B7
Hanging The SP5 . . . . **155** F1
Hangman's Stone *
RG17. . . . . **164** F4
Hanker Cl SN26. . . . . . .**20** D1
HANKERTON **15** C2
Hankerton Priory
SN16. . . . .**15** B4
Hankerton Rd SN16. . . .**16** C2
Hanks Cl SN16. . . . .**28** A5
Hannah Way SP4 . . . . **132** B1
HANNINGTON **22** B7
Hannington Cl SN2 . . . .**35** B6
HANNINGTON WICK . . .**11** A4
Hanover Cl BA14. . . . . **101** E4
Hanover Ct SN3. . . . . . .**51** D7
Hanson Cl 1 SN5. . . . . .**49** B8
Hanwell Cl 4 SN25 . . . .**34** D8
Ha'penny Bridge * GL7 .**2** C3
Happy Land SN6 . . . . . .**18** A8
Haragon Dr SP4 . . . . . **217** D1
Harbour Cl SN25. . . . . .**34** F3
Harbour Mdw SN2. . . . .**34** F3
Harcourt Mews 5
BA11. . . . . **110** A4
Harcourt Rd SN2 . . . . . .**50** A4
Harcourt Terr SP2 . . . **151** F8
Hardenhuish Ave
SN15. . . . .**70** C1
Hardenhuish La SN14 . .**70** B1
Hardenhuish Pk *
SN14. . . . .**70** C1
Hardenhuish Sch
SN14. . . . .**70** C2
Hardens Cl SN15. . . . . .**79** A5
Hardens Mead SN15 . . .**79** A6
Hardhams Rise SN13. . .**84** F1
Hardie Cl SN3 . . . .**36** A1
Harding St 6 SN1 . . . . .**50** B6
HARDWAY **122** A1
Hardwick Cl SN25 . . . . .**35** A5
Hardy Cl SN25 . . . .**34** D6
Hardyfair Cl 5 SP11. . **192** F1
Harebell Cl SN25 . . . . . .**34** D6
Harebell Rd 23 SP11 . **193** D5
Hare Cl SN2 . . . .**35** F5
Harefield Cres SP4 . . . **190** A2

Hare Knapp BA15 . . . . **100** B6
Harepit La
Kilmington BA12 . . . . . **123** F5
Kilmington BA12 . . . . . **124** A5
Harepit Way * SN11 . .**1**/**2** F7
Haresdown Hill
Rodmarton GL7 . . . .**3** F7
Rodmarton GL7 . . . .**4** A7
HARESFIELD **23** B8
Hares Patch SN14 . . . . .**70** B2
Hare St
Bremhill SN15 . . . .**72** C5
Pewsey SN9. . . . . **182** A7
Hare Warren Ct SP2 . . **144** C1
Harford Cl 4 SN15 . . . .**78** F5
Harford St 4 BA14 . . . **105** E8
Hargreaves Rd
Swindon SN25 . . . .**35** D6
Trowbridge BA14 . . . . . **105** E7
Harlech Cl SN5 . . . .**49** B4
Harlestone Rd SN3 . . . .**51** B8
Harley La SO51 . . . . . . **212** E3
HARNHAM **151** E6
Harnham CE Jun Sch
SP2 . . . . **151** F6
Harnham Inf Sch SP2 . **151** F6
Harnham Rd SP2 . . . . **151** F7
Harnham Trad Est
SP2 . . . . **151** D7
Harnham Trading Est
SP2 . . . . **151** D7
Harnish Way SN14 . . . .**70** B2
Harnwood Rd SP2 . . . . **151** E6
Harper Rd SP2 . . . . . . **145** D2
Harpers La 3 SN16 . . . .**28** A3
Harper's La SN16 . . . . .**27** F3
Harptree Cl SN5 . . . . . .**49** A8
Harrier Cl SN11. . . . . . .**81** A5
Harriers The SN3 . . . . .**51** C7
Harrington Dr 4
SP4. . . . . **198** E6
Harrington Wlk SN3 . . .**51** A7
Harris Cl
Frome BA11. . . . . **110** B4
5 Lambourn RG17 . . . **165** A2
Harris La SN9. . . . . **183** A7
Harris Rd
Ashton Keynes SN6 . . . . . .**7** A1
Calne SN11 . . . .**81** C5
Swindon SN2 . . . .**35** A2
Harroway La SP11 . . . . **193** B1
Harrow Cl
Swindon SN25 . . . .**35** F1
Swindon SN3 . . . .**36** A1
Harrow Gr SN5 . . . .**60** B2
Harrow Rd SP4 . . . . . . **197** E8
Harrow Way SP11 . . . . **193** B1
**Harrow Way Com Prim
Sch** SP10 . . . . **193** C1
Hart Cl
Royal Wootton Bassett
SN4 . . . .**61** F8
Wilton SP2 . . . . **144** E3
Hartfield SN10. . . . . . . **214** A2
Hartham La SN13 . . . . .**76** E5
Harthill Dro SP5 . . . . . **211** D7
Hartington Rd
Salisbury SP2. . . . . **145** E2
Swindon SN25 . . . .**34** C7
Hartland Cl SN3 . . . . . .**51** A5
Hartley
Winsley BA15. . . . .**90** E1
Winsley BA15. . . . .**99** E8
Hartley Way SP11. . . . **146** D5
Hartmoor Cl SN10 . . . . **214** A2
Hartmoor Rd SN10. . . . **214** A2
Harts Cl SN11. . . . . **166** A7
Harts La SN14 . . . .**76** E8
Hartsthorn Cl SN2 . . . . .**34** D3
Harvard Cl
16 Bower Hill SN12 . . .**178** B8
1 Salisbury SP2. . . . . **151** F5
Harvester Cl 7 SN5. . . .**48** F8
Harvest La SN5 . . . . . . **205** F4
Harvest Pl SN14 . . . . . .**78** A4
Harvey Gr SN2. . . . .**34** F2
Hassocks La BA10 . . . . **122** A7
Hastings Ave SN9. . . . **182** B2
Hastings Cl SN9 . . . . . **182** B2
Hastings Dr
Calne SN11 . . . .**81** D4
Lyneham SN15. . . . .**60** B2
Hastings Rd
Corsham SN13. . . . .**85** A8
Trowbridge BA14. . . . . . **102** B1
Trowbridge BA14. . . . . . **106** B8
Hatchbury La SP15. . . . **185** C3
Hatcher's Cres SN26. . .**21** B2
Hatches La SP1. . . . . . **152** D7
HATCHET GREEN **211** C6
Hatchet Hill SN4. . . . . **163** D6
Hatchet La SP11. . . . . **193** B5
Hatch La
Vernhams Dean SP11 . . **185** C4
West Tisbury SP3. . . . . **203** C8
Hatch Rd SN3 . . . .**36** B4
Hatfield Cl 4 SN25 . . . .**34** E6
Hatfields SN10. . . . . . . **181** A5
Hathaway Cl SP1 . . . . **145** F4
Hathaway Rd SN2. . . . .**35** E5
Hathaway Ret Pk
SN15. . . . .**78** E8
HATHERDEN **193** C5
Hatherden CE Prim Sch
SP11. . . . . **193** C5
Hatherell Rd SN15. . . . .**78** F4

Hatherhall Cl SN3 . . . . .**36** C2
Hatherleigh Ct SN3 . . . .**51** B6
Hatherley Rd SN3. . . . . .**51** B6
Hathersage Moor SN3 .**51** E2
Hattem Pl 22 SP10 . . . **193** D2
Hatton Gr SN3. . . . .**50** F6
Hatton Way SN13 . . . . .**76** E1
Haugh BA15. . . . .**90** D1
Havard Way 2 SP4. . . **217** D2
Havelock Sq SN1 . . . . . .**50** B6
Havelock St
Swindon SN1 . . . .**50** B5
Trowbridge BA14. . . . . . **105** E7
Haven Cl SN3. . . . .**51** B8
Havering La SN9. . . . . **182** E7
Havisham Dr SN25 . . . .**34** D6
Hawcroft BA14 . . . .**92** E1
Hawfinch Cl SN3. . . . . . .**51** E5
Hawker Ave SN4 . . . . . **132** B1
HAWKERIDGE **108** E8
Hawkeridge Pk BA13 . **108** E5
Hawkeridge Rd BA14 . **105** E2
Hawker Rd SN3. . . . .**51** C4
Hawkesdene 17 SP7 . . **202** C1
Hawkesdene La SP7 . . **202** C1
Hawkins Cl SN15 . . . . . .**78** F5
Hawkins Meadow
SN8. . . . . **213** B2
Hawkins Rd 16 SN8 . . **170** A6
Hawkins St
3 Swindon SN1 . . . .**49** F7
Swindon SN1 . . . .**50** A7
Hawksridge 4 SP2 . . . **152** A5
Hawkstreet SN15 . . . . . .**96** B2
Hawkswood SN3 . . . . . .**51** D8
Hawk's Worth Cl 6
BA11. . . . . **110** C7
Hawksworth Trad Est
SN2. . . . .**50** A8
Hawksworth Way SN2 .**50** A7
Hawthorn Ave SN3 . . . .**35** C2
Hawthorn Cl
Calne SN11 . . . .**81** D5
Pewsey SN9. . . . . **215** D5
Royal Wootton Bassett
SN4 . . . .**61** F8
1 Salisbury SP2. . . . . **145** F1
2 Shaftesbury SP7. . . **202** D2
Hawthorn Gr BA14. . . . **105** C5
Hawthorn Rd
Bowerhill SN12 . . . .**94** D3
Chippenham SN15 . . . . .**70** E1
Frome BA11. . . . . **110** A6
Tidworth SP9 . . . . **216** D7
Hawthorn Way SP2 . . . **151** D7
HAXTON **190** B4
Haybrook Rise SN9 . . . **215** B6
Haycombe Hill
Sutton Veny BA12 . . . . **194** A4
Sutton Veny SP3. . . . . . **121** F4
Tytherington SP3. . . . . . **194** A2
Haydock Cl 4 SN14. . . .**77** F5
Haydon Cl SN25 . . . . . .**34** E5
Haydon Ct Dr SN25 . . . .**34** E5
Haydon End La
Haydon Wick SN25. . . . .**34** D6
3 Swindon SN25 . . . . .**34** E5
Haydonleigh Dr SN25 . .**34** E4
Haydonleigh Prim Sch
SN25. . . . .**34** E5
Haydon St SN1 . . . .**50** C7
HAYDON WICK **34** E5
Haydon Wick Prim Sch
SN25. . . . .**34** E4
Haydown Leas SP11 . . **185** C3
Hayes Cl
Atworth SN12 . . . .**92** E8
Trowbridge BA14. . . . . . **101** E3
Hayesdown Fst Sch
BA11. . . . . **110** B5
HAYES KNOLL **19** E2
Hayes Knoll SN5. . . . . . .**33** F8
Hayes Knoll Sta SN5 . . .**19** F2
Haye's La GL9 . . . .**38** E2
Hayfield SN14 . . . .**74** A8
Hayfield Cl RG17. . . . . **171** C7
Haygrove BA12. . . . . . . **116** D6
Haygrove Farm Mws
BA12. . . . . **116** C6
Hay La SN5 . . . .**48** F6
Hayle Rd SN5. . . . .**49** F6
Hayman Cres SN3 . . . . .**50** E2
Haynes Cl SN3. . . . .**51** C4
Haynes Rd BA13 . . . . . **109** A3
Hay St SN14 . . . .**74** A8
Haystack Ave SN14 . . . .**78** A4
Haywain 6 SP4 . . . . . **217** B3
Haywain Cl SN25 . . . . . .**35** C6
Hayward Cl
Chippenham SN15 . . . . .**78** F5
Swindon SN25 . . . .**35** A6
Hayward Pl BA13 . . . . **108** F5
Haywards GL7. . . . .**10** E6
Haywards Pl SN10 . . . . **179** F2
Hazeland SN15 . . . .**80** C5
Hazelbury Cres SN3. . . .**51** C7
Hazelbury La SN13. . . . .**83** D6
Hazelbury Manor Gdns *
SN13. . . . .**83** F5
Hazel Cl
Marlborough SN8. . . . . **175** A7
Salisbury SP2. . . . . **145** B3
Hazel Copse 2 SN14. . .**77** F6
Hazeldon La SP3 . . . . . **203** D6
Hazel End SN4. . . . .**47** L1
Hazel Gr
Calne SN11 . . . .**81** B1

Hazel Gr *continued*
Swindon SN2 . . . .**35** C3
Trowbridge BA14. . . . . . **105** B5
Hazel Way
Colerne SN14. . . . .**75** A5
6 Corsham SN13 . . . . .**76** E1
Hazelwood Academy
SN5. . . . .**49** C4
Hazelwood Rd SN12 . . .**94** A3
Hazlemere Cl SN3 . . . . .**51** B4
Hazzard's Hill BA12. . . **139** B5
Headington Hts SN11. . .**89** B1
Headlands Gr SN2. . . . .**35** E3
Headlands Trad Est Rd
SN25. . . . .**35** E2
Headley Cl SN4 . . . .**64** D3
Headquarters Rd
8 Durrington/Bulford
SP4. . . . . **198** F6
Westbury BA13 . . . . . . **108** C6
Heale Gdn * SP4 . . . . **131** D5
Heath Ave SN15 . . . . . .**57** C2
Heath Barn SP11 . . . . **185** C6
Heath Cl BA12 . . . . **115** B8
Heathcote Cl SN5. . . . . .**49** B8
Heathcote Rd SN12 . . . .**94** C5
Heather Ave SN12 . . . . .**94** C4
Heather Cl BA13 . . . . . **108** F4
Heather Shaw
2 Trowbridge BA14. . . **101** E1
Trowbridge BA14. . . . . . **105** E8
Heather Way SN11. . . . .**81** C1
Heath Farm Pk SP3 . . **143** A1
Heathfield SN15 . . . .**70** E2
Heathfields Way 2
SP7 . . . . **202** C2
Heath Hill BA14. . . . . . **106** E5
Heath La
Buttermere SN8. . . . . . **185** C7
Great Somerford SN15 . .**43** D2
Heathlands The BA12 . **116** F5
Heath Plantation La
SP11. . . . . **185** B5
Heath Rd SP2. . . . . **145** D4
Heath Sq 4 SP4 . . . . . **197** E6
Heath View Dr SP2 . . . **145** C3
Heathway BA12. . . . . . **115** C8
Heath Way SN3 . . . .**51** B8
Heaton Cl SN25. . . . .**35** A6
Heaven Hill Rd SP1 . . . **185** C4
Heavens Rise SN16 . . . .**17** F7
Hebden Cl 5 SN25 . . . . .**34** E7
Hebden Rd BA15. . . . . . .**99** F3
Hector Rd 2 SN25. . . . .**34** C7
HEDDINGTON **89** B1
Heddington CE Prim Sch
SN11. . . . .**89** B1
Heddington Cl
Swindon SN2 . . . .**35** B5
Trowbridge BA14. . . . . . **105** C5
HEDDINGTON WICK . . .**88** E2
Hedgeditch La GL8 . . . .**26** D7
Hedge La SP9 . . . . **216** D8
Hedge Row SN15 . . . . . .**79** A4
Hedgerow La SN4 . . . . .**61** F8
Hedges Cl
1 Shipton Bellinger
SP9. . . . . **199** C8
Swindon SN3 . . . .**36** B3
Hedgesparrow La
SN13. . . . .**83** F8
Hedges The 4 SN4 . . . **163** A6
Heeks Cres 3 BA14. . . **101** F1
Heights The SN1. . . . . . .**50** A4
Hei-lin Way 2 SP11 . . **192** A5
Helena Rd SN25 . . . .**34** C8
Helena Terr 7 SP1 . . . **146** B1
Helliker Cl BA14 . . . . . **102** B1
Helmdon Rd BA14 . . . . **101** A1
Helmsdale SN25. . . . . . .**34** F4
Helmsdale Wlk SN3. . . .**51** A4
Helmsley Rd BA14 . . . **106** B8
Helps Well Rd BA14. . . **102** B2
Helston Rd SN3. . . . .**51** A5
Henchard Cres 7
SN2. . . . .**34** C5
Henderson Cl BA14 . . . **105** B7
Henford Cl BA12. . . . . . **117** A5
Henfords Marsh
BA12. . . . . **117** B4
Hengest Cl 5 SP10 . . . **193** C2
HENLEY
Box **83** C4
Buttermere **185** A6
Henley Ave SN11 . . . . . .**81** D3
Henley Dr SN6. . . . .**23** A7
Henley La
Box SN13 . . . .**83** C4
Henley SN8 . . . . **185** A5
Henley Mws BA12. . . . . **116** C6
Henley Rd 2 SN3. . . . . .**51** A4
Henloke Way SN16 . . . .**28** C2
Henman Cl
Devizes SN10. . . . . **214** B4
Swindon SN25 . . . .**35** A5
Henn La SN15 . . . .**57** C6
Henry's Garth 7
SN8. . . . . **183** D8
Henry St 9 SN1. . . . . . .**50** B6
Henset Village * SN8. **175** E7
Hensler Dr SP4 . . . . . . **146** C6
Hepworth Rd 5 SN25. . .**34** F6
Herbert Ludlow Gdns
SN15. . . . .**59** C3
Herbert Rd
3 Redlynch SP5 . . . . . **211** C7

Herbert Rd *continued*
Salisbury SP2. . . . . **145** C3
Horbleaze BA14 . . . . . **101** D5
Hercules Rd SN11 . . . . .**81** D4
Hercules View SN15 . . . .**59** F4
Hercules Way 1
SN12. . . . . **178** B8
Herdsman Cl SN14. . . . .**78** A4
Herd St SN8 . . . . **213** D4
Herdwick Rd 21 SP11 **193** F2
Hereford Cl SN14 . . . . . .**78** A5
Hereford Lawns SN3. . .**50** F3
Herepath SN8 . . . . **167** C1
Herepath or Green St
SN8. . . . . **168** C1
HERITAGE PARK **214** C1
Herman Miller Ind Est
SN14. . . . .**78** B5
Hermitage La SN2 . . . . .**35** E3
Hernsham St SP7. . . . . **203** C4
Heronbridge Cl 2
SN5. . . . .**49** C5
Heron Cl SN11 . . . .**81** D3
Herongate RG17 . . . . . **177** B8
Heronscroft SN3. . . . . . .**51** D7
Herons Ct 6 SN12. . . . **178** B8
Heronslade BA12 . . . . **117** D5
Heronswood SP2. . . . . **152** A5
Heron Way SN14. . . . . . .**77** F6
Heron Wlk 12 SP4 . . . **198** C7
Herridge SN8. . . . . **184** A1
Herschell Cl 7 SN25. . . .**34** B7
Hertford Cl
1 Fordingbridge
SP6. . . . . **210** D2
4 Swindon SN3 . . . . . .**50** F6
Hertford Rd SN8. . . . . **213** F1
Hesketh Cres SN1 . . . . .**50** D3
Hewers Cl SN4 . . . . . . **163** A6
Hewitt Cl
Swindon SN3 . . . .**51** C4
Trowbridge BA14. . . . . . **105** E7
Hewlett Cl SN15 . . . .**79** A5
Hexham Cl
4 Chippenham SN14 . . .**77** F6
Swindon SN5 . . . .**49** B5
Heyford Cl 8 SP4 . . . . **217** E3
Heygate SN25 . . . .**20** D1
HEYTESBURY **194** C5
Heytesbury BA12 . . . . **194** B3
Heytesbury CE Prim Sch
BA12. . . . . **194** C5
Heytesbury Pk BA12 . . **194** D5
Heytesbury Pk BA12. . . **194** C5
Heytsbury Gdns 4
SN5. . . . .**48** F4
HEYWOOD **109** A8
Heywood Cl SN2. . . . . . .**35** B5
Heywood Prep Sch
SN13. . . . .**77** A2
Hicks Cl SN4 . . . .**64** A6
Hidcot Cl SN25 . . . .**34** E7
High Bannerdown
BA1. . . . .**82** B4
Highbury Ave SP2 . . . . **145** E2
Highbury Cl 2 SP2 . . . **145** E2
Highbury Pk BA12 . . . . **117** C6
Highbury Prim Sch
SP2. . . . . **145** E2
Highclere Ave SN3. . . . .**50** F4
Highclere Cotts 4
BA12. . . . . **201** E8
Highdown La SP11. . . . **185** F6
Highdown Way SN25. . .**35** A7
Higher Barn Cl SP7 . . . **206** B7
Higher Blandford Rd
Cann Common SP7 . . . **206** A8
2 Shaftesbury SP7. . . **202** D1
Higher Mere Pk *
BA12. . . . . **202** A8
HIGHER PERTWOOD . . **127** E4
Higher Stavordale Farm
La BA9 . . . . **136** B5
Highfield SN15 . . . .**96** C7
Highfield Cl BA14 . . . . **102** F5
Highfield Cres SP5 . . . **149** B6
Highfield La 10 SP5 . . **211** C7
Highfield Rd
Amesbury SP4 . . . . **217** B3
Bradford-on-Avon
BA15. . . . . **100** D7
Salisbury SP2. . . . . **145** E2
Highfield Rise 1
SP3. . . . . **196** F6
Highfold SN4. . . . .**47** F1
Highgate Cottage SN4 .**46** F5
High Ground SN25. . . . .**20** B1
Highgrove Cl SN11. . . . .**81** D2
High La SP5. . . . . **205** B4
Highland Cl
8 Swindon SN5 . . . . . .**49** A7
Westbury BA13 . . . . . . **108** E1
Highlands SN10 . . . . . . **179** D5
Highlands Cl SN13 . . . . .**84** A8
Highlands Rd SP2 . . . . **152** A6
Highlands Way SP5 . . . **161** D4
Highland View
South Newton SP2. . . . **130** A2
South Newton SP2. . . . **130** B2
High Lane SP5 . . . . **204** F4
High Lawn SN10 . . . . . **179** D8
High Mead SN4 . . . .**47** F2
Highmoor Copse SN5 . .**34** A1
Highnam Cl SN3 . . . .**36** A1
High Post Bsns Pk
SP4. . . . . **132** B5

High Post Rd SP4 . . . . **131** E6
High Rd
Ashton Keynes SN6 . . . . . .**6** F1
Bishopstone SP5 . . . . . **205** E4
Britford SP5. . . . . **152** C4
Highridge Cl SN5 . . . . . .**33** A3
High St Brow SN8. . . . . **169** A6
High St
Alderbury SP5 . . . . **153** C5
Amesbury SP4 . . . . **217** A3
Ansty SP3. . . . . **203** F6
1 Ashbury SN6. . . . . . **164** A8
Ashmore SP5. . . . . **206** E4
Avebury SN8. . . . . **173** B8
Badminton GL9 . . . .**38** E2
Bath BA1 . . . .**82** D2
Berwick St James SP3. **196** F2
Bishopstone SN6. . . . . **163** E6
Bourton SP8. . . . . **137** F3
Box SN13 . . . .**83** C5
Broad Blunsdon SN26 . .**21** B1
Bromham SN15 . . . .**96** A7
Bulford SP4 . . . . **217** D8
Burbage SN8 . . . . **175** C1
Calne SN11 . . . .**81** B3
Chapmanslade BA13 . . **111** A4
Cheverell Magna SN10 **179** C1
Chippenham SN15 . . . . .**78** D7
Chiseldown SN4. . . . . . .**65** D4
Codford BA12. . . . . **195** A2
Codford St Mary BA12. **195** A3
Colerne SN14. . . . .**75** B3
Collingbourne Ducis
SN8 . . . . **191** E8
Compton Chamberlayne
SP3. . . . . **142** B1
Compton Chamberlayne
SP3. . . . . **205** A8
Corsham SN13. . . . .**77** A1
Cricklade SN6 . . . .**19** E8
Damerham SP6 . . . . . . **209** F3
Deptford BA12. . . . . . . **195** E1
Downton SP5. . . . . **211** B8
Durrington/Bulford
SP4. . . . . **198** B7
Erlestoke SN10 . . . . . . **187** A8
Farnham DT11 . . . . **207** C2
Figheldean SP4 . . . . . . **190** B1
24 Fordingbridge SP6 **210** D1
Fovant SP3. . . . . **204** E7
Great Bedwyn SN8 . . . **176** B3
Great Cheverell SN10 . **187** B8
Heytesbury BA12. . . . . **194** C5
Highworth SN6. . . . .**23** A5
Hindon SP3 . . . . **200** A4
Hinton Charterhouse
BA2 . . . .**98** E1
Hungerford RG17. . . . . **177** B7
Idmiston SP4 . . . . **133** D5
Kempsford GL7 . . . .**10** C7
Lacock SN15 . . . .**86** D5
Lambourn RG17. . . . . . **164** F3
Lechlade GL7 . . . .**2** C4
Limpley Stoke BA2. . . . .**99** B5
Little Bedwyn SN8 . . . . **176** D4
Littleton Panell SN10. . **187** C8
9 Ludgershall SP11 . . **192** A5
Maiden Bradley with
Yarnfield BA12. . . . . . **118** E3
Malmesbury SN16 . . . . .**28** A3
Market Lavington SN10 **179** F1
Marlborough SN8. . . . . **213** A1
Marshfield SN14 . . . . . .**74** A8
Melksham SN12 . . . .**94** A4
Meysey Hampton GL7 . . .**1** A5
Netheravon SP4 . . . . . . **190** A3
Ogbourne St George
SN8 . . . . **168** F5
Pewsey SN9. . . . . **215** D5
Pitton & Farley SP5 . . . **148** C3
Porton SP4 . . . . **133** D6
Purton SN5. . . . .**33** B4
Ramsbury SN8 . . . . **170** B2
Rode BA11. . . . . **103** F1
Rowde SN10 . . . .**96** D2
Royal Wootton Bassett
SN4 . . . .**47** D1
Salisbury SP1. . . . . **152** A8
Seend SN12 . . . . **178** E8
Semington BA14 . . . . . **102** F6
18 Shaftesbury SP7. . . **202** C1
Sherston SN16. . . . .**40** C8
Shipton Bellinger SP9 . **199** D8
Shrewton SP3 . . . . **196** E7
Sixpenny Handley SP5 . **208** A4
South Cerney GL7 . . . .**6** F6
Steeple Ashton BA14. . **178** A3
Stourton with Gasper
BA12. . . . . **123** F1
Sutton Benger SN15 . . .**57** C2
Sutton Veny BA12 . . . . **117** F1
Swindon SN25 . . . .**34** E4
Swindon SN3 . . . .**50** D4
Tilshead SP3 . . . . **188** B2
Tisbury SP3 . . . . **203** E8
Upavon SN9 . . . . **181** F2
Urchfont SN10 . . . . **180** C4
Vernhams Dean SP11 . . **185** C3
Wanborough SN4. . . . . **163** B6
Warminster BA12 . . . . . **117** A7
Westbury BA13 . . . . . . **109** A3
West Lavington SN10 . . **179** D1
Winterbourne Stoke
SP3. . . . . **197** A4
Woodgreen SP6. . . . . . **211** A4
Worton SN10 . . . . **179** B4
Wroughton SN4. . . . . . .**64** A5
Wylye BA12 . . . . **201** E8

High St continued
Yatton Keynell SN14 68 F5
Zeals BA12 138 A3
High View Cl SP3 203 E7
HIGHWAY 166 B5
Highway Comm
SN11 166 B6
Highway The SP5 158 F5
Highwood BA12 118 F8
Highwood Cl 4 SN2 34 D4
HIGHWORTH 23 B5
Highworth Ind Est
SN6 23 A7
Highworth Rd
Highworth SN6 22 D1
Shrivenham SN4 37 F8
Shrivenham SN6 23 E1
South Marston SN3 36 E6
Highworth Recn Ctr
SN6 22 F5
Highworth Warneford
Sch SN6 23 A4
HILCOTT 181 D5
Hillary Cl SN25 35 C4
Hill Beech Rd SP9 216 E7
Hillbourne Cl BA12 117 B7
Hill Cl 4 SP3 203 E8
Hill Cnr Rd SN15 70 E2
HILL CORNER 110 E7
Hillcote Hospl SP1 146 C1
Hillcrest
Colerne SN14 75 C6
Malmesbury SN16 28 B2
Hillcroft SN11 81 C2
HILL DEVERILL 120 F5
Hill Deverill Manor*
BA12 120 F5
Hill Deverill Medieval
Village of* BA12 120 F5
Hilldrop Cl 1 SN8 170 B2
Hilldrop La
Lambourn RG17 171 A6
Ramsbury SN8 169 F3
Hillfort Mews 1 SP4 132 C1
Hill Hayes SN14 41 D2
Hill Hayes La SN14 41 E1
Hillier Cres SN11 81 D3
Hillier Rd SN10 214 D6
Hilliers Yd SN8 213 D3
Hillingdon Rd SN3 51 B4
Hillmead Dr SN5 34 B1
Hillmead Ent Pk SN5 49 B8
Hillocks The SN4 60 B5
Hill Rd
Norton Bavant BA12 194 A4
Pewsey SN9 215 C3
Salisbury SP1 146 E2
Sutton Veny BA12 121 F6
Hill Rise SN15 70 E2
Hillside
Burcombe SP2 143 D2
Leigh SN6 18 C5
Nettleton SN14 53 A4
Hill Side SP3 129 E8
Hillside Ave SN1 50 A4
Hillside Cl
Heddington SN11 89 B1
Mere BA12 138 E5
West Tytherley SP5 155 F2
Hillside Ct SN1 50 A4
Hillside Dr
Frome BA11 110 B4
Winterbourne SP4 133 D3
Hillside Pk BA13 109 B3
Hillside Rd
4 Hungerford RG17 177 B6
South Newton SP2 130 B2
Hillside Villas SP10 193 D1
Hillside Way SN26 21 A1
Hill St BA14 101 C1
Hill The
Limpley Stoke BA2 99 C5
Little Somerford SN15 44 B6
Hill Top Ave SP9 216 C8
Hilltop Cl 2 SP3 196 F6
Hill Top Cl SP4 190 B2
Hilltop Rd BA9 137 A4
Hilltop Way SP1 146 A5
Hillview SP5 204 C3
HILL VIEW 215 B3
Hill View
Deanland SP5 208 A5
Stanton St Bernard
SN8 173 B1
Stanton St Bernard
SN8 181 B8
9 Swindon SN25 34 A2
Hillview Cl SP4 217 B4
Hill View Rd
6 Salisbury SP1 152 B8
Swindon SN3 36 C1
Hill Vw La SN15 59 D3
Hillwell SN16 15 B2
Hillwood Cl BA12 116 F5
Hillwood La BA12 116 F5
Hillwood Rd 15 SN8 170 A6
Hillworth Rd SN10 214 A2
Hillyard Cl 3 SN5 48 F4
Hilly Fields SN13 84 E8
HILMARTON 166 A6
Hilmarton Ave 1 SN2 35 C5
Hilmarton Prim Sch
SN11 166 A6
HILPERTON 102 A3
Hilperton CE VC Prim Sch
BA14 102 A3
Hilperton Dr BA14 102 A2
HILPERTON MARSH 101 F5
Hilperton Rd 1
BA14 101 E1
Hilton Cl SN1 50 D6
Hinde's Meadow SP3 196 F7
HINDON 200 B3
Hindon La
Codford St Mary
BA12 195 B2
Tisbury SP3 200 D1
Hindon Rd
Chilmark SP3 201 A4
Chilmark SP3 201 B3
East Knoyle SP3 141 C2
Kingston Deverill BA12 126 D7
Hinkson Cl SN25 34 F8
HINTON
CHARTERHOUSE 98 E1
Hinton Hill
Bishopstone SN4 163 D6
Hinton Charterhouse
BA2 98 A1
Hinton Ho* BA2 98 E1
Hinton La BA14 178 A5
HINTON PARVA 163 D6
Hinton Priory* BA2 98 F3
Hinton Springs SN6 163 D6
Hinton St SN2 50 D8
HISOMLEY 112 C7
Hitchings 4 SN6 19 D7
Hitchings Cl SN16 28 A6
Hitchings Skilling
SN14 75 B3
Hitch Rd SN25 35 B8
Hitcombe Bottom
Horningsham BA12 115 D1
Newbury BA12 119 D8
Hither Cl SN14 78 A8
Hither Spring SN13 84 F8
Hither Way SN15 86 D5
Hoadley Gn SP1 146 D4
Hobbes Cl SN16 27 F4
Hobbs Hill BA14 178 B5
Hobbs Wlk SN13 77 A1
Hobhouse Cl BA15 100 E4
Hobley Dr SN3 36 A3
Hocketts Cl SN15 60 A3
Hodds Hill SN5 34 B2
Hodge La SN16 27 F4
Hodges Barn Gdns*
GL8 26 F8
Hodges Dr 8 SN16 28 A5
HODSON 65 A5
Hodson Rd SN4 65 C4
HOGGINGTON 104 D4
Hoggington La BA14 104 D4
Hoggs La SN5 33 A4
Holbein Cl 6 SN5 49 A5
Holbein Ct SN5 49 A5
Holbein Field 12 SN5 49 A4
Holbein Mews 5 SN5 49 A4
Holbein Pl SN5 49 A5
Holbein Sq 10 SN5 49 A4
Holbein Wlk 11 SN5 49 A4
Holborn SN5 48 E8
Holborn Hill OX12 165 E8
Holbrook La BA14 105 D6
Holbrook Prim Sch
BA14 105 D6
Holbrook Vale SN12 93 F1
Holbrook Way SN1 50 B6
Holcombe La BA2 82 A1
Holdcroft Cl SN26 21 C2
Holden Cres SN25 35 A6
Holders Rd SP4 217 C4
Holford Cres GL7 10 E6
Holinshead Pl 4 SN5 49 A5
Holinshed Mews 3
SN5 49 A5
Holland Cl SN15 79 A4
Holland Dr 11 SP10 193 D2
Holliday Cl SN25 35 A6
Hollies La BA1 82 A6
Hollins Moor SN3 51 D2
Hollis Gdns SN14 39 E4
Hollis Way BA14 104 F3
HOLLOWAY 141 A1
Holloway SN16 28 A3
Holloway Cl
Amesbury SP4 217 D1
Swindon SN25 35 A8
Holloway Hill SN14 66 E8
Holloway La SP3 141 B1
Hollow La SN8 184 A7
Hollows Cl SP2 151 F6
Hollow St SN15 43 F2
Hollows The SP2 144 B4
Hollow The
Bratton BA13 186 A7
Chirton SN10 180 F4
Corsley BA12 111 B1
Dilton Marsh BA13 112 C8
Shrewton SP3 196 E7
Sixpenny Handley SP5 208 A4
Steeple Langford SP3 128 C5
Hollow Way SN15 59 D3
Hollybush BA12 119 D6
Hollybush Cl
Acton Turville GL9 53 A6
Chippenham Without
SN14 70 A2
Winsley BA15 99 E7
Hollybush La
Pewsey SN8 215 C8
Pewsey SN9 215 D6
Hollybush Rd BA12 117 A8
Holly Cl
Bower Chalke SP5 204 F2
Calne SN11 81 C1
Holly Cl continued
Pewsey SN9 215 D6
Swindon SN2 35 A2
Holly Cres 6 SN13 84 E8
Holly Ct BA11 110 B7
Holly Dr SN14 74 F6
Holmbury Cl BA11 110 C6
Holme La 7 BA13 186 B7
Holmeleaze BA14 178 A4
Holmes Cl SN15 78 F4
Holmes Rd SP1 146 D5
Holmfield
1 Littleton Panell
SN10 187 E8
Sherston SN16 25 C1
Holmleigh SN25 34 E4
Holmoak Ct 5 SN3 50 D4
Holne Rd SN1 50 A1
Holst Rd SN25 34 E8
HOLT 92 E1
Holt La
Tangley SP11 193 B8
Teffont SP3 201 C2
Witham Friary BA11 123 C8
Holt Rd
Bradford-on-Avon
BA15 100 E6
Bradford-on-Avon
BA15 101 A7
Witham Friary BA11 123 C8
Holt VC Prim Sch
BA14 92 F1
HOLWELL 139 B5
Holy Cross Catholic Prim
Sch SN3 50 D5
Holy Family Cath Prim
Sch SN3 51 B6
Holy Rd Church* SN3 50 E4
Holy Rood Cath Inf Sch
SN1 50 C5
Holyrood Cl BA14 105 B5
Holy Trinity CE Acad
SN11 81 C1
Holy Trinity CE Prim
Acad BA13 187 B8
Holy Trinity CE Prim
Acad The SN10 187 B8
Home Cl
Chiseldon SN4 65 C4
Fovant SP3 204 D8
Trowbridge BA14 105 D7
Homefarm SN6 22 F6
Home Farm Cl
Heddington SN11 89 B1
Mildenhall SN8 175 B8
Steeple Ashton BA14 178 A3
Home Farm Gdns 10
SP10 193 C2
Home Farm La SN6 22 B7
Home Farm Rd SP2 144 C1
Homefield
Mere BA12 138 F5
Motcombe SP7 202 C2
Royal Wootton Bassett
SN4 47 E2
Homefields
Longbridge Deverill
BA12 120 F6
Marlborough SN8 213 F2
Home Fields SN14 68 F5
Homefield Way RG17 177 B7
Home Gd
Cricklade SN6 19 C8
Royal Wootton Bassett
SN4 48 A2
Homelands The 1
BA12 116 E5
Home Mead 5 SN13 76 E1
Home Mill Bldgs
BA14 105 D8
Homes Mead 7 SN13 76 D1
Homestead Cl SN14 78 A4
HOMINGTON 151 D1
Homington Rd
Britford SP5 151 D3
Coombe Bissett SP5 151 A1
Coombe Bissett SP5 157 B8
Honeybone Cl GL7 1 F6
Honeybone Wlk SN3 51 E7
Honeybrook Cl SN14 78 B8
Honeybunch Cnr
SN8 164 C6
Honeyfields 10 RG17 177 B7
Honey Garston SN11 81 C3
Honey Hill 2 RG17 165 A2
Honey Knob Hill SN14 55 F1
Honey La
Norton SN16 41 E6
Westbury BA13 112 D8
Honeylight View 3
SN25 35 A6
Honeymans Cl BA14 105 F8
Honeymead SN11 81 C3
Honey Pot La BA11 118 B7
Honeysuckle Cl
Calne Without SN11 80 F4
Chippenham Without
SN14 70 B3
Melksham SN12 94 D4
1 Swindon SN25 34 D5
4 Trowbridge BA14 105 E7
Honiton Rd SN3 51 B5
HOOK 47 F6
Hook Cl SN5 34 A1
Hooks Hill SN5 33 C4
Hooks La SN10 179 A7
Hook St
Hook SN4 47 F6
Hook St continued
Swindon SN5 48 F4
HOOK STREET 48 B6
Hookwood La SP11 192 E8
Hoopers Pl SN1 50 D4
Hop Gdns The SP5 161 C3
Hopgood Cl SN10 214 F6
Hopkinson Way
SP10 193 B1
Hoppingstones SN11 166 B6
Hops Cl SP3 201 A3
Hopton Cl SN5 49 B3
Hopton Pk Ind Est
SN10 214 E7
Hopton Rd SN10 214 D6
Horace St SN2 49 F7
Horcott Rd
Fairford GL7 1 F6
Peatmoor SN5 34 B2
Swindon SN5 34 A2
Horder Mews SN3 50 D4
Horefield SP4 133 E7
Horham Cres SN3 51 A4
Hornbeam Cl 1
BA11 110 C6
Hornbeam Cres SN12 94 A3
Hornbeam Ct SN2 35 B2
Hornbeam Rd BA14 105 C5
Hornbury Cl SN16 17 A2
Hornbury Hill
Minety SN16 17 A2
Upper Minety SN16 16 E2
Hornchurch Rd 20
SN12 178 B8
Horne Cl SN25 20 D1
Hornell Cl 5 SP4 132 B1
Horne Rd SP4 198 E6
HORNINGSHAM 119 A7
Horningsham Prim Sch
BA12 119 B7
Hornsey Gdns SN2 36 A5
Horn's La SN4 167 B8
HORPIT 163 B7
Horsdown SN14 53 C4
Horse Barrow* SP4 133 D3
Horsebrook Pk SN11 81 B2
Horsebrook The SN11 81 C2
Horsefair La SN15 59 C3
Horse Fair La SN6 19 E8
Horse La SN15 96 C4
Horse Leaze SN10 214 F6
Horsell Cl 2 SN4 47 E2
Horseponds 8 SP7 202 B2
Horsepool SN15 96 B8
Horse Rd BA14 101 F4
Horseshoe Cl 1
BA14 102 B2
Horseshoe Cres SN5 34 A1
Horseshoe La SP11 193 F8
Horse Shoe La SP3 142 C3
Horseshoe Sq SN26 21 B1
Horsey Down SN6 19 C8
Horsington La SP8 139 B1
Horsley Cl 2 SN25 34 D8
Horta Cl SN26 20 D1
HORTON 172 C2
Horton Ave SN10 214 E6
Horton Cl BA15 100 E4
Horton Rd
Bishops Cannings
SN10 172 B2
Devizes SN10 214 F7
Swindon SN2 35 E6
Horton Way SN4 167 C7
Hospital of St John
BA12 194 C5
Hospital Rd BA13 109 A2
Hossil La SN6 22 B1
Houghton Cl BA12 117 C6
Houldsworth Ave
BA12 117 D8
House Field SN25 34 A3
Howard Cl SN3 50 F6
Howard-Vyse Rd
SP4 197 F7
Howgare Rd
Broad Chalke SP5 205 B2
Broad Chalke SP5 208 F8
Howse Gdn SN2 50 A8
Hreod Parkway Sch
SN2 34 E3
Hubble View SN25 34 B6
Hubert Hamilton Rd
SP4 198 E6
Huddleston Cl SN2 50 D8
Hudds Mill La BA13 186 B8
Hudson Rd
Amesbury SP4 217 C4
Malmesbury SN16 27 F4
Salisbury SP1 145 F3
Hudson Way SN25 35 A5
HUDSWELL 84 C8
Hudswell La SN13 84 C8
Hughes Cl SN8 213 A2
Hughes St SN2 49 F7
Hugo Dr SN25 35 A6
HUISH 174 A2
Hulbert Cl
Corsham SN13 76 E1
6 Trowbridge BA14 101 F1
HULLAVINGTON 41 E1
Hullavington Airfield
SN14 56 A7
Hullavington CE Prim Sch
SN14 41 F1
Hull Rd 4 SN2 34 E2
Hulse Rd SP1 146 A2
Humber La SP9 216 B4
Hummingbird Gdns
BA14 105 E6
Humphrey's La 3
RG17 171 E7
Hungerdown La SN14 78 A6
HUNGERFORD 177 A6
Hungerford Ave
BA14 105 A7
Hungerford Hill
Great Shefford RG17 171 F4
Lambourn RG17 165 A1
Hungerford La
Andover SP10 193 E3
Chute SP11 185 A1
Kintbury RG17 177 F6
Lake SP4 197 E1
Tangley SP11 193 A8
Hungerford Leisure Ctr
RG17 177 B6
HUNGERFORD
NEWTOWN 171 D2
Hungerford Prim Sch
RG17 177 B7
Hungerford Rd
Buttermere SN8 185 B7
Calne SN11 81 B4
Chippenham SN15 70 D1
Grafton SN8 184 A7
Hungerford RG17 177 D6
Kintbury RG17 177 F5
Hungerford Sta
RG17 177 C7
Hunsdon Cl SN3 51 A6
Hunt Cl The BA14 102 F5
HUNTENHULL
GREEN 111 C3
Huntenhull La BA13 111 D4
Hunter Cl SN11 81 D3
Hunters Chase BA13 108 F2
Huntersfield SN16 25 D1
Hunters Field SN14 78 A4
Hunter's Gr SN2 35 B1
Hunters Mead SP7 202 A5
Hunters Meadow
SN14 68 F5
Huntingdon Pl BA15 100 C7
Huntingdon Rise
BA15 100 C7
Huntingdon St BA15 100 C8
Huntingdon Way SN14 78 A6
Huntingfield BA14 106 A7
Huntingford Rd SP8 138 F1
Huntley Cl SN3 50 F7
Hunts Hill SN26 21 B2
Huntsland SN4 47 F2
Hunts Mead SN15 96 A7
Hunts Mill Rd SN4 61 A8
Hunts Rise SN3 36 C7
Hunt St SN1 50 C5
HURDCOTT 146 F8
Hurdcott Field SP4 132 D2
Hurdcott La
Winterbourne SP4 146 F8
Winterbourne Earls
SP4 133 A1
Hurley Cl 5 SP4 217 D3
Hurly La SN9 215 D4
Hurricane Dr SN11 81 D3
Hurricane Rd SN12 94 C1
Hurst Cres SN2 35 C3
Hurst's La SN9 181 C7
Hutton Cl
Trowbridge BA14 102 B1
Trowbridge BA14 106 B8
Huxley Ct GL7 7 A7
Hyam Cotts SN16 27 C4
HYDE 35 D7
Hyde Cross SP6 209 D1
Hyde La
Marlborough SN8 213 C3
Purton SN5 33 C4
Hyde Rd
Royal Wootton Bassett
SN4 47 F1
Swindon SN25 35 D6
Trowbridge BA14 101 C2
Hyde The SN5 33 D4
Hylder Cl SN2 34 D4
Hyson Cres 6 SP11 192 B5
Hysopp Cl SN2 34 C4
Hythe Rd SN1 50 B5

I

IBTHORPE 193 F8
Icknield Sch SP10 193 F1
Icknield Way
Andover SP10 193 E2
Bishopstone SN6 163 E6
Icomb Cl SN5 49 C4
Idlebush Barrow*
SN7 164 E7
IDMISTON 133 F8
Idmiston Rd SP4 133 E6
Idovers Dr SN5 49 C4
IDSTONE 163 F7
Idstone Hill SN6 163 F7
Idstone Rd SN6 164 A7
Iffley Rd SN2 49 F8
Iford Fields
Westwood BA15 99 E2
Westwood BA15 99 E3
Iford Hill BA15 99 E2
Iford La
Freshford BA15 99 D3
Westwood BA2 99 D2
Iford Manor* BA15 99 E3
Iles Ct SN11 73 F7
Ilett Cres SN25 20 B1
Ilkeston Rd SN25 34 C7
Ilynton Ave SP5 148 C7
Image Rd SN26 20 C1
IMBER 187 A3
Imber Ave
Amesbury SP4 217 D2
Warminster BA12 117 C7
Imber Pl SP3 188 B3
Imber Rd
Bratton BA12 186 C6
10 Shaftesbury SP7 202 D2
Warminster BA12 117 D8
Imber Wlk Rear SN2 35 B6
Imberwood Cl BA12 117 C7
Imby Cl BA12 117 F1
Imperial Way BA11 110 D7
India Ave SP2 145 E2
Indigo Gdns BA13 108 F3
Indigo La BA13 108 F3
Ingles Edge RG17 177 E2
INGLESHAM 2 B1
Inglesham Cl 3
BA14 105 D5
Inglesham Rd SN2 35 C4
Inglesham Village*
SN6 2 B1
Inglewood Rd RG17 177 E5
Ingram Pl BA13 108 F4
Ingram Rd SN12 94 D5
Ingram St SN16 28 A3
INKPEN 177 E3
Inkpen Community Prim
Sch RG17 177 E3
Inkpen Rd RG17 177 C5
Inlands Cl SN9 215 C5
Inmarsh La SN12 178 E7
Inmead BA13 186 C8
Innox Mill Cl BA14 101 B1
Innox Rd BA14 101 B1
Intercity Trad Est
SN12 94 A5
Interface Distribution Pk
SN4 47 F1
Inverary Rd SN4 64 A7
Ipswich St SN2 50 C8
IRELAND 105 B2
Ironstone Cl SN25 34 E7
Irston Way 4 SN5 49 B4
Irvine Cl SN26 20 D2
Irving Way SN8 213 C2
Isambard Com Sch
SN25 34 D7
Isambard Way SN25 34 D7
Isbury Rd SN8 213 E2
Isis Cl
Calne SN11 81 A4
Swindon SN25 35 A3
Islandsmead SN3 51 C6
Island The SN10 214 B3
Islay Cres SN6 22 F6
Isles Rd 6 SN8 170 B2
Islington BA14 101 D1
Islington St SN1 50 C6
Itchen Cl 2 SO51 212 F6
Ivies The SN9 181 F5
IVY CROSS 202 D2
Ivy Fields SN13 77 A2
Ivy La
Broad Blunsdon SN26 21 B2
Chippenham SN15 78 D7
South Wraxall BA15 91 E5
Ivy La Prim Sch SN15 78 D7
Ivy Mead BA12 139 B5
Ivy Rd SN15 78 D7
Ivy Rd Ind Est SN15 78 D7
Ivy St SP1 152 B8
Ivy Terr BA15 100 D7
Ixworth Cl 10 SN5 49 A7

J

Jackaments Barn GL7 4 B6
Jacklins Cl BA14 101 F5
Jack Paul Cl BA12 139 A6
Jack's Hedge Cnr
BH21 208 F2
Jacksom's La SN15 70 D5
Jackson Cl
3 Corsham SN13 84 F8
Devizes SN10 214 C2
Jack Thorne Cl 4
SN5 34 A2
Jacob Cl 22 SP11 193 F2
Jacob's Barrow*
SP5 211 E4
Jacobs Piece GL7 1 E6
Jacobs Wlk SN3 51 D4
Jacob Way BA12 116 D7
Jade Cl SN25 20 F1
Jagdalik Rd SP9 216 C4
Jaggards La SN13 84 D5
Jaggard View SP4 217 C3
Jagoda Ct 7 SN25 34 D6
James Ave SN11 81 D3
James Cl SN15 79 A4
James Rd SP4 217 C4
James's Hill BA10 122 A7
James St
Salisbury SP2 145 F1
Trowbridge BA14 101 D2
James Watt Cl SN2 50 A7
Jamrud Rd SP9 216 B5

Janesmoor Plain Rd
SO43. . . . . 212 B1
Janus Rd SN26 . . . . .21 A1
Jarvis St SN9 . . . . . . 181 F2
Jasmine Cl
Calne SN11 . . . . 81 B1
Chippenham SN14 . . . . 70 A1
Swindon SN2 . . . . 34 D4
Jasmine Way BA14 . . 105 E7
Jason Cl SN25 . . . . . .34 A7
Jasper Cl SN25 . . . . .20 F1
Javelin Cl ⑥ SP4 . . 217 D3
Jay Cl BA11. . . . . . . 110 B6
Jay Dr SP4 . . . . 132 C1
Jeanneau Cl ㉔ SP7. . 202 C2
Jebb Cl SN26 . . . . . . 20 D1
Jefferies Ave SN2. . . . 35 D2
Jefferies Cl SN8 . . . . 213 B2
Jeffreycl SN26. . . . . . 20 D1
Jekyll Cl SN25 . . . . . .20 C1
Jellicoe Ct SP10 . . . . 193 F1
Jenkins Cl SN26 . . . . . 21 D2
Jenkins St SN14 . . . . 101 C1
Jenner Cl SN4 . . . . . 163 A6
Jenner La ④ SN16 . . . .28 A5
Jenners Yard SN6 . . . .19 C8
Jenni Manners Ct ②
SN5. . . . . 49 D6
Jennings St SN2. . . . . 49 F6
Jenson Ave BA11 . . . . 110 D8
Jerram Gall The ★
SP1. . . . . 152 B8
Jersey Hill BA12 . . . . 116 D1
Jersey Pk SN5 . . . . . . 49 B8
Jervis Ct ⑪ SP10 . . . 193 F1
Jewel Cl ② SN5 . . . . .48 F5
Jewell Cl SN1 . . . . . . 146 D4
Joanna Cl ④ SP5 . . . 210 F8
Jockey La SN15. . . . . 96 A7
John Alder Cl SN4 . . . .65 C3
John Aubrey Cl SN14 . .68 F6
John Bentley Sch
SN11. . . . . 89 B8
John Betjeman Cl ⓵
SN16. . . . . .28 A5
John French Way
SP4. . . . . 217 E8
John Gay Rd ⑤ SP4. . 217 B3
John Herring Cres
SN3. . . . . .36 A1
John Ivie Ctr Pru
SP1. . . . . 152 B7
John of Gaunt Rd GL7. . 10 D6
John of Gaunt Sch The
BA14. . . . . 105 B8
John O'Gaunt Sch
RG17. . . . . 177 B6
John Rennie Cl
Bradford-on-Avon
BA15. . . . . 100 E4
Devizes SN10. . . . . . 214 A2
John Rumble Cl
SN10. . . . . 214 C3
John Ruskin Rd
Swindon SN25 . . . . . . 34 C8
Swindon SN26 . . . . . . 20 D1
Johnson Way ㉟
SP11. . . . . 192 A5
John St SN1. . . . . 50 B6
Joiner La SN1. . . . . . . 50 D4
Jole Cl SN2. . . . . 35 E5
Joles La BA11. . . . . . 110 F1
Jolliffe St ⑦ SN1. . . . .50 A5
Jones Cl SP2 . . . . . . 144 F4
Jones Hill BA15. . . . . 100 C5
Jones La SP9 . . . . . . 216 D8
Jone's Mill Nature
Reserve ★ SN9 . . . . 215 D7
Jopp Cl ⑨ SN25. . . . . .34 C5
Jordan Cl SN15 . . . . . .78 F5
Joseph St SN1 . . . . . .50 A5
Joule Rd ③ SP10 . . . 193 B1
Joyce Cl SN25 . . . . . .35 A6
Jubb's La SN8 . . . . . 169 A5
Jubilee Cl
Bermerton Heath
SP2. . . . . 145 C3
③ Sandleheath SP6 . . 210 C1
Westbury BA13 . . . . . 109 A3
Jubilee Ct
North Tidworth SP9 . . . 216 D7
③ Salisbury SP2 . . . . 145 F2
Jubilee Est SN5. . . . . .33 C5
Jubilee Gdns GL7. . . . . .6 F7
Jubilee Hill SP4 . . . . 197 F1
Jubilee Rd
Chippenham SN15 . . . . 70 E1
Devizes SN10. . . . . . 214 A3
Sandleheath SP6 . . . . 210 C1
Swindon SN2 . . . . . . 34 D3
Jubilee Terr SP2. . . . . 130 B2
Juggler's La SN11 . . . 166 C2
Juliana Cl ② SN5. . . . .49 A7
Jump Farm SN10 . . . . 214 C3
Jump Farm Rd SN10. . 214 C3
Junction Rd
Alderbury SP5 . . . . . 153 E3
Bradford-on-Avon
BA15. . . . . 100 C6
Juniper Cl
Calne SN11 . . . . 81 D5
Swindon SN3 . . . . . . .51 B8
Juniper Dr SP1 . . . . . 146 A5
Juniper Rd SP5. . . . . 148 C2

Juno Gdns SN6 . . . . . . .22 F4
Juno Way SN1. . . . . . . 49 F4
Jupiter Cl SN26 . . . . . .21 A1
Jutland Ave SN25 . . . . . 35 D3
Jutland Cres ③
SP10 . . . . 193 D2

K

Kandahar SN8. . . . . 170 A7
Kandy Rd ③ SP4. . . . 198 E6
Karachi Cl SP9 . . . . . 216 C7
Karslake Cl ⑥ SN3. . . .51 C4
Kashmir Rd ⑪ SP4 . . 198 E6
Katherine House Gall ★
SN8. . . . . 213 E2
Katherine's Wlk GL7 . . .2 D4
Katifer La SN14. . . . . .28 A3
Kavanagh Cl ⑩ SP7. . 202 D1
Keates Cl BA14 . . . . . 101 D1
Keats Cl
③ Melksham SN12. . . 94 B4
Royal Wootton Bassett
SN4 . . . . .47 B3
Keats Cres SN2 . . . . . 35 F4
Keats Mdw SP5. . . . . 208 B4
Keble Cl
Lechlade GL7. . . . . . . 2 D5
Swindon SN3 . . . . . . .51 C7
Keel Cl
Amesbury SP4 . . . . . 217 C1
Middle Winterslow SP5 149 B7
Keels SN3. . . . . 8 C1
Keepers Rd SN10 . . . . 214 C5
KEEVIL 178 C5
Keevil Airfield BA14. . 178 C4
Keevil Ave SN11 . . . . . .81 A3
Keevil CE Prim Sch
BA14. . . . . 178 B5
Kelham Cl ⑧ SN3. . . . .50 F4
Kelham Gdns SN8 . . . 213 E3
Kelk Cres SP9 . . . . . . 216 D8
KELLAWAYS 71 E4
Kellsboro Ave SN4. . . . 63 F7
Kelly Cl SN12 . . . . . . .93 F1
Kelly Gdns SN25 . . . . .34 F6
Kelmscot Rd SN25. . . . 35 C3
Kelmscott Rd GL7 . . . . 2 F3
Kelsey Rd SP1 . . . . . 146 B1
Kelso Ct ③ SN14. . . . .78 A5
Kelston Rd SN16 . . . . 176 C4
Kelvin Rd SN3 . . . . . . .51 A7
KEMBLE 4 E7
Kemble Bsns Pk GL7. . . .4 A3
Kemble Dr
Swindon SN2 . . . . . . .50 A7
Swindon SN5 . . . . . . .49 F7
Kemble Enterprise Pk
GL7. . . . . .4 A6
Kemble Rd GL7. . . . . . .4 F8
Kembles Cl SN16 . . . . .28 C2
Kemble Sta GL7 . . . . . .4 F8
KEMBLE WICK 4 E4
Kembrey Bsns Pk SN2. . 35 E2
Kembrey St SN2 . . . . . 35 D2
Kemerton Wlk SN3 . . . .51 A3
Kemmel Rd SP11 . . . . 191 F4
Kemp Cl SN10 . . . . . . 214 C3
Kempe La SN26. . . . . 20 D1
Kempsfield SN10 . . . . 214 C1
KEMPSFORD 10 E6
Kempsford CE Prim Sch
GL7. . . . . 10 C7
Kemp's La GL7 . . . . . . 4 F7
Kemp's Mill ⑩
SN14. . . . . .77 F6
Kencot Ct ⑤ SN2. . . . . 35 C6
Kendal SN5. . . . . 49 B4
Kendall La BA14. . . . . 102 E5
Kendrick Cl BA13. . . . 109 A3
Kendrick Ind Est SN2 . .49 E8
Kenilworth Gdns SN12 94 B3
Kenilworth Lawns
SN3. . . . . .50 F3
Kenley Cl SN12. . . . . .94 E1
Kennedy Ave SN12. . . .85 D1
Kennedy Dr SN3 . . . . . 51 D4
Kennedy Meadow
RG17. . . . . 177 B6
Kennel Dr GL9. . . . . . .38 E2
Kennet Ave SN25 . . . . 35 B3
Kennet Cl
Melksham SN12. . . . . 94 A6
Warminster BA12 . . . . 117 A5
Kennet Gdns BA15 . . . 100 D5
Kennet Mews SN8 . . . 213 E3
Kennet Pl SN8. . . . . . 213 E3
Kennet Rd
Devizes SN10. . . . . . 214 C2
South Tedworth SP9. . . 216 C6
Wroughton SN4 . . . . . 64 A7
Kennett Valley CE Prim
Sch SN8. . . . . 173 D8
Kennet Valley CE Prim
Sch SN8. . . . . 174 A6
Kennet Valley Mews
SN8. . . . . 169 D1
Kennet Way
Hungerford RG17. . . . 177 B8
Hungerford RG17. . . . 177 C8
Trowbridge BA14. . . . 101 D3
Ken Savage Cl SN4 . . .36 A1
Kensington Cl BA14. . . 101 D2
Kensington Fields
BA14. . . . . 104 F7

Kensington Rd ⓵
SP2. . . . . 145 F2
Kensington Way SN14 . 197 B4
Kent Cl SN14 . . . . .78 A6
Kent End SN6. . . . . 7 A1
Kent End Cl SN6 . . . . . .7 A1
Kent End Field SN6 . . . .7 A1
Kenton Cl SN3. . . . . . .51 B6
Kenton Dr BA14 . . . . . 101 F1
Kent Rd
Salisbury SP2. . . . . . 151 E6
Swindon SN1 . . . . 50 B4
Kents Hill SP3. . . . . . 201 A3
Kenwin Cl SN3. . . . . . .36 B2
Kenwood Rd BA14. . . . 105 F8
Keohler Cl SN26. . . . . .20 C2
KEPNAL 215 E5
Kerby Ave SP4. . . . . . 190 B3
Kerrs Way SN4 . . . . . . 64 A6
Kerry Cl
Derry Hill/Studley
SN11. . . . . .79 F2
Swindon SN5 . . . . 49 A7
Kershaw Rd SN3. . . . . .51 C4
Kestrel Ave BA14 . . . . 105 E6
Kestrel Cl
Calne SN11 . . . . .81 A5
Warminster BA12 . . . . 116 D6
Kestrel Dr
Swindon SN3 . . . . . . .51 E6
④ Winterbourne SP4 . 132 C1
Keswick Rd SN3 . . . . .51 B3
Kettle La BA14. . . . . . 106 A2
Ketton Cl BA14. . . . . . 101 A1
Kew Dr ④ BA14. . . . . . 105 A7
Kewlake La SO51. . . . 212 F1
Keyneston Rd
Swindon SN3 . . . . . . .50 F5
Swindon SN3 . . . . . . .51 A5
Keynsham Wlk SN3 . . .51 B4
Khyro Cl BA12 . . . . . . 116 F5
Kibblewhite Cl SN5 . . .33 B3
Kickdom Cl SP4 . . . . . 217 D2
Kidston Way SN13 . . . .84 A8
Kiel Dr SP10 . . . . 193 D2
Kilben Cl SN5. . . . . . . .48 F7
Kilby Cres SN25. . . . . .35 A8
Kilda Rd SN6 . . . . .22 E7
Kilford Ct SP4 . . . . . . 217 C1
Kill Barrow (Long
Barrow) ★ BA12 . . . 187 D3
KILMINGTON 123 E5
Kilmington Comm
BA12. . . . . 123 E5
KILMINGTON
COMMON. 123 D4
Kiln Cl
Alderbury SP5 . . . . . 153 F1
Devizes SN10. . . . . . 214 D3
Kiln La
Redlynch SP5 . . . . . . 211 D8
Swindon SN2 . . . . . . .34 F1
Kilns The SN1 . . . . . . .81 C4
Kilsby Dr SN3. . . . . . . .51 B8
Kilsyth Cl SN5 . . . . . . .49 B5
Kilve Cl SN3 . . . . .51 B6
Kilverts Cl SN14 . . . . . .78 A6
Kimber Cl SP9 . . . . . . 216 C7
Kimberley Rd SN3 . . . .51 A4
Kimbers Field ⑯
SN4. . . . . 163 A6
Kimbolton Cl ⑥ SN5. . .49 A4
Kimmeridge Cl SN3. . . .51 C6
KIMPTON. 192 C1
Kimpton Thruxton &
Fyfield CE Prim Sch
SP11. . . . . 192 C1
King Alfred Cl SN9. . . . 215 D5
King Alfreds Cl BA12. . 126 B7
King Alfred St SN15. . . .78 C8
King Alfred's Way
SP7. . . . . 202 C2
King Alfred Way BA15. 99 D7
King Arthur's Way
SP10. . . . . 193 E2
King Barrow ★
Bishopstone BA12. . . . 117 F5
Winterbourne Stoke
SP4. . . . . 197 C4
King Charles Rd SN5. . .49 B4
Kingdom Ave BA13 . . . 108 D5
Kingdom Cres ⓵
SN25. . . . . .24 D5
Kingdown Sch BA12 . . 117 D6
King Edward Cl SN1 . . .81 B4
Kingfisher CE Acad
SN1. . . . . .49 E3
Kingfisher Cl
Salisbury SP2. . . . . . 152 A5
Trowbridge BA14 . . . . 105 E6
Kingfisher Ct ⑦ SN11. .81 B5
Kingfisher Dr
Bower Hill SN12. . . . . 94 D1
Devizes SN10. . . . . . 214 E5
Kingfisher Pl GL7. . . . . 7 B7
Kingfishers ② SP9. . . 199 D8
Kingham Cl SN14 . . . . .78 C7
KINGHAY 202 F8
King Henry Dr
Chippenham SN15 . . . 79 A4
Swindon SN5 . . . . . . .48 C3
King John's House ★
SP5. . . . . 207 B4

King John St ③ SN1 . . 50 D4
King La BA12 . . . . . . 116 E5
King Oak ★ SN8. . . . 175 C4
Kings Ave
Chippenham Without
SN14. . . . . .77 F6
Corsham SN13. . . . . . .76 F2
Highworth SN6. . . . . . 23 A5
Kingsbere La ⑤ SP7. 202 D2
Kingsbourne Cl SP4 . . 133 B1
Kingsbury Cl SN12. . . .94 B3
Kingsbury Sq ③ SP2. 144 D3
Kingsbury St
Calne SN11 . . . . .81 B2
Marlborough SN8. . . . 213 D3
Kings Cl ③ SN6. . . . . 164 A8
Kings Cnr SN9. . . . . . 215 D4
Kingscote Cl ⓵ SN5. . .48 F8
Kings Ct ⑤ BA12 . . . 116 E5
KINGSDOWN
Box. 82 F3
Stratton St Margaret. . . 35 F5
Kingsdown Gr BA1. . . .82 F2
Kingsdown Ind Est
SN2. . . . . .36 A6
Kingsdown La SN25. . . 35 D8
Kingsdown Rd
Stratton St Margaret
SN2. . . . . 36 A6
Swindon SN2. . . . . . . 35 F5
③ Trowbridge BA14 . . 105 C5
Kingsdown Sch SN2 . . .35 F5
Kings Dr SN8 . . . . . . 175 C8
Kingsettle Hill BA10. . 122 C2
Kingsfield Cl BA15. . . 100 D7
Kingsfield Grange Rd
BA15. . . . . 100 E7
Kingsfield Leaze
BA15. . . . . 100 F6
Kingsford Cl ⑨ SP5. . 211 C7
Kings Gate SP2. . . . . 144 E4
Kings Gdns BA14 . . . . 101 E5
KINGSHILL. 50 B5
Kings Hill ⑱ SP7 . . . 202 C2
Kingshill Rd SN1. . . . . .50 A4
King's House ★ SP1. . 152 A7
King's La ⑦
SP3. . . . . 203 F5
⑦ Shaftesbury SP7. . 202 B2
Knap The BA14 . . . . . 102 A3
KNIGHTON 170 D2
Knighton Barrow (Long
Barrow) ★ SP4 . . . . 197 E8
Knighton Rd ⑤ SP5 . . 205 C4
Knightsbridge Rd
SP11. . . . . 193 F4
Knights Cl
⓵ Chippenham SN15 . .78 F4
West Overton SN8. . . . 173 F6
Kingsley Rd
Chippenham SN14 . . . 78 B6
Devizes SN10. . . . . . 214 C3
Kingsley Way SN2 . . . 35 D5
Kings Lodge Prim Sch
SN15. . . . . .79 A5
Kingsman Rd ⑱ SP7. 202 C1
Kingsmanor Wharf
SN10. . . . . 214 D5
Kingsmead
Lechlade GL7. . . . . . . .2 C7
Stoford SP2 . . . . 130 A3
Kingsmead House
SN15. . . . . .44 A5
Kingsmead Mill ★
SN15. . . . . .43 F6
Kings Meadow SN16. . . 14 D5
Kings Orch BA12. . . . . 116 E5
Kings Paddock SP5 . . 149 A5
Kings Rd
Easterton SN10 . . . . . 180 A2
Enham Alamein SP11. . 193 E4
Market Lavington
SN10 . . . . 179 F2
King's Rd SP1 . . . . . . 146 A2
Kings Rise BA12 . . . . 116 E5
King St
Melksham SN12. . . . . 94 A3
③ Swindon SN1 . . . . 50 B6
Warminster BA12 . . . . 116 E5
Wilton SP2. . . . . 144 D4
Kings Terr GL9 . . . . . . 24 B3
Kingsthorpe Gr SN3 . . .51 C8
Kingston SN16. . . . . . .43 F8
Kingston Ave BA15. . . 100 C5
KINGSTON
DEVERILL 126 B6
KINGSTONE
WINSLOW 164 A8
Kingston La
Kingston Deverill
BA12. . . . . 126 A7
Maiden Bradley BA12. 119 A2
Maiden Bradley with
Yarnfield BA12. . . . . 118 F2
Kingston Pk SO51. . . 212 F4
Kingston Rd
④ Bradford-on-Avon
BA15 . . . . 100 D6
Shalbourne SN8. . . . . 176 F1
Swindon SN3 . . . . . . .51 A4
Kings Wall SN16. . . . . .28 A3
King's Wall SN16 . . . . .28 A3
Kingsway
Preshute SN8. . . . . . 168 B1
Wilton SP2. . . . . 144 E5
Kingsway Bsns Ctr
SP2. . . . . 144 D4
Kingsway Cl ⓵ SN3. . . .50 F1
Kingswood
Trowbridge BA14. . . . 104 F6
Wroughton SN4 . . . . . 64 A5
Kingswood Ave SN3 . . .51 A5
Kington La SN14 . . . . .56 A4
King John's House ★
SP5. . . . . 207 B4
KINGTON LANGLEY. . 70 E7

KINGTON ST
MICHAEL 70 A8
Kington St Michael CE
Prim Sch SN14 . . . . 70 A8
Kingway View SN16. . . .42 E8
King William St CE Prim
Sch SN1. . . . . 50 C4
King William St SN1 . . .50 C4
Kinneir Cl SN13. . . . . .85 A8
Kintbury Rd RG17. . . . 177 F3
Kipling Gdns SN2 . . . . .35 E4
Kirby Cl SN3. . . . . .50 F4
Kirby Rd SN13 . . . . . . .76 E1
Kirkee Rd SP9 . . . . . . 216 C5
Kirkstall Cl SN5. . . . . .49 C4
Kirktonhill Rd SN5. . . .49 D6
Kishorn Cl SN5 . . . . . .34 B2
Kitchen Barrow ★
SN10. . . . . 172 E3
Kitchener Rd SP4. . . . 217 B4
Kitchener St SN2 . . . . .50 C8
Kitefield ② SN6 . . . . . 19 D8
Kite Hill SN4. . . . . . . 163 A5
Kite's Nest La SP8 . . . 137 E2
Kivel Ct SP2. . . . . 146 A2
Kiwi Prim Sch SP4. . . 198 E6
Kiwi Rd ⑥ SP4 . . . . . 198 F7
Kiwi The ★ SP4 . . . . 198 F6
Knap Barrow (Long
Barrow) ★ SP6 . . . . 209 D8
Knap Hill (Causewayed
Enclosure) ★ SN8. . 173 E2
KNAPP 205 A4
Knapp Cl
Swindon SN2 . . . . . . .35 A2
Westbury BA13 . . . . . 109 B5
KNAPP HILL 202 A5
Knapp Hill SP5 . . . . . 205 A4
Knapps Gate BA12. . . 115 C5
Knapps The BA14. . . . 102 F5
Knapp The
Calne SN11 . . . . .81 C3
Great Bedwyn SN8. . . 176 B3
Knap The BA14 . . . . . 102 A3
KNIGHTON 170 D2
Knighton Barrow (Long
Barrow) ★ SP4 . . . . 197 E8
Knighton Rd ⑤ SP5 . . 205 C4
Knightsbridge Rd
SP11. . . . . 193 F4
Knights Cl
⓵ Chippenham SN15 . .78 F4
West Overton SN8. . . . 173 F6
KNIGHTS ENHAM . . . 193 E3
Knights Enham Prim Sch
SP10. . . . . 193 E2
Knights Maltings
BA11. . . . . 110 A3
KNOCKDOWN 24 F5
Knockdown Rd
Sherston GL9. . . . . . . 25 B2
Sherston SN16 . . . . . . 25 C1
Knole Cl ④ SN25. . . . . .34 F7
Knoll Cl OX12. . . . . . 165 F8
Knoll The
⑫ Aldbourne SN8. . . 170 A6
Kempsford GL7 . . . . . 10 D7
Malmesbury SN16 . . . .28 B2
Westbury BA13 . . . . . 109 B4
Knolton Wlk SN3 . . . . .51 A4
KNOOK 194 D4
Knook Barrow (Long
Barrow) ★ BA12 . . . 194 D1
Knook Castle ★ BA12. 195 A1
Knook Manor ★
BA12. . . . . 194 D4
Knowlands SN6. . . . . .23 A7
KNOWLE. 215 C6
Knowledge Hill ②
SN8. . . . . 170 B2
Knowle The ⓵ SN13 . .84 F8
Knowsley Rd SN3. . . . .51 A4
Kohat Cl SP9 . . . . . . 216 B7
Komat Rd SP9 . . . . . . 216 C5
Kopernik Rd SN25 . . . .34 D6
Kyneton Way SN14. . . .70 C4
Kyte Cl BA12. . . . . . . 116 D5
Kyte Way BA14 . . . . . 105 E6

L

Labour-in-Vain Hill
SN11. . . . . 172 A8
Labrador Gdns ⑦
SP4. . . . . 217 F8
Laburnum Dr SN4 . . . .47 C3
Laburnum Cl ③
BA11. . . . . 110 B7
Laburnum Dr SN12 . . . .94 A3
Laburnum Gr BA14 . . . 105 B6
Laburnum Rd SN2 . . . .35 C3
Lacemakers Rd SN16 . .28 C5
Lackham Cir SN14 . . . .78 B6
Lackham Coll of
Agriculture SN15. . . .78 E1
Lackham Ctry Pk ★
SN15. . . . . .78 F1
Lackham Mus SN15 . . .78 F1
LACOCK 86 D5
Lacock Abbey ★ SN15 . 86 D6
Lacock CE Prim Sch
SN15. . . . . .86 D5
Lacock Gdns BA14 . . . 102 B2

Lacock Pottery ★
SN15. . . . . .86 D6
Lacock Rd
Corsham SN13. . . . . . .85 D8
Swindon SN2 . . . . . . .35 C4
Ladbrook La SN13 . . . .77 C1
Ladds La SN15. . . . . . .78 E7
Lady Coventry Rd
SN15. . . . . .78 F7
Lady Diana Ct ⑬
SP11. . . . . 192 A5
Ladydown
Calne SN11 . . . . .81 B4
Lower Chicksgrove
SP3. . . . . 201 B1
Lady Down View ⑤
SP3. . . . . 203 E8
Ladyfield Rd SN14 . . . .78 B7
Lady Godley Cl SP9 . . 216 C5
Lady Jane Wlk ㉒
SP11. . . . . 192 A5
Lady La
Broad Blunsdon SN25 . . 21 B1
Swindon SN2 . . . . . . .34 F7
Lady Margaret
Hungerford
Almshouse ★
SN13. . . . . .77 A1
Lady Mead SN6. . . . . . 19 D8
Ladysmith SP4 . . . . . 133 D3
Ladysmith Rd
Chiseldon SN4 . . . . . . 65 D1
Salisbury SP2. . . . . . 145 D3
Ladyway SP4 . . . . . . 134 A7
Ladywood ⑧ SN10. . . 179 F1
Lafranc Cl SP4. . . . . . 146 B7
Laggar The SN13 . . . . .77 A2
Lagos St ③ SN1 . . . . .50 C7
Lagpond La SP3. . . . . 204 B7
Lahore Cl SP9 . . . . . . 216 C7
Lahore Rd SP9. . . . . . 216 C5
Laines Head SN14 . . . .70 C2
Lainesmead Prim Sch
SN3. . . . . .50 E5
Lainey's Cl SN8. . . . . 213 D4
LAKE 197 F2
Lake Group (Tumuli) ★
SP4. . . . . 197 D3
Lake House ★ SP4 . . 197 D3
Lake Louise SN6. . . . . .8 C3
Lakeside
Fairford GL7. . . . . 1 F6
South Cerney GL7 . . . .7 B7
Swindon SN3 . . . . . . .50 E3
Lakeside Cl SP10 . . . . 193 C1
Lake View SN11 . . . . . 89 D8
Lake Vw SN4 . . . . 61 A7
Lalique Cl SN25. . . . . . 20 D1
Lamb Ale Gn BA14 . . . 105 D6
Lambdown App SP11 191 F3
Lambdown Terr
North Tidworth SP11. . 216 F6
Perham Down SP11. . . 191 F4
Lambe Cl GL7 . . . . 1 E6
Lambert Cl SN5. . . . . . 49 B3
Lamberts SN14 . . . . . .78 A8
LAMBOURN 165 B2
Lambourn Ave SN3 . . . 50 E3
Lambourn CE Prim Sch
RG17. . . . . 165 A1
Lambourne Cr ④
SN12. . . . . .94 B4
Lambourne Cres SN12 .94 B4
Lambourn La BA13. . . 186 C8
Lambourn Pl ⑩
RG17. . . . . 165 A2
LAMBOURN
WOODLANDS 171 A6
Lambrok Cl BA14 . . . . 104 F6
Lambrok Rd BA14. . . . 104 F6
Lammas SN11. . . . . . 166 A6
Lamora Cl ⑫ SN5. . . . .48 F8
Lampeter Rd SN25. . . .34 C4
Lamplighters Wlk
BA14. . . . . 105 C7
Lanac Rd SN3. . . . . . . 36 A1
Lancashire Dr SN1. . . .78 B3
Lancaster Cl ⑥ RG17 177 B6
Lancaster Mews SN3 . .36 C6
Lancaster Pl SN3 . . . . .36 C6
Lancaster Rd
Bower Hill SN12. . . . . 94 B1
Kempsford GL7 . . . . . 10 E6
Wroughton SN4 . . . . . 64 A6
Lancaster Sq
Hungerford RG17. . . . 177 B6
Lyneham SN15. . . . . . 60 D7
Lancefield Pl SN13. . . .76 E2
Landale Cl ③ SP11 . . 193 E4
LANDFORD 212 C6
LANDFORD WOOD. . . 212 D8
Landor Rd SN25 . . . . . 34 F8
Landsbury Dr SP9 . . . 216 D8
LANE END 115 A8
Lane's Cl SP4. . . . . . . 217 C4
Lanes End SN13 . . . . . 85 D5
Lanes End Hill
Corsley BA12. . . . . . . 115 A8
Lane End BA12. . . . . . 115 A8
Lane-side ⑨ SP7 . . . 202 C2
Lane The
④ Ashbury SN6 . . . . 164 A8
Bishopstone SN6 . . . . 163 C7
Lanfear Cl SP4. . . . . . 217 C4
Langale Dr SN5 . . . . . .49 B8
Langdean Rd ⑤ SN1. .50 B1
Langet GL7. . . . . .6 E6
Langfields SN8 . . . . . 170 A2

Langford Gr SN3. . . . . . .50 E6
Langford La
  Berwick St James
    SP3. . . . . 196 E2
  Downton SP5. . . . . . . 159 F2
  Downton SP5. . . . . . . 160 A3
Langford Rd
  Great Wishford SP2. . . 129 F4
  Little Langford SP3. . . 129 C5
  Trowbridge BA14. . . . . 101 C2
Langfords La 3 SP7. . . 202 B1
Langford Waie SP3. . . 196 D1
Langham Brake BA2. . 103 F2
Langham Pl BA11. . . . . 103 F1
Langholm Ave BA12. . 116 D6
Langholm Cl BA12. . . 116 B6
LANGLEY BURRELL. . . .71 A3
Langley Fitzurse CE Prim
  Sch SN15. . . . . .70 E6
Langley Gdn SP6. . . . 210 E2
Langley Pk SN15. . . . . .70 E1
Langley Pk SN15. . . . . .70 F1
Langley Rd
  Chippenham SN15. . . . 70 C1
  Swindon SN5. . . . . .34 B1
  Trowbridge BA14. . . . . 105 C5
Langley Wood National
  Nature Reserve ★
  SP5. . . . . 211 F7
Lang Mws SN26. . . . . . .21 C2
Langport 1 SN5. . . . . .49 B4
Langstone Way SN5. . .49 B4
Lanham's Cl BA13. . . 109 A2
Lanhill (Long Barrow) ★
  SN14. . . . . .69 B2
Lanhill View SN14. . . . 70 B2
Lanhydrock 9 SN5. .49 A4
Lansbury Dr SN2. . . . . .35 F4
Lansdown Cl
  Melksham SN12. . . . . . 94 D6
  Trowbridge BA14. . . . 105 B7
Lansdowne Cl
  Calne SN11. . . . . .81 A4
  Dilton Marsh BA13. . . .112 C8
Lansdowne Cres SN11 .79 F2
Lansdowne Terr
  SN10. . . . . 214 A3
Lansdown Gr SN15. . . .70 D1
Lansdown Rd SN1. . . .50 B4
Lapwing Cl 1 SN3. . . .51 E6
Lapwing Cres SN14. . . .70 E2
Lapwing Dr SP4. . . . . 132 C1
Lapwing Rd SN12. . . . .94 D5
Larch Cl
  Melksham SN12. . . . . . 94 A3
  Swindon SN25. . . . . . . .35 D2
Larchfield Cl BA11. . . .110 B7
Larch Gr BA14. . . . . . 105 B6
Larch Rd SN14. . . . . . .74 F6
Larchmore Cl SN25. . . .35 A3
Larch Row SP6. . . . . . 210 F1
Lark Cl SP9. . . . . 216 D7
Lark Down BA14. . . . . 101 E1
Larkham Rise SN15. . .78 F6
LARKHILL. 197 F6
Larkhill Prim Sch
  SP4. . . . . 197 E7
Larkhill Rd SP4. . . . . . 198 B7
Lark La 5 SP4. . . . . . 132 C1
Larkrise BA14. . . . . . . 105 F7
Larksfield SN3. . . . . . . .51 C8
Larkspur BA14. . . . . . 101 E1
Larkspur Dr SN11. . . . .81 D5
Larmer Tree Gdns ★
  SP5. . . . . 207 B3
Latchmoor Dro SP5. . 212 C6
Late Broads BA15. . . . .99 D7
Latham Rd SN2. . . . . . .35 B6
Latimer Gdns SN14. . . .41 E1
LATTON. 8 C4
Latton Cl SN2. . . . . . . .35 B6
Latton Wharf SN6. . . . . .8 E1
Laughton Way SN25. . .35 A6
Launcelot Cl 22 SP10. 193 E2
Laundry La 5 SP7. . . 202 B1
Laura Pl SN13. . . . . . . .83 F7
Laurel Dr
  Chippenham SN14. . . . .78 C6
  Colerne SN14. . . . . . . .74 F6
  Marlborough SN8. . . . 213 F2
Laurel Gr BA14. . . . . . 105 C6
Laurels The
  Hungerford RG17. . . . 177 C8
  Melksham Without SN12 86 A1
  Westwood BA15. . . . . .99 F3
Laurence Cl 10 SP11. 192 A5
Lavender Cl
  Melksham SN12. . . . . . 94 C3
  5 Trowbridge BA14. . . 105 F8
Lavender Ct BA11. . . . .110 B7
Lavender Dr SN11. . . . .81 B1
LAVERSTOCK. 146 E2
Laverstock Pk SP1. . . 146 D1
Laverstock Pk W
  SP1. . . . . 146 D2
Laverstock Rd SP1. . . 146 C1
Laverton Ct 1 BA13. . 109 A3
Laverton Gn 3 BA13. 108 F1
Laverton Rd BA13. . . 108 F1
Lavington Cl 10 SN8. 183 D8
Lavington Comp Sch
  SN10. . . . . 179 E1
Lavington Hill SN10. . 187 E8
Lavington La SN10. . . 187 E8
LAVINGTON SANDS. . 179 E2
LAWN. 50 F3
Lawn Farm Cl SN9. . . 182 E7

Lawn La SN6. . . . . .22 A5
Lawn Prim Sch SN3. . . .50 F2
Lawns The SN4. . . . . . 47 D2
Lawrence Cl
  4 Amesbury SP4 . . . 217 C3
  Devizes SN10. . . . . . . 214 C1
  Swindon SN3. . . . . . . .51 C4
Lawrence Dr SN11. . . . .81 D3
Lawrence Ind Est SN13 .84 E7
Lawrence Mead 3
  SN8. . . . . 170 B2
Lawrence Rd 3 SP4. . 197 F7
Lawson Rd 3 SP4 . . . 198 A6
Lawton Cl SN3. . . . . . . .51 A3
Layton Cl SP7. . . . . . . 202 C1
LEA. 28 F1
LEAFIELD. 84 E7
Leafield Ind Est SN13 .84 E6
Leafield Pl BA14. . . . . 100 F1
Leafield Rd SN13. . . . .84 E6
Leafield Way SN13. . . .84 E6
Leafy La SN13. . . . . . . .76 A1
Lea & Garsdon CE Prim
  Sch SN16. . . . . .28 A2
Lea House SN16. . . . . . 28 D1
Lea La SN6. . . . . .28 A2
Leamington Gr SN3. . .50 F2
Leap Gate
  Hilperton BA14. . . . . . 102 A1
  Trowbridge BA14. . . . 106 A7
  Trowbridge BA14. . . . 106 A8
Leatler Cl SP3. . . . . . 204 D8
Leaze Rd
  Marlborough SN8. . . . 213 C4
  Melksham SN12. . . . . . 94 C6
Leaze St SN1. . . . . .50 A2
Leaze The
  Ashton Keynes SN6. . . . .6 F1
  Durrington/Bulford
    SN4. . . . . 217 E8
  South Cerney GL7. . . . . .6 F6
LECHLADE-ON-
  THAMES. 2 D1
Lechlade Rd
  Buscot SN7. . . . . .2 E1
  Highworth SN6. . . . . . . 23 A7
  Lechlade-on-Thames GL7 .2 C1
  Little Faringdon GL7. . . .2 F7
Ledge Hill SN10. . . . . 179 E2
Ledger Hill Cl SP4. . . 217 D8
Leech La GL8. . . . . . . .25 C4
Lee Cres SN15. . . . . . . .57 C1
Leehurst Swan SP1. . 146 B2
Lees Ct SP2. . . . . 145 F2
Legate Cl SN15. . . . . . .79 B5
Legg Rd 12 SP7. . . . . 202 C1
Leicester Dr BA14. . . 106 B8
Leicester St SN1. . . . . 50 D6
LEIGH. 18 C5
Leigh Cl BA13. . . . . . 108 E1
LEIGH DELAMERE. . . .55 C3
Leighfield Cl 8 SN1. . 50 C5
Leigh Gr BA15. . . . . . . .91 E1
Leigh La
  East Knoyle SP3. . . . . 141 C1
  East Knoyle SP3. . . . . 202 E8
Leigh Pk Rd BA15. . . 100 D8
Leigh Pk Way BA13. . 108 E1
Leigh Rd
  Bradford-on-Avon
    BA15. . . . . 91 E1
  Holt BA14. . . . . .92 C1
  Swindon SN2. . . . . 35 C4
  Westbury BA13. . . . . . 108 F1
Leigh Rd W
  Bradford-on-Avon
    BA15. . . . . 91 D1
  Bradford-on-Avon
    BA15. . . . . 100 E8
Leigh Woods La
  SN10. . . . . 214 F6
Leisler Gdns BA14. . . 106 A8
Leland Cl 5 SN16. . . . .28 A5
Le Marchant Cl 2
  SN10. . . . . 214 D5
Lena Cl 26 SP11. . . . 192 A5
Lennards The GL7. . . . .7 A7
Lennox Dr SN3. . . . . . 50 F6
Lenta Bsns Ctr SN1. . 50 B6
Lenton Cl SN14. . . . . . 77 F7
Leonard Cheshire Cl 4
  SP4. . . . . 217 D2
Lesley Anne Skeete Ct
  SN3. . . . . .51 B4
Leslie Cl SN5. . . . . . . .49 A4
Leslie Rise BA15. . . . . .99 F3
LETCOMBE
  BASSETT. 165 F8
Lethbridge Prim Sch
  SN1. . . . . .50 C3
Lethbridge Rd SN1. . . .50 C3
Letterage Rd SN5. . . . .34 A2
Levell Ct 12 SP11. . . . 192 A5
Leven SN5. . . . . .49 A3
Leventon Pl BA14. . . . 102 B2
Leversedge Rd 2
  BA11. . . . . .110 A7
LEVERTON. 171 B1
Leverton Gate SN3. . . .50 F1

Leverton La RG17. . . . 171 B1
Lewington Cl SN12. . . .94 A3
Lewington Mews 14
  RG17. . . . . 177 B6
Lewis Cl
  Corsham SN13. . . . . . . 84 D8
  Swindon SN25. . . . . . . .34 F6
Lewis Ct BA14. . . . . . 105 A3
Lewisham Castle ★
  SN8. . . . . 169 E4
Lewisham Cl SN25. . . .34 F3
Leylands Rd
  Corsham SN13. . . . . . . 76 B1
Leys Hill BA11. . . . . . .110 A6
Leys La BA11. . . . . . . .110 A6
Leystone Cl BA11. . . . .110 A6
Ley The SN16. . . . . . . .27 F3
Lichen Cl 3 SN2. . . . . 34 D4
Lickhill Rd SN11. . . . . .81 A4
Lidbrook SN11. . . . . . . .81 B4
Liddell Gdns SN2. . . . 132 B1
Liddells Gn SN8. . . . . 168 F5
LIDDINGTON. 163 B4
  SN4. . . . . 163 A2
Liddington Castle (Fort) ★
  SN4. . . . . 163 A2
Liddington St SN2. . . . .35 C3
Liddington Way
  BA14. . . . . 105 D5
LIDEN. 51 D3
Lidenbrook 2 SN4 . . 163 A4
Liden Dr SN4. . . . . 51 D4
Liden Prim Sch SN3. . .51 D3
Light Cl SN13. . . . . . . .77 A2
Lightfoot Rd SP4. . . . 197 F7
Lightning Rd
  1 Amesbury SP4. . . . 217 D2
Light's La SP5. . . . . . 153 C2
Light The SN16. . . . . . .27 F3
Liguiel Cl 9 RG17. . . 177 B6
Lilac Ct SN2. . . . . .35 B2
Lilac Gr BA14. . . . . . . 105 B5
Lilac Way SN11. . . . . . .81 B1
Lilian Cl 8 SN25. . . . .34 C6
Lilian Lock Gdns SN2. .35 C5
Lillywhite Cres 1
  SP10. . . . . 193 E2
Lilypad St 5 SN3. . . . .51 B8
Lily Wlk 11 SP4. . . . . 198 C7
Lime Ave
  Badminton GL9. . . . . . 38 C1
  Melksham SN12. . . . . . 94 A3
Lime Cl
  Frome BA11. . . . . .110 B7
  Lyneham & Bradenstoke
    SN15. . . . . 60 C2
  Pewsey SN9. . . . . 215 D6
Lime Kiln SN4. . . . . . . 47 D3
Lime Kiln Cl BA12. . . . 113 A1
Limekiln Hill GL7 . . . . 4 B7
Limekiln La BA2. . . . . . 90 A5
Lime Kiln Rd SN11. . . 192 E6
Lime Kiln Sports Ctr
  SN4. . . . . 47 D3
Lime Kiln Way SP2. . . 152 A5
Lime Rd SN14. . . . . . . .75 A5
Limerick La BA11. . . . 107 A2
Limes Ave SN2. . . . . . .35 B3
Limes Pl SN6. . . . . .8 C4
Limes Rd GL7. . . . . .4 F7
Limes The
  Badminton GL9. . . . . . 38 E2
  Motcombe SP7. . . . . . 202 A4
  Porton SP4. . . . . 133 E6
  Shrewton SP3. . . . . . . 196 E7
  South Cerney GL7. . . . . .7 A6
Limestone Dr
  6 Corsham SN13. . . . .76 D1
  Corsham SN13. . . . . . . 84 D8
Lime Tree Cl SN11. . . . .81 A3
Lime Trees SN15. . . . . .58 A2
LIMPERS HILL. 139 D4
LIMPLEY STOKE. 99 A6
Limpley Stoke Rd
  BA15. . . . . 99 D6
Lincoln Gn SN12. . . . . .94 C7
Lincoln Gr SN12. . . . . .94 C7
Lincoln St SN1. . . . . . . 50 C6
Linden Ave SN2. . . . . . .35 C3
Linden Cl
  Calne SN11. . . . . .81 B2
  Colerne SN14. . . . . . . .74 C6
  Ludgershall SP11. . . . 192 B5
  Royal Wootton Bassett
    SN4. . . . . 47 E3
  Salisbury SP1. . . . . . . 146 D1
Linden Cres BA15. . . . 100 A3
Linden Gr 2 SN12. . . .94 A2
Linden Lea GL7. . . . . . 8 E8
Linden Pk SP7. . . . . . 202 D1
Linden Pl BA14. . . . . . 101 B1
Linden Way SN5. . . . . .34 A2
Lindford Rd SP1. . . . . 146 B6
Lindisfarne 1 SN4. . . .48 A1
Lindisfarne Cl BA15. . 99 E7
Lindlar Cl 13 SP7. . . . 202 C2
Lindley Cl SP9. . . . . . 216 D6
Lineacre Cl SN5. . . . . . 48 F4
Lingen Cl 12 SP10. . . 193 D2
Lingfield Cl 6 SN14. . 77 F6
Link Ave SN5. . . . . 49 B5
LINKENHOLT. 185 E5
Linkenholt Rd
  Little Down SP11. . . . . 185 D5
  Vernhams Dean SP11. 185 D3

Link La BA15. . . . . .83 A1
Link Leisure Ctr SN5. .49 B5
Link Rd BA13. . . . . . . 108 E7
Links The
  Corsham SN13. . . . . . . 84 B7
  Pewsey SN9. . . . . 215 B4
Link Way SP1. . . . . . . 146 C3
Linley Cl SN1. . . . . . . .50 C2
Linley Rd SN26. . . . . . .21 C2
Linnet Cl SN12. . . . . . .94 E5
Linnet Rd SN11. . . . . . .81 C5
Linnetsdene
  6 Salisbury SP2. . . . 152 A5
  Swindon SN3. . . . . . . .51 C8
Linnet Way BA11. . . . .110 B6
Linslade SN2. . . . . .50 A7
Linslade St SN2. . . . . . .49 F6
Linsvale Cl BA11. . . . . .110 C5
Linsvale Dr BA11. . . . . .110 C5
Lionel's Ave SP5. . . . . 207 C5
Lions Orch BA14. . . . . 101 E8
Lipgate SN10. . . . . . . 180 F8
Lipman Way SN16. . . . .28 C2
Liskeard Way SN5. . . . .49 B4
Lisle Cl SN5. . . . . .49 A5
Lismore Rd SN6. . . . . . .22 E6
Lister Gr BA15. . . . . . . .99 F3
Lister Rd SN4. . . . . . . .64 B7
Litchfield Cl 11 SP10. 193 C2
Litherland Cl SN14. . . .78 B6
Little Ashley BA15. . . . .91 A2
Little Ave SN2. . . . . . . .35 A1
LITTLE BADMINTON. . .38 E5
Little Badminton La
  SN16. . . . . .28 F2
LITTLE BEDWYN. . . . 176 D5
Little Brittox SN10 . . . 214 A3
Littlebrook 2 BA14. . 101 D5
LITTLE CHALFIELD. . . .92 C3
Little Chalfield Rd
  BA14. . . . . 92 B2
LITTLE CHEVERELL. . 187 D6
Little Clarendon ★
  SP3. . . . . 201 F2
Little Comm BA14. . . . 105 D3
Little Content La 17
  SP7. . . . . 202 C2
Littlecote SN11. . . . . . 166 B7
Littlecote Cl 3 SN5. . 49 D5
Littlecote Rd
  Chippenham SN14. . . . .78 A6
  Froxfield SN8. . . . . . . 176 D7
Littlecote Roman Villa ★
  RG17. . . . . 170 D1
LITTLECOTT
  Enford. 190 A6
  Hilmarton. 166 A7
Little Ct La BA13. . . . 186 D8
Little Cumberwell
  BA15. . . . . .91 B2
Littledown SP7. . . . . . 202 C2
LITTLE DOWN. 185 D4
Little Down SN14. . . . . .78 B7
Little Down La SP11. . 185 C5
Little Down View
  SP4. . . . . 131 F8
Little Dro SP5. . . . . . . 211 A4
LITTLE DURNFORD. . 131 D1
Little End SN14. . . . . . . 74 A8
Little Englands
  Chippenham SN14. . . . .78 E6
  Chippenham SN15. . . . .78 E6
LITTLE FARINGDON. . . .2 F8
Littlefield La SP5. . . . 208 A4
Little Ground 7 SN5. .34 A2
Little Hill BA12. . . . . . 116 E2
LITTLE HORTON. . . . 172 C1
Little Ingleburn SN16. .28 A2
Little Island SN9. . . . . 215 B5
Littlejohn Ave SN12. . .94 C6
LITTLE LANGFORD. . 129 A6
LITTLE LONDON. . . . 166 E2
Little London
  Heytesbury BA12. . . . 194 C5
  Mount Sorrel SP5. . . . 205 A3
  1 Swindon SN1. . . . . 50 D4
LITTLE MARSH. 102 F4
Littlemead SN13. . . . . .83 B5
Little Mead SN8. . . . . 176 F1
Littlemill La SP6. . . . . 209 F3
Little Parks BA14. . . . . .92 F1
Little Pk Cl SN15. . . . . .59 F1
Little Rose La SN26. . . .20 C5
Little Sands SN14. . . . .68 F5
LITTLE SOMERFORD. .44 B5
LITTLETON. 178 B7
Littleton
  Great Hinton BA14. . . 102 F4
  Semington BA14. . . . 102 E5
LITTLETON DREW. . . .53 E5
Littleton Drew La GL9. .53 A6
LITTLETON PANELL. . 179 D1
Little Woodbury ★
  SP5. . . . . 152 B4
Little Woodfalls Dr
  SP5. . . . . 211 C6
LITTLEWORTH. 182 E8
Littleworth La SN12. . .85 C2
Livery Rd
  West Dean SP5. . . . . . 155 B7
  Winterslow SP5. . . . . 149 B4
Livia Cl 13 SN10. . . . . 193 E2
Lockem Rd SN10. . . . . 214 E6
LOCKERIDGE. 174 A6
Lockeridge Cl BA14. . 105 D5

Lockeridge La SN8. . . 174 B7
Locke's Dro SP11. . . . 193 E6
Locking Cl SN12. . . . . 178 B8
Locks Cross SN5. . . . . .84 E5
Locksgreen Cres 1
  SN2. . . . . .34 E3
Lock's Hill BA11. . . . . . .110 A3
Lockside 1 SN15. . . . .78 F5
Locks La
  Purton SN5. . . . . 33 B5
  Widham SN15. . . . . . . 33 B6
Locks The SN10. . . . . 179 D8
Lockswell Cl SN15. . . . .79 A4
Loddon Way BA15. . . 100 E5
Lode Hill SP5. . . . . . . 211 B8
Loder La SP2. . . . . . . 144 E3
Loder's La 3 SP3. . . 204 D5
Lodge Cl SN11. . . . . . . .81 A3
Lodge Ct BA14. . . . . . 105 F8
Lodge Dr 6 SP11. . . . 192 F1
Lodge Dro SP5. . . . . . 211 C6
Lodge Fields BA12. . . 119 A8
Lodge Hill BA11. . . . . . .110 C5
Lodge La SP11. . . . . . 192 E6
Lodge Rd
  Chippenham SN15. . . . .79 A5
  Horningsham BA12. . . 119 A8
  Lodge Vw SP3. . . . . . 188 A2
Lodge Vw SP3. . . . . . 188 A2
Lodowicks SN11. . . . . .80 D7
Logan Cl 1 SN3. . . . . .50 E6
Loiret Cres
  Malmesbury SN16. . . . .27 F6
  Malmesbury SN16. . . . .28 A6
Lomond Cl SN5. . . . . . .34 B2
Londonderry Gdns
  SP4. . . . . 198 E7
London La SN5. . . . . . .17 C1
London Rd
  Amesbury SP4. . . . . . 217 B4
  Bishops Cannings
    SN10. . . . . 214 E6
  Box SN13. . . . . 83 D7
  Calne SN11. . . . . .81 B2
  Chippenham SN15. . . . .78 F6
  Firsdown SP4. . . . . . . 148 B8
  Laverstock SP4. . . . . . 147 B6
  Marlborough SN8. . . . 213 E2
  Meysey Hampton GL7. . .1 A5
  Salisbury SP1. . . . . . . 146 C3
  Shrewton SP3. . . . . . . 196 F3
London Rd E BA1. . . . .82 A3
London Ride SN8. . . . 176 A5
London St SN1. . . . . . 50 B6
Long Acre SN5. . . . . . .33 E4
Long Barn Rd 18
  SP11. . . . . 193 F2
Longbarrow Cross Roads
  SP4. . . . . 197 C4
Long Barrow Rd SN11. .81 A3
Long Bottom SP11. . . 192 D6
LONGBRIDGE
  DEVERILL. 120 F6
Long Cl
  Chippenham SN15. . . .78 A6
  Downton SP5. . . . . . . 211 A8
Long Cl Ave SN13. . . . .76 B1
Long Cl W SP5. . . . . . 211 A8
Longcombe Dr
  Corsley BA12. . . . . . . 115 C3
  Warminster BA12. . . . 116 A5
Longcot Cl SN3. . . . . . .36 A1
Longcroft Ave SN10. . 214 C3
Longcroft Cres SN10. . 214 C3
Longcroft Rd
  Berwick St John SP5. . 207 D6
  Devizes SN10. . . . . . . 214 C3
LONG CROSS. 138 E5
Long Cross
  Bramshaw SO43. . . . . 212 C2
  Shaftesbury SP7. . . . . 202 B2
Longcross Plain Rd
  SO43. . . . . 212 B2
LONG DEAN. 68 C4
Long Dro
  Burbage SN8. . . . . . . 183 D8
  Grimstead SP5. . . . . . 154 B4
Long Drove
  East Grimstead SP5. . 154 F5
  East Grimstead SP5. . 155 A5
Longfellow Cl 7 SN25 .35 A8
Longfellow Cres SN4. .47 F3
LONGFIELD. 105 E8
Longfield Cl 11 SP4. . 198 B7
Longfield Rd BA14. . . 105 D7
Longfields SN8. . . . . . 173 B8
Longfields Wlk SN10. 214 C2
Longford Castle ★
  SP5. . . . . 153 A2
Longford CE (VC) Prim
  Sch SP5. . . . . 152 D5
Longford Pk ★ SP5. . 152 E2
Longford Rd SN12. . . . .94 A2
Long Ground
  4 Corsham SN13. . . . .76 D1
  Corsham SN13. . . . . . . 84 D8
Long Harry SN8. . . . . 213 F1
LONGHEDGE. 115 D5
Long Hedge RG17. . . . 165 B1
Longhill Dr 1 SP2. . . 152 B5
Long Hollow BA13. . . 186 D7
Long La
  Bourton SP8. . . . . 137 B1

Long La continued
  Bourton SP8. . . . . 137 D2
  Cann SP7. . . . . 206 A8
  Kilmington BA12. . . . . 123 F3
  Stourton with Gasper
    BA12. . . . . 124 A3
Longland SP2. . . . . . . 145 E1
Longlands 5. . . . . .1 E7
Longlands Cl BA13. . . 186 C7
Longleat
  Longhedge BA12. . . . 115 A5
  Warminster BA12. . . . 114 F3
Longleat Gdns SN2. . . .35 C4
Longleat House ★
  BA12. . . . . 114 F3
Longleat Safari Pk ★
  BA12. . . . . 115 B4
Longleaze SN4. . . . . . . .47 E3
Long Leaze SN14. . . . . .53 C1
Long Leaze La SN12. . .94 C3
Longleaze Prim Sch
  SN4. . . . . .47 E3
Longleys Cl SN10. . . . 214 E2
Longmead SP7. . . . . . 202 C2
Long Meadow SP3. . . 201 D2
Longmeadow Prim Sch
  BA14. . . . . 105 E7
LONG NEWNTON. 13 C5
Long Ridings SN14. . . .70 C2
Long River Rd BA13. . 109 D2
Long Row SN6. . . . . . . 10 B4
Longsplatt SN13. . . . . .83 D3
Long St SN10. . . . . .81 A3
Long Steeple La SP6. 210 C6
Longstock Ct SN5. . . . .49 B6
Longstone Rd 1 SN8. .70 A1
LONGSTREET. 190 A6
Longs Yard 7 BA15. . 100 D6
Longthorpe Cl SN5. . . .49 D4
Lonsdale SN26. . . . . . .21 C2
Lonsdale Gdns
  Bowerhill SN12. . . . . . 94 E1
  Melksham SN12. . . . . . 94 A2
Loophill SN15. . . . . . . .96 A6
Loop Dro SN8. . . . . . . 175 A7
Lopcombe Cnr SP4. . 135 D3
LOPCOMBE
  CORNER. 135 D3
Lopes Way BA13. . . . . 108 F4
Lords Cl SN4. . . . . .64 E3
Lords Croft SP4. . . . . 217 B4
Lord's Hill SP3. . . . . . 121 C3
Lord's La SN15. . . . . . . .78 E7
Lord's Mead SN14. . . . .78 A8
Lordsmead Rd BA12. . 139 B4
Lorne St SP4. . . . . .50 A5
Lotmead 1 BA14. . . . 101 D5
Lottage Rd SN8. . . . . 170 A7
Lottage Way 2 SN8. . 170 A7
Lotts The SN6. . . . . . . .17 F8
Loughborough Cl 1
  SN5. . . . . .48 F4
Louise Rayner Pl SN14 78 E7
Lourdes Cres 15
  RG17. . . . . 177 B6
Louviers Way SN1. . . . .50 C2
Lovage La SN15. . . . . . .81 D5
Lovage Way BA12. . . . 139 B6
Loveage Cl 5 SN2. . . .34 D4
Lovegrove Acre 2
  SP3. . . . . 201 E2
Love La
  Box SN13. . . . . .83 F7
  Salisbury SP1. . . . . . . 152 B8
  4 Shaftesbury SP7. . . 202 B1
  Woodgreen SP6. . . . . 211 A4
Lovell Cl SN3. . . . . . . .51 D7
Lovel Rd BA12. . . . . . 194 E3
LOVER. 211 D6
Loveridge Cl
  5 Andover SP10. . . . 193 E2
  Swindon SN2. . . . . . . .35 E6
Loves La BA14. . . . . . 104 C7
Love's La SN8. . . . . . . 170 B3
Lovett Gn SP1. . . . . . 146 C4
Lowa Rd SP9. . . . . . . 216 B6
Lowbourne SN12. . . . . .94 B4
Lowden SN15. . . . . . . .78 C7
Lowden Ave SN14. . . . .78 C8
Lowden Hill SN15. . . . .78 C7
Lower Alma St BA14. . 105 E8
Lower Backway 7
  SP3. . . . . 196 E6
Lower Bartons 30
  SP6. . . . . 210 D1
Lower Blandford Rd
  Cann SP7. . . . . 206 A8
  5 Shaftesbury SP7. . . 202 D1
LOWER BLUNSDON. . .21 B3
LOWER BURGATE. . . 210 D2
LOWER
  CHICKSGROVE. . . . 201 B1
LOWER
  Churchfields
  SN8. . . . . 213 D2
LOWER CHUTE. 192 F8
Lower Ct BA14. . . . . . 101 D1
Lower Daggons La
  SP6. . . . . 209 F1
Lower Densome Wood
  SP6. . . . . 211 A4
LOWER EVERLEIGH. . 182 E1
Lower Folly SP2. . . . . 144 B1
Lower Goatacre
  SN11. . . . . 166 A7

Lower Gr SP6. . . . . . . **210** B5
LOWER GREEN **177** D3
Lower Ho SN16. . . . .**15** B8
Lower Kingsdown Rd
Box SN13. . . . .**83** A4
Kingsdown BA1. . . . . . **82** E2
Lower Marsh Rd
BA12. . . . .**117** A5
Lower Mill SN25. . . . . . .**34** B2
Lower Mill Est GL7. . . . . .**6** A1
Lower Mill La GL7. . . . . . .**6** A1
LOWER MOOR. **17** A4
Lower N Rd SP5 . . . . . **207** C5
Lower Pavenhill SN5. . . .**32** E5
Lower Prospect SN8. **213** E3
Lower Rd
Bratton BA13. . . . . . . **186** B7
Britford SP5. . . . . **152** C5
Coombe Bassett SP5 . .**151** C1
Downton SP5. . . . . . . **159** B4
Edington BA13. . . . . . **186** C8
Erlestoke BA13. . . . . . **178** F2
Netheravon SP4. . . . . **190** A3
Odstock SP5. . . . . **152** D4
Salisbury SP2. . . . . . . **144** F2
LOWER RUDGE. **107** D4
LOWER SEAGRY. **57** F7
Lower Shockerwick La
BA1. . . . .**82** D4
Lower Shute BA12. . . . **119** F6
Lower S Rd SP5 . . . . . **207** C4
Lower St
Donhead St Andrew
SP7. . . . .**203** B1
Netheravon SP4. . . . . **190** A4
Rode BA11. . . . . **103** E1
Salisbury SP2. . . . . . . **151** E7
LOWER STANTON ST
QUINTIN. **56** D6
Lower Stoke
Limpley Stoke BA2. . . . .**99** A6
Monkton Combe BA2. . . .**90** A1
LOWER STRATTON. **36** B2
LOWER STUDLEY. **105** E6
Lower Twinhoe BA2 . .**98** B4
Lower Upham
Draycot Foliat SN8. . . . **168** F8
Upper Upham SN8. . . . **169** A8
Lower Wadswick
SN13. . . . .**84** B3
LOWER
WANBOROUGH . **163** B6
Lower Westbury Rd
BA13. . . . . **109** E5
Lower Wharf SN10. . . **214** A4
Lower Whitbourne
BA12. . . . . **115** B7
Lower Widhill Farm La
SN26. . . . .**20** D3
LOWER WOODFORD. **131** C3
Lower Woodrow
Melksham Without
SN12. . . . .**86** F1
Melksham Without SN12 **87** A1
LOWER WRAXALL. **91** E5
LOWER ZEALS. **138** D5
Lowes Cl **2** SN5. . . . . .**34** B2
Low La SN11. . . . .**81** D2
Lowmead BA14. . . . . . **101** E1
Low Rd SN10 . . . . **179** C1
Loxley Cl SN12. . . . .**94** B6
Loxley Wlk SN3. . . . .**51** B3
Loyalty St SN14. . . . . . .**78** C7
Lubeck Dr **22** SP10. . . **193** C2
Luccombe Quarry
BA15. . . . . **100** E7
Lucerne Cl
Royal Wootton Bassett
SN4. . . . .**47** D4
10 Swindon SN5 . . . . .**48** F8
Lucetta Rise **6** SN25. . **34** D5
Lucewood La SP5. . . . **154** C7
Luckett Way SN11 . . . . .**81** C4
LUCKINGTON. **39** E4
Luckington Comm Sch
GL9. . . . .**38** E5
Luckington Com Sch
SN14. . . . .**39** E5
Luckington Ct* SN14. .**39** F5
Luckington Rd
Acton Turville GL9 . . . . .**53** B7
Luckington SN14 . . . . . .**39** D2
Sherston SN14. . . . .**40** B7
Lucknam Pk* SN14 . . .**75** B6
Lucknam Pk SN14 . . . . .**75** C7
Ludborne Pl BA13 . . . **108** D1
Luddesdown Rd SN5. . .**49** C4
LUDGERSHALL. **192** A5
Ludgershall Castle*
SP11. . . . . **192** A6
Ludgershall Rd
Collingbourne Ducis
SN8 . . . . **191** E8
4 Swindon SN1. . . . . .**49** F4
Tidworth SP9. . . . . . . **216** D7
Ludgershall Sports Club
SP11. . . . . **192** A5
Ludlow Cl
Chippenham SN15. . . . . .**79** A5
10 Frome BA11. . . . . **103** E1
Swindon SN3. . . . .**50** F4
Warminster BA12. . . . . **116** F6
Westbury BA13. . . . . . **108** F4
Ludmead Rd SN13 . . . . .**85** A8
LUDWELL. **203** A1

Ludwell Com Prim Sch
SP7. . . . . **203** A1
Ludwell Hill SP7. . . . . **203** A1
Lugbury (Long Barrow)*
SN14. . . . .**53** E2
Lukas Cl SN25 . . . .**34** F7
Luke St SP7 . . . . **203** E1
Lulworth Rd SN25 . . . . .**34** E3
Lumb Cl SN25 . . . .**20** C1
Lumley Cl
2 Swindon SN5 . . . . . .**49** A4
Westwood SP2. . . . . . **145** B5
Lumley Wlk **8** SP4 . .**217** D3
Luna Cl SN19 . . . .**34** B7
Lupin Cl SN11 . . . .**81** D5
Luxfield Rd BA12 . . . . **116** E7
Lyall Cl SN25 . . . .**34** F8
Lyburn Rd SP5. . . . . . **212** A5
Lycetts Orch SN13 . . . . .**83** D6
Lyddon Way SN25 . . . . .**34** F4
Lydford Cl **4** SN5. . . . .**49** A8
Lydiard Fields Bsns Pk
SN5. . . . .**48** E3
Lydiard Grn SN5. . . . . . .**33** A1
LYDIARD GREEN **48** B8
LYDIARD MILLICENT. . **33** D1
Lydiard Millicent CE Prim
Sch SN5. . . . .**48** B8
Lydiard Pk* SN5. . . . . . .**48** E6
Lydiard Pk Academy
SN5. . . . .**48** F5
LYDIARD PLAIN **32** E1
Lydiard Rd SN14 . . . . . .**78** A6
LYDIARD TREGOZE **48** E6
Lydiard Way BA14 . . . . **105** D5
Lye Comm SN15 . . . . . .**58** B2
Lye Gn BA15. . . . .**99** F4
LYE GREEN **100** A4
Lyes Gr BA13 . . . . **112** B8
Lyes Green BA12. . . . . **115** A8
LYE'S GREEN. **111** B1
Lye The SN12. . . . . . . **178** E8
Lyme Ave BA12 . . . . . **116** F6
Lymers The SN11 . . . . **166** E2
Lyme Way SN25 . . . .**35** A5
Lynch Cl BA12 . . . . . . **139** B5
Lynchet Cl **7** SN10 . . **179** F1
Lynchets Rd SP4 . . . . **217** B3
Lynchfield Rd **7** SP4 **217** B3
Lynch Field The **5**
SN4. . . . . **163** A5
Lynch La **6** RG17. . . . **165** A2
Lynch The SN8 . . . . . . **176** F1
Lynden Cl SN8 . . . . . . **184** A7
Lyndhurst Cres SN3. . . .**51** A6
Lyndhurst Rd
Amesbury SP4 . . . . . . **217** C3
Bramshaw SO51 . . . . . **212** D3
Brook SO43 . . . . **212** E1
Landford SP5 . . . . **212** C6
LYNEHAM. **60** B2
Lyneham Cl SN15. . . . . .**35** B6
Lyneham Prim Sch
SN15. . . . .**60** B2
Lyneham Way BA14. . . **105** F8
Lynmouth Rd SN5 . . . . .**49** F6
Lynt Farm Cotts SN6. . . .**12** B6
Lynt Farm La SN6. . . . . .**12** B6
Lynton Rd SN2. . . . .**34** E1
Lynt Rd SN6 . . . .**12** A5
Lynwood Gr SN2. . . . . . .**34** D3
Lynwood Rd BA14 . . . . **101** A1
Lyons Wlk **1** SP7. . . . **202** C1
Lypiatt SN13. . . . .**84** F6
Lypiatt Mead SN13 . . . . .**85** A8
Lypiatt Prim Sch SN13 . .**84** F6
Lypiatt Rd SN13. . . . .**85** A7
Lypiatt View SN6 . . . . . .**19** C7
Lysander Rd
Bower Hill SN12. . . . . . .**94** B1
Laverstock SP4 . . . . . **146** C8
Melksham Without
SN12 . . . . **178** B8
Lysley Cl SN15. . . . .**79** A5
Lyster Rd SP4 . . . . . . **210** E1
Lytchett Way SN3. . . . . .**51** C6
Lytham Cl SN15. . . . .**78** F7
Lywood Cl SP2 . . . . . . **151** E5

M

MacAdam Way SP10 . . **193** B1
MacCullum Rd SP11 . . **193** E4
Macie Dr SN13. . . . .**84** E8
Mackay Cres
Swindon SN25 . . . .**20** C1
Swindon SN25 . . . .**34** B8
MacKenzie Cl **1** SN3 . **51** D4
Mackintosh Davidson
Wood Nature Reserve*
BA12. . . . . **140** D3
MacKlin Cl **21** RG17. . **177** B7
MacKlin Rd SP2 . . . . . **145** E2
Mackmurdo Ave SN25 **20** D1
MacNeice Dr SN8. . . . **213** A2
MADDINGTON **196** E7
Maddington **2** SP3 . **196** E6
Maddington St **1** SP3 **196** E7
Maddle Rd RG17. . . . . **164** E4
Maddock's Hill **4**
BA12. . . . . **116** E5
Maddocks Rd BA14 . . . **101** D4
Magdalene Cl SN3. . . . . .**36** F4
Magdalene La* **7**
SP7. . . . . **202** C1
Magdalen La BA14. . . . **104** B7
Magdalen Rd SN4 . . . . **163** A6

Magic Rdbt SN1. . . . . . .**50** E6
Magister Rd SN12 . . . . .**94** D1
Magnolia Cl
1 Frome BA11. . . . . . **110** C7
Harnham SP2. . . . . . . **151** D7
Magnolia Ct SN2. . . . . . .**35** B2
Magnolia Gdns SN5. . . .**49** B7
Magnolia Rise
Calne SN11 . . . .**81** B1
Trowbridge BA14. . . . . **105** E7
Magnon Rd BA15. . . . . **100** B7
Magpie La SN3 . . . .**51** E6
Magpie Mews SN5. . . . **214** B3
Maida Vale **3** SN25. . . **34** D6
MAIDEN BRADLEY. . . . **118** D2
Maiden Bradley
Horningsham BA12 . . . **119** B4
Maiden Bradley BA12 . **118** F4
Maidencroft Cotts
GL7. . . . .**10** E6
Maiden La SN11. . . . . . **166** B1
Maidstone Rd SN1. . . . . .**50** B4
Main Dr
Swindon SN25 . . . .**34** F8
Westonbirt GL8 . . . .**25** C8
Main Rd
Amesbury SP4 . . . . . . **217** D2
Cherhill SN11. . . . . . . **166** B1
Christian Malford SN15. . **58** E5
Ogbourne St Andrew
SN8 . . . . **213** D8
St Paul Malmesbury Without
SN16 . . . .**42** E4
Sutton Benger SN15 . . . .**57** F2
Winterbourne Dauntsey
SP4. . . . . **133** B2
Main St E BA13 . . . . . . **108** C6
Main St
Great Hinton BA14. . . . **178** A6
Westbury BA13 . . . . . . **108** C6
Maisey Mws SN16 . . . . . .**17** F7
Maitland Cl SN15 . . . . . .**79** A4
Maitland Rd SN3. . . . . . .**51** A7
Maize Cl **6** SP11 . . . . **193** F2
Maizey Rd SN25 . . . .**20** D1
Majestic Cl **4** SN5. . . . .**49** A7
Malcolm Dr SP4 . . . . . **132** B1
Maldwyn Cl **9** SN5. . . .**48** F8
Mallard Ave SN15. . . . . .**60** B1
Mallard Cl
7 Bower Hill SN12. . . **178** B8
Calne SN11 . . . .**81** D2
Salisbury SP2. . . . . . . **151** F7
Trowbridge BA14. . . . . **105** E7
Westbury BA13 . . . . . . **109** B4
Mallards The
South Cerney GL7 . . . . . .**7** A5
20 West Tisbury SP3 . **203** E8
Mallory Pl SN1. . . . .**94** C2
Mallow Cl
2 Swindon SN2 . . . . . .**34** D4
4 Trowbridge BA14 . . **105** D6
Mall The
South Tedworth SP9. . . **216** A4
Swindon SN1 . . . .**50** B3
MALMESBURY. **28** B3
Malmesbury Abbey*
SN16. . . . .**28** A3
Malmesbury CE Prim Sch
Malmesbury SN16. . . . . .**27** F5
Malmesbury SN16 . . . . . .**28** A4
Malmesbury Gdns
SN3. . . . .**51** A5
Malmesbury House*
SP1. . . . . **152** A8
Malmesbury Ind Est
SN16. . . . .**28** A4
Malmesbury Primary
Care Ctr SN16. . . . .**28** B1
Malmesbury Rd
Chippenham SN15. . . . . .**70** C1
Kemble GL7 . . . .**4** C6
Leigh SN5. . . . .**17** E3
Lower Stanton St Quintin
SN14 . . . .**56** C8
Minety SN16. . . . .**17** A1
Minety SN16. . . . .**31** A8
Malmesbury Sch SN16 .**27** E3
Malmesbury Swimming
Pool SN16. . . . .**27** E4
Malmpit Hill
Codford BA12. . . . . . . **195** B2
Codford St Mary BA12. **195** C4
Malone Ave SN25 . . . . . .**35** B8
Malory Cl
Swindon SN25 . . . .**20** D1
Swindon SN25 . . . .**34** D8
Malthouse Cl
Ashbury SN6 . . . . **164** A8
Broad Blunsdon SN26 . .**21** C2
Malthouse La
Chute SP11. . . . . **192** E8
4 Salisbury SP2. . . . . **146** A1
Malt House La SP11. . . **193** F4
Maltings The
Malmesbury SN16. . . . . .**28** A3
Royal Wootton Bassett
SN4 . . . .**47** D1
Salisbury SP2. . . . . . . **146** A1
8 Wanborough SN4. . **163** B6
Warminster BA12. . . . . **116** F6
Yatton Keynell SN14 . . . .**68** F6
Malt Shovel La RG17. . **164** F2
Malvern Cl
Melksham SN12. . . . .**94** D4
7 Warminster BA12. . **117** A8
Malvern Rd SN2 . . . .**35** C1

Malvern Way SP4. . . . **133** D6
Malwayn Cl **5** BA14 . **101** F1
Mampitts La SP7 . . . . **202** D1
Manchester Rd SN1. . . .**50** C7
Mand Wood BA14. . . . **101** F8
Mane Way
Westbury BA13 . . . . . . **108** E2
Westbury Leigh BA13 . **108** D1
Manley Cl BA14 . . . . . . **101** C1
Manners Way SN4. . . . . .**63** E1
Manning Cl **8** SP1. . . **146** C5
MANNINGFORD
ABBOTS **182** A5
MANNINGFORD
BOHUNE. **181** F4
MANNINGFORD
BRUCE. **181** F5
Mannington La SN5. . . . .**49** D5
Mannington Pk SN2 . . . .**49** F5
Mannington Ret Pk
SN1. . . . .**49** E4
Mannock Field SP4 . . . **132** B1
Manor Ave GL7 . . . .**2** E3
Manor Bridge Ct
SP9. . . . . **216** D7
Manor CE VC Prim Sch
The SN12 . . . .**94** B4
Manor Cl
Broad Blunsdon SN26 . .**21** C2
28 Fordingbridge SP6 **210** D1
Semington BA14 . . . . . **102** F5
4 Shipton Bellinger
SP9. . . . . **199** D8
Trowbridge BA14. . . . . **105** A6
Wroughton SN4 . . . .**64** B5
Manor Copse SP11. . . **193** E4
Manor Cotts SN14 . . . . .**24** D1
Manor Cres SN2 . . . .**34** F2
Manor Ct SN9 . . . . **215** C4
Manor Dr BA1. . . . .**82** B2
Manor Farm Cl
Broad Chalke SP5 . . . . **205** C4
Upper Seagry SN15. . . . .**57** D5
Manor Farm Ct
East Kennet SN8 . . . . . **173** D6
Purton Stoke SN5 . . . . . .**19** C2
Manor Farm Dr SN15 . .**57** C2
Manor Farm La
Great Wishford SP2. . . . **129** F4
Patney SN10 . . . . **180** F5
Shorncote GL7 . . . .**6** B7
Manor Farm Rd
Salisbury SP1. . . . . **146** C1
1 Sandleheath SP6 . . **210** C1
Manor Fields **5**
BA13. . . . . **186** B7
Manor Fields Prim Sch
SP2. . . . . **145** E2
Manor Gdns
Bradford-on-Avon
BA15. . . . . **100** A4
Burbage SN8 . . . . **175** D1
Swindon SN2 . . . .**34** F1
Warminster BA12 . . . . . **117** A4
Manor Ho SN14. . . . .**68** C5
Manor House Cl SN4. . . .**47** D3
Manor House The*
SN9. . . . . **182** F7
Manor La
Baydon SN8 . . . . **170** C8
Broad Hinton SN4 . . . . **167** C4
Manor Mdws SN3. . . . . .**36** E4
Manor Orch SN6. . . . . . .**19** E8
Manor Pk
Froxfield SN8. . . . . **176** D6
Great Somerford SN15 . .**44** A2
South Marston SN3 . . . . .**36** E4
Manor Rd
Chippenham SN14. . . . . .**78** A8
Corsham SN13. . . . .**76** F2
7 Great Bedwyn SN8. **176** B3
Mere BA12 . . . . **138** F7
Mere BA12 . . . . **139** A6
Salisbury SP1. . . . . . . **146** C1
Swindon SN1 . . . .**49** F5
Trowbridge BA14. . . . . **105** A6
Upton Lovell BA12 . . . . **194** E3
Vernhams Dean SP11 . **185** D3
Manor The*
SN8. . . . . **213** A1
Keevil BA14 . . . . **178** A4
Longbridge Deverill
BA12 . . . . **120** F5
Manor View SN16. . . . . .**28** F2
Manor Vw SN4 . . . . . . **163** A4
Manor Yard BA12. . . . **120** E2
Mansion House Mews
SN13. . . . .**77** A1
Mantell Cl BA13 . . . . . **108** F4
Mantles La BA12. . . . . **194** C5
MANTON. **213** A1
Manton Cl
Marlborough SN8. . . . . **213** A1
Trowbridge BA14. . . . . **105** C6
Manton Dro SN8. . . . . **174** C6
Manton Hollow SN8 . . **213** A2
Manton Rd SN8. . . . . . **174** C7
Manton St SN2 . . . .**49** F7
Manvers St BA14 . . . . **101** C1
Maple Cl
Calne SN11 . . . .**81** B1
Harnham SP2. . . . . . . **151** D7
Melksham SN12. . . . .**94** D5
Pewsey SN9. . . . . **215** B6
Royal Wootton Bassett
SN4 . . . .**61** E2
Swindon SN3 . . . .**50** D3
Wroughton SN4 . . . .**64** B6
Maple Cres
7 Ludgershall SP11 . . **192** B5
Wilton SP2. . . . . **144** F3

Maplecroft **3** SP2. . . **152** A5
Maple Ct BA11. . . . . . . **110** A7
Maple Dr
Firsdown SP5. . . . . **148** C7
Royal Wootton Bassett
SN4 . . . .**47** E4
Maple Gr
Swindon SN2 . . . .**35** C2
Trowbridge BA14. . . . . **105** C6
Maple Terr **4** SP9 . . **216** E7
Maple Way
Amesbury SP4 . . . . . . **217** D4
Chippenham SN15. . . . . .**70** D2
3 Durrington/Bulford
SP4. . . . . **198** B7
Marbeck Cl SN3 . . . .**34** E7
Marbrean Cl **4** SP6. . **210** C1
Marchant's La BA2. . . . . .**98** F4
March Cl SN25 . . . .**35** A6
Marchment Cl SP2. . . . **144** F4
MARDEN. **181** A4
Marden Ave SN1. . . . . . .**49** E2
Marden Henge*
SN9. . . . . **181** B5
Marden Vale CE Acad
SN11. . . . .**81** C4
Marden Way SN11 . . . . . .**81** C4
Marden Wlk **2** BA14. **105** D6
Margaret Leckie Ct **5**
SN3. . . . .**50** F6
Margarets Cl SP4. . . . . **217** D2
Margaret Stancomb
Infants' Sch BA14 . . . . **101** C1
Margery Holroyd Rise
SN3. . . . .**27** F3
Margha Rd SP9. . . . . . **216** C6
Marie Ave **5** SP5 . . . **210** F8
Marigold Cl
Melksham SN12. . . . .**94** C3
Swindon SN2 . . . .**34** D4
Marina Dr BA14. . . . . . **101** D4
Marina Rd
Salisbury SP1. . . . . **152** C7
Marine Cl SN14 . . . .**64** B7
Mariner Rd SN25 . . . . . .**34** B7
Maristow St BA13. . . . . **109** A3
Marjoram Cl **4** SN2 . .**34** D5
Markan Rd SP4 . . . . . . **133** F7
Markay Est BA14 . . . . . **112** F1
Markenfield **2** SN5. . . .**49** D4
Market Hill SN11 . . . . . .**81** B3
Market La **4** SN16. . . . .**28** A3
MARKET
LAVINGTON. **179** E1
Market Lavington Mus*
SN10. . . . . **179** F1
Market Mead SN14 . . . . .**78** F8
Market Pl
Box SN13 . . . .**83** D6
Castle Combe SN14 . . . . .**68** A7
Chippenham SN15. . . . . .**78** E7
Colerne SN14. . . . .**75** B3
Lechlade GL7 . . . .**2** C4
18 Market Lavington
SN10 . . . . **179** F1
Marshfield SN14 . . . .**74** A8
Pewsey SN9. . . . . **215** C5
Warminster BA12 . . . . . **117** A7
2 Westbury BA13. . . . **109** A4
Market Pl The SN10. . . **214** A4
Market Sq The **3** SN3 **50** D4
Market St
Bradford-on-Avon
BA15. . . . . **100** D7
Swindon SN1 . . . .**50** B6
Trowbridge BA14. . . . . **105** D8
Markham Cl SN3 . . . .**50** F7
Markham Rd SN4 . . . . . .**63** E3
Markham Rd BA14 . . . . **105** A6
Markova Gr **9** SN25 . . .**34** C6
Markton Cl **3** SN25. . . .**34** C4
MARLBOROUGH. **213** F3
Marlborough Bsns Pk
SN8. . . . . **213** E1
Marlborough Cl
SN10. . . . . **214** F7
Marlborough Coll
SN8. . . . . **213** C2
Marlborough Craft Ctr*
SN8. . . . . **213** D2
Marlborough La SN1. . . .**50** D3
Marlborough Leisure Ctr
SN8. . . . . **213** C3
Marlborough Rd
5 Aldbourne SN8. . . . **170** A6
Bulford SP4 . . . . **198** E6
Burbage SN8 . . . . **175** C1
Chiseldon SN3 . . . .**51** C2
Collingbourne Ducis
SN8 . . . . **183** E1
Draycot Foliat SN4. . . . **168** F8
Everleigh SN8 . . . . **183** A1
Liddington SN4. . . . .**51** E1
Pewsey SN9. . . . . **215** B6
Royal Wootton Bassett
SN4 . . . .**61** E2
Swindon SN3 . . . .**50** D3
Wroughton SN4 . . . .**64** B6
Marlborough St **5**
SN1. . . . .**50** A5

Marlborough White
Horse* SN8 . . . . . **213** C1
Marl La SP6 . . . . **210** D1
Marlowe Ave SN3. . . . . .**50** F7
Marlowe Way SN4 . . . . . .**47** F3
Marlstones The SN1. . . .**50** B4
Marne Rd **3** SP4 . . . **198** F6
Marney Rd SN5. . . . .**49** A5
MARR GREEN **183** D7
Marshall Rd
Roundway SN10. . . . . . **214** D1
Swindon SN5. . . . .**49** B8
Marshall St SN14 . . . . . .**78** C7
Marshall Way BA11 . . . **110** D8
Marsh Cl SN25. . . . .**34** A3
Marsh Farm La SN1. . . . .**50** E7
MARSHFIELD. **74** A8
Marshfield Path GL9. . . .**38** A8
Marshfield Prim Sch
SN14. . . . .**74** B8
Marshfield Rd SN15. . . . .**78** C8
Marshfield Way SN3. . . .**36** A2
Marshgate SN1. . . . .**50** F8
Marsh Gr **6** SN13. . . . .**76** C1
Marsh La
Breamore SP6 . . . . **210** E4
Cherhill SN11. . . . . . . **166** A1
Coombe Bissett SP5 . . **150** F2
Hungerford RG17. . . . . **177** A7
Nettleton SN14 . . . .**53** C4
Pen Selwood BA9 . . . . **137** A4
Rowde SN10 . . . .**96** D2
Salisbury SP2. . . . . . . **145** F2
Marshmead BA14 . . . . . .**101** F4
Marshmead Cl SP5 . . . **152** E6
Marsh Rd
Berkley BA11. . . . . **107** C1
Rode BA11. . . . . **103** F1
Trowbridge BA14. . . . . **101** E5
Marsh St BA12. . . . . . . **117** A5
Marsh The SN4 . . . .**51** F3
Marshwood SP3. . . . . . **201** E3
Marsland Rd SN2 . . . . . .**35** D2
MARSTON. **179** A3
Marston Ave SN2 . . . . . .**35** D4
MARSTON HILL. **1** C4
Marston Hill GL7 . . . .**1** C5
Marston Hill Farm La
GL7. . . . .**1** D3
MARSTON MEYSEY. **1** B4
Marston Rd BA14 . . . . . **105** B4
Marsum Cl **1** SP10 . **193** D2
MARTEN. **184** C7
Martha's La SP3. . . . . . **140** F4
Marti Cl SN12. . . . .**94** C4
Martigny Rd SN12 . . . . . .**94** B3
MARTIN. **209** B6
Martinbushes Rd
SP4. . . . . **198** A7
Martin Cl SP9 . . . . **216** E6
Martin Crest BA12 . . . . **116** E5
MARTIN DROVE END. . **209** A8
Martinfield SN3 . . . .**51** D7
Martingale Rd SN8 . . . **183** D7
Martingate SN13 . . . .**77** A1
Martinique St SP9 . . . . **216** E6
Martin Rd SP6. . . . . . . **209** B6
Martins Cl
Chippenham SN15. . . . . .**79** A8
2 Salisbury SP2. . . . . **152** A5
Steeple Ashton BA14. . **178** C4
Martin's Cl SN9. . . . . . . **181** C4
Martins Croft SN14 . . . . .**75** B3
Martinsell Gn SN9 . . . . **215** D5
Martinsell Hill (Fort)*
SN8. . . . . **174** D2
Martins La BA14 . . . . . **178** C4
MARTINSLADE **178** E8
Martins Rd BA14 . . . . . **178** C5
Martins Rise SP5 . . . . . **161** C4
Martin's St **4** SP7 . . **202** C1
Martin Way SN11. . . . . . .**81** B3
Martlesham Rd SP4. . . **217** D2
Martlet Cl SN12. . . . .**94** D1
Martor Ind Est SN14 . . .**66** F2
Marvins Cl SP3 . . . . **188** B2
Mary Barters La SP3. . . **204** E8
Maryland Cl SP2. . . . . . **145** B5
Mascroft Rd BA14 . . . . **106** A8
Masefield SN4. . . . .**47** F3
Masefield Ave SN2. . . . . .**35** E3
Masefield Rd BA12. . . . **116** E6
Maskeleyne Way SN4. . .**63** F6
Maslen La SN13 . . . .**83** F7
Mason Rd SN25. . . . .**35** B6
Masons La BA15 . . . . . **100** D7
Masons The SN5. . . . . . .**33** A3
Masons Way SN11 . . . . . .**76** D1
Massey Cl SN15. . . . .**78** E5
Massey Rd **4** SN10 . . **214** D1
Massinger Wlk SN3. . . . .**50** F6
Matford Hill SN15. . . . . . .**79** A8
Mathews Cl SN25 . . . . . .**35** E3
Matilda's Piece **5** SN6 **19** D7
Matilda Way SN10 . . . . **214** D4
Matley Moor SN3 . . . .**51** E2
Matravers Cl BA13 . . . **108** F3
Matrons Cotts SP5. . . . **153** F1
Matthews Cl SN10 . . . . **172** F1
Mattocks Path **2** SN1 .**50** B1
Matty Hull Cl **19** SP7 **202** D1
Maud Cl SN10. . . . .**20** B1
Maud Heath Ct SN15. . . .**78** E8
Maud Heath's Cswy
Chippenham SN15. . . . . .**70** E1
Langley Burrell Without
SN15 . . . .**71** B3

Maud Heath's Mon ★
SN11 . . . . .80 C8
Maud Heath's Stone ★
SN11 . . . . .80 C8
Maulton Cl BA14 . . . . 101 D8
Maunders Dr BA14 . . . 101 D4
Maundrell Cl SN10 . . . . 96 D2
Maundrell Rd SN1 . . . . .50 C6
Maunsell Way SN4 . . . . .63 F7
Maur Cl SN15 . . . . .78 C7
Maurice Way SN8 . . . . 175 A7
Maurys La SO51 . . . . . 212 F6
Maxcroft La BA14 . . . . 101 E5
Maxey Cl SN5 . . . . .49 B8
Maxwell St SN1 . . . . . . .50 A6
Maybold Cres ⒏ SN2 . 34 D5
May Cl SN2 . . . . .35 C1
Mayenne Pl SN10 . . . . 179 C8
Mayfair Rd SN1 . . . . . 146 D1
Mayfield ⒈ SN4 . . . . . 163 A5
Mayfield Ave Ind. Pk
SP11 . . . . 192 E1
Mayfield Cl
⒋ Shipton Bellinger
SP9 . . . . 199 C8
Swindon SN3 . . . . .51 E7
Mayfield Rd ⒉ SP6 . . 210 C1
Mayflower Rd ⒈ SN3 . .51 B8
Mayfly Cl ⒋ SP6 . . . . 210 D1
Mayfly Rd SN25 . . . . . .34 A7
May La
Ebbesborne Wake
SP5 . . . . 204 D3
Yarnbrook BA14 . . . . . 105 F3
Mayo Cl SN13 . . . . . . .76 E2
Mays Dr BA13 . . . . . . 109 B5
Mays Firs SP6 . . . . . . 211 D5
May's La SN4 . . . . .65 D4
Maytree Cl ⒍ BA11 . . 110 B7
May Tree Rd ⒐
SP10 . . . . 193 C1
Mazurek Way SN25 . . . .34 E6
McArthur Glen Designer
Outlet Village SN2 . . .50 A6
McKie Rd ⒊ SP4 . . . . 217 D2
Mcnamara St SP4 . . . . 132 B1
McNeill Rd SP4 . . . . . 198 A4
Mead Com Prim Sch
The BA14 . . . . 102 B1
Mead Ct BA14 . . . . . . 105 D3
Meadens La SP5 . . . . 151 A1
Meade Rd ⒉ SN11 . . 192 B5
Meadland SN13 . . . . . .76 E1
Meadow Ave ⒑
SP6 . . . . 210 D1
Meadow Bridge Sch
SN5 . . . . .19 E8
Meadow Cl
Chippenham SN14 . . . .78 A7
⒈ Dinton SP3 . . . . . 201 E2
⒏ Fordingbridge
SP6 . . . . 210 D1
Upper Minety SN16 . . 16 D2
Yatton Keynell SN14 . . .68 F6
Meadowcroft SN2 . . . . .35 F3
Meadow Ct
⒒ Fordingbridge
SP6 . . . . 210 D1
Pewsey SN9 . . . . 215 C5
Trowbridge BA14 . . . . 101 D4
Whiteparish SP5 . . . . 161 E4
Meadow Dr SN10 . . . . 214 C3
Meadowfield BA15 . . . 100 B6
Meadow La
Little Somerford SN15 . .44 A5
Warminster BA12 . . . 116 D6
Westbury BA13 . . . . . 109 A4
Meadow Pk BA1 . . . . . .82 B3
Meadow Rd
Durrington/Bulford
SP4 . . . . 217 D2
Melksham SN12 . . . . . .94 C7
⒊ Salisbury SP2 . . . 145 F1
Meadow Rd (South) ⒌
SP2 . . . . 145 F1
Meadow Rise SN8 . . . 174 A6
Meadow Springs SN5 . .48 B8
Meadows The
Bourton SP8 . . . . 137 F2
Lydiard Tregoze SN5 . . .47 F5
Salisbury SP1 . . . . . . 152 D8
Meadowsweet Cl ⒉
SN25 . . . . .34 E6
Meadowsweet Dr
SN11 . . . . .80 D7
Meadow View
⒌ Fittleton SP4 . . . . 190 A4
Kempsford GL7 . . . . . 10 C7
Lechlade-on-Thames
GL7 . . . . 2 D5
Meadow Way
Chiseldon SN4 . . . . . . .65 E7
South Cerney GL7 . . . . .6 F7
Meadow Well SN8 . . . 183 C8
Mead Pk SN14 . . . . . . .84 F1
Meads Rd SP4 . . . . . . 198 B7
Meads The SN14 . . . . .53 B3
Mead The
Ashton Keynes SN6 . . . .17 F8
Warminster BA12 . . . 117 A7
Westbury BA13 . . . . . 109 A5
Winsley BA15 . . . . . . 99 E7
Meadway
⒋ Shrewton SP3 . . . 196 F6
Wingfield BA14 . . . . . 105 A8
Mead Way
⒒ Shaftesbury SP7 . 202 D1
Swindon SN5 . . . . 34 B2

Meares Dr SN5 . . . . . . .49 B8
Mears Rd ⒋ SP4 . . . . 198 A6
Medbourne SN14 . . . . 163 A4
Medbourne Rd SN4 . . 163 A4
Medgbury Pl SN1 . . . . .50 D6
Medgbury Rd SN1 . . . . .50 C6
Medicina St SP9 . . . . 216 D4
Medieval Hall Salisbury ★
SP1 . . . . 152 A8
Medina Way SN2 . . . . .35 F4
Medlar Ct SN2 . . . . . . .35 B2
Medway SN25 . . . . . . .34 F4
Medway Rd SN25 . . . . .34 F4
Meerut Rd SP9 . . . . . 216 C6
Melbourne St BA13 . . 186 B7
Melbourne Gdns ⒌
SP4 . . . . 198 F6
Melbourne St BA13 . . 186 B7
MELBURY ABBAS. . . . 206 B7
Melbury Abbas Mill ★
SP7 . . . . 206 A7
Melbury Down ★ SP5 206 C6
Melbury Way ⒓ SP7 . 206 B6
Melchet Cl SO51 . . . . 162 D1
Melchet Pk
Melchet Park and Plaitford
SO51 . . . . 162 C1
Plaitford SO51 . . . . . . 212 D8
Melchet Vw SO51 . . . . 162 D2
Melford Wlk SN3 . . . . .51 C7
Melfort Cl SN5 . . . . . . .34 E2
Meliot Rise ⒓ SP10 . . 193 E2
MELKSHAM. 94 A5
Melksham Blue Pool
SN12 . . . . .94 A4
Melksham Cl SN2 . . . . .35 B6
Melksham Com Hospl
SN12 . . . . .94 B3
MELKSHAM FOREST. . .94 D1
Melksham La SN12 . . . .93 C4
Melksham Oak Com Sch
SN12 . . . . .94 D1
Melksham Rd
Chippenham SN14 . . . .78 B5
Chippenham SN15 . . . .78 B5
Holt BA14 . . . . .92 F1
Holt SN12 . . . . .93 A2
Lacock SN15 . . . . .86 D5
Melksham Sta SN12 . . .94 A5
Mellow Gd SN25 . . . . .34 E5
Melrose Ave BA12 . . . 116 E6
Melrose Cl
Easterton SN10 . . . . . 180 A1
⒈ Swindon SN5 . . . .49 C6
⒋ Warminster BA12 . 116 E6
Melsome Rd SN15 . . . .59 F1
Melstock Rd SN25 . . . .34 C6
Melton Rd BA14 . . . . 101 D4
Melusine Rd ⒋ SN3 . . .51 B8
Melville Cl ⒊ SN3 . . . .50 F6
Melvin Cl SP1 . . . . . . 146 D1
Mendip Cl
⒊ Frome BA11 . . . . 110 A7
Melksham SN12 . . . . . .94 C4
Swindon SN25 . . . . . . .35 C3
⒍ Warminster BA12 . 117 A8
Mendip Dr BA11 . . . . 110 A7
Menham Cl SN2 . . . . . 35 D2
Mercer Cl SN25 . . . . . .20 C1
Merchants House The ★
SN8 . . . . 213 D3
Mercia Ave SP10 . . . . 193 C2
MERE 139 B5
Mere Ave SN14 . . . . . .41 F1
Mere By-Pass BA12 . . 139 A6
Mere Castle ★ BA12 . 138 F6
Mere Down
Kingston Deverill
BA12 . . . . 125 F3
Kingston Deverill BA12 126 A5
Mere Mus ★ BA12 . . . 139 A5
Mere Sch BA12 . . . . . 139 B5
Meriden Wlk SN3 . . . . .51 F4
Meridian Wlk BA14 . . 105 A8
Meriton Ave SN13 . . . .77 A1
Merlin Cl ⒓ SP10 . . . 193 E2
Merlin Rd ⒈ SN11 . . . .81 B5
Merlin Theatre BA11 . 110 A7
Merlin Way
Bower Hill SN12 . . . . . 94 B1
Stratton St Margaret
SN3 . . . . 51 D8
Swindon SN3 . . . . 36 D1
Merrifield Rd SP4 . . . 146 C6
Merrington Way SP9 . 216 C7
Merrivale Gr SN3 . . . . .50 E5
Merry Orch SO43 . . . . 212 D2
Mersey Cl SN1 . . . . . . 193 F1
Merton Ave SN2 . . . . . 35 D4
Merton Cl ⒍ SP6 . . . 210 D2
Merton St ⒉ SN1 . . . .50 C6
Mervyn Webb Pl SN2 . 50 D8
Mesh Pond SP5 . . . . . 210 B4
Methuen Ave SN12 . . . 94 B6
Methuen Cl BA15 . . . . 100 E4
Methuen Dr ⒈ SP1 . . 152 C8
Methuen Pk
Chippenham SN13 . . . .77 F4
Chippenham SN14 . . . .77 F4
⒌ Chippenham SN14 .77 F5
Methuen Way SN13 . . .76 F2
Metis Cl SN25 . . . . . . .34 F8
Mews The
Highworth SN6. . . . . . 23 A4
Lydiard Millicent SN5 . 48 D8
Warminster BA12 . . . 117 A7
Meynell Cl SN25 . . . . .34 F8

Meyrick Ave SP2 . . . . 152 A5
Meysey Cl GL7 . . . . . . .1 A5
MEYSEY HAMPTON. . . .1 A5
Michaelmas Dro
SP11 . . . . 192 E1
Middle Farm Cl SN15 . .45 B1
Middle Farm Ct GL7 . . 10 D7
Middle Field SN10. . . . 214 C3
Middle Gd
Cricklade SN6 . . . . 19 C8
Fovant SP3 . . . . 204 E7
Middle Green La SN15 . .45 B1
MIDDLEHILL. 83 A6
Middle La
Atworth/Whitley SN12 . .85 D1
Cherhill SN11 . . . . . . 166 B1
Martin SP5 . . . . 208 F6
Martin SP5 . . . . 209 A7
Trowbridge BA14 . . . . 101 F2
Middleleaze Dr SN5 . . .48 F7
Middlemass Gn SN9 . . 215 D5
Middlemead La
Hannington SN6. . . . . 22 B8
Hannington Wick SN6 . 11 A1
Middle St SP2 . . . . . . 151 E7
Middle Stoke BA2 . . . .99 A6
Middleton
Middle Winterslow
SP5 . . . . 149 B6
The Common SP5. . . . 149 B7
Middleton Cl
Swindon SN3 . . . . . . .50 F6
⒌ Warminster BA12 . 116 E6
Middleton Dr BA13 . . 100 E6
Middleton Medieval
Village of ★ BA12 . . 194 A7
Middleton Rd
Salisbury SP2 . . . . . . 145 F2
The Common SP5. . . . 149 B7
Middletons Cl RG17 . . 177 C8
Middleton Terr ⒍
SP4 . . . . 132 B1
MIDDLEWICK 76 D3
Middlewick La SN13 . . .76 D3
MIDDLE
WINTERSLOW 149 B7
MIDDLE
WOODFORD 131 B4
MIDFORD. 98 C6
Midford Hill BA2. . . . . .98 C4
Midford La
Limpley Stoke BA2. . . . 98 E7
Limpley Stoke BA2. . . . 98 F6
Midford Rd BA2 . . . . . .98 B7
Midhurst Rd SN3 . . . . .51 B5
Midlands Ind Est The
BA14 . . . . .92 E1
Mid Summer Pl SP4 . . 217 E5
Midwinter Cl SN5 . . . . .34 B2
Midwinter Gdns SN3 . . .36 A2
MILBOURNE 28 D4
Milbourne La SN16 . . . .28 C4
Milbourne Rd SN16 . . . .28 C4
Milbourne Way SN14 . .78 C5
MILDENHALL 175 A8
Mildenhall Way ⒈ SN2 .35 B6
Mildmay Cl ⒓ SN5 . . . .48 F5
Mile Dr SN15 . . . . .44 E1
MILE ELM 89 A7
MILE END 165 A3
Miles Field DT11. . . . . 206 A1
Miles Lane SP5 . . . . . 161 E5
Miles's La SP5 . . . . . . 161 E5
Milestone Way SN15. . .70 C2
MILFORD 152 E8
Milford Hill SP1 . . . . . 152 B8
Milford Hollow ⒍
SP1 . . . . 152 C8
Milford Ind Est SP1 . . 152 C8
Milford Manor Gdns
SP1 . . . . 152 D8
Milford Mill Rd SP1 . . 152 D8
Milford Pk SP1 . . . . . . 152 D8
Milford St
Salisbury SP1 . . . . . . 152 B8
Swindon SN1 . . . . 50 C6
Milford Way SN15 . . . .78 F4
MILKHOUSE WATER . . 215 E8
MILKWELL. 203 B2
Millais Cl SN25 . . . . . . .20 C1
Milland Cl SN25 . . . . . .35 B6
Millard Cl ⒉ SN15 . . . .78 F4
Millard Rd ⒌ SN25 . . .35 A8
Millards Cl BA14 . . . . 101 F4
Millards Way
Standerwick BA11 . . . . 107 B1
Upton Scudamore
BA12 . . . . 112 E4
Millbourn Cl BA15. . . . .99 D7
Millbrook ⒉ SP1 . . . . 146 B2
Millbrook La SP3 . . . . 141 C1
Millbrook Prim Sch
SN5 . . . . .49 A3
Millbuck Cl SN2 . . . . . .35 E1
Mill Cl
Devizes SN10 . . . . 214 C1
Great Bedwyn SN8 . . . 176 B2
Longbridge Deverill
BA12 . . . . 120 F6
South Cerney GL7 . . . . .7 A7
Winterbourne SP4 . . . 133 B4
Wroughton SN4 . . . . . 64 B6
Mill Ct ⒙ SP6 . . . . . . 210 D1

Millditch ⒖ BA13 . . . 186 B7
Mill Dro SN8 . . . . 183 C1
Mill End SP6 . . . . 209 F2
Millennium Cl ⒉
SP2 . . . . 152 B5
Millennium Visitor Ctr ★
GL7 . . . . .6 B4
Miller Cl
Chirton SN10 . . . . 180 F4
Salisbury SP2 . . . . . . 145 E5
Swindon SN5 . . . . .48 F8
Millers Cl SP8 . . . . . . 137 E2
Miller's La DT11 . . . . . 207 D1
Millfield ⒌ RG17 . . . . 165 A1
Millgreen Rd ⒈ SP4 . 217 C2
Millgrove St SN25 . . . . 34 D7
Millhand Villas BA14 . 105 E7
Mill Head SN10 . . . . . 179 A4
Mill Hill Ave SP9 . . . . 216 C8
Mill Hollow La SP7 . . . 206 A7
Milling Cl SN6 . . . . . . .7 A1
Millington Dr ⒊
BA14 . . . . 105 A7
Mill Island BA12 . . . . 117 E5
Mill La
Bishopstone SP5 . . . . 150 A1
Bishopstrow BA12 . . . 117 F4
Bourton SP8 . . . . 137 E2
Box SN13 . . . . .83 C7
Bradford-on-Avon
BA15 . . . . 100 D6
Broughton Gifford SN12 93 C3
Bulkington SN10 . . . . . 178 E5
Castle Eaton SN6 . . . . 10 A1
Cherhill SN11 . . . . . . 166 B1
Chilmark SP3 . . . . . . 200 F2
Fairford GL7 . . . . .1 F7
Fovant SP3 . . . . 204 D8
Gasper BA12 . . . . 137 C6
Hawkeridge BA13 . . . 108 E7
Heytesbury BA12 . . . . 194 C5
Lambourn RG17 . . . . 165 B1
Lechlade GL7 . . . . .2 C4
Little Somerford SN15 . .43 F5
Maiden Bradley BA12 . 118 D5
Malmesbury SN16 . . . 28 A3
Melbury Abbas SP7 . . 206 A7
Mere BA12 . . . . 139 B5
Monkton Combe BA2 . .98 E8
Poulshot SN10 . . . . . . 179 A5
Ramsbury SN8 . . . . . 170 B2
St Paul Malmesbury Without
SN16 . . . . 42 E5
Salisbury SP2 . . . . . . 145 E5
Selwood BA11 . . . . . . 114 F8
Shalbourne SN8 . . . . . 176 F2
Somerford Keynes GL7 . .6 A2
Stanton Fitzwarren SN6 22 A4
Swindon SN1 . . . . 49 E2
Swindon SN1 . . . . 50 A3
The Common SP5. . . . 149 E6
Westbury BA13 . . . . . 112 D8
West Lavington SN10 . 187 E8
Winterbourne Monkton
SN4 . . . . 167 C3
Winterslow SP5 . . . . . 149 D7
Zeale SP8 . . . . 137 F2
Mill Lake SP4 . . . . . . 132 E2
Mill Lane BA12 . . . . . 115 E4
Mill Path SP9 . . . . . . 216 A8
Mill Race SP2 . . . . . . 151 E8
Mill Rd
Devizes SN10 . . . . 214 C1
Netheravon SP4 . . . . . 190 A4
Potterne SN10 . . . . . . 179 D5
Salisbury SP2 . . . . . . 145 F1
Worton SN10 . . . . 179 A4
Mill Rise SP8 . . . . 137 E2
Mills Rd SN12 . . . . . . .94 C4
Mill St
Calne SN11 . . . . .81 B2
Fontmell Magna SP7 . . 206 A3
Heytesbury BA12 . . . . 194 C5
Trowbridge BA14 . . . . 105 D8
Millstone Cl SN4. . . . . .47 F1
Mill Stream App SP2 . 146 A1
Mills Way SP4 . . . . . . 217 D4
Milne Cres ⒊ SP4 . . . 197 E6
Milne Rd SP4 . . . . 198 E6
Milne Way SN3 . . . . . . .36 B5
MILSTON 198 B8
Milston Ave SN2 . . . . . .35 C5
Milston Down (Long
Barrows) ★ SP4 . . 198 E8
Milston Dro SP4 . . . . . 190 E1
Milston Rd
Bulford SP4 . . . . 198 C1
Durrington/Bulford
SP4 . . . . 217 D2
Milston View ⒉ SP4 . 198 C2
MILTON 141 B3
Milton Ave
⒍ Andover SP10 . . . 193 C1
Melksham SN12 . . . . . 94 B4
MILTON LILBOURNE . 182 F7
Milton Pl GL7 . . . . . . .1 F6
Milton Rd
Amesbury SP4 . . . . . . 217 E2
Pewsey SN9 . . . . 215 D5
Salisbury SP2 . . . . . . 152 B6
Swindon SN1 . . . . 50 B6
Milton St GL7 . . . . . . .1 F6
Milton's Way SN4 . . . . .47 C1
Milverton Ct SN3 . . . . .51 A5
MINCHINGTON. 207 D1
Minden ⒔ SP10 . . . . . 193 D2
Minden Way SP9 . . . . 216 D4
Minerva Hts SN26 . . . . .21 A1

MINETY 17 B2
Minety CE Prim Sch
SN16 . . . . .17 B2
MINETY COMMON 31 C8
Minety La SN16 . . . . . .16 A7
Minety Rd SN2 . . . . . . .35 B5
Minnow Cl
⒊ Calne SN11 . . . . . 81 B5
Swindon SN25 . . . . . . 34 A7
Minories Rd SN9 . . . . 216 E6
Minot Cl SN16 . . . . . . .28 A5
Minster CE Prim Sch The
BA12 . . . . 116 F7
Minster Cl SN25 . . . . . .34 F7
Minster St
⒎ Salisbury SP1 . . . 146 A1
Wilton SP2 . . . . 144 D3
Minster View BA12 . . 116 F7
Minster Way SN14 . . . .78 A5
Mint Cl SN2 . . . . .34 D4
Minton Distribution Pk
SP4 . . . . 217 C4
Minty's Top SN15 . . . . .96 A7
Mir Cres ⒊ SN25 . . . . .34 B7
MISSELFORE 204 F1
Mitchell Cl
Royal Wootton Bassett
SN4 . . . . 47 D1
Mitchell Dr
Bower Hill SN12 . . . . . 178 B8
Westonbirt GL8 . . . . . 25 D8
Mitchell Rd SP2 . . . . . 151 D8
Mitchells Cl ⒌ SP5 . . 211 C7
Mizmaze ★ SP6 . . . . . 210 D7
Moat Rd BA13 . . . . . . 108 D6
Moberly Rd SP1 . . . . . 146 B3
Model Farm La SP5 . . 148 C3
Moffat Rise SN16 . . . . .28 A5
Moggs La SN11 . . . . . 172 A8
Moldens The BA14 . . . 105 B4
Mompesson Ho ★
SP2 . . . . 152 A8
Monastery Rd BA13 . . 186 C8
Monet Cl SN25 . . . . . . .34 F7
Moneyer Rd ⒌ SP10 . 193 D2
Monkeys Jump SO51 . 212 F5
Monkley La
Rode BA11 . . . . 107 C8
Rode BA11 . . . . 104 C1
Monks Cl
North Tidworth SP9 . . 216 C7
Tidworth SP9 . . . . . . 216 C7
Monks Dr SN13 . . . . . .84 B8
Monk's La SN13 . . . . . .85 B6
Monks Pk SN16 . . . . . .28 D4
Monks Pk Gdns SN13 . .85 B5
Monks Way SN15 . . . . .79 A4
Monks Wlk GL7 . . . . . .2 C3
Monks Cl SN3 . . . . . . .51 B4
MONKTON COMBE 98 E8
MONKTON
DEVERILL 126 D7
MONKTON FARLEIGH. . .90 F7
Monkton Gdns ⒉ 126 D7
Monkton Hill SN15 . . . .78 D7
Monkton House ★
SN12 . . . . 93 C1
Monkton Pk SN15 . . . . .78 F7
Monkton Pk Prim Sch
SN15 . . . . .78 E7
Monmouth Cl ⒋ SN3 . .50 F4
Monmouth Dr BA11 . . 110 B5
Monmouth Rd SP3 . . . 203 D8
Mons Ave SP4 . . . . . . 198 E6
Mons La SN15 . . . . . . .86 D8
Montague Cl SN15 . . . .79 A7
Montague Ct BA14 . . . 102 A1
Montague Pl SN12 . . . .94 C5
Montague Rd SP2 . . . 151 D7
Montagu St SN2 . . . . . .49 F7
Monteagle Cl SN5 . . . . .49 A4
Montgomery Ave SN2. . .35 D2
Montgomery Gdns
SP2 . . . . 145 E2
Montgomery Rd
Enham Alamein SP11. . 193 E3
Warminster BA12 . . . 113 D1
Montreal Way ⒏
SP4 . . . . 217 E6
Montrose Cl SN2 . . . . .34 E2
Monument Hill SN10. . 214 E1
Monument View SN11 .89 C7
Monxton Cl ⒊ SP1 . . 146 D5
Moody's Hill SP5 . . . . 155 E2
Moon Cl SN14 . . . . . . .75 B3
Moonraker Rise
BA13 . . . . 109 B3
Moonrakers SN10 . . . . 214 D5
Moor Barton SN13 . . . .84 D6
Moore Cl SN14 . . . . . . .64 C8
Moore's Pl ⒓ RG17 . . 177 B7
Moores Yd BA14 . . . . 104 C6
Moorgate GL7 . . . . . . .2 B4
MOOR GREEN 84 D6
Moorhen Cl
Swindon SN3 . . . . 51 E6
Trowbridge BA14 . . . . 101 D4
Moor Hill SP3 . . . . . . 204 D8
Moorings The SN1 . . . .50 A5
Moor La
Charlton Heath SN16. . 29 D6
Whiteparish SP5 . . . . 161 A1
Moor Lane SP5 . . . . . 160 F1

Moormead Rd SN4 . . . .64 B6
Moor Pk SN13 . . . . . . .84 C6
Moors Cl SN15 . . . . . . .70 C5
Moot Cl
⒎ Andover SP10 . . . 193 E2
Downton SP5 . . . . . . 211 B7
Moot Gdns SP5 . . . . . 211 A7
Moot La SP5 . . . . 211 A7
Moot (Motte & Bailey)
The ★ 211 B8
Mopes La SN5 . . . . . . .33 C7
Moray Rd SN2 . . . . . . .35 E1
MOREDON. 34 E3
Moredon Pk SN2 . . . . .34 D3
Moredon Prim Sch
SN2 . . . . .34 E3
Moredon Rd SN25 . . . .34 D3
Moresby Cl SN5 . . . . . .49 C6
Morgan's La
Pentridge SP5 . . . . . . 208 E5
Winterbourne SP4 . . . 133 A2
Morgans Rd SN11 . . . .89 C8
Morgans Rise Rd ⒊
SP5 . . . . 211 C8
Morgans Vale SO43 . . 212 D2
Morgans Vale Rd
SP5 . . . . 211 C7
Morgan's Vale &
Woodfalls CE Prim Sch
SP5 . . . . 211 C8
Morie Cl SN5 . . . . .34 B1
Morley Field BA12 . . . 117 C7
Morley Pl ⒛ RG17 . . . 177 B7
Morley St SN1 . . . . . . .50 C5
Morris Cl BA1 . . . . . . .82 B3
Morris La
Bath BA1 . . . . 82 B3
Devizes SN10 . . . . 214 B3
Morrison St SN2 . . . . . .49 F7
Morris Rd SN8 . . . . . . 213 D2
Morris St SN5 . . . . . . .49 E6
Morse Cl
Chippenham SN15 . . . .78 E4
Malmesbury SN16 . . . 28 A4
Morse Gdns SN5 . . . . .49 C6
Morse St SN1 . . . . .50 B5
Morstone Rd SN4 . . . . 61 D8
Mortimer Cl ⒌ SN5 . . .49 B7
Mortimer St BA14 . . . 105 C7
Mortimores SN14 . . . . .75 B2
Moses Mead SN25 . . . .34 A3
Moss Mead SN14 . . . . .77 F8
MOTCOMBE 202 A4
Motcombe CE VA Prim
Sch SP7 . . . . 202 A4
Motcombe Rd SP7. . . . 202 B3
Moulton Dr BA15 . . . . 100 D4
MOUNTAIN BOWER . . .66 F4
Mountain Wood BA1. . .82 B2
Mount Carmel Rd
SP11 . . . . 199 F3
Mountford Manor Prim
Sch SN3 . . . . .50 F6
Mount Hts SP5 . . . . . . 211 C8
Mountings The SN4. . . .64 B8
Mount La
Barford St Martin
SP3 . . . . 143 B4
Warminster BA12 . . . 117 A5
Mountpleasant SP3 . . 203 D8
Mount Pleasant
Atworth SN12 . . . . . . 85 A1
Atworth/Whitley SN12 . 93 A8
⒋ Bishopstone SN6 . 163 E6
Bradford-on-Avon
BA15 . . . . 100 D7
Chippenham SN14 . . . .70 A1
Kilmington BA12 . . . . 123 F4
Lechlade GL7 . . . . .2 C4
South Newton SP2 . . . 130 A4
Mountsfield BA11. . . . . 110 A4
MOUNT SORREL 205 B3
Mount The BA14 . . . . . 101 D2
Mowlems The BA14 . . 104 F3
Moxhams ⒛ SP6 . . . . 210 D1
Moyle Pk BA14 . . . . . . 102 A1
Moyne Cl SN10 . . . . . . 179 D8
Moyne Gdns ⒎ SP4 . 217 D2
Mucha Cl SN25 . . . . . .20 D1
Muddyford Rd
Downton SP5 . . . . . . 159 F1
Redlynch SP5 . . . . . . 211 C8
Mud La SN5 . . . . .32 F2
Mudmead La BA14 . . . 106 E8
Muirfield SN25 . . . . . . .34 D7
Mulberry Cl SN14 . . . . .70 B1
Mulberry Ct
Frome BA11 . . . . 110 B7
Sixpenny Handley SP5 . 208 B4
Mulberry Gr
Swindon SN2 . . . . 35 A2
Swindon SN25 . . . . . . 35 A2
Mulcaster Ave SN5 . . . .48 F5
Mullins Cl SN14 . . . . . .75 A3
Mundy Ave SN3 . . . . . .51 C4
Munks Cl ⒊ SP2 . . . . 151 E7
Munnings Ct ⒉
SP10 . . . . 193 D1
Munro Cl SN3 . . . . . . .50 E6
MURCOTT. 14 F4
Murdock Rd SN3 . . . . .51 E6
Murhill BA2 . . . . .99 C6
Murrayfield SN15 . . . . .70 E1
Murray Rd BA14 . . . . 101 D2

Murray Wlk SN12 . . . . . **94** B5
Muscott Cl **3** SP9 . . . . **199** C8
Muscovey Cl SN15 . . . . . . **60** A2
Mustang Cl **1** BA13 . . **168** A5
Mustang Way SN5 . . . . **34** C2
Mustard Way **7**
  SP11 . . . . **193** F2
Mustons La **28** SP7 . . **202** C2
Mycroft Rd **2** SN25 . . **34** D6
Myrrfield Rd **7** SP1 . **146** D5
Myrtle La BA12 . . . . . **116** F6
Myrtle Gdns SN2 . . . . . . **35** C2
Mythern Meadow
  BA15 . . . . **100** E5

N

Nadder Cl **13** SP3 . . . . **203** E8
Nadder La SP2 . . . . . . **144** F2
Nadder Rd SP9 . . . . . . **216** D6
Nadder Terr SP2 . . . . . **144** C2
Nahalsen Cl SP4 . . . . . **133** D6
Naini Tal Rd SP9 . . . . . **216** C6
Nantwich SN5 . . . . **49** A3
Napier Cl SP2 . . . . **50** A7
Napier Cres SP1 . . . . . **146** D1
Napiers **1** SN8 . . . . . **176** B3
Napier Wlk SP10 . . . . . **193** F1
Narrow Wine St
  BA14 . . . . **105** D8
Nash Cl **3** SN25 . . . . . **35** A8
Nash La SN15 . . . . **56** B1
Nash Rd SN8 . . . . **173** A8
National Monuments
  Records Ctr ★ SN2 . . **50** A7
Naughton Ave SN10 . . **214** E6
Naunton Rd SN3 . . . . . . **51** A6
Navigator Cl SP4 . . . . . **101** E4
Neal Cl **1** SP1 . . . . . . **146** C5
Neale Ct SN13 . . . . **76** F1
Neale's Barrow ★
  SP2 . . . . **150** A6
Neeld Cl SN14 . . . . **68** F6
Neeld Cres SN14 . . . . . . **78** B8
Neighbridge GL7 . . . . **5** F1
Neigh Bridge Ctry Pk ★
  GL7 . . . . **5** F2
Nell Hill SN6 . . . . **22** A7
Nelson Cl **1** SP4 . . . . **198** F6
Nelson Rd SP2 . . . . . . **146** A2
Nelson St SN1 . . . . **49** F5
Nelson Wlk SP10 . . . . . **193** F1
Nepaul Rd SP9 . . . . . . **216** C7
Neptune Cres **2** SN3 . **51** B8
Neptune Rd BA13 . . . . **108** F5
Nery Rd SP9 . . . . **216** D4
Ness Cl **1** SN5 . . . . . . **34** B2
Nestings The BA14 . . . . **105** A5
Nestleton Cl SN11 . . . . . **81** B1
NESTON **84** E6
Neston Cres SN13 . . . . . **84** E6
Neston Gdns SN13 . . . . . **84** B7
Neston Pk ★ SN13 . . . . **84** E3
Neston Prim Sch
  SN13 . . . . **84** E5
NETHERAVON **190** A3
Netheravon Cl SP1 . . . **146** B3
Netheravon Rd
  Durrington SP4 . . . . . **198** B7
  Figheldean SP4 . . . . . **190** B1
  Salisbury SP1 . . . . . . **146** A3
Nethercote Hill SN15 . . . **86** D6
NETHERHAMPTON . . . **151** A8
Netherhampton Bsns Ctr
  SP2 . . . . **151** A8
Netherhampton Rd
  Netherhampton SP2 . . **150** F8
  Quidhampton SP2 . . . **144** F1
Nether Leaze SN9 . . . . **215** B6
Nethermore SN13 . . . . . **84** D6
Netherstreet SN15 . . . . . **96** D6
NETHERTON **185** F4
Netherton Cl SN3 . . . . . **51** B4
Netherton Hill SP11 . . **185** F4
Netherton House ★
  SP11 . . . . **185** F4
Netherton Rd SP11 . . . **185** F4
Nettlebed Nursery **14**
  SP7 . . . . **202** C2
Nettlecombe **6** SP7 . **202** D2
Nettlemead La
  Deptford BA12 . . . . . **195** F1
  Wylye BA12 . . . . **201** F8
NETTLETON **53** C1
NETTLETON GREEN **53** B1
Nettleton Rd SN14 . . . . . **53** B3
NETTLETON SHRUB **67** C7
NETTON **131** E6
Netton Cl SP5 . . . . **205** E4
Netton St SP5 . . . . **205** E4
Nett Rd SP3 . . . . **196** F6
Nevil Cl SP4 . . . . **217** D1
Neville Cl SP1 . . . . **146** C4
Neville Terr SN15 . . . . . . **57** D1
Nevis Cl SN5 . . . . **34** B2
Newall Tuck Rd SN15 . . **78** F7
Newark Cl SN5 . . . . **49** B3
New Bottom Rd SP4 . . **145** E7
Newbourne Gdns
  SN14 . . . . **56** D6
New Bridge Cl **4** SN1 . **50** C7
New Bridge Rd SP1 . . . **152** A7
New Bridge Sq **5**
  SN1 . . . . **50** C7

New Broughton Rd
  SN12 . . . . **94** A5
New Brunswick Cl **4**
  SP4 . . . . **217** F8
Newburgh Pl SN6 . . . . . **22** F6
Newburn Cres SN1 . . . . **49** F5
NEWBURY **119** C8
Newbury Ave SN11 . . . . **80** F4
Newbury Dr
  Chippenham SN14 . . . . **77** F5
  Swindon SN5 . . . . **49** B3
Newbury Rd
  Andover SP10 . . . . . . **193** E2
  Lambourn RG17 . . . . . **165** B1
Newbury St RG17 . . . . **165** A1
Newby Acre SN8 . . . . . **213** D4
Newby Cl **3** SN10 . . **187** E8
New Canal SP1 . . . . . . **152** A8
Newcastle St SN1 . . . . . **50** D6
New Cl
  Bourton SP8 . . . . **137** E2
  West Knoyle BA12 . . . **140** E7
  West Knoyle SP3 . . . . **141** A8
New Close Prim Sch
  BA12 . . . . **117** B6
New Coll SN3 . . . . **50** F5
New Coll Wlk SN3 . . . . . **50** F5
Newcombe Dr SN2 . . . . . **50** A7
Newcombe Trad Est
  SN2 . . . . **50** B7
New Cres SP1 . . . . **192** A5
Newcroft Cl SN11 . . . . . **81** B4
Newcroft Rd SN11 . . . . . **81** B4
New Cut BA12 . . . . **139** A6
New Dro SP11 . . . . **192** A5
Newfield Cl BA13 . . . . **108** F4
New Forest CE Prim Sch
  The SP5 . . . . **212** C4
NEWGROUNDS **211** B1
New Haig Rd **2** SP4 . **198** E6
New Hall Hospl SP5 . . . **158** F8
Newhall St SN1 . . . . **50** B5
New Harnham Rd
  SP2 . . . . **152** A6
New Hayward Bottom
  RG17 . . . . **171** C2
New House La SP11 . . . **192** E4
Newhurst Pk BA14 . . . . **102** A2
Newill Cl SN26 . . . . **20** D1
New King Barrows ★
  SP4 . . . . **197** F5
New La
  Cann SP7 . . . . **202** D1
  Cann Common SP7 . . **206** A8
  Seend SN12 . . . . **178** D7
Newland Rd SN25 . . . . . **35** A3
Newlands Cl SN15 . . . . . **70** E7
Newlands Rd SN13 . . . . . **77** A1
New Lawns SN12 . . . . . . **94** B4
Newleaze
  Steeple Ashton BA14 . . **178** A4
  Trowbridge BA14 . . . . **101** F4
Newleaze Pk SN12 . . . . . **93** B4
Newlyn Cl SN26 . . . . **20** D1
Newman Rd SN10 . . . . **214** C1
Newmans View SN5 . . . . **34** A2
Newmans Way SP4 . . . **217** E2
Newmarket Ave
  BA14 . . . . **105** A4
Newmarket Cl **9**
  SN14 . . . . **77** F6
Newmeadow Copse
  SN5 . . . . **34** A1
Newton Farm La GL8 . . . . **13** C4
Newton Gr SN16 . . . . . . **27** E4
Newton Rd GL8 . . . . **13** A5
Newopaul Way
  Warminster BA12 . . . . **112** F1
  Warminster BA12 . . . . **116** F8
Newpark Rd
  Charlton Musgrove
    BA9 . . . . **136** F6
  Penselwood BA9 . . . . **137** A5
New Pk Rd SN10 . . . . . **214** B4
New Pk St SN10 . . . . . **214** A4
Newport BA12 . . . . **117** A7
Newport St SN1 . . . . . . **50** D3
New Rd
  Bath BA1 . . . . **82** C2
  Bourton SP8 . . . . **137** D1
  Bradford-on-Avon
    BA15 . . . . **100** E7
  Bromham SN15 . . . . . . **96** A5
  Calne SN11 . . . . **81** B2
  Calne Without SN11 . . . **79** F3
  Chippenham SN15 . . . . **78** D7
  Chiseldon SN4 . . . . **65** D3
  Codford BA12 . . . . . . **195** A3
  Donhead St Andrew
    SP7 . . . . **203** B4
  Durrington/Bulford
    SP4 . . . . **198** A4
  East Knoyle SP3 . . . . **141** B3
  Erlestoke BA13 . . . . . **179** A2
  Kilmington BA12 . . . . **123** D6
  Landford SP5 . . . . . . **212** D5
  Limpley Stoke BA2 . . . . **99** B5
  Maiden Bradley with
    Yarnfield BA11 . . . . **123** D8
  Marlborough SN8 . . . . **213** D3
  Melksham Without SN12 . **94** E7
  Purton SN5 . . . . **33** C5
  Rockbourne SP6 . . . . **210** A3
  Royal Wootton Bassett
    SN4 . . . . **47** D1
  2 Shaftesbury SP7 . . **202** B2
  1 Trowbridge BA14 . **105** D7
  Zeale SP8 . . . . **138** A3

New Rd Ct BA15 . . . . . **100** E7
New Severalls The
  SN9 . . . . **182** C7
Newson Rd
  8 Swindon SN25 . . . . **34** C5
  5 Swindon SN25 . . . . **34** D5
New St
  16 Market Lavington
    SN10 . . . . **179** F1
  Salisbury SP1 . . . . . . **152** A8
  Winterbourne Stoke
    SP3 . . . . **196** F3
Newstead Cl **1** SN25 . . **34** F6
New Terr BA14 . . . . **101** D6
New Terrace BA14 . . . . **101** D6
Newth's La SN5 . . . . **19** D2
NEWTON **161** B2
Newton Abbot Cl **6**
  SP2 . . . . **130** E3
Newton Cl SP5 . . . . . . **161** C3
NEWTON GROVE **27** E4
Newton La SP5 . . . . . . **161** B3
Newton Rd SP2 . . . . . . **145** D1
Newtons Wlk SN8 . . . . **170** B8
NEWTON TONY **199** B3
Newton Tony CE Prim
  Sch SP4 . . . . **199** B3
Newton Way SN2 . . . . . . **35** C4
NEWTOWN
  Shalbourne **176** E2
  West Tisbury **203** B7
Newtown
  Bradford-on-Avon
    BA15 . . . . **100** C6
  Broad Chalke SP5 . . . **205** C4
  Heytesbury BA12 . . . . **194** C5
  Hullavington SN14 . . . . **41** F1
  Trowbridge BA14 . . . . **105** C8
  Westbury BA13 . . . . . **109** C3
NEW TOWN
  Alton **173** D3
  Farnham **207** C2
  Ramsbury **170** C2
  Sixpenny Handley **207** F6
  Swindon **50** D6
Newtown Com Prim Sch
  BA14 . . . . **105** C8
Newtown La
  Hinton Charterhouse
    BA2 . . . . **98** F1
  Hinton Charterhouse
    BA2 . . . . **103** A8
New Town La SN6 . . . . **163** E6
Newtown Rd SN8 . . . . **170** C2
New Ward Rd SP4 . . . . **198** E7
New Zealand Ave
  SP2 . . . . **145** D2
Niblett St BA15 . . . . . . **100** E6
Nicholas St SN1 . . . . . . **50** C2
Nicolson Cl **6** SP4 . . **217** E3
Nicolson Vale SP4 . . . . **132** B1
Niebull Cl SN16 . . . . **28** A5
Nightingale Ave
  Melksham SN12 . . . . . . **94** D4
  8 West Wellow SO51 . **212** F6
Nightingale Cl
  Melksham SN12 . . . . . . **94** D4
  8 West Wellow SO51 . **212** F6
Nightingale Dr BA13 . . **109** B4
Nightingale La
  South Marston SN3 . . . . **36** F4
  Tisbury SP3 . . . . **203** C6
Nightingale Rd BA14 . . **105** A8
Nightingale Way
  5 Calne SN11 . . . . . . **81** B5
  South Cerney GL7 . . . . . **7** A6
Nightingale Wlk SP2 . . **145** E2
Nightjar Cl SN12 . . . . . . **94** D4
Nightwood Copse **3**
  SN5 . . . . **34** A1
Nindum Rd SN3 . . . . **36** C1
Nine Acre Dr SN13 . . . . . **76** D1
NINE ELMS **49** A8
Nine Elms La SN5 . . . . . **48** F8
Nive Rd SN4 . . . . **168** E8
Noade St SP5 . . . . **206** E4
Nobles Pl **5** SN3 . . . . **76** C1
Noble St SN16 . . . . **40** C8
Nocton Rd SN4 . . . . **64** E3
Noctule Ave BA14 . . . . **106** A8
Nolan Cl **1** SN25 . . . . **34** B8
Nolands Rd SN11 . . . . **166** D2
NOMANSLAND **212** C4
Norbin
  South Wraxall BA15 . . . **83** F1
  South Wraxall BA15 . . . **91** F8
  South Wraxall BA13 . . . **84** A2
Norborne Rd SN4 . . . . **167** C2
Norcliffe Rd SN3 . . . . . . **51** B4
Noredown Way SN4 . . . . **47** E1
Noremarsh Com Jun Sch
  SN4 . . . . **47** E1
Nore Marsh Rd SN4 . . . . **47** E1
Norfolk Cl **1** SN3 . . . . **50** F6
Norfolk Rd SP2 . . . . . . **151** E7
NORLEAZE **108** F8
Norley La SN11 . . . . **80** C3
Norman Cl SN11 . . . . . . **79** A4
Norman Dr
  Old Sarum SP4 . . . . . . **146** C8
  Winterbourne SP4 . . . **132** C1
Normandy Rd
  Overtown SN4 . . . . **64** E3
  South Tidworth SP9 . . **216** D4
Normandy Way **14**
  SP6 . . . . **210** D1
Norman Rd SN2 . . . . **35** C1

NORMANTON **197** F3
Norney Rd BA13 . . . . . **179** A4
Norridge View **4**
  BA12 . . . . **116** E7
NORRINGTON
  COMMON **93** C6
Norrington Gate SN12 . **93** C5
Norrington Green
  SN12 . . . . **93** C6
Norrington La SN12 . . . **93** C6
Norrington Manor ★
  SP5 . . . . **204** A2
Norris Cl SN4 . . . . **65** C3
Norris Rd BA14 . . . . . . **102** B3
Northacre Ind Est
  BA13 . . . . **108** D5
Northampton St SN1 . . . **50** D6
North Bank Rise SN4 . . . **47** F2
Northbourne Rd SN25 . **35** A7
NORTH BRADLEY **105** D4
North Bradley CE Prim
  Sch BA14 . . . . **105** D2
NORTH BREWHAM **122** A6
NORTHBROOK **179** E1
Northbrook SN10 . . . . . **179** F1
Northbrook Cl **1**
  SN10 . . . . **179** F1
Northbrook Rd
  Melksham SN12 . . . . . . **93** F7
  Swindon SN25 . . . . **35** A1
North Cft SP3 . . . . **188** B3
NORTH CHARFORD . . . **211** C6
North Charford Crossing
  SP6 . . . . **210** F6
North Charford Dro
  SP6 . . . . **210** C8
North Comm La SP5 . . **212** B7
North Cote SN11 . . . . . . **81** A4
Northcote Cres **7**
  BA11 . . . . **110** A7
Northcroft Rd **1**
  SN13 . . . . **76** B1
North Down
  Hurstbourne Tarrant
    SP11 . . . . **185** F1
  Hurstbourne Tarrant
    SP11 . . . . **185** F2
North Dr **4** SN25 . . . . **34** F8
Northen Cl GL7 . . . . **10** E6
NORTHEND **82** A5
Northend BA1 . . . . **82** A5
NORTH END **6** E2
North End
  Ashton Keynes SN6 . . . . **6** E1
  Calne SN11 . . . . **81** A4
North End Gdns SN16 . . **25** C1
Northen Terr
  Durrington SP4 . . . . . **197** F7
  Larkhill SP4 . . . . **198** A7
Northern Rd SN2 . . . . . . **35** A1
North Farm Cl RG17 . . **165** B2
Northfield BA15 . . . . **99** F7
Northfield La SN14 . . . . . **66** A2
Northfields
  Bulkington SN10 . . . . **178** E5
  Calne SN11 . . . . **81** A4
Northfield Way SN3 . . . . **51** B7
Northgate Gdns
  SN10 . . . . **214** A4
Northgate St SN10 . . . **214** A4
North La
  Nomansland SP5 . . . . **212** C4
  Warminster BA12 . . . . **116** D4
  West Tytherley SP5 . . **149** F5
Northlands Ind Est
  BA12 . . . . **117** B7
Northleaze SN13 . . . . . . **76** D1
North Leaze Cl SN2 . . . . **34** F3
Northleigh BA15 . . . . **91** E1
Northleigh Terr SP2 . . . **144** D3
Northmoor La GL7 . . . . . . **6** B8
NORTH NEWTON **181** E4
North Rd
  Amesbury SP4 . . . . . . **217** E2
  Ashmore SP5 . . . . . . **206** E5
  Mere BA12 . . . . **139** A6
North Row BA12 . . . . . **117** A7
Northside SP4 . . . . **146** D8
North St
  Broad Chalke SP5 . . . **205** B4
  Calne SN11 . . . . **81** B4
  Mere BA12 . . . . **139** A5
  Pewsey SN9 . . . . **215** C5
  Salisbury SP2 . . . . . . **145** F1
  Swindon SN1 . . . . **50** C5
  Wilton SP2 . . . . **144** C3
North Standen Rd
  RG17 . . . . **177** A6
North Star Ave SN2 . . . . **50** B8
North Star Ind Est
  SN2 . . . . **50** B7
NORTH STREET **210** E5
NORTH TIDWORTH . . . **216** D8
Northview **20** RG17 . . **177** B7
North View
  Berwick St James
    SP3 . . . . **196** F2
  Highworth SN6 . . . . . . **22** F5
North View Hts RG17 . **177** C7
North View Pl SN8 . . . **213** D4
Northview Prim Sch
  SN6 . . . . **23** F5
North Wall SN6 . . . . **19** D8
Northway SP4 . . . . **134** B7

North Way
  Calne SN11 . . . . **81** A4
  Trowbridge BA14 . . . . **105** A7
North Wlk SP1 . . . . . . **152** A8
Northwood SN15 . . . . . . **70** E2
NORTH WRAXALL **67** B3
NORTH WROUGHTON . . **64** B8
NORTON **41** D5
NORTON BAVANT **194** A6
Norton Dr SP4 . . . . . . **146** D6
NORTON FERRIS **124** C4
Norton Gr SN3 . . . . **50** D5
Norton Rd
  Sutton Veny BA12 . . . **117** C1
  Sutton Veny BA12 . . . **194** A5
Norwood Castle (site
  of) ★ SN16 . . . . **4** F2
Norwood Cl **3** SN3 . . . **51** D4
NOTTON **86** B8
Notton House Sch
  SN15 . . . . **86** B8
Notton Pk
  Lacock SN14 . . . . **78** A1
  Notton SN15 . . . . **86** B8
  Thingley SN14 . . . . **77** F2
Nova Hroed Acad SN2 . **34** D2
Noyes Cl
  Chippenham SN14 . . . . **77** F8
  Haydon Wick SN5 . . . . . **34** C5
N Swindon District Ctr
  SN2 . . . . **34** E6
Nuffield Cl SN5 . . . . **49** B8
Nunns Pk SP5 . . . . **161** D4
NUNTON **152** D1
Nunton Dro SP5 . . . . . **152** D1
Nunwick Way **4** SN1 . **50** A2
Nurseries The
  Christian Malford
    SN15 . . . . **58** A2
  Swindon SN1 . . . . **50** B4
Nursery Cl
  4 Amesbury SP4 . . . **217** B3
  Atworth/Whitley SN12 . . **92** E8
  Trowbridge BA14 . . . . **102** A3
  Wroughton SN4 . . . . . . **64** A5
Nursery Gdns
  Corsham SN13 . . . . **85** A8
  Mere BA12 . . . . **139** A5
Nursery Rd
  Colerne SN14 . . . . **75** A3
  Salisbury SP2 . . . . . . **145** E1
  Siddington GL7 . . . . **6** B8
Nursery The SN16 . . . . . **27** F6
NURSTEED **214** E1
Nursteed Cl SN10 . . . . **214** D2
Nursteed Com Prim Sch
  SN10 . . . . **214** C1
Nursteed Pk SN10 . . . . **214** D2
Nursteed Rd SN10 . . . . **214** C2
Nursteed Rd Ind Est
  SN10 . . . . **214** C1
NUTBANE **193** A4
Nutbane La SP11 . . . . . **193** A4
Nuthatch Cl **4** SN3 . . . **51** E6
Nuthatch Rd SN11 . . . . . **81** B4
Nutley Ct **8** SN8 . . . . **183** D8
Nutmeg Cl **7** SN2 . . . . **34** D4
Nyland Rd SN3 . . . . **51** C7
Nyland Sch SN3 . . . . **51** B7
NYTHE **51** C7
Nythe Rd SN3 . . . . **36** B1

O

Oakapple Cl **4** SN4 . . **163** B6
Oak Ash Gn SP2 . . . . . **144** C2
Oak Ave GL8 . . . . **24** F7
Oakbournes The **5**
  SP1 . . . . **146** C5
Oak Cl
  Bishops Cannings
    SN10 . . . . **172** B2
  Calne SN11 . . . . **81** A3
  Pitton & Farley SP5 . . **154** E7
  South Newton SP2 . . . **130** B2
  Tidworth SP9 . . . . . . **216** E7
Oak Dr
  Alderbury SP5 . . . . . . **153** D2
  Highworth SN6 . . . . . . **22** F5
  Trowbridge BA14 . . . . **105** C3
Oakes Cl SP4 . . . . **133** C4
Oakes Ct **9** RG17 . . . **177** B7
Oakes La GL9 . . . . **52** B5
Oakford La SN14 . . . . . . **74** B2
Oakford Wlk SN3 . . . . . . **51** A6
Oak Gdns SN3 . . . . **36** A4
Oakham Cl SN5 . . . . **49** C5
Oak Hill SN8 . . . . **176** E6
Oakhurst Com Prim Sch
  SN25 . . . . **34** B7
Oakhurst Way
  Swindon SN25 . . . . **34** B8
  Swindon SN25 . . . . **34** C7
Oakie Cl SN25 . . . . **35** A5
Oak La
  Easterton SN10 . . . . . **179** F2
  Figheldean SP4 . . . . . **190** B2
  Mere BA12 . . . . **139** A4
Oaklands SN15 . . . . **70** D2
Oaklands Cl **12** SP6 . **210** D1
Oaklea La SP5 . . . . **153** E2
Oakleaze SN16 . . . . **17** B2
Oakleigh Dr SP5 . . . . . **212** C5
Oakley Bsns Pk SP3 . . **201** E5
Oakley Flats GL7 . . . . . . **10** D6
Oakley La
  Farnham DT11 . . . . . . **207** D2

Oakley La continued
  Sixpenny Handley SP5 . **208** B4
Oakley Rd SP2 . . . . . . **144** F4
Oak Lodge Cl SN14 . . . . **78** C8
Oak Pk BA14 . . . . **104** F5
Oak Pl SP4 . . . . **217** C4
Oak Rd
  Chippenham Without
    SN14 . . . . **77** B8
  Colerne SN14 . . . . **74** F5
  Down Ampney GL7 . . . . . **8** E6
OAKSEY **15** F7
Oaksey CE Prim Sch
  SN16 . . . . **16** A8
Oaksey Rd
  Minety SN16 . . . . **16** C4
  Somerford Keynes SN16 . **5** E1
  Swindon SN2 . . . . **35** C4
Oak St GL7 . . . . **2** C1
Oaks The
  Chippenham SN15 . . . . **70** D2
  Coate SN3 . . . . **51** A2
  Kemble GL7 . . . . **4** F7
  Warminster BA12 . . . . **117** A8
Oak Tree Ave SN2 . . . . . **35** D3
Oak Tree Bsns Pk SN3 . **36** C7
Oak Tree Cl BA14 . . . . **101** B1
Oak Tree Prim Sch
  SN3 . . . . **51** A4
Oak Way GL7 . . . . **6** F6
Oakwood Dr SN12 . . . . . **94** B4
Oakwood Gr SP5 . . . . . **153** D3
Oakwood Rd SN5 . . . . . . **49** C7
Oamaru Way SN10 . . . . **214** D3
OARE **174** B2
Oare Hill SN8 . . . . **174** C2
Oare Prim Sch SN8 . . . **174** B2
Oasis Acad BA14 . . . . **105** D7
Oasis Leisure Ctr SN2 . **50** B7
Oasthouse Cl **3** SN5 . . **49** A8
Oate Hill SN15 . . . . **78** F6
Oatfields BA14 . . . . . . **101** D4
Oathill La GL7 . . . . **3** B8
Oathills SN13 . . . . **84** F8
Oatlands SN5 . . . . **48** F4
Oatmeal Row **5** SP1 . **152** A8
Oat Rd **12** SP1 . . . . . **193** F2
Oatway Rd SP9 . . . . . . **216** D8
Obelisk Terr **6** BA12 . **116** F7
Oberon Way SN25 . . . . . **35** A5
Ocotal Way SN1 . . . . . . **50** D8
Oddford Vale **17** SP3 . **203** E8
O'Donnell Cl SN15 . . . . . **70** E1
ODSTOCK **152** A1
Odstock Rd
  Britford SP2 . . . . **152** B4
  Swindon SN2 . . . . **35** C6
Offerton Rd **3** SN1 . . . **50** A2
Ogbourne SN14 . . . . **75** B3
OGBOURNE MAIZEY . . **213** C7
Ogbourne Rd SN8 . . . . **169** E6
OGBOURNE ST
  ANDREW **168** F3
OGBOURNE ST
  GEORGE **169** A5
Ogbourne St George & St
  Andrew CE Prim Sch (Controlled)
  SN8 . . . . **168** F5
Ogbury Camp ★ SP4 . . **198** A1
Ogilvie Sq SN11 . . . . . . **81** C3
Okebourne Pk SN3 . . . . **51** C3
Okeford Cl SN3 . . . . **51** C7
OKUS **50** A4
Okus Gr SN2 . . . . **35** D4
Okus Rd SN1 . . . . **49** F3
Okus Trad Est SN3 . . . . . **50** A4
Olaf Cl **10** SP10 . . . . **193** E2
Old Alexander Rd
  SN16 . . . . **27** F4
Old Bakery Cl SN16 . . . . **28** F2
Old Barn BA15 . . . . **91** E8
Old Batch The BA15 . . **100** B8
Old Bath Rd
  Cherhill SN11 . . . . **166** D1
  Cherhill SN11 . . . . **172** D8
Old Beasants SN8 . . . . **174** A6
Old Blandford Rd
  SP2 . . . . **151** F6
Old Boundary Rd **5**
  SP7 . . . . **202** C1
Oldbrick Fields BA14 . . **105** A5
Old Brickyard Rd
  SP6 . . . . **210** B1
Old Broughton Rd
  SN12 . . . . **94** A5
Oldbury Castle (Hill
  Fort) ★ SN11 . . . . . . **172** C8
OLDBURY ON THE
  HILL **24** B5
Oldbury Prior SN11 . . . . **81** C1
Oldbury Way SN11 . . . . . **81** A3
Old Castle Rd SP1 . . . . **146** A5
Old Chapel Cl SP5 . . . . **153** D3
Old Chase Rd SN8 . . . . **169** A4
Old Coach Rd
  Durrington/Bulford
    SP4 . . . . **217** D2
  North Wraxall SN14 . . . . **67** D2
  Shipton Bellinger SP11 . **191** F1
Old Coach Works **19**
  RG17 . . . . **165** A1
Old Comm Way **13**
  SP11 . . . . **192** A5
Old Cranborne Rd
  BH21 . . . . **209** B3
Old Cranbourne Rd
  SP6 . . . . **209** C5

Old Ct SN4 47 D1
Old Dairy Cl
Bermerton Heath SP2 145 C3
Swindon SN2 35 E3
Old Dairy Ct SN12 94 C5
Old Dairy Dr The SN14 68 B7
Old Dairy La SN4 167 B2
Old Dairy The
Amesbury SP4 217 C5
Nunton SP5 152 D1
Old Derry Hill SN15 79 D2
Old Dilton BA13 112 D6
Old Dilton Rd BA13 112 E7
Old Down Rd GL9 52 C8
Olde Fairfield SP8 138 A2
Oldenburg Cl SN5 34 C2
Oldenburgh Rd 3 BA13 108 E1
Old English Dr 2 SP10 193 D2
Old Estate Yd The GL7 8 D7
Old Farm Cl
Hankerton SN16 15 C2
Hullavington SN14 41 F1
Old Farmhouse / Cotswold Community The SN6 6 C4
Old Farmhouse The SN10 214 C1
Old Farm Rd BA14 105 F7
Oldfield Pk BA13 108 E3
Oldfield Rd
Salisbury SP1 146 C5
Westbury BA13 108 E4
Oldford Hill BA11 110 A8
Old Forge Cl
Brinkworth SN15 45 E6
Heytesbury BA12 194 C5
Old Granary La SP4 217 B3
Old Hardenhuish La SN14 70 B1
Oldhat Barrow★ SN9 183 A3
Old Hayward La RG17 171 B1
Old Hollow BA12 139 B6
Old Hospl Rd SN9 215 B6
Old Hungerford La SP11 185 C5
Old Jockey SN13 83 F3
Old King Barrows★ SP4 197 F5
Old Lady La SN26 21 B1
Oldlands Wlk SN3 51 A3
Old Malmesbury Rd SN4 47 E4
Old Malthouse La SP4 147 B7
Old Manor House★ BA12 194 A4
Old Mdws Wlk SP2 151 E7
Old Midford Rd BA2 98 A7
Old Mill Farm La GL7 5 E4
Old Mill Gdns SP2 151 E7
Old Mill La SN3 50 D3
Old Oak Cl 5 SP11 193 F2
Old Orch The SN16 28 A6
Old Post Office La 5 SP4 190 A3
Old Pound Ct SP8 137 D1
Old Railway Cl GL7 2 D5
Old Rd
Alderbury SP5 153 C4
Chippenham SN15 78 D8
Derry Hill/Studley SN11 80 B2
Old Rly Cl 1 SN16 28 A4
Old Ropeworks The★ SN8 213 E2
Old Sarum★ SP1 145 F6
Old Sarum Barracks SP4 146 C8
Old Sarum Bsns Pk SP4 146 C8
Old Sarum Pk SP4 146 D8
Old Sarum Prim Sch SP4 146 C8
Old Sawmills The RG17 177 F3
Old Sawmill The BA12 123 F5
Old Sch Cl SN15 96 C7
Old Sch Ct SN3 51 B6
Old School Cl SP4 190 A3
Old School Ct SN14 74 A8
Old School Dr 33 SP11 192 A5
Old Sch Yd SN13 85 A8
Old Severalls The SN9 182 E7
Old Shaftesbury (Shaston) Dro
Bishopstone SP2 150 A6
Harnham SP2 151 D5
Netherhampton SP2 151 A5
Old Shaftesbury (Shaston) Drove SP5 150 E5
Old Shaw La SN5 48 F8
Oldsodbury Rd GL9 52 F6
Old Sodbury Rd GL9 52 F6
Old Sodom La SN15 59 B8
Old St SP2 152 A6
Old Sta Yd The 14 RG17 165 A1
Old Surgery Cl SN5 33 C4
OLD TOWN 50 D3
Old Track BA2 98 F7
Old Vicarage La
Alderbury SP5 153 C1
Kemble GL7 4 F7
Swindon SN3 36 F4
Old Vineries The 10 SP6 210 C1
Old Wardour Castle★ SP3 203 D5
Old Ward Rd 5 SP4 198 E6
Old Were Ct 3 BA12 117 A7
Old Yard SN10 187 D8
Olive Gr SN2 35 B3
Olivemead La SN15 45 C1
Oliver Ave SN13 76 F2
Oliver Cl SN5 48 F6
Oliver's Castle (Fort)★ SN10 97 C6
Olivers Cl SN11 166 B1
Olivers Ct SN11 89 C8
Olivers Hill SN11 166 B1
Oliver's La 5 SN16 28 A3
Oliver Tomkins CE Jun & Inf Sch SN5 49 B5
Olivier Cl SP2 145 C5
Olivier Rd
Swindon SN25 35 B6
Wilton SP2 144 B5
Olympiad L Ctr★ SN15 78 E8
Olympian Rd SN9 215 B5
Olympia The SN8 168 E3
Olympic Pk Rd 30 SP11 193 E2
Omar Rd SN13 84 F6
Omdurman St SN2 35 B1
One Sch Global Salisbury Campus SP2 144 B4
Ontario Way 6 SP4 217 F8
Onyx Cl 2 SN25 34 F8
Opal Rd SN26 21 A1
Orange Cl SN6 23 A6
Orbital Rd
Wroughton SN4 63 F3
Wroughton SN4 167 F8
Wroughton SN4 168 A8
Orbital Sh Pk SN25 34 E6
Orchard Cl
Calne SN11 81 C2
Devizes SN10 214 B1
34 Fordingbridge SP6 210 D1
Kemble GL7 4 F7
Lechlade GL7 2 B4
5 Ramsbury SN8 170 B2
2 Wanborough SN4 163 A6
Warminster BA12 117 B8
West Ashton BA14 106 B4
Westbury BA13 112 C8
Westwood BA15 99 F3
Orchard Cres SN14 78 B7
Orchard Ct
17 Bratton BA13 186 A7
St Paul Malmesbury Without SN16 28 A2
Orchard Dr BA14 104 E2
Orchard End SP4 217 D8
Orchard Gdns
6 Bradford-on-Avon BA15 100 D6
Melksham SN12 94 A3
Purton SN5 33 A3
Orchard Gr
Bromham SN15 96 D7
Swindon SN2 35 D3
Orchard Mead 3 SN4 48 A2
Orchard Pk Cl 3 RG17 177 B6
Orchard Pl SN10 187 E8
Orchard Rd
Chippenham SN14 78 B7
Corsham SN13 77 A2
Marlborough SN8 213 E2
Redlynch SP5 211 C8
Salisbury SP2 145 D2
Trowbridge BA14 105 D7
Westbury BA13 109 A3
Orchard Terr 3 SP3 201 E2
Orchard The
Chirton SN10 180 F4
Chiseldown SN4 65 E4
Kington St Michael SN14 70 A8
Limpley Stoke BA2 99 C5
Salisbury SP1 146 C2
Semington BA14 102 F6
Sixpenny Handley SP5 208 B4
Upton Scudamore BA12 112 F4
Orchard Way
Amesbury SP4 217 C3
Longbridge Deverill BA12 116 E1
Trowbridge BA14 105 C3
ORCHESTON 196 D8
Orchid Cl SN25 35 C3
Orchid Dr 30 SP11 192 A5
Orchids The SN15 70 E2
Orchid Vale Prim Sch SN25 34 D6
Orchid Vw 17 SP7 202 D1
Ordnance La SP11 192 E1
Ordnance Rd SP9 216 D6
Orford Rd SP4 217 D2
Oriel Cl BA14 102 A4
Orkney Cl SN5 49 B7
Orlando Cl 4 SN5 48 F5
Orpen Cl SN3 50 E2
Orpington Way BA14 102 B1
Orrin Cl SN5 34 B1
Orwell Cl
Malmesbury SN16 28 A5
Orwell Cl *continued*
Swindon SN25 35 A5
Osborne Rd BA14 101 E3
Osborne St SN2 50 B8
Oslings La BA1 82 B2
Osmund Cl SN10 214 D3
Osmund Rd SN10 214 D2
Osprey Cl
Bower Hill SN12 94 D1
Swindon SN3 51 E6
Osprey Rd BA12 116 D5
Osterley Rd SN25 34 E6
Otford Cl SN5 48 F4
Otter Row 7 SN3 51 B8
Otter Way SN4 47 F2
OUTMARSH 102 F7
OUTWICK 210 D4
Overbrook SN3 51 C3
Overhouse Dr 12 SP3 203 E8
Over St SP3 129 D7
Overton Gdns SN3 36 B2
OVERTOWN 64 D4
Overtown Hill SN4 64 C5
Overway La SP7 203 B2
Owen Cl SN10 214 D3
Owen Ct SN3 36 A1
Owl Cl
Swindon SN3 51 E6
Warminster BA12 116 D5
Owlets The SN3 51 E6
Owlswood 9 SP2 152 A5
Ox Dro
Ashmore SP5 206 D7
Ashmore SP5 206 E7
Barford St Martin SP3 143 A6
Berwick St John SP5 207 B7
Bishopstone SP5 205 F2
Bower Chalke SP5 208 A8
Broad Chalke SP5 205 C1
Kimpton SP11 192 A1
Teffont SP3 201 C5
Wilton SP2 144 A5
Ox Drove
Alvediston SP5 207 F8
Chicklade SP3 200 B5
Dinton SP3 142 C7
Dinton SP3 201 E5
Homington SP5 157 A3
Oxencroft 8 SP7 202 C2
Oxenden Cl BA13 109 B5
Oxendene BA12 113 F2
OXENWOOD 184 E6
Oxford Ct SN11 81 B3
Oxford Gdns BA14 101 F1
Oxford Mws 6 BA13 109 A3
Oxford Rd
Calne SN11 81 B3
Swindon SN3 36 A1
Upavon Down SN9 182 B2
Oxford St
Aldbourne SN8 170 A6
Deanend SP5 207 E5
Hungerford RG17 177 C8
Lambourn RG17 165 A1
Malmesbury SN16 28 A3
Marlborough SN8 213 D3
Ramsbury SN8 170 B2
Swindon SN1 50 B6
Oxleaze La SN16 15 B2
Oxon Pl SN6 163 E6
Ox Path The SN8 174 B2
Ox Row 4 SP1 152 A8
Oxyard BA12 195 B2
Ox Yd GL7 3 C8

P

Pack Hill SN4 51 F2
Pack Horse SN5 33 D8
Packhorse Bridge★ SN15 86 E5
Packhorse La SN5 33 E8
Pack Horse La BA2 98 A7
Packington Cl SN5 49 B7
Packway The
Durrington SP4 197 D7
Shrewton SP3 197 A7
Paddington Dr SN5 49 E5
Paddock Cl
Enford SN9 190 A6
Great Somerford SN15 44 A2
4 Shaftesbury SP7 202 D1
Sixpenny Handley SP5 208 A3
Swindon SN25 34 E5
Winterbourne SP4 133 B2
Paddock End SN14 70 A7
Paddock La
Chilmark SP3 200 F2
Corsham SN13 84 D8
Paddocks The
10 Aldbourne SN8 170 A6
Chippenham SN15 78 E6
Mere BA12 139 A5
14 Ramsbury SN8 170 B2
5 Swindon SN3 36 A2
Westbury BA13 109 A4
Paddock The
5 Bradford-on-Avon BA15 100 D6
Highworth SN6 23 A5
Market Lavington SN10 180 A1
8 Tisbury SP3 203 E8
Paddock Way SP1 146 E2
Paddock Wood 13 SP4 198 B7
Padfield Gdns SN12 93 F1
Padstow Rd SN5 49 F5
Page Cl
Calne SN11 81 C3
Chippenham SN14 78 A7
Paget Cl SP9 216 B8
Pagnell La SN10 179 D1
Pagoda Pk SN5 49 D7
Pains Hill SO51 162 F7
Pains Way 8 SP4 217 C2
Painters Mead BA14 102 A2
Pakenham Rd SN3 51 B4
Palairet Cl BA15 100 D4
Palestine Rd SP11 199 F3
Palmer Dr BA15 100 D8
Palmer Gr BA14 102 F6
Palmer Rd
Devizes SN10 214 C5
Salisbury SP2 145 E2
Trowbridge BA14 101 D2
Palmer St SN14 78 C7
Palmerston Meadow SN9 190 A6
Palmers Way 11 SN4 163 A6
Palm Rd SN14 75 A5
Palomino Pl
Swindon SN5 34 B2
7 Westbury Leigh BA13 108 E1
Pampas Ct 1 BA12 116 E6
Pans La SN10 214 B2
Panters Rd SP3 204 C8
Pantiles The 12 SP6 210 C1
Pantry Bridge BA14 178 D5
Parade The
Marlborough SN8 213 D3
Swindon SN1 50 C6
Paradise La
Longbridge Deverill BA12 116 E1
Rowde SN10 96 E2
Parham La SN10 179 E2
Parhams Ct SN4 47 E2
Parhams Hill SP7 203 B1
Parham Wlk 7 SN5 48 F5
Park Ave
Chippenham SN14 78 B8
Corsham SN13 84 A8
Highworth SN6 23 A5
Park Cl
Calne SN11 81 C2
Malmesbury SN16 27 F4
Salisbury SP1 146 A4
Trowbridge BA14 105 D3
PARK CORNER 99 A4
Park Dr SP3 201 B3
Park End SN6 17 F8
Parkers Cl SP5 159 A1
Parkers La SN15 70 D6
Park Field SN10 214 C5
Park Fields SN15 78 C8
Parkhouse Cnr SP4 199 D6
Parkhouse Rd SP9 199 C8
Park La
Castle Combe SN14 68 A7
Cherhill SN11 166 C1
Chippenham SN15 78 D8
Corsham SN13 76 D1
Great Somerford SN15 44 A2
Heytesbury BA12 194 D5
Heywood BA13 109 C7
Lea & Cleverton SN16 29 D3
Lydiard Millicent SN5 48 D7
Malmesbury SN16 27 E5
North Wraxall SN14 68 A2
Odstock SP5 152 D4
Salisbury SP1 146 A3
Sutton Benger SN15 57 D2
Swindon SN1 50 A6
West Dean SP5 149 F1
Parklands
Malmesbury SN16 27 E4
Trowbridge BA14 101 D2
Parklands Rd SN3 50 D5
Parklands The SN14 55 E8
Parkland Way SP4 133 D6
Park Mead SN16 27 F4
PARK NORTH 51 A5
Park Pl SN6 6 F1
Park Rd
Fordingbridge SP6 210 D1
Malmesbury SN16 27 F4
Market Lavington SN10 179 E1
Rushall SN9 181 F3
Salisbury SP1 146 D2
Shrewton SP3 196 F6
Shrewton SP3 197 A6
Tidworth SP9 216 D5
Tisbury SP3 203 E8
Trowbridge BA14 105 D8
Westbury BA13 112 B8
Parkside
Chippenham SN15 78 D8
Swindon SN3 36 A3
PARK SOUTH 51 A4
Park Springs SN5 49 C5
Park St
Charlton SN16 29 A6
Heytesbury BA12 194 C5
Hungerford RG17 177 B7
Salisbury SP1 146 B2
Swindon SN3 36 C2
Trowbridge BA14 105 C7
Parkstone Wlk SN3 51 B3
Park Terr SN15 78 C8
Park The
Erlestoke SN10 179 A1
8 Lambourn RG17 165 A2
Park View
Chirton SN10 180 F4
Devizes SN10 179 D8
Park View Dr
Lydiard Millicent SN5 48 D8
1 Westbury BA13 108 F1
Park Vw Point DT11 207 A3
Parkwater Rd SP5 161 E1
Park Way RG17 177 B6
Parliament Row SN16 28 A2
Parliament St SN14 78 B7
Parr Cl SN5 49 A6
Parsley Cl SN2 34 D5
Parsloes Cl SN4 64 E3
Parsonage Cl
31 Fordingbridge SP6 210 D1
Salisbury SP1 145 E5
Parsonage Down National Nature Reserve★ SP3 196 D5
Parsonage Gn SP2 151 E6
Parsonage Hill SP5 154 D7
Parsonage La
Charlton Musgrove BA9 136 C2
Hungerford RG17 177 B7
9 Lambourn RG17 165 A1
20 Market Lavington SN10 179 F1
Parsonage Pk Dr 3 SP6 210 D1
Parsonage Pl 9 RG17 165 A2
Parsonage Rd
Amesbury SP4 217 B3
Swindon SN3 36 A3
Trowbridge BA14 102 A1
Parsonage The SP5 208 B4
Parsonage Vale SN8 183 D2
Parsonage Way SN15 70 F1
Parsons Cl SP4 133 D5
Parsons Gn 4 SP3 196 E6
Parsons La BA12 116 E2
Parson's La SN6 22 B7
Parsons Pl SN26 20 B1
Parsons Pool 19 SP7 202 C2
Parsons Way SN4 47 E1
Partridge Cl
Chippenham SN14 70 B2
4 Corsham SN13 76 E1
Swindon SN3 51 E6
Partridge Hill SP5 212 E6
Partridge Way SP4 146 C8
Passmore Cl SN3 51 E7
Pasteur Dr SN1 50 A3
Pasture Cl SN2 49 E7
Pastures The BA15 99 E3
Pasture Wlk 19 SP11 193 F2
Patchway SN14 78 B8
Patchway The SN10 214 D3
Pathfinder Way
Bowerhill SN12 94 C2
5 Swindon SN25 34 B7
PATNEY 180 F5
Patney Rd SN10 180 F5
Paton Cl GL7 1 E7
Pat-yat GL7 4 B5
Paulet Cl 3 SN5 49 A4
Pauls Croft SN6 19 D7
Paul's Dene Cres SP1 146 A5
Paul's Dene Rd SP1 146 A5
Paul St SN13 76 F1
Paveley Cl BA13 108 E3
Pavely Cl SN15 78 C6
Pavely Gdns BA14 102 A1
Paven Cl SN5 33 A4
Pavenhill SN5 33 A4
PAXCROFT 102 C3
Paxcroft Prim Sch BA14 101 F1
Paxcroft Way BA14 105 F8
Paxmans Rd BA13 108 E5
Payne Cl SN15 78 E4
Payne's Hill 2 SP1 152 B8
Peacock SN8 173 E6
Peaks Down SN5 34 B2
Peak The SN5 33 B3
Pealsham Gdns 6 SP6 210 D1
PEAR ASH 137 C4
Pear Ash La
Penselwood BA9 137 B4
Pen Selwood BA9 137 C4
Pearce Cl SN2 35 E6
Pearce Way SP1 146 D5
Pearl Cl BA14 101 D2
Pearl Rd SN5 49 A7
Pearson Rd SN25 20 C1
Peartree Cl
Atworth/Whitley SN12 85 C1
Purton SN5 33 C5
7 West Wellow SO51 212 F6
Pear Tree Dr SP5 212 C5
Pear Tree La SN10 187 B8
Pear Tree Orch 2 BA13 186 B7
PEATMOOR 34 B1
Peatmoor Com Prim Sch SN5 34 A2
Peatmoor Way SN5 34 A1
PECKINGELL 71 B2
Peel Cir SN13 84 D8
Peel Ct SN12 94 A3
Pegasus Way SN12 94 C1
Peglars Way SN1 49 F3
Pekin Way SP9 216 D4
Pelch La SN12 178 D8
Pelham Ct
Broad Chalke SP5 205 B4
Marlborough SN8 213 E3
Pembridge Rd SP6 210 E1
Pembroke Cl 1 BA14 105 D6
Pembroke Ctr SN2 34 E1
Pembroke Gdns SN25 34 E3
Pembroke Gn SN16 28 F1
Pembroke Park Prim Sch SP2 145 D4
Pembroke Rd
Chippenham SN15 79 A4
Melksham SN12 94 B4
Salisbury SP2 145 C2
Upavon Down SN9 182 B2
Pembroke St SN1 50 B4
Pencarrow Cl 6 SN25 34 E6
Pen Cl SN25 35 A4
Pendennis Rd SN5 49 A3
Penfold Gdns SN1 50 C4
PENHILL 35 C5
Pen Hill
Brixton Deverill SP3 127 A5
Monkton Deverill BA12 126 E6
Stourton with Gasper BA10 122 F1
Penhill Dr SN2 35 C4
PENKNAP 112 E8
Penknap Rd BA12 112 D8
PENLEIGH 108 D2
Penleigh Cl SN13 84 F8
Penleigh Rd BA13 108 D2
Pen Mill Hill BA9 137 E3
Penn Comm Rd SO51 212 E3
Penn Ct SN11 81 C3
Penneys Piece 2 BA11 110 C6
Penn Hill Rd SN11 81 C3
Pennine Cl SN12 94 D4
Pennine Way SN25 34 F7
Penning Rd SP2 145 B4
Pennings Dro
Coombe Bissett SP5 151 A1
Coombe Bissett SP5 157 A8
Pennings Rd
North Tidworth SP9 191 D5
Tidworth SP9 216 C8
Penn Marsh SO51 212 E3
Pennycress Cl SN25 34 E4
Pennycress Dr SN12 94 C3
Penny Farthing Cl RG17 177 A7
Pennyfarthing St SP1 146 B1
Penny Hill SN8 191 E8
Penny La
Amesbury SP4 217 D1
Chippenham SN15 78 F4
Swindon SN3 50 F7
Penny Royal Cl SN11 80 F3
Penny's Cl 3 SP6 210 D2
Penny's Cres 4 SP6 210 D2
Pennys La SP6 210 D2
Penny's La
Pitton & Farley SP5 154 E7
2 Wilton SP2 144 D3
Penrose Wlk SN3 51 A5
Penruddock Cl SP2 145 C3
PENSELWOOD 137 B4
Penselwood Loop BA9 137 A3
Pensford Way BA11 110 D6
PENTON CORNER 193 A1
PENTON GRAFTON 193 A2
Penton La SP11 193 A3
PENTON MEWSEY 193 B2
PENTRIDGE 208 E4
Pentridge Cl SN3 51 C7
Pentylands Cl SN6 22 F7
Penzance Dr
Swindon SN5 49 F5
Swindon SN5 49 F6
Pepperacre La BA14 101 F1
Pepperbox Hill SN5 34 B2
Pepperbox Rise SP5 153 E2
Pepperbox The★ SP5 160 C6
Peppercombe Cl 6 SN10 180 B4
Peppercombe Wood Nature Reserve★ SN10 180 B4
Peppercorn Orch BA14 178 A6
Pepper Pl BA12 117 D7
Perch Cl 8 SN11 81 B5
Percheron Cl 11 SN5 49 A7
Percheron Pl BA13 108 D2
Percy St SN2 49 F7
Peregrine Cl SN3 51 D8
Peregrine Cl 2 SN11 81 B5
Perham Cres 1 SP11 192 B5
PERHAM DOWN 191 F4
Perhamdown Rd SP9 216 E6
Peridot Cl SN25 34 F8
Periwinkle Cl SN2 34 C3
Perrinsfield GL7 2 D6
Periwinkle Cl BA12 116 D6
PERRY GREEN 29 B7
Perry's La
Seend SN12 178 D8
Wroughton SN4 64 A6

Perth Rd SP11........ 191 F4
Peshawar Cl SP9 .... 216 B7
Peter Furkins Ct SN1 . 50 A5
Petersfield Green
SP9............... 216 C6
Petersfield Rd SN3....51 B4
PETERSFINGER 152 E7
Peters Finger Rd
SP5............... 152 E7
Peto Gdn The★ BA15 . .99 E2
Petter Cl SN4........64 B7
Petticoat La
Redlynch SP5......211 D8
Westbury BA13 .....112 C8
Pettridge La BA12 ... 139 A5
PETTY FRANCE........38 B8
Petty France Farm La
GL9...............38 B8
Petty La SN11 ....79 F3
Pevensey Way SN5 ....49 C5
Pew Hill SN15 ....70 E2
PEWSEY 215 D4
Pewsey Downs National
Nature Reserve★
SN8............... 173 C2
Pewsey Prim Sch
SN9............... 215 B5
Pewsey Rd
Marlborough SN8.....213 D2
Rushall SN9 .... 181 E2
Pewsey Sports Ctr &
Swimming Pool
SN9............... 215 B5
Pewsey Sta SN9 ..... 215 B5
Pewsey Vale Sch
SN9............... 215 B5
PEWSEY WHARF 215 B7
Pewsey White Horse★
SN9............... 215 E1
Pewsham Lock SN15...78 E5
Pewsham Rd SN2.....35 D5
Pewsham Way SN15 ..78 E4
Pheasant Bsns Pk
SN14...............78 B5
Pheasant Cl
8 Chippenham Without
SN14...............77 F6
Swindon SN3........51 E5
Pheasant Dr
Old Sarum SP4.......146 B8
Trowbridge BA14.....105 E6
Pheasantry The GL7...8 E7
Philip Cl SN12........94 C6
Philip Ct SP2....... 145 D3
Philipps House & Dinton
Pk★ SP3.......... 201 E2
Philip Rd
21 Durrington/Bulford
SP4................198 B7
Wilton SP2.......... 144 B5
Phillip Cl SN10 ...... 214 C4
Phillips Cl SN14 ......77 F7
Phillips Gr SN14 ......68 F6
Phillips La
Salisbury SP4........145 E6
Swindon SN1 ....50 D4
Phillips Way BA14 ... 105 E2
Phipps Cl BA13 ..... 108 F4
Phoebe Way SN25 ....34 B7
Phoenix Cl SN14 ......78 F6
Phoenix Gdns 20 SN25 .34 B7
Phoenix Rise BA13... 108 E3
Phoenix Sq SN9 ..... 215 C4
Piccadilly SN8....... 184 C8
Picked Mead 1 SN13 .84 E8
Pickernell Rd SP9 ... 216 D8
Picket Cl SN5....... 210 D1
Picket Cnr SP6 ...... 211 F3
Picketleaze SN14 .....78 A7
Picket Post
Corsley BA12........116 A3
Longbridge Deverill
BA12..............115 E3
Picket Post Gate
BA12..............116 A4
Pickford Way 2 SN25 .35 B6
PICKWICK 76 E2
Pickwick SN13........76 F2
Pickwick Cl SN2......35 E5
Pickwick Rd SN13.....76 F2
Picquet The 12 BA13 .186 B7
Picton Rd SN5.......149 A5
Pictor Cl SN13....... 76 D1
Pierce Rd SP9.......216 D8
Piernik Cl SN25.......34 E6
Pigeon House La SN3 .36 A3
Pig La
Bishops Cannings
SN10..............172 C1
Hullavington SN14.....41 A3
Pigott Cl 4 SP4 .....190 A4
Pigtrough La SP7.....203 B4
Pike Cl BA14........102 B1
Pike Cnr SN16........17 D7
Pikefield Cres SN16....29 A6
Pike House Cl SN6....19 C8
Pilgrim Cl SN5........49 A7
Pilgrims Ct SP1......146 E2
Pilgrims Mead SP1 ..146 C5
Pilgrims Way SP1 ...146 E2
Pill Hill SP5 ....161 C4
Pilots View SP4......217 D3
Pilton Cl SN5.........49 A8
Pimperleaze Rd
Charnage BA12.......139 E5

Pimperleaze Rd continued
Mere BA12.........139 F1
PINCKNEY GREEN 90 E5
Pinckneys Way 13
SP4...............198 B7
Pine Cl
Corsham SN13........76 A1
Landford SP5........212 C5
Melksham SN12.......94 A3
Pinecroft La SP5....149 C8
Pine Ct 2 BA11......110 B7
Pine Ct SN2..........35 E2
Pine Gr BA14........105 C6
Pinehurst........... 35 D3
Pinehurst Rd SN2.....35 C2
Pinehurst Sports Ctr
SN25..............35 B3
Pines Rd SN10......214 C2
Pines The SP6.......211 A1
Pinetree Rise SN2.....35 B3
Pinetum Cl SN10....214 A2
Pineview Cl SP5.....211 C6
Pine Wlk
Amesbury SP4.......217 D3
Trowbridge BA14.....105 C3
Pinewood Sch SN4 ....37 F2
Pinewoods Cl SP2 ...145 B4
Pinewood Way
Colerne SN14.........74 F7
Salisbury SP2........145 B4
Pinfield La SN15......78 F4
Pinhills SN11.........81 A2
Pink La SN16.........29 C5
Pinkney Pk★ SN16....25 F1
Pinnegar Way SN3....51 E6
Pinnocks Pl SN2......35 F4
Pintail Ct SN15.......60 B1
Pintail Way BA13....109 B4
Pinto Cl SN2.........34 C3
Pioneer Cl 3 SN5.....49 A7
Pioneer Rd SN25......34 B7
Pipehouse La SN4.....37 F2
Pipehouse La BA2.....98 A4
Pipers Cl SN4........61 D8
Pipers Way SN1......50 C1
Pipistrelle Cres SN4 106 A8
Pipitdene SN3........51 D7
Piplar Gd BA15......100 D4
Pippins The 3 BA12 .116 F7
Pippin The SN11......81 B3
Pippit Pl 5 SN12......94 D5
Pips Field Way GL7....1 F6
Pipsmore Rd
5 Chippenham SN14 ..70 A1
Chippenham SN14 ....78 A8
Pitchens End SN4....167 C7
Pitchens The SN4.....64 B5
Pitch Pan La BA12...139 B4
Pitman Ave BA14 ....105 B7
Pitman Ct BA14......105 B6
Pit Mead La BA12 ...117 E4
Pitt Cl 3 SN1.........50 E7
PITTON.............148 C3
Pitton CE (VA) Prim Sch
SP5...............148 B3
Pitton Rd
Firsdown SP5........148 E6
Pitton & Farley SP5....154 D8
Winterslow SP5.......134 F1
Pitts Croft SN13......84 E5
Pittsfield SN6.........19 D7
Pitts La
Bishopstone SP5.....205 F4
Chitterne BA12......195 D7
Sedgehill & Semley
SP7...............202 B7
PITTS THE 205 F5
Pix Mead Gdns 1
SP7...............202 A1
Pk La
Corsham SN13........85 A3
Neston SN13.........84 F4
Pk Rd GL9............38 E7
Place Rd SN12........94 A4
PLAITFORD 212 E6
PLAITFORD GREEN .212 F8
Plane Tree Cl SN12 ...85 C1
Planks The SN3.......50 D4
Plantation Rd
Chippenham SN14 ....78 C8
Tidworth SP9.......216 D5
Wellow SO51........212 F4
Plantation The SP5 ..149 A5
Plants Gn BA12......117 B6
Plassey Rd SP9......216 C7
Platford St SN11......81 B2
Platt Cl RG17.......177 C6
Plattes Cl SN5........49 B8
Platt La RG17.......170 E7
Play Cl SN5..........33 C4
Player Ct 8 SP6.....210 D2
Playhouse Salisbury★
SP2...............146 A1
Pleydell Rd SN1......50 C2
Pleydells 3 SN6.......19 D8
Plough La
Kington Langley SN15 ..70 C5
Marston SN10.......179 A3
Plough Way 9 SN1 ..193 F2
Plume of Feathers La
SN8...............213 E3
Plum La SN10.......180 E4
Plummer Cl SN4......64 A6
Plumpton Cl SN14 ....77 F6
Plymouth St SN1 .....50 D6
Poachers Way SN25 ..34 F7
Pochard Way GL7.....6 F6

Pockeredge Dr SN13...84 C7
Pockeridge Rd SN13...84 E7
Pointers Way SP4 ...217 D3
Polaris Way SN2......50 B7
Polden Rd SP1......152 C7
Polebarn Rd BA14 ...105 D8
Pollen Cl SP4.......190 B2
Pollen Rd SP4.......190 B2
Polonez Ct SN25......34 D6
Poltondale SN3.......51 D7
Pomeroy La BA14....104 B6
Pond House La SP11 .185 D3
Pond La
Charlton SN16........29 F4
Charlton SN16........30 A4
Purton SN5..........19 B1
Pond St SN25........34 F5
Pontefract Ave BA14 .106 B7
Ponting's Cl SN26 ....21 C2
Ponting St SN1.......50 C7
Poole Gn SN13.......84 C6
Pool Gastons Rd SN16 .27 F3
Pool Gn SN13........84 C6
Poores Rd 17 SP4....198 B7
Poor St SN5..........33 A3
Pope Cl SN25........34 F5
Popham Ct SN15......78 E6
Poplar Ave SN2......35 C2
Poplar Cl SP2........151 C2
Poplar Coll SN15......78 E8
Poplar La BA14......101 C1
Poplars The
Chippenham SN14 ....70 A1
Fovant SP3.........204 D8
Trowbridge BA14.....105 B7
Poplar Tree La BA14 .104 B3
Poplar Way
Colerne SN14........74 F5
Colerne SN14........75 A5
Salisbury SP1........146 C5
Popplechurch Dr 5
SN3................51 E7
Poppy Cl SN11........80 F4
Poppy Fields SN25....35 E3
Porchester Cl 8
SP10..............193 C2
Portal Ave SN13......84 B8
Portal Cl SN15.......70 C1
Portal Pl SN15........60 A1
Portal Rd SN2........35 A2
PORTASH...........201 B2
Port Down RG17.....177 C7
Porte Marsh Ind Est
SN11..............81 C5
Porte Marsh Rd SN11 .81 C5
Porters Mead SN13 ...76 F1
Portfield Rd SP5.....150 A4
Porth Cl 3 SN5.......34 C7
Port Hill SN8........213 D5
Portland Ave
Britford SP2........151 F5
Swindon SN1 ....50 A4
Portland Pl BA13 ....109 B5
Portland Rise SN13 ..84 E7
Portland Way SN11...81 C2
Portman Rd SN12.....94 A6
Portmore Cl SN5......34 C2
Portnell's La BA12...137 F4
PORTON............133 D6
Porton Rd
Amesbury SP4.......217 D3
Porton SP4.........132 E8
Porton SP4.........133 B8
Port Regis Prep Sch
SP7...............202 A3
Portsmouth St SN1 ..50 D6
Portway
Chippenham SN14 ....78 B6
Frome BA11........110 A4
Laverstock SP4.......146 B7
Warminster BA12 ....117 A7
Port Way BA13......186 A6
Portway Gdns 10
BA11..............110 A4
Portway Ind Est SP10 193 B1
Portway La BA12....117 A8
Portway The SP1 ...145 E4
Portwell 3 SN6.......19 D7
Poseidon Cl SN25.....34 B6
Postmill Dr SN4.......47 F1
Postoffice La SN9 ...215 C5
Post Office La
Atworth/Whitley SN12 .92 F8
Broad Hinton SN4 ....167 C7
Corsham SN13........77 A1
Culkerton GL8........3 A4
Post Office Rd RG17 .177 F3
Poston Way BA15.....99 D7
Pot La BA11.........110 F8
Potley La SN13........84 C7
Potterdown Rd 3
SN2...............35 C5
POTTERNE..........179 D5
Potterne Rd SN10...214 A1
POTTERNE WICK 179 E4
Potters Way SP1....152 D8
Pottery La RG17 ....177 E3
Pottle St BA12......119 A6
Potts Field SN11.....166 B1
Poulsen Cl BA12.....117 A5

POULSHOT 179 B6
Poulshot Rd SN10 ..179 A5
Poulton BA15.......100 C5
Poulton La BA15.....100 C5
Poulton La BA15.....100 E5
Poulton St SN2.......50 C8
Pouncette Cl SP4....217 D1
Pound Cl
Lyneham SN15.......60 A3
Semington BA14......102 F6
Pound Farm Cl BA14 .101 E4
Pound Hill
Landford SP5........212 C7
Melchet Park & Plaitford
SO51..............212 F7
St Paul Malmesbury Without
SN16...............43 A3
Pound La
Bradford-on-Avon
BA15..............100 C5
Damerham SP6 .....209 E3
Melchet Park & Plaitford
SO51..............212 F7
Semington BA14......102 E6
Shaftesbury SP7.....202 D2
Swindon SN2........35 B2
Wilcot SN8.........174 B2
Pound Mead 5 SN13 .84 F8
Pound Piece
Ashbury SN6........164 A8
5 Hungerford RG17...177 B7
Pound Pill SN13.......77 A1
Pound Rd SN6........22 F7
Pound Row BA12....116 F6
Pound St
Ebbesbourne Wake
SP5...............204 D3
Warminster BA12 ....116 F6
Pound The
Bromham SN15.......96 B7
Mere BA12.........139 B5
Poveys Pl 1 SN6....163 E6
Powell Pl 3 SN2......34 E2
Powell Rise SN16.....28 B5
Power Rd SP4.......197 E7
Pownall Rd SP4.....198 A6
Poynder Pl SN11.....166 A6
Poynder Rd SN13.....76 E1
Poynings Way SN5....48 F4
Pragnell Ct SP4.....133 E6
Prescombe Down
National Nature
Reserve★ SP5.....204 C4
Preshute CE Prim Sch
SN8...............213 A1
Preshute La SN8.....213 B2
Prestbury Dr BA12...117 C5
Prest Grove SN14.....67 D2
Prestly Wood 3
SN13..............76 B1
PRESTON
Aldbourne..........170 B4
Lyneham and
Bradenstoke........60 D1
Preston La SN15......60 B1
Pretoria Rd 13 SP11 .192 B5
Priddy Cl SN11......110 C7
Prideaux Dr SP7.....202 A5
Priestley Gr SN11.....81 C2
Priestley Prim Sch
SN11..............81 C2
Priestly Wood Rd 6
SN13..............76 B1
Primmers Pl BA13 ..108 F5
Primrose Cl
Calne SN11..........81 B5
Swindon SN2........34 D5
Primrose Cnr BA14 ..101 D4
Primrose Dr SN12 ....94 C4
Primrose Hill
Tockenham SN4.......60 D6
Wilton SN8.........144 D4
Primrose La
Manningford SN9.....181 F6
Redlynch SP5........211 C7
Primrose Pl 26 SP4 ..198 B7
Primrose Rd
24 Ludgershall SP11 ..192 A5
Salisbury SP2........145 C4
Primrose Way SN14...70 B2
Primrose Wlk 1
BA12..............116 E7
Prince Charles Cl 14
SP11..............192 A5
Prince Charles Dr
SN11..............81 C3
Princecroft County Prim
Sch BA12..........116 E6
Princecroft La 3
BA12..............116 E6
Princes Cl SP5......211 D8
Princes Hill SP5.....211 D8
Princess Anne Rd 9
BA11..............110 A7
Princess Gdns
Trowbridge BA14.....101 E4
Warminster BA12 ....117 D6
Princess Margaret Hospl
SN3................51 D1
Princess Mary Gdns 19
SP11..............192 A5
Princes St 4 SN1.....50 C5
Priorsfield SN8.......213 E2
Prior's Hill SN4........64 B5
Priors Wlk GL7........2 E3
Priory Ave RG17.....177 B6
Priory Cl
Alderbury SP5.......153 F2

Priory Cl continued
Bradford-on-Avon
BA15..............100 C7
5 Hungerford RG17...177 B6
5 Shrewton SP3......196 E6
Wilton SP2.........144 C2
Wilton SP2.........144 B2
Priory Coll SN1......50 C4
Priory Gn SN6........23 A6
Priory La SN16........28 B2
Priory New Rd SN13 ..76 F2
Priory Pk BA15......100 D7
Priory Pl 1 RG17.....177 B6
Priory Rd
Hungerford RG17....177 B6
Swindon SN3........51 A4
Priory Sq 5 SP2.....146 A1
Priory St SN13........76 F2
PRIORY VALE 34 C8
Priory Way 1 BA14 ..28 B2
Pritchard Cl SN2.....35 F5
Privet La SN11.......192 D2
Privet Way 2 SN13...84 E8
Proby Pl BA14.......102 A1
Professions Cnr SP5 .206 D6
Pro Logis Pk SN3.....36 C6
Prospect
Box SN13...........83 B4
Corsham SN13........85 A7
Prospect Fields SN12 .92 F8
Prospect Hill SN1.....50 C5
Prospect Pl
Bathford BA1........82 D2
Mere BA12.........138 F5
Swindon SN1 ....50 C4
Trowbridge BA14.....101 D1
Prospect Rd RG17 ..177 B7
Prospect Sq 3 BA13 .109 A3
Prospero Way
7 Swindon SN25......34 C6
Swindon SN25.......34 D6
Proud Cl SN5.........33 B3
Providence La SN13 ..76 F1
Providence Terr SN15 78 D7
Provis Mead SN15 ....79 A4
Provost St 23 SP6...210 D1
Pub La SN10........180 F8
Pucklands SN10......180 E5
Puck Well Nature
Reserve★ BA12 ...140 C4
Pudding La SN14 .....78 B5
Puddlesloosh La SP6...210 C2
Pugin Cl SN25........34 B8
Pullman Dr SP2 .....145 B3
Pulsar Rd 14 SN25 ...34 B7
Pump La
Bathford BA1........82 B1
Long Newnton GL8 ....13 C4
Purbeck Cl SN3......51 C7
Purbeck Pl SN11.....81 D2
Purcell Rd SN25.....34 E8
Purleigh Rd SN13.....76 E1
Purley Ave SN3......51 B3
Purley Rd SN4........51 F1
Purley Way SO51 ...212 E6
PURLPIT.............93 A8
Purlpit SN12.........85 A1
Purlyn Acre SN8.....213 D4
Purslane Cl SN2......34 C3
PURTON.............33 B4
PURTON COMMON ...33 A5
Purton Mus★ SN5 ....33 C4
Purton Rd
Cricklade SN6.......19 D7
Haydon Wick SN2.....34 C3
Swindon SN25.......34 C3
PURTON STOKE......19 C1
Purvis Cl 4 SN4.....217 E3
Pyatts Cnr BA14.....178 C4
Pye La SN4.........167 A8

Q

Quadrangle The SN15..78 C6
Quakers La SN11.....73 F7
Quakers Rd SN10 ...214 C5
Quakers Wlk SN11...73 F7
Quantock Cl
Melksham Without
SN12..............94 D4
5 Warminster BA12 ..117 A8
Quarr Barton SN11...81 B3
Quarries The SN11....50 C3
Quarrybrook Cl SN3 ..36 E5
Quarry Cl
Corston SN16........42 E5
Winsley BA2.........99 D6
Quarry Cres SN16.....22 F6
Quarryvale Cl SN11...81 B2
Quarry Field SN25....34 A3
Quarry Fields Ind Est
BA12..............138 C5
Quarry Hill SN13......83 C6
Quarry Ho SN16......42 F5
Quarry La
Colerne SN14........75 B3
Melbury Abbas SP7...206 A7
Quarry Mews SN1....50 C3
Quarry Rd
Bratton BA12.......186 B6
Swindon SN1 ....50 C4
Quartermaster Rd
BA13..............108 D6
Quarterway La BA14 .101 E1
Quavey Rd SP5......211 D7
Quebec Rd
Bulford SP4.........217 F8

Quebec Rd continued
Chiseldon SN4.......168 E8
Queen Alexandra Rd
SP2...............145 D3
Queenborough SN5...49 C4
Queen Elizabeth Dr
SN2................34 C4
Queen Manor Rd
Clarendon Park SP5...147 B3
Clarendon Park SP5...147 B3
Laverstock SP5.....152 E8
Queen Mary Rd SP2 .145 D3
QUEEN OAK 138 A3
Queen Oak★ SN8...175 C4
Queen Oak Rd SP8...138 A3
Queens Ave
Corsham SN13........76 F3
Highworth SN6.......23 A6
Queen's Barrow★
BA12..............201 A7
Queensberry Rd
Amesbury SP4.......217 C4
Salisbury SP1........146 A3
Queens Chase BA12..117 A8
Queens Cl
27 Ludgershall SP11 ..192 A5
Sutton Benger SN15 ...57 D2
Queens Club Gdns
BA14..............105 A8
Queens Cres SN14....78 A6
Queen's Crescent Prim
Sch SN14...........78 A6
Queen's Dr SN3.......51 B2
Queen's Dr SN3.......50 E6
Queensfield SN2......35 D5
Queens Gdns
32 Fordingbridge
SP6...............210 D1
Trowbridge BA14.....101 E4
Queens Gr BA9......137 C3
Queens Rd
Hannington SN6......21 F8
Mere BA12.........139 B6
Salisbury SP1........146 B2
7 Tisbury SP3.......203 E8
Trowbridge BA14.....101 C2
Queen's Rd
Devizes SN10.......214 A2
Royal Wootton Bassett
SN4................47 E2
Westbury BA13 .....108 E3
Westbury BA13 .....108 F2
Queens Sq
Box SN13...........83 D5
Chippenham SN15 ....78 F6
Westbury BA13 .....108 E3
Queen St
Hale SP6...........211 B5
Salisbury SP1........146 A1
Swindon SN1 ....50 B6
Wilton SP2.........144 D4
QUEEN STREET 31 B3
Queensway
Andover SP10 ......193 F1
Melksham SN12......94 C4
2 Netheravon SP4...190 A3
Warminster BA12 ....117 D6
Queens Way SN8 ...213 F2
Quentin Rd SN1......50 D3
QUEMERFORD 89 D8
Quemerford
Calne SN11..........81 C1
Quemerford SN11......89 E8
QUEMERFORD GATE
SN11..............172 A8
QUIDHAMPTON 145 A2
Quidham St SP5.....204 F2
Quilling Cl BA14.....105 E7
Quinton Pl BA12.....195 A3

R

Rabley Wood View
SN8...............213 E4
Race Plain Rd SP2...150 D7
Rackham Cl SN25.....34 C8
Radcliffe Rd SP2.....152 A6
Radcot Cl SN5........34 A1
Radley Bottom
Hungerford Newtown
RG17..............171 D2
Hungerford Newtown
RG17..............171 E1
Kintbury RG17......177 F7
Radley Cl SN3........51 C7
Radnor Cl SN10.....214 C2
Radnor Pk SN16......42 E4
Radnor Pl 3 SN1.....94 A2
Radnor Rd SP1......146 A3
Radnor St SN1........50 A5
Radstock Ave SN3....51 B6
Radway Rd SN3......35 F3
Radways Cl GL7.......1 F6
Raffin La SN9.......215 C4
RAGGED
APPLESHAW.......192 F3
Raggett St SN1.......50 C5
Raglan Cl SN3........50 E2
Ragleth Gr BA14.....101 E2
Rag Ride SN8.......184 B2
Rail Road La SN4......61 F8
Railway Cl BA13 ....108 F3
Railway Village Mus★
SN1................50 B6
Railway Wlk 9 BA11 .110 A4
Rainer Cl SN3........36 B3
Rainham Rd 2 SN25...34 F7

Rake Way [10] SP11 . . . . 193 F2
Raleigh Ave SN3 . . . . . 50 F6
Raleigh Cres SP4 . . . . 217 E3
RAM ALLEY 175 B2
Rambler Cl
  Trowbridge BA14 . . . . . 101 A1
  Trowbridge BA14 . . . . . 105 A8
Rambridge Cres SP2 . 145 B5
Ramleaze Dr
  Salisbury SP2 . . . . . 145 C5
  Swindon SN5 . . . . . 49 A7
Ramnuggur Rd SP9 . 216 D3
Rampart Rd SP1 . . . . . 146 B1
Ramsay Rd SN11 . . . . 81 D3
RAMSBURY 175 A2
Ramsbury Ave SN2 . . . 35 B6
Ramsbury Dr
  Hungerford RG17 . . . 177 C7
  Old Sarum SP4 . . . . . 146 B7
Ramsbury Manor*
  SN8 . . . . . 169 F1
Ramsbury Prim Sch
  SN8 . . . . . 170 B2
Ramsbury Terr RG17 . 177 C7
Ramsbury Wlk BA14 . 105 D6
Ramscliff SN10 . . . . 187 F7
Ramscombe La BA1 . . . 82 A6
Ramsden Rd SN1 . . . . 48 F3
Ramshill Dro
  East Winterslow SP5 . . 149 F8
  Winterslow SP5 . . . . 134 F1
Ramsthorn Cl SN2 . . . 34 D4
Randall Cl SN13 . . . . 76 D1
Randall Cres SN5 . . . . 49 A8
Randall's Croft Rd
  SP2 . . . . . 144 B2
Randolph Cl SN3 . . . . 50 F5
Rank The BA14 . . . . 105 C3
Rannoch Cl [4] SN5 . . 34 B2
Ransome Cl SN5 . . . . 49 B8
Ransome Terr BA13 . . 108 E3
Raspberry La [8] SP7 . 202 B1
Ratcliff's Gdn [15] SP7 202 C1
RATFORD 80 E5
Ratford Hill SN11 . . . . 80 D5
RATFYN 217 C5
Ratfyn Rd SP4 . . . . 217 B4
Rat Hill SN14 . . . . 54 E2
Raven Cl SP9 . . . . . 216 D6
Ravenglass Rd SN5 . . . 49 C6
Ravenhurst SN16 . . . . 14 E6
Ravenscroft
  [7] Salisbury SP2 . . . 152 A5
  Swindon SN3 . . . . . 51 C8
Ravenscroft Gdns
  BA14 . . . . . 101 F1
Ravensdale [7] SN1 . . 50 A2
Ravensroost Wood &
  Mdws Nature Reserve*
  SN16 . . . . . 31 A5
Ravens Wlk SN4 . . . . 48 A2
Rawlence Rd
  Salisbury SP2 . . . . . 145 B2
  Wilton SP2 . . . . . 144 C2
Rawlings Cl SN3 . . . . 36 E4
Rawlings Ct SP11 . . . 192 A5
Rawlingswell La
  SN8 . . . . . 213 E3
Rawlinson Rd SP4 . . . 198 E6
Rawlins Pk SN8 . . . . 167 C1
Rawlins Rd SN9 . . . . 215 C5
Rawston Cl SN3 . . . . 51 C6
Raybrook Cres SN2 . . . 49 E6
Ray Cl
  Chippenham SN15 . . . . 78 F5
  Swindon SN25 . . . . . 34 A2
  Swindon SN25 . . . . . 35 A4
Rayfield Gr
  Swindon SN2 . . . . . 50 B8
  Swindon SN25 . . . . . 35 B1
Reading St [4] SN4 . . . 50 B6
Read St SN1 . . . . . 50 A5
Rea Rd SN13 . . . . 84 F6
Recreation Rd
  [10] Durrington/Bulford
  SP4 . . . . . 198 B7
  Ludgershall SP11 . . . 192 A6
Rectory Cl
  Alton SN8 . . . . . 181 C8
  North Tidworth SP9 . 216 C7
  Overtown SN4 . . . . . 64 E3
  Stanton St Quintin SN14 56 B4
  [11] Warminster BA12 . 117 A8
Rectory Ct SP4 . . . . 133 F7
Rectory Hill SP5 . . . . 155 F3
Rectory La
  Alderbury SP5 . . . . 153 E2
  Breamore SP6 . . . . 210 E4
  Charlton Musgrove
  BA9 . . . . . 136 B1
  Cricklade SN6 . . . . . 19 E8
  Letcombe Bassett
  OX12 . . . . . 165 F8
Rectory Pl [4] SP11 . . 192 F1
Rectory Rd
  Alderbury SP5 . . . . 153 E2
  Clarendon Park SP5 . 153 D8
  Salisbury SP2 . . . . . 151 E8
  Sutton Mandeville SP3 . 204 C7
Rectory Wood [1]
  SN8 . . . . . 170 A6
Reculver Way [6]
  SP10 . . . . . 193 C2
Red Barn La SN1 . . . . 49 F4
Redbridge Cl [1] SN1 . . 49 F4
Redcap Gdns SN5 . . . . 49 A7
Redcliffe St SN2 . . . . 49 F6

Red Cross House*
  SN10 . . . . . 214 B4
REDENHAM 191 E4
Redenham Dro SP11 . 192 E4
Redford Cl SP1 . . . . 146 D3
Red Gables Cl SN5 . . . 33 A3
Redhill Cl SN11 . . . . . 79 F2
Redhills SN4 . . . . . 62 B1
Redhorn Gdns SN10 . 214 B2
Red House Cl SP7 . . . 202 A5
Redhouse Gdns [2]
  SN25 . . . . . 34 D7
Redhouse Way
  Swindon SN25 . . . . . 34 B7
  Swindon SN25 . . . . . 34 C7
  Swindon SN25 . . . . . 34 D7
Red La
  East Winterslow SP5 . 149 C7
  Mildenhall SN8 . . . . 169 B2
  Sixpenny Handley SP5 . 208 A3
Redland SN14 . . . . . 78 B8
Redland La BA13 . . . 108 F2
Redland Prim Sch
  SN14 . . . . . 78 B8
REDLANDS 22 F3
Redlands [3] BA13 . . 186 B7
Redlands Cl SN6 . . . . 23 A4
Red Lion La SN6 . . . . 19 E8
Red Lion Mews SN6 . . 23 A6
Red Lodge Cl SN4 . . . 61 E8
REDLYNCH 211 D8
Redlynch Cl SN2 . . . . 35 C5
Redman Rd SN11 . . . . 81 C6
Redmans La SP7 . . . . 206 A7
Red Oaks Prim Sch
  SN25 . . . . . 34 D7
Red Pit BA13 . . . . 112 A8
Red Post La SP11 . . . 192 F1
Redposts Dr SN1 . . . . 49 F4
Redruth Cl SN3 . . . . . 51 B5
REDSTOCKS 95 A2
Redstocks La SN12 . . . 95 A2
Red Way The BA12 . . 115 F3
Redwing Ave SN14 . . . 70 B2
Redwing Rd SN12 . . . 94 D5
Redwood Way SN14 . . . 75 A5
Redworth Dr SP4 . . . 217 C2
Redworth Wlk SP4 . . 217 C2
Reed Cl SN5 . . . . . 36 C1
Reed Pl SN15 . . . . . 96 F1
Reeds SN6 . . . . . 19 E8
Reeds Farm Rd SN16 . . 28 A4
Reeds Gd SN8 . . . . 213 F3
Reed Wlk [10] SP4 . . . 198 C7
Rees Dr SP4 . . . . . 132 B1
Reeves Cl [2] SN3 . . . 51 C4
Reeves Piece [14]
  BA13 . . . . . 186 B7
Reeves Rd SN10 . . . . 214 D1
Regal Ct
  [3] Trowbridge BA14 . 105 C8
  Warminster BA12 . . . 117 A6
Regent Circus [6] SN1 . 50 C5
Regent Cl
  [15] Hungerford RG17 . 177 B7
  Swindon SN5 . . . . . 50 C6
Regents Pl
  Bradford-on-Avon
  BA15 . . . . . 100 D5
  Studley Green BA14 . 104 F6
Reid's Piece SN5 . . . . 33 B3
Reith Way [2] SP10 . . 193 B1
REME Museum*
  SN15 . . . . . 60 A1
Rendall's Barn GL7 . . . 4 E5
Rendells Ct SN10 . . . 214 B3
Renoir Cl [2] SN25 . . . 35 A8
RESTROP 33 A2
Restrop Rd SN5 . . . . 33 A3
Restrop View SN5 . . . 33 A4
Retingham Way SN2 . . 36 A5
Reto Gr BA15 . . . . 99 F3
Retreat The
  Frome BA11 . . . . 110 B4
  Highworth SN6 . . . . . 22 F6
Revell Cl SN2 . . . . . 35 E4
REYBRIDGE 86 D7
Reynolds Ct [4] SP10 . 193 D1
Reynolds Rise [18]
  SP7 . . . . . 202 D1
Reynolds Way SN25 . . 35 A8
Rhine Cl SN1 . . . . . 49 F4
Rhodes Moorhouse Way
  [1] SN14 . . . . 132 B1
Rhuddlan SN5 . . . . . 49 B4
Rhymes La GL7 . . . . 1 E3
Ricardo Rd SN15 . . . . 78 D8
Richard Jefferies Mus*
  SN3 . . . . . 51 E2
Richards Cl SN4 . . . . 47 D1
Richards Dr SN14 . . . . 66 E1
Richardson Rd SN25 . . 35 A8
Richards Way SP2 . . . 151 E7
Richard Webb Mews
  SN1 . . . . . 50 B3
Richborough Dr [3]
  SP10 . . . . . 193 C2
Richmond Cl [2]
  BA14 . . . . . 105 D6
Richmond Cres SP9 . . 216 E6
Richmond Ct SN6 . . . . 6 F1
Richmond Rd
  Calne Without SN11 . . 81 A4
  [2] Salisbury SP2 . . . 145 F2
Rickbarton [2] SN10 . 187 E7
Rickfield BA15 . . . . 100 B6
Rickworth Pl BA12 . . 195 A3

Rickyard The [9] SP7 . 202 D1
Riddell Way SP2 . . . . 151 D7
RIDGE 200 F2
Ridge SP3 . . . . . 200 F4
Ridge Gn SN5 . . . . . 49 B7
Ridgemead SN11 . . . . 81 B4
Ridge Nether Moor
  SN3 . . . . . 51 D2
Ridge The
  Broad Blunsdon SN26 . . 21 B2
  Redlynch SP5 . . . . 211 C7
Ridge Way SP3 . . . . 201 A3
Ridge Way SP7 . . . . 202 C3
Ridgeway Cl SN2 . . . . 34 F2
Ridgeway Ct BA12 . . . 117 B6
Ridgeway Farm CE Acad
  Sch SN25 . . . . 34 B3
Ridgeway La
  Dauntsey SN15 . . . . 44 E1
  Latton SN6 . . . . . 9 D3
Ridgeway Rd
  Salisbury SP1 . . . . . 146 B2
  Swindon SN2 . . . . . 35 E5
Ridgeway Sch The
  SN4 . . . . . 64 B7
Ridgeway The
  Chiseldon SN4 . . . . 65 D2
  Crudwell SN16 . . . . 14 E6
  Liddington SN4 . . . . 163 A2
  Warminster BA12 . . . 117 B6
Ridgmount [6] SP4 . . 198 B7
Ridings Mead SN14 . . . 70 C2
Ridings The SN14 . . . . 70 A8
Rifles La SP7 . . . . . 202 D1
Rigel Cl SN25 . . . . . 34 C7
Rigsby's La
  Minety SN16 . . . . . 16 F5
  Upper Minety SN16 . . 16 A5
Ringsbury Camp*
  SN5 . . . . . 32 E2
Ringsbury Cl SN5 . . . . 32 F3
Ringwood Ave [5]
  SP4 . . . . . 217 C3
Ringwood Cl SN3 . . . . 51 B6
Ringwood Rd [27]
  SP6 . . . . . 210 D1
Rinsdale Cl SN5 . . . . . 34 B1
Ripley Rd SN1 . . . . . 50 C4
Ripon Cl SN14 . . . . . 78 A5
Ripon Way SN3 . . . . . 51 A3
Ripple Field SN5 . . . . 49 B4
Rise Rd BA12 . . . . 194 C4
Rise The SN11 . . . . . 89 C8
Risingham Mead SN5 . . 49 C5
Ritter Cl SP4 . . . . 132 B1
RIVAR 184 F8
Rivar Rd
  Rivar SN8 . . . . . 184 F8
  Shalbourne SN8 . . . 176 F1
Rivenhall Rd SN5 . . . . 49 C5
Riverbourne Rd
  Laverstock SP1 . . . . 146 D1
  Salisbury SP1 . . . . . 152 D8
Riverdale Cl
  [9] Fordingbridge
  SP6 . . . . . 210 D1
  Swindon SN1 . . . . . 50 C2
Riverdale Wlk SN1 . . . 50 C2
Rivergate SN5 . . . . . 49 C8
Rivermead [4] BA14 . . 133 F8
Rivermead Dr SN5 . . . 49 C7
Rivermead Ind Est
  SN5 . . . . . 49 C7
River Mead Sch SN12 . . 94 B5
River Par SN15 . . . . . 78 D7
River Pk SN8 . . . . 213 D2
River Ray Ind Est SN2 . . 49 E7
Riverside
  Calne SN11 . . . . . 89 D8
  Wilton SP2 . . . . . 144 D3
Riverside Cl
  Salisbury SP1 . . . . . 146 D2
  South Newton SP2 . . 130 A4
Riverside Dr
  Chippenham SN15 . . . . 79 A8
  Melksham SN12 . . . . 94 A6
Riverside Pk SN15 . . . . 44 A2
Riverside Pl SP6 . . . . 210 E1
Riverside Rd SP1 . . . 146 D2
Riverside Terr SP3 . . . 129 E7
Rivers Reach [6]
  BA11 . . . . . 110 A4
River St
  Chippenham SN15 . . . . 78 E7
  Pewsey SN9 . . . . . 215 C5
Rivers Way SN6 . . . . . 22 F6
River View SN25 . . . . 34 B3
River Way
  [5] Durrington/Bulford
  SP4 . . . . . 198 C7
  South Cerney GL7 . . . . 6 F7
  Trowbridge BA14 . . . 101 C1
Rixon Gate
  Ashton Keynes SN16 . . 17 F8
  Ashton Keynes SN6 . . 18 A1
  Ashton Keynes SN6 . . 18 A8
Roach's La GL9 . . . . 38 C1
Robbers' Stone*
  SN10 . . . . . 187 E6
Robbins Ridge SP4 . . 217 C2
Robert Franklin Way
  GL7 . . . . . 7 A7
Robert Le Kyng Prim Sch
  SN1 . . . . . 50 A5
Roberts Cl SN4 . . . . . 64 B5
Roberts of Kandahar Rd
  BA12 . . . . . 113 F1

Roberts Rd
  North Tidworth SP11 . 192 A5
  Salisbury SP2 . . . . . 145 D3
Robin Cl BA12 . . . . 117 C6
Robin Hill La SP4 . . . 217 C8
Robin Hood's Ball*
  SP4 . . . . . 189 C1
Robin Hood's Bower*
  BA12 . . . . . 117 B1
Robinia Cl SN9 . . . . 215 D5
Robin Rd SP4 . . . . . 132 C1
Robins Cl
  Chippenham SN14 . . . . 70 B2
  Royal Wootton Bassett
  SN4 . . . . . 48 A2
Robinscroft SN26 . . . . 21 A1
Robinsgreen SN3 . . . . 51 D7
Robins Hill RG17 . . . . 177 C5
Robinson Cl SN3 . . . . 51 D6
Robinson Gr [2] SP4 . 132 B1
Rochdale Ave SN11 . . . 81 B4
Roche Cl SN3 . . . . . 51 D4
Rochelle Ct [19] SN10 . 179 F1
Rocher Cl BA13 . . . . 108 F3
Rochester Cl [5] SN5 . . 49 B4
Rochford Cl
  East Winterslow SP5 . 149 D7
  Swindon SN5 . . . . . 49 A5
ROCKBOURNE . . . 210 A4
Rockbourne La SP6 . . 209 F3
Rockbourne Mus*
  SP6 . . . . . 210 A4
Rockbourne Rd SP6 . . 156 C3
Rockbourne Roman
  Villa* SP6 . . . . 210 A4
Rockdown Cl SN2 . . . . 35 D4
Rocker Bench SN6 . . . 163 E6
Rockfel Rd RG17 . . . . 165 A1
Rockfield SN14 . . . . . 75 B3
Rock La BA12 . . . . 117 C6
ROCKLEY 168 C2
Rockley SN8 . . . . . 168 D2
Rockley Rd SN8 . . . 213 C7
Rockmoor La SP11 . . 185 C5
Rock Rd BA14 . . . . 105 B7
RODBOURNE
  St Paul Malmesbury
  Without 43 A3
  Swindon 35 A1
RODBOURNE
  BOTTOM 43 A2
RODBOURNE
  CHENEY 35 B2
Rodbourne Cheney Prim
  Sch SN25 . . . . 35 A3
Rodbourne House
  SN16 . . . . . 43 B4
Rodbourne Rd
  Corston SN16 . . . . . 42 F4
  Rodbourne SN15 . . . . 43 C3
  Rodbourne SN16 . . . . 43 A3
  St Paul Malmesbury Without
  SN16 . . . . . 42 F4
  Swindon SN2 . . . . . 49 F7
Roddenbury Cl BA11 . 110 B5
Roddenbury View
  BA12 . . . . . 115 A8
Rodden Manor*
  BA11 . . . . . 110 D4
Rodden Rd BA11 . . . 110 A5
Rode Bridge* BA11 . 103 E1
Rode Comm BA11 . . . 107 A8
Rode Common BA14 . 104 B1
RODE HILL 103 F1
Rode Hill
  Box SN13 . . . . . 82 F8
  Colerne SN14 . . . . . 74 D1
  Ditteridge SN13 . . . . 83 A8
  Rode BA11 . . . . . 103 F1
RODMARTON 3 C8
Rodmarton Cl SN25 . . 20 B1
Rodmarton La GL7 . . . 3 C8
Rodney Ct SP10 . . . . 193 F1
Rodsleigh BA14 . . . . 104 F6
Rodway [13] SN4 . . . 163 A6
Rodway Cl BA14 . . . . 101 E2
Rodwell Cl [3] SN3 . . . 51 A4
Rodwell Pk BA14 . . . 101 E2
Roebuck Cl SN4 . . . . 47 F2
Roger Penny Way
  SP6 . . . . . 211 C3
Rogers Cl
  Quidhampton SP2 . . 145 A3
  Swindon SN3 . . . . . 51 A7
Rogers Meadow SN8 . 213 D5
Rogers's La RG17 . . . 171 D7
Roger Way
  Old Sarum SP4 . . . . 146 C8
  [8] Winterbourne SP4 . 132 C1
ROLLESTONE 196 F6
ROLLESTONE CAMP . 197 B7
Rollestone Crossroads
  SP3 . . . . . 197 B8
Rollestone Rd SP3 . . . 196 E6
Rollestone St [1] SP1 . 146 B1
Rolleston St [1] SN1 . . 50 C5
Roman Cres SN1 . . . . 50 B3
Roman Meadow SP5 . .
  211 A8
Roman Rd
  Salisbury SP2 . . . . . 145 D2
  West Tytherley SP5 . . 149 F6
Roman Way
  Andover SP10 . . . . 193 E2
  Chippenham SN15 . . . . 79 B5
  Highworth SN6 . . . . . 22 F6

Roman Way continued
  [15] Market Lavington
  SN10 . . . . . 179 F1
  Warminster BA12 . . . 112 F1
  Warminster BA12 . . . 116 F8
Roman Way Prim Sch
  SP10 . . . . . 193 E2
Romer Rd SP2 . . . . . 152 A6
Romney Cl BA12 . . . . 116 D7
Romney Rd [23] SP11 . 193 F2
Romney Way SN5 . . . . 49 A6
Romsey Rd
  Amesbury SP4 . . . . 217 D2
  Cowesfield Gate SP5 . 162 C3
  Whiteparish SP5 . . . 162 B3
Romsey Road SP5 . . . 162 A3
Romsey St SN2 . . . . . 34 D5
Ron Golding Cl SN16 . . 28 A5
ROOD ASHTON . . . 106 C4
Rood Ashton Pk
  BA14 . . . . . 106 C4
Rookery Cottages
  SP5 . . . . . 155 F4
Rookery La
  Ansty SP3 . . . . . 203 F6
  Breamore SP6 . . . . 210 D5
  Swallowcliffe SP3 . . 204 A6
Rookery Meadow
  SN8 . . . . . 174 A6
Rookery Pk
  Calne SN11 . . . . . 89 C7
  Quemerford SN11 . . . 89 B8
Rookes La SN10 . . . . 179 D5
Rooks La BA11 . . . . 110 E6
Rooks Nest Cl SN15 . . . 78 F4
Rook St BA12 . . . . 139 A4
ROOK STREET . . . 139 A4
Rookwood Gdns [9]
  SN5 . . . . . 210 C1
Ropewind SN8 . . . . 176 F1
Rope Wlk SN12 . . . . . 94 B3
Rope Yd SN4 . . . . . 47 D1
Rorkes Drift Dr SP9 . . 216 D4
Rosary The SN4 . . . . . 47 E2
Rose Ave BA12 . . . . 117 C6
Rosebery St SN1 . . . . 50 D7
Rosebrock Gdns
  SN12 . . . . . 94 C3
Rosedale Gdns BA14 . 101 A1
Rosedale Rd SN3 . . . . 51 B4
Rosefield Way BA13 . . 108 F4
Rosehill Cl SN15 . . . . 59 D3
Roseland Ave SN10 . . 214 C3
Rosemary Cl
  Great Bedwyn SN8 . . 176 B3
  Laverstock SP1 . . . . 146 D1
  [2] Swindon SN2 . . . 34 D5
Rosemary La
  Freshford BA2 . . . . . 99 B4
  Lacock SN15 . . . . . 86 B6
  [2] Salisbury SP1 . . . 152 A8
Rosemary Way SN12 . . 94 D4
Rosenheim Rise [1]
  BA13 . . . . . 186 B7
Rose St SN2 . . . . . 49 F7
Rosetta Cl [6] SN25 . . 34 B7
Rosewood Ct SN3 . . . 51 D3
Rossett Gdns BA14 . . 105 A8
Rossetti La SN25 . . . . 34 D8
Ross Gdns SN2 . . . . . 36 A4
Ross Rd SP4 . . . . . 197 E2
Rother Cl SN25 . . . . . 34 F5
Rothe Rise BA13 . . . 108 F1
Rotherstone SN10 . . 214 A4
Rotten Row SN4 . . . . 163 A6
Rougemont Cl SP1 . . 146 B1
Roughmoor Farm Cl
  SN5 . . . . . 33 F1
Roughmoor Way SN5 . . 34 A1
Rough St SN13 . . . . . 84 F5
Roundaway La SP11 . . 193 A5
Round Barrow Cl
  SN14 . . . . . 75 B3
Round Hill
  [25] Fordingbridge
  SP6 . . . . . 210 D1
  Maiden Bradley BA12 . 118 F3
  Maiden Bradley BA12 . 118 F5
  Round Hill* SN14 . . . . 67 A7
Roundhills Mead SN6 . . 23 B6
Round House SN11 . . . 81 D1
Round House La GL7 . . . 2 B3
Roundpond SN12 . . . . 93 F6
Roundponds SN12 . . . 93 F6
Roundstone St BA14 . 101 D1
ROUNDWAY 214 D7
Roundway Cl SN11 . . . 89 B1
Roundway Down SN5 . . 49 B3
Roundway Gdns
  SN10 . . . . . 214 C6
Roundway Ind Est
  SN10 . . . . . 214 C5
Roundway Pk SN10 . . 214 C6
Roundway Rise SN11 . . 89 C8
Roundwood View
  SN15 . . . . . 58 A3
Roundwood Way
  SN25 . . . . . 34 C6
Rovers Farm & Visitor
  Ctr* SN6 . . . . 37 B6
Roves La SN6 . . . . . 23 B1
Rowan Cl
  Colerne SN14 . . . . . 75 A5
  [5] Durrington/Bulford
  SP4 . . . . . 198 B7
  Salisbury SP2 . . . . . 145 B4

Rowan Ct
  Frome BA11 . . . . 110 B7
  Melksham SN12 . . . . 94 A3
Rowan Dr
  Bishops Cannings
  SN10 . . . . . 214 F6
  Royal Wootton Bassett
  SN4 . . . . . 47 E1
Rowan La SN13 . . . . . 84 C5
Rowan Rd SN2 . . . . . 35 A3
Rowans The SN16 . . . . 27 F4
Rowbarrow SP2 . . . . 152 B5
Rowbarrow Cl [3]
  SP2 . . . . . 152 B5
Rowbarrow La [4]
  SP2 . . . . . 152 B5
ROWDE 96 D2
Rowde CE Prim Acad
  SN10 . . . . . 96 C1
Rowde Ct Rd SN10 . . . 96 D1
Rowdeford Sch SN10 . . 96 D3
Rowden Hill SN15 . . . . 78 C6
Rowden La
  Bradford-on-Avon
  BA15 . . . . . 100 D4
  Chippenham SN15 . . . . 78 C5
Rowden Rd SN15 . . . . 78 C6
Rowe Mead SN15 . . . . 78 C5
Rowes Hill BA12 . . . . 119 C8
Rowe's Hill BA12 . . . 119 C8
Rowhill SO43 . . . . . 212 D2
Row La SN12 . . . . . 178 C7
Rowland Hill Cl SN3 . . . 51 E4
Rowlands Cl BA1 . . . . 82 B2
Rowley Medieval Village
  of* BA15 . . . . 99 F1
Rowley Pl SN12 . . . . . 94 B4
Row The SP5 . . . . . 211 C8
Rowton Heath Way
  SN5 . . . . . 49 A4
Royal Crescent The
  SP9 . . . . . 216 D7
Royal Cl SN15 . . . . . 78 D6
Royal Field Cl SN14 . . 55 E8
Royal Oak Cl SN15 . . . 78 F6
ROYAL WOOTTON
  BASSETT 47 C2
Royal Wootton Bassett
  Acad SN4 . . . . 47 D3
Royal Wootton Bassett
  Inf Sch SN4 . . . . 47 C1
Royal Wootton Bassett
  Mus* SN4 . . . . 47 D1
Royce Cl [5] SP10 . . . 193 B1
Royston Rd SN3 . . . . 51 A4
Rubens Cl SN25 . . . . 34 F8
Ruby Cl SN26 . . . . . 20 F1
Ruckley Gdns SN3 . . . 36 B2
Rudd Rd [6] SN11 . . . . 81 B5
RUDGE 107 D5
Rudge Hill BA11 . . . 107 D5
Rudge La
  Beckington BA11 . . . 107 B6
  Lower Rudge BA11 . . 107 D5
  Wilcot SN8 . . . . . 174 B1
Rudge Rd BA11 . . . . 107 B2
RUDLOE 76 B1
Rudman Pk SN14 . . . . 78 D7
Rumble Dene SN15 . . . 78 E5
Rune Dr SP4 . . . . . 193 D2
Runnymede Gdns [6]
  BA14 . . . . . 105 D6
RUSHALL 181 E2
Rushall CE Prim Sch
  SN9 . . . . . 181 E3
Rushall Cl SN2 . . . . . 35 B5
Rushall Dro SN9 . . . . 181 D1
Rushall Rd SN9 . . . . 181 F3
Rushcroft Cl SN16 . . . 28 F1
Rushey La BA15 . . . . . 91 F3
Rushmead La
  Marshfield SN14 . . . . 66 A3
  South Wraxall BA15 . . 91 C5
Rushmere Path SN25 . . 34 E5
Rushmore Down La
  SP11 . . . . . 185 C1
Rushmore Pk* SP5 . 207 C5
Rushton Rd SN3 . . . . 51 A4
Rushworth Row SP4 . . 217 C2
Rushy Platt Ind Est
  SN5 . . . . . 49 E4
Rushy Platt Nature
  Reserve* SN1 . . . 49 F4
Ruskin Ave
  Melksham SN12 . . . . 94 B4
  Swindon SN2 . . . . . 35 F3
Ruskin County Jun Sch
  SN2 . . . . . 35 F4
Ruskin Dr
  Royal Wootton Bassett
  SN4 . . . . . 47 F3
  Warminster BA12 . . . 116 D6
Russel Cl GL9 . . . . . 24 B3
Russell Mill La SN10 . 179 D1
Russell Rd SP2 . . . . 145 E2
Russell St SP2 . . . . . 144 D3
Russell Wlk SN3 . . . . 50 E6
Russet Ave GL7 . . . . . 2 E3
Russet Cl BA12 . . . . 116 F7
Russley Cl
  Swindon SN5 . . . . . 33 F1
  Swindon SN5 . . . . . 33 F2
Russley Gn [3] SN8 . . 164 C1
Russley Pk* SN8 . . . 164 A3
Rusty La SN12 . . . . 178 E8

Rutherford Cl SN11 . . . 81 D3
Rutland Cl SN12 . . . . . .94 C3
Rutland Cres BA14 . . . 105 C6
Rutland Rd [1] SN3 . . . . .50 F5
Rutter Cl [16] SP7 . . . . 202 D1
Rutts La [3] SN10 . . . . 187 E7
Ruxley Cl SN4 . . . . 47 D1
Ryan Ave SN14 . . . . . . .78 A7
Ryan Cl SN5 . . . . .34 B2
Rybury Camp (Hill Fort) ★
SN10 . . . . 173 A2
Rycote Cl SN5 . . . . . . .49 A6
Rydal Cl SN25 . . . . . . .34 F5
Rye Cl SN5 . . . . .49 A7
Rye Hill BA12 . . . . . . 120 B6
Ryeland Way
[26] East Anton SP11 . . 193 F2
Trowbridge BA14 . . . . 105 E7
Ryeleaze SN10 . . . . . . 179 D5
Rye Way [14] SP11 . . . 193 F2
Rylands Way SN4 . . . . .47 E2
Rylane SN1 . . . . .50 B1
Ryles La SN8 . . . . 174 B6
Rymer's La SP11 . . . . . 185 E4
Ryon Cl [11] SP10 . . . . 193 E2
Rysy Ct [3] SN25 . . . . .34 E6

S

Sack Hill BA12 . . . . . . 113 F1
Sackville Cl SN5 . . . . . .50 F7
Saddleback Cl SN11 . . .81 C2
Saddleback La SN10 . 179 E5
Saddleback Rd SN5 . . . .49 A7
Saddlers Mead SP2 . . 144 C3
Saddlers Mews SP11 . 192 D1
Saddlers Way SN8 . . . 183 D7
Sadlers Field SN6 . . . . . 6 F1
Sadlers Mead SN15 . . . .78 E8
Sadlers Rd RG17 . . . . 177 C3
Sadler Wlk SN3 . . . . . .50 F5
Saffron Cl
Royal Wootton Bassett
SN4 . . . . 47 E4
[2] Swindon SN2 . . . . 34 E3
Saffron Meadows
SN11 . . . . .80 F3
Sage Cl SN2 . . . . 34 D5
St Albans Cl
Salisbury SP1 . . . . . . 146 D5
Swindon SN2 . . . . . . 49 E7
St Aldhelm Rd BA15. . 100 E5
St Aldhelms Cl SN16 . .27 F4
St Aldhelms Rd SN16 . .27 F4
St Alphege Gdns [7]
SP10 . . . . 193 D1
St Ambrose Cl SN3 . . .51 D6
ST ANDREW RIDGE . . .35 A8
St Andrews SN1 . . . . . . 6 F1
St Andrew's CE VA Prim
Sch SP1 . . . . 146 E3
St Andrews Cl SN4 . . . .64 B7
St Andrew's Cl
Wilton SP2 . . . . 144 B2
Wooton Rivers SN8 . . 174 A1
St Andrews Gn SN3 . . .51 E7
St Andrews Rd
Tidworth SP9 . . . . . 216 C6
Warminster BA12 . . . 116 D6
St Andrew's Rd
Melksham SN12 . . . . . 94 C5
Salisbury SP2 . . . . . . 145 C2
South Newton SP2 . . 130 B2
St Andrews Ridge [4]
SN25 . . . . .35 A8
St Annes Cl
Amesbury SP4 . . . . . 217 C4
Southwick BA14 . . . . 105 A4
St Ann Pl SP1 . . . . . . 152 B8
St Ann St SP1 . . . . . . 152 B8
St Arild's Rd GL9 . . . . .24 B4
St Athan Cl BA14. . . . 178 B8
St Augustine's RC Coll
BA14 . . . . 105 B8
St Augustine's Rd [5]
BA14 . . . . 105 B8
St Austell Way SN5 . . .49 F6
St Barbara's Rd SN13 . 84 D8
St Barnabas CE Sch
SN10 . . . . 179 F1
St Bartholomew's CE
Prim Sch SN4 . . . . .47 E2
St Bartholomew's St
SP7 . . . . 203 B4
St Bedes Cl [5] SP1 . . 146 D5
St Birinus Ct GL7 . . . . . 2 C5
St Birinus Gdns SP10 193 D2
St Birinus Rd [4] SP5 . 211 C7
St Birstan Gdns [9]
SP10 . . . . 193 D1
St Brendans Cl SP1 . . 146 C5
St Catherine La
St Catherine BA1 . . . .74 A1
St Catherine BA1 . . . . 82 A8
St Catherines Cl SN11. .81 C4
St Catherines RC Prim
Sch SN2. . . . . .35 C4
St Christophers Cl [4]
SP1 . . . . 146 D5
St Clair Rd SP2 . . . . . 152 B6
St Clements Cl SN3 . . .51 A4
St Clements Way
SP1 . . . . 146 C5
St Davids Cl SP1 . . . . 146 D5

St David's Way SN8 . . 213 D3
St Dennis Rd [7] SN16. .28 A3
St Dunstan Cl SN11 . . .81 A5
ST EDITH'S 96 D5
St Edith's Cl SP2. . . . 144 C1
St Edith's Marsh SN15 96 D5
St Edmund's Church St [2]
SP1. . . . . 146 B1
St Edmund's Girls' Sch
SP1. . . . . 146 E3
St Edmund's RC Prim Sch
SN11. . . . . 81 C4
St Edwards [12] SP7. . 202 C2
St Edwards Meadow
SP4. . . . . 133 B2
St Edwards Sch
SO51. . . . . 162 B2
Saintes Cl [1] SP1 . . . 146 D5
St Francis Ave SN15 . .78 C6
St Francis CE Prim Sch
SN25. . . . . .34 C5
St Francis Cl SN9 . . . 215 D5
St Francis Rd SP1. . . . 146 A4
St Francis Sch SN9 . . 215 B6
St George's CE Prim Schl
BA14. . . . . 102 E6
St Georges CE Sch
SP8. . . . . 137 E1
St George's Cl
Ogbourne St George
SN8 . . . . 169 A5
Warminster BA12 . . . 117 E5
St Georges Ct BA14 . . 102 E5
St Georges Pl BA14 . . 102 E5
St Georges RC Prim Sch
BA12. . . . . 117 D5
St Georges Rd
[35] Fordingbridge
SP6. . . . . 210 D1
Tidworth SP9 . . . . . . 216 C6
St George's Rd
Salisbury SP2. . . . . . 151 D7
Semington BA14 . . . . 102 E5
[11] Shaftesbury SP7. . 202 C1
St Giles Cl SN16 . . . . .29 A2
St Gregory's Ave SP2 145 D2
St Helens Gdns SN4. . .64 B5
St Helens View SN1. . .49 F4
St Ives Cl SN3 . . . . . .51 B7
St James SN15 . . . . . .59 A7
St James Cl SN2 . . . . . 34 D5
St James Dr [5] SN13. .84 B8
St James Gdns
Devizes SN10. . . . . . 214 B4
Trowbridge BA14. . . . 101 D1
St James's Cl SP1 . . . 146 D5
St James's St SP7 . . . 202 B1
St Martin's St SP11 . . 192 A5
St James Gdns
[10] Swindon SN2 . . 49 E7
St John Rd SN4. . . . . .64 A6
St Johns Alley SN10. . 214 A3
St John's Catholic Prim
Sch BA14. . . . . 105 B8
St John's CE Prim Sch
SP3. . . . . 203 D8
St John's CE Sch
BA12. . . . . 117 C6
St Johns Churchyard
SN10. . . . . 214 A3
St Johns Cl
Pewsey SN9. . . . . . . 215 D5
[19] Tisbury SP3. . . . 203 E8
St John's Cl
Donhead St Mary SP7. 203 A1
Marlborough SN8. . . 213 D4
[2] Salisbury SP1. . . . 152 D8
St John's Cres BA14. . 104 F6
St Johns Ct SN10 . . . 214 A3
St John's Ct SP2. . . . . 144 C3
St John's Hill SP7. . . . 202 B1
St John's Marlborough
SN8. . . . . 213 D1
St John's Priory Pk
GL7. . . . . 2 E3
St John's RC (Aided)
Prim Sch BA14 . . . . 105 A8
St John's Rd
Frome BA11. . . . . . . 110 B5
Warminster BA12 . . . 117 C5
St Johns Sq SP2 . . . . 144 C3
St John's St
Devizes SN10. . . . . . 214 A3
Lechlade GL7. . . . . 2 C4
Malmesbury SN16 . . . .28 B2
Salisbury SP1. . . . . . 152 B8
St John's Way SN16. . .29 A6
St Joseph's Catholic
College SN3. . . . . . . .50 E7
St Joseph's Catholic Prim
Sch SN10. . . . . 179 D8
St Joseph's Catholic Sch
SP1. . . . . 146 C5
St Josephs Cl SP1 . . . 146 C4
St Joseph's Dr SN15 . .78 C6
St Josephs RC Prim Sch
SN16. . . . . .28 B2
St Josephs Way SN15. .60 B2
St Judes Cl SN3 . . . . . 36 E4
St Julians Cl SN3 . . . .36 F4
St Just Cl SN4 . . . . . . 199 B3
St Katharine's CE (VC)
Prim Sch SN8 . . . . . 175 E4
St Katherine Gn [2]
SN3. . . . . .51 E7
St Katherines SN4 . . . 167 C6
St Katherine's Pl [17]
SN4. . . . . 163 A6

St Laurence CE Prim Sch
GL7. . . . . 2 D3
St Laurence Rd BA15. 100 E5
St Laurence Sch
BA15. . . . . 105 C7
St Lawrence Cl SP1. . 145 E5
St Lawrence Cres [6]
SP7. . . . . 202 C2
St Lawrence Rd GL7 . . 2 C4
St Lawrence Sq [8]
RG17. . . . . 177 B7
St Lawrence CE Prim
Acad SN26 . . . . .21 C1
St Leonard's Church*
St Leonards Cl SN16 . . 16 D3
St Leonard's Cl SP4. . 217 D8
St Leonard's Row
SN16. . . . . 16 D3
St Lukes Cl [8] SP1. . . 146 D5
St Lukes Dr SN15 . . . .78 C6
St Luke's Sch SN2 . . . 35 D5
St Margarets Cl SN11 . .81 A4
St Margaret's Cl [2]
SP1. . . . . 152 C8
St Margarets Gdns
SN15. . . . . .78 C6
St Margaret's Gdns
SN12. . . . . .94 C5
St Margaret's Gn [1]
SN13. . . . . .36 B2
St Margaret's Hill [1]
BA15. . . . . 100 D6
St Margarets Hospl
SN3. . . . . .36 B4
St Margaret's Mead
SN8. . . . . 213 F2
St Margaret's Pl [2]
BA15. . . . . 100 D6
St Margaret's Rd SN1. 50 D3
St Margarets Ret Pk
SN4. . . . . 36 D2
St Margaret's St
BA15. . . . . 100 D6
St Margaret's Villas [3]
BA15. . . . . 100 D6
St Mark's Ave SP1 . . 146 B3
St Marks CE Jun Sch
SP1. . . . . 146 B3
St Mark's Rd SP1 . . . 146 B2
St Martins SN8 . . . . . 213 E3
St Martin's CE VA Prim
Sch SP1. . . . . 152 C8
St Martins SP3 . . . . . 143 A4
St Martin's Cl SP3 . . . 143 A4
St Mary's BA14 . . . . . 178 A3
St Mary's Broughton
Gifford (VC) CE Prim
Sch SN12. . . . . .93 B3
St Mary's CE Inf Sch
SN8. . . . . 213 E2
St Marys CE Prim Sch
SN5. . . . . .33 C4
St Mary's Church
(remains of)* SP7. 206 A5
St Mary's Cl
Chitterne SP3. . . . . . 195 D6
Dinton SP3. . . . . 201 E2
Kempsford GL7 . . . . . 10 E6
Lyneham SN15. . . . . . 59 C3
Potterne SN10. . . . . . 179 D5
Redlynch SP5. . . . . . 211 D7
Sixpenny Handley SP5. 208 A4
Trowbridge BA14. . . . 101 E4
Wilton SP2. . . . . 144 C1
[1] Wylye BA12. . . . . 201 E8
St Mary's Ct BA12. . . 112 E4
St Marys Field GL7. . . 1 A5
St Marys Gdns SN10 . 214 B4
St Marys Gdns BA14. 101 E4
St Marys Gr SP2 . . . . .35 B1
St Marys La
Dilton Marsh BA13. . . 108 B1
Westbury BA13 . . . . 112 C8
St Mary's La [2] SN6. .28 A3
St Mary's Pl SN15. . . .78 D8
St Mary's RC Prim Sch
SN15. . . . . .78 C6
St Mary's Rd
Dinton SP3. . . . . 201 E2
Frome BA11. . . . . . . 110 B5
[12] Market Lavington
SN10 . . . . 179 F1
Salisbury SP2. . . . . . 151 F7
St Mary's Roman Catholic
Prim Sch SN2 . . . . .35 A1
St Mary's Sch
Calne SN11 . . . . 81 B3
Coombe SP7. . . . . . . 202 E1
St Mary's St [1] SN16. .28 A3
St Mary St SN15 . . . . .78 E7
St Matthews Cl
Rowde SN10 . . . . 96 D2
[6] Salisbury SP1. . . . 146 D5
St Mellion Cl SN15. . . .78 F7
St Michaels Ave SP9 . 216 C5
St Michael's CE Aided
Prim Sch SN8 . . . . . 170 A4
St Michael's CE Prim Sch
SP4. . . . . 190 B2
St Michaels Cl SN15 . . 59 F4
St Michael's Cl
[8] Aldbourne SN8. . . 170 A6

St Michael's Cl *continued*
Brinkworth SN15 . . . . 45 E6
[3] Lambourn RG17. . . 165 A1
Trowbridge BA14 . . . 102 A3
Wilton SP2. . . . . 144 B1
St Michael's Ct BA2. . .98 E8
St Michael's Rd
Melksham SN12. . . . . 94 A3
Salisbury SP2. . . . . . 145 C4
St Michael's View
SP9. . . . . 216 E7
St Michaels Vw BA12 138 F5
St Nicholas CE Prim Sch
SP4. . . . . 133 B6
St Nicholas CE VC Prim
Sch SN15. . . . . .96 A7
St Nicholas Cl
Calne SN11 . . . . 81 C4
[11] Ludgershall SP11. . 192 B5
Porton SP4. . . . . 133 D6
Trowbridge BA14 . . . 105 D3
Wilton SP2. . . . . 144 B1
Winsley BA15. . . . . . 99 D7
St Nicholas' Rd SP1. . 152 A7
St Nicholas Sch SN14 . .70 C2
St Osmund's Catholic
Prim Sch SP1 . . . . . 152 A7
St Osmund's Cl SP1. . 146 A5
St Patricks Ave SP9. . 216 B5
St Patrick's Catholic Prim
Sch SN15. . . . . .77 A1
St Paul's Dr SN3. . . . . .51 E6
St Paul's Prim Sch
SN15. . . . . 70 D2
St Paul's Rd SP2 . . . . 145 F1
St Paul's St SN15 . . . . .35 C1
St Paul St SN15 . . . . . 78 D8
St Peter's CE Academy
SN14. . . . . .78 A8
St Peter's CE Prim Sch
SP11. . . . . 192 E4
St Peter's Church*
SP3. . . . . 127 D4
St Peters Cl
Chippenham SN15 . . . 78 C6
[5] Shipton Bellinger
SP9. . . . . 199 D8
St Peter's Cl
Wilton SP2. . . . . 144 B2
Winterbourne Stoke
SP3. . . . . 196 F3
St Peter's Pump*
BA12. . . . . 123 C3
St Peters Rd SP1 . . . 146 C5
St Philip's Rd SN2 . . .35 E4
St Philip St [3] SN13. . 84 B8
St Quentin Cl SN3 . . . .36 B4
St Rumbold's Rd [9]
SP7. . . . . 202 C1
St Sampson's CE Prim
Sch SN6. . . . . 216 D4
St Stephen's Pl BA14. 105 D8
St Swithin Way [8]
SP10. . . . . 193 D1
St Teresas Cl [7] SP1 . 146 C5
St Teresa's Dr SN15. . .78 C7
StThomas à Becket C of
E (Aided) Prim Sch
SP3. . . . . 188 B3
St Thomas Cl [14]
SP10. . . . . 193 D2
St Thomas' Rd BA14 . 101 D1
St Thomas's Sq SP1. . 146 A1
St Thomas's Way
SP1. . . . . 146 C5
St Ursula's Cl [9] SP1. 146 D5
Salamanca Dr SP9 . . 216 D3
Salamander Ct SP9 . . 216 D7
Salcombe Gr SN3. . . . .50 E5
SALISBURY 152 C7
Salisbury Arts Ctr*
SP1. . . . . 146 B1
Salisbury Bsns Pk
SP1. . . . . 152 D7
Salisbury Cath* SP1 152 A8
Salisbury Cath Sch
SP1. . . . . 152 A7
Salisbury Cl
[1] Chippenham SN14 . . 78 A6
[8] Westbury Leigh
BA13 . . . . 108 E1
Salisbury District Hospl
SP5. . . . . 152 B3
Salisbury Hill SN8 . . 213 E1
Salisbury Hollow
BA13. . . . . 186 D8
Salisbury Medieval Hall*
SP1. . . . . 152 A8
Salisbury Mus &
Stonehenge Gallery*
SP1. . . . . 152 A7
Salisbury Racecourse
SP2. . . . . 150 E5
Salisbury Rd
Amesbury SP4 . . . . . 217 B3
Breamore SP6 . . . . . 210 F5
Cobley SP5. . . . . 208 E7
Codford St Mary BA12. 195 B2
Coombe Bissett SP5 . 150 F1
Coombe Bissett SP5 . 151 A2
Coombe Bissett SP5 . 151 B6
Downton SP5. . . . . . 211 A8
Fordingbridge SP6. . . 210 E1
Hungerford RG17. . . . 177 B6
Lopcombe Corner SP5. 134 E4
Marlborough SN8. . . . 213 D2
Netheravon SP4. . . . . 190 A3
Pewsey SN9. . . . . . . 215 B3

Salisbury Rd *continued*
Pewsey SN9. . . . . . . 215 C3
Plaitford/Landford
SO51. . . . . 212 E6
Sherfield English SO51 162 E2
Shipton Bellinger SP9 . 199 D7
[3] Shrewton SP3. . . . 196 E6
South Tedworth SP9. . 216 C3
Steeple Langford SP3 . 128 D8
Steeple Langford SP3 . 128 D8
Steeple Langford SP3 . 128 E5
Upton Lovell BA12. . . 194 F3
Wilton SP2. . . . . 144 B3
Salisbury Rd Ind Est
SN9. . . . . 215 B3
Salisbury Sch of English
SP1. . . . . 152 B8
Salisbury Sixth Form Coll
SP1. . . . . 152 B8
Salisbury St
Amesbury SP4 . . . . . 217 A3
Devizes SN10. . . . . . 179 D8
[26] Fordingbridge SP6 210 D1
Mere BA12. . . . . 139 A5
[3] Shaftesbury SP7. . 202 C1
Swindon SN1 . . . . . . .50 B7
Salisbury Sta SP2 . . . 145 F1
Salisbury & S Wiltshire
Mus & Stonehenge
Gall* SP1 . . . . 152 A7
Salisbury Swimming
Baths SP1 . . . . 146 B2
Sally In the Wood BA1 .90 C6
Sally Kings La [5]
SP7. . . . . 202 B2
Salmons Leap SN11. . .81 A5
Saltash Rd SN5 . . . . . .49 F5
Salter Cl BA14 . . . . . . 105 E7
Saltersford La SN14. . .78 A5
Salters Hill BA9. . . . . 137 A1
SALTERTON. 131 D4
Salt La
Salisbury SP1. . . . . . 146 B1
Winterbourne SP4. . . 133 C3
Saltram Cl SN3 . . . . . .51 C6
Salt Spring Dr SN4. . . .47 C1
Salzgitter Dr SN25. . . .35 A8
SAMBOURNE. 116 F5
Sambourne Chase
BA12. . . . . 117 A7
Sambourne Gdns
BA12. . . . . 117 A6
Sambourne Rd
Minety SN5. . . . . 17 D2
Warminster BA12 . . . 117 A6
Sambre Rd
Chiseldon SN4 . . . . . . 65 D1
Draycot Foliat SN4. . . 168 E8
Sams La SN10 . . . . .21 C1
Samson St SP9 . . . . . 216 D4
Sanctuary The* SN8. 173 D6
Sandacre Rd
[1] Swindon SN5 . . . . 34 A1
[3] Swindon SN5 . . . . .48 F8
Sandalwood Rd [1]
BA13. . . . . 108 E1
Sandbourne Rd [7]
SN25. . . . . 34 D5
Sanden Cl RG17 . . . . 177 B7
Sanders Cl SN2 . . . . . .35 F4
Sanders Rd BA14 . . . 101 C2
Sandes Cl SN15. . . . . .78 C7
Sandfield
Littleton Panell SN10. . 187 E8
Sutton Veny BA12 . . . 194 A5
Sandford Pk BA14 . . . 104 F7
Sandgate SN3. . . . . . . .36 B1
Sandhills Rd SP3 . . . . 142 A4
Sandholt Cl SN11. . . . .81 A4
Sandpit La BA12 . . . . 112 D5
Sandpit Rd SN11. . . . . 81 D4
Sandpits La
Sherston SN16. . . . . . 25 C1
Steeple Ashton BA14. . 106 E6
Sandpitts La
Gastard SN13. . . . . . . .85 E5
Lacock SN15. . . . . . . 86 A5
Sandquarry La BA9. . . 137 B1
Sandridge Comm
SN12. . . . . .94 D5
Sandridge Hill SN12 . .95 A6
Sandridge La SN12. . . .95 C7
Sandridge Pk* SN12. .95 B6
Sandridge Rd SN12. . .94 D5
Sandringham Rd
Swindon SN3. . . . . . . .50 F3
Trowbridge BA14. . . . 105 B5
Sandringhams The
SP5. . . . . 153 E1
Sandroyd Sch SP5 . . . 207 C5

Sands Cl SN10 . . . . . . 96 D1
Sands' La SP7 . . . . . . 203 C3
Sands' La SN10 . . . . . . 96 D1
Sand St
Longbridge Deverill
BA12 . . . . 121 A6
Longbridge Deverill
BA12 . . . . 121 A7
Longbridge Deverill
BA12 . . . . 121 B7
Sands The SN9 . . . . . 181 C7
Sandstone Rd SN25. . .34 F7
Sandwood Cl SN5 . . . .34 B2
Sandy La
Edington BA13 . . . . . 186 C7
Marten SN8 . . . . 184 D8
Redlynch SP5. . . . . . 211 D8
Swindon SN1 . . . . . . .50 B4
SANDY LANE. 88 B4
Sandy Lea Ave [5]
SN13. . . . . .76 B1
Sandy Leaze BA15 . . . 100 C6
Sandy Ridge SN11 . . . .81 C1
Sanford St [3] SN1. . . .50 C6
Sangster Ave SN12 . . .94 B4
SANHAM GREEN 177 B5
Sapphire Rd SN26 . . . .21 A1
Sarsen Cl SN1 . . . . . . .49 F4
Sarson La SP11 . . . . . 192 E1
Sarum Ave SN12. . . . . .94 B2
Sarum Cl
Salisbury SP2. . . . . . 145 E3
Shipton Bellinger SP9 . 199 C8
Sarum Dr SN10 . . . . . 214 C2
Sarum Gdns BA13 . . . 109 A4
Sarum Rd SN14. . . . . .78 A6
Sarum St Paul's CE Prim
Sch SP2. . . . . 145 F2
Sarum Way
Calne SN11 . . . . 81 A3
[2] Hungerford RG17. . 177 B6
Sasson Cl SP2 . . . . . . 145 C3
Sassoon Cl BA12. . . . 116 D6
Saunders Ave SP4 . . . 146 C6
Saunders Gr SN13 . . . 76 D1
Saunders Meadow
SN8. . . . . 183 E1
Savernake Ave SN12. . .94 C6
Savernake Cl [4]
BA12. . . . . 117 A8
Savernake Cres SN8. . 213 F2
Savernake Ct SN8 . . . 213 E2
Savernake Hospl
SN8. . . . . 175 A7
Savernake Rd
Burbage SN8 . . . . . . 175 D1
Corsham SN13. . . . . . 84 D8
Hudswell SN13. . . . . . 84 D8
Savernake St SN1. . . . .50 B5
Savill Cres SN4 . . . . . .63 F7
Sawpit Dr SN8. . . . . . 175 C5
Sawpit Hill BA12. . . . 140 B4
Sawyer Cl SP9. . . . . . 216 D8
Sawyer Rd SN25 . . . . .35 B6
Sawyers Cl SN16. . . . . 17 A2
Sawyers Cres [3] SN13 76 D1
SAWYERS HILL. 17 A2
Sawyers Hill SN16 . . . .17 A2
Saxby Rd SN15 . . . . . .70 E1
Saxifrage Bank SN12. .94 C3
Saxon Cl
Cricklade SN6 . . . . . . 19 D7
[14] Market Lavington
SN10 . . . . 179 F1
Sherston SN16. . . . . . 25 C1
Westbury BA13 . . . . 109 A4
Saxon Ct
North Tidworth SP9 . . 216 D7
[8] Swindon SN3. . . . 50 D4
Saxon Dr BA14. . . . . . .78 A8
Saxonhurst [4] SP5. . . 211 B8
Saxon Leas SP5. . . . . 149 C6
Saxon Meadow SP5. . 211 A8
Saxon Mill
Chiseldon SN4. . . . . . 65 D5
Swindon SN25. . . . . . 34 B2
Saxon Rd SP2 . . . . . . 151 F6
Saxon Rise SN8. . . . . 183 E1
Saxons Acre BA12. . . . 116 E6
Saxon Spur [10] SP7. . 202 C2
Saxon St SN14. . . . . . .78 B8
Saxon Way
Andover SP10 . . . . . 193 D2
Fairford GL7. . . . . 1 C6
Winsley BA15. . . . . . 99 F7
Saxton Wlk SN5 . . . . .49 B8
Scallows La [16] SN8 170 B2
Scamblers Mead
SP11. . . . . 193 A3
Scamell's Rd SP2 . . . 146 A2
Scarborough Rd SN2 . .49 F8
Scarlet Cl [8] SN25 . . .34 F7
Scholard's La SN16. . . 17 A2
Scholars Cl [34] SP11. 192 A5
Scholars Pk SN10 . . . .96 C2
Scholars Way SN13. . .93 F6
School Cl
Chiseldon SN4. . . . . . 65 E4
Keevil BA14 . . . . 178 B5
St Paul Malmesbury Without
SN16 . . . . 28 A1
Vernhams Dean SP11 . 185 C3
School Dr [25] SP4 . . . 198 B7
School Hill
Alderbury SP5 . . . . . 153 C2
Brinkworth SN15. . . . . 45 E5
School La
All Cannings SN10. . . 180 F8

School La continued
[1] Amesbury SP4 .... 217 B3
Badminton GL9 .... 38 E2
Bromham SN15 ...... 96 A7
Castle Combe SN14.... 68 A7
Castle Eaton SN6..... 10 B4
East Garston RG17.. 171 E8
Grittleton SN14...... 54 E5
Hindon SP3 .... 200 B3
Lea SN16 .... 29 A2
Little Bedwyn SN8 .. 176 C5
Marlborough SN8.... 213 A2
Melbury Abbas SP7.. 206 B7
Melksham Without
SN12 .... 93 D8
Meysey Hampton GL7 ...1 A4
South Cerney GL7 .... 6 F7
Staverton BA14...... 101 D5
Westbury BA13 ...... 108 E1
Wroughton SN4...... 64 A6
School Rd
Calne SN11 .... 81 A4
[1] Durrington/Bulford
SP4............... 198 C7
Kemble GL7 .... 4 F7
Nomansland SP5 .... 212 C4
Redlynch SP5....... 211 E6
Seend SN12........ 178 D8
School Wlk SN14......78 A7
Scimitar Way SN3....36 B5
Scorhill La SN1......50 A2
Scotby Ave SN3.....50 E2
Scotchel Gn SN9.... 215 D5
Scotland BA14....... 105 B2
Scotland Hill
Clanville SN15.......56 F5
Seagry SN15......... 57 A5
Scotland La
Beckington BA11..... 107 C4
Landford SP5........ 212 B8
Scotland Rd SN12.....94 A6
Scotney Cres [2] SN25..34 F6
Scots La SP1 .... 146 A1
Scott Cl
Burbage SN8 .... 183 C8
Swindon SN25 .... 34 C8
Scotts Cl SN11.......89 B2
Scott's Cl SP5....... 211 A8
Scott's Hill SP7..... 203 C4
Scott Thomlinson Rd
GL7.................1 F6
Scott Way SN1......49 E3
Scouts La SP5 ...... 149 F4
Scratchbury Camp*
BA12.............. 194 B7
Scrubbity Barrows*
SP5................ 207 E4
Scythe Cl [12] SP11... 193 F2
Seacole Cres SN1......50 A3
Seaford Cl SN5.......49 A6
Seagrim Rd SP2 .... 144 C2
Seagry CE Prim Sch
SN15............... 57 D6
Seagry Ct SN2........35 B5
Seagry Heath
Great Somerford SN15 .43 F1
Great Somerford SN15 . 44 A1
Lower Seagry SN15....57 F7
Seagry Hill SN15......57 D3
Seagry Rd
Hullavington SN14....56 D6
Sutton Benger SN15 ...57 D2
Seaton Cl SN25.......34 F5
Second Broad Dr
SP3................ 128 C2
Secret Gdn The GL7 ...6 F7
Sedgefield Gdns
SN10.............. 214 B4
Sedgefield Way SN14 .78 F4
SEDGEHILL......... 202 C7
Sedge Rd [20] SP11 ... 193 F2
SEEND............. 178 E7
Seend CE Prim Sch
SN12.............. 178 D8
SEEND CLEEVE..... 178 C7
Seend Hill SN12 .... 178 F8
Sefton La SN8 ...... 168 B1
Sefton Rd [4] SN25....34 C7
Sefton Way SN25......34 C7
Selby Cres SN5.......49 B4
Seldon Cl [4] SN3.....50 E6
Selions Cl SN14.......70 B2
SELLS GREEN......95 E1
Selwood Cl [1] SN1....50 E7
Selwood Cres [1]
BA11.............. 110 A7
Selwyn Rd SN25......20 C1
SEM HILL.......... 202 E5
SEMINGTON........ 102 E5
Semington Bypass
BA14.............. 102 F4
Semington Rd
Berryfield BA14........94 A1
Melksham Without
BA14.............. 178 A8
Semington Strand
SN1.................49 F3
Semington Turnpike
BA14.............. 102 F5
SEMLEY............ 202 F5
Semley Ceva Prim Sch
SP7................ 202 F5
Semley Wlk SN3.....35 C4
Senior Dr SP2....... 152 A5
Sergeant Rogers Way
Devizes SN10........ 172 A2

Sergeant Rogers Way
continued
Roundway SN10...... 214 E7
Serotine Cres BA14.. 106 A7
SERRINGTON........ 129 D7
Seth Ward Dr SP1 .. 146 D4
Seven Barrows*
Lambourn RG17...... 165 A5
South Tedworth SP9... 191 B3
Sevenfields SN6......23 A7
Seven Fields Nature
Reserve* SN25.....35 B5
Seven Fields Prim Sch
SN2................35 B4
SEVENHAMPTON.....23 B2
Severn Ave SN25.....35 A4
Severn Cl SN11.......81 A5
Severn Rd SN12......94 A6
SEVINGTON..........55 A2
Sexton Cl SN25.......20 B1
Seymour Ct BA14.... 101 C1
Seymour Gdns SP4 .. 217 A3
Seymour Rd
Chippenham SN15 .....78 F8
Swindon SN3.........50 F6
Trowbridge BA14..... 101 C2
Seymours Ct* BA11. 107 A6
Shackleton Cl SN12...94 D1
Shackleton Rd SN10. 214 D2
Shackleton Sq SP10 . 193 F2
Shady Bower SP1.... 152 C8
Shady Bower Cl SP1. 152 C8
SHAFTESBURY...... 202 A1
Shaftesbury Ave SN3 .51 B4
Shaftesbury CE Prim Sch
SP7................ 202 D2
Shaftesbury Ct BA14. 105 A6
Shaftesbury Dro SP2. 151 E5
Shaftesbury Leisure Ctr
SP7................ 202 C1
Shaftesbury Mus*
SP7................ 202 C1
Shaftesbury Rd
Barford St Martin
SP3................ 143 B3
Compton Chamberlayne
SP3................ 205 A8
East Knoyle SP3..... 141 C1
Fovant SP3......... 204 F8
Mere BA12.......... 139 B4
Mere BA12.......... 139 C2
Motcombe SP7....... 202 A3
Wilton SP2.......... 144 B3
Shaftesbury St* SP2. 144 C1
Shaftesbury St [19]
SP6................ 210 D1
Shaftesbury Cl SN5...33 C5
Shails La
Melksham Without
SN12.............. 178 A8
Trowbridge BA14..... 101 C1
Shakespeare Ave
SP10.............. 193 C1
Shakespeare Dr SN8. 213 C2
Shakespeare Path
SN3................35 F3
Shakespeare Rd
Royal Wootton Bassett
SN4.................47 F3
Salisbury SP1....... 145 F4
SHALBOURNE...... 176 F2
Shalbourne CE Prim Sch
SN8................ 176 F2
Shalbourne Cl
Hungerford RG17.... 177 A7
Swindon SN2 ....35 B5
Shalford La BA9 .... 136 A3
Shallowbrooks La
Luckington SN14......39 F7
Sherston SN14.......39 F8
Sherston SN14.......40 A6
Shallows The SP6 ... 210 F4
Shallow Wagon La
BA13.............. 108 F6
Shambles The BA15. 100 D7
Shanklin Rd SN2......34 E4
Shapland SN25.......20 C1
Shaplands [4] SN3....36 A2
Shapwick Cl SN3.....51 C7
SHARCOTT......... 182 A6
Sharcott Dro SN9.... 215 A4
Share La SP3........ 203 C6
Sharp Cl SN5........49 B7
Sharplands
Sutton Benger SN15 ...57 D2
Sutton Benger SN15 ...57 E1
Sharpley Cl SP6..... 210 D2
SHARPSTONE.......99 A4
Sharpstone La BA2....99 A4
Sharratt Ave [4] SP1.. 146 C5
Shaston Ct SP2...... 144 C3
Shave La BA10....... 122 A4
SHAW
Melksham Without.....93 D7
Swindon............49 B7
Shaw CE(VC) Prim Sch
SN12...............93 D8
Shawgrove SN8..... 176 B3
Shaw Hill
Collingbourne Ducis
SN8............... 191 E7
Melksham Without
SN12...............93 D7
Shaw Rd SN5........49 B7
Shaw Ridge Leisure Pk*
SN5................49 B6
Shaw Ridge Prim Sch
SN5................49 B7

Shaw Village* SN8. 173 F4
Shear Cross BA12... 116 E1
Shearings The SN1....50 C4
Shearman St BA14... 105 D7
Shears Dr
Amesbury SP4...... 217 C1
Amesbury SP4...... 217 D1
Shearwater
Horningsham BA12 .. 119 F6
Longbridge Deverill
BA12.............. 120 A7
Shearwater Way SN13 84 D7
Shearwood Rd SN5....34 A1
Sheasby Cl SP5..... 208 A3
Sheen Cl
Salisbury SP2....... 145 B5
[4] Swindon SN3.....49 A4
Sheepbridge Rd SP4. 198 E7
Sheepcote Barton [3]
BA14.............. 105 C7
SHEEPDROVE...... 165 B2
Sheepdrove Rd
RG17.............. 165 B2
Sheep Fair Way [13]
RG17.............. 165 A1
Sheepridge SN8 .... 168 E3
Sheepscroft SN14.....70 B2
Sheep St
Devizes SN10....... 214 B3
Highworth SN6.......23 A6
Sheepwash La [2]
BA12.............. 201 E8
Sheerwold Cl SN3....36 B3
Sheffield La SN13....76 D1
Sheffield Dr SN15.....60 A1
SHEFFORD
WOODLANDS...... 171 E4
Shelburne Rd SN11...81 C1
Shelburne Way SN11 .79 F2
Sheld Dr SN15.......60 A1
Sheldon Bsns Pk
SN14...............77 D8
Sheldon Manor & Gdns*
SN14...............69 D1
Sheldon Rd SN14.....78 B7
Sheldon Sch SN14....70 B1
Shelfinch SN5........49 D4
Shelley Ave [2] SN4...47 F3
Shelley Dr SN15..... 145 F4
Shelley Gdns SN12....94 B4
Shelley St SN1.......50 B5
Shelley Way BA12... 116 D6
Shelly's Wlk GL7.......2 D4
Shenton St SN3......36 B3
Shepherds SN3.......84 D6
Shepherds Breach [1]
SN4.................47 E2
Shepherds Cl
Coombe Bissett SP5 .. 151 A1
Odstock SP5........ 152 A1
Odstock SP5........ 158 A8
Shepherds Croft SN14. 106 C3
Shepherds Dro BA14. 106 C3
Shepherd's La
Donhead St Andrew
SP7................ 203 B2
Selwood BA11...... 114 D6
Shepherds Mead
BA13.............. 112 A8
Shepherd Spring Jun &
Inf Sch [33] SP10..... 193 E2
Shepherds Rise SP11 185 C3
Sheppard Cl SN15....78 F5
Sheppard's Acre SN15 .46 B7
Sheppards Rise SN15 .46 B7
Sheppard St SN1.....50 B7
Shepperd St SP9.... 216 D8
Shepperton Way SN25 .34 F6
Sherborne Pl SN3....51 B7
Sherborne Rd BA14.. 101 A1
Sherborne St GL7......2 C4
Sherbourne Dr
Old Sarum SP4...... 146 B8
Winterbourne SP4... 132 C1
Sherfield SP4....... 133 A2
Sherfield English La
SO51.............. 212 F7
Sherfield English Rd
SP5................ 212 E6
Sherfields SN4.......47 E1
Sherford Rd SN25....34 E4
Sheridan Dr SN4......47 F3
Sheringham Ct SN3.. 51 D3
Sherington Mead
SN15...............79 B4
Sherrer La SN26......20 C2
SHERRINGTON...... 194 F1
Sherrington La BA12. 195 A2
Sherrington Mead
SN15...............79 B4
SHERSTON......... 25 B1
Sherston Ave SN2....35 C5
Sherston CE Prim Sch
SN16...............25 C1
SHERSTON PARVA
OR PINKNEY....... 25 E2
Sherston Rd
Brokenborough SN16 . 27 E4
Luckington SN14......39 E5
Sherston SN14.......40 A6
Sherwood Ave SN2...94 C6
Sherwood Cl [3]
BA12.............. 117 A8
Sherwood Rd SN3....51 B4
Shetland Cl
Swindon SN5........49 B7
Westbury BA13 ..... 108 D2
Shetland Gdns SN5...49 A7
Shipley Dr SN25......34 F6

SHIPTON
BELLINGER........ 199 D8
Shipton Bellinger Prim
Sch............... 199 C8
Shipton Gr SN3......50 E5
Shipton Hill [3] SN16...28 A4
SHIPTON MOYNE.....26 E8
Shiptons La SN15.....43 F2
Shire Cl SN5.........49 A7
Shire Ct [2] SN1......50 A5
Shire Hill SN14......66 A7
Shires Sh Ctr The
BA14.............. 105 C8
Shire Way BA13 .... 108 E2
Shirley Cl SN3.......50 F7
SHOCKERWICK......82 E5
Shockerwick Farm La
BA1................82 E6
Shockerwick La BA1...82 E5
Shoddesden La SP11. 192 B4
Shoemaker La SN15...45 F6
SHOE THE..........66 F1
Shop La
Badminton GL9 ......38 E2
Wingfield BA14...... 104 C6
Shoreland Cl BA13... 108 F3
Shore Pl BA14....... 100 F1
SHORNCOTE...........6 A6
Short Dro SN4...... 163 C6
Short La
Andover SP11....... 193 B1
Barford St Martin SP3. 143 A4
Shortlands SP3...... 143 A4
Short River Rd BA13. 109 D2
Short St
Dilton Marsh BA13... 112 A6
Ludgershall SP11.... 192 A5
Melksham SN12......94 C6
Shoscombe Gdns [3]
BA11.............. 110 C7
Shoscombe Gn SN3...51 B6
Showfield SN4.......47 D3
Shrapnel Rd [1] SP4.. 197 E7
Shrewsbury Rd SN3...50 F6
SHREWTON......... 196 E6
Shrewton CE(VC) Prim
Sch SP3........... 196 E7
Shrewton Cl BA14... 105 D6
Shrewton Rd BA12... 195 E6
Shrewton Wlk SN25...35 C5
Shripple La SP5..... 149 D6
Shrivenham Rd
Highworth SN6.......23 B4
South Marston SN4...37 C3
Swindon SN1........50 E7
Swindon SN3........36 E2
Shropshire Cl
Salisbury SP2....... 145 C5
[1] Swindon SN5....49 B7
Shurnhold SN12.......93 F5
Shute End SN5...... 153 B2
Shute End Rd SP5... 153 B4
Shuter Gr SN25......35 B8
Shutts La
Coombe Bissett SP5 .. 151 A1
Coombe Bissett SP5 .. 157 A8
Sidbury Circular Rd
SP9................ 216 B7
Sidbury Hill Ave SP9. 216 C8
Siddal St
Swindon SN25 ....34 D8
Swindon SN5 ....20 D1
Sidings The [2] SP5.. 211 B8
Sidmouth Par SN10.. 214 B3
Sidney Cl
[3] Swindon SN3....50 E6
Swindon SN5........48 F4
Sidney St SP2....... 145 F1
Sidney Wood Ct SN14 .78 C7
Sigerson Rd [2] SN25. 34 C5
Signal St SP4....... 198 E6
Signal Way
Chippenham SN14.....78 B8
Swindon SN1........50 D3
Silbury Cl
Chippenham SN14.....78 A6
Westbury BA13 ..... 108 F4
Silbury Hill* SN8... 173 C7
Silbury Mews SN5....34 E3
Silbury Rd SN11......81 A3
Silchester Way SN5...49 C6
Silk Houses BA12... 123 E4
Sillars Green SN16....27 F6
Sillen La SP6....... 209 B6
Sillington La SN10... 179 B7
Silman Cl SN13......76 D1
Silton Rd
Bourton SP8........ 138 A2
Zeale SP8.......... 137 F2
Silver Barrow*
SP3................ 188 D2
Silver Birch Rd BA14. 105 B5
Silver Cl SN16.......17 B2
Silver La
Compton Bassett
SN11.............. 166 B4
Selwood BA11...... 114 C6
Silverless St SN8 ... 213 D3
Silver Meadows
BA14.............. 105 A5
Silver Rd SN9...... 215 B5
Silver St La
Brokerswood BA13... 107 E6
Bromham SN15 ......87 D1
Trowbridge BA14.... 105 B5
Silver St
Alderbury SP5...... 153 B2

Silver St continued
Bradford-on-Avon
BA15.............. 100 D6
Calne SN11 ....81 B1
Calne Without SN11...89 B8
Colerne SN14........75 B3
Corsham SN13.......85 C6
Kington Langley SN15 ..70 F7
Malmesbury SN16 ....28 A3
Minety SN16.........17 B2
Potterne SN10...... 179 D5
Salisbury SP1....... 152 A8
Sherston SN16.......40 C8
South Cerney GL7 ......6 F7
Steeple Ashton BA14.. 178 A3
Trowbridge BA14.... 105 D8
Warminster BA12 ... 117 A7
Westbury BA13 ..... 112 C8
Wilton SP2......... 144 D3
Silverton Rd SN3.....51 B6
Silver Wood SN5.... 153 C3
Silverwood Dr SP1... 146 E2
Silverwood Sch BA14 101 E1
Silveston Way SN16...27 A8
Simmance Way SP4.. 217 C3
Simnel Cl SN5........48 F5
Simonds Rd [17] SP11. 192 A5
Sir Bernard Lovell Rd
SN16...............28 C1
Siren Cl [8] SN3......51 B8
Six Acre La
Charnage BA12 ..... 139 F5
Shalbourne RG17.... 176 F3
West Knoyle SP3.... 140 A4
SIXPENNY
HANDLEY.......... 208 A3
Sixpenny Handley Fst Sch
SP5................ 208 A4
Skew Bridge Cl SN4...47 C1
Skew Bridge Rd SP2. 145 D2
Skew Rd SP2........ 145 B2
Skinner's Cl SN6......22 B7
Skye Cl SN6.........22 F7
Skylark SN26........21 B1
Skylark Rd [3] SN12...94 D5
Skylark Rise [11] SN6...19 D8
Skynet Dr SN13......84 B8
Slab La SP5......... 211 C7
Slade Dr SN3.........36 B1
Sladesbrook BA15... 100 E8
Sladesbrook Cl BA15. 100 D8
Slade St SN2........34 E2
Slades The SN11......81 C3
Slag La BA13....... 108 F5
Slaite La SN14......66 C5
Slater Rd SN9...... 215 C5
Slate Way SP5...... 148 B3
SLAUGHTERFORD....76 A8
Slaughterford Rd
SN14...............68 C1
Slay Barrow* SP4... 189 A6
Sleightholme Ct [2]
BA14.............. 105 C7
Sleight La SN10..... 179 F6
Sleight Rd SN10 .... 214 E1
Slessor Rd
Lyneham SN15.......60 A1
Lyneham & Bradenstoke
SN15.............. 166 A8
Slim Rd BA12....... 113 E1
Sling Orch SP3..... 204 E7
Sling Rd SP4....... 198 E7
Slipper La SN4.......65 D4
Slipway The BA14.... 101 D4
Slodbrook La SP8... 138 E1
Slowgrove Cl BA14.. 105 F8
Smallbrook Gdns [3]
BA14.............. 101 D5
Smallbrook La BA12. 117 D5
Smallbrook Mdws Nature
Reserve* BA12..... 117 C5
Smallbrook Rd BA12. 117 B5
Small La SN10...... 180 F4
Smannell Rd SN1 ... 193 F2
Smart Cl SN25.......34 E8
Smay Down La SN8. 184 E6
Smeaton Rd
[1] Andover SP10.... 193 B1
Smitan Brook SN3....51 D6
Smith Bridge Rd
RG17.............. 177 B7
Smithfield St [2] SP4. 217 D3
Smithmead La SN5 ...33 F6
Smiths Cl SN9...... 215 B5
Smith's Cl SN5.......33 C5
Smith's Hill OX12.... 165 F7
Smith St
Nettleton SN14......67 A6
West Kington SN14...66 F7
Smiths Yd SN13......77 A2
Smithy La SN9...... 181 C6
Smithys La SN5..... 181 C6
Smithwell Cl BA14... 105 F8
Snail-Creep Hanging*
SP3................ 200 E7
Snails' La SN10..... 214 A3
Snappersnaps BA13. 109 A3
Snapps Cl SN4.......64 B5
Snap Village* SN8 . 169 C7
Snarlton La SN12.....94 D5
Snell Ave SN14......28 A5
Snoddington Rd
Fyfield SP11........ 192 D1
Shipton Bellinger SP9. 199 E7
Snowberry La SN12...94 C3
Snowdon Pl SN2......35 E4
Snowdrop Cl [2] SN25 . 34 D5

Snow Hill
Dinton SP3........ 201 F2
Hilmarton SN11......73 F5
Snowshill Cl SN25....34 F5
Snowswick La SN7....12 E7
Snuff St SN10...... 214 A4
Sobers Sq SP11..... 193 F2
Sodbury Rd GL9......52 F7
SODOM.............59 C7
Sodom La SN15......59 C7
Solar Way SP4...... 217 F4
Soldier's Ring* SP6. 209 D4
Solstice Pk Ave SP4. 217 D4
Solstice Pk Bsns Park
SP4................ 217 D4
Solstice Rise SP4 .. 217 B3
Somerbrook SN15....44 B2
Somerdale Cl [6] SN5 .49 C6
Somerford Cl SN2....35 C4
SOMERFORD KEYNES .. 5 F3
Somerford Lakes
Reserve* GL7........5 D2
Somerfords Walter
Powell VA CE Prim Sch
SN15...............44 B2
Somerleyton Cl
SN10.............. 187 D8
Somerset Cl [1] RG17. 177 B7
Somerset Cres SN2...94 B3
Somerset Ct [11] SN4. 163 B6
Somerset Dr BA13... 109 A5
Somerset Rd
Salisbury SP1....... 146 B3
Swindon SN2........34 F1
Somerset Way BA14. 102 F6
Somerton Gdns
BA11.............. 110 C7
Somerville Ct [2]
SP10.............. 193 F1
Somerville Rd SN3....50 F6
Somme Rd SP11..... 191 F4
Soprano Way SN4 .. 106 A8
Sopwith Pk [7] SP10. 193 C1
SOPWORTH.........24 D1
Sopworth La SN14....39 E6
Sopworth Rd SN14....39 E5
Sorley Cl SN8....... 213 B3
Sorrel Cl
Melksham SN12.......94 B3
Royal Wootton Bassett
SN4.................47 E4
Trowbridge BA14.... 105 D5
Sorrel Dr SN14......70 B3
Sorrel St SN15.......81 D5
Sound Copse SN5....34 B2
Southall Cl SN5......49 C7
South Alley [6] BA12. 116 E5
Southampton Rd
Alderbury SP5...... 153 A5
Alderbury SP5...... 153 D3
Fordingbridge SP6... 210 E1
Landford SP5....... 212 C7
Landford SP5....... 212 D6
Salisbury SP1....... 152 C7
Southampton St SN1 . 50 D6
Southay SN3........ 186 B7
South Bank SN8 .... 174 F2
SouthBank Gdns
RG17.............. 165 B1
Southbank Glen SN4.. 47 F2
Southbourne Way
SP4................ 133 D6
SOUTH BREWHAM . 122 A4
SOUTHBROOK..... 139 B4
Southbrook BA12... 139 C4
Southbourne Gdns
BA12.............. 139 B4
Southbrook La BA13. 178 B1
Southbrook Rd SN12. 93 F6
Southbrook St SN2...35 B1
Southbrook Infs Sch
SN10.............. 214 C2
Southbroom Rd
SN10.............. 214 B3
Southbroom St James
Church Academy
SN10.............. 214 C2
SOUTH CERNEY......7 A6
South Charford Dro
SP6................ 210 D6
South Cliffe Rd [6]
SN6................ 179 F1
SOUTHCOTT....... 215 D3
Southcott Rd
Pewsey SN9........ 215 D4
Pewsey SN9........ 215 F2
Southcroft Dr BA13.. 111 D4
Southcroft Rd [2]
SN13...............76 B1
South Cross La SN10. 179 C3
Southdown [3] SN4.. 163 A5
South Down Way
BA12.............. 116 D7
South Dr
South Tedworth SP9... 216 C4
Swindon SN25 ....34 F8
SOUTHEND......... 168 F4
Southernwood Dr
SN2................34 C4
Southerwicks SN13...84 F8
Southey Cl [3] SN25...34 F8
Southfield
[2] Aldbourne SN8... 170 A6
Southwick BA14.... 104 F2

Southfield *continued*
West Overton SN8.... **173** F6
Southfield Jun Sch
SN6........................**23** A5
Southfields BA11.... **110** A3
Southfield Way BA11 **110** A3
Southgate
Devizes SN10....... **214** B2
Stonebridge BA11.... **110** D7
Southgate Cl SN10... **214** B2
South La
Downton SP5....... **211** A8
Nomansland SP5..... **212** C4
Southleigh BA15..... **100** C5
Southleigh View
BA12.................. **117** C5
SOUTH MARSTON **36** F5
South Marston CE Prim
Sch SN3............... **36** C6
South Marston Park
SN3..................... **36** C7
South Mdw La SN5.... **19** F3
Southmead SN14...... **78** B6
South Mill Cl SP4.... **217** B2
Southmill Hill SP4.... **217** B1
South Mill Rd SP4.... **217** B2
SOUTH NEWTON **130** B2
South Newton Hospital
SP2.................... **130** B2
South Pk★ SP11.... **192** B4
South Pl
Calne SN11.......... **81** B2
Corsham SN13....... **77** A1
Southside
Laverstock SP4..... **146** D8
Shipton Moyne GL8.. **26** E7
Southside Cl SN16.... **42** E4
South St
Aldbourne SN8..... **170** A6
Avebury SN8........ **173** B8
Broad Chalke SP5... **205** B4
Corsham SN13....... **77** A1
Great Wishford SP2.. **130** A3
8 Salisbury SP2.... **145** F1
Swindon SN1........ **50** C4
Warminster BA12.... **116** E5
Wilton SP2.......... **144** C1
SOUTH TIDWORTH .. **216** D4
South Ugford Medieval
Village of★ SP2.... **144** A2
South View RG17.... **177** B7
South View Ave SN3... **50** E5
South View Pl SN8.... **213** E3
Southview Rd BA14... **105** D6
Southville Cl BA15... **100** E5
Southville Rd BA15... **100** E5
Southward La SN8.... **170** A6
Southwark Cl SP9.... **216** E6
Southway SP4........ **134** B7
South Way
Alderbury SP5....... **153** E2
Trowbridge BA14.... **105** D7
Southway Rd BA15... **100** D4
Southwell Cl **2** SN14..**78** A5
South Western Rd
SP2.................. **145** F1
SOUTHWICK **104** F3
Southwick Ave SN2... **35** F6
Southwick CE Prim Sch
BA14.................. **104** F3
Southwick Ctry Pk★
BA14.................. **104** F5
Southwick Mws **5**
BA14.................. **105** C5
Southwick Rd BA14... **105** C2
South Wilts Grammar
School for Girls
SP1.................. **146** A3
Southwold Cl SN25 ...**34** B6
Southwood Rd BA14.. **105** F8
SOUTH WRAXALL **91** D6
Sovereign Ct SP2.... **145** F1
Soyuz Cres **12** SN25...**34** B7
Spackman La SN13 ....**84** F8
Spa Cl SN6............**23** B6
Spa Ct SN12..........**94** B2
Spanbourn Ave SN14 ..**78** D7
Spaniels Bridge Rd
SN10.................. **172** C1
Sparcells Dr SN5......**34** B2
Spa Rd SN12..........**94** B3
Sparkes Dr SP5...... **153** F1
Sparrow St BA14..... **105** E6
SPA THE..............**94** C2
Spa The BA14.........**92** E1
Speedwell Cl
Melksham SN12...... **94** C2
1 Swindon SN25 ..... **34** B5
3 Trowbridge BA14.. **105** D6
Spencer Cl
Melksham SN12...... **94** A4
Swindon SN5..........**48** F7
Spencers Orch
Bradford-on-Avon
BA15................. **100** D5
Wroughton SN4......**64** B6
Spenser Cl SN3........**51** A7
Spereshott SN5.......**49** D4
Spey Ct SP10........ **193** F1
Spiders Island SP5.... **153** F2
Spiers Piece BA14 ... **178** B3
Spindle Tree Ct
Swindon SN2........**35** B2
1 Swindon SN25 ... **35** B2
Spine Rd GL7..........**7** E7

Spine Rd (East) GL7 ....**7** C4
Spine Rd W GL7........**6** A2
Spine Rd West GL7 ....**5** F2
Spine Rd (East) SN6...**6** F3
Springfield Rd BA12 .. **139** B5
Spin Hill SN10....... **179** E1
Spinners Croft **5**
BA14................. **105** D7
Spinners Way BA12... **139** B6
Spinney Cl
Chippenham SN14.....**78** A6
3 Liddington SN4.... **163** A4
Spinney Rd SP11..... **192** A5
Spinney The
Lechlade GL7..........**2** C4
3 Littleton Panell
SN10.................. **187** E8
Trowbridge BA14.... **105** F8
SPIRTHILL..............**73** B4
Spitalcroft Rd SN10.. **214** C4
Spital La SN6..........**19** E7
Spitfire Rd
Calne SN11...........**81** D3
Laverstock SP4......**146** D8
Spitfire Way SN3......**36** C7
Spode Cl SN25........**34** D7
Spout La SN12....... **178** F8
Spouts La SO51...... **212** F7
Spracklands SP3 .... **201** F2
Spratsgate La GL7.....**6** B4
Spray Leaze **10** SP11.. **192** B5
Spray Rd RG17...... **177** C2
Sprays **9** SN8....... **183** D8
Spread Eagle Hill
SP7.................. **206** B6
Spreckley Rd **1**
SN11.................. **166** A1
Spring Bottom SP4 .. **197** E2
Spring Cl SN1.........**50** C6
Springers Cl SN10... **214** D4
Springfield BA15..... **100** E6
Springfield Bldgs
SN15..................**78** D8
Springfield Cl
Corsham SN13........**84** A8
7 Shaftesbury SP7... **202** C2
Trowbridge BA14.... **101** E2
Springfield Cres
11 Redlynch SP5..... **211** C7
Royal Wootton Bassett
SN4....................**47** D2
Springfield Dr SN11...**81** A3
Springfield Gdns
SN12...................**85** C1
Springfield Pk
18 Tisbury SP3...... **203** E8
Trowbridge BA14.... **101** E1
Springfield Rd
Rowde SN10..........**96** D1
Swindon SN1..........**50** C3
Westbury BA13...... **108** F2
Springfields Acad The
SN11...................**81** A3
Springfield Sports Ctr
SN13...................**76** F1
Spring Gdns
Corsham SN13........**77** A2
Lechlade GL7..........**2** C4
Swindon SN1..........**50** C6
Springhead BA12.... **194** A4
Springhill Cl **3** SN5 ...**49** C5
Spring La SN13........**84** C7
Springlines **10** SN4 .. **163** B6
Spring Meadow SN8 . **191** D8
Spring Meadows
BA14.................. **105** A5
Spring Rd BA11...... **110** A6
Spring The **5** SN10.. **187** E8
Spring Tining SN13 ...**76** F1
Spruce Ct **2** SN25 ....**35** B2
Spur Off Maury's La **9**
SO51.................. **212** F7
Spur The BA13....... **112** D8
Spur Way SN2.........**35** E3
Spye Pk SN12..........**87** E2
Squalls La SP3....... **203** F6
Square The
Calne SN11...........**81** B3
Mere BA12.......... **139** A5
Pewsey SN9......... **215** C5
7 Swindon SN3......**50** D4
Squarey Cl SP5...... **211** A7
Squires Copse SN5 ....**34** A1
Squires Hill Cl
4 Royal Wootton Bassett
SN4....................**47** F2
7 Royal Wootton Bassett
SN4....................**48** A2
Squirrel Cres **1** SN4...**47** F2
Squirrel's Cnr BH21.. **208** D1
Stable Cl SP11....... **192** A5
Stables Rd SP9...... **216** C4
Stacey's La SN4..... **163** B5
Stackpole Cres **4**
SN25...................**34** C8
Stadium View SN25....**35** B8
Stafford St SN1........**50** B5
Stag Hill RG17....... **171** A1
Stainers Mead SP7 .. **202** A5
Staldon Rd SN1........**50** B2
Stallard St BA14..... **105** C8
Stalls The BA12...... **114** F5
Stambrook Pk BA1.....**82** A5
Stamford Cl SN2........**35** C6
Stanbridge Pk **9** SN5..**49** A7
Stanbury Rd SP11.... **192** C1
Stancomb Ave BA14 . **101** E1

Stancombe Pk **1** SN5 **49** D5
Standen Way SN25.....**35** A7
STANDERWICK....... **107** B2
Standerwick BA13.... **107** E3
Standings Cl **6** SN5...**49** A8
Stanford Rd SN25.....**34** C7
Stanier Cl BA11...... **110** D6
Stanier Rd SN11......**81** C6
Stanier St SN1........**50** B5
STANLEY...............**80** A6
Stanley Cl **9** SN4.... **163** B6
Stanley Ct SP2...... **151** E8
Stanley Honey Ct **7**
SN3.....................**50** F6
Stanley La SN15......**79** D6
Stanley Little Rd SP2. **145** B3
Stanley St SN1........**50** C5
Stanley Terr SN10... **214** B2
Stanmore SN1.........**50** A5
Stannon La SN1........**50** B2
Stansfield St SN5 ....**49** D4
Stanton Cl BA14..... **105** D5
STANTON
FITZWARREN........**22** B1
Stanton La SN14......**56** A1
Stanton Pk Farm★
SN6....................**36** B8
Stanton Pk Nature
Reserve★ SN6.......**36** B8
STANTON ST
BERNARD **173** A1
STANTON ST
QUINTIN..............**56** B4
Stanton St Quintin Com
Prim Sch SN14.......**56** B4
Stanway Cl **5** SN3.....**51** A4
Staplefield Rd SP5 .. **207** E6
STAPLEFORD **129** E7
Stapleford Castle Ring &
Bailey★ SP3........ **129** C8
Stapleford Cl SN15 ....**78** E4
Stapleford Rd
Stapleford SP3...... **129** C8
Stapleford SP3...... **196** D1
Stapleford Way SN2 ...**35** B6
Stapler's La SN6......**22** B5
Staples Hill BA2.......**99** C3
Stapleton Cl SN6......**22** F5
Stardust Cres **13** SN25 **34** B7
Star Ground BA14 ... **101** F8
Staring Cl **6** SN5......**48** F8
Star La SN14...........**74** D8
Star The BA14....... **101** E7
STARTLEY.............**43** D1
Station App
9 Bradford-on-Avon
BA15.................. **100** D6
4 Frome BA11....... **110** A4
32 Ludgershall SP11... **192** A5
Melksham SN12.......**94** A6
Minety SN16..........**17** C2
Swindon SN1..........**50** D3
1 Trowbridge BA14 .. **105** C8
Westbury BA13...... **108** E4
Station Hill SN15......**78** D8
Station Ind Est SN1 ...**50** B6
Station Rd
Ashbury SN6........ **164** A8
Badminton GL9.......**38** F1
Calne SN11...........**81** B2
Chiseldown SN4......**65** D4
Christian Malford SN15. **58** A2
Codford BA12....... **194** F3
Corsham SN13........**77** A1
Devizes SN10....... **214** A3
East Garston RG17 .. **171** E7
Great Wishford SP2.. **129** F3
Great Wishford SP2.. **130** A2
Heytesbury BA12.... **194** C4
Highworth SN6........**22** F6
Holt BA14............**92** E1
19 Hungerford RG17.. **177** B7
Kemble GL7...........**4** F7
10 Lambourn RG17... **165** A1
Lechlade GL7..........**2** D5
Limpley Stoke BA2.....**99** C5
Minety SN16..........**17** C1
Purton SN5............**33** C5
Royal Wootton Bassett
SN4....................**47** D1
Sandleheath SP6.... **210** C1
Sedgehill & Semley
SP7.................. **202** D5
South Cerney GL7.....**7** B7
Swindon SN1..........**50** B7
Tidworth SP9....... **216** D5
Warminster BA12.... **117** B7
Westbury BA13...... **108** E5
Station Road SN15....**58** A3
Station Terr **4** SP2... **145** F1
Station Way SN14... **105** C8
STAVERTON **101** C6
Staverton CE (VC) Prim
Sch BA14............ **101** C5
Staverton Way **2** SN2 **35** C6
Stavordale Priory★
BA9.................. **136** D5
Stavordale Priory La
BA9.................. **136** C4
Steadings The
Royal Wootton Bassett
SN4....................**47** F1
Salisbury SP4...... **146** D6
STEAM Mus of the Great
Western Railway★
SN2....................**50** A6
Stedham Wlk SN3.....**51** B4

Steele Cl SN10....... **214** D4
Steels Dro SP6...... **211** A4
Steels La SP5........ **209** F2
Steel's La
Penselwood BA9.... **136** F3
Pen Selwood BA9.... **137** A3
Steepe Way SN8..... **175** C1
Steep Hollow SP3... **201** E3
STEEPLE ASHTON ... **178** B3
Steeple Ashton Rd
BA13.................. **186** C8
STEEPLE
LANGFORD **128** D8
Steeple Vw SN1.......**50** D4
Steep St BA12....... **139** A6
Steiner Academy Frome
BA12.................. **111** D2
Steinlen Cl SN25......**20** D1
Stenbury Cl SN25.....**35** A7
Stenness Cl SN5......**34** C2
Stephen Martin Gdns **7**
SP6.................. **210** D1
Stephens Cl
Lechlade-on-Thames
GL7.....................**2** B4
1 Salisbury SP2.... **151** E7
Stephenson Dr BA11. **110** C6
Stephenson Rd
Salisbury SP2....... **145** E1
Swindon SN25.......**35** C7
The Ham BA13...... **108** D5
Stephens Rd SN3......**36** A1
Stephens Way BA12.. **116** F8
Steplake La
Sherfield English
SO51.................. **162** C1
Sherfield English SO51 **212** F8
Steplake Rd SO51.... **212** F8
Step Stones SN25.....**34** A3
Sterling Pk **1** SP10.. **193** C1
STERT................. **180** B6
Stert Valley La SN10. **180** A6
Stevenson Rd SN2....**34** C5
Stewart Cl
Chippenham SN15.....**78** F4
3 Swindon SN25 .... **35** B6
Steway La BA1.........**82** B6
STIBB GREEN **175** D1
Stibb Hill SN10...... **187** F7
Stickleback Rd SN1...**81** B6
Stickley Cl SN26......**20** B1
Stickway SP5........ **206** F3
Still Man Cl BA14.... **101** E8
Stirling Cl
3 Bower Hill SN12... **178** B8
Wroughton SN4......**64** A7
Stirling Rd
Market Lavington
SN10.................. **180** A1
South Marston Park SN3 **36** C4
Stirling Way BA11.... **110** C6
STITCHCOMBE...... **175** D8
Stitching's La SN9.... **181** D5
Stobberts Pl **4** SN10 **179** F1
Stobberts Rd **3**
SN10.................. **179** F1
Stockbridge Copse **2**
SN5....................**34** A2
Stockbridge Rd SP5 . **135** F3
Stockham Cl SN6......**19** D4
Stockham Gdns SN6 ..**19** F8
Stock La
Aldbourne SN8...... **169** D4
Landford SP5....... **212** C7
STOCKLEY.............**89** C4
Stockley Hollow SN11. **89** C4
Stockley La
Calne Without SN11...**89** C6
Quemerford SN11.....**89** C8
Stockley Rd SN11.....**89** C2
Stockport Rd SP4.... **217** D1
Stocks Bridge La
SP5.................. **151** A1
Stock's Cross SO43.. **212** D2
Stock St BA12....... **139** B4
STOCKS THE **178** C7
STOCKTON **195** B1
Stockton Earthworks★
BA12.................. **201** A6
Stockton House★
BA12.................. **195** B1
Stockton Rd SN2......**35** C4
Stockwell Rd SN10... **214** C4
Stockwood Cl SP1... **146** C3
Stockwood Rd SN14...**78** B6
STOFORD.............. **130** A3
Stoford Bottom SP2. **130** A4
Stoke Comm La SN5...**19** A2
Stoke Common La
SN6....................**18** E1
Stoke Common Mdws
Nature Reserve★
SN6....................**18** E1
STOKE FARTHING .. **205** D4
Stokehill BA14....... **106** A8
Stoke Mdw SN11......**81** B1
Stoke Mead BA2.......**98** F7
Stokesay Dr SN5......**49** C4
Stokes Rd SN13.......**85** A8
Stonar Sch SN12......**92** B8
Stone Ave★ SN8..... **173** C8
STONEBRIDGE....... **110** C7
Stonebridge Cl SN8.. **213** F3
Stonebridge Dr BA11 **110** B7
Stone Cl
Half Way Firs SN13 ...**76** C1
The Common SP5.... **149** C6

Stonecrop Way SN25 ...**34** E5
Stonefield Cl SN5......**49** C7
Stonefield Dr SN6.....**23** A5
Stonehenge★ SP4.... **197** E5
Stonehenge Cursus★
SP4.................. **197** C6
Stonehenge Rd
Amesbury SP4...... **198** A4
Swindon SN1..........**50** A2
West Amesbury SP4 . **197** F4
Stonehenge Sch The
SP4.................. **217** B4
Stonehenge Visitor Ctr★
SP4.................. **197** C5
Stonehill SN16.........**30** B7
Stonehill Barn GL8.....**3** C6
Stonehill Gn SN5......**49** D6
Stonehill La GL8........**3** C6
Stone La
Lydiard Millicent SN5. **33** E1
Ramsbury SN8...... **175** D8
Stonelea Cl SN14......**78** E7
Stoneleigh Rise
BA11.................. **110** A6
Stoneover La
Lydiard Tregoze SN4 ..**48** A3
Royal Wootton Bassett
SN4....................**47** F2
Stone (site of King's
Elm)★ SP3.......... **142** B1
Stones La SN6..........**8** B1
Stonewall Terr BA11. **110** A3
Stoneworks The SN13 **84** C6
Stoney Bridge BA12.. **140** D5
Stoney Cross **20**
SP11.................. **192** A5
Stoney Dro SP11..... **185** D4
Stoney La
Bromham SN15.......**88** A1
Bromham SN15.......**96** A8
Stoneywell SN25......**20** B1
Stonybeck Cl SN5.....**49** D6
Stony Gutter BA14... **102** D1
Stony La
Damerham SP6...... **209** E2
Lambourn RG17..... **171** D6
St Catherine BA1......**82** A8
Stoppers Hill SN15....**46** B7
Stops Hill SP3....... **200** B3
Stop St SP3.......... **200** C2
Storey Mws SN16......**28** A1
Stork House Dr **18**
RG17.................. **165** A1
STORMORE........... **112** A8
Stormore BA13....... **111** F8
Storms Farm Rd
SO51.................. **212** F1
Storridge Rd BA13... **108** C6
Stour Cl SO51....... **212** F6
Stourhead House &
Gdns★ BA12........ **123** F1
STOURTON **123** F1
Stourton Bushes
BA13.................. **107** E4
Stourton House Flower
Gdn★ BA12......... **123** F1
Stourton La BA12.... **123** E3
Stourton Pk BA14.... **102** B3
Stour Wlk SN25.......**35** B4
Stowell Pk★ SN8.... **182** A8
Stradbrook BA13.... **186** B7
Straight La
Dean SP5............ **207** E3
Lambourn RG17..... **171** C6
STRAIGHT SOLEY.... **171** A3
STRAND THE......... **178** B6
Strand The
Calne SN11...........**81** B3
Steeple Ashton BA14. **178** A3
STRANGWAYS....... **198** A6
Strangways SP4..... **197** F6
Stranks Cl SN6........**23** A4
Strap La BA10........ **122** C8
Stratford Cl SN5......**49** D5
Stratford Rd SP1.... **146** A3
STRATFORD SUB
CASTLE **145** F5
Stratford Sub Castle CE
Prim Sch SP1....... **145** D5
STRATFORD TONY .. **150** C2
Stratford Tony Rd
SP5.................. **150** E2
Stratton Orch **1** SN3...**36** A2
Stratton Rd
Pewsey SN9......... **215** C4
Swindon SN1..........**50** F8
Swindon SN25.......**35** F1
Stratton Rd & Marshgate
Ind Est SN1..........**50** F8
STRATTON ST
MARGARET..........**36** A3
Strattons Wlk SN12...**94** B4
Strawberry Hill SN10. **187** E7
Strawberry La GL7.....**1** A4
Street La
Brewham BA10..... **122** A4
Sedgehill & Semley
SP7.................. **202** C4
Street The
All Cannings SN10... **172** F1
Alvediston SP5..... **204** B2
Bishops Cannings
SN10.................. **172** B3
Brinkworth SN15......**45** F6
Broughton Gifford SN12 **93** B4
Castle Combe SN14...**68** A7
Charlton SN16........**29** B6

Street The *continued*
Cherhill SN11....... **166** B1
Chilmark SP3....... **201** A3
Chirton SN10....... **180** F4
Crudwell SN16.......**14** E5
Didmarton GL9.......**24** C3
East Knoyle SP3.... **141** C1
Holt BA14............ **101** D8
Hullavington SN14....**41** F1
Kilmington BA12.... **123** F4
Latton SN6............**8** C4
Lea SN16.............**28** F1
Liddington SN4..... **163** A4
Little Somerford SN15. **44** C5
Luckington SN14......**39** E4
Lydiard Millicent SN5. **48** D8
Marden SN10....... **181** A4
Marston Maisey SN6...**9** D6
Milton Lilbourne SN9. **182** E7
Nettleton SN14.......**53** B4
Oaksey SN16.........**15** F8
Pitton & Farley SP5. **154** E7
Shipton Moyne GL8... **26** E8
Swindon SN25.......**34** E3
West Knoyle BA12... **140** D5
Winterslow SP5..... **149** A5
Yatton Keynell SN14...**68** F6
Stroma Way SN6..... **22** E7
Strongrove Hill RG17 **177** A7
Strongs Cl
Sherston SN16.......**25** C1
Steeple Ashton BA14. **178** C4
Stroud La SN10...... **179** F5
Stroud's Hill SN4......**65** D4
Stuart Cl
2 Swindon SN3......**50** F6
Trowbridge BA14.... **101** E4
Stuart Gn BA12...... **117** A6
Stubbs Ct **3** SP10 .. **193** D1
Stubbs La SN14.......**70** A7
Stubhampton Bottom
DT11.................. **206** C3
Stubsmead SN3.......**51** C5
Stuckton Rd SP6.... **210** E1
Studd St SP9......... **216** D8
Studio Theatre★
SP2.................. **146** A2
Studland Cl SN3.......**51** B3
Studland Pk BA13.... **109** B2
STUDLEY..............**80** B3
Studley Castle★ SP6. **211** F3
Studley Cnr SN11......**80** B4
Studley Gdns SN11....**80** A3
Studley Gn Prim Sch
BA14.................. **105** A6
STUDLEY GREEN ... **104** F7
Studley Hill SN11......**80** A4
Studley La SN11.......**80** A3
Studley Rise BA14... **105** D6
STURFORD........... **115** E6
Sturford La BA12.... **115** D6
Styles Ave BA11..... **110** C4
Styles Cl
Frome BA11......... **110** B4
Porton SP4......... **133** D5
Styles Hill BA11..... **110** B4
Styles Pk BA11...... **110** B4
Styles The SP5...... **205** F4
Sudeley Dr GL7........**6** F6
Sudeley Way SN5......**49** A5
Sudley Way SN5.......**48** F5
Suffolk Cl SN16.......**29** A7
Suffolk Pl GL7..........**8** D7
Suffolk Rd
Salisbury SP2....... **151** E6
Westbury BA13...... **112** D8
5 Westbury Leigh
BA13.................. **108** C1
Suffolk St SN2.........**50** C8
Sully BA15........... **100** D6
Sumbler Dr SN11......**81** D3
Summerdown Ct
BA13.................. **109** A4
Summer Down Wlk
BA14.................. **105** C5
Summerhouse Rd SN4 **63** F7
Summer La
Castle Combe SN14... **53** F3
Castle Combe SN14... **68** D7
Monkton Combe BA2... **98** D8
Summerleaze
2 Corsham SN13..... **76** D1
Trowbridge BA14.... **105** A6
Summerlock App **2**
SP2.................. **146** A1
Summerlug SP4..... **133** A3
Summer Oaks SP7... **202** A5
Summer Rd BA13.... **108** F4
Summers La SN4.... **167** C7
Summers St SN2.......**49** F7
Sumsions Dr **8** SN13. **76** D1
Sunbeam Dr SN14.....**78** B5
Sundays Hill
Brinkworth SN15......**30** B1
Brinkworth SN15......**30** D1
Brinkworth SN15......**45** C8
Sunderland Cl **14**
SN12.................. **178** B8
Sunflower Way **1**
SP11.................. **193** F2
Sunhill Cl GL7..........**1** E7
Sun La SN13..........**76** C1
Sunningdale Cl SN15 ..**78** F7
Sunnybank Rd BA13. **109** A5
Sunnyhill SN8....... **191** D8
Sunnyhill La SN8.... **174** C1

Sunnyhill Rd SP1 . . . . . 146 A4
Sunnyside SN10 . . . . . 187 E8
Sunnyside Av SN1 . . . . 50 A4
Sunnyside Cl SP10 . . . 193 C1
Sunrise Way SP4 . . . . 217 D4
SUNTON 183 E1
Surrendell Cottage
SN14 . . . . . 55 B8
Surrey Pl
  Trowbridge BA14 . . . . 105 B7
  ■ Trowbridge BA14 . . . . 105 C7
Surrey Rd SN2 . . . . . 35 A1
Sussex Rd SP2 . . . . . 151 E6
Sussex Sq SN3 . . . . . 50 E6
Sussex Wlk ■ BA14 . . 101 F1
Sutherland Cresent
SN14 . . . . . 70 B3
Sutherland Ct ■
SP10 . . . . . 193 D1
Suthmere Dr SN8 . . . . 183 D8
SUTTON BENGER 57 C2
Sutton Benger CE Prim
Sch SN15 . . . . . 57 D2
Sutton Bottom SP3 . . 141 B5
Sutton Gdns SN15 . . . . 57 C1
Sutton Hill
  Sherrington BA12 . . . . 195 A2
  Sutton Mandeville SP3 . 204 C7
  Sutton Waldron SP7 . . . 206 A3
Sutton La
  Langley Burrell Without
  SN15 . . . . . 71 C5
  Sutton Benger SN15 . . . 57 D1
SUTTON
MANDEVILLE 204 C8
Sutton Parva BA12 . . . 194 A4
Sutton Pk SN26 . . . . . 21 C1
Sutton Rd
  Fovant SP3 . . . . . 204 D7
  Kington Langley SN15 . . 70 F7
  Swindon SN3 . . . . . 51 C4
SUTTON ROW 204 D7
SUTTON VENY 117 F1
Sutton Veny CE Sch
BA12 . . . . . 194 A4
Suvla La ■ SP4 . . . . . 198 E6
Swaddon St SN11 . . . . 81 B4
Swainsford BA12 . . . . 139 A1
Swaledale Rd BA12 . . . 116 D6
Swallet House SN15 . . 58 D5
SWALLETT GATE 59 A6
Swallow Cl
  Tidworth SP9 . . . . . 216 D6
  ■ Warminster BA12 . . 116 E5
SWALLOWCLIFFE 204 A6
Swallowdale SN3 . . . . 51 D7
Swallow Dr
  Frome BA11 . . . . . 110 B6
  ■ Trowbridge BA14 . . . 105 B7
Swallowfield Ave SN3 . 50 F5
Swallowmead ■
SP2 . . . . . 152 A5
Swallows Mead ■
SN4 . . . . . 48 A2
Swallows Rise BA13 . . 108 E4
Swanage Wlk SN5 . . . . 48 E6
Swan Barton SN16 . . . . 40 C8
SWANBOROUGH 22 C4
Swanborough Cl ■
SN15 . . . . . 78 F4
Swanborough Tump*
SN9 . . . . . 181 E6
Swanbrook SN3 . . . . 51 D8
Swan Cl
  ■ Durrington/Bulford
  SP4 . . . . . 198 C7
  Lechlade GL7 . . . . . 2 C4
  Salisbury SP2 . . . . . 152 A6
  South Cerney GL7 . . . . 7 A6
  ■ Swindon SN3 . . . . 51 C8
Swan Ct BA14 . . . . . 104 F3
Swan Dr BA14 . . . . . 101 D5
Swangate RG17 . . . . . 177 B8
Swangrove La GL9 . . . . 38 D8
Swan La SN6 . . . . . 17 F7
Swan Meadow SN9 . . . 215 D3
Swan Rd
  Corsham SN13 . . . . . 76 E1
  Pewsey SN9 . . . . . 215 C4
Swan's Bottom ■
SN8 . . . . . 170 B2
Swan's Cl ■ SN8 . . . . 170 B2
Swansfield GL7 . . . . . 2 D6
Swans Mdw GL7 . . . . 2 E3
Swattons Cl SP4 . . . . . 217 E8
Swayne Cl ■ SN15 . . . 78 F5
Swayne Rd SP2 . . . . . 144 C2
Swaynes Cl ■ SP1 . . . 146 B2
Sweetapplecl SP9 . . . . 216 D8
Sweet Briar Rd SN12 . . 94 C3
Sweetmans Rd SP7 . . . 202 C2
Swift Ave SN25 . . . . . 35 A7
Swiftdown ■ SP2 . . . 152 A5
Swift Dr BA14 . . . . . 105 E6
Swift Link GL7 . . . . . 7 A6
Swift Mead BA14 . . . . 116 E5
Swillbrook Lakes Nature
Reserve* SN16 . . . . . 16 F8
Swinburne Pl SN4 . . . . 47 E3
SWINDON 50 E4
Swindon Acad SN25 . . 35 C5
Swindon Academy
SN2 . . . . . 35 B2
Swindon Arts Ctr*
SN1 . . . . . 50 C4
Swindon Coll
  Marlborough SN8 . . . . 213 D3
  Swindon SN2 . . . . . 50 B8

Swindon & Cricklade
Rly* SN25 . . . . . 33 F8
Swindon Mus & Art Gall*
SN1 . . . . . 50 D4
Swindon Rd
  Avebury SN8 . . . . . 167 C1
  Cricklade SN6 . . . . . 19 F7
  Cricklade SN6 . . . . . 20 A8
  Highworth SN6 . . . . . 22 F3
  Highworth SN6 . . . . . 23 A4
  Hilmarton SN11 . . . . . 73 F3
  Kington Langley SN15 . . 70 F5
  Lea SN16 . . . . . 28 A3
  Lydiard Tregoze SN4 . . . 48 C2
  Lydiard Tregoze SN5 . . . 48 D2
  Malmesbury SN16 . . . . 28 C1
  Royal Wootton Bassett
  SN4 . . . . . 47 F3
  Swindon SN1 . . . . . 36 A1
  Wroughton SN4 . . . . . 64 C7
Swindon St SN6 . . . . . 23 A5
Swindon Sta SN2 . . . . 50 B7
Swindon Town Football
Club SN1 . . . . . 50 D7
Swinford Paddocks
SN16 . . . . . 27 E2
Swinley Dr SN5 . . . . . 34 A5
Sword Gdns ■ SN1 . . . 49 F4
Swynford Cl GL7 . . . . . 10 D6
Sycamore Cl
  Long Newnton GL8 . . . . 13 B4
  Lyneham & Bradenstoke
  SN15 . . . . . 60 C2
  North Tidworth SP9 . . . 216 E6
  Sixpenny Handley SP5 . . 208 A4
Sycamore Dr
  Calne SN11 . . . . . 81 D5
  ■ Frome BA11 . . . . . 110 B7
  Salisbury SP1 . . . . . 146 C5
Sycamore Gr
  Swindon SN2 . . . . . 35 C2
  Trowbridge BA14 . . . . . 105 C5
  Westbury BA13 . . . . . 108 F3
Sydnalls La BA12 . . . . . 115 D6
Sylvester Dr ■ BA14 . 101 F1
Symonds SN5 . . . . . 49 B3
Symons Cl SP9 . . . . . 216 D8
Syon Cl
  Corsham SN13 . . . . . 84 E8
  ■ Swindon SN25 . . . . 34 F6
Syringa Cl SP2 . . . . . 145 D1
Sywell Rd SN3 . . . . . 51 C8

T

Tadpole Farm CE Prim
Acad SN26 . . . . . 20 C1
Tadpole Farm CE Prim
Sch SN25 . . . . . 20 C1
Tadpole La
  Blunsdon St Andrew
  SN25 . . . . . 34 C8
  Purton SN5 . . . . . 33 F8
  Swindon SN25 . . . . . 34 A8
Talavera Rd SN4 . . . . . 168 E8
Talavera Way SP9 . . . . 216 D3
Talbot Cl
  Melksham SN12 . . . . . 94 D5
  Salisbury SP1 . . . . . 146 C4
Talbot Rd BA14 . . . . . 105 A7
Talboys (Medieval Hall
House)* BA14 . . . . . 178 B4
Tallis Wlk SN5 . . . . . 49 A5
Tallow La ■ SN4 . . . . 163 A6
Tall Trees SN14 . . . . . 78 D7
Tallys La BA9 . . . . . 136 E1
Tamar Cl SN25 . . . . . 35 A4
Tamar Rd SN12 . . . . . 94 A6
Tamesis Dr GL7 . . . . . 4 F7
Tame Way GL7 . . . . . 1 E6
Tamworth Dr SN5 . . . . 49 A7
Tanarisk Cl SN11 . . . . . 81 C1
Tangier Cl BA12 . . . . . 117 A8
Tangley Bottom Rd
SP11 . . . . . 185 A1
Tangmere Cl ■
SN12 . . . . . 178 B8
TANIS 96 F2
Tankard La ■ SN8 . . . 170 B2
Tankey's Cl ■ BA11 . . 110 A7
Tan La SP5 . . . . . 205 B4
Tan La
  Bourton SP8 . . . . . 137 F2
  Bourton SP8 . . . . . 138 A2
Tanner Cl SN15 . . . . . 78 F5
Tanners Cl
  Royal Wootton Bassett
  SN4 . . . . . 47 D2
  Winterbourne SP4 . . . . 133 A4
Tanners Field SP4 . . . . 217 D3
Tanners Hill SN16 . . . . 40 C8
Tanners La
  Sandleheath SP6 . . . . . 210 A1
  Shrewton SP3 . . . . . 196 E7
  Winterbourne SP4 . . . . 133 A4
Tansley Moor SN5 . . . . 34 B1
Tanyard La ■ SP7 . . . 202 B1
Tanyard Way BA13 . . . 112 D8
Taplow Wlk SN3 . . . . . 51 A4
Taramah Gdns ■
SP3 . . . . . 203 E8
Targetts Mead SP3 . . . 203 E8
Tarka Cl SN25 . . . . . 34 F7
Tarragon Cl SN2 . . . . . 34 C4
Tarrant's Hill ■
RG17 . . . . . 177 B7

Tarters The SN16 . . . . . 40 D8
Tascroft BA12 . . . . . 116 B5
Tasker Cl SN13 . . . . . 84 E8
Tasker La SN8 . . . . . 183 D8
Tatry Rd ■ SN25 . . . . 34 D6
Tattershall SN5 . . . . . 49 C3
Taunton Cl ■ SN14 . . 77 F5
Taunton St SN1 . . . . . 50 A6
Tavinor Dr SN15 . . . . . 78 E4
Tavistock Rd SN3 . . . . 51 B5
Tawny Cl SN13 . . . . . 84 C6
Tawny Owl Cl SN3 . . . . 51 C8
Taylor Cres SN3 . . . . . 36 A4
Taylors Cl SN16 . . . . . 17 B1
Taylors Gn SN4 . . . . . 174 A7
Taylors La SN8 . . . . . 168 B1
Taylors View BA14 . . . 101 D1
Teachers Way SN12 . . . 93 F7
Teal Ave SN15 . . . . . 60 A1
Teal Cl BA13 . . . . . 109 B4
Tealgate RG17 . . . . . 177 B8
Tealsbrook SN3 . . . . . 51 D7
Teal Way GL7 . . . . . 7 A6
Teapot St BA12 . . . . . 201 E8
Teasel Cl
  Devizes SN10 . . . . . 214 E2
  ■ Ludgershall SN1 . . 192 A5
Teasels The BA12 . . . . 116 F6
Techno Ind Est SN2 . . . 35 E1
Tedder Ave SN13 . . . . 84 A8
Tedder Cl SN2 . . . . . 35 B2
Tees Cl SN25 . . . . . 35 A4
Teeswater Cl SN5 . . . . 49 A6
TEFFONT EVIAS 201 C2
Teffont Field Bldgs*
SP3 . . . . . 201 D4
TEFFONT MAGNA 201 C3
Teffont Manor* SP3 . . 201 D2
Teichman Cl BA12 . . . 117 C6
Telegraph SP5 . . . . . 212 A4
Telford Pool SN2 . . . . 49 F8
Telford Rd SN2 . . . . . 50 A8
Telford Way SN1 . . . . 49 E4
Tellcroft Cl SN13 . . . . 84 F8
Tellings Orch SN16 . . . 16 D3
TELLISFORD 103 E4
Tellisford La BA2 . . . . 103 C4
Tellisford Rd BA2 . . . . 103 E7
Tempest Rd ■ SP4 . . 217 D3
Templar's Firs SN4 . . . 61 E8
Templars Way Ind Est
SN4 . . . . . 61 D7
TEMPLE 115 C6
Temple St SN1 . . . . . 50 C5
TEMPLETON 177 D5
Ten Acres SP7 . . . . . 202 C2
Tenby Cl SN3 . . . . . 50 F3
Tench Rd SN11 . . . . . 81 B5
Tennis Cnr Dro BA12 . . 107 D2
Tennyson Cl BA12 . . . 116 E6
Tennyson Rd SN4 . . . . 47 F3
Tennyson St SN1 . . . . . 50 B5
Tenzing Gdns SN25 . . . 35 C3
Teo Cl SN25 . . . . . 35 B8
Tern Cl SN11 . . . . . 81 D2
Terncliff SN3 . . . . . 51 D7
Tetbury Hill SN16 . . . . 27 F6
Tetbury Hill Gdns
  Malmesbury SN16 . . . . 27 F5
  ■ Malmesbury SN16 . . 28 A5
Tetbury La
  Charlton SN16 . . . . . 14 F1
  Charlton SN16 . . . . . 29 A7
  Crudwell SN16 . . . . . 14 D6
Tetbury Rd
  Brokenborough SN16 . . 27 E7
  Culkerton GL8 . . . . . 3 A5
  Didmarton GL9 . . . . . 24 A3
  Sherston SN16 . . . . . 25 D2
Tethering Dro SN11 . . . 211 C6
Tewkesbury Way
  Lydiard Millicent SN5 . . 48 E2
  Swindon SN5 . . . . . 49 A6
Thackeray Cl SN3 . . . . 51 D4
Thackeray Cres SN4 . . 94 B4
Thames Ave SN25 . . . . 34 E5
Thames Cl
  South Cerney GL7 . . . . 6 F6
  Warminster BA12 . . . . 117 A5
Thames Cres SN12 . . . 94 A6
Thamesdown Dr
  Haydon Wick SN25 . . . . 34 B7
  Swindon SN25 . . . . . 35 A7
  Swindon SN25 . . . . . 35 B8
Thames La SN6 . . . . . 19 E8
Thames St GL7 . . . . . 2 C3
Thames View
  Ashton Keynes SN6 . . . 17 F8
  Broad Blunsdon SN26 . . 21 A2
  Ewen GL7 . . . . . 5 C8
Thatcham SN11 . . . . . 81 A4
Thatchers The SN25 . . . 35 C7
The Arc ■ SN25 . . . . 35 A8
Theatre Sq SN1 . . . . . 50 C6
The Ave
  Odstock SN3 . . . . . 158 B7
  Swindon SN3 . . . . . 36 C8
The Bank SN3 . . . . . 133 B2
The Banks SN15 . . . . . 59 E4
The Belt SP3 . . . . . 142 D3
The Brook SN25 . . . . . 34 A3
The Buffer SN25 . . . . . 34 B2
The Causeway BA14 . . 101 C7
The Chase Pk SN14 . . . 55 D4
The City BA13 . . . . . 186 C7
The Cl
  Hilmarton SN11 . . . . . 73 F3
  South Cerney GL7 . . . . 7 A7

The Cl continued
  Winterbourne Bassett
  SN4 . . . . . 167 C5
The Clay SN10 . . . . . 188 A8
The Comm
  Damerham SP6 . . . . . 209 F2
  Heddington Wick SN11 . . 88 E3
The Common SN15 . . . . 96 A2
The Copse
  Batheaston BA1 . . . . . 82 A3
  Broad Blunsdon SN26 . . 21 B2
The Cres
  Dilton Marsh BA13 . . . . 112 B8
  Lea SN16 . . . . . 43 E8
  Swindon SN25 . . . . . 34 A2
The Crossing SN16 . . . . 16 F3
The Deanery CE Acad
SN1 . . . . . 49 E3
The Drive SO51 . . . . . 162 C1
The Drove
  Coulston BA13 . . . . . 186 E8
  Stourton with Gasper
  BA12 . . . . . 124 B2
  Upton Scudamore
  BA12 . . . . . 112 A8
The Druck BA12 . . . . . 116 E1
The Elms SP3 . . . . . 204 D8
The Farm SN25 . . . . . 34 A3
The Folly SN11 . . . . . 80 A2
The Forum ■ SN1 . . . 49 C5
The Garretts GL7 . . . . . 1 E7
The Gdns SN11 . . . . . 81 B4
The General's Ave
SP5 . . . . . 207 D6
The Gibb SN14 . . . . . 54 A2
The Gn BA12 . . . . . 116 F2
The Green
  Broughton Gifford
  SN12 . . . . . 93 B2
  Christian Malford SN15 . . 58 A2
  Goatacre SN11 . . . . . 73 F6
  Luckington SN14 . . . . . 39 E4
The Halve BA12 . . . . . 116 D6
The Hollows SP4 . . . . 131 C3
The Island BA12 . . . . . 119 B7
The Kennels BA12 . . . . 117 F1
The La SP4 . . . . . 133 D6
The Landings GL7 . . . . . 7 B6
The Laurels
  Castle Eaton SN6 . . . . . 10 B4
  Midford BA2 . . . . . 98 C5
The Leasowes SN25 . . . 20 B1
The Link GL8 . . . . . 25 B7
The Lotts SN6 . . . . . 6 F1
The Lynch SN12 . . . . . 139 B5
The Marsh
  Longbridge Deverill
  BA12 . . . . . 120 F6
  Longbridge Deverill
  BA12 . . . . . 121 A6
  Mount Sorrel SP5 . . . . 205 A3
The Matravers Sch
BA13 . . . . . 108 F8
The Mdws
  Bourton SN4 . . . . . 37 F3
  Luckington SN14 . . . . . 39 F4
The Mead Com Prim Sch
BA14 . . . . . 104 C6
The Moor
  Leigh SN16 . . . . . 17 F3
  Minety SN16 . . . . . 17 B3
The New Forest CE Prim
Sch SP5 . . . . . 212 C6
THEOBALD'S GREEN . . 172 A4
Theobald St SN1 . . . . . 50 B6
The Old Barnyard
BA12 . . . . . 112 F4
The Old Orch SN15 . . . 100 E7
The Old Turnpike
SN11 . . . . . 88 E1
The Orch
  Bradford Leigh BA15 . . 91 F1
  Cherhill SN11 . . . . . 166 B1
  Lydiard Millicent SN5 . . 48 D8
  Swindon SN3 . . . . . 36 E4
The Paddock BA12 . . . 117 C6
The Philip Green
Memorial Sch BH21 209 B1
The Plantation SP5 . . . 149 A5
The Portway
  Winterbourne SP4 . . . . 132 F2
  Winterbourne SP4 . . . . 133 A3
The Pry SN5 . . . . . 33 F5
The Pyghtell SN14 . . . . 39 E5
The Quarry SN11 . . . . . 81 B1
The Race Plain SP5 . . . 150 D6
The Reeds SP3 . . . . . 201 B3
The Ridge SN9 . . . . . 215 C5
The Ridgeway SN4 . . . . 168 C8
The Row Service Rd
SN25 . . . . . 35 D1
The Royal Cres SP9 . . . 216 D7
The Sidings SN5 . . . . . 33 D5
The Spinney
  Malmesbury SN16 . . . . 28 C1
  Trowbridge BA14 . . . . . 106 A8
The Spitfire Retail Pk
BA14 . . . . . 105 D5
The Springs SN14 . . . . 78 F6
The St
  Acton Turville GL9 . . . . 52 E6
  Alderton SN14 . . . . . 39 F7
  Alderton SN14 . . . . . 40 A3
  Castle Combe SN14 . . . 67 F5
The Stables GL7 . . . . . 2 D8
Thestfield Dr BA14 . . . 101 B4
The Stones SN25 . . . . . 34 A2
The Street SP5 . . . . . 148 F5

The Sunflowers SN25 . . 35 E3
The Tannery BA14 . . . . 92 E1
The Thetford Way SN25 . 34 C5
The Turnpike SN11 . . . 88 D2
The Village Gn BA13 . . 109 A8
The Wern GL7 . . . . . 2 B4
The Wharf SN15 . . . . . 86 E5
Thickets Rd SN8 . . . . . 169 C1
THICKWOOD 75 D6
Thickwood La SN14 . . . 75 C6
THINGLEY 77 F1
Thingley Top SN3 . . . . 85 D8
Thirsk Cl SN14 . . . . . 78 A5
Thirsk Dr BA14 . . . . . 106 B8
Thistlebarrow Rd
SP1 . . . . . 146 A4
Thistledown ■ SN4 . . 163 A6
Thomas Bunn Cl
BA11 . . . . . 110 A7
Thomas Byron Rd
SN10 . . . . . 214 C1
Thomas Ct SN1 . . . . . 81 C1
Thomas Hardy Dr ■
BA11 . . . . . 110 A7
Thomas Mead SN15 . . . 78 C5
Thomas St SN2 . . . . . 49 F7
Thomas Wyatt Rd
SN10 . . . . . 214 B1
Thompson Cl SP2 . . . . 151 F5
Thompson Ct SN5 . . . . 33 A3
Thompson Rd SP9 . . . . 216 C7
Thompsons Hill SN16 . . 40 C7
Thomson Way SN8 . . . . 213 B2
Thorley Ct SN25 . . . . . 35 A6
Thornbank SN12 . . . . . 94 A3
Thornbridge Ave SN3 . . 51 A4
Thornbury Rd BA13 . . . 108 F4
Thorne Cl SP5 . . . . . 150 F1
THORNEND 58 C5
Thorne Rd
  ■ Netheravon SP4 . . 190 A4
  Swindon SN3 . . . . . 51 C4
Thorneydown Rd
SP4 . . . . . 133 C1
Thorney Pk SN3 . . . . . 64 B3
Thornford Dr SN5 . . . . 49 C5
THORNHILL 61 F1
Thornhill Dr SN25 . . . . 35 A8
Thornhill Ind Est SN2 . . 35 E1
Thornhill Mews SN16 . . 27 E2
Thornhill Rd
  Swindon SN3 . . . . . 36 C4
  Swindon SN3 . . . . . 36 E4
  Warminster BA12 . . . . 116 D6
Thorns The SN8 . . . . . 213 D5
Thornton Cres SP2 . . . 144 F4
Thornycroft La SN10 . . 172 E1
Thoulstone BA12 . . . . . 112 A4
Threadgill Way ■
SP9 . . . . . 199 C8
Threadneedle St SN14 . . 78 C5
Three Barrows*
SN8 . . . . . 164 B3
Three Cuppes La ■
SP1 . . . . . 146 B1
Three Horseshoes Wlk ■
BA12 . . . . . 117 A7
Three Oak Hill Dr
SN8 . . . . . 175 D4
Three Post La ■
RG17 . . . . . 165 A2
Three Shire Stones*
SN14 . . . . . 74 D1
Three Sisters Rd ■
SN4 . . . . . 163 B6
Thresher Dr SN25 . . . . 35 C6
Thrushel Cl SN25 . . . . 34 E4
Thurlow Cl ■ SP4 . . . 217 E3
Thursday St SN25 . . . . 34 D6
Thyme Cl SN2 . . . . . 34 C3
Thyme Rd SN12 . . . . . 94 D3
Tibb's Meadow SP11 . . 192 D8
Tiberius Rd ■ SP10 . . 193 E2
TIDCOMBE 184 C5
Tidcombe (Long
Barrow)* SN8 . . . . . 184 D4
TIDDLEYWINK 69 A4
Tidford Cts GL7 . . . . . 2 C1
Tidling Cnr SN16 . . . . 16 C5
TIDPIT 209 C6
TIDWORTH 216 E7
Tidworth Cl ■ SN1 . . 49 F4
Tidworth Coll SP9 . . . . 216 D6
Tidworth Leisure Ctr
SP9 . . . . . 216 D6
Tidworth Oval* SP9 . . 216 C5
Tidworth Rd
  Bulford SP4 . . . . . 199 A7
  Collingbourne Ducis
  SN8 . . . . . 191 D7
  Idmiston SP4 . . . . . 133 E8
  Ludgershall SP11 . . . . . 191 F5
  Milston SP4 . . . . . 191 B1
  Porton SP4 . . . . . 133 C4
Tiffany Cl SN25 . . . . . 20 D1
Tile Hill BA10 . . . . . 122 A5
Till Cl ■ SP11 . . . . . 193 F2
Tilley's La SN3 . . . . . 36 A2
TILSHEAD 188 B3
Tilshead Wlk SN2 . . . . 35 B5
Timandra Cl ■ SN25 . . 35 A4
Timberley La SP5 . . . . 211 E2
Timbers Hill BA12 . . . . 114 D5
Timber St SN15 . . . . . 78 C6
Timbrells Cl GL7 . . . . . 6 F7

Timbrells Pl SN14 . . . . 78 C6
Timbrell St BA14 . . . . 101 D1
Timbrells The GL7 . . . . . 5 C8
Timbrell View BA15 . . . 100 C6
Timoney Pl ■ SN1 . . . 50 B5
Timor Rd SN3 . . . . . 108 E2
Tinhead Hill BA12 . . . . 186 D6
Tinhead Rd BA13 . . . . 186 C8
Tinings The SN5 . . . . . 79 A8
Tinkers Field SN4 . . . . 47 D2
Tinkers Mead SN9 . . . . 215 D4
Tinneys Cl SP5 . . . . . 211 C6
Tin Pit SN8 . . . . . 213 E4
Tintagel Cl
  ■ Andover SP10 . . . . 193 E2
  Swindon SN25 . . . . . 49 B4
Tintern Rd SN10 . . . . . 214 B1
Tippett Ave ■ SN25 . . 34 E7
TISBURY 203 D8
Tisbury Cl ■ SN2 . . . . 35 C6
Tisbury & District Sports
Ctr SP3 . . . . . 203 D8
Tisbury Rd SP3 . . . . . 204 D8
Tisbury Row SP3 . . . . . 203 F8
Tisbury Sta SP3 . . . . . 203 E7
Tismeads Cres SN1 . . . 50 C2
Titchfield Cl ■ SN5 . . 48 F5
Tithe Barn Cres SN1 . . 49 F3
Tittymouse La SP11 . . . 192 F1
Tiverton Rd SN2 . . . . . 35 C1
Tobruk Cl ■ SP11 . . . 193 E4
Tobruk Rd SP11 . . . . . 191 F3
Tobys Ct ■ SP7 . . . . . 202 C2
TOCKENHAM 60 E3
Tockenham Cnr SN4 . . 60 D6
Tockenham Way SN2 . . 35 B6
TOCKENHAM WICK . . . 60 D7
Toghill Cres SN13 . . . . 76 B1
Tokes La SP7 . . . . . 202 E6
Tollard Cl SN3 . . . . . 51 C6
TOLLARD FARNHAM . 207 B2
TOLLARD ROYAL 207 B4
Toll Down Way SN14 . . 53 A4
Tollgate Cl SP4 . . . . . 217 A5
Tollgate Pk SP7 . . . . . 202 C3
Tollgate Rd
  Andover SP10 . . . . . 193 C1
  Salisbury SP1 . . . . . 152 B8
Tombs Rd SP4 . . . . . 198 A6
Tomlinson Cl GL7 . . . . . 1 E7
TOOTHILL 49 C4
Topaz Cl SN25 . . . . . 34 F8
Topcliffe Rd BA14 . . . . 106 B8
Top Farm GL7 . . . . . 4 F7
Top La
  Atworth/Whitley SN12 . . 85 C1
  Stourton with Gasper
  BA12 . . . . . 137 D7
Toppers Cl SN25 . . . . . 35 A3
Top Rd
  Ebbesbourne Wake
  SP5 . . . . . 204 C3
  Kempsford GL7 . . . . . 10 C7
Top St SN15 . . . . . 44 A4
Tor House ■ BA13 . . . 109 A3
Tormarton Rd
  Acton Turville GL9 . . . . 52 E6
  Marshfield SN14 . . . . . 66 A2
Tornado Cl SN11 . . . . . 81 D3
Tornio Cl SN10 . . . . . 214 D4
Toronto Rd SP4 . . . . . 217 F8
Torr Cl SN14 . . . . . 70 B2
Torridge Cl SN25 . . . . 34 F4
Torrington Ct SN3 . . . . 51 A5
Torun Way SN25 . . . . . 34 D6
Tottenham Ho* SN8 . . 175 F4
Tottenham Pk* SN8 . . 175 F5
Totterdown Cl ■ SN3 . 51 E7
Totterdown La GL7 . . . . 1 F3
Totts La SN14 . . . . . 75 B7
Totworth Rd SN25 . . . 34 C8
Toucan St SN14 . . . . . 105 E6
Touchorne La SP3 . . . . 141 A4
Tournament Rd SP2 . . 145 C3
Tout Hill SP7 . . . . . 202 B2
Tovey Ct ■ SP10 . . . . 193 F1
Tovey Rd SN2 . . . . . 35 B2
Tow Barrow (Long
Barrow)* SN8 . . . . . 184 B4
Towcester Cl SN14 . . . 77 F5
Towcester Pl ■ SN14 . 77 F5
Towcester Rd
  North Bradley BA14 . . . 105 E4
  Swindon SN3 . . . . . 51 C8
Towell Rd ■ SP4 . . . . 198 A6
Tower Cl
  Andover SP10 . . . . . 193 C2
  Trowbridge BA14 . . . . . 105 A7
Tower Hill
  Dilton Marsh BA13 . . . . 112 D7
  Iwerne Minster DT11 . . 206 A1
Tower Mews SP1 . . . . . 146 B2
Tower Rd
  Melksham SN12 . . . . . 94 C5
  Stourton with Gasper
  BA10 . . . . . 122 F3
Tower View SN10 . . . . 96 D2
Town Bridge BA14 . . . 101 C1
Town Bridge Bradford-
on-Avon BA15 . . . . . 100 C6
Town Farm Pl SP5 . . . . 208 B4
Townfield ■ SN8 . . . . 170 B2
Town Gdns* SN1 . . . . . 50 C4

Town Mill SN8...... 213 D2
Town Path SP2...... 151 E7
TOWNSEND
  Poulshot.......... 179 A6
  Urchfont.......... 180 C3
Townsend
  Allington SN10..... 172 F1
  Chitterne BA12.... 195 D7
  Great Cheverell SN10. 187 C8
  Pitton & Farley SP5.. 148 C4
Town's End BA12.... 138 F5
Townsend Cl BA12... 138 F5
Townsend La
  Martin SP5......... 208 F6
  Martin SP6......... 209 A6
Townsend Pl SN14... 77 F8
Townsend Rd SN4.... 37 F5
Towpath Rd BA14.... 101 D4
Toyd Down SP6...... 209 C6
Toynbee Ave
  Swindon SN25....... 20 D1
  Swindon SN25....... 34 C8
Tozer Way SP5...... 153 F1
Tracy Cl SN25....... 35 A6
Trafalgar Cl **11** SN13.. 76 C1
Trafalgar Ho ★ SP5.. 159 D4
Trafalgar Sch at Downton
  The SP5........... 211 A8
Trafalgar Sq SP4.... 133 B2
Trajan Rd SN3....... 36 C1
Tramways SN13...... 84 F8
Transfer Bridges Ind Est
  SN1.............. 50 D8
Travellers Rest SN13.. 76 C1
Travers Cl SN11..... 81 D3
Trecastle Rd **1** SN1.. 50 A2
Tree Courts Rd **3**
  SN25............. 35 B2
Treforest Cl **1** SN25.. 34 C7
Tregantle Wlk SN3... 51 C6
Tregoze Prim Sch
  SN5.............. 49 A6
Tregoze Way SN5.... 48 F6
Trellis St SN25...... 20 C1
Trenchard Ave
  Box SN13.......... 84 A8
  Calne Without SN11.. 81 F1
  4 Corsham SN13.... 76 B1
  Winterbourne SN4... 133 C2
Trenchard Cl **5** SN14. 78 A6
Trenchard Rd
  Lyneham SN15...... 60 A1
  Stanton Fitzwarren SN6 22 B2
Trent Cres SN12..... 94 A6
Trentham Cl SN3.... 51 A4
Trent Rd SN25...... 35 A4
Trevello Rd SN1..... 50 B2
Trevithick Cl **5**
  BA11............. 110 C6
Triangle The SP5.... 161 D4
Trigg Cres SP4...... 132 B1
Trimm's Dro SP6.... 211 A4
Trimnells SN14...... 75 B3
Trinity Cl SN3....... 51 A3
Trinity Pk SN11...... 81 C1
Trinity Rd
  14 Shaftesbury SP7... 202 D1
  Shrewton SP3....... 196 F7
Trinity Rise SP11.... 193 A2
Trinity St SP11...... 152 B8
Trinity VA CE Prim Sch
  SN10............. 214 C5
Trinity View Rd SP9.. 216 C2
Trollope's Hill BA2... 90 A1
Tropenell Cl **2** SN13.. 76 C1
Trout La SN13....... 84 B7
TROWBRIDGE...... 101 E3
Trowbridge Cl SN2... 35 D4
Trowbridge Com Hospl
  BA14............. 101 D2
Trowbridge Lodge Pk
  BA14............. 105 F8
Trowbridge Mus ★
  BA14............. 105 D8
Trowbridge Rd
  Bradford-on-Avon
  BA15............. 100 E5
  Bratton BA13....... 186 A8
  Farleigh Hungerford
  BA2.............. 103 D7
  Seend SN12........ 178 C7
  Trowbridge BA14.... 102 A2
  Westbury BA13...... 109 B5
Trowbridge Sports Ctr
  BA14............. 105 B6
Trowbridge Sta
  BA14............. 105 C8
Trow La
  Brinkworth SN15..... 59 F8
  Maiden Bradley with
  Yarnfield BA12..... 118 E4
Trowle BA14........ 101 A2
TROWLE COMMON... 100 F2
Truman Cl SN3...... 51 C4
Truro Wlk SN14...... 77 F6
Truscott Ave SN25... 34 E8
Trusloe Cotts SN8... 173 B8
Tryhorn Dr SP1..... 146 C5
Tryon Cl SN3........ 51 D2
Tubbs Farm Cl **6**
  RG17............. 165 A1
Tucker Cl **5** SP4.... 217 C2
Tuckers La SN4..... 163 D6
TUCKINGMILL....... 203 D8
TUCKING MILL....... 98 D8

Tucking Mill Cotts
  BA2.............. 98 D8
Tucking Mill La BA2... 98 C7
Tuckwell Rd GL7...... 10 E6
Tudor Cl SN15....... 79 A4
Tudor Cres SN3...... 36 B1
Tudor Dr BA14...... 101 E4
Tudor Wlk SN3...... 50 F6
Tugela Rd SN15...... 70 E1
Tuggy's La BA2...... 98 E1
Tulse Hill
  Zeale BA12......... 138 A4
  Zennor BA12........ 137 F3
Tumlins SN10....... 180 F8
Tunball La SN8...... 184 F4
Tuners La SN14...... 14 E6
Tunnel Hill SP5...... 153 C2
Tunnicliffe Cl SN3.... 50 E2
Tupman Rd SN13.... 76 E2
Turf Ho La SN11...... 72 D1
Turin Ct **17** SP10.... 193 E2
TURLEIGH.......... 99 F6
Turleigh Hill BA15... 99 E6
Turl St SN1......... 50 C6
Turnball SN4........ 65 D4
Turnberry Cl SN15... 78 F7
Turner Cl **2** SP2.... 151 E7
Turner Ct SP10...... 193 D1
Turner St SN1....... 50 A5
Turnham Gn SN5..... 49 A4
Turnpike **4** SN8.... 170 A6
Turnpike Cl BA14.... 102 F5
Turnpike Ct **5** BA12.. 117 A7
Turnpike Rd
  Blunsdon St Andrew
  SN26............ 35 C8
  Broad Blunsdon SN26.. 21 B1
  Highworth SN6...... 23 A6
Turnpike The
  Chippenham SN15.... 79 B5
  East Knoyle SP3.... 202 D8
Turnstile Wlk **3**
  BA14............. 105 C7
Turntable Pl BA13... 108 F5
Turpin Way SN4...... 77 F7
Tuscan Rd SN25...... 34 D7
Tutton Hill
  Colerne SN14....... 75 B3
  Colerne SN14....... 75 C1
  Ditteridge SN13..... 83 C8
Twatley Cotts SN16... 27 C4
Tweed St SN25...... 34 F4
Twickenham Cl SN3... 51 B8
Twickenham Way
  SN15............. 70 E1
Twineham Gdns SP5.. 153 F2
Twineham Rd SN25.. 34 C8
Twyford Cl SN3...... 51 A6
Twynham Cl SP5.... 211 A7
Twynnoy Cl SN16.... 28 A5
Tyburn Cl SN5....... 49 B5
Tydeman St SN2..... 35 D1
Tye Gdns SN5....... 48 F5
Tylees Ct SN10...... 214 B3
Tylers Cl SP2....... 151 D7
Tyndale Gdns SN3... 51 C6
Tyndales Meadow
  SP3.............. 201 F2
Tyneham Rd SN3.... 51 B6
Tyning Cl **1** BA14... 105 A7
Tyning La **9** BA13... 186 B7
Tyning Pk SN11...... 81 C1
Tyning Rd
  Bathampton BA2..... 82 A2
  Winsley BA15........ 99 E7
Tynings La BA1....... 82 A7
Tynings The
  Biddestone SN14..... 76 D7
  Westbury BA13...... 108 F2
Tynings Way BA15... 99 F3
Tyning The BA2...... 99 B4
Tyrone Ave SP4..... 198 E7
Tythe Cl **17** SP11... 193 E2
TYTHERINGTON.... 194 B4
Tytherington Rd
  Corton BA12....... 194 C3
  Heytesbury BA12.... 194 C5
Tytherley Rd SP5... 149 E6
Tytherly La BA2...... 98 E1
TYTHERTON LUCAS.. 71 D1

U

Uddens Rd SP5...... 207 C4
UFFCOTT........... 167 E8
Uffington Pl BA13... 109 A5
UGFORD........... 144 A3
Ugford Pl SP2....... 144 A3
Ullswater Cl SN3..... 51 E3
Ulysses Rd **2** SN25.. 34 B7
Umbers Hill **2** SP7.. 202 B1
Uncles La BA14...... 100 E6
Underacre Cl **1**
  BA14............. 106 B8
Underdown Cl **12**
  SN4.............. 163 A6
UNDERHILL......... 140 F2
Underhill
  East Knoyle SP3.... 141 A4
  Mere BA12......... 138 F5
  Pen Selwood BA9... 137 B2
Underwood Dr SP4.. 217 D2
Union Rd
  Chippenham SN15.... 78 D3
  Tisbury SP3........ 203 E7
Union Row SN1...... 50 D4

Union St
  Melksham SN12...... 94 A4
  Ramsbury SN8...... 170 B2
  Swindon SN1....... 50 C5
  Trowbridge BA14.... 101 D1
Unity St SN14........ 78 C7
UPAVON........... 181 F2
Upavon Airfield SN9.. 182 B1
Upavon Ct SN2....... 35 C5
Upcott SN6.......... 8 C4
Upcott Ct SN6....... 8 D4
Upfield SN3......... 51 D3
Upham Rd SN3...... 50 E5
Upham Village ★
  SN8.............. 169 C8
Upland Rise BA13... 109 B2
Uplands **28** BA12... 177 B7
Uplands Cl BA2...... 98 F7
Uplands Sch SN25... 34 D8
Uplands The BA12... 117 C7
Upnor Cl SP11...... 191 F4
Upper Backway SP3.. 193 A2
Upper Broad St BA14. 101 C1
UPPER BURGATE.... 210 E3
UPPER CASTLE
  COMBE........... 68 B8
UPPER
  CHICKSGROVE.... 201 A1
Upper Church Fields
  SN8.............. 213 E1
UPPER CHUTE..... 192 D8
Upper Cocklebury La
  SN14............. 78 F8
Upper Dro SP10..... 193 C1
Upper Eddington
  RG17............. 177 C8
UPPER ENHAM..... 193 F4
Upper Folly SP2.... 144 B1
Upper Garston La **8**
  BA13............. 186 B7
UPPER GREEN..... 177 E2
UPPER INGLESHAM.. 12 B5
Upper Isbury SN8... 213 E2
Upper La SN13....... 84 D7
UPPER LAMBOURN.. 164 F3
Upper Lambourn Rd
  RG17............. 165 A2
Upper Ley SN13...... 83 D5
Upper Marsh La
  BA12............. 117 A5
Upper Marsh Rd
  BA12............. 117 A6
UPPER MINETY..... 16 D3
Upper Mount Pleasant
  BA2.............. 99 A4
Upper Noremarsh SN4 47 F1
Upper North Rd SP5.. 207 C5
Upper Ox Hill SN3.... 50 F6
Upper Pavenhill SN5.. 32 F4
UPPER PICKWICK... 76 C3
Upper Potley SN13... 84 E7
Upper Regents Pk
  BA15............. 100 D6
UPPER SEAGRY..... 57 D6
Upper St SP2....... 151 D7
UPPER STRATTON... 35 E4
UPPER STREET..... 210 D5
UPPER STUDLEY... 105 A5
Upper Studley BA14.. 105 A6
UPPER TOWN....... 58 D4
UPPER UP........... 6 E6
UPPER UPHAM..... 169 C8
Upper Waterhay Nature
  Reserve ★ SN6...... 18 D7
Upper Water St SN12. 139 B5
Upper Westwood Rd
  Westwood BA15..... 99 F4
  Westwood BA15.... 100 A3
UPPER WOODFORD.. 131 C7
UPPER WRAXALL.... 66 E2
Uppington La SP3... 129 E8
Up St BA12......... 194 E4
UPTON
  East Knoyle........ 141 A5
  Vernhams Dean..... 185 D2
Upton Cl
  Swindon SN25....... 34 F5
  5 Warminster BA12.. 116 E7
Upton Folly BA12.... 194 E4
Upton
  SCUDAMORE..... 112 E5
Upton Pl SP11...... 185 D2
Upton Pl SP11...... 185 E1
UPTON
  SCUDAMORE..... 112 C5
URCHFONT......... 180 C4
Urchfont CE Prim Sch
  SN10............. 180 B4
Urchfont Way SN2... 35 C4
Ursa Way **16** SN25... 34 B7
Utah Cl SN1......... 49 F4
Utah Ct SN6......... 29 A2
UTC Swindon SN1.... 50 A6
Utterson View SN15.. 78 C7
Uxbridge Rd SN5.... 49 A3

V

Vaggs Hill BA2...... 103 F4
Vale Leaze SN15..... 44 C5
Valens Terr SN13.... 83 C6
Valentia Ct **19** SN12.. 178 B8
Vale Rd SP5......... 211 C7

Vale View SN4....... 47 D1
Vale View Rd SP2... 130 B2
Valiant Cl SN12..... 178 B8
Valletta Gdns SN14... 56 B5
Valley Cl SP5....... 211 C7
Valley Rd SN13...... 76 E1
Valleyside SN1...... 50 A4
Valley The SP2..... 145 C5
Valley View SN11..... 81 A2
Valley Vw **18** SN8... 170 A6
Valley Way SN4...... 75 C6
Vanbrugh Gate SN3.. 50 F1
Vancouver Dr **7** SN8. 213 C2
Van Diemen's Cl SN8. 213 C2
Van Erp Cl SN25..... 20 B1
Vanessa Ave SP1... 146 D1
VASTERN........... 60 F8
Vasterne Cl SN5..... 33 B5
Vasterne Hill SN5.... 33 B5
Vastern Wharf SN4... 61 A7
Vaughan Williams Way
  SN25............. 34 D7
Vega Cl **10** SN25.... 34 B7
Velley Hill SN13...... 85 C5
Venice Ct **30** SP11... 193 E2
Venn The **11** SP7... 202 C2
Ventnor Cl SN24..... 34 E4
Ventry Cl **3** SP1.... 146 B2
Ventry The SP1..... 146 B2
Verden Way **19** SP10. 193 D2
Verney Cl SN3....... 51 D6
VERNHAM BANK... 185 B3
VERNHAM DEAN... 185 C3
Vernham Dean Gullum's
  Prim Sch SP11..... 185 C3
VERNHAM ROW.... 185 B4
Vernham Row La
  SN8.............. 185 A4
Vernham St SP11.... 185 A4
VERNHAM STREET.. 185 D4
Vernon Cl **2** SP4... 217 E3
Verona Rd SP1..... 145 F4
Verulam Cl SN3...... 51 D8
Verwood Cl SN3..... 51 B4
Vespasian Cl SN3... 51 C8
Vespasian Rd
  19 Andover SP10... 193 E2
  Forest Hill SN8.... 175 A7
Vesta Cl SN26....... 21 A1
Vetch Way **27** SP11.. 193 F2
Vicarage Cl
  Calne SN11......... 81 B3
  Marlborough SN8... 213 B3
Vicarage Cotts SN15.. 57 F6
Vicarage Gdns
  Dilton Marsh BA13... 112 B8
  Malmesbury SN16.... 28 B2
  3 Netheravon SP4.. 190 A3
Vicarage La
  Charlton SN16....... 29 B7
  Colerne SN14....... 75 C3
  Easterton SN10..... 179 F2
  Hankerton SN16..... 15 B1
  Highworth SN6....... 23 A6
  Steeple Ashton BA14. 178 A3
  Upavon SN9........ 181 F2
Vicarage Mews BA12. 116 F7
Vicarage Pk **1** SP5.. 211 C7
Vicarage Rd
  Redlynch SP5...... 211 E7
  Swindon SN2....... 34 F1
  Tisbury SP3........ 203 E8
Vice La SO51....... 212 E2
Victoria Cl
  Lyneham SN11....... 73 E8
  Wilton SP2......... 144 C4
Victoria Cross Rd
  SN4.............. 63 F7
Victoria Ct SP1..... 146 A3
Victoria Dr
  10 Bulford SP4.... 217 F8
  Pewsey SN9........ 215 D5
  Rowde SN10........ 96 D1
  Sutton Veny BA12... 121 F8
Walnut Dr SN14..... 74 F6
Victoria Gdns
  14 Sandleheath SP6. 210 C1
  Trowbridge BA14.... 101 E2
Victoria Mws BA12... 116 E6
Victoria Pk SN10.... 187 B8
Victoria Rd
  Devizes SN10....... 214 B4
  Frome BA11........ 110 A4
  Salisbury SP1...... 146 A2
  Sandleheath SP6... 210 C1
  Swindon SN1....... 50 C5
  Trowbridge BA14.... 101 E3
  Warminster BA12... 116 B5
  Wilton SP2......... 144 C4
Victoria St **21** SP7.. 202 C2
Victoria Terr SN11.... 81 B3
Victory Rd BA13..... 108 C6
Viking Cl SN25....... 34 F7
Viking Way
  Andover SP10....... 193 E2
  Salisbury SP2...... 152 B5
Vilett St SN1........ 50 B6
Village Mus the Castle
  Combe ★ SN14...... 68 A7
Village St
  Alton SN8.......... 173 D1
  Upton SP11......... 185 D2
Villiers Cl
  Chippenham SN15... 78 F7
  Lydiard Tregoze SN5.. 48 F7
Vimoutiers Ct **16**
  SP6.............. 210 D1
Vimy Cres
  Bulford SP4........ 217 F8

Vimy Cres continued
  8 Durrington/Bulford
  SP4.............. 198 E6
Vincent Cl SN12..... 94 C4
Vincients Rd SN14... 69 F1
Vincients Wood Nature
  Reserve ★ SN14..... 77 F7
Viner's La SP1g...... 53 B5
Vinescroft **4** BA14.. 101 D5
Vines Ct **3** SN12.... 94 D5
Virginia Cl **1** SP4... 217 E3
Virginia Dr BA12.... 116 F3
Virginia Way SP4.... 132 C1
Viscount Way SN3... 36 C6
Vista Ct **4** BA13.... 109 A3
Vistula Cres **2** SN25.. 34 E6
Vize La SN4......... 167 B7
Vockins Cl SP9...... 216 C8
Volpe Cl SN5........ 48 F4
Volta Rd SN1........ 50 C6
Vorda Rd SN6....... 23 A7
Vowley View SN4..... 47 F1
Voyager Dr SN25.... 34 B7

W

Wade Hill SN6....... 22 F5
Wade Mews SN15.... 70 E1
Wade Rd **3** SN25.... 34 D7
Wadleys Drove BH21. 209 B1
WADSWICK........ 84 B4
Wadswick La SN13... 84 B3
Wadworth Rd SN10.. 214 C4
Waggoner Cl SN25... 35 B5
Wagtail Cl SN3...... 51 C8
Waiblingen Way
  SN10............. 214 A4
Wain-a-Long Rd
  SP1.............. 146 C1
Wains Way SN4..... 190 A3
Wainwright Cl **4** SN3. 51 D4
Wainwright Dr **5**
  BA11............. 110 C7
Wainwright Mews
  SN4.............. 64 B6
Waite Meads Cl SN5.. 33 C4
Wakefield Cl
  Kempsford GL7...... 10 E6
  Swindon SN5........ 49 A4
Walbury Hill (Fort) ★
  RG17............. 185 F8
WALCOT EAST...... 50 E6
Walcot Rd SN3...... 50 E5
WALCOT WEST..... 50 C5
Walden Lodge Cl
  SN10............. 214 B2
Waldron Cl **3** SN3... 51 C4
Waleran Cl SP5..... 153 E2
Walker Rd BA11..... 110 A3
Walker's La **3** RG17. 165 A2
Walkinshaw Rd **5**
  SN2.............. 34 C2
Wallbridge BA11.... 110 A4
Wallbridge Ave **2**
  BA11............. 110 A4
Wallbridge Gdns **1**
  BA11............. 110 A4
Wallbridge Mills
  BA11............. 110 B4
Waller Rd SN10..... 214 C2
Wallingford Cl SN5... 49 C3
Wallingtons Rd RG17. 177 F4
Wallis Dr SN25...... 35 A8
Wallsworth Rd **4** SN3. 51 A4
Walmesley Chase
  1 Trowbridge BA14. 101 E1
  Trowbridge BA14... 102 A1
Walnut Cl
  Harnham SP2...... 151 D7
  3 Netheravon SP4.. 190 A4
  Pewsey SN9........ 215 D5
  Rowde SN10........ 96 B1
  Sutton Veny BA12... 121 F8
Walnut Dr SN14..... 74 F6
Walnut Gr BA14..... 105 B6
Walnut Rd BA12..... 139 B4
Walnut Tree Cl SN3... 36 B2
Walnut Tree Gdns
  SN5.............. 48 D8
Walnut Trees Hill
  SN6.............. 164 A8
Walnut Wlk **1** BA11.. 110 B7
Walronds Cl SN8.... 170 C8
Walsingham Rd SN5.. 50 F6
Walter Cl SN5....... 49 A6
Walter Sutton Cl SN11. 80 F3
Walter Way **2** SP4... 132 C1
Walton Cl **3** SN1..... 50 F4
Walwayne Ct Prim Sch
  BA14............. 105 B8
Walwayne Ct Sch
  BA14............. 101 B1
Walwayne Field SN2.. 36 A5
Walworth Rd SP10... 193 F1
WANBOROUGH..... 163 A5
Wanborough Prim Sch
  SN4.............. 163 A6
Wanborough Rd
  Swindon SN3....... 36 C1
  Wanborough SN4.... 51 F6
Wansdyke ★ SN11... 172 C5
Wansdyke Com Sch
  SN10............. 214 B1
Wansdyke Dr SN1.... 81 A3
Wansdyke Rd SN8... 176 B4
Wantage Rd RG17... 165 B2
Waram Cl RG17..... 177 C8

Warbeck Gate **11** SN5. 48 F5
Warbler Cl **1** BA14... 105 B8
Warburton Cl BA14.. 105 A6
Ward Cl SN5......... 33 A3
Wardley Cl SN3...... 51 A4
WARDOUR.......... 203 D6
Wardour Cl SN3...... 50 E3
Wardour Pl **4** SN12.. 94 A2
Wardour RC Prim Sch
  SP3.............. 203 C6
Wardour Rd **4** SN14.. 78 A6
Wardrobe Mus ★
  SP1.............. 152 A8
Wareham Cl SN5..... 49 B5
WARLEIGH......... 90 D5
Warleigh Dr BA1..... 82 A3
Warleigh La BA1..... 82 B1
War Meml Ave **13**
  RG17............. 177 B6
Warmer's Inn La SN16. 217 F7
WARMINSTER..... 116 E7
Warminster Ave **2**
  SN2.............. 35 C5
Warminster Bypass
  Norton Bavant BA12. 194 A5
  Sutton Veny BA12... 117 F3
  Upton Scudamore
  BA12............. 112 E2
  Warminster BA12... 116 D5
Warminster Coll
  BA12............. 117 A7
Warminster Com Hospl
  BA12............. 117 A7
WARMINSTER
  COMMON........ 116 E5
Warminster La
  Upton Scudamore
  BA12............. 112 E2
  Warminster BA12... 113 A2
Warminster La N
  BA12............. 112 F3
Warminster Mus ★
  BA12............. 117 B7
Warminster Old Rd
  Upton Scudamore
  BA12............. 112 F5
  Upton Scudamore
  BA12............. 112 C5
  Upton Scudamore
  BA12............. 113 A5
Warminster Rd
  Claverton BA2...... 90 B4
  Edington BA13..... 186 E3
  Frome BA11........ 110 B4
  Heytesbury SN10... 187 B3
  Hinton Charterhouse
  BA2.............. 98 F3
  Hinton Charterhouse
  BA2.............. 99 A2
  Norton Bavant BA12. 194 A6
  South Newton SP2.. 130 B1
  Stapleford SP3..... 129 C6
  Upton Scudamore
  BA12............. 112 F3
  Westbury BA13..... 108 F1
  Wilton SP2......... 144 D5
Warminster Sambourne
  CE Prim Sch BA12.. 116 F6
Warminster Sch
  BA12............. 116 F7
Warminster Sports Ctr
  BA12............. 117 D6
Warminster Sta
  BA12............. 117 B7
Warneage Gn **2**
  SN4.............. 163 A5
Warneford Cl **4** SN5. 49 D4
Warneford Cres **4**
  SP4.............. 132 B2
Warner Cl **2** SN3.... 36 B3
Warrener Cl SN25... 35 B7
Warren Bsns Pk GL8.. 24 F5
Warren Cres SN11... 81 C4
Warren Rd BA14.... 101 D5
Warrens La SP5..... 159 A4
Warwick Cl
  Chippenham SN14... 77 F5
  Salisbury SP1...... 145 F3
Warwick Cres SN12... 94 B3
Warwick Rd SN1..... 50 C5
Washbourne Rd SN4.. 47 E1
Washern Cl SP2..... 144 C1
Washers Pit ★ DT11.. 206 D3
Washington Rd BA13. 108 C6
Washmeres SN14.... 75 B2
Washpool
  Lydiard Millicent SN5.. 33 F1
  Swindon SN5........ 48 F8
Washpool La
  Kemble GL7........ 5 B7
  Kempsford GL7...... 10 E8
  Kempsford GL7...... 11 A7
Wason Rd **5** SP4... 197 E6
Waste Dr GL8....... 25 A8
Wastfield SN13...... 84 F8
Watercrook Mews **2**
  SN5.............. 49 D5
Water Ditchampton
  SP2.............. 144 C4
Waterdown Cl **2** SN2. 34 C4
Water Field SN5..... 33 A3
Waterford Beck
  BA14............. 104 F6
Water Furlongs **2**
  SN6.............. 19 D7
Watergate La SP4... 217 C7
Watergates SN14.... 75 C3
WATERHAY......... 18 C7

Waterhole Ave 1
SN13. . . . . .76 C1
Waterhouse La BA2. . . .98 F8
Water La
Collingbourne Ducis
SN8 . . . . 184 B1
Enford SN9. . . . . 190 B6
Horningsham BA12. . . . 119 A8
Salisbury SP1. . . . . . . 152 A8
Somerford Keynes GL7 . . .6 A1
Water Lily Cl BA14. . . . 101 D4
Waterloo Rd SP1 . . . . . 152 C7
Watermead SN3. . . . . . . 36 C2
Watermeadow La
BA12. . . . . 195 C1
Water Meadows SN16. .28 A2
Watermint Way SN11 . .80 F4
Waters Bank Rd
Box SN13. . . . . 84 B8
1 Rudloe SN13. . . . . . 84 B8
Waters Edge SN15. . . . .78 E5
Waterside SN14 . . . . . .68 A7
Waterside Pk Ind Est
SN2. . . . . .49 E8
Waterside Way SN3. . . .51 A1
Watersmeet Rd SP2 . . 152 A6
Waters Rd SP1 . . . . . . 146 A4
Water St
Berwick St John SP7 . . 203 E1
Durrington/Bulford
SP4. . . . . 217 D8
Mere BA12. . . . . 139 B6
Upton Lovell BA12. . . . 194 E3
Waters View GL7 . . . . . . .6 F6
Waterworks Rd BA14 105 B7
Watery La
Corsham SN15. . . . . . . 85 A3
Donhead St Mary SP7 . 203 A3
Shaftesbury SP7 . . . . . 202 C1
Shipton Bellinger SP9 . 216 C1
Sutton Veny BA12. . . . 117 F4
Swindon SN5. . . . . . . .48 F7
Watling Cl SN2 . . . . . . .49 E6
Watson Rd SP4. . . . . . . 197 E7
Watson's Ct 2 SN12. . .94 B4
Watt Cl 4 SP10. . . . . . 193 C1
Watt Rd SP2. . . . . 151 D8
Watts La SN14. . . . . . . .41 F1
Watt's Way 22 SN10. . 179 F1
Wavell Rd
Salisbury SP2. . . . . . . 152 A6
Swindon SN2 . . . . .35 B2
Tidworth SP9 . . . . 216 B8
Warminster BA12 . . . . 113 D1
Waverley Cl
7 Fordingbridge
SP6. . . . . 210 D2
Frome BA11. . . . . 110 C6
Waverley Ct
4 Corsham SN13. . . . .84 F8
Corsham SN13. . . . . . .85 A8
Waverley Gdns SN12. . .94 A3
Waverley Rd
Fordingbridge SP6 . . . 210 D2
Swindon SN3 . . . . .36 C1
Waylands
Cricklade SN6 . . . . . . .19 E7
Devizes SN10. . . . . . . 214 D3
Wayne Cl SN25 . . . . . . .35 A5
Wayside Cl
Frome BA11. . . . . 110 C6
Kington Langley SN15 . .70 E7
Swindon SN2 . . . . .49 E7
Wayte St 5 SN25. . . . . .34 E3
Weaveland Rd 2
SP3. . . . . 203 B8
Weavern Ct SN14. . . . . .78 A7
Weavern La SN13. . . . . .76 A5
Weavers Cl
Chippenham SN14 . . . . .77 F7
3 Malmesbury SN16. . .28 A5
Weavers Crofts SN12. . .94 A5
Weavers Dr BA14. . . . . 105 D7
Weavers La RG17. . . . . 177 E3
Weavers Mead SN10 . 179 C1
Weavers The SN3. . . . . .50 D4
Webb Cl SN15 . . . . .78 E5
Webbers Ct BA14. . . . . 105 A6
Webbington Rd SN15 . .78 E5
Webb La SN25. . . . . . . .34 D8
Webbs Ct SN15. . . . . . .60 A3
Webb's La SN10 . . . . . 179 D8
Webbs Pl SN25. . . . . . .34 A3
Webbs Way
Burbage SN8 . . . . 183 D8
Malmesbury SN16. . . . .28 A5
Webbs Wood SN5. . . . . .34 A2
Wedgewood Cl SN2. . . .50 A7
WEDHAMPTON 180 E4
Wedmore Ave SN15. . . .70 C6
Wedmore Cl BA11. . . . 110 C7
Wedmore Dr BA13. . . . 109 A5
Weedon Rd SN3. . . . . . .51 B8
Weeke Cl 1 SP5. . . . . 210 F8
Weir Heyes Ave 7
SN13. . . . . .76 B1
Weir La SN14. . . . . .74 A8
Weirside Ave SN4 . . . . .64 B6
Weir The BA13. . . . . . . 186 C8
Welbeck Cl SN3 . . . . . . .50 F5
Welby Cl SN25. . . . . . . .34 B8
Welcombe Ave SN3. . . .51 A5
Welford Cl SN3. . . . . . .51 C8
WELL BOTTOM 206 E3
Well Cl SN4 . . . . .65 D4
Weller Rd SN13. . . . . . .76 F2
Welle Sley Cl 18
SN12. . . . . 178 B8

Wellhead BA12 . . . . . . 139 A6
Wellhead Dro BA13. . . 109 A1
Well House Cl SP6. . . . 210 B6
Wellington Academy The
SN11. . . . . 191 F5
Wellington Dr
Bishops Cannings
SN10 . . . . 214 F7
Bower Hill SN12. . . . . .94 C1
Wellington Lions Prim
Acad SP9 . . . . 216 D8
Wellington Pl SN14. . . .55 F8
Wellington Rd
5 Durrington/Bulford
SP4. . . . . 198 F7
South Marston SN3 . . . .36 C6
Wellington Sq SN12 . . .94 C1
Wellington St SN1. . . . .50 C7
Wellington Way SP2 . 145 D3
Well La
Godshill SP6. . . . . 211 A1
Hawkesbury GL9 . . . . . .38 E5
4 Shaftesbury SP7. . . 202 B2
Wellow Dr BA11. . . . . . 110 C7
Wellow La BA2 . . . . . . .98 D1
Wellow Wood Rd
SO51. . . . . 212 F8
Wells Cl
Chippenham SN14 . . . . .78 A5
Durrington SP4 . . . . . . 198 A6
Wellscote Gdns 7
BA14. . . . . 105 D6
Wells Rd SP4 . . . . 198 A6
Wellsted Cl SN5 . . . . . 149 F4
Wellworthy Dr SP2 . . 151 D7
Welsh Way GL7. . . . . . . .1 D8
Welton Rd SN5 . . . . . . .49 D6
Wembley St SN2. . . . . .49 F8
Wenhill Hts SN11. . . . .81 B2
Wenhill La SN11. . . . . .81 A1
Wensleydale Cl SN5 . . .49 B6
Wentworth Cl SN15. . . .78 F7
Wentworth Pk 1 SN5. .49 A4
Were Cl 3 BA12. . . . . . 116 E7
Werg SN8 . . . . 175 B8
Wesley Cl BA14. . . . . . 104 E2
Wesley La BA14. . . . . . 104 E2
Wesley Rd BA14 . . . . . 105 C7
Wesley St SN1. . . . . . . .50 C4
Wessex Cl
Calne SN11 . . . . .81 C3
Chippenham SN14 . . . . .78 B8
2 Hungerford RG17. . 177 B1
Melksham SN12. . . . . .94 B3
Semington BA14 . . . . . 102 E5
Wessex Pl 29 RG17. . 177 B1
Wessex Rd
Chippenham SN14 . . . . .78 B8
Salisbury SP1. . . . . . . 146 C1
Wilton SP2 . . . . 144 C1
Wessex Way SN6. . . . . .23 B7
Wessex Wlk BA13. . . . 109 A4
Wessington Ave SN11 .81 C1
Wessington Ct SN11. . .81 C1
Wessington Pk SN11. . .81 C1
West Allcourt GL7 . . . . .2 C4
WEST AMESBURY . . . 198 A4
West Ashton CE (VA)
Prim Sch SN14 . . . . . 106 B4
West Ashton Rd
BA14. . . . . 105 E8
Westbourne CE SP1 . . 152 C8
Westbourne Gdns 6
BA14. . . . . 105 B8
Westbourne Mws
BA14. . . . . 105 B8
Westbourne Rd
Trowbridge BA14. . . . . 105 B8
Westbury BA13. . . . . . 109 A3
West Bourton Rd
SP8. . . . . 137 D1
WESTBROOK. 95 E8
Westbrook SN15. . . . . .96 A8
Westbrook Cl
Chippenham SN14 . . . . .78 A7
14 Hungerford RG17. . 177 B7
Westbrook Gn SN15 . . .95 E8
Westbrook Rd
Bromham SN15 . . . . . . .88 A1
Swindon SN2 . . . . .35 A1
WESTBURY 109 B2
Westbury CE Jun Sch
BA13. . . . . 108 F3
Westbury Ind Est
BA13. . . . . 108 E5
Westbury Infants' Sch
BA13. . . . . 108 F3
WESTBURY LEIGH . . . 108 E1
Westbury Leigh
BA13. . . . . 108 E1
Westbury Leigh CE Prim
Sch BA13. . . . . 108 E1
Westbury Pk SN4 . . . . .47 D1
Westbury Rd
Bratton BA13. . . . . . . 186 A7
Cheverell Magna
SN10 . . . . 179 C1
Great Hinton BA14. . . . 102 F3
Heywood BA13. . . . . . 109 A8
North Bradley BA14. . . 105 E3
Semington BA14 . . . . . 102 F3
Swindon SN2 . . . . .35 B5
Warminster BA12 . . . . 113 A2
Westbury Sta BA13. . . 108 E5
Westbury View SN12. . .94 C1

Westbury Visitor Ctr ★
BA13. . . . . 109 A3
Westbury White Horse ★
BA13. . . . . 109 F1
West Cepenway SN14. .69 F1
West Cepen Way
Chippenham SN14 . . . . .70 B3
Chippenham Without
SN14. . . . . .77 F5
WEST CHISENBURY . 189 F7
Westcombe La BA12. . 195 E1
Westcott Cl 9 BA11. . 110 C6
Westcott Pl SN1. . . . . . .50 A5
Westcott St SN1. . . . . . .50 A5
Westcroft SN1. . . . . . . .50 A5
Westcroft St BA14. . . . 101 C1
WEST CRUDWELL 14 D7
WEST DEAN. 155 F3
West Dean Rd SP5. . . . 149 F5
West Ditch La
West Ashton BA14. . . . 106 E3
West Ashton BA14. . . . 106 E4
West End
Bishops Cannings
SN10 . . . . 172 B3
Ebbesbourne Wake
SP5. . . . . 204 C3
Foxham SN15. . . . . . . .72 B7
Melksham SN12. . . . . .94 A3
Westbury BA13. . . . . . 109 A3
West End Cl SN14. . . . . .78 C8
West End Gdns GL7. . . .1 E7
West End Hill BA11. . . 123 C8
West End La
Bishopstone SN6 . . . . . 163 E6
Donhead St Andrew
SP7. . . . . 203 B3
West End Rd
Salisbury SP2. . . . . . . 145 E2
Swindon SN3 . . . . .36 A1
West Ennox La SN13 . .84 A6
Westerham Wlk SN11. .81 C2
Westerleigh Cl BA14. . .78 B6
Western Downland CE
Aided Prim Sch
SP6. . . . . 210 A5
Western Downland CE
(VA) Prim Sch (Infant
Site) SP6. . . . . 209 F2
Westergate SN5. . . . . . .34 B1
Western St SN1. . . . . . .50 C5
Western Way
Melksham SN12. . . . . .93 F3
Salisbury SP2. . . . . . . 145 B3
Westfield BA15 . . . . . 100 B7
Westfield Chase 13
SN8. . . . . 170 A6
Westfield Cl
15 Durrington/Bulford
SP4. . . . . 198 B7
Laverstock SP1 . . . . . . 146 D2
Trowbridge BA14. . . . . 105 A6
Westfield Rd BA14. . . . 105 A7
Westfields BA14. . . . . 137 F4
Westfield Way SN2 . . . .34 D4
WEST GRAFTON. 183 E7
WEST GRIMSTEAD . . 154 C2
Westgrove 17 SP6 . . . 210 D1
WEST HATCH 203 C7
West Hay Gr GL7. . . . . . .4 F7
West Highland Rd
SN25. . . . . .34 F7
WEST HILL. 85 B1
West Hill
Broad Blunsdon SN26 . .21 B2
Heytesbury BA12. . . . . 194 D7
Melksham Without SN12 85 B1
Westhill Cl SN6. . . . . . .22 C7
Westinghouse Pk
SN14. . . . . .78 B8
WEST KENNETT 173 D7
West Kennett Long
Barrow ★ SN8 . . . . . 173 C6
WEST KINGTON 66 F7
West Kington Rd
SN14. . . . . .67 B8
WEST KINGTON
WICK. 67 B6
WEST KNOYLE 140 E6
West La
Kemble GL7 . . . . .2 A4
Melbury Abbas SP7 . . . 206 A7
Westlake Pl SN15. . . . . .57 D1
Westland Cl 3 BA12. . 217 D3
Westlands 2 BA12 . . 194 C5
Westlands La SN12 . . . .85 F2
WEST LAVINGTON. . . 187 E8
WESTLEA. 49 D5
Westlea Campus SN5 . .49 C7
Westlea County Prim Sch
SN5. . . . . .49 C6
Westlea Dr SN5. . . . . . .49 C6
Westlecot Rd SN1 . . . . .50 B3
Westleigh BA12. . . . . . 116 E6
West Manton SN8 . . . 174 C7
Westmead Cres
BA14. . . . . 105 B4
Westmead Dr SN5. . . . .49 D7
Westmead Ind Est
SN5. . . . . .49 D6
Westmead La SN15. . . .78 D7
Westmead Terr SN15 . .78 E6
West Mill La SN6 . . . . . .8 C1
Westminster Cl
Dunkirk SN10. . . . . . . 179 D8
1 Shaftesbury SP7. . . 202 B7
Westminster Gdns
SN14. . . . . .78 B7

Westminster Meml Hospl
SP7. . . . . 202 B1
Westminster Rd
Salisbury SP2. . . . . . . 145 F2
Swindon SN5. . . . . . . .49 B4
Westmorland Rd SN1 . .50 D5
WESTONBIRT 25 D8
Westonbirt Arboretum ★
GL8. . . . . .25 B8
Westonbirt Rd
Westonbirt GL8. . . . . . .25 E6
Westonbirt GL8. . . . . . .26 A6
Westonbirt Sch GL8. . .25 E8
Weston Cl SN11. . . . . . .81 D6
Weston Ct 1 SP11. . . . 193 E4
Weston La SP5 . . . . . . 149 B5
WEST OVERTON. 173 F6
West Par BA12. . . . . . . 116 F6
West Pk SP1. . . . . 192 E3
West Pk ★ SP6. . . . . . . 210 A3
West Pk Dr SP6. . . . . . 209 F3
West Pk La SP6. . . . . . 209 F3
West Pk Rd SN13 . . . . .76 C1
Westpoint Bsns Pk
SN14. . . . . .70 A1
West Portway SP10 . . 193 C1
WESTROP. 77 C1
Westrop SN6 . . . . .23 A6
Westrop Prim Sch
SN6. . . . . .22 F6
West St Pl BA12 . . . . . 116 E6
Westside SP4. . . . . . . 199 A2
Westside Cl SP4 . . . . . 146 C8
West St
Aldbourne SN8 . . . . . . 169 F6
Aldbourne SN8. . . . . . 170 A6
Barford St Martin SP3. 143 A4
Castle Combe SN14. . . .67 F7
Castle Combe SN14. . . .68 A7
22 Fordingbridge SP6 210 D1
Great Somerford SN15 . .43 F2
Great Wishford SP2. . . 129 F4
Lacock SN15 . . . . .86 D5
1 Malmesbury SN16. . .28 A3
Salisbury SP2. . . . . . . 145 F1
Trowbridge BA14. . . . . 105 C8
Warminster BA12 . . . . 116 E6
Wilton SP2 . . . . 144 C3
WEST STOWELL 173 F1
West Swindon Sh Ctr
SN5. . . . . .49 B5
West View SN3 . . . . . . .51 B7
West View Cotts
SP11. . . . . 185 D5
West View Cres
SN10. . . . . 214 A3
Westview Orch BA2. . . .99 B5
West View Rd BA1. . . . .82 A3
West Vw Rd SN8. . . . . 191 A8
West Way GL7 . . . . .2 C5
Westway Cl SN14 . . . . .68 B7
WESTWELLS. 84 C6
Westwells SN13. . . . . . .84 C6
Westwells Rd SN13. . . .84 B7
West Wick 6 SP5 . . . . 210 F8
West Wiltshire Craft Ctr ★
BA13. . . . . 108 D6
West Wilts Trading Est
BA13. . . . . 108 D7
WEST
WINTERSLOW . . . 148 F5
West Wlk SP1 . . . . 152 A7
WESTWOOD
Salisbury 145 B5
Westwood. 99 F2
Westwood Manor
House ★ BA15. . . . . 100 A3
Westwood Rd
Corsham SN13. . . . . . . .84 B8
Farleigh Hungerford
BA2 . . . . 103 E8
Salisbury SP2. . . . . . . 145 B4
Swindon SN2 . . . . .35 C6
Trowbridge BA14. . . . . 101 A1
Westwood BA15 . . . . . .99 F1
Wingfield BA15 . . . . . 100 D2
Westwoods BA1. . . . . . .82 B3
Westwood St Thomas
Sch SP2. . . . . 145 A4
Westwood-with-Iford
Prim Sch BA15 . . . . . .99 F3
WEST YATTON. 68 D3
West Yatton Rd SN14 . .68 E5
Wetherby Cl 1 SN14. .78 A5
Wetherby Gdns 24
SP10. . . . . 193 D2
Wet La BA12. . . . . 139 D2
Wet Pits La SN8. . . . . . 168 E3
WEXCOMBE 184 B6
Wexland Ave SP4. . . . . 189 F3
Wey Cl SN25. . . . . .35 A4
WEYHILL 192 F1
Weyhill Cl SN3 . . . . . . .51 B5
Weyhill Gdns 7
SP11. . . . . 192 F1
Weyhill Rd 1 SP11. . . 193 A1
Weymouth St BA12 . . 117 A6
WHADDON
Alderbury 153 E1
Hilperton 102 C7
Whaddon Bsns Pk
SP5. . . . . 153 F1
Whaddon La
Hilperton BA14 . . . . . . 102 B5
Trowbridge BA14. . . . . 102 A3
Whall Cl SN26 . . . . . . .20 B1
Whalley Cres SN4. . . . .63 F6
Wharf Ct SN12. . . . . . . .94 B3

Wharf Ctr The ★
SN10. . . . . 214 A4
Wharfings The GL7 . . . .10 D6
Wharf La
Kempsford GL7 . . . . . . .10 D6
Lechlade GL7 . . . . .2 D3
Wharf Rd SN4 . . . . .49 C1
Wharf St SN10. . . . . . . 214 A4
Wharf The SN13. . . . . . .83 D6
Wharf Theatre & Ctr The
SN10. . . . . 214 A4
Wharncliffe St 3
SN25. . . . . .34 D8
Whatcombe Brow
SP3. . . . . 196 D8
Whatley Dr SN9 . . . . . 215 C5
Whatleys Cl SN10 . . . . 179 A4
Whatleys Orch SN6 . . 163 E6
Wheat Cl BA14. . . . . . . 105 A7
Wheatcroft Way SN1. . .50 E7
Wheatfield Ave SN14 . .78 A4
Wheatlands SN25. . . . .34 E4
Wheatley Cl SP9 . . . . . 216 D8
Wheatsheaf Gdns
SN25. . . . . .35 E3
Wheatsheaf La SN16. . .16 A8
Wheatstone Rd SN3. . .51 E4
Wheeler Ave SN2 . . . . .35 D2
Wheeler Cl SN9. . . . . . 215 B5
Wheeler Pl SN10. . . . . .96 E5
Wheelers La BA12. . . . 117 B5
Wheeler Way SN16 . . . .28 A5
Wheelwright's Cl
SP5. . . . . 208 A4
Whelford Rd GL7 . . . . . .10 D7
Whilestone Way SN3. . .36 C1
Whinyates Rd 2 SP4 197 E1
Whistley Rd SN10. . . . 179 C8
Whitbourne Ave SN3. . .50 F5
WHITBOURNE
MOOR 115 C7
WHITBOURNE
SPRINGS 115 E5
Whitbred Cl 2 SN5. . . .49 B7
Whitbred Rd SP2 . . . . 145 C5
Whitby Gr SN2. . . . . . . .34 F1
Whitchers Meadow
SP5. . . . . 153 D4
Whitcombe Cl SN15. . . .73 F8
White Barrow (Long
Barrow) ★ SP3 . . . . 188 B1
White Beam Ct SN12. . .35 B2
Whitebridge Rd SP1 . 146 D1
White Castle SN5 . . . . .49 C3
White Cliff ★ BA13. . . . 186 B6
WHITE CROSS 137 E5
White Eagle Rd SN25 . .34 D5
White Edge Moor
SN3. . . . . .51 D2
White Enox La SN13 . . .83 F7
White Farm La SN8 . . . 185 C7
Whitefield Cl BA1. . . . . .82 B4
Whitefield Cres SN5 . . .34 A1
Whitefriars La SN6 . . . . .6 E1
Whitefriars Rd 1
SP1. . . . . 152 B7
Whitegates SN14 . . . . .68 A8
White Hart La 12
SP7. . . . . 202 C1
Whiteheads La BA15 . 100 D7
Whitehead St SN1 . . . . .50 B5
Whitehill
Bradford-on-Avon
BA15 . . . . 100 D7
Hindon SP3. . . . . 200 B3
White Hill BA13. . . . . . 139 C2
White Hill
Bishopston SN4 . . . . . 163 D5
Farley SP5 . . . . 154 D8
Pitton SP5 . . . . 148 C2
Pitton & Farley SP5 . . . 148 C3
Whitehill Cl 11 SN8 . . 170 B2
Whitehill Ind Pk SN4. . .47 B1
Whitehill La SN4. . . . . .47 B2
Whitehill Way SN5. . . . .48 F3
Whitehorn Cl SN14 . . . .47 E4
Whitehorn Dr SP5 . . . . 212 C5
White Horse Bsns Pk
BA14. . . . . 105 B4
White Horse Cl BA14. . 105 D6
Whitehorse Dr SN9 . . 215 B4
White Horse Dr 8
BA11. . . . . 110 C6
White Horse Rd
Cricklade SN6 . . . . .19 D8
Forest Hill SN8. . . . . . 175 A4
Winsley BA15. . . . . . . .99 E7
Wroughton SN4. . . . . . 167 F8
White Horse Sports Ctr
SN11. . . . . .81 C1
White Horse Way
Calne SN11 . . . . .81 B1
Devizes SN10. . . . . . . 214 B5
Devizes SN10. . . . . . . 214 D6
Westbury BA13 . . . . . . 109 A4
Whitehouse La GL8. . . .26 B4
Whitehouse Rd SN2 . . .50 B8
White La SN8. . . . . 184 B1
Whiteland Rise BA13. 109 B2
Whitelands Rd SN3. . . .36 A1
Whitelawn La BA14. . . 106 F4
White Lion Pk SN16. . . .27 E4
Whitelocks Piece
RG17. . . . . 171 A1
Whiteman St SN2. . . . . .50 C8
Whitemarsh BA12 . . . 139 B4
WHITEPARISH 161 D4

Whiteparish All Saints CE
Prim Sch SP5 . . . . . . 161 D3
White Pit La SP7. . . . . 206 B6
WHITEPITS 126 A7
White Rd
Mere BA12. . . . . 139 B6
Savernake SN8 . . . . . . 175 A6
White Row Hill BA14. . 105 A5
Whiterow Pk BA14. . . . 105 A6
Whitesbury Rd SP5. . . 152 B5
Whites Cnr SN12. . . . . .85 D1
White Sheet Castle ★
BA12. . . . . 124 E1
Whitesheet CE(VA) Prim
Acad BA12. . . . . 138 A4
Whitesheet CE (VA) Prim
Sch BA12. . . . . 123 C8
White Sheet Hill Nature
Reserve ★ BA12. . . . 124 C2
White Sheet La BA12. 124 C3
White's Hill SN8 . . . . . 169 F2
Whiteshoot SP5 . . . . . 211 D6
Whiteshoot Hill SP5 . 211 D6
White Shute RG17 . . . 171 A8
White St
Easterton SN10 . . . . . 180 A1
Horningsham BA12 . . . 119 B8
21 Market Lavington
SN10 . . . . 179 F1
Whitestone Rd BA11. . 110 B6
Whites Way SN15. . . . . .57 C2
White Way
Broad Town SN4 . . . . . 167 A8
Pitton SP5 . . . . 148 B4
Pitton & Farley SP5. . . 148 C3
Whitgift Cl SN5. . . . . . .48 F6
WHITLEY. 85 C1
Whitley Rd 14 SN8 . . 170 A6
Whitlock Rise SP5 . . . 205 F5
Whitmarsh 7 SP4 . . . 190 A4
Whitmore Cl SN5. . . . . .48 F6
Whitney St SN1. . . . . . .50 C5
WHITSBURY 210 B5
Whitsbury Rd
Fordingbridge SP6. . . . 210 D2
Odstock SP5. . . . . 158 A7
Whittingham Dr SN4. . .64 C3
Whittington Rd SN5 . . .49 C6
Whittle Ave SN11. . . . . 166 A1
Whittle Cl SN14. . . . . . .78 A7
Whittle Rd
4 Andover SP10. . . . . 193 B1
Salisbury SP2. . . . . . . 145 C1
Whittle Ride SN8 . . . . 184 B1
Whittocks La BA12. . . 116 C5
WHITTONDITCH. 170 D3
Whittonditch Rd SN8 170 C2
Whitworth Rd SN5 . . . .35 A3
Wichelstok Cl SN1. . . . .50 C3
Wichel Way
Swindon SN1 . . . . .49 B2
Swindon SN1 . . . . .49 E2
WICK 210 F8
Wick Ball Camp ★
SP3. . . . . 201 D3
Wickdown Ave SN25. . .34 F3
Wicker Hill 2 BA14. . . 105 C8
Wickfield SN10 . . . . . . 214 B2
Wickhill SN11. . . . . . . .80 C8
Wick Hill SN15. . . . . . .72 B1
Wick La
Devizes SN10. . . . . . . 214 B1
Downton SP5 . . . . 210 E8
Lacock SN15 . . . . .85 F4
Manningford SN9. . . . . 181 F5
Wanborough SN4. . . . . .51 F6
Wick Rd
Oaksey GL7. . . . . .4 F3
Oaksey SN16. . . . . .5 A1
Oaksey SN16. . . . . . . .16 A8
Wicks Cl SN25. . . . . . . .34 E5
Wicks Dr SN15. . . . . . . .78 F5
Wickwater La GL7 . . . . .7 C4
WIDBROOK 100 E4
Widbrook Meadow
BA14. . . . . 105 A8
Widbrook View SN15 100 E5
Widdenham SN14 . . . . .75 D2
WIDHAM. 33 C5
Widham SN5. . . . . .33 C6
Widhill La SN26. . . . . . .21 A1
Wigmore Ave SN3 . . . . .50 F3
WILCOT 182 A7
Wilcot Ave SN2. . . . . . .35 D5
Wilcot Cl
Amesbury SP4. . . . . . . 217 D2
Trowbridge BA14. . . . . 105 C6
Wilcot Rd
Pewsey SN9. . . . . 215 B5
Pewsey SN9. . . . . 215 C5
Wilcox Cl SN2 . . . . .35 C2
Wild Acre 9 SN4 . . . . 163 A6
Wild Cross
Little Chalfield BA15 . . .92 B6
South Wraxall SN12. . . .91 F6
Wilderness The
BA15. . . . . 100 C1
Wildern Sq SN3 . . . . . .36 A4
WILDHERN. 193 D5
Wildmoorway La GL7 . . .7 B7
Wiley Terr SP2 . . . . . . 144 D4
Wilkins Cl SN2. . . . . . . .35 F5
Wilkinson Cl SN12. . . . .94 C5
WILLESLEY 25 C6

Willesley Dr GL8.......25 B7
William Cl SP1 ...... 146 D1
William Morris Prim Sch
SN26................20 E2
William Morris Way
Swindon SN25..... 34 D8
Swindon SN26 ...... 20 D2
William Rd SN10.... 214 D2
William Robbins Ct
SN25................34 F3
Williams Cl 6 SN12...94 B4
Williams Gr SN13....85 A8
Williamson Cl 3
SP11..............192 A5
William St
Calne SN11 ...... 81 C4
Swindon SN1 ...... 50 A4
William Stumpes Cl 7
SN16...............28 A5
Willis Cl
5 Chippenham SN15...78 F4
Great Bedwyn SN8 .. 176 C3
Willis Way SN5.......33 B3
Willoughby Cl BA13.. 108 E2
Willoughby Rd SP4 .. 197 E6
Willow Ave 5 SP6.. 210 D1
Willowbank SN14.....70 A2
Willowbrook SN5.....33 C4
Willowbrook End
SN15................57 D2
Willow Cl
Laverstock SP1 .....146 D2
Melksham SN12.......94 A3
Willow Cres
Broughton Gifford
SN12 ....93 A5
Warminster BA12.....117 C5
Willow Dr
Devizes SN10........214 E5
4 Durrington SP4.. 198 B7
Willow Gr
Chippenham SN15.....70 E2
South Cerney GL7 .....7 A6
Trowbridge BA14.....105 B5
Westbury BA13.....108 E3
Willow Gro 9 SN6....19 D8
Willowherb SN25....34 E5
Willowmead Cl SP5.. 150 F2
Willows Ave SN2 .....35 C3
Willows The
Calne SN11 ...... 89 E8
Highworth SN6........23 A5
Swindon SN5 ...... 34 A2
Willow View BA14.. 105 C3
Willow View SN16....27 F4
Willow Way SP7.... 202 A4
Willow Wlk SN4 .....64 B6
Wills Ave SN1 ....50 E8
Wilmot Cl SN5........48 F6
WILSFORD
Wilsford............181 B4
Wilsford cum Lake... 197 F2
Wilsford Group
(Tumuli) *
SP4...............197 D2
Wilsford Rd SN9.... 181 C5
Wilson Rd
Larkhill SP4 ...... 197 E6
Swindon SN25.......34 F6
Wilson Sq BA12..... 117 C7
WILTON
Grafton.............184 A8
Wilton.............144 C3
Wilton and Barford CE
Prim Sch SP2 .... 144 B2
Wilton Carpet Factory *
SP2...............144 D4
Wilton Dr BA14.... 105 D6
Wilton Ho* SP2.... 144 D2
Wilton Pk* SP2.... 144 D1
Wilton Rd
Barford St Martin
SP3...............143 C3
East Grafton SN8.... 184 A7
Quidhampton SP2 .. 144 F3
Wylye BA12 .... 201 F8
Wilton Windmill*
SN8...............184 B8
Wilton Wlk SN2......35 C6
Wiltshire Ave SN2....50 A8
Wiltshire Cl
Bulford SP4 ...... 217 F8
3 Hungerford RG17.. 177 B7
Wiltshire Coll
Chippenham SN15.....78 E1
Chippenham SN15.....78 E8
Devizes SN10........214 B3
Trowbridge BA14.....105 C8
Westbury BA13.....109 A3
Wiltshire Coll & Univ Ctr
BA14..............105 B6
Wiltshire Cres
Melksham SN12.......94 C3
Royal Wootton Bassett
SN4
Wiltshire Dr BA14.. 105 D5
Wiltshire Gall The*
SP1..............145 F1
Wiltshire Heritage Mus*
SN10..............214 A3
Wiltshire Music Ctr
BA15..............100 B8

Wiltshire Path SN14...24 C2
Wiltshire Rd SP2 ... 151 E6
Wiltshire Way BA13.. 109 A4
Wimpole Cl SN3.......51 B4
Winchcombe Ave
SN10................97 D1
Winchcombe Cl SN5...48 F7
Winchcombe Gdns GL7.6 F6
Winchester Cl
Amesbury SP4 ...... 217 D2
2 Chippenham SN14... 78 A6
North Bradley BA14.. 105 C2
Swindon SN3 ...... 36 B1
Winchester St SP1.. 146 B1
Wincombe Bsns Pk
SP7...............202 C3
Wincombe La SP7.. 202 D3
Wincombe Pk* SP7. 202 D3
Windbrook Meadow
SN2.................36 A4
Windermere SN3 .... 51 D3
Windermere Rd
BA14..............101 E2
Windflower Rd SN25...34 E5
Winding Way SP2..... 145 B3
Windlass Way SN10...36 B4
Windlesham Rd SP1. 146 B4
Windmill Cl
3 Aldbourne SN8.... 170 A7
Alderbury SP5 ...... 153 E2
4 Shaftesbury SP7... 202 C2
Windmill Dr SP9.... 216 D8
Windmill Hill Bsns Pk
SN5.................48 F3
Windmill Hill
(Causeway
Enclosure) *
SN4...............167 A2
Windmill La
Hurstbourne Tarrant
SP11..............193 F8
Kemble GL7 ....4 F8
Winterbourne SP4.... 133 B4
Windmill Piece SN4 .. 65 D4
Windmill Rd
Kemble GL7 ....4 F8
Royal Wootton Bassett
SN4...............47 F1
WINDMILLS.........193 F7
Windmill Tump (Long
Barrow) * GL7........3 A7
Windrush SN6.........22 E5
Windrush Rd SN25....35 A3
Windsor Ave SN12....94 B3
Windsor Cl
Chippenham SN14.... 78 A6
Lydiard Tregoze SN4 .. 47 F6
Windsor Cres BA11.. 110 A5
Windsor Dr
Devizes SN10........214 D3
1 Trowbridge BA14.. 105 B5
Westbury BA13.....109 B4
Windsor Mews 8
SP4...............198 B7
Windsor Rd
Calne Without SN11...81 F1
9 Durrington/Bulford
SP4...............198 B7
North Bradley BA14.. 105 E4
9 Salisbury SP2..... 145 F1
Swindon SN3 ...... 50 F2
Windsor St 10 SP2.. 145 F1
Windwhistle Cnr
SP7...............202 E2
Windwhistle La
Alderbury SP5 ...... 160 B7
Grimstead SP5.......154 B1
Windwhistle Way
SP5...............153 F2
Windyridge BA15.....99 F3
Wine St
Bradford-on-Avon
BA15 ....100 C6
Devizes SN10........214 B3
Wingate Par SN2.....35 A2
WINGFIELD.........104 C6
Wingfield SN2........36 A5
Wingfield Ave SN2....35 C6
Wingfield Rd BA14.. 105 A7
Win Gn View 7 SP7. 202 D7
Wing Rd SP4 ...... 198 E6
Winifred St SN1 .... 50 D3
Winkelbury Hill (Hill
Fort) * SP7 ...... 207 C8
Winkins La SN15......44 A2
Winkworth Cottage
SN16................29 C2
Winlaw Cl SN5........49 C7
Winnipeg Rd 1 SP4. 217 F8
Winscombe Ct BA11.. 110 B5
WINSLEY.............99 E7
Winsley Bypass BA15..99 E7
Winsley CE VC Prim Sch
BA15..............99 E7
Winsley Cl SN2.......35 C4
Winsley Hill BA2......99 B6
Winsley Rd BA15.....100 B7
Winstanley Cl 8 SN5..49 A4
Winston Rd SN12.....93 F1
WINTERBOURNE
BASSETT............167 B5
WINTERBOURNE
DAUNTSEY.........133 B2
WINTERBOURNE
EARLS.............133 A1
Winterbourne Earls CE
Prim Sch SP4 ..... 133 A1

WINTERBOURNE
GUNNER........... 133 D3
WINTERBOURNE
MONKTON.........167 B3
Winterbourne Rd 9
SN25.............. 34 D5
WINTERBOURNE
STOKE 196 F4
Winterbourne Stoke
Group (Tumuli) *
SP4...............197 C4
Winter Gn SN11.....80 F3
Winter's Dro SN9... 215 E2
Winterslow CE (Aided)
Prim Sch SP5 ..... 149 B6
Winterslow Rd
Idmiston SP4........198 C1
Porton SP4.........133 D6
2 Trowbridge BA14.. 105 B5
Winton Cl SP9...... 216 D4
Winton Rd SN3.......36 B4
Winwick Rd SN5......49 B4
Wirral Way SN25.....34 F7
Wirr The SP3.......128 D7
Wise Cl SN2..........35 E3
Wise La SP4........141 A2
Wiseman Cl 2 SN3...51 E6
Wishart Way SN15... 78 F5
Wishford Rd
Great Wishford SP2.. 130 A1
Middle Woodford SP4. 130 E6
Wilton SP2.........144 B5
Woodford SP4.......131 A5
Witan Cl 8 SP10... 193 E2
Witchcombe Cl 1
SN10..............187 B8
Witchcombe La SN10 179 B1
Witchell La SN10.... 180 B3
Witfield Cl SN5........33 B5
Witham Way SN2.....35 F4
Withering Rd SN1....50 A3
Witherington Rd
Alderbury SP5 ...... 153 C2
Downton SP5........159 C5
Witherington Ring (Field
System) * SP5 .... 159 D7
Witheys The 10 SN4. 163 A6
Withies The SN8.... 175 D1
Withy Bed
Bushton SN4 ...... 166 E8
Clyffe Pypard SN4 .....61 C1
Withybed La RG17... 177 F5
Withy Cl
Royal Wootton Bassett
SN4...............47 D3
Trowbridge BA14.....101 E3
Withymead Rd SN14...74 A8
Wittenham View 7
SP4...............217 C2
Wittensford La SO51.. 212 F1
Witt Rd SP5........149 D5
Witts La SN5.........33 B5
Wivenhoe Ct 7
BA11..............110 C6
Wizard Education SN1.50 C5
Woburn Cl
Swindon SN25.......34 F6
Trowbridge BA14.....105 A8
Wolferstan Dr SP1... 146 D5
Wolfhall Rd SN8.... 183 D8
Wolsely Ave SN3......51 A4
WOLVERTON.........138 B4
Wolverton Cl SN14....77 F6
WOODBOROUGH... 181 D6
Woodborough CE Aided
Prim Sch SN9 ..... 181 C6
Woodborough Cl
BA14..............105 D5
Woodborough Rd
Beechingstoke SN9 .. 181 B6
Corsham SN13.......85 B7
Pewsey SN9........215 A5
Woodbridge Rd
BA13..............186 B8
Woodbury RG17.....165 B1
Woodbury Cl 2 SN5...49 A8
Woodbury Gdns SP2. 152 A5
Woodbury La SP2.... 152 B5
Woodbury Rise SP2.. 152 B5
Woodbury Yd 5 SP2. 152 B5
Woodchester SN5.....49 C5
WOODCOCK.........117 C6
Woodcock Cl SP9... 216 D6
Woodcock Gdns
BA12..............117 C6
Woodcock Ind Est
BA12..............117 D7
Woodcock La SP4... 117 B7
Woodcock Pk
Warminster BA12 .... 117 C6
Warminster BA12 .... 117 C7
Woodcock Rd BA12.. 117 C6
Woodcock Ride GL8 .. 25 B7
Woodcombe SN12.....94 C6
Woodcote Rd SN8 .. 185 B8
Woodcutters Mews
SN25...............35 C6
WOODCUTTS....... 207 D4
WOODFALLS....... 211 D7
Woodfern SP6.......210 F1
Woodfolds SN16......15 F7
Woodford Cl
Devizes SN10........214 C1
3 Swindon SN2 .... 35 C6
Woodford Valley CE
Primary Acad SP4.. 131 C5

WOODGREEN 211 A4
Wood Hall Dr SN2... 34 D3
++Woodhayes Rd BA11 110
C6
Woodhenge* SP4.... 217 A7
Woodhill Ave SN11 ...81 C3
Woodhill Pk* SN4.. 166 E7
Woodhill Rise SN11...81 C4
Woodhill Village *
SN4...............166 D8
WOODHOUSE 193 F3
Woodhouse Castle (rems
of) * BA12 ...... 114 E1
Woodhouse Gdns
BA14..............102 B2
Woodhouse La DT11. 206 F1
Woodhouse Rd 3
SN3.................50 F5
Wood La
Brinkworth SN15 .... 46 D7
Chapmanslade BA13 . 111 D4
Chippenham SN15 ...78 E6
Fonthill Gifford SP3.. 200 C3
Lydiard Millicent SN5.. 32 A1
Nettleton SN14 ...... 67 B8
Purton SN5.........31 E1
Sherston GL8.......25 B5
Woodland Cl SN3......36 A6
Woodland Dr SN5.... 149 B6
Woodland Heritage Ctr
The * BA13.......107 F5
Woodland Ind Est
BA13..............108 F2
Woodland Pk SN11...81 B2
Woodland Rd
Patney SN10 ...... 180 F5
2 Warminster BA12.. 116 E6
Woodlands SN13......76 C2
Woodlands Bglws
SN14................78 B7
Woodlands Cl SN15...58 A3
Woodlands Dr BA2 ...99 B6
Woodlands Edge
BA14..............105 F7
Woodlands La SP7... 203 E1
Woodlands Manor*
BA12..............139 A3
Woodlands Prim Sch
SP2...............145 B4
Woodlands Rd
Chippenham SN14.... 78 C8
Gillingham SP8.......138 F1
Mere BA12.........139 B2
Mildenhall SN8.......169 A1
Pewsey SN9........215 D4
Woodlands Rd Ind Est
BA12..............139 B4
WOODLANDS ST
MARY.............171 B6
Woodlands The
BA12..............113 A1
Woodland View
Calne SN11 ...... 81 B1
South Newton SP2.... 130 B2
Westbury BA13.....112 B8
Wroughton SN4.......50 B1
Woodland Way
Devizes SN10........214 A1
Salisbury SP1.......146 E2
Stonebridge BA11.... 110 D7
Woodlea SN14.......75 C6
Woodlea Grange
SP5...............153 E2
Wood Leaze SN10... 214 F6
Woodley La SP5..... 206 E5
Woodling Cres SP6.. 210 F1
Woodman Mead 5
BA12..............116 F7
Woodmarsh BA14 .. 105 D4
WOODMINTON..... 204 E1
Woodpecker Cl SN12. 93 C4
Woodpecker Dr
BA14..............105 E6
Woodpecker Mews
SN14................70 B2
Wood Rd SP4 ...... 198 A6
Woodroffe Sq SN11...81 C2
Woodrow
Durnford SP4........132 C8
Great Durnford SP4.. 197 F1
Melksham Without
SN12................94 D7
Woodrow Rd SN12....94 C6
Woodsage Way SN11..80 F3
Woods Cl SN16........25 C1
WOODSEND........169 C7
WOODSHAW........48 A2
Woodshaw Mead 8
SN4.................48 A2
Woods Hill BA2.......99 A6
Woodside Ave SN3....50 E5
Woodside Bottom Rd
SP5...............212 C4
Woodside Rd
Salisbury SP2.......145 C3
South Marston Park SN3.36 C7
Woodsman Rd SN25...35 B6
Woods's La SP3 .... 200 F2
Wood St
Calne SN11 ...... 81 B3
Clyffe Pypard SN4 .....61 D1
Royal Wootton Bassett
SN4...............47 D2
Swindon SN1 ...... 50 A4
Woodstock Gdns
SN12................94 B3

Woodstock Rd SP1 .. 146 B2
Woodvill Rd SP1..... 146 D4
Woodward's Way
SP5...............207 C4
Woodway Cotts GL9 .. 24 E5
WOODYATES....... 208 D6
Woolands La 1 SP7. 202 B2
Woolcott La GL8......26 D8
Wooley Dr BA15 .... 100 E7
Woolford Grange 2
SN4.................48 A2
Wool House Gdns
BA12..............195 A2
Woollaton Cl SN5.....49 A5
WOOLLEY............100 E7
Woolley Cl BA15.... 100 E7
Woolley Dr BA15.... 100 E7
WOOLLEY GREEN. 100 F8
Woolley Orch BA15.. 100 E7
Woolley Pk BA15.... 101 A3
Woolley St BA15.... 100 E6
Woolley Terr BA15... 100 E7
Woolmer Dro SN8 .. 168 F6
Woolner Rd
Swindon SN25 ...... 20 C1
Swindon SN25 ...... 34 C8
Woolpack Meadows
BA14..............105 E7
WOOLVERTON 103 C1
Wootton Bassett Rd
SN5.................49 C5
WOOTTON RIVERS. 174 C2
Wor Barrow (Long
Barrow) * SP5 .... 208 C4
Worcester Lodge*
GL9.................24 A3
Wordsworth Cl 1 SN4 47 F3
Wordsworth Dr SN2.. 35 F4
Wordsworth Rd SP1. 146 B2
Workway Dro SN8 .. 173 E2
Worlidge Dr SN5.....49 B8
Wormcliff La SN13.... 83 A4
Wormwell La GL8.....26 C8
Wormwood SN13.....84 B3
Worsley Rd SN5......49 A4
Worsted Cl BA14.... 105 E7
Wortheys Cl SN16 .... 28 A5
Worthies La SN16.... 28 A4
Worthington Cl 2
SN3.................51 B7
WORTON 179 B4
Worton & Marston Prim
Sch SN10...........179 B4
Worton Rd SN10.... 179 C4
Wouldham Cl SP11.. 191 F4
Wrag View SN6.......23 A4
Wren Cl
Frome BA11........110 B7
3 Warminster BA12.. 116 E5
Wren Ct
Calne SN11 ...... 89 E8
Trowbridge BA14.....105 B4
Wrenscroft 8 SP2... 152 A5
Wrenswood SN3......51 D8
Wright Cl 9 SN25....35 A4
Wright's La RG17.... 185 E8
WROUGHTON.........64 A5
Wroughton Airfield
SN4.................63 F2
Wroughton Inf Sch
SN4.................64 A6
Wroughton Jun Sch
SN4.................64 A7
Wroughton Science
Musuem* SN3.......64 B1
Wych Elm Rd BA11.. 110 C6
Wych Gn SO51.......212 D3
Wychurch Rd SN16...28 A5
Wyck Village* SP3.. 203 E7
Wycombe Cl SN11....79 F2
Wycombe La SN10... 172 F1
Wyke Rd BA14.......101 E4
Wyld Ct SN25........34 E8
Wyle Down National
Nature Reserve*
BA12..............201 E7
WYLYE 201 F8
Wylye Cl
Quidhampton SP2 ... 144 F2
Swindon SN25.......34 F4
Warminster BA12 .... 116 F5
Wylye Rd
Steeple Langford SP3. 128 B7
Tidworth SP9.......216 D7
Warminster BA12 .... 117 A5
Wylye BA12 .... 201 F8
Wylye Valley CE VA Prim
Sch BA12..........195 B3
Wymans Field SN8... 173 F6
Wyncies The 2 SN6. 163 E6
Wyndham Cl SN15....79 A8
Wyndham La SP4.... 199 A2
Wyndham Pk SP1.... 146 B2
Wyndham Pk Inf Sch
SP1...............146 B3
Wyndham Rd
Salisbury SP1.......146 A2
Swindon SN2 ...... 50 A7
Wyndhams Pl SP3... 200 E1
Wyndham Terr SP1.. 146 B2
Wynd The SN11.......81 B4
Wynford Rd BA11.... 110 B6
Wynndale SN12.......36 A4
Wynsome St SN14... 104 F3
Wynwards Rd SN25...35 A5
Wythburn Rd BA11.. 110 C5
Wyvern Ave SN11.....81 C3

Wyvern Cl SN1........50 C2
Wyvern Coll SP1.... 146 E3
Wyvern Rd
Bowerhill SN12 ...... 94 D1
Bulford SP4 ...... 198 E6
Wyvern Theatre & Arts
Ctr* SN1 ...... 50 C6
Wyvern Wlk SN1.... 108 E3
Wyville Rd BA11.... 110 C6

Y

Yard Ct BA12....... 117 B6
Yard La SN15.........96 D7
Yardlee Wlk 2 SN1...50 A2
Yardley Cl SN2.......34 F2
Yard's La SN9......181 C5
Yarmley La SP5......149 B6
Yarmouth Cl SN5.....49 B4
YARNBROOK........105 F3
Yarnbrook Gdns 4
BA14..............105 C5
Yarnbrook Rd
Steeple Ashton BA14.. 102 E1
West Ashton BA14... 105 F2
Yarnbrook Road
BA14..............106 C7
Yarnbury Castle (Fort)*
BA12..............196 B3
Yarnton Cl SN5.......49 A8
Yarrow Cl
East Anton SP11 .... 193 F2
Swindon SN2 ...... 34 C3
YATESBURY 166 E2
Yatesbury La
Winterbourne Bassett
SN11 ....167 A5
Yatesbury SN11..... 166 E4
YATTON KEYNELL.....68 E6
Yatton Rd SN14.......68 E1
Yeates Field Vw
BA12..............117 D5
Yeatmans Cl 6 SP7. 202 B2
Yeatmans La 3 SP7 . 202 B2
Yeats Cl SN25........35 A8
Yelland Wlk 4 SN1...50 B1
Yellowhammer Cl 2
SN3.................51 C8
Yellow Way Rd BA11. 118 A5
Yells Way GL7 ...... 1 F6
Yeoman Cl
5 Market Lavington
SN10 ....179 F1
Swindon SN5 ...... 49 A7
Yeoman Way BA14.. 105 C7
Yeovil Ct SN3.........51 B5
Yerbury St 1 BA14.. 105 E8
Yew Bank Cott Triangle
BA9.................137 A4
Yews The BA12...... 139 A6
Yewstock Cres W
SN15................70 C1
Yewtree Cl 8 SP4.. 198 C7
Yew Tree Cl
Calne SN11 ...... 81 A3
Chirton SN10 ...... 180 F4
The Common SP5.... 149 B6
Yew Tree Dr SN4.... 167 B8
Yew Tree Gdns SN3...36 E4
Yew Tree La SN14... 167 C7
Yew Way SN13........84 E8
Yiewsley Cres SN3....36 B2
Yockney Cl SN13......76 E1
Yonder Way 7 SN4.. 163 A6
York Bldgs SN14.... 101 D1
York Cl
Chippenham SN14.... 78 A6
Corsham SN13.......76 F2
York Dro SP5....... 212 C4
York La SN15.........46 A7
York Rd
Calne SN11 ...... 81 D4
7 Hungerford RG17.. 177 B6
Lyneham SN15.......60 B2
Salisbury SP2.......145 F1
Stapleford SP3......197 B1
Swindon SN1 ...... 50 D6
Upavon Down SN9... 182 B1
Youngs Cl BA13.... 109 A4
Youngs Paddock
SN5...............149 C6
Ypres Rd SN4....... 168 F8
Yule Hill SP3....... 203 F6

Z

Zakopane Rd 4 SN25. 34 D6
Zander Rd
Calne SN11 ...... 81 A5
Calne SN11 ...... 81 B5
ZEALS................137 F4
Zeals Bypass BA12... 138 B5
Zeals Gn Dr BA12... 138 A4
Zeals Rise BA12 .... 137 F4
Zig Zag Hill SP7.... 206 C7
Zion Rd SP11....... 199 F3
Zoar Cl SN4..........64 A6
Zouch Ave SP9 .... 216 C7
Zouch Cl SP9........216 C7
Zouch Farm Rd
North Tidworth SP9... 216 C7
Tidworth SP9.......216 C7
Zouch Prim Sch SP9. 216 B8